LOSS AND TRAUMA

LOSS AND TRAUMA

General and Close Relationship Perspectives

edited by

John H. Harvey, Ph.D.
Eric D. Miller, Ph.D.

 **Routledge**
Taylor & Francis Group
New York   London

Published in 2000 by
Routledge
Taylor & Francis Group
270 Madison Avenue
New York, NY 10016

Published in Great Britain by
Routledge
Taylor & Francis Group
2 Park Square
Milton Park, Abingdon
Oxon OX14 4RN

Printed in the United States of America on acid-free paper
10 9 8 7 6 5 4 3

International Standard Book Number-10: 1-58391-013-1 (Softcover)
International Standard Book Number-13: 978-1-58391-013-9 (Softcover)
Library of Congress Card Number 00-025633

Library of Congress Cataloging-in-Publication Data

Loss and trauma : general and close relationship perspectives / edited by John H. Harvey,
    Eric D. Miller.
    p. cm.
    Includes bibliographical references and index.
    ISBN 1-58391-012-3 (case : alk. paper) — ISBN 1-58391-013-1 (pbk. : alk paper)
    1. Loss (Psychology) 2. Grief. 3. Adjustment (Psychology) 4. Life change events.
    5. Bereavement—Psychological aspects. I. Harvey, John. H., 1943- II. Miller, Eric D., 1972-
BF575.D35 L67 2000
155.9'3—dc21
                                                            00-025633

Taylor & Francis Group
is the Academic Division of T&F Informa plc.

Visit the Taylor & Francis Web site at
http://www.taylorandfrancis.com

and the Routledge Web site at
http://www.routledge-ny.com

CONTENTS

4

Helping Victims of Loss and Trauma: A Social Psychological Perspective

Louis A. Penner, John F. Dovidio, Terrance L. Albrecht   **62**

5

Victim Thinking

Roy F. Baumeister, Ellen Bratslavsky   **86**

6

The Ranking of Personal Grief: Death and Comparative Loss

Harvey Peskin   **102**

7

Parallel Selves as the End of Grief Work

Aurora Liiceanu   **112**

PART II
LOSS AND TRAUMA ASSOCIATED WITH SPECIFIC POPULATIONS

PART IV
CONCLUSION

PREFACE

This collection represents a follow-up set of contributions to Harvey's (1998) edited volume entitled *Perspectives on Loss: A Sourcebook* (also published by Brunner/Mazel). In their breadth and depth, the combined set of volumes could comprise the first comprehensive handbook of loss and trauma. The idea behind both of these volumes is to reflect a sampling of the wide array of phenomena and research programs that may be classified as part of the loss and trauma field. While trauma by definition is an unusual type of loss, there are many types of loss that do not constitute trauma. Loss may be defined as a reduction in resources in which a person has an emotional investment. Such resources may include the presence of and interaction with significant others, loss of personal identity, self-esteem, loss of trust, hope, health, opportunity, and the like (Harvey, 1996). In his seminal work on hope under the most inhumane and degrading circumstances, Frankl (1959) suggested that the greatest loss a human can suffer is that of the ability or will to find meaning and to realize personal potential. He suggested that in their devastating impact, such losses—including those he observed in Nazi death camps—far transcended the loss of nutrition and bodily strength and health.

Many of the losses we experience in life are what Viorst (1986) referred to as natural losses, such as the loss of friends, health issues, and the like. Harvey and Miller (1998) have suggested that major losses (e.g., death, divorce, loss of employment, brain injury, chronic disease, political repression) and the pile up of such losses are the events that most tax us as humans. Ironically, though, it is these same major losses that sometimes lead to growth and the quest to give back to others based on our learning (Erikson, 1963). Harvey and Miller (1998) and Harvey (in press) have argued for the value of a broad field of the psychology of loss that subsumes topics pursued in related fields as traumatology, death and dying, stress and coping, and the study of suicide. Beyond the "psychology" of loss, this broad field needs to be interdisciplinary and international in scope. Both of those qualities are found in the writings in this present volume.

☐ Organization and Foci of Chapters of This Volume

We believe that the chapters in the present volume along with those in *Perspectives on Loss: A Sourcebook* provide a good selection of the types of phenomena that are a part of this broad field of loss. Three main types of chapters are presented in the first three sections in this volume. The first concerns general analyses of loss and trauma concepts; these are general, far-reaching theoretical statements. The second concerns analysis of loss and trauma in specific populations. The populations include patient populations (e.g., cancer patients), and the treatments address specific loss and coping issues for these populations. The third pertains to loss and trauma in close, personal relationships—both romantic and familial. These chapters speak to the importance of loss in relationships, a type of loss that Weiss (1998) suggested is the most daunting that humans face. The final section is a commentary on the volume's chapters and loss and trauma work in general by Robert A. Neimeyer. Neimeyer, a pioneering worker in this field and a leading scholar, clinician, and editor, addresses the overall pros and cons of the collection and directions in the field of loss and trauma.

The eight general analysis chapters in Part I cover the gamut from positive gains and growth from loss and trauma (Updegraff & Taylor; Janoff-Bulman & Berger) to behavior and aspects of the victim of loss (Penner, Dovidio, & Albrecht; Baumeister & Bratslavsky) to family members' ranking of grief and the nature of grief work (Peskin; Raphael & Dobson; Liiceanu), and to rational suicide (Mayo). Some unusual features of this section are the emphasis on growth and gain from the chapters by Updegraff and Taylor, Janoff-Bulman and Berger, Raphael and Dobson, and Liiceanu, and the treatments of the nature of being a victim and what victims can do to help their situations by Penner and colleagues and Baumeister and Bratslavsky. In discussing the issue of taking one's own life to alleviate great suffering, Mayo presents aspects of the dilemma surrounding this moment of truth. In many cases, the person's decision to take her or his life at this point reflects courage and acceptance in letting go of life, while the individual still possesses a modicum of personal control.

There are other special features of these general statements. The theoretical analysis of Updegraff and Taylor builds on Taylor's (1983) influential theory of cognitive adaptation, that emphasizes people's active attempts to restore meaning, mastery, and self-esteem in their coping behavior. Similarly, Janoff-Bulman and Berger build on Janoff-Bulman and Berg's (1998) conception of how people try to create new values and meaning after having their assumptions of reality shattered—a concept that Janoff-Bulman (1992) introduced that has had an enormous impact on the field. Raphael and Dobson's chapter follows up on Raphael classic work on the anatomy of bereavement (Raphael, 1983). She is both a distinguished scholar and clinician who played a principal role in the development of the field when it began to flourish in earnest in the 1970s. It is interesting to note the convergence of the first three chapters as Updegraff and Taylor, Janoff-Bulman and Berger, and Raphael and Dobson all suggest that surviors may eventually grow and experience great gains in perspective and resiliency based on their losses.

Penner and colleagues provide probably the first analysis of how the extensive literature on altruism in social psychology represents a natural interface with work on loss and coping. Ironically, there has been little interplay between work on helping behavior and loss. Finally, Baumeister and Bratslavsky ask unique questions about being a victim, questions that are related to Baumeister's well-regarded work on the nature of evil (Baumeister, 1997) and on the construction of meaning (Baumeister, 1991).

The nine chapters in Part II focus on specific populations. Again, diversity is found in this set. Thompson and Kyle deal with perceived control as a key concept across different types of chronic illness. The enhancement of perceived control is a principal strategy for dealing with major losses and stresses. Two chapters focus on cancer.

Ferring and Filipp present a general conception of coping, basing their analysis on work with cancer patients. Their analysis brings to mind Taylor's (1983) theory of cognitive adaptation. Leedham and Meyerowitz are concerned with loss, adjustment, and growth by children of cancer patients. Note again the emphasis on growth from loss by Leedham and Meyerowitz. Additionally, this chapter is unique in pointing to the dynamics of children's reactions to their parents' life-threatening situation. On the other side of the growth argument is Farina's chapter on the few gains and the many losses for those stigmatized by psychiatric disorders. In a similar vein, Lerner addresses the topic of costs and losses that are the consequence of organizational downsizing. He uses this context to present a theoretical analysis of the role of the justice motive in the behavior of managers, dismissed workers, and survivors. It should be emphasized that Farina and Lerner also were key players in the development of work on stigma and justice, respectively, two invaluable concepts in the field of loss and trauma.

The growth theme is again suggested by Ramsey and Blieszner's treatment of spirituality in old age and how the women they studied transcended a lifetime of losses. Their chapter is provocative in its display of the challenge to live long and deal with loss with grace and courage. The chapter by Toth, Stockton, and Browne concerns issues in grief and loss experienced by college students. As these authors suggest, there is an amazing amount of loss and grief found among college students, who often are stereotyped as relatively care-free and free of such concerns. The final chapter in this section by Morse focuses on homelessness and mental illness. This chapter continues Morse's important contributions to the loss literature and introduces such fascinating new terms as "compassion fatigue," in referring to the general inattention to the homeless and their needs.

Seven chapters dealing with a variety of close relationship loss issues constitute the third part. Hobfoll, Ennis, and Kay provide a general analysis of loss, resources, and resiliency in close relationships. This analysis amplifies Hobfoll's (1988) influential theory of conservation of resources in understanding stress and adaptation. Ellis uses the context of impending loss of a close other to provide a unique communication, collusion, and coalition in caregiving. She presents new perspectives on her powerful story and analysis of loss of a loved one after a long battle with emphysema. This story, initially presented in her book *Final Negotiations* (Ellis, 1995), concerns her 9-year relationship with sociologist Eugene Weinstein—a relationship that occurred in Ellis' 20s and 30s. *Final Negotiations* is a work that has affected thousands of students taking loss and trauma courses. Some students have even decided to enter the field after reading Ellis' compelling story and listening to her penetrating voice of wisdom.

Caregiving is also the topic of Williamson and Shaffer's chapter. They show the relevance of the theory of communal relationships to caregiver behavior and feelings. Williamson and Shaffer show the value of sound theory in helping us understand data from one of the most important and productive research programs in the United States on caregiving for Alzheimer's patients. In her chapter, Abbey treats the topic of adjusting to infertility. Infertility may lead to a type of disenfranchised grief in that it often is associated with less support than are other types of loss such as death. Abbey's work in this area is unique. In their chapter, Hansson and Hayslip address widowhood in later life. This chapter follows up on the ideas generated in Hansson's invaluable work on aging and widowhood (e.g., Hansson & Carpenter, 1994). Their chapter has relevance for Ramsey and Blieszner's chapter in the previous section. Hansson and Hayslip also focus in part on dealing with losses over the life span and successful aging. Two chapters deal with relationship loss issues in romantic close relationships. Boekhout, Hendrick, and Hendrick focus on the impact of infidelity. Their work is novel in its breadth of analysis of theory on infidelity and data from their own research. The reader will learn nuances of the decision process that characterizes people's decision to engage in infidelity. With the perspective of practitioners who have witnessed the travail of families breaking up, Karkazis and Lazaneo focus on custody disputes and describe some of the powerful loss experiences that children and parents encounter in these disputes. Agnew deals with dissolution issues and provides a valuable linkage between dissolution and interdependence theory.

In the concluding chapter in the book, Neimeyer and Levitt provide a compelling commentary about people's narratives of loss. In this commentary, they also provide insights about chapters in this volume. Neimeyer and Levitt emphasize the value of people's constructive activities in developing and revising their stories and discuss dimensions of narratives. They conclude with the cogent point that narrative has everything to do with our coping with the anguish of losing a loved one (or some other important loss). Narrative, while not a perfect antidote, is our best tool in coping with major losses.

☐ Transcending Themes in This Volume

Seligman (1998), Snyder (in press), and other prominent psychologists have recently called for greater emphasis in psychology on what is positive about human behavior. They suggest that the history of psychological research to date has put too much attention on negative aspects of human behavior, character, and potential. We believe that, ironically, a better understanding of the depth and breadth of a new field of work on loss will provide this new field of positive psychology with some of its greatest lessons.

As can be seen from the above sketches of the chapters in this book, scholars and researchers of loss and trauma are positing growth and gain as a part of the field of study of the impact of loss and trauma, just as they have long studied the devastating effects of loss and trauma. Central to this emphasis on growth is an emphasis on finding meaning (Frankl, 1959), or what Neimeyer (in press) has called meaning reconstruction. The process of searching for and creating meaning is pervasive in our moments of living and may be found in each and every chapter in this book.

> "A single moment can retroactively flood an entire life with meaning."
> —Viktor Frankl (1946, p. 44)

John H. Harvey
Eric D. Miller

☐ References

Baumeister, R. F. (1997). *Evil: Inside human violence and cruelty*. New York: Freeman.
Baumeister, R. F. (1991). *Meanings of life*. New York: Guilford.

Ellis, C. (1995). *Final negotiations*. Philadelphia: Temple University Press.

Erikson, E. (1963). *Childhood and society* (2nd ed.). New York: Norton.

Frankl, V. (1946). *The doctor and the soul* (R. & C. Winston, Trans.). New York: Knopf.

Frankl, V. (1959). *Man's search for meaning*. New York: Washington Square Press.

Hansson, R. O., & Carpenter, B. N. (1994). *Relationships in old age*. New York: Guilford.

Harvey, J. H. (1996). *Embracing their memory: Loss and the social psychology of story-telling*. Needham Heights, MA: Allyn & Bacon.

Harvey, J. H. (Ed.) (1998). *Perspectives on loss: A sourcebook*. Philadelphia: Brunner/Mazel.

Harvey, J. H. (in press). The psychology of loss as a lens to a positive psychology. *American Behavioral Scientist*.

Harvey, J. H., & Miller, E. (1998). Toward a psychology of loss. *Psychological Science, 9*, 429–434.

Hobfoll, S. E. (1988). Conservation of resources: A new attempt at conceptualizing stress. *American Psychologist, 44*, 513–524.

Janoff-Bulman, R. (1992). *Shattered assmuptions: Towards a new psychology of trauma*. New York: Free Press.

Janoff-Bulman, R., & Berg, M. (1998). Disillusionment and the creation of value: From traumatic losses to existential gains. In J. H. Harvey (Ed.), *Perspectives on loss: A sourcebook* (pp. 35–47). Philadelphia: Brunner/Mazel.

Neimeyer, R. A. (Ed.). (in press). *Meaning reconstruction and the experience of loss*, Washington, DC: APA Books.

Raphael, B. (1983). *The anatomy of bereavement*. New York: Basic Books.

Seligman, M. E. P. (1998, August). Call for a new discipline: Positive psychology. *APA Monitor*, pp. 1 & 15.

Snyder, C. R. (Ed.). (in press). *Handbook of positive psychology*. New York: Oxford University Press.

Taylor, S. E. (1983). Adjustment to threatening events: A theory of cognitive adaptation. *American Psychologist, 38*, 1161–1173.

Viorst, J. (1986). *Necessary losses*. New York: Fawcett.

Weiss, R. S. (1998). Issues in the study of loss and grief. In J. H. Harvey (Ed.), *Perspectives on loss: A sourcebook* (pp. 343–352). Philadelphia: Brunner/Mazel.

CONTRIBUTORS' LIST

ANTONIA ABBEY, Ph.D., is an Associate Professor in the Department of Community Medicine at Wayne State University. She is interested in how people cope with health problems such as infertility and sexual assault.

CHRISTOPHER R. AGNEW, Ph.D., is an Assistant Professor of Psychological Sciences at Purdue University. As a social psychologist his research primarily focuses on interpersonal relations, the social/psychological dimensions of health, and the biases of individuals and couples regarding contraception use and HIV/AIDS. He has published widely, including articles in the *Journal of Personality and Social Psychology, Personality and Social Psychology Bulletin* and *AIDS and Behavior.* Currently, he has written chapters for the forthcoming *Blackwell Handbook of Social Psychology* and *Advances in Population: Psychological Perspectives.*

TERRANCE L. ALBRECHT, Ph.D., is Professor in the department of Community and Family Health, College of Public Health at the University of South Florida. Her research areas include the study of real-time strategic interaction patterns between oncologists and patients during accrual to clinical trials, the role of social support networks in health and well being. She is currently principal investigator of a major federal grant that involves the study of the social, behavioral and organizational barriers to access and utilization of prenatal care of low-income pregnant women. She has authored over 100 books, articles, and chapters in these areas and has received numerous university and professional research awards.

ROY F. BAUMEISTER, Ph.D., holds the Elsie B. Smith chair in the liberal arts department at Case Western University. After receiving his doctoral degree from Princeton, and following a brief postdoctoral fellowship at UC Berkeley, he came to CWRU as an assistant professor in 1979. He has also held visiting appointments at the University of Virginia, the University of Texas and the Max-Polanck-Institute in Munich, Germany. Dr. Baumeister has over 200 scientific publications covering multiple topics, including self and identity, emotion, sexuality, aggression, self-control the need to belong and performance under pressure. His most recent book is *Evil: Inside Human Violence and Cruelty* (W. H. Freeman).

ANDREA R. BERGER is a doctoral student in the personality and social psychology program at the University of Massachusetts, Amherst. Her research focuses primarily on value creation in close relationships.

ROSEMARY BLIESZNER, Ph.D., is a Professor in the Department of Human Development and Associate Director of the Center for gerontology at Virginia Polytechnic Institute. Her research focuses on family and friend relationships, life events and psychological well being in adulthood and old age. She is a fellow of the American Psychological Association, Association for Gerontology in Higher Education and Gerontological Society of America. She was a co-editor of *Older Adult Friendship: Structure and Process and Handbook of Aging and the Family*. She was also co-author of *Adult Friendship* and *Spiritual Resiliency in Older Women: Models of Strength for Challenges through the Life Span*.

BROCK BOEKHOUT is a Psychology intern at Kansas State University. His research interests are in the area of close relationships, particularly with regard to exclusivity, infidelity, and communication issues. He has published work in the *Journal of Personal and Interpersonal Loss* and *Contemporary Development*.

ELLEN BRATSLAVSKY is a graduate student in the social psychology program at Case Western University in Ohio. She is interested in the causes of self-control failure, mood control, and close relationships. She is currently working on her dissertation examining downward mood regulation in anticipation of self-relevant feedback.

FREDRICK BROWNE is a doctoral student in the department of Counseling and Educational Psychology, School of Education, Indiana University.

MATTHEW DOBSON, Ph.D., is a research psychologist with extensive experience in the field of war-related trauma. His research interests have generated a number of articles that span the fields of stress, trauma, public health, and psychiatric epidemiology. He is currently working as a Senior Policy Analyst in the Centre for Mental Health.

JOHN F. DOVIDIO, Ph.D., is a Charles A. Dana Professor and Chair of the Department of Psychology at Colgate University. Former editor of *Personality and Social Psychology Bulletin*, Dr. Dovidio is currently Associate Editor of *Group Processes and Intergroup Relations*. Dr. Dovidio's research interests are in stereotyping, prejudice and discrimination; social power and nonverbal communication; and altruism and helping. He has published over 100 books, articles, and chapters on these topics. He shared the 1985 and 1998 Gordon Allport Intergroup Relations Prize with Samuel L. Gaertner for their work on aversive racism and ways to reduce bias.

CAROLYN ELLIS, Ph.D., is a Professor of Communication and Sociology and co-director of the Institute for Interpretive Human Studies at the University of South Florida. She is the author of *Final Negotiations: A Story of Love, Loss and Chronic Illness* and *Fisher Folk: Two Communities on Chesapeake Bay*. She is also co-editor of *Composing Ethnography, Investigating Subjectivity, Social Perspectives on Emotion Vol. III* and the AltaMira series *Ethnographic Alternatives*. Her current research focuses on illness narratives, autoethnography, and emotional sociology.

NICOLE ENNIS is a doctoral candidate in Clinical Psychology whose interests are in stress and ethnic minority well-being. She has published a number of articles and book chapters on stress in the lives of inner-city women.

AMERIGO FARINA, Ph.D., is a Professor emeritus in the in the Department of Psychology at the University of Connecticut. His teaching and research have focused on societal and interpersonal factors in stigmas. He has studied how society both responds to and affects stigmatized people and has also published journal articles and books on the subject.

DIETER FERRING, Ph.D., is a Professor of Psychology at the University of Trier, Germany. Her research interests include: coping with physical illness, quality of life, life satisfaction in old age, psychological measurement, measurement of change, and structural equation modeling.

SIGURN-HEIDE FILIPP, Ph.D., is a Professor of Psychology at the University of Trier, Germany. Research interests include self-concept, coping with crises and loss experiences, life satisfaction in old age, age stereotypes, and intergenerational relationships.

ROBERT O. HANSON, Ph.D., is a Professor of Psychology at the University of Tulsa. His current research interests focus on successful aging, aging families and coping with stressful life events in old age. His books include *Relationships in Old Age* and *The Handbook of Bereavement.*

JOHN H. HARVEY, Ph.D., is a Professor of Psychology at the University of Iowa. He formerly taught at Vanderbilt, Ohio State, and Texas Tech Universities. He was also Educational Affairs Officer at the American Psychological Association from 1981–82. He is a social psychologist specializing in the study of close relationships, attribution and account making, and loss and trauma phenomena. He is a Fellow of Division 8 of the APA and was a Fulbright Research Fellow. He has been an author or editor for more than 20 books and has published over 130 articles and chapters. In addition to being the editor of Contemporary Psychology 1992–98, he was also founding editor of the *Journal of Social and Clinical Psychology* and the *Journal of Personal and Interpersonal Loss.*

BERT HAYSLIP, JR., Ph.D., is a Regents Professor of Psychology at the University of North Texas. He is the current editor of the *International Journal of Aging & Human Development* and has co-authored and co-edited several books including *Hospice Care, Adult Development and Aging* and *Grandparents Raising Grandchildren: Theoretical, Empirical and Clinical Issues.*

SUSAN S. HENDRICK, Ph.D., is a Professor of Psychology at Texas Tech University. She is also a counseling psychologist and marriage and family therapist. Her research focuses on intimate relationships with emphases on love, sexual attitudes, and relationship satisfaction. She has published numerous books, chapters, and articles and has served as President of the International Network on Personal Relationships.

CLYDE HENDRICK, Ph.D., is a Paul Whitfield Horn Professor of Psychology at Texas Tech University. He has published research in a variety of areas in social psychology. For the past several years he has co-authored and edited books on close relationships and has conducted empirical research in this area. He is a co-editor of the Sage Series on *Close Relationships* and *Close Relationships: A Sourcebook.*

STEVAN E. HOBFALL, Ph.D., is a Professor of Psychology and Director of the Applied Psychology Center at Kent State University. His principal interests are in stress and in health promotion during stressful circumstances. He has published 10 books and over 120 articles and book chapters. His has received critical acclaim for his books *The Ecology of Stress* and *Stress Culture, and Community: The Psychology and Philosophy of Stress.*

RONNIE JANOFF-BULMAN, Ph.D., is a Professor of Psychology at the University of Massachusetts, Amherst. Her present research interests are the motivational bases of perceived obligations and the psychological processes underlying value creation. Among her publications is *Shattered Assumptions: Towards a New Psychology of Trauma*.

JACQUELINE L. KARKAZIS and *SHARON L. LAZANEO* have been working with families in crisis since 1965. They share a private practice in conducting child custody mediations and evaluations. Both have a wealth of experience in teaching, training, and consulting with other mental health professionals and law enforcement personnel. Other areas of expertise include high-conflict divorce, domestic violence, child abuse, crisis intervention, and dispute resolution as it relates to mediating parental conflict over children.

JENNIFER KAY is a doctoral candidate in Clinical Psychology whose interests are in stress and women's well-being. Currently, she has been examining the role of cognitive loss on the stress process.

DIANA J. KYLE is an Assistant Professor at Fullerton College. She is a fourth-year social psychology doctoral student at Claremont Graduate University. Her research interests focus on areas of health psychology related to illusions of control and perceptions of HIV risk. She has published articles in *Psychology of Women Quarterly* and *Contemporary Issues in Psychology*.

BETH LEEDHAM is an Assistant Researcher in the Division of Cancer Prevention and Control at the Jonsson Comprehensive Cancer Center. Her research focuses generally on quality-of-life issues among cancer patients and their families. More specifically, her interests include the impact of cancer on family relationships, the psychological effects of genetic testing for cancer on patients and families, and adjustment and quality of life among long-term cancer survivors. She has published several book chapters on these topics.

MELVIN J. LERNER, Ph.D., is a distinguished Professor emeritus at the University of Waterloo and a Visiting Scholar at Florida Atlantic University. He has conducted research on the origins, forms, and consequences of the justice motive and the social and psychological processes involved in coping with life crises. In addition to his professional publications he is also editor of the series *Critical Issues in Social Justice* (Plenum Press) and is founding editor of the journal *Social Justice Research*.

AURORA LIICEANU, Ph.D., is a Professor at the International Faculty of Human Sciences and Senior Researcher at the Institute of Psychology at the Romanian Academy. She was named International Woman of the Year in 1992 and was also a guest professor at L'Ecole des Hautes Etudes in Sciences Sociales (Paris) 1994.

HEIDI M. LEVITT, Ph.D., is an Assistant Professor in Clinical Psychology at the University of Memphis. Although she has conducted research on the processes of wisdom, on metaphor usage in Psychotherapy, and on the semiotics of eating disorders, her dominant concentration has been on the role of narrative in Psychotherapy. She is a co-author of the *Narrative Process Coding System* and her research has focused on the development and utilization of this system to analyze narrative processes and structures.

DAVID J. MAYO, Ph.D., is a Professor of Philosophy at the University of Minnesota and Faculty Associate of the University's Center for Bioethics. For the last twenty years the issues of rational suicide and physician aid-in-dying have been his primary research interests. He currently serves on the board of both the Hemlock Society USA and the Death with Dignity National Center.

BETH E. MEYEROWITZ, Ph.D., is a professor in the Department of Psychology at the University of Southern California. She has published widely on topics related to quality of life and coping among cancer patients and their families. Recent publications have been on subjects such as sexuality and intimacy following cancer, the relationship of ethnicity to cancer outcomes, and quality of life following different treatments for cancer. Her current projects include randomized clinical trials designed to test the effectiveness of brief psychosocial interventions for cancer patients and their partners.

ERIC D. MILLER, Ph.D., is an Assistant Professor of Psychology at Kent State University in East Liverpool, Ohio. With a Ph.D. in personality/social psychology, Dr. Miller's research interests include the interface of social, personality, clinical, and health psychology with a particular emphasis on the study of coping with major loss.

GARY A. MORSE, Ph.D., is Executive Director of Community Alternatives: Innovations in Behavioral Care, and Adjunct Professor of Psychology and Gerontology at the University of Missouri, St. Louis. He is also Principal Investigator of a current project supported by NIMH to develop and study effective methods of helping homeless people with serious mental disorders and substance abuse disorders.

ROBERT A. NEIMEYER, Ph.D., is a Professor of Psychology at the University of Memphis where he also maintains a clinical practice. Dr. Neimeyer has published 17 books including *Lessons of Loss: A Guide to Coping, The Constructions of Disorder,* and *Dying: Facing the Facts.* Also the author of over 200 articles and book chapters he is currently helping advance a more adequate theory of grieving as a process of meaning reconstruction. Dr. Neimeyer is the editor of the international journal *Death Studies* and has also served as President of the Association for Death Education and Counseling. In recognition of his scholarly contributions, Dr. Neimeyer has been granted both the Distinguished Teaching Award and he has been made a Fellow of the Clinical Psychology Division of the American Psychological Association. He was also given the Research Recognition Award by the Association for Death Education and Counseling.

LOUIS A. PENNER, Ph.D., is a Professor of Psychology at the University of South Florida. He was also chair of the Psychology Department from 1985–92. In addition to numerous articles and book chapters, Dr. Penner has authored, co-authored, or edited seven books. Most recently, *The Psychology of Helping and Altruism* (with David Schroeder, John Dividio, and Jane Pilivin) and *Psychology, Fifth Edition* (with Douglas Bernstein, Alison Clarke-Stewart, Edward Roy, and Christopher Wickens). His primary research interests concern individual differences in pro-social personality orientations, volunteerism, and pro-social behavior in organizations. He is also a consulting editor for the *Personality and Social Psychology Bulletin* and the *Journal of Social and Clinical Psychology.*

HARVEY PESKIN, Ph.D., is a former president of the Psychoanalytic Institute of Northern California, professor emeritus in the Psychology Department at San Francisco

State University, clinical professor in the Psychiatry Department at the University of California San Francisco, and visiting scholar at the Institute of Human Development at UC Berkeley. He is a clinical psychologist in private practice in Berkeley and serves on the board of the Bay Area Holocaust Oral History Project.

BEVERLEY RAPHAEL has extensive experience and research interests in the fields of bereavement, trauma, and disaster. She has published and edited a number of books on these subjects as well as articles and chapters. She is currently Director of the Centre for Mental Health in New South Wales, Australia and is responsible for the management of the mental health aspects of disaster at a national and state level. She is also a consultant to the World Health Organization on the Mental Health Aspects of Disasters.

JANET L. RAMSEY, is a Marriage and Family therapist at the Pastoral Counseling Center of the Roanoke Valley. Her clinical practice focuses on issues related to aging, caretaking and chronic illness. She has written articles and given numerous presentations on issues related to spirituality and coping and is a co-author of *Spiritual Resiliency in Older Women: Models of Strength for Challenges Through the Life Span.*

DAVID R. SHAFFER, Ph.D., is a Professor and Chair of the Social Psychology Program at the University of Georgia. He has published more than 75 articles investigating various topics in social psychology such as self-disclosure, attitudes, attitude change, pro-social behavior, and psychological issues. He is author of three major textbooks in the field of human development.

REX STOCKTON, Ph.D., is a professor in the department of Counseling and Educational Psychology, School of Education, Indiana University. He has numerous articles published in the area of group psychotherapy and cognitive self-talk. Dr. Stockton is a fellow in Divisions 17 and 49 of the American Psychological Association and in the Association for Specialists in Group Work of the American Counseling Association. Currently he is president of Division 49 of the APA.

SHELLEY E. TAYLOR, Ph.D., is a Professor of psychology at UCLA. Dr. Taylor completed her Ph.D. at Yale University in 1972. Her work focuses on behavioral and neuroendocrine moderators of stress responses. She has published several books and over 120 articles on these and related topics.

SUZANNE C. THOMPSON, Ph.D., is a Professor of Psychology at Pomona College. Her research focuses on perceptions of control, coping with chronic illness, and caregiving relationships. She has published extensively on control issues including the role of perceived control in coping with chronic illness and illusions of control.

PAUL L. TOTH is a staff psychologist and coordinator of evaluation and research at the Counseling and Psychological Service at the Indiana University Health Center. He is also a part-time Assistant Professor in the Counseling and Educational Psychology Department. Current research interests include group process and college student grief and loss. He has articles published in the following journals: *Journal of Personal and Interpersonal Loss, Journal for Specialists in Group Work, Journal of Counseling and Development.*

JOHN A. UPDEGRAFF has an MA in Social Psychology from UCLA. His research focuses on the processes of resilience and growth in the face of stressful experiences such as community disaster and HIV-infection (in collaboration with Shelley Taylor). He is currently a National Institute of Mental Health trainee and is working towards his Ph.D. in social psychology.

GAIL M. WILLIAMSON, Ph.D., is an Associate Professor and Chair of the Life-Span Developmental Psychology program at the University of Georgia. She is presently the Principal Investigator on a grant from NIA for a multi-site longitudinal project investigating mental health and quality of care in medically compromised older adults. She has served on the editorial boards of *Journal of Gerontology, Psychology and Aging* and *Contemporary Psychology*.

GENERAL PERSPECTIVES ON LOSS, TRAUMA, COPING, AND THE POSITIVE IMPACTS OF LOSS

CHAPTER 1

John A. Updegraff
Shelley E. Taylor

From Vulnerability to Growth: Positive and Negative Effects of Stressful Life Events

Severely stressful life events can have a substantial impact on those who experience them. For some, experience with a traumatic life event can leave them confused, withdrawn, depressed, and increasingly vulnerable to the next stressful situation that arises. The clinical literature, for example, has found various stressful life events to be risk factors for the development of depression, anxiety, and in extreme cases, posttraumatic stress disorder (PTSD). For other individuals, a traumatic experience can serve as a catalyst for positive change, a chance to reexamine life priorities or develop strong ties with friends and family. Recent research has explored the immediate and long-term positive effects of similarly severe life events, such as cancer, bereavement, and HIV-infection, to identify the factors and processes that appear to contribute to resilience and growth. These two lines of research, however, have developed largely independent of each other and a number of questions remain to be explored in their integration. For example, do the roots of these apparently divergent patterns lie in the events themselves or in the people who experience them? Do some experiences typically lead to negative outcomes, whereas others contribute to the development of positive changes? What psychological factors appear to moderate these outcomes? How do positive outcomes, such as perceptions of stress-related growth and benefit, relate to measures of negative adjustment?

To address these questions, we begin with a review of positive outcomes that have been reported in response to stressful life events, such as the perceptions of stress-related growth and benefit, and theories that help to explain these changes. We then

Preparation of this manuscript was supported by a grant to the second author from the National Institute of Mental Health (MH 056880) and by funding from the MacArthur Foundation's SES and Health Network. The first author was supported by a training grant from the National Institute of Mental Health (MH 15750).

look at some of the negative outcomes associated with stressful life experiences, such as depression, anxiety, and posttraumatic stress disorder, and discuss theoretical perspectives on these outcomes. Psychological factors that may moderate the relationship between these stressors and the outcomes, such as coping style, optimism, and control, are then addressed. Finally, we address characteristics of stressful events that may contribute to the nature of their long-term impact, and conclude by noting limitations of existing research and directions for future work.

☐ Positive Effects of Stressful Life Experiences

For decades, philosophers and psychologists have written about the paradoxical positive effects that may occur in the wake of severely traumatic events, such as the Holocaust, serious illness, natural disasters, and other traumatic events (e.g., Chodoff, Friedman, & Hamburg, 1964; Frankl, 1963; Mechanic, 1977; Visotsky, Hamburg, Goss, & Lebovits, 1961). Although relatively understudied scientifically in comparison to the negative effects, the positive effects of stressful life events have increasingly come under the scrutiny of theorists and researchers. Studies exploring a variety of stressful events have found that typically over half of individuals who experience a traumatic life event report some degree of positive outcomes as a result, including changes in self-perceptions, social relationships, and life perspective (Dhooper, 1983; Taylor, 1983; Wallerstein, 1986; Yarom, 1983). For example, in a study of bereavement, Calhoun and Tedeschi (1990) found that most participants reported positive changes resulting from the deaths of their spouses, with the most prevalent benefits being reported in the domain of self-perception. Two-thirds of the participants in Thompson's (1985) study of residential fire victims and over half of the participants in Affleck, Tennen, and Gershman's (1985) study of parents with children in neonatal intensive care units reported that they perceived benefits from their experiences. Similarly, in a study of cancer patients, Collins, Taylor, and Skokan (1990) found that the changes reported in the domains of social relationships, priorities, and activities were primarily positive, but that changes in the their views of themselves and the world were mixed; on balance, reported changes were positive. Two studies have explicitly compared the quality of life reported by cancer patients with a normal sample free of chronic disease, and found quality of life experienced by the cancer sample to be higher than that of the non-ill sample (Danoff, Kramer, Irwin, & Gottlieb, 1983; Tempelaar et al., 1989). Other studies have shown that, both during the immediate aftermath of traumas such as bereavement and disability and over the course of a long-term stressor such as AIDS caregiving, positive emotions are as prevalent as negative emotions (Folkman, 1997; Silver, 1982; Wortman & Silver, 1987), suggesting that adjustment to stressful events may be far less distressing and much more variable than commonly assumed (Wortman & Silver, 1989).

Across the studies that have examined the benefits that people perceive as resulting from severely stressful life events, three important and consistent domains of change have appeared (Taylor, 1983): (1) self-concept, (2) relationships with social networks, and (3) personal growth and life priorities. The positive changes in self-concept following severe life stressors typically include the belief that one is a stronger person for the experience and is better able to handle the blows that life will inevitably deal. For example, in Calhoun and Tedeschi's (1990) bereavement study, over two-thirds of the participants described themselves as stronger and more competent people, and over 80% felt that they were wiser, stronger, more mature, and better able to cope with other crises (see also Thomas, DiGiulio, & Sheehan, 1991). Sledge and colleagues documented similar changes in self-concept in repatriated prisoners of the Vietnam War (Sledge, Boydstun, & Rabe, 1980). Taylor (1983) found that breast cancer survivors often reported a stronger sense of self as a result of their illness, and as did individuals infected with HIV (Taylor, Kemeny, Reed, & Aspinwall, 1991).

A second area in which individuals commonly perceive posttraumatic benefits is in their social relationships. Life crises can force people to take a dependent and receptive stance toward their external environment (Stewart, Sokol, Healy, & Chester, 1986) that may necessitate the solicitation of help from family and friends. Thus, if an individual is overwhelmed by an unanticipated threat and feels that the world is falling apart, having a supportive and stable social network to rely on can increase one's appreciation of friends and family and lead to the perception that these social ties have been strengthened as a result. Indeed, research does bear out such a claim. In Calhoun and Tedeschi's (1990) and Thompson's (1985) studies, the most common benefit that victims cited was the realization that other people were available to help and rely upon. Similarly, in Mendola and colleagues' (1990) study of women with impaired fertility and Schwartzberg's (1993) study of men with AIDS, close to half of the respondents reported improved social relations and a stronger sense of belonging. Evidence is mounting that when stressful events occur in conjunction with high levels of social support, they can have positive influences on mood (Caspi, Bolger, & Eckenrode, 1987) and on psychological growth (Park, Cohen, & Murch, 1996).

A third general area in which people often perceive stress-related benefits is in their personal growth and life priorities. In a study of HIV-positive men, Schwartzberg (1993) reported that three-quarters of the participants viewed their HIV-infection as a catalyst for personal growth, including reprioritizing values and time commitments, becoming more understanding with friends and family, and accomplishing goals that would have otherwise been delayed (see also Reed, 1989). In a study of cancer patients (Collins et al., 1990), more than 90% of respondents reported at least some beneficial changes in their lives. Further, Baumeister (1994) reviewed evidence suggesting that a negative life change, even a relatively minor one, can serve to link together other existing problems, conflicts, and dissatisfactions in a person's life, resulting eventually in a broad restructuring of attitudes and priorities that can have positive long-term effects.

Mounting evidence suggests that these reordered priorities may translate into changes in activities. For example, in studies of women with breast cancer, Taylor and colleagues (Taylor, 1983; Taylor, Lichtman, & Wood, 1984) reported that over 75% of the participants made health-related behavioral changes as a result of their condition. Affleck and colleagues' (Affleck, Tennen, Croog, & Levine, 1987) research on heart attack patients found that perceptions of stress-related benefits were associated with better long-term physical health and lower levels of mortality, suggesting that perceptions of benefit might have been associated with the adoption of more healthy behaviors (see also Bar-On, 1987).

Finding benefits in traumatic events is not unexpectedly associated with better psychological adjustment to those events. Park and colleagues (1996) found that college students who reported high degrees of perceived growth in response to a stressful life event also showed pre-event to post-event increases in optimism and positive affectivity. Other studies of women with impaired fertility (Mendola et al., 1990) and disaster victims (McMillen, Smith, & Fisher, 1997; Thompson, 1985) have reported similar findings. Lehman and colleagues (Lehman et al., 1993), however, reported no relationship between perceived benefits and psychological adjustment, and suggested that a balanced recognition of the positive and negative aspects of a traumatic event contributes best to psychological functioning, a position supported by other studies (Taylor, Kemeny et al., 1991).

Indeed, the question of whether positive changes, or a mix of positive and negative changes, are associated with optimal adjustment following stressful events is an issue that remains unresolved. Some research (Taylor, Kemeny et al., 1991) has shown that a mix of changes proved to be more beneficial. However, more recent research on women with AIDS found exclusively positive changes to be associated with best adjustment (Updegraff, Taylor, Kemeny, & Wyatt, 2000). It may be that, for ongoing traumatic events that require a major life readjustment, positive changes better predict adjustment, because the sheer stress of the event may be otherwise overwhelming; in contrast, people reporting on events that are in the past and for which the full ramifications are known may be more likely to acknowledge a mix of changes which may be associated with adjustment (cf. Updegraff et al., 2000).

Taken together, these studies suggest that stressful life events can have long-term positive effects and can help people to understand more about themselves, their social network, their priorities, and their lives in general. It should be noted, however, that much of this research has been based on self-report data, so it is unclear how valid these changes may actually be. To date, only a few studies have linked these reported changes to behavioral outcomes (Taylor et al., 1984) or to corroborated perceptions by friends or relatives (Park et al., 1996). A few studies have begun to tie such positive changes to physiological, neuroendocrine, and immune functioning (Epel, McEwen, & Ickovics, 1998; Kamen-Siegel, Rodin, Seligman, & Dwyer, 1991) and to health (Affleck, Tennen, Croog et al., 1987). For example, a study by Bower, Kemeny, Taylor, and Fahey (1998) found that the ability to find meaning in an AIDS-related bereavement experience was associated with a slower course of AIDS among men infected with HIV. Given that these perceptions of stress-related growth may have such salutatory effects on behavior and health, it is important for future research to tie these reports of benefits to tangible outcomes.

Because stressful life events create the potential for positive change as well as negative change, it is important for theories to be able to explain both positive changes as well as the overall variability in response to stressful life events. A number of theories have been proposed to explain the positive effects that people report from stressful life events, such as Taylor's (1983) theory of cognitive adaptation, Aldwin's (Aldwin, Sutton, & Lachman, 1996) deviation amplification model of stress and coping, Hobfoll's (1988) conservation of resources theory, and Meichenbaum's (1985) stress inoculation approach. These theories will be presented in light of evidence noted.

Taylor's Cognitive Adaptation Theory

Taylor's (1983) theory of cognitive adaptation conceptualizes individuals as active agents in restoring psychological equilibrium in the aftermath of a traumatic life event. According to the theory, traumatic life events initially take their toll by challenging people's sense of meaning, their sense of mastery, and their self-esteem. As a result, people are motivated to restore their self-esteem and sense of meaning and mastery by the production of self-enhancing cognitions (Taylor & Brown, 1988). For example, a sense of meaning can be regained by understanding why a traumatic event occurred and what its role in a person's life will be, and a sense of meaning is typically produced by either a causal attributional search or a rethinking of attitudes and life priorities. Similarly, individuals can preserve their sense of mastery by believing that they can exercise control over the event. However, different events allow for different amounts of control, and if an individual's attempts at control in one domain are thwarted, Taylor (1983) suggests that individuals will preserve their sense of control and mastery by focusing on domains of their life where they do have control; empirical research supports this prediction (Taylor, Helgeson, Reed, & Skokan, 1991). An individual's self-esteem can also be preserved by focusing on aspects in which one's self-concept is relatively unaffected or improved, or by comparing oneself to less fortunate others in an effort to cast oneself in a more positive light (Taylor & Lobel, 1989; Taylor, Wood, & Lichtman, 1983).

Thus, Taylor's theory of cognitive adaptation posits that positive reinterpretation and selective focus and evaluation are mechanisms by which individuals restore their views of themselves and the world. Within this perspective, perceptions of stress-related growth are likely to be the natural and inevitable products of a person's motivation to enhance his or her self-perceptions, which creates some speculation as to the validity of people's reports of stress-related growth (Affleck & Tennen, 1996; Lehman et al., 1993). It is important to note, however, that even though Taylor's basic model focuses almost exclusively on the production and maintenance of people's positive beliefs about themselves and their situations, it may have implications for guiding adaptive behavior, because research suggests that these positively-biased beliefs can motivate people towards active goal attainment (Taylor & Gollwitzer, 1995; Taylor et al., 1992).

On the whole, evidence supports predictions from Taylor's framework with a few exceptions. The evidence relating causal attributions for the victimizing event to successful adjustment is mixed (Bulman & Wortman, 1977; Taylor et al., 1984; but see Bar-On, 1987). Evidence concerning the predictions regarding social comparisons is largely supportive but are somewhat more complex than the theory originally proposed. For example, comparison of one's situation with less fortunate others appears to more benefit those coping with traumatic events, but actual contact with and information from people who have managed those events successfully seems to be more beneficial (Taylor & Lobel, 1989). As noted, the question of whether the recognition of primarily positive changes or a mix of positive and negative changes following a traumatic event is optimal for adjustment remains unresolved.

Aldwin's Deviation Amplification Model and Hobfoll's Conservation of Resources Theory

Whereas Taylor's theory of cognitive adaptation focuses on the processes by which people faced with traumatic life events restore their positively-biased beliefs by the use of cognitive reinterpretation and selective focus, other theorists have focused on the differential resources and skills that people may bring to traumatic events that may be more or less likely to help them find long-term benefits in those events. Aldwin's

(Aldwin et al., 1996) deviation amplification model of stress and coping proposes that coping is "a process that extends across situations by resulting in general changes in coping resources, such as management skills, and, as such, can affect personality processes such as mastery and self-esteem" (p. 842). As Aldwin's theory proposes, the changes that occur in response to traumatic life events may be subject to positive feedback processes, in which small changes for the worse can trigger maladaptive spirals, such as increases in intrusive thoughts and avoidant coping strategies, and small changes for the better can trigger adaptive spirals, such as increases in mastery and the use of active coping strategies.

Whether a particular event triggers a maladaptive or adaptive cycle may depend on a person's personal and coping resources, such as socioeconomic status, social network, self-esteem, optimism, and mastery (Hobfoll, 1988; Holahan & Moos, 1987), as well as the nature and severity of the event itself. Both Hobfoll's (1988) conservation of resources theory and the deviation amplification model predict that individuals who have higher levels of initial personal and coping resources should use more adaptive coping strategies and perceive more advantages from a traumatic events, which in turn should predict more positive long-term effects and subsequent increases in mastery. In contrast, individuals with lower levels of initial resources should rely more on maladaptive coping strategies, which should predict more negative long-term effects and subsequent decreases in mastery. Consistent with these predictions, Aldwin and colleagues (Aldwin et al., 1996) found that coping strategies differentially predicted perceived positive effects (such as strengthened coping skills) or negative effects (such as learning about their own weaknesses) in a large sample that reported on a significant stressful life event, and these effects predicted current mastery and depression levels. Research by Holahan and Moos (1990) also shows that improvements in self-confidence and an easygoing disposition over the course of high stress were predicted by higher initial resources, which appeared to be mediated by the use of more adaptive coping strategies.

Although Aldwin's deviation amplification model is a useful conceptual tool in understanding how stressful events may lead to both positive and negative long-term consequences, it is difficult to test the cyclical effects that it predicts. The above findings, however, are consistent with other studies that suggest positive long-term effects for individuals who perceive benefits from traumatic life events. For example, in Aldwin, Levenson, and Spiro's (1994) study of war veterans, beneficial appraisals of combat experience moderated the relationship between combat exposure and PTSD development, even after controlling for depressive symptomatology.

Both Aldwin's theory and Hobfoll's resource analysis suggest a personality-based explanation for the perception of benefits in traumatic events. Specifically, both models suggest that the ability to find benefits in a stressful situation may result from a stable coping style (Park, 1998a), dispositional optimism (Scheier & Carver, 1985), or some other dispositional resource. Some support for such a personality-based cause comes from a study by Park et al. (1996) that found moderately high within-person correlations of reported growth over different events in a six-month period.

In certain respects, the Taylor perspective and the Aldwin and Hobfoll perspective might be seen as providing alternative explanations for the relation of perceived benefits in traumatic events to psychological adjustment. It is possible, however, that the perspectives are compatible. Specifically, Aldwin and Hobfoll suggest that dispositional resources may predispose people to find benefits in stressful or traumatic events

(Aldwin et al., 1996; Hobfoll, 1988), and Taylor's perspective emphasizes the dynamic adaptive mechanisms whereby these benefits may be obtained. As such, the two approaches may represent complementary perspectives on a fundamentally similar set of outcomes.

Meichenbaum's Stress Inoculation Approach

An additional positive effect of traumatic life events, understudied but potentially important, is the experience it may give people to draw from in appraising and dealing with subsequent stressful life events. This potential benefit of stressful life events forms the basis of Meichenbaum's (1985) stress inoculation approach, which proposes that experience in dealing effectively with moderate-level stressors may inoculate individuals against the potentially pathogenic effects of subsequent stressful events. This inoculation may result from knowledge of and more use of adaptive coping strategies, confidence in one's ability to deal with events, or a less threatening appraisal of potential threats. Some support for this proposition is offered by Aldwin and colleagues (Aldwin et al., 1996) in their qualitative study of adults coping with a variety of stressful life events. Nearly all of their participants reported drawing from previous experiences in dealing with a current problem, although only 22% of the participants reported drawing from similar experiences. The other specific experiences that the participants drew from included work experience, illnesses and deaths of others, military experience, and childhood problems.

More concrete evidence in support of this inoculation perspective comes from studies of rape victims (Burgess & Holmstrom, 1978), war veterans (Elder & Clipp, 1989), and Holocaust survivors (Shanan & Shahar, 1983). In Burgess and Holmstrom's (1978) study, women who had experienced the death of a family member more than two years before a rape victimization recovered more quickly than women who had not. Shanan and Shahar (1983) also found that Holocaust survivors coped more actively and reported more life satisfaction and more long-term stability than a matched control group of people who did not directly experience the Holocaust. Further, Elder and Clipp (1989) found that veterans with heavy combat experience became more resilient and less helpless over time when compared to veterans with less severe combat experience (see also Sledge et al., 1980). The veterans with more heavy combat experience were also more likely to report that they had learned to cope with adversity, learned self-discipline, and had a clearer sense of direction than those with less heavy combat experience (but see Lee, Vaillant, Torrey, & Elder, 1995; McCarroll, Fagan, Hermsen, & Ursano, 1997).

Although all of the above studies suggest that experience with traumatic life events may, in some cases, actually improve one's ability to deal with subsequent life events, they may be limited by selection bias and, thus, are only suggestive of the inoculative effects of stressful experiences. Moreover, several of the events hypothesized to inoculate people against stress (such as the Holocaust and combat experience) are extremely traumatic stressors that have been associated with negative outcomes as well. For example, one of the chief risk factors for posttraumatic stress disorder is a prior intense stressful event, such as combat experience or sexual abuse, and so the point at which a prior stressor inoculates an individual against subsequent stressors versus renders that individual more vulnerable to adverse consequences of stress remains unclear. Most of these studies do not specify the processes or factors that may affect how such experiences inoculate individuals against the effects of future life stressors or specify which individuals will show positive versus negative effects. Inasmuch as prior experience with stressful life events has been posited both to inoculate against adverse effects of stress and to exacerbate adverse effects of stress, the factors that determine the inflection point at which the effects of prior stressful experiences begins to reverse requires delineation; as yet, there is little suggestion other than the magnitude of the stressor of what such boundary conditions might be. Some of the factors that may determine this range of outcome will be discussed later, although further research is needed to understand how individuals may actually benefit and ultimately thrive as a result of their experiences with traumatic life events.

☐ Negative Effects of Stressful Life Experiences

Some widely researched effects of stressful life events include negative reactions, such as depression and anxiety (Nolen-Hoeksema & Morrow, 1991; Stewart & Salt, 1981), and cognitive disruptions such as intrusive thoughts and ruminations that can interfere with a person's normal activities and successful adjustment (Horowitz, 1976; Shaham, Singer, & Schaeffer, 1992). Much of this research has been guided by cognitive processing theories of adjustment, such as Horowitz's (1976) theory of stress responses and Janoff-Bulman's (1992) assumptive world theory.

More extreme negative responses to traumatic events have been chronicled in posttraumatic stress disorder, a syndrome characterized by extensive, long-lasting, and severe responses to stress. These after-effects of a stressful experience can include physiological arousal, distractibility, and other negative effects that last for days, months, or even years after the event has terminated. Such symptoms have most clearly been documented among soldiers exposed to combat—indeed, before PTSD was acknowledged as a psychological disorder, it was called "shell shock"—but PTSD responses may also occur in response to assault, rape, domestic abuse, a violent encounter with nature, such as an earthquake or flood (Ironson et al., 1997), or a technological disaster, such as a nuclear accident (Norris, 1990). The person suffering from PTSD typically shows several symptoms of psychic numbing, such as reduced interest in once-enjoyable activities, detachment from friends, or constriction in emotions. In some cases, the person will relive aspects of the trauma. In addition, PTSD appears to be a risk factor for extremely negative responses to subsequent stressful events (American Psychiatric Association [APA], 1994).

Horowitz's and Silver's Perspectives on Cognitive Reworking

Theories developed by Horowitz (1976) and by Silver and her associates (Silver, Boon, & Stones, 1983; Tait & Silver, 1989) propose that many of the negative effects of traumatic events result from an individual's difficult attempts to rework distressing thoughts of the traumatic event into a viable cognitive framework. Horowitz and Silver suggest that this cognitive reworking is brought about by repetitive cycles of intrusive thoughts and denial (Horowitz, 1979; Tait & Silver, 1989), which serve to gradually fit the event-related thoughts into a stable and viable cognitive framework. Further, Silver proposes that this cognitive reworking is intimately tied with the processes of finding meaning in the event and dealing with the ongoing social and personal implications of the event (Tait & Silver, 1989). In cases of severely negative experiences, this cognitive integration can be extremely difficult and the cycles of intrusive and avoidant thoughts can lead to long-term distress (Lepore, Silver, Wortman, & Wayment, 1996; Miller, Rodoletz, Schroeder, Mangan, & Sedlacek, 1996), and can contribute to the development of PTSD symptomatology (Horowitz, Wilner, & Alvarez, 1979). Indeed, level of intrusive thoughts has been shown to be a strong predictor of overall distress following a traumatic event (Creamer, Burgess, & Pattison, 1992). In their study of incest survivors, Silver and her associates (Silver et al., 1983) found that many of the women were unable to make sense of the event, to find meaning in it, or to understand why the incest had happened and, decades later, reported that the events were as intense, disruptive, and disturbing as they had been at the time of occurrence. Those women who had been able to resolve the events in their minds were less likely to be troubled by rumination. Similar results were also found in Tait and Silver's (1989) study of elderly community members. A majority of the participants in their study experienced frequent, intense, and intrusive thoughts of their most negative experience (which had occurred, on average, over 20 years earlier), and these ruminations were also associated with lower life satisfaction and the inability to find meaning in the event (see also Holman & Silver, 1996).

Although the theoretical perspective on cognitive reworking has considerable data to support it (e.g., many individuals ruminate following stressful events), there is little evidence that the need to cognitively rework a stressful event is what gives rise to rumination. It is possible that rumination is a symptom of poor adjustment, such as depression, rather than the manifestation of the causal process that leads to adverse coping with stressful events. Further, other researchers suggest that it is this difficult reworking process that ultimately leads to long-term benefit rather than decline (Tedeschi & Calhoun, 1995), a perspective that, although consistent with Silver's idea that ruminations are tied to the process of finding meaning in traumatic events, requires some empirical reconciliation with research showing the long-term drawbacks of these ruminative processes. Nonetheless, it is clear that adverse life events can have a long-term negative impact on the individual, and that the thoughts and images of the event may last long after the actual event has subsided. To the extent that these distressing thoughts are ongoing and intense, an individual's ability to effectively cope with subsequent stressors may be significantly diminished, leaving the individual even more vulnerable to the negative effects of later stressful events.

Janoff-Bulman's Assumptive World Theory

Janoff-Bulman's (1992) assumptive world theory is an alternative cognitive theoretical perspective for understanding the negative impact of traumatic events. The theory proposes that untraumatized individuals maintain positive perceptions of themselves and others, and hold a belief in a just, meaningful, and benign world. One of the negative effects of traumatic life events is the shattering of these fundamental assumptions (Janoff-Bulman, 1989, 1992; cf. Beck & Clark, 1988), and a major task of recovery is the reestablishment of viable beliefs with which to understand oneself and the world.

Janoff-Bulman's research suggests that traumatic life events such as bereavement, incest, rape, and disaster can and do shatter these beliefs, and leave individuals with a less positive self-concept and less likely to believe in a benevolent and meaningful world (Janoff-Bulman, 1989; Schwartzberg & Janoff-Bulman, 1991). Other research has similarly documented negative effects of war involvement on self-efficacy (Solomon, Benbenishty, & Mikulincer, 1991) and Holocaust survival on beliefs in the benevolence of the world (Prager & Solomon, 1995). Little research, however, has examined the long-term effects of these changes in fundamental assumptions, so it is unclear what effects these disconfirmations may have on people's future functioning and ability to handle later life stressors.

To the extent that traumatic events bring people's cognitions more in line with reality, such changes may aid in the processing of future threatening events by facilitating a less threatening appraisal and easier cognitive integration of adverse experiences (Wortman & Silver, 1987). From this perspective, shattered assumptions may actually have a beneficial effect on subsequent coping, although research to support this possibility remains to be done. On the other hand, it is possible that these shattered assumptions may contribute to the distress that is often reported following severely stressful life events (Nolen-Hoeksema & Morrow, 1991; Stewart & Salt, 1981). For example, research has shown that experiencing a severely stressful life event such as a loved one's death, a health threat, or a loss of employment, can lead to a significantly increased risk of developing clinical depression and anxiety within a one-year period (Bifulco & Brown, 1996; Finlay-Jones & Brown, 1981), and these psychological effects may be due in part to the interaction of negative events with a person's maladaptive cognitions about themselves and the world (Beck & Clark, 1988). Other research has found low belief in a just world to be related to more threatening appraisal of stressful events and greater stress-related autonomic reactivity (Tomaka & Blascovich, 1994). It must be noted, however, that these effects of shattered assumptions are suggestive and there is little research indicating that these changes in beliefs drive the process of adjustment, affect coping behavior, or determine adjustment to subsequent stressful events.

☐ Factors That May Influence Growth and Vulnerability

Although the previous theoretical perspectives allow us to understand how adverse experiences can have both positive and negative effects, they do less to specify why some people benefit from stress while others become debilitated. As Park (1998b) notes, the prediction of positive versus negative outcome is a challenge for this broader conceptualization of stress and coping (see also O'Leary & Ickovics, 1995). Accordingly, this section will focus on some of the potential determinants of stress-related growth and vulnerability. These factors include an active coping style, optimism, perceptions of control over life events, a strong sense of self, as well as the nature of the stressful experience itself. Correspondingly, a personality marked by negativity, a severe prior traumatic experience, such as victimization, disaster, combat experience, and physical or sexual abuse, may act as vulnerability factors leading to a greater likelihood of stress-related maladaptive symptoms and poor adjustment.

Coping Style

The ways in which an individual copes with a traumatic life event are important predictors of how well a person adjusts to it. Although a number of possible coping strategies have been identified and examined in the literature (Carver, Scheier, & Weintraub, 1989; Lazarus & Folkman, 1984), for this discussion they will be grouped into three general categories: active coping, acceptance and positive reinterpretation, and avoidance coping. Active coping refers to strategies that are directed at problem solving, and entails taking direct action to confront a stressor and reduce its effects. In Carver et al.'s (1989) typology of coping strategies, active coping strategies include problem-solving, planning, suppression of competing activities, restraint coping, and seeking support for instrumental reasons. Acceptance and positive reinterpretation refer to acceptance of a stressor as real and unavoidable and attempts to focus on the positive aspects of a situation. Avoidance coping refers to primarily emotion-focused strategies, which may reduce the distress associated with a stressful event by denial or withdrawal from the situation, without reducing the noxious aspects of the situation itself. In Carver et al.'s (1989) typology, avoidance coping strategies include mental and behavioral disengagement, alcohol-drug disengagement, and denial.

Active coping can lead to adjustment and improvement by both reducing the distress and the impact of a traumatic event, as well as by contributing to perceptions of stress-related growth. In general, an active coping style is highly effective in the management of severe stressors and future threats (Suls & Fletcher, 1985; Taylor & Clark, 1986). Research suggests that the use of active coping strategies in dealing with a stressful life event can contribute to lower levels of depression (Aldwin, 1991) and less distress and PTSD symptomatology (Solomon, Mikulincer, & Flum, 1988). Further, the use of active, problem-focused coping strategies may contribute to positive outcomes, such as greater resolution of the event (Aldwin & Revenson, 1987; Thoits, 1994), stable psychological functioning (Holahan & Moos, 1990), positive psychological states (Folkman, 1997), motivation (Aspinwall & Taylor, 1992), and perceptions of benefits and growth (Collins et al., 1990; Holahan, Moos, & Schaefer, 1996; Park et al., 1996). Consistent with theories presented earlier, an active coping style may also be determined by psychosocial factors such as perceptions of control over the stressful event (Taylor et al., 1984; Thompson, 1981), a confidence in one's ability to manage the event (Bandura, 1977), and the availability and effective seeking of social support (Folkman, Lazarus, Dunkel-Schetter, DeLongis, & Gruen, 1986).

While an active coping style may be most adaptive in situations that are controllable and modifiable, acceptance and positive reinterpretation coping may be most adaptive in situations that are not controllable by direct action. As Carver et al. (1989) note, positive reinterpretation and acceptance coping may be important in situations where a stressor is essentially unchangeable, requiring accommodation. Positive reinterpretation can be used to manage one's emotions in an uncontrollable situation and to motivate the use of active coping strategies in a controllable situation. Most important, positive reinterpretation and acceptance coping appear to be significant determinants of stress-related growth. By allowing individuals to accept a situation and focus on its positive aspects and implications, these coping strategies may be the most responsible for contributing to people's beliefs that they have benefited from a stressful life event. Accordingly, Park et al.'s (1996) research with college students does, in fact, show positive reinterpretation and acceptance coping to be among the best predictors of stress-related growth.

Research suggests that strategies of positive reinterpretation may also contribute to better adjustment across a variety of stressful experiences. Folkman's (1997) study of caregivers of men with AIDS shows that positive reappraisal of the experience was associated with greater positive psychological states. Likewise, positive reinterpretation coping has been associated with better psychological well-being in chronic fatigue syndrome patients (Moss-Morris, Petrie, & Weinman, 1996) and decreased depression and anxiety in first year medical students (Stewart et al., 1997). Similarly, acceptance has also been shown to predict lower distress in breast cancer patients (Carver et al., 1993), better adjustment in HIV-infected men (Thompson, Nanni, & Levine, 1994), and better physical functioning over a variety of events (Gall & Evans, 1987). Taken together, these studies suggest that positive reinterpretation and acceptance can be important contributors to long-term adjustment, particularly in situations that may not be amenable to active, problem-focused coping.

In contrast, an avoidant coping style appears to be a less adaptive response to a stressful life event and can ultimately lead to greater long-term distress and disruptive cycles of intrusion and avoidance. Although avoidance coping may reduce short-term distress and may be an effective strategy for dealing with a short-term stressor, it can lead to more maladaptive functioning in response to more severe, long-term stressors (Holahan & Moos, 1987; Suls & Fletcher, 1985). The research of Miller and colleagues (Miller et al., 1996) and Wegner (1994) shows that efforts to avoid the unpleasant thoughts and emotions associated with a traumatic event are often unsuccessful. The thoughts and emotions that are avoided frequently resurface in the form of intrusive and distressing thoughts that, when met by further avoidance, can lead to maladaptive cycles of intrusion and avoidance discussed earlier (Horowitz, 1976; Miller et al., 1996; Tait & Silver, 1989). A number of studies indicate these intrusion/avoidance cycles frequently mediate the relationship between stressful life events and long-term distress (Bifulco & Brown, 1996; Creamer et al., 1992; Holahan & Moos, 1986; Hovanitz, 1986) and even the development of PTSD (Sutker, Davis, Uddo, & Ditta, 1995). Other research suggests that the use of avoidant coping strategies is most common in individuals with fewer personal and social resources, poorer mental health, more recent stressful life events and higher levels of chronic stress (Aldwin & Revenson, 1987; Baum, Cohen, & Hall, 1993; Holahan & Moos, 1987). Avoidant coping strategies are also more likely to be used in response to events that are perceived as significant threats, as opposed to challenges or potentially beneficial experiences (Carver & Scheier, 1994).

Although there is some evidence that the types of coping strategies used in response to a stressful event depend upon characteristics of the event itself, such as its controllability, chronicity, and severity (Felton & Revenson, 1984; McCrae, 1984, 1992; Paterson & Neufeld, 1987), other research suggests that a person's characteristic style of coping may be fairly consistent across a variety of situations. For example, McCrae (1992) estimated that a person's coping strategies were determined largely by personality and personality-situation interactions, which explained 13% and 11% of the variance in coping behaviors, respectively. In contrast, situational factors alone explained only 2% of the variance in coping behaviors. Further, in Folkman, Lazarus, Gruen, and DeLongis' (1986) study of coping across situations, positive reappraisal emerged as the most stable intra-individual coping strategy. Finally, Carver and colleagues (Carver et al., 1989) found that people's dispositional style of coping was fairly consistent with their style of coping with a specific stressor, with the exception that an active coping style was more likely to be used in a situation that was perceived as controllable.

Optimism

Research has shown that dispositional optimism and pessimism can influence how a person deals with a stressful life experience, and may also affect a person's long-term adjustment. The basis for this research comes from expectancy-value theories (for a discussion, see Scheier & Carver, 1985), which propose that people remain engaged in efforts to deal with difficult or adverse events to the degree that they expect that success will be likely. In simple terms, optimists, or people with positive expectations for themselves and the future, should be more likely to persevere in the face of adverse events than those with more negative expectations of themselves and the future. Although optimism and pessimism may appear to be opposite sides of the same coin, research suggests that measures of these two dimensions may be relatively unassociated with each other (Marshall, Wortman, Kusulas, Hervig, & Vickers, 1992; Mroczek, Spiro, Aldwin, Ozer, & Bosse, 1993) but may begin to show negative associations under situations of significant stress (Robinson-Whelen, Kim, MacCallum, & Kiecolt-Glaser, 1997). Further, as will be noted, both optimism and pessimism may independently predict positive and negative outcomes and the use of both adaptive and maladaptive coping strategies, and may be driving forces in understanding how some people may grow and benefit from experience with traumatic life events, while others succumb to them.

In general, optimism predicts better adjustment to stressful life events. Some specific effects of optimism on adjustment include greater well-being and less perceived stress (Aspinwall & Taylor, 1992), less psychological symptomatology (Scheier & Carver, 1985) and more perceived growth and benefits in college students (Affleck & Tennen, 1996; Park et al., 1996), and less distress in women with breast cancer (Carver et al., 1993) and HIV-positive men (Taylor et al., 1992). The effects of optimism on adjustment, however, appear to be mediated by the coping strategies that optimistic people rely on for dealing with stress. For example, Taylor and colleagues (Aspinwall & Taylor, 1992; Taylor et al., 1992) and Hart and Hittner (1995) found optimism to be associated with greater use of active coping strategies and less reliance on avoidant strategies. Further, Park et al.'s (1996) research suggests that the relationship between optimism and stress-related growth may be mediated by the use of positive reframing and acceptance strategies. Likewise, Scheier and Carver's research (Carver et al., 1993; Scheier, Weintraub, & Carver, 1986) shows that optimistic people are more likely to use positive reframing and humor in dealing with stressful events in general, and acceptance coping in dealing with uncontrollable stressors. Thus, optimism may contribute to better adjustment to a stressful life event by promoting the use of an active, problem-focused coping style (for controllable events) and to the use of positive reinterpretation and acceptance coping strategies (for uncontrollable events), which should both predict overall adjustment as well as perceptions of stress-related growth and benefits.

In contrast, research indicates that pessimism, or negative expectancies for the self and the future, is associated with greater vulnerability to stressful life events and the use of maladaptive coping strategies. In particular, the relationship between stressful life events and the onset of depression appears to be mediated by pessimistic expectations (Bifulco & Brown, 1996; Nolen-Hoeksema, Parker, & Larson, 1994). Further, in a sample of adult caregivers, pessimism was found to predict greater levels of both physical and psychological symptomatology over time (Robinson-Whelen et al., 1997).

Although these studies do not investigate how pessimism may lead to these negative effects, other research suggests that pessimism may contribute to negative outcomes through the use of avoidant coping strategies. In particular, Scheier et al. (1986) found pessimism to be associated with greater use of denial and distancing in response to a stressful life event. Thus, the research presented here suggests that pessimism may be an important predictor of negative outcomes such as distress and depression, as well as a predictor of avoidant coping, which may lead to the maladaptive intrusion and avoidance cycles described previously.

Perceptions of Control over Life Events

Numerous studies have indicated that the amount of control individuals feel they have over a particular event or events in general can influence their ways of dealing with stressful life events and their long-term adjustment. In the stress literature, control has been most commonly conceptualized in three ways: mastery (Pearlin & Schooler, 1978), locus of control (Rotter, 1966), and perceived control over a particular life event (Rothbaum, Weisz, & Snyder, 1982; Thompson, 1981). All of these conceptualizations provide evidence that control is associated with better adjustment in response to stressful life events, and they will be discussed in light of supporting research below.

Mastery is the most general conceptualization of the three, and refers to the degree to which people feel that they have control over the their life, their problems, and their future (Pearlin & Schooler, 1978). Mastery can promote adjustment to and resolution of stressful life events (Thoits, 1994), and may also be substantially correlated with optimism (Marshall & Lang, 1990). Hobfoll and colleagues have shown a high degree of mastery to be associated with less depression and anxiety in studies of college students during a military conflict (Hobfoll, London, & Orr, 1988), women undergoing cancer biopsies (Hobfoll & Walfisch, 1984, 1986), mothers of ill children (Hobfoll & Lerman, 1988), and families of men recruited into the Israel-Lebanon military conflict (Hobfoll & London, 1986). Further, Hobfoll and colleagues showed mastery to be a moderating factor in the relationship between stressful life events and depression (Hobfoll & Walfisch, 1986). Other research, however, has examined the reciprocal effects of stressful life events on people's sense of mastery, and found that ongoing stressful life experiences can be important determinants of a person's overall sense of mastery. For example, research by Pearlin and colleages (Pearlin, Menaghan, Lieberman, & Mullan, 1981) suggests that stressful experiences can diminish people's mastery, which can, in turn, lead to a greater likelihood of depression. Similarly, other research on Alzheimer's caregivers (Skaff, Pearlin, & Mullan, 1996) showed decreases in mastery levels for participants who continued to give care to their relatives, stability in mastery levels for participants who placed their relatives in a care facility, and increases in mastery for participants who experienced the death of their relatives over the course of the study. In light of Aldwin's deviation amplification model described earlier, these studies suggest that the initial effects of a negative experience on a person's perception of control may be subject to positive feedback processes, which may contribute in part to either long-term growth or vulnerability.

Locus of control is a concept developed by Rotter (1966), and refers to people's beliefs in whether events are controlled by themselves (internal locus of control) or by outside forces such as other people, chance, or luck (external locus of control). Similar to a high sense of mastery, an internal locus of control can moderate the relationship between stressful life events and psychological distress (Sandler & Lakey, 1982; Taylor et al., 1984). Werner's longitudinal research on children from high-risk environments has shown an internal locus of control to be a factor associated with long-term resiliency (Werner, 1986; Werner & Smith, 1982). Further, Aspinwall and Taylor (1992) found that an internal locus of control predicted better adjustment in a longitudinal sample of college freshman, and that this relationship was moderated by the use of active coping strategies and the nonuse of avoidant coping strategies.

The third common conceptualization of control is a person's perceived control over a particular experience, and this conceptualization is often broken down into primary control and secondary control (Rothbaum et al., 1982). Primary control refers to people's beliefs that they can take direct action to bring an event or experience in line with their wishes and expectations. If an event is resistant to primary control attempts, then attempts at secondary control may emerge. Secondary control refers to people's attempts to fit in with the experience and "flow with the current" (Rothbaum et al., 1982, p. 8), and can include attempts to seek an understanding of the event and derive meaning from the experience. In a study of parents of high-risk infants, perceptions of both primary and secondary control were shown to be related to better mood and less intrusive thoughts and avoidance of the experience (Affleck et al., 1985). Taylor, Helgeson et al. (1991) found that primary control may be more adaptive for men, but that either primary or secondary control may be adaptive for women coping with stressful events. In a study of HIV-positive men, perceptions of both primary and secondary control were associated with better adjustment, but perceptions of secondary control were found to be most beneficial at low levels of primary control, suggesting that secondary control may be most effective in situations that may be resistant to direct attempts at control (Thompson et al., 1994). Further, research on women with impaired fertility found that as women's expectations of conception decreased, perceptions of secondary control and benefit from the experience increased (McLaney, Tennen, Affleck, & Fitzgerald, 1995), suggesting that secondary control is associated with perceptions of benefits and growth.

Strong Sense of Self

Since the inception of research on coping with trauma, philosophers and researchers have suggested that a strong sense of self may provide the basis for resilience in the face of traumatic events. A sense of coherence about one's life (Antonovsky, 1979), a sense of purpose in life (Visotsky et al., 1961), and a hardy personality (Kobasa, 1979) have all been described as valuable resources for coping with trauma. High self-esteem may enable people to cope more successfully with stressful events (Whisman & Kwon, 1993) and may help to protect against some of the debilitating physiological consequences that are sometimes seen in response to stressful events (e.g., Seeman et al., 1995). A cluster of personality qualities called ego strength—dependability, trust, and lack of impulsivity—appear to represent coping resources that also help people manage the stresses of daily life over time (e.g., Friedman et al., 1995; Holahan & Moos, 1990). Holahan & Moos (1990) have suggested that these resources may improve coping by increasing the likelihood of the use of active coping behaviors.

Preexisting Vulnerabilities

A counterpoint to these findings is the observation that preexisting vulnerabilities represent risk factors for poor adjustment to stressful events. Some of this work has focused on negative affectivity (Watson & Clark, 1984), a pervasive dispositional negative mood marked by anxiety, depression, and hostility. Individuals high in negative affectivity express distress, discomfort, and dissatisfaction across a wide range of situations (Brett, Brief, Burke, George, & Webster, 1990; Watson & Clark, 1984). Negative affectivity appears to be associated with poor responses to stressful events, including elevations in neuroendocrine activity (e.g., cortisol) that may presage health problems in response to stressful events (van Eck, Berkhof, Nicolson, & Sulon, 1996). The adverse effects of negative affectivity on coping may be mediated, in part, by behavioral avoidance coping. For example, people who are high in negative affectivity are more prone to drink heavily (Francis, Franklin, & Flavin, 1986), to be depressed (Francis, Fyer, & Clarkin, 1986), and to engage in suicidal gestures or even suicide (Cross & Hirschfeld, 1986) in response to stress. Preexisting dispositional vulnerabilities have also been tied to a higher likelihood of PTSD in the face of intensely stressful or traumatic events. Research suggests that those who exhibit the symptoms of PTSD in response to stress were disproportionately likely to have preexisting psychological problems, such as depression or anxiety (APA, 1994; Keane & Wolfe, 1990).

Related dispositional vulnerabilities include neuroticism (Boland & Cappeliez, 1997; McCrae & Costa, 1986) and pessimistic explanatory style (Burns & Seligman, 1989; Peterson, Seligman, & Vaillant, 1988). Neuroticism appears to be linked to avoidant coping behavior and less reliance on growth-related coping style (McCrae & Costa, 1986). Pessimistic explanatory style refers to a tendency that some people have to characteristically explain the negative events of their lives in terms of internal, stable, and global qualities of themselves. In so doing, they may lay the groundwork for depression and poor health (e.g., Kamen-Siegel et al., 1991). The extent to which pessimistic explanatory style is independent of depression and the degree to which these three preexisting vulnerabilities cohere or maintain relative independence has not been formally ascertained. Nonetheless, research has related all three to risk for adverse adjustment to stressful life events.

Event Characteristics

In addition to personality resources as determinants of positive and negative outcomes of traumatic events, the characteristics of events themselves may influence whether people derive long-term positive or negative consequences. The severity of the adversity, for example, appears to be related to greater risk for the negative effects of depression (Frank, Tu, Anderson, & Reynolds, 1996; Kendler, Karkowski, & Prescott, 1998), anxiety (Kendler et al., 1998), and PTSD (Yehuda, Southwick, & Giller, 1992). On the other hand, greater severity also appears to be related to increased reports of stress-related growth (Elder & Clipp, 1989; McMillen et al., 1997; Park et al., 1996; Sledge et al., 1980). As these studies of stress-related growth are based on retrospective accounts, one possible explanation is that the greater the initial disruption and distress that an event creates, the greater the potential that benefit will later be found. This perspective is consistent with Tedeschi and Calhoun's (1995) process model of posttraumatic growth, which argues that the more an individual needs to work through a traumatic event and its painful after-effects, the more an individual will subsequently benefit from the experience. To date, however, there is little evidence examining how stress-related growth develops over time, and the processes by which initial distress is transformed to later growth. An alternate view—but not necessarily contrary one—is that the more an event disrupts a person's life, the more potential it has to change the person, with some individuals ultimately benefiting from the experience and others succumbing to it. Evidence from McMillen et al.'s (1997) study of disaster victims lends support to this individual differences perspective, in that levels of stress-related benefit moderated the effect of severity on long-term change in mental health. For individuals who reported high levels of perceived benefits, increased severity was associated with subsequent decreases in psychopathology; for individuals who reported low levels of perceived benefit, increasing severity was associated with increases in psychopathology. A final perspective, suggested by Carver (1998), is that the actual relationship between severity and outcome may be curvilinear: low level stressors may not be disruptive enough to have significant effects, either positive or negative; more severe stressors may be disruptive enough to elicit some negative effects, but manageable enough to allow for ultimate benefit; finally, extremely severe stressors— such as those that commonly are associated with the development of PTSD—may be beyond the range of effective management and may contribute to more long-term decrement.

Another event characteristic that may be related to the nature of the response is the controllability of the event. The previous discussion of secondary control perceptions and positive reinterpretation strategies leads to the intriguing hypothesis that experiences most resistant to direct control and coping attempts may be most likely to contribute to perceptions of benefit and growth. Such events may be dealt with through positive reinterpretation and acceptance coping strategies, which may contribute to perceptions of positive consequences. Indeed, many of the experiences that were discussed earlier as contributors to perceptions of growth are essentially unmodifiable experiences that typically follow a long course of adaptation, such as bereavement, cancer, HIV infection, and impaired fertility. In contrast, experiences that are modifiable by direct control and active coping attempts may contribute to a person's sense of mastery and self-efficacy (see Bandura, 1977), but may not generate high perceptions of stress-related growth or meaning. Thus, it may be that the less a person feels that he or she can take direct control over a negative event, the more the person may engage in the coping strategies that appear to lead to perceptions of benefit and growth.

The specific nature of the event itself may also influence the ability to derive benefits from traumatic events, specifically, whether the event represents a significant loss such as a death, a separation, a loss of employment or possession, or a significant threat such as a health threat, combat experience, or victimization. In one line of research, Finlay-Jones and Brown (1981) showed differential effects of loss events and threat events. Events that represented severe losses, in general, were related to the subsequent onset of depression, but not anxiety. In contrast, events that represented severe threats or dangers were related to the subsequent onset of anxiety, but not depression (Finlay-Jones, 1989; Finlay-Jones & Brown, 1981). While this research suggests some specificity between the nature of the event and the nature of the negative response, it is not known how the distinction between severe losses and threats may relate to positive outcomes. Perhaps positive reinterpretation and acceptance are more likely to be used as coping strategies in dealing with severe losses than severe threats, so it may be useful to examine losses as a distinct class of events that may dispropor-tionately contribute to the phenomena of growth and meaning (see also Harvey & Miller, 1998). In contrast, severe threats may elicit the more typical "fight or flight" response, and may be responded to with more attempts at either direct action or avoidant coping strategies, rather than the positive reinterpretation that contributes to perceptions of stress-related growth.

Other dimensions of stressful events may also influence whether responses to them are primarily positive or predominantly negative. Some researchers have suspected that impersonal events, such as those that result from natural disasters or illness, may be more amenable to finding benefits than events that represent the malevolent ac-tion of another individual, such as rape or assault. Although there is insufficient re-search comparing responses across events to justify such a conclusion, one study exam-ined responses to three community traumas and found a natural disaster to result in greater reports of perceived benefit, in comparison to a shooting and a technological disaster (McMillen et al, 1997). Also potentially consistent with this hypothesis is the finding that, when people blame another person for a stressful event, their psycho-logical adjustment is worse (Affleck, Tennen, Pfeiffer, & Fifield, 1987; Taylor et al., 1984); however, such attributions may themselves be characteristics of the people making them, rather than characteristics of the events, and so this issue remains un-resolved.

☐ Conclusion

Traumatic events are known to produce many adverse psychological outcomes, in-cluding depression, anxiety, and rumination. Yet most people derive at least some benefits from these intensely stressful events as well, including positive changes in the self-concept, beneficial changes in relationships with others, and personal growth and alteration of life priorities. The last two decades have provided manifold evidence of the many mechanisms by which people can construe benefit from stress or trauma, including selective perceptions, selective evaluation, and selective social comparisons. In this chapter, we have examined the processes of finding benefits versus adversity in stressful events, and the personal resources and the characteristics of events that are conducive to finding benefits or that predispose people to negative psychological outcomes.

Overall, the process of achieving growth versus enhancing vulnerability in the wake of traumatic events appears to be heavily predicted by personal resources. People with a strong sense of self, who cope actively, are optimistic, and perceive more con-trol over life events can thrive in the face of adversity. On the other hand, people who rely more on avoidant coping strategies, have more pessimistic expectancies, have low perceptions of control, and have preexisting dispositional vulnerabilities may suc-cumb to the negative effects of stressful life events and become more vulnerable to subsequent stresses.

A number of qualifications of a dispositional analysis should be noted, however. First, some of these dispositional factors may be substantially correlated with each other in individuals, and these general orientations may be driven in part by outcome expectancies (Aspinwall & Taylor, 1992) or even a genetic basis (e.g., Kendler, Kessler, Heath, Neale, & Eaves, 1991; Plomin et al., 1992). Second, much of research reviewed here is cross-sectional, raising the possibility that some of the personal resources associated with finding benefits or adversities in stressful events may be outcomes of the process, rather than causes of it; hence, it is important to conduct longitudinal studies to identify the predictors of a positive versus negative trajectory. Last, whether or not a stressful experience triggers a cycle of growth or vulnerability may depend on the resources a person initially has available to use in dealing with a stressful life event (Hobfoll, 1988). In this light, resources such as supportive social relations, self-confidence, and a sense of control may be outgrowths of prior and more fundamental resources, such as income and education, which may profoundly determine who is able to turn a threatening situation to their advantage and who will become increasingly vulnerable as a result (Taylor & Seeman, 2000). Thus, although the general model discussed here is primarily personality-based, other factors outside the individual may influence the nature of the response.

Relative to characteristics of the person, research has focused somewhat less on characteristics of the traumatic events that may lead disproportionately to finding meaning versus sustaining negative outcomes in the face of traumatic events. Rather, some intriguing dimensions, such as whether the event is a loss or threat, and whether an event is perceived to be an intentional or motivated act of another versus a random, impersonal event, may be important. However, research has not yet sustained the importance of these distinctions, so additional work is needed.

In sum, this review highlights the importance of taking into account both the positive and the negative changes reported by people who are confronted with adversity. Research clearly shows that there is a wide variety in people's responses to severely stressful life events, and future research may profit from greater attention to both the scope of people's responses as well as the processes and factors that influence this range of outcomes. We also stress that, although experience with adversity can lead to a number of the vulnerabilities described earlier, it can also serve as an opportunity for personal change, growth, reassessment, and a chance to deepen people's appreciation of themselves, their life, and their loved ones. This ability to transform adversity into opportunity is perhaps the most impressive finding across the studies reviewed here, and highlights a human resiliency that is by no means rare. Such resiliency is reflected in the observations of Viktor Frankl (1963), who drew from his own experiences in a Nazi concentration camp, when he wrote, "When we are no longer able to change a situation . . . we are challenged to change ourselves" (p. 135).

☐ References

Affleck, G., & Tennen, H. (1996). Construing benefits from adversity: Adaptational significance and dispositional underpinnings. *Journal of Personality, 64,* 899–922.

Affleck, G., Tennen, H., Croog, S., & Levine, S. (1987). Causal attribution, perceived benefits, and morbidity after a heart attack: An 8-year study. *Journal of Consulting and Clinical Psychology, 55,* 29–35.

Affleck, G., Tennen, H., & Gershman, K. (1985). Cognitive adaptations to high-risk infants: The search for mastery, meaning, and protection from future harm. *American Journal of Mental Deficiency, 89,* 653–656.

Affleck, G., Tennen, H., Pfeiffer, C., & Fifield, C. (1987). Appraisals of control and predictability in adapting to a chronic disease. *Journal of Personality and Social Psychology, 53,* 273–279.

Aldwin, C. M. (1991). Does age affect the stress and coping process? Implications of age differences in perceived control. *Journal of Gerontology, 46,* 174–180.

Aldwin, C. M., Levenson, M. R., & Spiro, A. (1994). Vulnerability and resilience to combat exposure: Can stress have lifelong effects? *Psychology and Aging, 9,* 34–44.

Aldwin, C. M., & Revenson, T. A. (1987). Does coping help? A reexamination of the relation between coping and health. *Journal of Personality and Social Psychology, 53,* 337–348.

Aldwin, C. M., Sutton, K. J., & Lachman, M. (1996). The development of coping resources in adulthood. *Journal of Personality, 64,* 837–871.

American Psychiatric Association. (1994). *Diagnostic and statistical manual of mental disorders* (4th ed.). Washington, DC: Author.

Antonovsky, A. (1979). *Health, stress, and coping.* San Francisco: Jossey-Bass.

Aspinwall, L. G., & Taylor, S. E. (1992). Modeling cognitive adaptation: A longitudinal investigation of the impact of individual differences and coping on college adjustment and performance. *Journal of Personality and Social Psychology, 63,* 989–1003.

Bandura, A. (1977). Self-efficacy: Toward a unifying theory of behavioral change. *Psychological Review, 84,* 191–215.

Bar-On, D. (1987). Causal attributions and the rehabilitation of myocardial infarction victims. *Journal of Social and Clinical Psychology, 5,* 114–122.

Baum, A., Cohen, L., & Hall, M. (1993). Control and intrusive memories as possible determinants of chronic stress. *Psychosomatic Medicine, 55,* 274–286.

Baumeister, R. F. (1994). The crystallization of discontent in the process of major life change. In T. F. Heatherton & J. L. Weinberger (Eds.), *Can personality change?* (pp. 281–297). Washington, DC: American Psychological Association.

Beck, A. T., & Clark, D. A. (1988). Anxiety and depression: An information processing perspective. *Anxiety Research, 1,* 23–36.

Bifulco, A., & Brown, G. W. (1996). Cognitive coping response to crises and onset of depression. *Social Psychiatry and Psychiatric Epidemiology, 31,* 163–172.

Boland, A., & Cappeliez, P. (1997). Optimism and neuroticism as predictors of coping and adaptation in older women. *Personality and Individual Differences, 22,* 909–919.

Bower, J. E., Kemeny, M. E., Taylor, S. E., & Fahey, J. L. (1998). Cognitive processing, discovery of meaning, CD 4 decline, and AIDS-related mortality among bereaved HIV-seropositive men. *Journal of Consulting and Clinical Psychology, 66,* 979–986.

Brett, J. F., Brief, A. P., Burke, M. J., George, J. M., & Webster, J. (1990). Negative affectivity and the reporting of stressful life events. *Health Psychology, 9,* 57–68.

Bulman, R. J., & Wortman, C. B. (1977). Attributions of blame and coping in the "real world": Severe accident victims react to their lot. *Journal of Personality and Social Psychology, 35,* 351–363.

Burns, M. O., & Seligman, M. E. P. (1989). Explanatory style across the life span: Evidence for stability over 52 years. *Journal of Personality and Social Psychology, 56,* 471–477.

Burgess, A. W., & Holmstrom, L. L. (1978). Recovery from rape and prior life stress. *Research in Nursing and Health, 1,* 165–174.

Calhoun, L. G., & Tedeschi, R. G. (1990). Positive aspects of critical life problems: Recollections of grief. *Omega, 20,* 265–272.

Carver, C. S. (1998). Resilience and thriving: Issues, models, and linkages. *Journal of Social Issues, 54,* 245–266.

Carver, C. S., Pozo, C., Harris, S. D., Noriega, V., Scheier, M. F., Robinson, D. S., Ketcham, A. S., Moffat, F. L., & Clark, K. C. (1993). How coping mediates the effect of optimism on distress: A study of women with early stage breast cancer. *Journal of Personality and Social Psychology, 65,* 375–390.

Carver, C. S., & Scheier, M. F. (1994). Situational coping and coping dispositions in a stressful transaction. *Journal of Personality and Social Psychology, 66,* 184–195.

Carver, C. S., Scheier, M. F., & Weintraub, J. K. (1989). Assessing coping strategies: A theoretically based approach. *Journal of Personality and Social Psychology, 56,* 267–283.

Caspi, A., Bolger, N., & Eckenrode, J. (1987). Linking person and context in the daily stress process. *Journal of Personality and Social Psychology, 52,* 184–195.

Chodoff, P., Friedman, P. B., & Hamburg, D. A. (1964). Stress, defenses and coping behavior: Observations in parents of children with malignant disease. *American Journal of Psychiatry, 120,* 743–749.

Collins, R. L., Taylor, S. E., & Skokan, L. A. (1990). A better world or a shattered vision? Changes in life perspectives following victimization. *Social Cognition, 8,* 263–285.

Creamer, M., Burgess, P., & Pattison, P. (1992). Reaction to trauma: A cognitive processing model. *Journal of Abnormal Psychology, 101,* 452–459.

Cross, C. K., & Hirschfeld, M. A. (1986). Psychosocial factors and suicidal behavior. *Annals of the New York Academy of Sciences, 487,* 77–89.

Danoff, B., Kramer, S., Irwin, P., & Gottlieb, A. (1983). Assessment of the quality of life in long-term scenarios after definitive radiotherapy. *American Journal of Clinical Oncology, 6,* 339–345.

Dhooper, S. S. (1983). Family coping with the crisis of heart attack. *Social Work in Health Care, 9,* 15–31.

Elder, G. H., & Clipp, E. C. (1989). Combat experience and emotional health: Impairment and resilience in later life. *Journal of Personality, 57,* 311–341.

Epel, E. S., McEwen, B. S., & Ickovics, J. R. (1998). Embodying psychological thriving: Physical thriving in response to stress. *Journal of Social Issues, 54,* 301–322.

Felton, B. J., & Revenson, T. A. (1984). Coping with chronic illness: A study of illness controllability and the influence of coping strategies on psychological adjustment. *Journal of Consulting and Clinical Psychology, 52,* 343–353.

Finlay-Jones, R. (1989). Anxiety. In G. W. Brown & T. O. Harris (Eds.), *Life events and illness* (pp. 95–112). New York: Guilford Press.

Finlay-Jones, R., & Brown, G. W. (1981). Types of stressful life event and the onset of anxiety and depressive disorders. *Psychological Medicine, 11,* 803–815.

Folkman, S. (1997). Positive psychological states and coping with severe stress. *Social Science and Medicine, 45,* 1207–1221.

Folkman, S., Lazarus, R. S., Dunkel-Schetter, C., DeLongis, A., & Gruen, R. J. (1986). Dynamics of a stressful encounter: Cognitive appraisal, coping, and encounter outcomes. *Journal of Personality and Social Psychology, 50,* 992–1003.

Folkman, S., Lazarus, R. S., Gruen, R. J., & DeLongis, A. (1986). Appraisal, coping, health status, and psychological symptoms. *Journal of Personality and Social Psychology, 50,* 571–579.

Francis, R. J., Franklin, J., & Flavin, D. (1986). Suicide and alcoholism. *Annals of the New York Academy of Sciences, 487,* 316–326.

Francis, R. J., Fyer, M., & Clarkin, J. (1986). Personality and suicide. *Annals of the New York Academy of Sciences, 487,* 281–293.

Frank, E., Tu, X. M., Anderson, B., & Reynolds, C. F. (1996). Effects of positive and negative life events on time to depression onset: An analysis of additivity and timing. *Psychological Medicine, 26,* 613–626.

Frankl, V. E. (1963). *Man's search for meaning.* New York: Washington Square Press.

Friedman, H. S., Tucker, J. S., Schwartz, J. E., Tomlinson-Keasey, C., Martin, L. R., Wingard, D. L., & Criqui, M. H. (1995). Psychosocial and behavioral predictors of longevity: The aging and death of the "Termites." *American Psychologist, 50,* 69–78.

Gall, T. L., & Evans, D. R. (1987). The dimensionality of cognitive appraisal and its relationship to physical and psychological well-being. *The Journal of Psychology, 121,* 539–546.

Hart, K. E., & Hittner, J. B. (1995). Optimism and pessimism: Associations to coping and anger-reactivity. *Personality and Individual Differences, 19,* 827–839.

Harvey, J. H., & Miller, E. D. (1998). Toward a psychology of loss. *Psychological Science, 9,* 429–434.

Hobfoll, S. E. (1988). *The ecology of stress.* New York: Hemisphere.

Hobfoll, S. E., & Lerman, M. (1988). Personal relationships, personal attributes, and stress resistance: Mother's reactions to their child's illness. *American Journal of Community Psychology, 16,* 565–589.

Hobfoll, S. E., & London, P. (1986). The relationship of self-concept and social support to emotional distress among women during war. *Journal of Social and Clinical Psychology, 4,* 189–203.

Hobfoll, S. E., London, P., & Orr, E. (1988). Mastery, intimacy, and stress resistance during war. *Journal of Community Psychology, 16,* 317–331.

Hobfoll, S. E., & Walfisch, S. (1984). Coping with a threat to life: A longitudinal study of self-concept, social support, and psychological distress. *American Journal of Community Psychology, 12,* 87–100.

Hobfoll, S. E., & Walfisch, S. (1986). Stressful events, mastery, and depression: An evaluation of crisis theory. *Journal of Community Psychology, 14,* 183–195.

Holahan, C. J., & Moos, R. H. (1986). Personality, coping, and family resources in stress resistance: A longitudinal analysis. *Journal of Personality and Social Psychology, 51,* 389–395.

Holahan, C. J., & Moos, R. H. (1987). Personal and contextual determinants of coping strategies. *Journal of Personality and Social Psychology, 52,* 946–955.

Holahan, C. J., & Moos, R. H. (1990). Life stressors, resistance factors, and improved psychological functioning: An extension of the stress resistance paradigm. *Journal of Personality and Social Psychology, 58,* 909–917.

Holahan, C. J., Moos, R. H., & Schaefer, J. A. (1996). Coping, stress resistance, and growth: Conceptualizing adaptive functioning. In M. Zeidner & N. S. Endler (Eds.), *Handbook of Coping: Theory, Research, Applications* (pp. 24–43). New York: Wiley.

Holman, E. A., & Silver, R. C. (1996). Is it abuse or the aftermath? A stress and coping approach to understanding responses to incest. *Journal of Social and Clinical Psychology, 15,* 318–339.

Horowitz, M. J. (1976). *Stress response syndromes.* New York: Jason Aronson.

Horowitz, M. J. (1979). Psychological response to serious life events. In V. Hamilton & D. M. Warburton (Eds.), *Human stress and cognition: An information processing approach* (pp. 235–263). New York: Wiley.

Horowitz, M. J., Wilner, N., & Alvarez, W. (1979). Impact of Events Scale: A measure of subjective stress. *Psychosomatic Medicine, 41,* 209–218.

Hovanitz, C. A. (1986). Life event stress and coping style as contributors to psychopathology. *Journal of Clinical Psychology, 42,* 34–41.

Ironson, G., Wynings, C., Schneiderman, N., Baum, A., Rodriguez, M., Greenwood, D., Benight, C., Antoni, M., LaPerriere, A., Huang, H. S., Klimas, N., & Fletcher, M. A. (1997). Post-traumatic stress symptoms, intrusive thoughts, loss, and immune function after Hurricane Andrew. *Psychosomatic Medicine, 59,* 128–141.

Janoff-Bulman, R. (1989). Assumptive worlds and the stress of traumatic events: Applications of the schema construct. *Social Cognition, 7,* 113–136.

Janoff-Bulman, R. (1992). *Shattered assumptions: Towards a new psychology of trauma.* New York: Free Press.

Kamen-Siegel, L., Rodin, J., Seligman, M. E. P., & Dwyer, J. (1991). Explanatory style and cell-mediated immunity in elderly men and women. *Health Psychology, 10,* 229–235.

Keane, T. M., & Wolfe, J. (1990). Comorbidity in post-traumatic stress disorder: An analysis of community and clinical studies. *Journal of Applied Social Psychology, 20,* 1776–1788.

Kendler, K. S., Karkowski, L. M., & Prescott, C. A. (1998). Stressful life events and major depression: Risk period, long-term contextual threat and diagnostic specificity. *Journal of Nervous and Mental Disease, 186,* 661–669.

Kendler, K. S., Kessler, R. C., Heath, A. C., Neale, M. C., & Eaves, L. J. (1991). Coping: A genetic epidemiological investigation. *Psychological Medicine, 21,* 337–346.

Kobasa, S. C. (1979). Stressful life events and health: An inquiry into hardiness. *Journal of Personality and Social Psychology, 37,* 1–11.

Lazarus, R. S., & Folkman, S. (1984). *Stress, appraisal, and coping.* New York: Springer.

Lee, K. A., Vaillant, G. E., Torrey, W. C., & Elder, G. H. (1995). A 50-year prospective study of the psychological sequelae of World War II combat. *American Journal of Psychiatry, 152,* 516–522.

Lehman, D., Davis, C., DeLongis, A., Wortman, C., Bluck, S., Mandel, D., & Ellard, J. (1993). Positive and negative life changes following bereavement and their relations to adjustment. *Journal of Social and Clinical Psychology, 12,* 90–112.

Lepore, S. J., Silver, R. C., Wortman, C. B., & Wayment, H. A. (1996). Social constraints, intrusive thoughts, and depressive symptoms among bereaved mothers. *Journal of Personality and Social Psychology, 70,* 271–282.

Marshall, G. N., & Lang, E. L. (1990). Optimism, self-mastery, and symptoms of depression in women professionals. *Journal of Personality and Social Psychology, 59,* 132–139.

Marshall, G. N., Wortman, C. B., Kusulas, J. W., Hervig, L. K., & Vickers, R. R., Jr. (1992). Distinguishing optimism from pessimism: Relations to fundamental dimensions of mood and personality. *Journal of Personality and Social Psychology, 62,* 1067–1074.

McCarroll, J. E., Fagan, J. G., Hermsen, J. M., & Ursano, R. J. (1997). Posttraumatic stress disorder in U.S. Army Vietnam veterans who served in the Persian Gulf War. *Journal of Nervous and Mental Disease, 185,* 682–685.

McCrae, R. R. (1984). Situational determinants of coping responses: Loss, threat, and challenge. *Journal of Personality and Social Psychology, 46,* 919–928.

McCrae, R. R. (1992). Situational determinants of coping. In B. N. Carpenter (Ed.), *Personal coping: Theory, research, and application* (pp. 65–76). Westport, CT: Praeger.

McCrae, R. R., & Costa, P. T., Jr. (1986). Personality, coping, and coping effectiveness. *Journal of Personality, 54,* 385–405.

McLaney, A., Tennen, H., Affleck, G., & Fitzgerald, T. (1995). Reactions to impaired fertility: The vicissitudes of primary and secondary control appraisals. *Women's Health: Research on Gender, Behavior, and Policy, 1,* 143–160.

McMillen, J. C., Smith, E. H., & Fisher, R. H. (1997). Perceived benefit and mental health after three types of disaster. *Journal of Consulting and Clinical Psychology, 65,* 733–739.

Mechanic, D. (1977). Illness behavior, social adaptation, and the management of illness. *Journal of Nervous and Mental Disease, 165,* 79–87.

Meichenbaum, D. (1985). *Stress inoculation training.* New York: Pergamon.

Mendola, R., Tennen, H., Affleck, G., McCann, L., & Fitzgerald, T. (1990). Appraisal and adaptation among women with impaired fertility. *Cognitive Therapy and Research, 14,* 79–93.

Miller, S. M., Rodoletz, M., Schroeder, C. M., Mangan, C. E., & Sedlacek, T. V. (1996). Applications of the monitoring process model to coping with severe long-term medical threats. *Health Psychology, 15,* 216–225.

Moss-Morris, R., Petrie, K. J., & Weinman, J. (1996). Functioning in chronic fatigue syndrome: Do illness perceptions play a regulatory role? *British Journal of Health Psychology, 1,* 15–25.

Mroczek, D. K., Spiro, A., Aldwin, C. M., Ozer, D. J., & Bosse, R. (1993). Construct validation of optimism and pessimism in older men: Findings from the normative aging study. *Health Psychology, 12,* 406–409.

Nolen-Hoeksema, S., & Morrow, J. (1991). A prospective study of depression and posttraumatic stress symptoms after a natural disaster: The 1989 Loma Prieta earthquake. *Journal of Personality and Social Psychology, 61,* 115–121.

Nolen-Hoeksema, S., Parker, L. E., & Larson, J. (1994). Ruminative coping with depressed mood following loss. *Journal of Personality and Social Psychology, 67,* 92–104.

Norris, F. H. (1990). Screening for traumatic stress: A scale for use in the general population. *Journal of Applied Social Psychology, 20,* 1704–1718.

O'Leary, V. E., & Ickovics, J. R. (1995). Resilience and thriving in response to challenge: An opportunity for a paradigm shift in women's health. *Women's Health: Research on Gender, Behavior, and Policy, 1,* 121–142.

Park, C. L. (1998a). Implications of growth for individuals. In R. G. Tedeschi, C. L. Park, & L. G. Calhoun (Eds.), *Posttraumatic growth: Positive change in the aftermath of crises* (pp. 153–177). Mahwah, NJ: Erlbaum.

Park, C. L. (1998b). Stress-related growth and thriving through coping: The roles of personality and cognitive processes. *Journal of Social Issues, 54,* 267–277.

Park, C. L., Cohen, L. H., & Murch, R. L. (1996). Assessment and prediction of stress-related growth. *Journal of Personality, 64,* 71–105.

Paterson, R. J., & Neufeld, R. W. J. (1987). Clear danger: Situational determinants of the appraisal of threat. *Psychological Bulletin, 101,* 404–416.

Pearlin, L. I., Menaghan, E. G., Lieberman, M. A., & Mullan, J. T. (1981). The stress process. *Journal of Health and Social Behavior, 22,* 337–356.

Pearlin, L. I., & Schooler, C. (1978). The structure of coping. *Journal of Health and Social Behavior, 19,* 2–21.

Peterson, C., Seligman, M. E. P., & Vaillant, G. E. (1988). Pessimistic explanatory style is a risk factor for physical illness: A thirty-five-year longitudinal study. *Journal of Personality and Social Psychology, 55,* 23–27.

Plomin, R., Scheier, M. F., Bergeman, C. S., Pedersen, N. L., Nesselroade, J. R., & McClearn, G. E. (1992). Optimism, pessimism and mental health: A twin/adoption analysis. *Personality and Individual Differences, 13,* 921–930.

Prager, E., & Solomon, Z. (1995). Perceptions of world benevolence, meaningfulness, and self-worth among elderly Israeli holocaust survivors and non-survivors. *Anxiety, Stress, and Coping: An International Journal, 8,* 265–277.

Reed, G. M. (1989). *Stress, coping, and psychological adaptation in a sample of gay and bisexual men with AIDS.* Unpublished doctoral dissertation, University of California, Los Angeles.

Robinson-Whelen, S., Kim, C., MacCallum, R. C, & Kiecolt-Glaser, J. K. (1997). Distinguishing optimism from pessimism in older adults: Is it more important to be optimistic or not to be pessimistic? *Journal of Personality and Social Psychology, 73,* 1345–1353.

Rothbaum, F., Weisz, J. R., & Snyder, S. S. (1982). Changing the world and changing the self: A two-process model of perceived control. *Journal of Personality and Social Psychology, 42,* 5–37.

Rotter, J. B. (1966). Generalized expectancies for internal versus external control of reinforcement. *Psychological Monographs, 80,* 1–28.

Sandler, I., & Lakey, B. (1982). Locus of control as a stress moderator: The role of control perceptions and social support. *American Journal of Community Psychology, 10,* 65–80.

Scheier, M. F., & Carver, C. S. (1985). Optimism, coping, and health: Assessment and implications of generalized outcome expectancies. *Health Psychology, 4,* 219–247.

Scheier, M. F., Weintraub, J. K., & Carver, C. S. (1986). Coping with stress: Divergent strategies of optimists and pessimists. *Journal of Personality and Social Psychology, 51,* 1257–1264.

Schwartzberg, S. S. (1993). Struggling for meaning: How HIV-positive gay men make sense of AIDS. *Professional Psychology: Research and Practice, 24,* 483–490.

Schwartzberg, S. S., & Janoff-Bulman, R. (1991). Grief and the search for meaning: Exploring the assumptive worlds of bereaved college students. *Journal of Social and Clinical Psychology, 10,* 270–288.

Seeman, T. E., Berkman, L. F., Gulanski, B. I., Robbins, R. J., Greenspan, S. L., Charpentier, P. A., & Rowe, J. W. (1995). Self-esteem and neuroendocrine response to challenge: MacArthur studies of successful aging. *Journal of Psychosomatic Research, 39,* 69–84.

Shaham, Y., Singer, J. E., & Schaeffer, M. H. (1992). Stability/instability of cognitive strategies across tasks determine whether stress will affect judgmental processes. *Journal of Applied Social Psychology, 22,* 691–713.

Shanan, J., & Shahar, O. (1983). Cognitive and personality functioning of Jewish Holocaust survivors during the midlife transition (46–65) in Israel. *Archiv fur die Gesamte Psychologie, 135,* 275–294.

Silver, R. L. (1982). *Coping with an undesirable life event: A study of early reactions to physical disability.* Unpublished doctoral dissertation, Northwestern University, Evanston, IL.

Silver, R. L., Boon, C., & Stones, M. H. (1983). Searching for meaning in misfortune: Making sense of incest. *Journal of Social Issues, 39,* 81–102.

Skaff, M. M., Pearlin, L. I., & Mullan, J. T. (1996). Transition in the caregiving career: Effects of sense of mastery. *Psychology and Aging, 11,* 247–257.

Sledge, W. H., Boydstun, M. C., & Rabe, A. J. (1980). Self-concept changes related to war captivity. *Archives of General Psychiatry, 37,* 430–443.

Solomon, Z., Benbenishty, R., & Mikulincer, M. (1991). The contribution of wartime, pre-war, and post-war factors to self-efficacy: A longitudinal study of combat stress reaction. *Journal of Traumatic Stress, 4,* 345–361.

Solomon, Z., Mikulincer, M., & Flum, H. (1988). Negative life events, coping responses, and combat-related psychopathology: A prospective study. *Journal of Abnormal Psychology, 97,* 302–307.

Stewart, A. J., & Salt, P. (1981). Life stress, life-styles, depression, and illness in adult women. *Journal of Personality and Social Psychology, 40,* 1063–1069.

Stewart, A. J., Sokol, M., Healy, J. M., & Chester, N. L. (1986). Longitudinal studies of psychological consequences of life changes in children and adults. *Journal of Personality and Social Psychology, 50,* 143–151.

Stewart, S. M., Betson, C., Lam, T. H., Marshall, I. B., Lee, P. W. H., & Wong, C. M. (1997). Predicting stress in first year medical students: A longitudinal study. *Medical Education, 31,* 163–168.

Suls, J., & Fletcher, B. (1985). The relative efficacy of avoidant and nonavoidant coping strategies: A meta-analysis. *Health Psychology, 4,* 249–288.

Sutker, P. B., Davis, J. M., Uddo, M., & Ditta, S. B. (1995). War zone stress, personal resources, and PTSD in Persian Gulf War returnees. *Journal of Abnormal Psychology, 104,* 444–452.

Tait, R., & Silver, R. C. (1989). Coming to terms with major negative life events. In J. S. Uleman & J. A. Bargh (Eds.), *Unintended thought* (pp. 351–382). New York: Guilford.

Taylor, S. E. (1983). Adjustment to threatening events: A theory of cognitive adaptation. *American Psychologist, 38,* 1161–1173.

Taylor, S. E., & Brown, J. D. (1988). Illusion and well-being: a social psychological perspective on mental health. *Psychological Bulletin, 103,* 193–210.

Taylor, S. E., & Clark, L. F. (1986). Does information improve adjustment to noxious events? In M. J. Saks & L. Saxe (Eds.), *Advances in applied social psychology* (Vol. 3, pp. 1–28). Hillsdale, NJ: Erlbaum.

Taylor, S. E., & Gollwitzer, P. M. (1995). Effects of mindset on positive illusions. *Journal of Personality and Social Psychology, 69,* 213–226.

Taylor, S. E., Helgeson, V. S., Reed, G. M., & Skokan, L. A. (1991). Self-generated feelings of control and adjustment to physical illness. *Journal of Social Issues, 47,* 91–109.

Taylor, S. E., Kemeny, M. E., Aspinwall, L. G., Schneider, S. G., Rodriguez, R., & Herbert, M. (1992). Optimism, coping, psychological distress, and high-risk sexual behavior among men at risk for acquired immune immunodeficiency syndrome (AIDS). *Journal of Personality and Social Psychology, 63,* 460–473.

Taylor, S. E., Kemeny, M. E., Reed, G. M., & Aspinwall, L. G. (1991). Assault on the self: Positive illusions and adjustment to threatening events. In J. Strauss & G. R. Goethals (Eds.), *The self: Interdisciplinary approaches* (pp. 239–254). New York: Springer-Verlag.

Taylor, S. E., Lichtman, R. R., & Wood, J. V. (1984). Attributions, beliefs in control, and adjustment to breast cancer. *Journal of Personality and Social Psychology, 46,* 489–502.

Taylor, S. E., & Lobel, M. (1989). Social comparison activity under threat: Downward evaluations and upward contacts. *Psychological Review, 96,* 569–575.

Taylor, S. E., & Seeman, T. E. (2000). Psychosocial resources and the SES/health relationship. In N. Adler, M. Marmot, & B. McEwen (Eds.), *Socioeconomic status and health in industrial nations: Social, psychological, and biological pathways* (pp. 210–225). New York: New York Academy of Sciences.

Taylor, S. E., Wood, J. V., & Lichtman, R. R. (1983). It could be worse: Selective evaluation as a response to victimization. *Journal of Social Issues, 39,* 19–40.

Tedeschi, R. G., & Calhoun, L. G. (1995). *Trauma and transformation: Growing in the aftermath of suffering.* New York: Sage.

Tempelaar, R., de Haes, J. C. J. M., de Ruiter, J. H., Bakker, D., van den Heuvel, W. J. A., & van Nieuwenhuizen, M. A. (1989). The social experiences of cancer patients under treatment: A comparative study. *Social Science and Medicine, 29,* 635–642.

Thoits, P. A. (1994). Stressors and problem-solving: The individual as psychological activist. *Journal of Health and Social Behavior, 35,* 143–159.

Thomas, L. E., DiGiulio, R. C., & Sheehan, N. W. (1991). Identifying loss and psychological crisis in widowhood. *International Journal of Aging and Human Development, 26,* 279–295.

Thompson, S. C. (1981). Will it hurt less if I can control it? A complex answer to a simple question. *Psychological Bulletin, 90,* 89–101.

Thompson, S. C. (1985). Finding positive meaning in a stressful event and coping. *Basic and Applied Social Psychology, 6,* 279–295.

Thompson, S. C., Nanni, C., & Levine, A. (1994). Primary versus secondary and central versus consequence-related control in HIV-positive men. *Journal of Personality and Social Psychology, 67,* 540–547.

Tomaka, J., & Blascovich, J. (1994). Effects of justice beliefs on cognitive appraisal of and subjective, physiological, and behavioral responses to potential stress. *Journal of Personality and Social Psychology, 67,* 732–740.

Updegraff, J. A., Taylor, S. E., Kemeny, M. E., & Wyatt, G. E. (2000). *The positive and negative effects of HIV-infection in women with low socioeconomic resources.* Manuscript submitted for publication.

van Eck, M., Berkhof, H., Nicolson, N., & Sulon, J. (1996). The effects of perceived stress, traits, and mood states and stressful daily events on salivary cortisol. *Psychosomatic Medicine, 58,* 447–458.

Visotsky, H. M., Hamburg, D. A., Goss, M. E., & Lebovits, B. Z. (1961). Coping behavior under extreme stress. *Archives of General Psychiatry, 5,* 423–448.

Wallerstein, J. S. (1986). Women after divorce: Preliminary report from a ten-year follow-up. *American Journal of Orthopsychiatry, 56,* 65–77.

Watson, D., & Clark, L. A. (1984). Negative affectivity: The disposition to experience aversive emotional states. *Psychological Bulletin, 96,* 465–490.

Wegner, D. M. (1994). The ironic processes of mental control. *Psychological Review, 101,* 34–52.

Werner, E. E. (1986). Resilient offspring of alcoholics: A longitudinal study from birth to age 18. *Journal of Studies on Alcohol, 47,* 34–40.

Werner, E. E., & Smith, R. S. (1982). *Vulnerable but invincible: A longitudinal study of resilient children and youth.* New York: McGraw-Hill.

Whisman, M. A., & Kwon, P. (1993). Life stress and dysphoria: The role of self-esteem and hopelessness. *Journal of Personality and Social Psychology, 65,* 1054–1060.

Wortman, C. B., & Silver, R. C. (1987). Coping with irrevocable loss. In G. R. VandenBos & B. K. Bryant (Eds.), *Cataclysms, crises, and catastrophes: Psychology in action* (pp. 189–235). Washington, DC: American Psychological Association.

Wortman, C. B., & Silver, R. C. (1989). The myths of coping with loss. *Journal of Consulting and Clinical Psychology, 57,* 349–357.

Yarom, N. (1983). Facing death in war: An existential crises. In S. Breznitz (Ed.), *Stress in Israel* (pp. 3–38). New York: Van Nostrand Reinhold.

Yehuda, R., Southwick, S. M., & Giller, E. L. (1992). Exposure to atrocities and severity of chronic posttraumatic stress disorder in Vietnam combat veterans. *American Journal of Psychiatry, 149,* 333–336.

Ronnie Janoff-Bulman
Andrea R. Berger

The Other Side of Trauma: Towards a Psychology of Appreciation

Were we asked to predict the psychological impact of traumatic life events, most of us would no doubt focus on negative reactions such as intense anxiety, depression, and disorientation. We would not be entirely incorrect, for these surely are common responses to traumatic events. However, we would be only partially correct, because we would have failed to recognize another, quite different, set of reactions. This other side is the positive impact of trauma. In recent years much attention has been devoted to survivors' reports of benefits following their traumatic experience (see, e.g., Affleck & Tennen, 1996; Affleck, Tennen, & Gershman, 1985; Collins, Taylor, & Skokan, 1990; Janoff-Bulman, 1985, 1992; Lehman et al., 1993; Schwartzberg, 1996; Taylor, 1983; Taylor, Lichtman, & Wood, 1984; Tedeschi & Calhoun, 1995, 1996; Tennen & Affleck, 1999; Thompson, 1985; Thompson & Janigian, 1988; Wortman & Silver, 1987). Researchers no longer regard these perceived benefits as the responses of just a few, or the minor responses of many, but as a powerful reaction reported by the majority of survivors.

Our own erroneous, or at least limited, prediction in failing to recognize the positive impact of trauma is consistent with recent work by Gilbert and his colleagues (Gilbert, Pinel, Wilson, Blumberg, & Wheatley, 1998), which demonstrated that people overestimate the duration of negative affect following negative events and fail to take into account the "psychological immune system" that actively operates to "convert adversity into prosperity" (p. 619). Whether we recognize it or not, however, the psychological immune system of survivors is thankfully very active and effective in the aftermath of traumatic life events. A closer look at the diverse benefits reported by survivors finds that essentially all represent instances of increased appreciation; in the face of painful losses, survivors discover and create greater value in their lives.

The psychological literature is essentially silent on the topic of appreciation, and thus a study of the responses of trauma survivors can serve to provide not only a greater understanding of the coping processes following extreme negative events, but of the psychological processes potentially involved in producing greater appreciation in the lives of nonvictims as well. Our primary task, then, is to explore the ways in which appreciation is experienced in the aftermath of trauma. However, in order to understand survivors' experiences of appreciation—the positive side of trauma—we must familiarize ourselves with the negative side, with the losses that accompany traumatic experiences, for the two sides of trauma are closely linked. We will then focus more specifically on the psychological processes or mechanisms that underlie instances of value creation, in order to provide a basis for understanding, more generally, the psychology of appreciation.

☐ The Negative Side of Trauma: Loss and Vulnerability

The losses most readily associated with trauma are those that are physical or evident in the survivor's external circumstances. Examples include the absence created by the death of a loved one, decreased health or physical harm resulting from disease, accident, or physical violation by another, and the destruction of a home by fire. These are the losses that are most apparent to others and consequently seem to define the essence of the traumatic experience. Yet there is another kind of loss that characterizes the aftermath of extreme, negative events; this is the psychological loss that results from fundamental changes in survivors' world-views and feelings of safety and security. This is the loss of invulnerability, which so readily, yet typically unknowingly, underlies the daily activities of nonvictims.

In years of studying survivors' responses, the phrase heard most often was, "I never thought it could happen to me." We generally navigate our life-course with a sense of security and invulnerability. Somehow, we know that bad things happen, but deep in our psyches and deep in our guts we don't believe they will happen to us (see, e.g., Lifton, 1967; Perloff, 1983; Weinstein, 1989; Wolfenstein, 1957). We feel protected, yet we are generally unaware of this assumption until we are victimized. For some, this sense of safety derives from an ability to ignore or underestimate general base-rates of negative events; for others, there is a recognition of misfortune, but a simultaneous belief that they are somehow protected because they are careful people who take adequate precautions. Thus, if we eat well, exercise, and avoid too much stress we can avoid disease, as can our loved ones; if we drive carefully and attend to the road we can avoid auto accidents; if we are cautious about where and when we walk in the big city, we can avoid assaults, and the list goes on, specifying personal and societally-shared heuristics for avoiding negative outcomes. Yet good, careful, caring people contract life-threatening diseases, are raped or physically assaulted, and get into disabling accidents. All of the precautions one might consider will not decrease the likelihood of misfortune to zero. Yet we live our lives feeling secure and protected. Our mind "tries to protect us by enslaving us to false illusions that absolute safety is possible" (Gould, 1978, p. 218).

This sense of invulnerability is a natural and expected consequence of a set of fundamental assumptions about ourselves and our world that are built up over years of experience and constitute the core of our inner world. At the foundation of our cognitive-emotional systems are theories or working models that guide our interactions and typically go unchallenged (Bowlby, 1969; Epstein, 1973, 1991; Janoff-Bulman, 1985,

1992; McCann & Pearlman, 1990). Three of these core assumptions regarding ourselves, the external world, and the relationship between the two are the belief that the world is meaningful, the world is benevolent, and we are worthy, competent people (Janoff-Bulman, 1985, 1992).

Most fundamentally, we believe that our world is meaningful in the sense that events are not random; rather, there is a comprehensible relationship between people and what happens to them. The world makes sense because there is a person-outcome contingency. Just as in science phenomena are comprehensible if they fit certain accepted laws or theories, so in our daily lives outcomes make sense if they fit accepted social laws or theories. In Western cultures, these are generally theories of justice or control. When we invoke justice, we believe people get what they deserve and deserve what they get (Lerner, 1980); thus, good, decent caring people will experience good fortune, whereas bad, morally corrupt people will experience misfortune. These theories of justice and deservingness are often the basis for religious beliefs about the distribution of outcomes (e.g., Pargament, Ensing, Falgout, Olsen, Reilly, Van Haitsma, & Warren, 1990).

When we invoke control to explain the relationship between people and their outcomes, we focus on actions and behaviors, rather than character. We assume that by engaging in the "correct" behaviors, we can bring about positive outcomes and avoid negative ones. Yet researchers have consistently demonstrated that we overestimate our control over events (e.g., Gilovich, 1991; Henslin, 1967; Langer, 1975; Wortman, 1975). Those who think they can eliminate the threat of heart disease by running, of an auto accident by driving carefully, of assault by walking in the "right" neighborhoods are assuming they can prevent misfortune through their own actions. Theories of control and justice are the most common means of making sense of events in Western culture; other cultures have developed other theories to account for the selective incidence of events—why they happen to particular people. Among the Azande of the Sudan, for example, witchcraft is invoked to explain the death of a child whose boat was overturned by a hippopotamus (Gluckman, 1944). Across different cultures, people strive to believe that harm and misfortune are not arbitrary, random events, but rather that their world makes sense.

This belief in the meaningfulness of the world coexists with two other related assumptions that reflect positive views of the world and the self. In general, we believe the world is a good place, or more specifically, that *our* world is a good place. It is not that we are unaware of misery, pain, and oppression, but rather that we make a psychological distinction between the world in general and the world in which we live. The people and events that touch us constitute our world, and it is these people and events we expect to be benevolent rather than malevolent. Thus, people are typically very optimistic about their own outcomes (Taylor, 1990), even if they are pessimistic about the fate of their nation or the larger world (e.g., Watts & Free, 1978). We expect others to care about us and treat us well, reflecting what Maya Angelou has called an "unconscious innocence" (Weller, 1973). This is in part related to a third assumption: the belief that we are worthy, good, competent people. This global self-evaluation largely reflects our ability to focus on our positive qualities, ignore our weaknesses, overvalue our strengths, and exaggerate our responsibility for positive outcomes (Brown, 1986; Greenwald, 1980; Snyder, Higgins, & Stucky, 1983; Taylor, 1990; Taylor & Brown, 1988). In terms of justice we are the kind of people who deserve good outcomes; in terms of control, we engage in careful, precautionary behaviors. Our world is a good place, and outcomes are not randomly distributed. Surely, we believe, bad things won't happen to us.

Yet traumatic events happen in spite of our deepest feelings of safety and security, and they happen to the good, the bad, the careful, and the careless. When tragedy strikes, our fundamental assumptions are shattered (Janoff-Bulman, 1985, 1992), our protective illusions are destroyed, and survivors are forced to confront their own vulnerability and fragility. Diseases, accidents, and assaults force survivors to acknowledge the possibility of their own annihilation and they experience "a jarring awareness of the fact of death" (Lifton, 1967, p. 35). Stripped of their illusions, they see themselves as helpless inhabitants of a malevolent, meaningless world and consequently experience intense anxiety, depression, and disorientation. Terror characterizes the immediate aftermath of trauma, for the universe is now perceived as threatening and frightening, and their disintegrated inner world no longer provides a road map for negotiating daily life.

As survivors cope in the aftermath of extreme negative events, they rebuild their inner worlds (Janoff-Bulman, 1985, 1992; Schwartzberg & Janoff-Bulman, 1991; see also Horowitz, 1976; Tait & Silver, 1989). Although the terror of the experience subsides, and survivors typically rebuild viable, more comfortable self- and world-views, they nevertheless retain a fundamental awareness of the fragility of existence and the possibility of loss. No longer can they say, "I never thought it could happen to me"; survivors know it happened to them and could happen again. Yet it is this very acknowledgment of loss and vulnerability that lays the groundwork for the work of value creation and the positive effects of trauma.

☐ The Positive Side of Trauma: Appreciation and Value Creation

Posttrauma, the experience of survivors is not simply more negative, reflecting inconsolable and all-encompassing anxiety and depression, but positive as well. It is not a case of either-or, of losses versus gains, but rather of losses and gains coexisting (e.g., Collins et al., 1990; Harvey, Orbuch, Weber, Merbach, & Alt, 1992; Janoff-Bulman, 1985, 1992; Lehman et al., 1993; Tedeschi & Calhoun, 1996). With its pain and disillusionment, trauma provides an unexpected opportunity for survivors to create greater value in their lives, or more accurately, to increase the value of particular aspects of their lives. They experience greater *appreciation*, which by definition involves an appraisal of increased value or worth (see Singer, 1996). Thus, from an economic perspective, when goods appreciate, they increase in value; from a psychological perspective, when we appreciate something, we increase its perceived value in our eyes. Interestingly, according to philosopher Irving Singer (1994), love is a process of bestowing value on another; as such, it is actually a form of appreciation. Created by an act of the imagination, love, according to Singer (1994), augments not only the beloved, but the lover as well.

We typically don't value the ordinary; we only do so by regarding it somehow as extra-ordinary. And thus appreciation entails an attribution of specialness. It is this perceived specialness that leads us to the perception of value and worth. In the aftermath of trauma, survivors typically report newfound appreciation in one or more of the following domains: greater appreciation of others, greater appreciation of the self, and greater appreciation of life itself. These domains parallel the three areas that constitute the foci of our fundamental assumptions pre-victimization: the assumption of benevolence in others, the assumption of self-worth, and the assumption of contingent outcomes (i.e., meaningfulness) in life insuring against unpredictability and randomness.

It is particularly ironic that in the aftermath of trauma, when the meaningless of the world becomes all too apparent, another type of meaning-making takes hold, that associated with the creation of value in survivors' lives. At issue are two very different understandings of meaning: meaning as comprehensibility and meaning as significance (Janoff-Bulman & Frantz, 1997). Whereas the first addresses questions about whether an outcome makes sense, the second is concerned with value and worth. It is meaning as comprehensibility that gets shattered by the experience of trauma, leaving the survivor all too aware of randomness and human vulnerability. Yet, in the face of this newfound awareness, survivors create their own meaning in life. They are less concerned with questions about the meaningfulness of life in general than questions about meaning in their own life, and they minimize their existential crisis by generating significance through appraisals of value and worth. In other words, they engage in a re-"valuation" of their lives and in doing so experience a newfound sense of appreciation.

☐ The Importance of Attending and Noticing

The real voyage of discovery consists not in seeing new landscapes, but in having new eyes.

Marcel Proust

Most of us move through life largely in automatic mode, paying little attention to numerous aspects of our lives. In the interests of conserving mental energy, we do a great deal automatically via a process of overlearning. Thus, we are well aware of the phenomenon of driving to a destination and arriving without any awareness of how we got there, although we know we were at the wheel of the car. Alfred North Whitehead once noted that civilization advances by increasing the number of important operations we can perform without thinking about them, and thus such automatic behaviors are sometimes regarded as accomplishments (Whitehead, 1911). When there is little need to devote mental resources to particular behaviors or stimuli, we don't pay attention; and the more things stay the same, the more routinized the behaviors, the less likely we are to notice and pay attention to specifics. We are simply not motivated to attend, although we are certainly capable of more highly controlled, effortful mental processing.

Researchers typically operationalize our automatic mode by creating conditions of overload in experiments; participants are asked to memorize minute details of a passage, leaving few mental resources available to attend to other aspects of the experiment. Such overload is intended largely to parallel our daily lives, in which there is so much going on that we notice little; only when we are highly motivated to attend to a particular stimulus or feature of our lives do we truly attend. Overall, then, the routinization, pace, and complexity of our lives typically account for an automatic style of existence and information processing. In other words, we rarely stop to smell the roses, because they are not apt to be noticed along the busy path we walk daily.

To increase the value of something—to appreciate it—we must perceive it as special and recognize its worth, rather than simply take it for granted. Routinization and constancies are enemies of appreciation, for by definition they seem to deny the perception of specialness. And appreciation is certainly not a necessary consequence of good fortune, which is all the more likely to generate an attitude of blind acceptance and inattentiveness. This, of course, is the essence of Emily's poignant realization in Thornton Wilder's (1975) play, *Our Town*. She is given the opportunity to witness daily life in Grover's Corners after her own death and tearfully admits, "I didn't realize. So all that was going on and we never noticed? . . . Oh, earth, you're too wonderful for anybody to realize you" (p. 138). This sentiment is echoed by another deceased character who notes, "Yes, now you know. Now you know! That's what it was to be alive. To move about in a cloud of ignorance . . . To spend and waste time as though you had a million years" (pp. 139–140).

Survivors no longer operate on automatic, for they have been shaken from the comfort and complacency of their pretrauma existence. Their lives have been dislodged from any routine, and their disintegrated inner worlds require intense attention to daily existence, for things are no longer as they had seemed. It is a time of exquisite, if painful, sensitivity to the pushes and pulls of life. For trauma survivors, the mundane and everyday are no longer "just business as usual," but rather experiences all the more remarkable because of their natural contrast to their extreme negative experience. The traumatic event serves as a salient touchstone, an ever-available comparison against which to perceive and appraise daily experiences (for different explanations of this contrast effect, see, e.g., Brickman, Coates, & Janoff-Bulman, 1978, and Helson, 1964, on adaptation level theory; Kahneman & Miller, 1986, on norm theory; Kahneman & Tversky, 1982, and Taylor & Schneider, 1989, on simulation processes; and Kahneman & Tversky, 1973, on anchoring and adjustment processes). Trauma survivors take little for granted; they are motivated to live life differently—to pay attention and consciously notice what is around them—and attending and noticing are necessary elements of value creation. Yet, although necessary, attending and noticing are not sufficient. In the process of noticing, we must make an attribution of specialness in order to experience appreciation, and this process of value creation is most apparent in survivors' appraisals of life, other people, and their own strengths.

Appreciating Life Itself: Mortality as a Basis for Valuing

Most of us unwittingly may live, as Wilder's character proposes, as if we believed we had a million years, but survivors surely do not. They have been forced to confront their own fragility and to acknowledge their own vulnerability. Survivors live with an awareness of mortality and the real constraints imposed by death. And yet it is this very awareness of the ever-present possibility of loss that reveals what it is to be alive (see Singer, 1996). Once the reality of death intrudes, life can no longer be taken for granted. Not surprisingly, then, survivors commonly report a newfound appreciation for life itself (e.g., Affleck, Tennen, & Gershman, 1985; Collins, Taylor, & Skokan, 1990; Janoff-Bulman, 1992; Joseph, Williams, & Yule, 1993; Schwartzberg, 1996; Schwartzberg & Janoff-Bulman, 1991; Taylor, 1983; Taylor, Lichtman, & Wood, 1984;

Taylor, Wood, & Lichtman, 1983; Tedeschi & Calhoun, 1996; Thompson, 1985; Thompson & Janigian, 1988). Comments such as "I never knew I was alive before . . . ", "I now know that life is precious . . . ", and "Before I was just going through the motions, whereas now I appreciate being alive" are commonly voiced by survivors.

Once confronted head-on with the possibility of nonexistence, survivors become aware of the amazing fact of existence. Often they seem to experience something akin to Joseph Campbell's (1988) "rapture of living" or Wittgenstein's sense of "astonishment that anything exists" (see Singer, 1996). For many philosophers, ontological anxiety and ontological wonder often exist side by side, for the recognition that "I may die" and that everything adds up to nothingness also allows individuals to intuit the mystery and wonder of what it means to be alive (see Singer, 1996, for a review of philosophical perspectives on this topic).

For survivors, the anxiety associated with vulnerability remains but does not wholly define their emotional life. Rather, more positive emotions and appraisals coexist with the awareness of vulnerability, and these include a profound sense of appreciation of life. It is this recognition of the value of life itself that leads survivors to take seriously their new choices and commitments. They often establish new goals and new priorities; by valuing life itself, they create renewed meaning in their own lives through these choices. Life is to be lived fully, based on deliberate choices, in essence demonstrating Sartre's (1964, 1966) proposition that in the face of absurdity and dread, we must make our choices about what matters and thereby create our own values out of nothingness. Thus survivors frequently report the importance of spending more time with family and friends, turning to spiritual pursuits, or engaging in altruistic activities. Life is now perceived as precious, and it is not to be wasted.

The particular value accorded life itself is poignantly illustrated by the account of a woman who recently approached the first author to tell of her traumatic experience. Now in her mid-40s, she had lost her husband while in her late 30s. He, too, was in his late 30s and died from a brain tumor. She had been devastated. Left with two young children, she experienced intense anxiety, depression, and a sense of utter vulnerability. She went through the motions of daily life, cared for her children, and slowly but surely got back on her feet and reestablished a life for herself and two children. Then another catastrophe struck—her house was burned to the ground, and virtually all of her physical possessions were destroyed. She proceeded to calmly tell me that she was unfazed by the fire. She noted with surprise that friends and neighbors marveled at her stoicism and strength. Yet, she said, given what she had gone through with the death of her husband, a house meant little. She and her children were safe, they had their lives, and she knew that was all that mattered. It was her appreciation of life itself—her own and her children's—that enabled her to minimize the impact of the fire, and this appreciation of life was a legacy of her husband's early death.

Psychological Processes. Psychologically, what is the appraisal process or strategy that best accounts for this valuation of life in the face of death and loss? It seems likely that the attribution of specialness and value follows from a recognition of potential unavailability. That which we may lose suddenly is perceived as valuable. The powerful role of potential future loss is no doubt related to a "scarcity principle" (see Cialdini, 1993), by which we accord greater value to objects and opportunities that are less available. Thus, lay notions of economic value include beliefs that scarce commodities should and do cost more (Lynn, 1992). Similarly, Cialdini (1993) compellingly argues that retailers make use of the scarcity principle through a "limited number" tactic to increase the value—and thus sales—of their products.

The lack of availability may exist in the present, in that there are few items attainable at the time, or it may be perceived to exist in the future. Potential unavailability is a particularly powerful motivational mechanism. As Kahneman & Tversky (1982) have demonstrated in the area of decision-making, we are more motivated by the thought of losing something than we are of gaining something of equal value. Thus unavailability of objects and opportunities can be defined by number or time; items can be regarded as special and valuable because they are numerically scarce (i.e., there are few of them). They can also be considered special because their existence is temporally limited. In both cases the object is not apt to be taken for granted and is regarded as valuable. For trauma survivors, the harsh realization that life itself can end at any time creates a profound appreciation for being alive.

Appreciating Others: The Role of Reciprocal Valuing

In the aftermath of victimization, as survivors struggle to rebuild their assumptive world, the reactions of other people play a crucial role in the coping process. The psychological literature provides strong evidence to support the powerful association between social support and positive posttraumatic adjustment (see, e.g., Burgess & Holmstrom, 1978; Cohen & Wills, 1985; Dunkel-Schetter, 1984; Erikson, 1976; Silver & Wortman, 1980; Wallston, Alagna, DeVellis, & DeVellis, 1983). Whether struck by serious disease, accident, crime, war, natural catastrophe, or death of a loved one, survivors are considerably more likely to evidence psychological health and well-being when they receive sensitive, supportive responses by close friends and family; the absence of such support is typically regarded as a serious obstacle to adjustment.

Psychologists have recognized the multidimensional nature of social support in specifying different types of resources provided by others (e.g., Cohen & Wills, 1985; Silver & Wortman, 1980). Helpful family and friends provide emotional support and companionship, which serve to demonstrate acceptance and approval of the survivor, encourage open expression of feelings and beliefs, and acknowledge the appropriateness of such feelings and beliefs. Support may also be instrumental, material, or informational, involving financial assistance or tangible resources as well as advice and knowledge about available services. No doubt all of these resources contribute to survivors' psychological adjustment. However, they fall short of providing an understanding of the special role of social support posttrauma, a role that becomes more apparent as one considers survivors' efforts to rebuild their inner world.

In the aftermath of traumatic events, most survivors are engaged in the arduous process of constructing a more positive, less threatening view of the world and themselves than that implied by the extreme experience (Janoff-Bulman, 1992). Just as our assumptive worlds were first created in the context of other people, specifically early caregivers, survivors' assumptive worlds are reconstructed within an interpersonal context as well. Through their interactions with others close to them, survivors are provided with powerful information about the world and themselves—not only about the benevolence of others, but about their own self-worth in the eyes of others. Posttrauma, when questions of benevolence and self-worth are so pivotal and pervasive, others' reactions take on particularly potency (Janoff-Bulman, 1992). Harsh, rejecting responses by close friends and family offer strong evidence not only of the malevolence of the world, but of one's own unworthiness. On the other hand, warm, supportive reactions provide emotionally rich evidence not only of the fundamental goodwill and kindness of close others, but of one's own value in their eyes as well. Many survivors report that the support of others forced them to realize how much others really do care—in other words, how much others appear to value the survivor.

It is in the context of this sensitivity to others' reactions posttrauma that survivors come to more fully appreciate those close to them. Survivors commonly express a newfound appreciation for loved ones in their lives, as family members and close friends take on new value and meaning in the aftermath of the trauma; close relationships are far more important to them now. Again, there is appreciation—a perceived increase in value—of caring family and friends. For many this is a deliberate choice about priorities in their lives. Yet, for large numbers of survivors, this sense of appreciation is also directly related to the support they received. Close friends and family were there for the survivor and are now more fully acknowledged for their significance in the survivor's life.

Psychological Processes. From the perspective of a psychology of appreciation, how can we best understand the psychological process underlying this increased valuing of others often reported by survivors? In part, it may relate to the greater value accorded life itself, as discussed above, for it is likely that the lives of close family and friends are more highly valued. Further, the scarcity principle surely plays an important role, for the supportive reactions of others stand in marked contrast to the posttraumatic perception of malevolence in the world in general. Supportive, caring, sensitive responses are apt to be regarded as relatively scarce and special. In addition, however, a primary basis for the survivor's greater appreciation of others seems to lie in a process best described as reciprocal valuing—we value others who value us.

Most simply, when others make us feel special, they become special to us. Survivors posttrauma suddenly become strikingly aware of the fact that others value them; this may not have been readily apparent in the past, perhaps because relationships were taken for granted or not thought about a great deal, or because there were limited opportunities for others to demonstrate the lengths to which they would go for their friend or loved one. Posttrauma, survivors' perceived importance and meaning to others becomes the basis for a profound sense of appreciation—a valuing of these others as well. These close friends and family are special because their kindness and caring have been directed towards the survivor, and in the aftermath of trauma, when malevolence seems to define the universe, such positive attention is particularly noteworthy and valued; surely those who rejected and ignored the survivor are not appreciated. The process of reciprocal valuing does not demean the outcome; it is not a foolhardy, egotistical response. Rather, to value others who value us is a fundamental and extremely important psychological process that serves to bind individuals in communities of caring. The literature on liking and loving provides strong support for the reciprocal nature of these processes (Berscheid & Walster, 1978), and it is the realization that we are valuable to supportive others posttrauma that becomes the basis for an increased appreciation of close friends and family.

Appreciating the Self: Effort-Based Discovery of Personal Strength

Given the helplessness and vulnerability survivors experience, it is little wonder that they undergo considerable self-questioning about their abilities and deficiencies, strengths and weaknesses. Now that they know all too well about randomness and unpredictability, survivors profoundly realize that they may not be able to prevent future misfortune. Yet in the face of this new stark reality, they also recognize a new sense of personal strength: a belief that they can cope with whatever comes their way (e.g., Collins, Taylor, & Skokan, 1990; Janoff-Bulman, 1992; Taylor, 1983; Tedeschi & Calhoun, 1996; Thomas, DeGiulio, & Sheehan, 1991). Survivors' limits have been tested and they have passed, often with flying colors. Thus, survivors commonly assert that they went through agony and are stronger for it. The world may be regarded as more dangerous, now that their rose-colored lenses have been removed, but it can be confronted without the acute anxiety of the helpless; rather, survivors feel a greater sense of personal strength and competence. This new self-perception is apparent in the words of a rape victim: "I feel much stronger now, even though I feel vulnerable to being raped in this culture. Part of that rape was to dominate and humiliate me and he didn't succeed at that. I came through with my integrity—I got through those months of hell" (Janoff-Bulman, 1992, p. 137).

This reaction to trauma seems to parallel the old adage suggesting that whatever doesn't kill us makes us stronger, a message also implicit in the redemptive value of suffering taught in many religions. Ultimately we do not have control over what happens to us in terms of life's outcomes, but we retain considerable control over our own attitudes and choices. This is the message of concentration camp survivor Victor Frankl (1978), who maintains that people can choose an attitude of dignity and integrity, even in the face of great suffering. For trauma survivors, a core piece of this attitude of dignity is a newfound sense of their own competencies and abilities. Survivors often learn to better appreciate themselves—to recognize and value their own strengths—even in the face of impotence in preventing misfortune.

Psychological Processes.   What appraisal mechanisms account for the increased appreciation of the self in the aftermath of victimization? To some extent the attribution of specialness accorded to the self and its newfound competencies derive from a belief in the uniqueness, or scarcity, of this special strength. In other words, the survivor's personal strength is perceived as unusual—not ordinary—both in terms of other people (i.e., what would be expected of most people) and in terms of the survivor's own past history. After all, we expect people to be defeated by traumatic life events (see Gilbert et al., 1998), yet the survivor has successfully coped. The psychological strength of survivors was not recognized before, because their coping resources had never been called on to the extent demanded by the traumatic experience. It is as if the trauma provided an opportunity for survivors to learn about their own strengths, which had previously gone untested. As noted by a survivor of a debilitating accident: "I never knew I had it in me."

Trauma provided the occasion for discovering personal strength, a quality no doubt perceived as unusual, and yet an understanding of the appraisal processes accounting for the survivor's appreciation of self would be incomplete without ample recognition of the role of effort. It is not simply that survivors learn about themselves—and about their strengths—through the trauma, but that they learn about themselves in the course of expending incredible effort and determination in the coping process. It is through the commitment of time, energy, and emotional resources that survivors come to better understand themselves, and it is the effort that ultimately teaches them what they are capable of accomplishing. Survivors learn about themselves, not by being told, but by going through the pain of surviving; and in turn they develop a far greater appreciation of their special qualities and strengths.

The importance of effort and work for developing appreciation of the self is implicit in outdoor leadership programs such as Outward Bound and survival living courses. These are based on the recognition that through hard work and struggles, people come to better understand and recognize their own strengths. Interestingly, the role of effort and learning—albeit far less agonizing effort and learning—has been noted in the development of art and music appreciation. Scholars note the importance of devoting time and effort to learning about the elements of a piece of music or a painting. Thus, it is assumed that we can only truly appreciate a great symphony if we comprehend the thematic structure and know how to listen appropriately. We understand the music better. Thus, when we appreciate music or art, it is largely because we are able to perceive the complexity, beauty, or coherence of particular works, having expended the time and effort to learning how to listen or look. Admirable qualities inherent in the works are recognized via an effortful process. In a parallel fashion, admirable qualities inherent in survivors are recognized via an effortful process, although undeniably a far harsher, more painful process of coping in the aftermath of trauma.

☐ Towards A Psychology of Appreciation

Survivors' newfound experience of appreciation represents a remarkable accomplishment, given the trials and terrors generated by traumatic life events. Yet it is the trauma itself that increases the likelihood of appreciation. Trauma survivors do not experience appreciation *in spite of* their losses and sense of vulnerability, but *because* of them. They are more apt to recognize what matters and to create value and meaning in a universe now largely perceived as meaningless. Perhaps it is not surprising, then, that trauma researchers have concluded that "there is emerging evidence that more intense experience with trauma may produce greater benefits" (Tedeschi & Calhoun, 1996, p. 464). These researchers investigated changes in a general population over the course of a year and found that the perception of positive change was associated with the experience of severe trauma. In particular, Tedeschi and Calhoun (1996) found that those who had experienced traumatic life events were more apt to report a greater appreciation of life, better relationships with others, and perceptions of increased personal strengths. Trauma survivors experience greater appreciation of life, others, and themselves. Of all people, they are far from pollyannaish—they know all too well that dread lives next door and can strike at any time. And yet they are able to see the good with the bad—or more accurately, the good because of the bad.

A sense of appreciation enables us to discover what's valuable—in fact to create value—where others might not even notice it. It enriches people's lives, and yet for most of us, appreciation is not a defining feature of our daily existence; as Yale English Professor William Phelps (1932) noted earlier in the century, "The curse of modern life, the poison that turns honey into gall, the cause of the dull, stupid, despondent mood in which so many people live and move and have their being is a lack of appreciation" (pp. 16–17). Given the psychological rewards of a sense of appreciation, why isn't it a more common element in our lives?

The psychological processes underlying survivors' appreciation—perceptions of scarcity and potential unavailability, reciprocal valuing, and effort-based discovery of special qualities—suggests the potential role of these strategies in maximizing appreciation in nonvictims' lives. By expending effort to learn about ourselves, others, or new endeavors, we are apt to discover and better appreciate these aspects of our lives. Perhaps doing something special and unsought for a close friend or family member would initiate a cycle of reciprocal valuing and increase the appreciation each feels for the other. These behaviors would provide a basis for recognizing the value and worth accorded one another, but which are generally overlooked in the course of daily living. By looking at aspects of our lives with new eyes, we could perceive specialness in the ordinary, as poets whose rich images enable us to see our mundane world in new and wonderful ways.

Further, based on principles of scarcity and potential unavailability, we could construct alternative negative outcomes and imagine losses so as to enhance the value of a particular object or opportunity. People do, in fact, engage in downward social comparisons and imagine worse worlds (Taylor & Lobel, 1989; Wills, 1981; Wood, 1989), but we tend to do so when we already feel threatened or perceive an outcome negatively. These processes enable us to perceive ourselves, the stimulus, or the event less negatively, but they do little to enhance the value of our everyday experiences. One key to appreciation would be to get people to imagine loss and negative alternatives when all is going fine, so that more typical experiences—an interaction with a friend, a meal with close family, a walk on a beautiful day—are nevertheless perceived as worthy of appreciation. Yet some of these imagined alternatives, such as the loss of family or friends, are apt to be extremely uncomfortable and threatening and are therefore likely to be avoided.

Further, and perhaps more important, when things are going along just fine, there is little motivation to break the routine flow of our daily life. Psychologically, we are more attuned to negative feedback and emotions than positive ones, for the former call for behavioral change, whereas the latter do not (Schwarz, 1990). As Emily of *Our Town* makes evident, habituation and routine are natural barriers to appreciation. It is not surprising, then, that in a recent study we conducted, the extent to which participants experienced appreciation loaded on a factor with the extent to which they experienced grief, rather than happiness. Nonvictims are typically not motivated to engage in the processes that will maximize appreciation. For survivors, the traumatic experience provides both the motivation and the opportunity to perceive the ordinary as extraordinary.

It remains an open question whether years after the traumatic experience survivors will retain their sense of appreciation. Perhaps they get rehabituated, as the days and years pass. Yet, it is also possible that the traumatic experience, which was so emotionally powerful, remains etched in the psyche so as to serve as an ever-available reminder of the past pain and the possibility of future losses. In this sense, the trauma may remain a touchstone for the recognition of value in survivors' lives long after the initial negative event.

Survivors' Fundamental Ambivalence

In the course of coping, survivors often experience an unexpected change in their perception of the traumatic experience. No longer is it regarded as wholly tragic, all-pervasive in its negativity, and offering no solace from the terror of its implications for the world and oneself. Instead, a more ironic view prevails, one that entails a realization of unexpected gains. Survivors now maintain a more fundamental ambivalence about the traumatic experience. Yes, the trauma was painful, terrifying, unchosen, and unwanted; and survivors would surely not choose the experience if given the option (see, e.g., Kushner, 1981). Yet, having been forced to go through the losses associated with the trauma—not only visible losses, but those associated with long-held illusions of vulnerability and safety—survivors emerge simultaneously stripped and enriched by the experience. The traumatic event is no longer solely negative, but is seen as partially positive as well. Survivors' experiences suggest the vital bond that often exists between gains and losses (Viorst, 1986).

In recognizing the positive and the negative in their experience—confronting the good and the bad—survivors emerge with a more complex and flexible view of not only their experience, but also their lives. Nonvictims rarely recognize the extent of their own vulnerability, but rather work to maintain their benign assumptions so as to feel protected psychologically against misfortune. Pretrauma we are like young children who naturally engage in splitting, seeing our parents as all-good, for example, in order to defend against the anxiety associated with recognizing the bad. In the course of transforming the traumatic experience, survivors learn to live with ambivalence. From the singular event that so disrupted and devastated their lives, they nevertheless recognize gains. Theirs is now a world in which value has been created because they have faced up to the grim fact of misfortune and the real possibility of future loss.

The survivor's ambivalence is a healthy ambivalence, reflecting a more complex and flexible world-view. Their new assumptions incorporate the new and the old, the good and the bad, for they are far less absolutist than they had been. Thus, the world is benevolent and meaningful, but not always; the self is competent, but not always. More specifically, life is not assured, but is more valuable. Evil exists, but those closest to the survivor are good. The survivor may not be able to prevent misfortune, but will be able to cope if it strikes again. No longer is there a simple expectation that "bad things won't happen to me"; this naive form of optimism is gone, but has been replaced by a more mature form that is characterized by a belief that life is worth living—and living deeply—and all can be handled (see Carver & Scheier, 1999). The legacy of survivors' traumatic experience is not wholly negative, as might be expected, for a heightened sense of both vulnerability and appreciation emerge. By being forced to confront harsh reality, survivors discover the means to enrich it.

☐ References

Affleck, G., & Tennen, H. (1996). Construing benefits from adversity: Adaptational significance and dispositional underpinnings. *Journal of Personality, 64,* 899–922.

Affleck, G., Tennen, H., & Gershman, K. (1985). Cognitive adaptations to high-risk infants: The search for mastery, meaning, and protection from future harm. *American Journal of Mental Deficiency, 89,* 653–656.

Berscheid, E., & Walster, E. H. (1978). *Interpersonal attraction.* Reading, MA: Addison-Wesley.

Bowlby, J. (1969). *Attachment and loss: Attachment* (Vol. 1). London: Hogarth.

Brickman, P., Coates, D., & Janoff-Bulman, R. (1978). Lottery winners and accident victims: Is happiness relative? *Journal of Personality and Social Psychology, 36,* 917–927.

Brown, J. D. (1986). Evaluations of self and others: Self-enhancement biases in social judgments. *Social Cognition, 4,* 353–376.

Burgess, A. W., & Holmstrom, L. L. (1978). Recovery from rape and prior life stress. *Research in Nursing and Health, 1,* 165–174.

Cialdini, R. B. (1993). *Influence: Science and practice.* New York: Harper Collins.

Carver, C. S., & Scheier, M. F. (1999). Optimism. In C. R. Snyder (Ed.), *Coping: The psychology of what works* (pp. 182–204). New York: Oxford University Press.

Cohen, S., & Wills, T. A. (1985). Stress, social support, and the buffering hypothesis. *Psychological Bulletin, 98,* 310–357.

Collins, R. L., Taylor, S. E., & Skokan, L. A. (1990). A better world or a shattered vision: Changes in life perspectives following victimization. *Social Cognition, 8,* 263–285.

Dunkel-Schetter, C. A. (1984). Social support and cancer: Findings based on patient interviews and their implications. *Journal of Social Issues, 40,* 77–98.

Epstein, S. (1973). The self-concept revisited, or a theory of a theory. *American Psychologist, 28,* 404–416.

Epstein, S. (1991). The self-concept, the traumatic neurosis, and the structure of personality. In D. Ozer, J. M. Healy, Jr., & A. J. Stewart (Eds.), *Perspectives on personality* (Vol. 3, pp. 63–98). London: Jessica Kingsley.

Erikson, K. T. (1976). *Everything in its path: Destruction of community in the Buffalo Creek flood.* New York: Simon & Schuster.

Frankl, V. E. (1978). *Man's search for meaning: An introduction to logotherapy.* New York: Washington Square Press.

Gilbert, D. T., Pinel, E. C., Wilson, T. D., Blumberg, S. J., & Wheatley, T. P. (1998). Immune neglect: A source of durability bias in affective forecasting. *Journal of Personality and Social Psychology, 75,* 617–638.

Gilovich, T. (1991). *How we know what isn't so: The fallibility of human reason in everyday life.* New York: Free Press.

Gluckman, M. (1944, June). The logic of African science and witchcraft: An appreciation of Evans-Pritchard's "Witchcraft Oracles and Magic among the Azande" of the Sudan. *The Rhodes-Livingstone Institute Journal,* 61–71.

Gould, R. (1978). *Transformations.* New York: Simon & Schuster.

Greenwald, A. G. (1980). The totalitarian ego: Fabrication and revision of personal history. *American Psychologist, 35,* 603–618.

Harvey, J. H., Orbuch, T. L., Weber, A. L., Merbach, N., & Alt, R. (1992). House of pain and hope: Accounts of loss. *Death Studies, 16,* 1–26.

Helson, H. (1964). *Adaptation level theory: An experimental and systematic approach to behavior.* New York: Harper.

Henslin, J. M. (1967). Craps and magic. *American Journal of Sociology, 73,* 316–330.

Horowitz, M. J. (1976). *Stress response syndromes.* New York: Jason Aronson.

Janoff-Bulman, R. (1985). The aftermath of victimization: Rebuilding shattered assumptions. In C. Figley (Ed.), *Trauma and its wake: The study and treatment of post-traumatic stress disorder* (pp. 15–35). New York: Brunner/Mazel.

Janoff-Bulman, R. (1992). *Shattered assumptions: Towards a new psychology of trauma.* New York: Free Press.

Janoff-Bulman, R., & Frantz, C. M. (1997). The impact of trauma on meaning: From meaningless world to meaningful life. In M. Power & C. Brewin (Eds.), *The transformation of meaning in psychological therapies.* London: Wiley.

Joseph, S., Williams, R., & Yule, W. (1993). Changes in outlook following disaster: The preliminary development of a measure to assess positive and negative responses. *Journal of Traumatic Stress, 6*, 271-279.

Kahneman, D., & Miller, D. T. (1986). Norm theory: Comparing reality to its alternatives. *Psychological Review, 93*, 136-153.

Kahneman, D., & Tversky, A. (1973). On the psychology of prediction. *Psychological Review, 80*, 237-251.

Kahneman, D., & Tversky, A. (1982). The simulation heuristic. In D. Kahneman, P. Slovic, & A. Tversky (Eds.), *Judgment under uncertainty: Heuristics and biases* (pp. 201-208). New York: Cambridge University Press.

Kushner, H. S. (1981). *When bad things happen to good people.* New York: Schocken Books.

Langer, E. J. (1975). The illusion of control. *Journal of Personality and Social Psychology, 32*, 311-328.

Lehman, D. R., Davis, C. G., DeLongis, A., Wortman, C. B., Bluck, S., Mandel, D. R., & Ellard, J. (1993). Positive and negative life changes following bereavement and their relations to adjustment. *Journal of Social and Clinical Psychology, 12*, 90-112.

Lerner, M. J. (1980). *The belief in a just world.* New York: Plenum.

Lifton, R. J. (1967). *Death in life: Survivors of Hiroshima.* New York: Simon and Schuster.

Lynn, M. (1992). Scarcity's enhancement of desirability: The role of naive economic theories. *Basic and Applied Social Psychology, 13*, 67-78.

McCann, I. L., & Pearlman, L. A. (1990). *Psychological trauma and the adult survivor: Theory, therapy, and transformation.* New York: Brunner/Mazel.

Pargament, K. I., Ensing, D. S., Falgout, K., Olsen, H., Reilly, B., Van Haitsma, K., & Warren, R. (1990). God help me: I. Religious coping efforts as predictors of outcomes to significant negative life events. *American Journal of Community Psychology, 18*, 793-824.

Perloff, L. S. (1983). Perceptions of vulnerability to victimization. *Journal of Social Issues, 39*, 41-62.

Phelps, W. L. (1932). *Appreciation.* New York: E. P. Dutton & Co.

Sartre, J. P. (1964). *Nausea.* Norfolk, CT: New Directions.

Sartre, J. P. (1966). *Being and nothingness: A phenomenological study of ontology.* New York: Washington Square Press.

Schwartzberg, S. S. (1996). *A crisis of meaning: How gay men are making sense of AIDS.* New York: Oxford University Press.

Schwartzberg, S. S., & Janoff-Bulman, R. (1991). Grief and the search for meaning: Exploring the assumptive worlds of bereaved college students. *Journal of Social and Clinical Psychology, 10*, 270-288.

Schwarz, N. (1990). Feelings as information: Informational and motivational functions of affecive states. In R. Sorrentino & E. T. Higgins (Eds.), *Handbook of motivation and cogntion: Foundations of social behavior.* (Vol. 2, pp. 527-561). New York: Guilford.

Silver, R. L., & Wortman, C. B. (1980). Coping with undesirable life events. In J. Garber & M. E. P. Seligman (Eds.), *Human helplessness: Theory and application* (pp. 279-375). New York: Academic Press.

Singer, I. (1994). *The pursuit of love.* Baltimore: Johns Hopkins University Press.

Singer, I. (1996). *The creation of value.* Baltimore: Johns Hopkins University Press.

Snyder, C. R., Higgins, R. L., & Stucky, R. J. (1983). *Excuses: The masquerade solution.* New York: Wiley.

Tait, R., & Silver, R. C. (1989). Coming to terms with major negative life events. In J. S. Uleman & J. A. Bargh (Eds.), *Unintended thought* (pp. 351-382). New York: Guilford.

Taylor, S. E. (1983). Adjustment to threatening events: A theory of cognitive adaptation. *American Psychologist, 38*, 1161-1173.

Taylor, S. E. (1990). *Positive illusions: Creative self-deception and the healthy mind.* New York: Basic Books.

Taylor, S. E., & Brown, J. D. (1988). Illusion and well-being: A social-psychological perspective on mental health. *Psychological Bulletin, 103*, 193–210.

Taylor, S. E., Lichtman, R. R., & Wood, J. V. (1984). Attributions, beliefs about control, and adjustment to breast cancer. *Journal of Personality and Social Psychology, 46*, 489–582.

Taylor, S. E., & Lobel, (1989). Social comparison activity under threat: Downward evaluations and upward contacts. *Psychological Review, 96*, 569–575.

Taylor, S. E., & Schneider, S. K. (1989). Coping and the simulation of events. *Social Cognition, 7*, 176–196.

Taylor, S. E., Wood, J. V., & Lichtman, R. R. (1983). It could be worse: Selective evaluation as a response to victimization. *Journal of Social Issues, 39*(2), 19–40.

Tedeschi, R. G., & Calhoun, L. G. (1995). *Trauma and transformation: Growing in the aftermath of suffering.* Newbury Park, CA: Sage.

Tedeschi, R. G., & Calhoun, L. G. (1996). The posttraumatic growth inventory: Measuring the positive legacy of trauma. *Journal of Traumatic Stress, 9*, 455–471.

Tennen, H., & Affleck, G. (1999). Findings benefits in adversity. In C. R. Snyder (Ed.), *Coping: The psychology of what works* (pp. 279–304). New York: Oxford University Press.

Thomas, L. E., DeGiulio, R. C., & Sheehan, N. W. (1991). Identifying loss and psychological crisis in widowhood. *International Journal of Aging and Human Development, 26*, 279–295.

Thompson, S. C. (1985). Finding positive meaning in a stressful event and coping. *Basic and Applied Social Psychology, 12*, 81–96.

Thompson, S. C., & Janigian, A. S. (1988). Life schemes: A framework for understanding the search for meaning. *Journal of Social and Clinical Psychology, 7*, 260–280.

Tversky, A., & Kahneman, D. (1981). The framing of decisions and the psychology of choice. *Science, 211*, 453–458.

Viorst, J. (1986). *Necessary losses.* New York: Simon & Schuster.

Wallston, B. S., Alagna, S. W., DeVellis, B. M., & DeVellis, R. F. (1983). Social support and physical health. *Health Psychology, 2*, 367-391.

Watts, W., & Free, L. A. (1978). *State of the nation III.* Lexington, MA: Lexington Books.

Weinstein, N. D. (1989). Optimistic biases about personal risks. *Science, 246*, 1232–1233.

Weller, S. (1973). Work in progress: Maya Angelou. *Intellectual Digest, June*, 11–12, 14.

Whitehead, A. (1911). *An introduction to mathematics.* London: Williams and Norgate.

Wilder, T. (1975). *Our town.* New York: Avon Books.

Wills, T. A. (1981). Downward comparison principles in social psychology. *Psychological Bulletin, 90*, 245–271.

Wilson, J. P., & Krauss, G. E. (1985). Predicting post-traumatic stress disorders among Vietnam veterans. In W. E. Kelly (Ed.), *Post-traumatic stress disorder and the war veteran patient.* New York: Brunner/Mazel.

Wolfenstein, M. (1957). *Disaster: A psychological essay.* Glencoe, IL: Free Press.

Wood, J. V. (1989). Theory and research concerning social comparisons of personal attributes. *Psychological Bulletin, 106*, 231–248.

Wortman, C. B. (1975). Some determinants of perceived control. *Journal of Personality and Social Psychology, 31*, 282–294.

Wortman, C. B., & Silver, R. C. (1987). Coping with irrevocable loss. In G. R. Van den Bos & B. K. Bryant (Eds.), *Cataclysms, crises, and catastrophes: Psychology in action* (pp. 189–235). Washington, DC: American Psychological Association.

Beverley Raphael
Matthew Dobson

Bereavement

The term bereavement is used variously—to describe the reaction to loss, the loss itself, and as an experience more generally. It will be used in this chapter to describe the whole process of anticipation (where this occurs), and reaction to the loss of a person to whom the individual is attached in the sense of human affectional bonds. In this sense it will encompass both the inner psychological processes and their outer expression, for instance grief and psychological mourning, as well as the external, socially sanctioned behaviors and rituals. Bereavement may occur also for many other losses: the loss of love; the loss of home, community, country; the loss of work; the loss of health, body part, or function. It may also include less concrete but still meaningful losses—the loss of hoped-for futures, of personal integrity, of belief in social institutions. However, the key phenomena will be described here as they apply to the loss of loved ones, by death, and the loss of primary attachment figures and the processes that follow. How these understandings may apply to other losses will only be discussed more generally. The factors that influence the nature of bereavement reactions will also be considered, as well as the complexities that may arise. Bereavement as it can be understood in terms of biological, psychological, social, and cultural contexts will also be explored and finally bereavement and its relation to trauma, and as a model for human response to adversity will be analyzed. Bereavement may also contribute significantly to human growth and development, and the strengths from grieving and mastering loss, and the internalizations of those loved, may all contribute to the character and adaptability of the individual.

While bereavement and the processes of grief and mourning are widely described in the classical literature, attention to the psychology of grief and mourning owes much to Freud's classic essay on mourning and melancholia (Freud, 1917). Freud drew attention to the psychological processes of undoing the bonds with the loved one, the processes of internalization, and the affects of sadness. He differentiated mourning from melancholia, where the internalization of the ambivalently loved object was seen to contribute to the evolution of depression.

☐ Attachment, Separation, and Loss

Much of our current understanding of human reaction to loss has been built from the framework of attachment theory. John Bowlby (1969, 1973, 1980) described the nature of human attachments, first in the paradigm of the mother-infant relationship and subsequently in that of adult attachment or pair-bonding. Other "affectional bonds" bring similar patterns to these, but usually differing intensities, although the key element is the interactional and affectional nature of these mutual relationships. Within the basic paradigm of the mother-infant relationship, separation induces specific forms of anxiety, separation anxiety, distress, and protest. With reunion these affects settle, but when reunion does not occur, the processes of mourning do, with feelings of sadness and a sense of loss. It is this conceptualization that is the basis for the understanding of reactions to loss. While there may be an initial brief period of shock, numbness, and disbelief, this gives way to intense separation distress or anxiety with yearning and longing for the return of the lost person. Angry protest is diffuse, but really toward the deceased who may be perceived as abandoning the bereaved. The bereaved person is highly aroused and scans the environment for signs of the lost one, perhaps seeing his or her face or hearing the loved one's voice, or even experiencing hallucinatory phenomena of the loved one's voice, touch, or image. Gradually over the days and weeks following the loss, the reality and finality of the absence of the loved one, of the death, is progressively accepted, even though it may have been known intellectually before. This progressive emotional recognition of finality opens into the psychological mourning process where the lost relationship takes on a new focus with remembering or nostalgia. It is as though what has been lost is reviewed and memories of the person and the relationship are sorted through, just as clothes and possessions may be. There is pervasive sadness with heightened affect related to specific memories—which may roll before the eyes like glimpses of a movie. As human relationships are inevitably ambivalent, some of these memories may also be fraught with anger and guilt, others with the bittersweetness of nostalgia. Progressively this intense focus is relinquished, affect returns to "normal" and the person returns to the world and relationships—the phase of resolution and reorganization progresses.

This theoretical paradigm has been substantiated by a significant body of research in different settings (Middleton, Burnett, Raphael, & Martinek, 1996). Parkes (1986) was the first to demonstrate this pattern in a study of widows, and recent studies have extended the understanding of adult bereavement phenomenology in systematic ways. For instance, Jacobs, in a study of bereaved adults, has shown dimensions of numbness, separation distress, and mourning (Jacobs, 1993). Middleton et al. in a number of studies showed the dimensions of separation anxiety, grief, and mourning, and made comparisons between adults facing different bereavements—the death of a child, parent or spouse—with the former leading to greatest distress (Middleton, Raphael, Burnett, & Martinek, 1998).

In examining these dimensions of grief and bereavement reaction, a measure of bereavement phenomena, the Core Bereavement Items or CBI scale has been developed for measurement of these elements in systematic ways (Burnett, Middleton, Raphael, & Martinek, 1997). It has been applied to other bereaved populations such as older adults (Byrne & Raphael, 1994) and families (Kissane & Bloch, 1994) and shown to be a valid and useful measure of these phenomena.

Consistently throughout these studies is the ubiquity of the pattern in different bereavements and at different stages of the life cycle. This pattern is intense in the first weeks and months after the loss but settles progressively within this time. Throughout the first year after major loss, periods of intense grief may reappear, especially with triggers or reminders of the loss, and at the anniversaries. Similar patterns may continue into the second year but with diminishing intensity. Some memories and distress may persist, but to a much lesser degree over the years that follow, and become more intense with acute reminders or with a subsequent loss. Nevertheless, for the majority of people, these reactions progressively settle and the loss and memories are incorporated into life (Raphael, 1983).

Furthermore, in studies of adults, it has been possible to identify patterns of abnormal bereavement reaction, both in terms of consensus (Middleton, Moylan, Raphael, Burnett, & Martinek, 1993) and in terms such as measurement—for instance the pattern of "chronic grief" which is a prolonged and intense level of normal bereavement phenomena lasting over a year and occurring in about 9% of a community population of bereaved people (Raphael & Minkov, 1999). Others using different methods have also put forward criteria for Complicated Grief Disorder (Horowitz et al., 1997) and what is called Traumatic Grief (Prigerson, Shear, Jacobs, & Reynolds, 1999). All of these studies demonstrate the centrality of separation distress and yearning for the lost person plus preoccupation with the deceased as the pathognomonic phenomena of bereavement, both normal and abnormal.

While these studies of adults have confirmed the value of attachment theory in understanding and describing certain bereavements, there has been a shortage of similar studies in childhood and adolescent bereavement although both the work of Worden (1991) and other contributions (Raphael, Field, & Kvelde, 1980) have highlighted the presence of many of the phenomena discussed above. Separation anxiety has been systematically demonstrated by attachment theorists such as Ainsworth (1982) and Main (1985) but requires further systematic research in terms of its patterns and significance in bereaved children, where it is likely to be both more intense and potentially very significant for development. Patterns of behavioral distress and change do encompass separation phenomena however, in both younger and older children, and the capacity of even quite young children to mourn psychologically has been demonstrated (Raphael et al, 1980; Pynoos, Nader, Frederick, Gorda, & Stuber, 1987). Children frequently show regression in the face of loss—for instance, the death of a parent—and may demonstrate externalizing or internalizing behavior patterns that cloud the picture of bereavement, or indeed may indicate that the child is not able to grieve.

Bereavement in childhood may impact on development; much will depend on the continuity and security of the child's life, and whether they will be supported in their adaptation. Particularly stressful to the child is the death of a parent and this may lead to subsequent vulnerabilities in childhood, adolescent, or adult life. These may include risk of depression (Brown, Harris, & Copeland, 1977; Van Erdewegh et al, 1985) antisocial behaviors, early pregnancy, and difficulties in attachment (Main, 1985). Surviving parents may not recognize the child's grief and loss, because of immersion in their own distress. This, plus family insecurity, may mean the child's issues are unresolved.

☐ Biological Correlates of Bereavement

Significant research effort has attempted to address some of the biological correlates of grief and bereavement reactions. A recent review by Biondi and Picardi (1996) has summarized much of this research.

The neuroendocrine system has been investigated in a range of studies. Studies of the early period of bereavement have shown increased adrenocortical activity among bereaved persons. In general this activity appears not to be found in all those who are bereaved, but rather to be associated with intense grief, high levels of anxiety, or depressed mood (Biondi & Picardi 1996, p. 235). A recent study highlights the relationship of higher levels of separation anxiety distress in a one month period after the loss, with higher urinary free cortisol excretion (Jacobs et al, 1987). This suggests that the continuing high distress may be associated with such dysregulation and higher adrenocortical activity. This dysregulation of the hypothalamic pituitary axis may be evidenced by the descamethosone nonsuppression which is associated with separation anxiety distress in the early stages, or depression later (Schucter, Zisook, Kirkorowicz, & Risch, 1986; Weller, Weller, Fristad, & Bowes, 1990). These findings are of interest in highlighting the biological significance of intense distress as reflected both in separation anxiety and depressive reactions in the postbereavement period.

Brain neurotransmitters have been studied in animal research that looked at separation responses in infants that may reflect responses similar to those that would occur in humans (Biondi & Picardi, 1996, p. 238–239). Separation of infant monkeys from their mothers produces a similar set of separation reactions to those observed in humans. In the initial acute phase, catecholamine and serotonin are released in the central nervous system. Other evidence supports the hypothesis that biogenetic amine systems are involved in the separation response (Kling et al., 1992) and may be sensitive to bendiazepines (Valium) while the despair response may be sensitive to antidepressants (McKinney, 1995). These findings suggest directions for further research as studies become more sophisticated and also imply relevance to immune system change.

Immune system changes have also been found in a number of studies that have shown decreased immunocompetence in bereaved subjects (e.g., Bartrop, Lazarus, Luchkurst, Kiloh, & Penny, 1977; Schleifer, Keller, Camerino, Thornton, & Stein, 1983). The suppression of mitogen-induced leucocyte proliferation was associated with actual loss of the spouse, rather than the long-term stress of terminal illness. These findings showing that T cell sub-populations and natural killer cell activity that were altered in the bereaved were associated with increased experiences of stressful life events and more severe depressive symptoms (Irwin, Daniels, Bloom, Smith, & Weiner, 1987). Neuroendocrine changes may be associated with the changes in numerous functions, or they may occur through the profound psychobiological impact of the loss, with disruptions of biological rhythms (Biondi & Picardi, 1996; Hofer, 1984). The degree to which immune changes in the bereaved relate to the level of depression remains to be clarified.

Of great interest is recent work looking at brain imaging findings with experimentally induced sadness, which is one of the principal affects of bereavement (George et al., 1995). Increases in regional cerebral blood flow were found in the ventrolateral limbic and paralimbic sites, and decreases were found in the dorsal central regions, inferior parietal, and other areas (Mayberg, Liotti, Brannan, McGinnis, & Mahurin, 1999). In this study changes were contrasted with recovery from depression. These findings highlight the biological responses that are gradually being understood as research extends in these areas. The findings also identify different responses in terms of separation, and later phases involving despair or depressive phenomena. The biological research mirrors the psychological in highlighting the utility of Bowlby's (1980) attachment model. But it also helps explain the confusion between the misery and sadness of 'normal' grief and the depression that may occur in association with it.

☐ Social and Cultural Parameters of Bereavement

Social parameters of bereavement are likely to be defined in terms of both the role of the bereaved person, and the sanctions for response. For instance, the person who is defined as the primary bereaved person, who is seen as appropriately defined as bereaved may influence the capacity of other persons to express their grief and have their grief recognized. The nature of the death may also influence the societal response to the loss, for instance the particular sensitivities surrounding death from HIV; the violence of death through homicide where the investigation process may further complicate social response; or the deaths of babies and their meaning, to name a few such socially determined contexts. In addition, there are likely to be role requirements on the bereaved both in terms of funeral practice, and subsequent social expectations and behaviors. These may include sanctions regarding sexual behaviors for the widow, and the period of grieving. Such requirements may also be strongly culturally based. There is often a change in social status following bereavement, too. For instance, the bereaved may have decreased access to resources, or a disadvantaged social position, although this is not necessarily the case. The person may move into a new social group—for instance, that of widows (Lopata, 1979).

Social movements of mutual support such as self-help associations provide a framework for bereaved people. They provide a network of others who have had similar experiences, mutual support by those who have "been through the same thing," and frequently provide identity, roles, and pathways to altered states and often to psychosocial 'recovery' (Silverman, 1986).

Changes in family structure following bereavement may impact adversely on children, particularly if there is a break-up or discontinuity of a nurturing environment and the loss of other attachments. Thus, for the child, continuity of affectional bonds and social structures to support these bonds, are very important for his or her capacity to deal with a bereavement such as the death of a family member, particularly a parent (Worden, 1991).

A recent work has examined the sociology of dying and bereavement (Seale, 1998). Seale argues that rather than being a society that denies death, social and cultural life involves turning away from the inevitability of death, which is contained in the fact of our embodiment, towards life" (p. 1). He suggests, too, that knowledge of one's body, humanity, and inevitable mortality leads to human social activity, with an "orientation towards continual meaningful existence" (p. 1). With respect to grief he suggests that the narratives of mourning serve a variety of resurrective practices which allow the recovery from bereavement. He goes on to suggest that mourning practices, whether they be the mortuary rites of tribal and traditional practices or the micro-interventions of grieving individuals are helpful to the "ontological security of the mourners" through engendering hope in the survivors for the continuing life of the deceased in community, an imagined community which is a form of resurrection and ongoing life—thus, he lives in the discussion and memory of him in this community. Seale also describes the physicalization of grief in the work of Parkes (1986) and others when bereavement is linked to increased mortality, and physical and psychiatric morbidity. Seale (1998) also suggests that the concept of grief is of hard work with normal grief the ultimate reward (Seale, 1998, p. 196). Work with self-help groups and examination of the grief process leads to the conclusion that it is "a structure for publicly expressing grief" that may apply for these groups and bereavement counseling more generally. This narrative helps in providing a life for the deceased, but helps those bereaved to reclaim community membership "and restore a damaged social bond". How much bereavement counseling fits with ritual or with other cultural prescriptions is not known. However, as Seale notes, these rituals may or may not be helpful to those bereaved.

The social construction of grief, Seale contests, may require certain rituals or behaviors which demonstrate weeping, mourning, righteous sign, penitence and so forth, or behavior relevant to the treatment of the corpse. Weeping was seen as universal but other emotions varied, suggesting a degree of cultural influence on how many emotions are externally expressed. In this context Western psychiatric ideas about grief are viewed as culturally bound.

Specific contributions describing different cultural practice include Rosenblatt, Walsh, and Jackson's (1976) work on grief and mourning in a cross-cultural perspectives and more recently, Parkes (1986). These and other works provide valuable descriptions of specific cultural practices and requirements. However an analysis of how these practices change over time and the significance of commonalities and differences require much further attention.

It can be concluded however that the social and cultural meanings of loss, death, and bereavement and the relationship of psychobiology to social prescription and cultural practice will be important pathways to explore. Some workers have taken such theory into the modality of cultural bereavement (Eisenbruch, 1991) which encompasses the cultural aspects of both bereavement and loss. This research highlights the complexity of this field.

A further key theme is that of spiritual interpretations and meaning. Here in either broader spiritual contexts or in terms of specific religions or theological understandings, meaning and response in bereavement may be powerfully influenced. This may range from the "rites de passage" identified by Van Gennep (1960) to the broader specialized frameworks. It is suggested, when considering this with indigenous communities, a ritual elder may create a safe space where grief can be safely sampled. This may provide holistic and healing processes that are at the same time spiritual. This seeking of spirituality and spiritual meaning in the face of loss is widespread and a significant social parameter that should also be encompassed in understanding grief.

☐ Bereavement as a Stressor

Bereavement has also been seen as a model of life adversity, of stress, and of human response to these. Such response may encompass both a stimulus for personal growth and a stressor that may negatively impact on well-being, social functioning, or health.

Research makes it clear that the majority of people adjust to the death of a loved one successfully. Despite remembering the deceased with nostalgia, and sometimes psychological pain, the bereaved move on in their lives. Nevertheless, this experience is stressful and may lead to adverse consequences.

Bereavement Pathologies

These pathologies have been identified with some consensus—for instance absent, chronic, or delayed grief (Middleton et al., 1993). Research studies have provided evidence to date only on chronic grief (Byrne & Raphael, 1994; Middleton et al., 1998; Raphael & Minkov, 1999). Recent work has identified a Complicated Grief Disorder with criteria of distressing yearnings, pangs of severe separation anxiety, intense intrusive thoughts, feelings of increasing aloneness and emptiness, excessive avoidance of tasks related to the deceased, loss of interest in personal activities, and some sleep disturbance, present more than a year after the loss (Horowitz et al., 1997). Traumatic grief is a form of pathological grief that has been identified in a consensus process and research studies and is reported by Prigerson et al. (1999). It also encompasses intense and prolonged separation distress, and yearning, as well as preoccupation with the deceased. These patterns are very similar to those of chronic grief described by Middleton and Byrne and all represent prolonged separation distress and failure to psychologically mourn the loss (Middleton et al., 1993; Byrne and Raphael, 1994). They are likely to be very disabling for the bereaved, both in terms of social existence as well as ongoing distress.

Social Pathologies

Social pathologies may also arise following bereavement, such as, patterns of acting-out sexually or in other ways, aggressive behaviors, excessive intake of alcohol or other drugs, or antisocial behaviors. Impairment of the capacity to work, and of social, family, and personal relationships may also occur (Raphael, 1983). Loss of role and identity may add further impairments. These behaviors may not be recognized as related to the loss, and are often the pattern in adolescence. They should be dealt with alongside other pathologies of bereavement.

Bereavement and Health

Bereavement has been shown to be associated with an increase in health care utilization, increased usage of alcohol and sometimes other drugs, and, for widowers at least, with increased mortality (Jacobs & Ostfield, 1977; Kaprio, Koskenvko, & Rita, 1987). The pathways by which bereavement exerts such effects are not established. Morbidity, which may occur in association with the stressor of bereavement, includes the development of anxiety disorders and depressive disorders (Jacobs, 1993). A number of possibilities may explain these vulnerabilities, including preexisting psychiatric disorder or other relevant risk factors, the particular nature of the lost relationship, personality, response styles, and degree of perceived social support, as well as the values and circumstances of the death. Biondi and Picardi (1996) suggest a psychosomatic process may lead from loss to depression, whereas Brown's conceptualization links adult depression to earlier losses and recent precipitation by another loss. Whatever the pathways, and the growing science of genetic contributions, environmental stressors such as loss still play a part.

It has been suggested that effects may arise through impact or immune function, neuroendocrine positively, altered health behaviors, or neurophysiological mechanisms. Nevertheless, these pathways are not established (e.g., Byrne & Raphael, 1994). It is likely that risk will be heightened if the circumstances of the death are particularly difficult, if the relationship which has been lost has been very complex (e.g., highly ambivalent, dependent) and more particularly, if the bereaved perceives the social network as nonsupportive for his or her grieving (Maddison & Walker, 1967). These broad-brush findings need a great deal of further research to clarify how it may be that some bereaved persons are more vulnerable to these particular adverse health outcomes than others.

Bereavement and Depression

Early discussion of the phenomena of bereavement frequently equated bereavement to depression, a "reactive depression." A more sophisticated appraisal has shown that normal bereavement phenomena are distinct from those of depression—a fact well recognized by bereaved people who will see themselves as "sad" not "depressed," and make clear that these are not the same experiences. There is an increased risk of depression developing in the postbereavement period, however, and this is relevant for both prevention and management. It is more likely for those with a previous history of depression (Zisook, Shuchter, Sledge, Paulus, & Judd, 1994). It is frequent in circumstances where the relationship that has been lost is one of high levels of ambivalence. There may then be more complex processes to resolve the loss which may increase the likelihood of depression. Lack of support to deal with these issues increases such vulnerability although focussed counseling to deal with this may prevent some level of depression (Raphael & Maddison, 1976). In addition, the experience of loss in childhood, for instance the death of a mother before the age of five, may predispose a woman to depression in adult life: a depression which is more likely in those with young children and who lack a supportive partner when they face another loss (Brown et al., 1977). It seems that loss as an adverse life experience is more likely to lead to depressive reactions, whereas other stressors such as life-threat may be more likely to lead to anxiety syndromes. Nevertheless, there is frequently overlap in reactions, and the genetic vulnerability that may increase risk by increasing reactiveness to the stressors of adverse life experience may be part of the mechanism by which bereavement may lead to depression.

Bereavement and Trauma

Loss is not a traumatic stressor in the true sense. True traumatic stressors are more related to personal life threat although Horowitz initially described loss as a traumatic stressor in his model of stress response syndromes (Horowitz, 1976). Deaths may, however, be so traumatic in their circumstances that those bereaved are exposed to either personal life threat, shock, and helplessness, or to gruesome and horrific death. Violent deaths such as those from suicide, homicide, terrorism, or war may also be particularly traumatic for the bereaved, as may the sudden, unexpected, and untimely deaths caused by motor vehicle accidents. Such deaths are of themselves a death encounter, and meet the criterion for a traumatic stressor (Criterion A of PTSD, DSM-IV) so that those bereaved in this way may also be at risk of developing posttraumatic stress disorder. Thus, the bereaved person will suffer additional stress which may complicate the capacity to grieve. Two sets of phenomena—those of traumatic stress reactions and those of bereavement—may overlap (Raphael & Martinek, 1997; Schut et al., 1991).

Studies of those bereaved due to disasters (Lundin, 1984; Singh & Raphael, 1981) or through homicide (Rynearson, 1984) show clearly the particular difficulties that then arise. In addition, in disasters there may be dislocation, chaos, lack of information, uncertainty about how the person died, and even greater difficulties if the body cannot be found. Studies examining intervention in these settings show it is usually necessary to focus initially on the traumatic stress effects, with their intrusive and avoidant phenomena, before the person may be able to move on to grieve in the bereavement process (Lindy et al., 1982; Raphael & Minkov, 1999).

Bereavement Across Generations

Descriptive work has suggested that the impact of loss in one generation of a family or group may affect the next. This has been described in Holocaust survivors and their families (e.g., Danieli, 1982) and also in groups who have experienced extensive trauma and loss across many generation (e.g., indigenous populations; Raphael & Swan, 1997). The pervasiveness of grief, the protectiveness of attachments, and the fearfulness of loss may influence behaviors for generations to come (e.g., Ober, Peeters, Archer, & Kelly, 1999). In families the mourning and transfer of identity, for example from a lost parent or sibling to a new replacement child, may influence expectations and adaptation in unconscious and subtle ways (Cain, Fast, & Erickson, 1964). Families also have particular patterns of response to loss and family grief (Kissane & Bloch, 1994), which will contribute to and are influenced by transgenerational issues.

☐ Responses to Those Bereaved

There are basic human comforting responses to those who are distressed, and who have lost those they love. These may be demonstrated in personal and social situations such as the rituals of funeral and the provision of social support to families, neighbors, and friends. But the need to respond is quite powerful and has lead to developments beyond these normal interactions and adaptations.

Self-Help Groups for the Bereaved

Among the many victim movements, self-help programs for the bereaved are in the forefront. These are both generic and specific to certain losses. Such groups provide crisis support, role models for survival and adaptation pathways, and social networks. They are effective because of the value of sharing with those who have been through the same thing. Some examples include groups for stillbirth and neonatal deaths, sudden infant deaths, deaths of children, for the death of a spouse, or for the survivors of motor vehicle deaths, suicide, or homicide. Groups may also arise spontaneously about particular mass deaths, for instance following a disaster, a plane crash, and so forth. These movements are an important part of the response to bereavement as a stressor, and there is evidence of their effectiveness as social and healing processes (e.g., Silverman, 1986; Vachon, Lyall, & Rogers, 1980).

Health System Responses to the Bereaved

While it is now fully agreed that grief is not a disease (Engel, 1961), the health system has a number of levels of interactions with the bereaved. These may be part of the work of the health system, such as the provision of certification of death, the treatment of the dying, and the conveying of the news of the death to the bereaved. These tasks may be carried out in ways which encompass and are supportive of the bereaved, or they may add additional stress if carried out in negative ways. This can be exemplified in the explanation of the death given, time spent with the bereaved, and empathy in the conveying of the "bad news" of the death. Sudden, unexpected deaths create the greatest difficulty for both the bereaved and those dealing with them. New forms of practice may include family members during the resuscitation process and this has been found to be helpful in many instances—for the family sees that all that was possible has been done. The engagement of the health system is of course, more relevant where this is part of the institutionalized management of death and dying, as noted above.

A further important issue for the health system and perhaps the funeral system, is the capacity of the bereaved to see and say goodbye to the deceased—to touch and hold the body if desired, and to spend time with the dead person. This is relevant for all deceased, from the stillborn, to the aged. If the body is severely disfigured the bereaved may need extra support, but will usually still find this opportunity for goodbye a vital element in their recovery process. It is also a particularly relevant practice for sudden and unexpected deaths (e.g., Singh & Raphael, 1981).

New aspects of death and dying are relevant in that the definition of death is more complex, and the bereavement process may commence before death occurs. Particularly difficult for the bereaved may be the turning off of life-support systems, the giving of permission for organ donation and transplant, and the knowledge that another lives because their loved one died. The ways in which the health system deals with such issues may make a significant positive or negative contribution to the well-being of those bereaved.

Intervention with the Bereaved

The risks of adverse outcome following bereavement have set a context in which interventions are provided for bereaved people. The aims of such interventions vary from prevention to the treatment of pathologies that have arisen. A significant body of research supports the provision of such programs, although there is a need for a more systematic dissemination and uptake of this. Bereavement Counseling is a commonly used term to describe what is provided, but such counseling may vary substantially in both quality and effectiveness, for it is not necessarily informed by the knowledge base that exists, nor provided by skilled and qualified persons. Nevertheless, like the self-help movement described earlier, it represents the wish to care and help, to make better, and as such represents a positive and compassionate human endeavor and a culturally derived practice in Western society at least.

Evidence-based intervention and guidelines for best practice are needed to ensure that outcomes sought in lessening bereavement related morbidity are achieved and that the provision of counseling is related to need and not provided in ways that medicalize normal human adaptation. Formalized intervention programs for bereaved people fall into two main categories: prevention and treatment.

Preventive Intervention for Bereaved at Risk of Adverse Outcomes. As in other areas of preventive intervention, scientific studies show that efforts are most relevant when they are targeted at populations who are at higher risk. Nevertheless, more broadly-based programs directed towards the whole community may be helpful: for instance, education about normal bereavement processes, how to help others, and when to seek professional assistance. Stakeholders such as the clergy, the funeral industry, and health and welfare organizations will also benefit from information that describes what is helpful and how not to harm by behaviors or practices that could add to psychological distress. Also important are programs in schools that provide supportive education to children and adolescents on key issues regarding death, dying, and bereavement, and what is normal. Those facing a loss directly may require not only support, but also information on what is normal and helpful, for themselves, children, and others. A significant number of popular literature and programs have addressed these generic issues.

Bereaved people have been shown to be at higher risk of the range of adverse outcomes listed above when a number of factors are present. These factors include personal characteristics of the bereaved individual, such as traits of high levels of reactiveness to adverse life experiences (Andrews, 1996); biological/genetic or other vulnerabilities to psychiatric disorder; traumatic circumstances of the death, especially deaths that are untimely, unexpected, shocking, or violent; difficulties in the preexisting relationship with the deceased, such as high levels of dependence or ambivalence; other current adverse life experiences; and perceptions that the social network is not supportive of the person's need to grieve (Raphael, 1977; Parkes & Weiss, 1983). It is also true that previous losses, for instance the death of a parent in childhood may increase vulnerability, as may overwhelming or repeated losses in a close timeframe. Those who are intensely distressed following the loss may also be at higher risk of delay in resolution (Vachon et al., 1980). Developmental issues are vital for children facing bereavement in terms of the impact the stressor may have, the disruptions of family and nurturing environments, and the lack of role models. Families may also be at greater risk if there are sullen, hostile, and conflictual dynamics which may disrupt adaptation (Kissane, 1998).

Preventive interventions are those aimed at decreasing these risks. They have been shown to be effective for the crisis of conjugal bereavement (Raphael, 1977; Parkes, 1980); for older people who are bereaved (Casserta, Lund, Perry, & Talbott, 1993; Gerber, Wiener, & Battin, 1975) and for parents following the death of an infant (e.g., Murray, 1998). These interventions generally take the form of focussed counseling applied in the early weeks following the death, or even beforehand if the death is anticipated. This may be provided by professionals or by skilled self-help workers such as widows, but these workers require significant training to achieve effectiveness (e.g., Parkes, 1980). Key themes in these preventive approaches include providing information; facilitating the discussion of the circumstances of the death and the bereaved's efforts to deal with these; facilitating the expression of affects of separation, longing, yearning, and angry protest as elements of grief; encouraging a history or review of the lost relationship in both its positive and negative aspects to facilitate the psychological processes of mourning; facilitating a reorientation to relationships and the world, including enhancing social support networks and the bereaved's capacity to utilize these. If issues relevant to earlier losses appear, they are dealt with in terms of the current loss, for these preventive interventions are focused on this loss, and are not psychotherapy. Dealing with these issues usually involves 4–8 sessions, more or less. The principle task of these programs is to facilitate normal grieving and diminish risk factors, but these programs do not complete the tasks of the grief. Grieving may occur over months and years to come and can be facilitated by these earlier interventions.

Treatment of Bereavement-related Pathologies.   In circumstances involving bereavement-related pathologies, intervention ideally encompasses both the facilitation of the normal grieving process, and specific therapy for the established disorders.

First, with bereavement pathologies the emphasis must be on the return of the grieving process to normal, and the cessation of excessive grief (Raphael, 1983). Psychotherapy is the basic process for the majority of these circumstances (Marmar et al., 1988; Raphael, 1983). Resolution is frequently difficult to achieve, but can involve guided mourning or other more behavioral techniques that support the bereaved person in reconfronting the loss, dealing with tasks and affect, and reengaging in the life roles (Sireling, Cohen, & Marks, 1988). These pathologies are distinct from depression in the bereaved, and from PTSD, but may co-occur. If the person cannot be moved from his or her role of grief-stricken victim, support, rehabilitation and engagement in other roles may be necessary for ongoing quality of life. The pathologies described above—chronic grief, complicated grief disorder, and traumatic grief—all have at their core continuing and excessive separation anxiety, and they all represent an avoidance of giving up the deceased. These issues need to be understood in any treatment proposed, for the key to success is being able to move the bereaved out of ongoing engagement with the deceased, which persists as a core dynamic despite the external trappings to the contrary.

Bereavement and Ill Health

Bereavement and ill health management should encompass whatever health problems exist, for these are likely to be real, while at the same time providing an opportunity, even if delayed, to work through the grief and loss. This requires the principles outlined above for both prevention and treatment and the understanding that the illness may also symbolically represent the deceased and his or her symptoms. It may represent adverse health behaviors perhaps (unconsciously) motivated by guilt. If appropriate the link to illness may be made directly, but this is not always necessary. The central issue is the facilitation of, and focus on, the loss and its resolution.

Bereavement and Depression

A careful clinical assessment is necessary to establish the difference between the sadness and emptiness of the *bereaved*, their feelings of not being able to go on without the deceased, and the despair, withdrawal, sleep disturbance, and even biological symptoms of the *depressed* person. This differentiation is often difficult, for the person is both bereaved and depressed. The management of depression in association with bereavement is that which is most appropriate for the depression that has been identified, and is usually a combination of interpersonal or cognitive behavioral psychotherapy and appropriate antidepressant medication. Risk of suicide is a particular issue that must be dealt with, and carefully monitored, for it is increased in both the bereaved and the depressed, especially if the bereavement is for a suicide death, or in the elderly. At the same time it will be necessary to deal with the grief that is experienced, which may require a specific focus in psychotherapy or counseling (Reynolds, 1997). To some degree there may need to be a specific focus on reviewing ambivalence and dependence in the lost relationship that may contribute specifically to the depressive constellation. There is evidence that such a plan has value (e.g., Raphael & Maddison, 1976). If depression is very severe and nonresponsive, then it may be necessary to consider hospitalization or even electroconvulsive therapy. Nevertheless, the key principles are to deal with both the depressive disorder and the bereavement.

Bereavement and Trauma

For the person who is both traumatized and bereaved there are likely to be specific needs. It is likely that the trauma will need to be dealt with first and in ways that also recognize the bereaved's grief. For instance, it is inappropriate to consider debriefing in such acute situations. Dealing with the traumatic stress effects will involve reviewing what has happened and reconfronting the experience in ways which do not overwhelm the traumatized and bereaved person, such as with the "dosing of affect" (Lindy, Green, Grace, & Tichener, 1983) in ways that will make it possible for the person to work through his or her issues. Decreasing arousal, preventing retraumatization, using cognitive behavioral interventions focused on the trauma (Solomon, 1999), and perhaps using medication such as anxiolytics or antidepressants are likely to be necessary if posttraumatic stress disorder becomes established. It is only as the focus on the traumatic circumstances of the death is lessened that the person may feel secure enough to commence the grieving process. Therapy in these instances, involving as it does both the trauma and the loss, must be carefully staged, and tuned to the individual's needs, but with clear end points in mind, particularly those that will enable the person to live with what has happened, and what cannot be altered (Raphael & Martinek, 1997).

Bereavement Across Generations and in Families

The recognition of the ongoing effects of loss in earlier generations is complex. When this has been large scale, restitution, apology, and recognition are likely to be helpful as are culturally appropriate memorialization and counseling or other interventions. Kissane et al. have developed a model of family grief and demonstrated the effectiveness of intervention with this model (Kissane et al., 1993). A family genogram of loss can be of value as can more individual counseling that allows for the recognition of themes and allows the person, family, or group to move on.

☐ Bereavement and Personal Growth

It has long been recognized that the majority of people deal with bereavement satisfactorily, adapt well, and continue their lives in new and positive ways. As loss is an inevitable aspect of human existence, the ways in which children learn to master it are important to their future development. For instance, learning of loss and grief, the normality and appropriateness of these feelings and their expression, can be a significant process for the child. Being able to bear separation distress and being secure in the knowledge of ongoing nurturance are key elements. If grief follows the loss of a primary attachment figure, then this will require extra resources for the child and the young person. While vulnerabilities related to loss at this stage of life have been identified above, it is also true that bereaved children in such circumstances may go on to greater creativity and enhanced development (but not a precocious maturity which is ultimately unhelpful to the child). Learning to master loss, to value oneself, to trust and express emotion, and to go on into the future, incorporating such changes are important processes, and ultimately helpful.

Vaillant (1988) has written of the positive aspects of internalization that occur in the adjustment of the bereaved. These internalizations are frequently positive, and build new aspects into the nature of the bereaved person. The phrase "it is better to have loved and lost, than never to have loved at all" is a recognition of the importance of attachments, and that the pain of loss does not destroy, but can contribute to the richness of human experience.

Ultimately, grief and bereavement are a testimony to human love and attachment—the former only occurs because of the latter. These bonds, and the pain of separation are seen to be essential to the social nature of society (e.g., Averil, 1968) and without them there would be little human growth, or social development. Bereavement is the other side of attachment—and both contribute to the social capital.

☐ References

Ainsworth, M. (1982). Attachment: Retrospect and prospect. In C. M. Parkes & J. Stevenson-Hinde (Eds.), *The place of attachment in human behavior* (pp. 3–30). New York: Basic Books.

Andrews, G. (1996). Comorbidity and the general neurotic sundrome. *British Journal of Psychiatry, 168* (Suppl. 30), 76–84.

Averill, J. (1968). Grief: Its nature and significance. *Psychological Bulletin, 70,* 721–748.

Bartrop, R. W., Lazarus, L., Luckhurst, E., Kiloh, L. G. & Penny, R. (1977). Depressed lymphocyte function after bereavement. *Lancet I,* 834–836.

Biondi, M., & Picardi, A. (1996). Clinical and biological aspects of bereavement and loss-induced depression: A reapraisal. *Psychotherapy and Psychosomatics, 65,* 229–245.

Bowlby, J. (1969). *Attachment and loss.* Vol. 1. *Attachment.* London: Hogarth/New York: Basic Books.

Bowlby, J. (1973). *Attachment and loss.* Vol. 2. *Separation: Anxiety and anger.* New York: Basic Books/London: Hogarth Press.

Bowlby, J. (1980). *Attachment and loss*. Vol. 3. *Loss: Sadness and depression*. London: Hogarth Press/New York: Basic Books/Harmondsworth: Penguin Books.

Brown, G., Harris, T., & Copeland, J. (1977). Depression and loss. *British Journal of Psychiatry, 30*, 1–18.

Burnett, P., Middleton, W., Raphael, B., & Martinek, N. (1997). Measuring core bereavement phenomena. *Psychological Medicine, 7*, 49–57.

Byrne, G. J., & Raphael, B. (1994). A longitudinal study of bereavement phenomena in recently widowed elderly men. *Psychological Medicine, 24*, 411–421.

Cain, A. C., Fast, I., & Erickson, M. E. (1964). Children's disturbed reactions to the death of a sibling. *American Journal of Orthopsychiatry, 34*, 741–752.

Casserta, M. S., Lund, D. A., Perry, S. W., & Talbott, J. A. (1993). Intrapersonal resources and the effectiveness of self-help groups for bereaved older adults. *Gerontologist, 33*, 619–629.

Danieli, Y. (1982). Families of survivors of the Nazi Holocaust: Some short- and long-term effects. In C. D. Spielberger, I. G. Sarason, & N. A. Milgram (Eds.), *Stress and anxiety*. Washington, DC: Hemisphere.

Eisenbruch, M. (1991). From post-traumatic stress disorder to cultural bereavement: Diagnosis of South East Asian refugees. *Social Science and Medicine, 33*, 673–680.

Engel, G. L. (1961). Is grief a disease? *Psychosomatic Medicine, 23*, 18–22.

Freud, S. (1917/1975). Mourning and melancholia. In *Collected papers* (Vol. IV). London: Hogarth Press.

George, M. S., Ketter, T. A., Parekh, P. I., Horwitz, B., Herscovitch, P., & Post, R. M. (1995). Brain activity during transient sadness and happiness in healthy women. *American Journal of Psychiatry, 152*, 341–351.

Gerber, I., Wiener, A., & Battin, D. (1975). Brief therapy to the aged bereaved. In B. Schoenberg & I. Gerber (Eds.), *Bereavement: Its psychosocial aspects*. New York: Columbia University Press.

Hofer, M. A. (1984). Relationships as regulators: A psychobiological perspective on bereavement. *Psychosomatic Medicine, 46*, 183–197.

Horowitz, M. (1976). *Stress response syndromes*. Northvale, NJ: Aronson.

Horowitz, M. J., Siegel, B., Holen, A., Bonnanno, G., Milbrath, C., & Stinson, C. H. (1997). Diagnostic criteria for complicated grief disorder. *American Journal of Psychiatry, 154*(7), 904–910.

Irwin, M., Daniels, M., Bloom, E., Smith, T. L., & Weiner, H. (1987). Life events, depressive symptoms, and immune function. *American Journal of Psychiatry, 144*, 437–441.

Jacobs, S. C. (1987). Measures of the psychological distress of bereavement. In S. Zissook (Ed.), *Biopsychosocial aspects of bereavement* (pp. 127–138). Washington, DC: American Psychiatric Association.

Jacobs, S. C. (1993). *Pathologic grief: Maladaptation to loss*. Washington, DC: American Psychiatric Press.

Jacobs, S., & Ostfeld, A. (1977). An epidemiological review of the mortality of bereavement. *Psychosomatic Medicine, 39*, 344–357.

Kaprio, J., Koskenvko, M., & Rita, H.H. (1987). Mortality after bereavement: A prospective study of 96,647 widowed persons. *American Journal of Public Health, 77*, 283–287.

Kissane, D. (1998). A controlled trial of family intervention to promote health family functioning in at-risk palliative care families. *Australian and New Zealand Journal of Psychiatry, 32* (Suppl.).

Kissane, D., & Bloch, S. (1994). Family grief. *British Journal of Psychiatry, 164*(60), 728–740.

Kling, A., Llioyd, R., Tachiki, K., Prince, H., Klimenko, V., & Korneva, E. (1992). Effects of social seperation on immune function and brain neurotransmitters in cebus monkey (C. apella). *Annals of New York Academy of Science, 650*, 257–261.

Lindy, J. D., Green, B. L., Grace, M., & Tichener, J. (1983). Psychotherapy with survivors of the Beverley Hills Supper Club fire. *American Journal of Psychotherapy, 37*, 593–610.

Lopata, H. Z. (1979). *Women as widows*. New York and Amsterdam: Elsevier.

Lundin, T. (1984). Morbidity following sudden and unexpected bereavement. *British Journal of Psychiatry, 144*, 84–88.

Maddison, D. C., & Walker, W. L. (1967). Factors affecting conjugal bereavement. *British Journal of Psychiatry, 113*, 1057–1067.

Main, M. (1985). An adult attachment classification system. Paper presented at the biennial meeting of the Society for Research in Child Development, Toronto.

Marmar, C. R., Horowitz, M. J., Weiss, D. S., Wilner, N. R., & Kaltreider, N. B. (1988). A controlled trial of brief psychotherapy and mutual-help group treatment of conjugal bereavement. *American Journal of Psychiatry, 145*, 203–209.

Mayberg, H. S., Liotti, M., Brannan, S. K., McGinnis, S., & Mahurin, R. K. (1999). Reciprocal limbic-cortical function and negative mood: Converging PET findings in depression and normal sadness. *American Journal of Psychiatry, 156*, 675–682.

McKinney, W. T. (1995). Animal research and its relevance to psychiatry. In H. I. Kaplan & B. J. Sadock (Eds.), *Comprehensive textbook of psychiatry*, Edition 6. Baltimore: Williams & Wilkins.

Middleton, W., Burnett, P., Raphael, B., & Martinek, N. (1996). The bereavement response: A cluster analysis. *British Journal of Psychiatry, 169*, 167–171.

Middleton, W., Moylan, A., Raphael, B., Burnett, P., & Martinek, N. (1993). An international perspective on bereavement-related concepts. *Australian & New Zealand Journal of Psychiatry, 27*, 457–463.

Middleton, W., Raphael, B., Burnett, P., & Martinek, N. (1998). A longitudinal study comparing bereavement phenomena in recently bereaved spouses, adult children and parents. *Australian & New Zealand Journal of Psychiatry, 32*, 235–241.

Murray, J. (1998). Bereavement after infant death. *Grief Matters, 1*(3).

Ober, C., Peeters, L., Archer, R., & Kelly, K. (2000). Debriefing in different cultural frameworks: Experience with indigenous populations. In B. Raphael & J. Wilson (Eds.), *Stress debriefing: Theory, practice and challenge*. London: Cambridge University Press.

Parkes, C. M. (1980). Bereavement counselling: Does it work? *British Medical Journal, 281*, 3–10.

Parkes, C. M. (1986). *Bereavement: Studies of grief in adult life*. New York: International Universities Press.

Parkes, C. M., & Weiss, R. S. (1983). *Recovery from bereavement*. New York: Basic Books.

Prigerson, H. G., Shear, K., Jacobs, S., & Reynolds, C. (1999). Consensus criteria for traumatic grief: A preliminary empirical test. *British Journal of Psychiatry, 174*, 67–73.

Pynoos, R. S., Nader, K., Frederick, C., Gonda, L., & Stuber, M. (1987). Grief reactions in school-age children following a sniper attack at school. *Israeli Journal of Psychiatry and Related Sciences, 24*, 53–63.

Raphael, B. (1977). Preventive intervention with the recently bereaved. *Archives of General Psychiatry, 34*(12),1450–1454.

Raphael, B. (1983). *Anatomy of bereavement*. New York: Basic Books.

Raphael, B., Field, J., & Kvelde, H. (1980). Childhood bereavement: A prospective study as a possible prelude to future preventive intervention. In E. J. Anthony & C. Chiland (Eds.), *Preventive psychiatry in an age of transition*. New York: Wiley.

Raphael, B., & Maddison, D. C. (1976). Care of bereaved adults. In O. W. Hill (Ed.), *Modern Trends in Psychosomatic Medicine-3* (pp. 491–506). London: Butterworths.

Raphael, B., & Martinek, N. (1997). Assessing traumatic bereavement and PTSD. In J. Wilson & T. Keane (Eds.), *Assessing Psychological Trauma and PTSD* (pp. 373–395). New York: Guilford Press.

Raphael, B., & Minkov, C. (1999). Abnormal grief. *Current Opinion in Psychiatry, 12*, 99–102.

Raphael, B., & Swan, P. (1997). The mental health of Aboriginal and Torres Strait Islander people. *International Journal of Mental Health, 26*(3), 9–22.

Reynolds, C. F. (1997). Treatment of major depression in later life: A life cycle perspective. *Psychiatry Quarterly, 68*(3), 221–246.

Rosenblatt, P. C., Walsh, R. P. & Jackson, D. A. (1976). *Grief and mourning in a cross-cultural perspective.* New Haven: Human Relations Area Files Press.

Rynearson, E. K. (1984). Bereavement after homicide: A descriptive study. *American Journal of Psychiatry, 141,* 1452–1454.

Schleifer, S. J., Keller, S. E., Camerino, M., Thornton, J. C., & Stein, M. (1983). Suppression of lymphocyte stimulation following bereavement. *Journal of the American Medical Association, 250,* 374–377.

Schut, H. A. W., Keijser, J. D., Van Den Bout, J., & Dijhuis, J. H. (1991). Post-traumatic stress symptoms in the first years of conjugal bereavement. *Anxiety Research, 4,* 225–234.

Seale, C. (1998). *Constructing death: The sociology of dying and bereavement.* Cambridge, UK: Cambridge University Press.

Shuchter, S. R., Zisook, S., Kirkorowicz, C., & Risch, C. (1986). The dexamethazone test in acute grief. *American Journal of Psychiatry, 143,* 879–881.

Silverman, P. R. (1986). *Widow-to-widow.* New York: Springer.

Singh, B., & Raphael, B. (1981). Postdisaster morbidity of the bereaved. A possible role for preventive psychiatry? *Journal of Nervous and Mental Disease, 169,* 203–212.

Sireling, L., Cohen, D., & Marks, I. (1988). Guided mourning for morbid grief: A controlled replication. *Behavior Therapy, 19*(2), 121–132.

Solomon, Z. (1999). Interventions for acute trauma response. *Current Opinion in Psychiatry, 12,* 175–180.

Vachon, M. L., Lyall, W. A., & Rogers, J. (1980). A controlled study of self-help interventions for widows. *American Journal of Psychiatry, 137*(11), 1380–1384.

Vaillant, G. E. (1988). Attachment, loss and rediscovery. *Hillside Journal of Clinical Psychiatry, 10*(2), 148–164.

Van Eerdewegh, M. M., Clayton, P. J., & Van Eerdewegh, P. (1985). The bereaved child: Variables influencing early psychopathology. *British Journal of Psychiatry, 147,* 188–194.

Van Gennep, A. (1960). *The rites of passage.* Chicago: University of Chicago Press.

Weller, E. B., Weller, R. A., Fristad, M. A., & Bowes, J. M. (1990). Dexamethasone suppression test and depressive symptoms in bereaved children: A preliminary report. *Journal of Neuropsychiatry and Clinical Neuroscience, 2,* 418–421.

Worden, W. (1991). *Grief counselling and grief therapy.* London: Routledge.

Zisook, S., Shuchter, S. R., Sledge, P. A., Paulus, M., & Judd, L. L. (1994). The spectrum of depressive phenomena after spousal bereavement. *Journal of Clinical Psychiatry, 55* (Suppl.), 29–36.

Louis A. Penner
John F. Dovidio
Terrance L. Albrecht

Helping Victims of Loss and Trauma: A Social Psychological Perspective

The primary goal of this chapter is to apply the social psychological literature on prosocial behavior to the topic of helping people who have experienced a loss or trauma. Specifically, we first discuss why people are motivated to help people who are victims of such circumstances. Then we examine a particular kind of helping that seems especially effective during times of loss and trauma—social support. Next we consider the factors that may affect a person's willingness to ask for help at the time of a personal loss or trauma. Finally, we attempt to integrate the three major sections of the chapter and outline some of the conceptual relationships among the occurrence of personal loss or a traumatic event, the emotional and behavioral reactions, and the affective and behavioral responses of others who are available to help or offer social support.

Before reviewing the relevant research literatures in these three areas, we present the conceptual definitions that guide this chapter and identify some of the important parameters of helping in the context of loss and trauma. We conceive of loss as an instance in which one person loses the companionship of a valued other because that person dies or voluntarily or involuntarily terminates the relationship. Thus, examples of loss would include the death of individuals such as a family member, close friend, or lover; the end of a platonic or romantic relationship; or the undesired physical separation of people who previously lived in close proximity (e.g., a job change that required a move to a distant location). There could also be losses that involve a substantial decline in the quality of an ongoing relationship (e.g., the impact of Alzheimer's disease or some similar disorder on the relationship between a child and parent). A trauma, as it is conceptualized here, would involve some extremely severe, unpleasant, and perhaps life-changing event that a person has survived but with some considerable physical and/or psychological consequences. Examples of this would include being the victim of some natural disaster, such as a hurricane, being stricken with a severe and debilitating illness, and being the victim of a violent crime.

Experiences of loss and trauma are much more common than one might suppose. Calhoun and Tedeschi (1998) reported that 21% of the respondents sampled in a four city survey had had a traumatic event in the past year and "69 percent reported the occurrence of one such event in their lifetime" (p. 357). Of course, most personal losses are also extremely traumatic events. For example, Wortman and her colleagues (e.g., Wortman, Battle, & Lemkau, 1997) have found that the unexpected death of a spouse or child may traumatize the surviving family members for years after the death.

Next, there is the matter of the kinds of help that we consider. We focus primarily on nonprofessional helping. This is assistance provided by people who are not employed in a helping profession, or at least who are not operating in a professional capacity at the time they come to another's aid. There are a number of different kinds of nonprofessional helping. McGuire (1994) asked college students to list the different kinds of help they had received from and given to friends, casual acquaintances, and strangers. Based on their responses, she identified four kinds of helping: 1) casual helping—doing some small favor for a casual acquaintance, such as lending the person a pen; 2) substantial personal helping—expending some considerable effort to provide a friend with tangible benefit, such as helping the friend move into an apartment; 3) emotional helping—providing emotional or personal support to a friend, such as listening to a friend's personal problems; and 4) emergency helping—coming to the aid of a stranger with an acute problem, such as helping the victim of an accident. It would seem reasonable that in those instances when the person in need has experienced a loss or trauma, the aid offered would be substantial and often involve the provision of both emotional and personal support. We discuss this in more detail in the section on social support in response to loss and trauma.

Finally, there is the context in which the helping occurs. Clark and her associates (e.g., Clark & Mills, 1993; Clark & Pataki, 1995) distinguish between *exchange* and *communal* relationships. In an exchange relationship, there is an expectation that whatever benefits one party provides to the other, will be reciprocated. Failure to do this can impair or even end the relationship. In contrast, parties to a communal relationship do not expect repayment, because they have feelings of "responsibility for the other's well-being [and] . . . benefits are given in response to others' needs or simply to please the other" (Clark & Pataki, 1995, p. 290). Thus, the relevant motives and norms that govern offering and seeking help may differ as a function of whether a relationship is exchange or communal. We note at this point, however, that much of the work on helping, although it may identify differences in responses to friends and strangers, does not explicitly consider whether these relationships are communal or exchange. In the next section, we explore the different motivations that can underlie helping.

☐ Motives for Helping

There is an extensive body of social psychological research concerned with the situational variables that make it likely that help will be offered (see Batson, 1998; Dovidio, 1984; Dovidio & Penner, in press; Schroeder, Penner, Dovidio, & Piliavin, 1995). People are more likely to help others when the problem is clear and severe, when the person has great need for assistance, when the bystander and the person in need share a close relationship, when the bystander is more likely to conclude that he or she is responsible for helping, and when helping is less "costly" for the benefactor. These principles also apply directly to helping in situations of actual or potential loss or trauma (Otten, Penner, & Waugh, 1988; Rabow, Newcomb, Monto, & Hernandez, 1990). In this section, however, we focus on the processes that ultimately motivate people's actions to help. Affect plays a prominent role in these processes.

Affect and Helping

Awareness of another's loss or experience of a traumatic event often initiates a social comparison process in which people compare their own situation to the plight of the other person. Depending on one's focus of attention, this comparison can produce different emotional reactions and decisions about whether to help (Thompson, Cowan, & Rosenhan, 1980). For instance, when people focus on their own fortunate situation, relative to that of another person, they often experience feelings of guilt. Guilt is a powerful motivator of helping (Salovey, Mayer, & Rosenhan, 1991). Simply anticipating guilt can also motivate helping. That is, people may offer assistance because they believe, probably through past experience, that they will feel guilty if they do not help. Such guilt is most strongly and commonly experienced in communal relationships (Baumeister, Stillwell, & Heatherton, 1994). Alternatively, when people focus their attention on the other person's loss in their social comparison, the predominant emotion may be sadness. Feelings of sadness also promote helping (Cialdini, Kenrick, & Baumann, 1982).

How do personal negative reactions, such as guilt and sadness motivate helping? Cialdini and his colleagues (Cialdini et al., 1982; Cialdini et al., 1987) have proposed a general model, the *negative state relief model*, to explain the effects of guilt and sadness on helping. This theory of what motivates helping begins with the well-documented premise that, through socialization and experience, people have learned helping can serve as a secondary reinforcer (Williamson & Clark, 1989; Yinon & Landau, 1987); the good feelings derived from helping may therefore relieve their negative mood. Thus, negative moods, such as guilt or sadness, may motivate people to help because helping produces the reward of making them feel better. The negative state relief model proposes that people are motivated primarily to feel good rather than to look good. This motivation for helping is essentially egoistic. That is, the primary motive for helping another person is that helping improves the helper's own situation. Thus, the negative state relief model might posit that the personal sadness or guilt caused by the awareness of another's loss might motivate the observer to offer help. But the primary motive underlying the helping is the alleviation of the helper's own sadness (Cialdini, Darby, & Vincent, 1973). (For a critique of the negative state relief model see Carlson & Miller, 1987.)

In addition to experiencing personal negative emotions to another person's loss, people also commonly feel bad *for* the other person. Even the most stoic victim of some loss or trauma is likely to display some overt indication of his or her distress. People who witness this reaction are autonomically aroused by the distress and experience some sort of emotional response (see Eisenberg, Cumberland, & Spinrad, 1998). This phenomenon is so strong and universal that some researchers have proposed that empathic arousal, arousal generated vicariously by another person's distress, has a biological and evolutionary basis (Harris, 1998; also see Schroeder et al., 1995).

Although most researchers agree that empathic arousal is important and fundamental in helping (see Dovidio, 1984), there is much less agreement about the nature of this emotion and how it actually motivates people to help. Empathic arousal may produce different emotions. In severe situations, potential helpers may become upset and distressed; in less critical, less intense problem situations, observers may feel sad (Cialdini et al., 1987), tense (Hornstein, 1982), or concerned and compassionate (Batson, 1991). Thus, in contrast to the negative state relief model, other affective models of helping focus more on the empathic arousal people experience in response to another person's problem, plight, or distress.

The *arousal: cost-reward model* is a tension-reduction model that proposes that empathic arousal motivates bystanders to take action, and a cost-reward analysis shapes the direction that this action will take. More specifically, this model proposes that empathic arousal is generated by witnessing the distress of another person. When the bystander's empathic arousal is attributed to the other person's distress, it is emotionally experienced by the observer as unpleasant and the bystander is therefore motivated to reduce it. One normally efficient way of reducing this arousal is by helping to relieve the other's distress, but if another, nonhelpful action (e.g., leaving the scene) provides the same result at a lower overall cost, people will choose this course of action.

There is substantial evidence for the fundamental proposition of this model that people are emotionally responsive to the distress of others (see Fabes, Eisenberg, & Eisenbud, 1993). Adults and children not only report feeling empathy, but they also become physiologically aroused by the pain and suffering of others. Moreover, observers may not just feel bad about the pain or distress of another person, but they may also begin to experience what the other person is feeling (Vaughan & Lanzetta, 1980). Also supportive of the arousal: cost-reward model, empathic arousal attributed to the other person's situation motivates helping. Facial, gestural, and vocal indications of empathically induced arousal, as well as self-reports of empathically induced anxiety, have consistently been found to be positively related to helping (see Dovidio, Piliavin, Gaertner, Schroeder, & Clark, 1991; Eisenberg & Miller, 1987; Marks, Penner, & Stone, 1982). Finally, although this model was specifically developed to explain bystanders' reactions in emergency situations, it appears to be applicable to the provision of psychological help by friends in response to psychological distress (Otten et al., 1988).

Although this model of helping, like the negative state relief model, posits an egoistic motive for helping, the two models differ in two basic respects. First, in the arousal: cost-reward model only arousal attributed to the plight of the other person will motivate helping. In contrast, the negative state relief model posits that negative states regardless of their source (particularly guilt and sadness) can motivate helping. Second, the arousal: cost-reward model is a tension-reduction model, in which the victim's need produces an arousal state in the potential helper; and the benefactor intervenes to alleviate his or her own aversive state by eliminating the victim's distress. According to the negative state relief model, however, people in negative moods are looking for ways to eliminate or neutralize their negative mood. Thus, any event, even one that would not benefit the person in distress, could improve the emotional state of the observer.

In contrast to these egoistic models of helping is the *empathy-altruism hypothesis*, developed by Batson and his colleagues (see Batson, 1991; Batson, 1998; Batson et al., 1997). These researchers acknowledge that egoistically motivated helping occurs, but they also argue that true altruism also exists. Altruism is defined as helping with the primary and exclusive goal of improving the other person's welfare. Specifically, according to the empathy-altruism hypothesis, witnessing another person in need can produce a range of emotional experiences, such as sadness, personal distress (e.g., upset, worry), and empathic concern (e.g., sympathy, compassion). However, whereas sadness and personal distress produce egoistic motivations to help, empathic concern creates altruistic motivation.

Batson (1987, 1991) suggests that under some circumstances, for example if there is a special bond between the potential helper and the person in need, the primary affective response will not be sadness or personal distress but rather empathy or empathic concern, which he defines as, "an other-oriented emotional response (e.g., sympathy, compassion) congruent with the . . . welfare of another person" (Batson & Oleson, 1991, p. 63). In contrast to sadness and personal distress, which as noted above generate an egoistic desire to reduce one's own distress, Batson (1987, 1991) proposes that empathic concern produces an altruistic motivation to reduce the other person's distress. The altruistically motivated person will then help if helping is possible; helping is perceived to be ultimately beneficial to the person in need; and helping personally will provide greater benefit to the person in need than would assistance from another person also able to offer it. Thus, empathic concern is hypothesized to produce greater concern for the welfare of the other person.

In numerous experiments, conducted over a 20-year period, Batson and his colleagues have produced impressive empirical support for the empathy-altruism hypothesis (Batson, 1991, 1998). Participants who experience relatively high levels of empathic concern (and who presumably are altruistically motivated) show high levels of helpfulness. However, several researchers have proposed alternative explanations that challenge Batson's contention that helping may be altruistically motivated. Perhaps the alternative explanations of most relevance to an understanding of helping in a time of loss or trauma are those proposed by Cialdini and his colleagues (Cialdini et al., 1987; Schaller & Cialdini, 1988).

They have argued that empathic people may have a greater motivation to help because empathy has aroused sadness as well as empathic concern, and it is the egoistic need to relieve this sadness that is really motivating helping. The data relevant to this argument are inconsistent and contradictory. Cialdini and his colleagues found that empathy produced high levels of sadness as well as empathic concern (Cialdini et al., 1987, Study 1) and that empathically concerned people showed high levels of helpfulness only when they believed that their sad mood could be improved by helping (Cialdini et al., 1987, Study 2). But in two subsequent studies, Batson et al. (1989) demonstrated, consistent with altruistic motivation, that anticipating a mood-enhancing event did not lead people high in empathic concern to be less helpful. Other studies have revealed that empathically-aroused participants exhibit a high level of helping even when they are led to believe that helping could not improve their mood (Schroeder, Dovidio, Sibicky, Matthews, & Allen, 1988) and that their motivation is directed at helping the particular person for whom they feel empathy, not helping just anyone (which would also presumably improve their mood; Dovidio, Allen, & Schroeder, 1990).

More recently, Cialdini, Brown, Lewis, Luce, and Neuberg (1997) have argued that the conditions that typically lead to empathic concern for another person may also create a greater sense of self-other overlap, or "oneness" between the potential helper and the recipient of the help. This raises the possibility that empathy-related helping may not be selfless, because helping would also indirectly improve at least the psychological well-being of the helper. Cialdini et al. obtained results that supported this thesis. However, in response to this challenge, Batson et al. (1997) conducted a series of studies in which they directly manipulated empathy and shared group membership (which, presumably affects self-other overlap). Contrary to Cialdini's argument, Batson et al. reported that the empathy helping relationship was "unqualified by group membership" (p. 495). (For further discussion of these studies see also Batson, 1997; Neuberg et al., 1997.)

The issue of whether true altruism is possible remains unresolved, but the theoretical arguments between Cialdini and Batson serve to highlight one of the difficulties in specifying the motivations that underlie helping in a time of a personal loss. On the one hand, it is reasonable to assume that often the "special bond" of which Batson speaks often exists between the helper and the recipient; thus empathic concern is likely to exist. At the same time, it is also likely that the potential helper, like the potential recipient, is directly and negatively affected by the loss or trauma, is greatly saddened or distressed by the recipient's displays of grief and sorrow, or both. Thus, in a real world context parsing out the motivational processes that underlie the prosocial action may be difficult, if not impossible.

Motivations for helping include cognitive as well as affective components. That is, people learn through socialization what is expected and socially valued. In addition, they internalize these values as personal standards for behavior. We examine these motivational factors in the next section.

Social Norms and Personal Standards

People often help others because they have expectations based on previous social learning or by learning through the current behavior of others that helping is the socially appropriate response. That is, helping results from "pressure to comply with shared group expectations about appropriate behavior that are backed by social sanctions and rewards" (Schwartz & Howard, 1982, p. 346). Researchers have identified two classes of social norms involving helping. One class relates to feelings of fairness; the other relates to very general norms of aiding, such as the social responsibility norm (Berkowitz, 1972).

One major kind of fairness norm is the norm of reciprocity—people should help those who have helped them, and they should not help those who have denied them help for no legitimate reason (Gouldner, 1960). Consistent with this proposition, people normally reciprocate assistance to others who have helped them. This is particularly true when the person expects to see the helper again (Carnevale, Pruitt, & Carrington, 1982), although it can also occur when there is no expectation of future interaction (Goranson & Berkowitz, 1966). Also, the more assistance a person receives, the more help he or she subsequently gives (Kahn & Tice, 1973). Reciprocity involving the repayment of specific benefits is particularly strong for most casual relationships, but it may be weaker in more intimate communal relationships (Clark & Mills, 1993). In communal relationships, however, a broader type of reciprocity may be involved in which people are generally mutually responsive to the needs of the other person, if needs arise. People involved in such relationships are primarily concerned about the welfare of their partner and anticipate that kindnesses will be reciprocated if such actions are ever needed (Webley & Lea, 1993). Consequently, they monitor the needs of their partner more closely than the immediate exchange of assistance, and thus helping is tied more directly to responsiveness to these needs than to a desire to repay specific assistance previously received. However, these circumstances notwithstanding, the norm of reciprocity appears to be a basic and fundamental aspect of human social exchanges.

The norm of social responsibility, however, it is based on the notion that people are expected to help others who are dependent on them, even when there is no tangible gain for the benefactor (Berkowitz & Daniels, 1964). In general, the greater the need, the more likely people are to help (Piliavin, Dovidio, Gaertner, & Clark, 1981). This norm exerts less influence, however, if the person in need is responsible for creating his or her own plight through a lack of effort (Frey & Gaertner, 1986) or through immoral conduct (Weiner, Perry, & Magnusson, 1988). There are also cultural differences, with individualistic cultures having weaker social responsibility norms than collectivistic cultures (Ma, 1985).

Norms of social responsibility may be general and societal or they may be personal—that is, held personally by the individual. Whereas general norms provide only a vague guide for behavior in concrete situations, personal norms and standards are valuable for accounting for how a particular person will behave in a specific situation. Personal norms typically predict both incidental helping and assistance to victims of trauma (e.g., bone marrow donation; Schwartz, 1970) better than general social norms (Schwartz & Howard, 1982), particularly when attention is focused inward on these personal standards (Hoover, Wood, & Knowles, 1983). Personal norms and standards and affective reactions can also influence longer-term forms of helping.

Sustained Helping

One recent trend in the study of the motives that underlie helping is the functional approach of Snyder, Clary, and their associates (e.g., Clary & Snyder, 1991; Clary et al., 1998; Omoto & Snyder, 1995). This approach attempts to identify the "personal and social needs, plans, goals, and functions that are being served by . . . [these] actions." (Clary & Snyder, 1991, p. 123). The personal goals that underlie helping may differ as a function of the context in which the helping occurs.

These researchers have focused primarily on a particular form of helping—volunteerism, or sustained helping without obligation (Omoto & Snyder, 1995). Clary et al. (1998) identified six motives that might lead a person to offer help: 1) value-expressive—expressing values related to altruistic and humanitarian concerns; 2) understanding—gaining knowledge or exercising existing knowledge, skills, and abilities; 3) social—being among friends and engaging in activities that might win their approval; 4) career—pursuing activities that might directly or indirectly benefit one's career; 5) protective—protecting one's ego from negative features of the self and helping to address personal problems; and 6) enhancement—enhancing positive feelings about oneself and furthering personal growth and development.

Omoto and Snyder (1995; see also Snyder & Omoto, 1992) have conducted longitudinal studies of the motives of volunteers at organizations that serve people experiencing a particular kind of trauma—individuals with a HIV infection or AIDS, for instance. Omoto and Snyder (1995) found that three self-serving motives—understanding, personal development, and esteem enhancement—were all positively associated with tenure as a volunteer, but the value-expressive motive was not. These findings were consistent with earlier findings by Snyder and Omoto (1992), and led Omoto and Snyder (1995) to conclude, "it appears that the opportunity to have personal, self-serving, and perhaps even selfish functions served by volunteering was what kept volunteers actively involved" (p. 683).

Other studies have also found that personal motives play a significant role in volunteerism, but sometimes these are not the same motives identified Omoto and Snyder. For example, Penner and Finkelstein (1998) also studied AIDS volunteers but did not find any significant relationships involving the self-serving or selfish motives. However, among male volunteers they did find significant positive correlations between the value-expressive motive and willingness to directly aid a person with HIV or AIDS. Similarly, Clary and Orenstein (1991) found a positive association between altruistic motives and the length of service of crisis counseling volunteers.

Although the study of specific motives that may underlie helping would seem to be a fruitful line of research to pursue, some might question whether it will help us to better understand helping in response to another person's loss or trauma. As noted above, Omoto and Snyder (1995) conceive of volunteerism as a nonobligated form of helping. They distinguish it from obligated kinds of helping, such as caring for a disabled or impaired family member, in which case they believe that personal and familial obligations rather any personal needs or goals may drive the sustained helping. Certainly, in many instances of loss and trauma such obligations would be present. But at the same time, there are many other instances in which people offer nonobligated help in response to a person's loss or trauma. Thus, an understanding of the helper's specific motives or the functions that helping serves for her or him may further our understanding of helping under these circumstances. Some researchers have suggested that at least some of the most basic functions of helping may have evolutionary and biological bases.

Biological Bases of Helping

Although biologists and ethologists have long argued for a biological basis of helping, the extension of these arguments to prosocial actions among humans is a relatively recent and sometimes controversial development (Buss & Kenrick, 1998). However, the following findings lend credence to a biological approach to helping. First, as noted earlier, empathy plays a critical role in helping and it appears that there is a specific part of the human brain—the limbic system—that gives humans the capacity to empathize with other people (Carlson, 1998). Moreover, this brain structure was present very early in human evolutionary history (MacLean, 1985). Indeed, it may have been present in the earliest mammals, over 180 million years ago. Second, studies of identical twins have consistently suggested the heritability of empathy (Davis, Luce, & Kraus, 1994; Rushton, Fulker, Neale, Nias, & Eysenck, 1986; Zahn-Waxler, Robinson, & Emde, 1992). Thus, although there may be individual differences in empathic tendencies (Penner, Fritzsche, Craiger, & Freifeld, 1995), humans appear to be generally inherently empathic. Lastly, there is the fact that in all known cultures the principle of reciprocity exists in some form (Moghaddam, Taylor, & Wright, 1993), suggesting to some researchers that there is a biological basis for this behavior (Sober & Wilson, 1998).

Trivers (1971) used the term *reciprocal altruism* to refer to a genetic tendency for mutual helping that increases inclusive fitness, the likelihood that one's genes will be transmitted to future generations. One important component of inclusive fitness is a form of helping known as kin selection. A well-documented phenomenon among animals, kin selection refers to the strong positive association between biological (i.e., genetic) relatedness and the incidence of mutual helping (Alcock, 1989). Kin selection makes evolutionary sense because saving the lives of relatives (sometimes even at the sacrifice of one's own life) can increase the incidence of one's own genes in subsequent generations (Buss & Kenrick, 1998).

Cunningham (1985/1986) reviewed the research on kin selection and reciprocal altruism in humans and found, supportive of the biological perspective, that the closer the kinship relationship the greater the expectations that help would be given to them, the greater the resentment if help were withheld, the greater the willingness to provide aid to the other person, and the more they expected that help would be reciprocated. More recently, Burnstein, Crandall, and Kitayama (1994) used a simulation methodology with college students and found that helping increased as a function of biological relatedness (see also Segal, 1993). With respect to specifically helping victims of trauma, Borgida, Conner, and Manteufal (1992) found that people were about three times more likely to donate a kidney to a relative than to a nonrelative (73% vs. 27%). Taken together, these studies would lead one to conclude that at least some portion of the help that people provide to one another in times of loss or trauma may have its roots in human's evolutionary history. Indeed, one might conjecture that helping people—especially during times of loss or trauma—might have considerable evolutionary value for both the helper and the recipient.

Helping often occurs in less dramatic forms than organ donation, involving more sustained efforts at providing material, emotional, and psychological support. These efforts are often embedded in ongoing relationships. In the next section we consider this type of assistance—social support.

☐ Social Support

Among the different kinds of help that could be offered to someone who has suffered a loss or trauma, the kind that is most likely to be offered is social support (see Pierce, Lakey, Sarason, & Sarason, 1997; Pierce, Sarason, & Sarason, 1996). We begin this section with a discussion of the characteristics and functions of social support and social support networks.

The Nature of Social Support

Social support is a form of communication that occurs among people during ordinary, but also extraordinary, life events such as after divorce (Bretherton, Walsh, & Lependorf (1996) and among care givers to persons with Alzheimer's disease (Pillemer & Suitor, 1996). Supportive relationships between intimates, acquaintances, work associates, friends, relatives, extended kin, and, at times, strangers affect many aspects of emotional and physical well-being (Albrecht, Burleson, & Goldsmith, 1994). Early definitions of support were primarily based in individual perceptions of acceptance and caring. For example, Cobb (1976) defined support as the "individual's perception of being esteemed and valued, of belonging to a network of communication and mutual obligation" (p. 1300). In contrast, Tolsdorf (1976) and Eyres and MacElveen-

Hoehn (1983) viewed support as an action or behavior that facilitates coping, mastery or control. Later definitions were broadened to include processes of exchange between people. Currently, researchers view social support as an interactional process of helping, comforting, caring for, aiding, and responding to the needs of others (Albrecht & Adelman, 1987; Albrecht, Burleson, & Sarason, 1992; Burleson, Albrecht, Goldsmith, & Sarason, 1994; Cutrona, 1996; Cutrona, Suhr, & MacFarlane, 1990; Duck & Silver, 1990; Sarason, Pierce, & Sarason, 1990). When framed as a communication process, social support has been described as verbal and nonverbal behaviors that influence how both parties to the interaction view themselves, the situation, the other person, and the relationship. Social support functions to help those in need manage personal and situational uncertainty and increase the perception of personal control (see also Albrecht & Adelman, 1987; Ford, Barrow, & Stohl, 1996).

We must also note that although this chapter focuses primarily on helping in dyads, supportive relationships and interactions never exist in a vacuum. Individuals are part of social networks and social support is provided by members of such collectives (Wills, 1990). Thus, supportive individual interactions occur within the context of larger support networks; further individual interactions and social support networks are involved in reciprocal relationships. That is, social support networks shape and sustain supportive behaviors among individuals and reflect and reinforce the values and structures of support in the larger community.

Networks can be characterized by several structural properties, including size, density, homogeneity or heterogeneity, and multiplexity. Typically, the larger the size of the network, the more options one has for seeking help from close relationships (e.g., family, kin, and friends) and more distant ones as well (e.g., acquaintances, familiar strangers, friends of friends). Nurturing, caring, and tangible assistance are likely to be provided almost immediately in close relationships; in more distant ones, the support is likely to come in the form of external referrals and needed information. Density (the relative interconnectedness of one's ties) and multiplexity (the degree to which multiple role relationships connect people, such as being neighbors, and coworkers, or being cousins, teammates, and close friends) are operationalizations of the level of connection, bonding, and emotional ties existing among people. Close, integrated ties can provide a sense of stability and belongingness. Such networks are more reactive, pliable structures in that information may travel more quickly, thus mobilizing needed resources and aid in a relatively shorter time frame. There is an upper limit, however, to this. Overly dense and multiplex relationships can be stifling, less prone to act if conflict exists, provide group pressure, and retain a collective memory of trauma and loss in ways that may delay recovery, fresh starts and cognitive reframing (Albrecht, 1994; Albrecht & Adelman, 1987; Albrecht et al., 1994).

Benefits of Social Support

Social support can take both tangible and intangible forms. Tangible support includes activities such as offering resources (e.g., money, skills, services, food, shelter, childcare, transportation, hygiene, safety, task sharing) and referrals. Less tangible emotional support involves expressions of love, caring, concern, inclusion or belongingness, approval, respect, and reassurance about one's self-worth and emotional state. In addition, social support may come in the form of providing models or instruction for coping, responding to threat, and shifting perspectives on cause-effect contingencies that may enable victims to begin to reduce their uncertainty and recover a sense of control (Albrecht & Adelman, 1984; Shumaker & Brownell, 1984). Finally, encouraging ventilation of one's emotions can help reduce the intensity, provide a safe situation or "sink" for one's hidden terrors, a way to ease internal pressures, and "create through talk imagery that crystallizes somewhat unknown cognitions into known and shared entities" (Albrecht & Adelman, 1987, p. 33).

Research suggests that there are two ways in which social support could benefit an individual. First, people with high levels of social support may simply lead happier, healthier, and less traumatic lives (Wills, 1992). Second, effective social support may also provide a buffer for a person when he or she experiences stressful or negative life events (e.g., a physical illness, a divorce, the death of a loved one, losing a job; Cohen & Wills, 1985). Thus, social support does not make it less likely that a person will experience a loss or trauma, but when such stressors occur, social support helps the person effectively deal with them.

There are findings to indicate that social support produces both benefits. People with adequate social support networks experience fewer and less severe stressful life events, and they are more likely to resolve small problems effectively before they evolve into major problems (Wills, 1992). With regard to buffering, Baron, Cutrona, Hicklin, Russell, and Lubaroff (1990), studied people who were undergoing severe stress because their spouse had developed cancer. Baron et al. examined the immune responses of these people and found that those who reported high levels of social support were more resistant to certain kinds of diseases and infections than those who reported low levels of support.

Why is it that social support is often an effective form of helping in times of loss and trauma? Trauma and loss generally induce acute emotional distress in people's lives. One of the central ways in which social support aids distressed individuals is by enabling them to talk about their situation in ways that assist them in improving how they feel. Emotions such as sadness, grief, anxiety, fear, anger, shame, and embarrassment may be managed by supportive behaviors involving both emotional and physical assistance (Albrecht et al., 1994).

One possible explanation of these effects is provided by *appraisal theory* (Lazarus, 1991), in which emotions are viewed as the result of an individual's interpretation of an event. Support may assist the individual to reframe or reinterpret the situation and its consequences in ways that improve his or her affective state. For example, an irrevocable loss such as a death may induce grief and sadness. Supportive interpersonal messages may help the individual to accept the reality of the loss, legitimize feelings associated with this loss, acknowledge its irreversibility, engage in behaviors that demonstrate the acceptance of the loss, and help place it in a larger context of what is gone but also what remains (Lazarus, 1991).

Trauma and loss may also induce feelings of fear, anxiety, and personal threat to one's well-being. This is particularly associated with situations that are perceived as uncertain and possibly uncontrollable such as a divorce or life-threatening illness. Effective support efforts are interpersonal messages that assist the individual with managing uncertainty about the situation, and enhance the person's sense of personal control and efficacy, such as helping the individual to specify the extent of the threats, generate options, clarify consequences, develop plans, calculate appropriate risks, and envision outcomes (Albrecht et al., 1994).

Yet another emotion that may be associated with loss and trauma is anger. In such instances, social support is not always effective. Indeed, discussing the person's circumstances may exacerbate the victim's sense of outrage, particularly when perceptions of injustice, unfairness, and protectiveness are triggered. However, acknowledging the legitimacy of these feelings, elucidating injustices, setting goals in response to the situation, devising strategies for meeting those goals, and diminishing the appeal of unrealistic goals form a complement of communication tactics for addressing the anger supportively (Albrecht & Adelman, 1987).

Finally, shame, embarrassment, and face threat (i.e., impression management) are also possible responses to certain types of loss and trauma. Humiliation, a sense of failure, and the damage to one's public identity are serious threats to self-esteem, efficacy, and personal control. Messages of caring, acceptance, reassurance, and affirmation often form the basis for most emotional support strategies to comfort another (Burleson, 1994).

Moderators of the Effects of Social Support

A growing body of research is showing that different types of supportive messages are more or less effective depending on the types of situations in which they are communicated. For example, the "optimal matching model" (Cutrona, 1996; Cutrona & Russell, 1990; Cutrona & Suhr, 1992) shows a relationship between the controllability of stress and types of support. When stress is uncontrollable, supportive messages that express comfort, love, caring, and acceptance are most helpful; when stress is controllable, tangible assistance and esteem support are most useful. Social support can also have different effects as a function of where the other person is in the experience of traumatic events. Some experiences, such as the deterioration of health from HIV infection, increasingly limit individuals from actively engaging others who can provide social support. As a consequence, they receive less social support, which accelerates the effects of the infection and interferes with their psychological ability to cope (Kaplan, Patterson, Kerner, Grant, & the HIV Neurobiological Research Center, 1997). Social support provided under these conditions of deteriorating health can thus have particularly beneficial consequences.

Work on understanding the helpful nature of support has been strengthened by research on well-intentioned, but unhelpful acts (see Albrecht & Adelman, 1987; Lehman, Ellard, & Wortman, 1986). For example, Lehman et al. (1986) interviewed individuals who had unexpectedly lost a spouse or child in a motor vehicle accident and asked about the kinds of support they found helpful and nonhelpful. In the former category were attempts to put the people in contact with a similar other and providing them with the opportunity to express their feelings. In the latter category was giving advice and encouraging quick recovery from the loss and trauma.

Providers who are perceived to be more trustworthy, credible, and possess greater expertise related to the problem are often likely to be judged by recipients as most helpful (Cutrona & Suhr, 1992; Goldsmith & Parks, 1990). However, the actual behavior of the person providing support could temper these effects. Behaviors that show regard for the other's face needs (being liked and accepted, desire for privacy, autonomy, etc.) are typically helpful; those that threaten these needs are unhelpful (see Albrecht et al., 1994; Goldsmith, 1992). This may explain the results of a study of social support among cancer patients conducted by Dakof and Taylor (1990). In their study Dakof and Taylor found that when the relationship with the person providing support was more distant—a friend or acquaintance—giving emotional support was often seen as unhelpful relative to informational support and tangible aid. However, when the person providing the support was an intimate other (e.g., a spouse or sibling), esteem and emotional support was seen as more helpful and valued. Presumably, this was because the person in need was more comfortable expressing his or her fears, concerns, and emotions to a family member than a person with whom they had more distant ties.

In summary, under many circumstances effective social support at an individual and a network level can do much to mitigate the psychological and perhaps even physical impact of trauma and loss on an individual. However, one must guard against what Cohen and Smyme (1985) have succinctly described as the "magic bullet" view of social support. That is, it works for all people in all circumstances irrespective of the specific problem. Rather, as this brief review has suggested, one must consider the needs of the person who would receive the support, the circumstances surrounding his or her loss or trauma, and the relationship between the recipient and the provider of social support. And as the following portion of the chapter suggests, we should not assume that people in distress will always seek or want help from others.

☐ Seeking Help

Given the severity of a loss or trauma and the beneficial effects of social support, one would suppose that people in such circumstances would invariably seek help, but the available literature suggests otherwise (Fisher, Nadler, & DePaulo, 1983). Why would people *not* seek such aid? According to Nadler (1991), decisions about help seeking are influenced by 1) the characteristics of the person in need—some people are more inclined to seek help than are others; 2) the specific kind of assistance needed—there are some problems for which people readily seek help, there are other types that they prefer to deal with alone; and 3) the relationship with the potential helper.

Characteristics of the Person in Need

Both demographic variables (i.e., gender, race, age, socioeconomic status) and personality characteristics (e.g., self-esteem) have been found to play important roles in determining whether a person will request aid. We examine the demographic variables first. The research literature suggests that women are significantly more likely to seek help than are men, even when the need for assistance is the same (Cutrona, 1996; Schroeder et al., 1995). It appears that gender or gender roles rather than biological sex are responsible for male-female differences in help seeking.

For example, Barbee and her associates (Barbee et al., 1993; Derlega, Barbee, & Winstead, 1994) have examined how gender roles affect seeking social support. Barbee et al. believed that social support involves a dynamic, interactive process between the person who seeks this kind of help and those who provide it. The actions of the person who needs social support play a major role in the quantity and the quality of the support she or he receives. Gender roles affect both of these. Men are more likely than women to worry about people's reactions if they ask for help with a problem (Bruder-Mattson & Hovanitz, 1990). Because strength, competence, and autonomy have traditionally been associated with the male gender role and dependence and naivete have been associated with the feminine gender role, a man who subscribes to the traditional male gender role may estimate that the social costs of asking for social support (even from close associates) are too high. Rather than suffer the potential embarrassment of asking for assistance, he decides to forego the help that he may need. A woman seeking social support, however, may be perceived as satisfying her gender role requirements, while also securing the help that she may need (Barbee et al. 1993; Derlega et al., 1994)

It also appears that women may simply be better than men at eliciting support from others (Cutrona, 1996). Reviews of the research literature indicate that the more feminine a person's gender role orientation, the more empathic, socially skilled, emotionally expressive, and skilled at sending and receiving nonverbal messages the person will be (Eagly, 1987; Eagly & Wood, 1991). Barbee et al. argued that these kinds of gender-related differences result in women being better than men at letting other people know when they need social support.

Turning to personality traits (see also Nadler, 1997), self-esteem is particularly relevant to help seeking behavior. However, the relationship between self-esteem and help seeking appears to be moderated by the relationship between the help seeker and the target helper. If the target helper is a stranger, people with high self-esteem are often less willing than people with low self-esteem to ask for help (e.g., Miller, 1985; Nadler & Fisher, 1986; Weiss & Knight, 1980; Wills & DePaulo, 1991). For instance, abused women with low self-esteem are more likely to seek treatment or counseling (Frieze, 1979). Maintaining self-esteem seems particularly important to people who have a very positive self-image. Because of the potential damage of help seeking to their image of competence and control, these people are hesitant to seek assistance from others.

When there is a close relationship with the potential provider of support, the relationship between help seeking and self-esteem reverses. For example, Caldwell and Reinhart (1988) found that students with high self-esteem were somewhat more likely to receive social support from their families than were students with low self-esteem. It is reasonable to surmise that the students with high self-esteem had good relations with their families and did not feel that their self-esteem would be threatened by asking their parents or siblings for help.

The Nature of the Problem

Some problems make it less likely that people will ask for help. For example, the controllability of the problem is critical. People are motivated to seek help when they believe that they are losing control of an important aspect of their life that is ultimately controllable. However, if problems persist and become so serious that people come to believe that they are uncontrollable, they will no longer be motivated to seek help. People may simply decide to give up. For example, Wolcott (1986) surveyed nearly 300 recently divorced people about their help-seeking actions prior to divorce. The primary factor that differentiated those couples that did seek help from those that did not was their beliefs about whether they could do anything to avoid a divorce. The people who did not seek help believed that the relationship could not be saved and that "things" could not be changed. Thus, there was no need to seek help.

A second important issue is how the problem relates to a person's self-concept or self-identity. Tesser and his associates (see Tesser, 1988) have found that when people compare themselves to others on a dimension that is important to their self-concept, it is much more threatening to feel inferior to a comparable or similar person than a dissimilar person. Thus, people confronted with losses that might be seen as reflecting their self-worth (e.g., being abandoned by a spouse or lover) might be more reluctant to seek help than those whose problems are unrelated to such considerations (e.g., the unexpected death of a spouse or lover). Nadler (1987) has found this pattern among students seeking help for academic problems. Further, the reluctance to ask for help with ego-central problems was greatest among the students who were high in self-esteem.

It is, perhaps, for these reasons that people with problems sometimes turn to impersonal sources for help. Seeking impersonal help can reduce the psychological costs of requesting aid (e.g., embarrassment, threat to self-esteem), because little or no social comparison takes place when impersonal help is used (Tesser, 1988). The success of crisis hotlines for providing aid to victims' of trauma or to those considering suicide has been attributed, in part, to the anonymity that such programs provide to the callers (Hill & Harmon, 1976; Raviv, Raviv, & Yunowitz, 1989). Despite the advantage of minimizing psychological costs, the disadvantages of impersonal sources involves the quality of help provided. Because of the nature of these sources, communication is less open and interactive. The help received may therefore not be satisfying. Thus, although there are some circumstances under which impersonal help may be preferable, in many cases those in need prefer help from personal contacts if the problem to be solved is a significant one.

The closeness of the relationship between the potential helper and recipient moderates the effects of the kind of problem on help seeking. Studies of social support suggest that people are more willing to ask similar others (i.e., relatives and friends) for help with problems than they are to ask dissimilar others (i.e., professionals). For example, Wills (1992) reported that people with personal or emotional problems were two to three times more likely to ask for informal help from people in their social support network than to ask for help from a professional. Even when people seek organized formal support for a specific problem, they are as likely to join a "self-help" group comprised of people with the same problem (e.g., an alcoholic joining Alcoholics Anonymous) as they are to go to a professional who treats such problems.

The explanation of the moderating effects of closeness probably lies in the differences between the dynamics of a communal versus an exchange relationship, which we discussed earlier in this chapter. Whereas the people in Nadler's (1987) experiment probably (correctly) saw themselves as in an exchange relationship with the similar stranger, people are likely to see their relationship with similar friends and relatives as a communal one. In such relationships, help seekers may feel that they can expose their weaknesses and problems to others without a great deal of fear that they will be ridiculed or rejected. Studies of homosexual men coping with their concerns about HIV and AIDS are supportive of this interpretation (e.g., Hayes, Catania, McKusick, & Coates, 1990; Pryor, Reeder, & McManus, 1991). And laboratory studies of help seeking find that when the relationship involves close friends, similarity between the requestor and potential provider typically does not inhibit a person's willingness to seek help (see Barbee, 1990; Barbee et al., 1993; Derlega et al., 1994). Thus, it appears that similarity is likely to inhibit help seeking when the potential provider is a stranger or the parties are in an exchange relationship; however, it is likely to facilitate helping in a communal relationship.

In general, people who are in need of assistance often choose not to seek help. This decision is not necessarily irrational. People weigh the tangible benefits of immediate assistance against the short- and long-term effects on their image to others and on their own esteem and self-worth. This judgment process is greatly affected by the nature of the problem and characteristics of both the person in need and potential helpers. Often, immediate concerns about one's image and esteem outweigh the objective benefits of receiving help. Thus one's overall well-being may be sacrificed because of immediate needs and concerns.

☐ Conclusion

Research on helping behaviors has traditionally focused on spontaneous, instrumental forms of assistance—typically among strangers. People experiencing personal loss do have immediate material needs, but the type of assistance they most often need is psychological support. The experience of loss and trauma can have dramatic effects on psychological and emotional well-being. As a consequence, emotional reactions of both the person victimized by loss and by potential helpers play a particularly important role in help giving, help seeking, and recipient reactions to aid under these circumstances. In Figure 1 we present a conceptual model that summarizes our view of the nature of these relationships. The model is intended to provide a theoretical integration of the major ideas presented in this chapter; hopefully, it will serve as a conceptual framework for future research on helping at times of loss and trauma.

The model begins with the impact of the loss or trauma on the victim and individuals who might provide him or her with help. The experience of loss can produce a wide range of emotional reactions, depending upon the nature and importance of the loss, individual differences in coping style, and the individual's stage of coping and adjustment. Emotional reactions may involve, for example, sadness, depression, an-

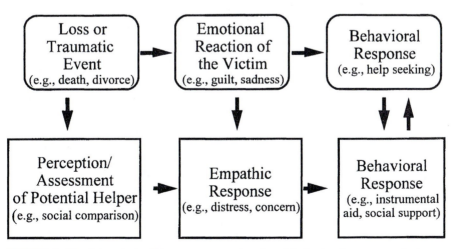

FIGURE 1. The interrelationship among emotional and behavioral responses to loss or traumatic events and the affective reactions and actions of others.

ger, guilt, or even hopelessness. Depending on the emotion experienced, people develop different needs and exhibit different behavioral responses. As a consequence, different types of social support may be more or less effective. For example, when the event is perceived as uncontrollable (such as with a divorce or life-threatening illness), people may experience fear, anxiety, and threat. Their interactions with others may be impaired by feelings of loss of control and helplessness. Social support that provides assistance with managing uncertainty and enhancing a sense of efficacy is one of the most helpful types under these circumstances In general, when stress is perceived as uncontrollable, supportive messages that express caring and acceptance are most effective; when stress is controllable, tangible assistance and esteem support are most useful.

The responses of potential helpers are, in turn, determined by their perceptions of the situation of loss and their reactions to the emotional response of the person experiencing the loss. In particular, potential helpers who are aware of the other's loss or traumatic event may engage in social comparison. This process may increase the salience of general norms of social responsibility or feelings of obligation based on personal standards, and thereby motivate assistance. In addition, this social comparison process can have affective consequences, producing negative personal emotions to the person's less fortunate situation. If, in this social comparison process, people focus on the other's plight they are likely to experience sadness; if they focus on their more fortunate circumstances, they are likely to experience feelings of guilt. Both sadness and guilt can then motivate helping. As noted in the chapter, however, this will be egoistically-motivated helping with the primary goal of making oneself feel better. As a consequence, helping may be relatively short-term.

Alternatively, through the process of empathy—which may have biological and evolutionary bases—people may respond directly to the emotions of the person experiencing the loss. Empathy may also produce personal negative states, such as distress and upset, leading to other kinds of egoistic motivations for helping. However, under certain circumstances (e.g., when there is a close relationship between the potential helper and the person in need) empathy may generate the other-oriented emotion of empathic concern. Empathic concern produces altruistic motivation with the ultimate goal of improving the other person's welfare.

Returning to the person in need, others may not be aware of his or her circumstances, or aware of them but reluctant to help without a request to do so. So, people who experience a traumatic loss may sometimes need to seek help. However, often they do not. Whether or not a person seeks assistance is a function of the characteristics of the person in need, the nature of the problem, and who the potential helpers are. For example, with respect to demographic characteristics, women are much more likely to ask for help than men. With regard to the nature of the problem, people are less likely to seek help for problems they see as uncontrollable or for losses they perceive as reflecting their self-worth. In terms of the characteristics of potential helpers, people are most likely to turn to others with whom they already have a close personal relationship and whom they perceive as most efficacious. However, if a request for assistance from a friend or similar other makes a person feel inferior on a dimension that is important to one's self-concept, he or she may be more likely to seek help from a stranger or an anonymous source. Thus, individuals are motivated to regain a sense of control while maintaining feelings of self-worth, and they will choose the source of assistance that they perceive as representing the best balance between instrumental value for improving the situation and threats to self-esteem for acknowledging their need for help.

In conclusion, the type of assistance offered to victims of loss and trauma is not the form that has received the most attention in social psychological research (i.e., relative to spontaneous instrumental interventions); however, the principles and processes that have been identified in this research are directly relevant to this kind of helping. These social psychological approaches recognize the importance of the situation (e.g., the nature of the loss); the personalities and characteristics of the individuals involved (i.e., of the person who experiences the loss and of potential helpers) and their interpersonal relationships; and the perceptions, motives, and needs of those involved. Application of social psychological theories of helping can have important practical as well as conceptual benefits. An understanding of the factors that independently and jointly determine whether victims of traumatic events and personal loss receive assistance can guide interventions that most effectively balance the material, emotional, and psychological needs of the recipients while also increasing the likelihood that available resources will be optimally utilized. In turn, a consideration of the unique needs, adaptations, and vulnerabilities of victims of loss and trauma can inform current social psychological theory, present new conceptual challenges, and ultimately facilitate the development of a more comprehensive understanding of human needs.

☐ References

Alcock, J. (1989). *Animal behavior* (4th ed.). Sunderland, MA: Sinauer Press.

Albrecht, T. L. (1994). Epilogue: Social support and community. An historical account of the rescue networks in Denmark. In B. R. Burleson, T. L. Albrecht, & I. G. Sarason (Eds.), *Communication of social support: Messages, interactions, relationships, and community* (pp. 267–280). Thousand Oaks, CA: Sage.

Albrecht, T. L., & Adelman, M. B. (1984). Social support and life stress: New directions for communication research. *Human Communication Research, 11*, 3–32.

Albrecht, T. L., & Adelman, M. B. (1987). *Communicating social support*. Newbury Park, CA: Sage.

Albrecht, T. L., Burleson, B. R., & Goldsmith, D. (1994). Supportive communication. In M. L. Knapp & G. R. Miller (Eds.), *Handbook of interpersonal communication* (2nd ed., pp. 419–449). Thousand Oaks, CA: Sage.

Albrecht, T. L., Burleson, B. R., & Sarason, I. G. (1992). Meaning and method in the study of communication and support: An introduction. *Communication Research, 19*, 149–153.

Barbee, A. P. (1990). Interactive coping: The cheering up process in close relationships. In S. Duck (Ed.), *Personal relationships and social support* (pp. 45–65). London: Sage.

Barbee, A. P., Cunningham, M. R., Winstead, B. A., Derlega, V. J., Gulley, M. R., Yankeelov, P. A., & Druen, P. B. (1993). Effects of gender role expectations on the social support process. *Journal of Social Issues, 49*, 175–190.

Baron, R. S., Cutrona, C. E., Hicklin, D., Russell, D. W., & Lubaroff, D. M. (1990). Social support and immune function among spouses of cancer patients. *Journal of Personality and Social Psychology, 59*, 344–352.

Batson, C. D. (1987). Prosocial motivation: Is it ever truly altruistic? In L. Berkowitz (Ed.), *Advances in experimental social psychology* (Vol. 20, pp. 65–122). New York: Academic Press.

Batson, C. D. (1991). *The altruism question: Toward a social-psychological answer*. Hillsdale, NJ: Erlbaum.

Batson, C. D. (1997). Self-other merging and the empathy-altruism hypothesis: Reply to Neuberg et al. *Journal of Personality and Social Psychology, 73*, 517–522.

Batson, C. D. (1998). Altruism and prosocial behavior. In D. T. Gilbert, S. T. Fiske, & Lindzey (Eds.), *The handbook of social psychology* (4th ed., Vol. 2, pp. 282–315). New York: McGraw-Hill.

Batson, C. D., Batson, J. G., Griffitt, C. A., Barrientos, S., Brandt, J. R., Sprengelmeyer, P., & Bayly, M. J. (1989). Negative-state relief and the empathy-altruism hypothesis. *Journal of Personality and Social Psychology, 56,* 922–933.

Batson, C. D., & Oleson, K. C. (1991). Current status of the empathy-altruism hypothesis. In M. S. Clark (Ed.), *Review of personality and social psychology: Vol. 12. Prosocial behavior* (pp. 62–85). Newbury Park, CA: Sage.

Batson, C. D., Sager, K., Garst, E., Kang, M., Rubchinsky, K., & Dawson, K. (1997). Is empathy-induced helping due to self-other merging? *Journal of Personality and Social Psychology, 73,* 495–509.

Baumeister, F. F., Stillwell, A. M., & Heatherton, T. F. (1994). Guilt: An interpersonal approach. *Psychological Bulletin, 115,* 243–267.

Berkowitz, L. (1972). Social norms, feelings, and other factors affecting helping behavior and altruism. In L. Berkowitz (Ed.), *Advances in experimental social psychology* (Vol. 6, pp. 63–108). New York: Academic Press.

Berkowitz, L., & Daniels, L. R. (1964). Affecting the salience of the social responsibility norm: Effect of past help on the responses to dependency relationships. *Journal of Abnormal and Social Psychology, 68,* 275–281.

Borgida, E., Conner, C., & Manteufal, L. (1992). Understanding living kidney donation: A behavioral decision-making perspective. In S. Spacapan & S. Oskamp (Eds.), *Helping and being helped* (pp. 183–212). Newbury Park, CA: Sage.

Bretherton, I., Walsh, R., & Lependorf, M. (1996). Social support in postdivorce families. In G. R. Pierce, B. R. Sarason, & I. G. Sarason (Eds), *Handbook of social support and the family* (pp. 345–373). New York, Plenum.

Bruder-Mattson, S. F., & Hovanitz, C. A. (1990). Coping and attributional styles as predictors of depression. *Journal of Clinical Psychology, 46,* 557–565.

Burleson, B. R. (1994). Comforting messages: Significance, approaches, and effects. In B. R. Burleson, T. L. Albrecht, & I. G. Sarason (Eds.), *Communication of social support: Messages, interactions, relationships, and community* (pp. 3–28). Thousand Oaks, CA: Sage.

Burleson, B. R., Albrecht, T. L., Goldsmith, D. J., & Sarason, I. G. (1994). Introduction: The communication of social support. In B. R. Burleson, T. L. Albrecht, & I. G. Sarason (Eds.), *Communication of social support: Messages, interactions, relationships, and community* (pp. ix–xxx). Thousand Oaks, CA: Sage.

Burnstein, E., Crandall, C., & Kitayama, S. (1994). Some neo-Darwinian decision rules for altruism: Weighing cues for inclusive fitness as a function of the biological importance of the decision. *Journal of Personality & Social Psychology, 67,* 773–789

Buss, D. M., & Kenrick, D. T. (1998). Evolutionary social psychology. In D. T. Gilbert, S. T. Fiske, & G. Lindzey (Eds.), *Handbook of social psychology* (Vol 2, 4th ed., pp. 982–1026). Boston: McGraw-Hill.

Caldwell, R. A., & Reinhart, M. A. (1988). The relationship of type of personality to individual differences in the use and type of social support. *Journal of Social and Clinical Psychology, 6,* 140–146.

Calhoun, L. G., & Tedeschi, R. G. (1998). Beyond recovery from trauma: Implications for clinical practice and research. *Journal of Social Issues, 54,* 357–372.

Carlson, M., & Miller, N. (1987). Explanation of the relation between negative mood and helping. *Psychological Bulletin, 102,* 91–108.

Carlson, N. R. (1998). *Physiology of behavior.* Boston: Allyn Bacon.

Carnevale, P. J. D., Pruitt, D. G., & Carrington, P. I. (1982). Effects of future dependence, liking, and repeated requests for help on helping behavior. *Social Psychology Quarterly, 45,* 9–14.

Cialdini, R. B., Brown, S. L., Lewis, B. P., Luce, C., & Neuberg, S. L. (1997). Reinterpreting the empathy-altruism relationship: When one into one equals oneness. *Journal of Personality and Social Psychology, 73,* 481–494.

Cialdini, R. B., Darby, B. K., & Vincent, J. E. (1973). Transgression and altruism: A case for hedonism. *Journal of Experimental Social Psychology, 9,* 502–516.

Cialdini, R. B., Kenrick, D. T., & Baumann, D. J. (1982). Effects of mood on prosocial behavior in children and adults. In N. Eisenberg (Ed.), *The development of prosocial behavior* (pp. 339–359). New York: Academic Press.

Cialdini, R. B., Schaller, M., Houlihan, D., Arps, K., Fultz, J., & Beamen, A. L. (1987). Empathy-based helping: Is it selflessly or selfishly motivated? *Journal of Personality and Social Psychology, 52,* 749–758.

Clark, M. S., & Mills, J. (1993). The difference between communal and exchange relationships: What it is and is not. *Personality and Social Psychology Bulletin, 19,* 684–691.

Clark, M. S., & Pataki, S. P. (1995). Interpersonal processes influencing attraction and relationships. In A. Tesser (Ed.), *Advanced social psychology* (pp. 283–331). New York: McGraw-Hill.

Clary, E. G., & Orenstein, L. (1991). The amount and effectiveness of help: The relationship of motives and abilities to helping behavior. *Personality and Social Psychology Bulletin, 17,* 58–64.

Clary, E. G., & Snyder, M. (1991). A functional analysis of altruism and prosocial behavior: The case of volunteerism. In M. S. Clark (Ed.), *Review of personality and social psychology: Vol. 12. Prosocial behavior* (pp. 119–148). Knobbier Park, CA: Sage.

Clary, E. G., Snyder, M., Ridge, R., Copeland, J., Haugen, J., & Miene, P. (1998). Understanding and assessing the motivations of volunteers: A functional approach. *Journal of Personality and Social Psychology, 74,* 1516–1530.

Cobb, S. (1976). Social support as a moderator of life stress. *Psychosomatic Medicine, 38,* 300–314.

Cohen, S. & Smyme, S. L. (1985). Issues in the study and application of social support. In S. Cohen, & S. L. Smyme (Eds.), *Social support and health* (pp. 3–22). Orlando, FL: Academic Press.

Cohen, S., & Wills, T. A. (1985). Stress, social support, and the buffer-hypothesis. *Psychological Bulletin, 98,* 310–357.

Cunningham, M. R. (1985/1986). Levites and brother's keepers: A sociobiological perspective on prosocial behavior. *Humboldt Journal of Social Relations, 13,* 35–67.

Cutrona, C. E. (1996). *Social support in couples.* Thousand Oaks, CA: Sage.

Cutrona, C. E., & Russell, D. W. (1990). Type of social support and specific stress: Toward a theory of optimal matching. In B. Sarason, I. Sarason, & G. Pierce (Eds.), *Social support: An interactional view* (pp. 319–366). New York: Wiley.

Cutrona, C. E., & Suhr, J. A. (1992). Controllability of stressful events and satisfaction with spouse support behaviors. *Communication Research, 19,* 154–174.

Cutrona, C.E., Suhr, J., & MacFarlane, R. (1990). Interpersonal transactions and the psychological sense of support. In S. Duck & R. Silver (Eds.), *Personal relationships and social support* (pp. 30–45). London: Sage.

Dakof, G. A., & Taylor, S. E. (1990). Victims' perceptions of social support: What is helpful from whom? *Journal of Personality and Social Psychology, 58,* 80–89.

Davis, M. H., Luce, C., & Kraus, S. J. (1994). The heritability of characteristics associated with dispositional empathy. *Journal of Personality, 62,* 369–391

Derlega, V. J., Barbee, A. P., & Winstead, B. A. (1994) Friendship, gender and social support. In B. R. Burelson, T. L. Albrecht, & I. G. Sarason (Eds.), *The communication of social support: Messages, interactions, relationships, and community* (pp. 136–150). Newbury Park, CA: Sage.

Dovidio, J. F. (1984). Helping behavior and altruism: An empirical and conceptual overview. In L. Berkowitz (Ed.), *Advances in experimental social psychology* (Vol. 17, pp. 361–427). New York: Academic Press.

Dovidio, J. F., Allen, J., & Schroeder, D. A. (1990). The specificity of empathy-induced helping: Evidence for altruism. *Journal of Personality and Social Psychology, 59,* 249–260.

Dovidio, J. F., & Penner, L. A. (in press). Helping and altruism. In G. Fletcher & M. S. Clark (Eds.), *Blackwell Handbook of Social Psychology: Interpersonal Relations*. London: Blackwell.

Dovidio, J. F., Piliavin, J. A., Gaertner, S. L., Schroeder, D. A., & Clark, R. D., III (1991). The arousal: Cost-reward model and the process of intervention: A review of the evidence. In M. S. Clark (Ed.), *Review of personality and social psychology: Vol. 12. Prosocial behavior* (pp. 86–118). Newbury Park, CA: Sage.

Duck, S., & Silver, R. C. (Eds.). (1990). *Personal relationships and social support*. London: Sage.

Eagly, A. H. (1987). *Sex differences in social behavior: A social-role interpretation*. Hillsdale, NJ: Erlbaum.

Eagly, A. H., & Wood, W. (1991). Explaining sex differences in social behavior: A meta-analytic perspective. *Personality and Social Psychology Bulletin, 17*, 306–315.

Eisenberg, N., Cumberland, A., & Spinrad, T. L. (1998). Parental socialization of emotion. *Psychological Inquiry, 9*, 241–273.

Eisenberg, N., & Miller, P. (1987). The relation of empathy to prosocial and related behaviors. *Psychological Bulletin, 101*, 91–119.

Eyres, S. J., & MacElveen-Hoehn, P. (1983, April*). Theoretical issues in the study of social support*. Paper presented at the Conference on Social Support, University of Washington School of Nursing, Seattle.

Fabes, R. A., Eisenberg, N, & Eisenbud, L. (1993). Behavioral and physiological correlates of children's reactions to others in distress. *Developmental Psychology, 29*, 655–664.

Fisher, J. D. Nadler, A., & DePaulo, B. (Eds.). (1983). *New directions in helping: Vol. 1. Recipient reactions to aid*. San Diego, CA: Academic Press.

Ford, L. A., Barrow, A. S., & Stohl, C. (1996). Social support messages and the management of uncertainty in the experience of breast cancer: An application of problematic integration theory. *Human Communication Research, 63*, 189–207.

Frey, D. L., & Gaertner, S. L. (1986). Helping and the avoidance of inappropriate interracial behavior: A strategy that perpetuates a nonprejudiced self-image. *Journal of Personality and Social Psychology, 50*, 1083–1090.

Frieze, I. H. (1979). Perceptions of battered wives. In I. H. Frieze, D. Bar-Tal, & J. S. Carroll (Eds.), *Attribution theory: Applications to social problems* (pp. 79–108). San Francisco: Jossey-Bass.

Goldsmith, D. (1992). Managing conflicting goals in supportive interaction: An integrative theoretical framework. *Communication Research, 19*, 264–286.

Goldsmith, D., & Parks, M. (1990). Communicative strategies for managing the risks of seeking social support. In S. Duck & R. Silver (Eds.), *Personal relationships and social support* (pp. 104–121). London: Sage.

Goranson, R.., & Berkowitz, L. (1966). Reciprocity and responsibility reactions to prior help. *Journal of Personality and Social Psychology, 3*, 227–232.

Gouldner, A. (1960). The norm of reciprocity: A preliminary statement. *American Sociological Review, 25*, 161–178.

Harris, J. R. (1998). The trouble with assumptions. *Psychological Inquiry, 9*, 294–296.

Hayes, R. B., Catania, J. A., McKusick, L., & Coates, T. J. (1990). Help-seeking for AIDS-related concerns: A comparison of gay men with various HIV diagnoses. *American Journal of Community Psychology, 18*, 743–755.

Hill, F. E., & Harmon, M. (1976). The use of telephone tapes in telephone counseling program. *Crisis Intervention, 7*, 88–96.

Hoover, C. W., Wood, E. E., & Knowles, E. S. (1983). Forms of social awareness and helping. *Journal of Experimental Social Psychology, 18*, 577–590.

Hornstein, H. A. (1982). Promotive tension: Theory and research. In V. J. Derlega & J. Grezlak (Eds.), *Cooperation and helping behavior: Theories and research* (pp. 229–248). New York: Academic Press.

Kahn, A., & Tice, T. (1973). Returning a favor and retaliating harm: The effects of stated intention and actual behavior. *Journal of Experimental Social Psychology, 9*, 43–56.

Kaplan, R. M., Patterson, T. L., Kerner, D., Grant, I., & the HIV Neurobiological Research Center (1997). Social support: Cause or consequence of poor health outcomes in men with HIV infection? In G. R. Pierce, B. Lakey, I. G. Sarason, & B. R. Sarason (Eds), *Sourcebook of social support and personality* (pp. 279–301). New York: Plenum.

Lazarus, R. S. (1991). *Emotion and adaptation.* New York: Oxford University Press.

Lehman, D. R., Ellard, J. H., & Wortman, C. B. (1986). Social support for the bereaved: Recipients' and providers' perspectives on what is helpful. *Journal of Consulting and Clinical Psychology, 54,* 438–446.

Ma, H. (1985). Cross-cultural study of altruism. *Psychological Reports, 57,* 337–338.

MacLean, P. D. (1985). Evolutionary psychiatry and the triune brain. *Psychological Brain, 15,* 219–221.

Marks, E., Penner, L. A., & Stone, A. V. (1982). Helping as a function of empathic responses and sociopathy. *Journal of Research in Personality, 16,* 1–20.

McGuire, A. M. (1994). Helping behaviors in the natural environment: Dimensions and correlates of helping. *Personality and Social Psychology Bulletin, 20,* 45–56.

Miller, W. R. (1985). Motivation for treatment: A review with a special emphasis on alcoholism. *Psychological Bulletin, 98,* 84–107.

Moghaddam, F. M., Taylor, D. M., & Wright, S. C. (1993). *Social psychology in cross-cultural perspective.* New York: W.H. Freeman and Co.

Nadler, A. (1987). Determinants of help seeking behavior: The effects of helper's similarity, task centrality and recipient's self esteem. *European Journal of Social Psychology, 17,* 57–67.

Nadler, A. (1991). Help-seeking behavior: Psychological costs and instrumental benefits. In M. S. Clark (Ed.), *Review of personality and social psychology: Vol. 12. Prosocial behavior* (pp. 290–311). Newbury Park, CA: Sage.

Nadler, A. (1997). Personality and help seeking: Autonomous versus dependent help seeking. In G. R. Pierce, B. Lakey, I. G. Sarason, & B. R. Sarason (Eds.), *Sourcebook of social support and personality* (pp. 379–407). New York: Plenum.

Nadler, A., & Fisher, J. D. (1986). The role of threat to self-esteem and perceived control in recipient reaction to help: Theory development and empirical validation. In L. Berkowitz (Ed.), *Advances in experimental social psychology* (Vol. 19, pp. 81–122). San Diego, CA: Academic Press.

Neuberg, S. L., Cialdini, R. B., Brown, S. L., Luce, C., Sagarin, B. J., & Lewis, B. P. (1997). Does empathy lead to anything more than superficial helping? Comment on Batson et al. (1997). *Journal of Personality and Social Psychology, 73,* 510–516.

Omoto, A., & Snyder, M. (1995). Sustained helping without obligation: Motivation, longevity of service, and perceived attitude change among AIDS volunteers. *Journal of Personality and Social Psychology, 68,* 671–687.

Otten, C. A., Penner, L. A., & Waugh, G. (1988). That's what friends are for: The determinants of psychological helping. *Journal of Social and Clinical Psychology, 7,* 34–41.

Penner, L. A., & Finkelstein, M. A. (1998). Dispositional and structural determinants of volunteerism. *Journal of Personality and Social Psychology, 74,* 525–537.

Penner, L. A., Fritzsche, B. A., Craiger, J. P., & Freifeld, T. R. (1995). Measuring the prosocial personality. In J. Butcher & C. D. Spielberger (Eds.), *Advances in personality assessment* (Vol. 10, pp. 147–163). Hillsdale, NJ: Erlbaum.

Pierce, G. R., Lakey, B., Sarason, I. G., & Sarason, B. R. (Eds.). (1997). *Sourcebook of social support and personality.* New York: Plenum.

Pierce, G. R., Sarason, B. R., & Sarason, I. G. (Eds.). (1996). *Handbook of social support and the family.* New York: Plenum.

Piliavin, J. A., Dovidio, J. F., Gaertner, S. L., & Clark, R. D. III (1981). *Emergency intervention.* New York: Academic Press.

Pillemer, K., & Suitor, J. (1996). Family stress and social support among care givers to persons with Alzheimer's disease. In G. R. Pierce, B. R. Sarason, & I. G. Sarason (Eds), *Handbook of social support and the family* (pp. 467–494). New York: Plenum.

Pryor, J. B., Reeder, G. D., & McManus, J. A. (1991) Fear and loathing in the workplace: Reactions to AIDS infected co-workers. *Personality and Social Psychology Bulletin, 17,* 133–139.

Rabow, J., Newcomb, M. D., Monto, M. A., & Hernandez, A. C. R. (1990). Altruism in drunk driving situations: Personal and situational factors in helping. *Social Psychology Quarterly, 53,* 199–213.

Raviv, A., Raviv, A., & Yunovitz, R. (1989). Radio psychology and psychotherapy: A comparison of client attitudes and expectations. *Professional Psychology: Research and Practice, 20,* 1–7.

Rushton, J. P., Fulker, D. W., Neale, M. C., Nias, D. K. B., & Eysenck, H. J. (1986). Altruism and aggression: The heritability of individual differences. *Journal of Personality and Social Psychology, 50,* 1192–1198.

Salovey, P., Mayer, J. D., & Rosenhan, D. L. (1991). Mood and helping: Mood as a motivator of helping and helping as a regulator of mood. In M. S. Clark (Ed.), *Review of personality and social psychology: Vol. 12. Prosocial behavior* (pp. 215–237). Newbury Park, CA: Sage.

Sarason, B. R., Pierce, G. R., & Sarason, I. G. (1990). Social support: The sense of acceptance and the role of relationships. In B. R. Sarason, I. G., Sarason, & G. R. Pierce (Eds.), *Social support: An interactional view* (pp. 9–25). New York: Wiley.

Schaller, M., & Cialdini, R. B. (1988). The economics of empathic helping: Support for a mood management motive. *Journal of Experimental Social Psychology, 24,* 163–181.

Schroeder, D. A., Dovidio, J. F., Sibicky, M. E., Matthews, L. L., & Allen, J. L. (1988). Empathy and helping behavior: Egoism or altruism. *Journal of Experimental Social Psychology, 24,* 333–353.

Schroeder, D. A., Penner, L. A., Dovidio, J. F., & Piliavin, J. A. (1995). *The psychology of helping and altruism: Problems and puzzles.* New York: McGraw-Hill.

Schwartz, S. H. (1970). Elicitation of moral obligation and self-sacrificing behavior: An experimental study of volunteering to be a bone marrow donor. *Journal of Personality and Social Psychology, 10,* 243–250.

Schwartz, S. H., & Howard, J. (1982). A normative decision-making model of helping behavior. In J. P. Rushton & R. M. Sorrentino (Eds.), *Altruism and helping behavior* (pp. 189–211). Hillsdale, NJ: Erlbaum.

Segal, N. L. (1993). Twin sibling and adoption methods: test of evolutionary hypotheses. *American Psychologist, 48,* 943–956.

Shumaker, S., & Brownell, A. (1984). Toward a theory of social support, *Journal of Social Issues, 40,* 11-36.

Snyder, M., & Omoto, A. M. (1992). Who helps and why? In S. Spacapan & S. Oskamp (Eds.), *Helping and being helped* (pp. 213–239). Newbury Park, CA: Sage.

Sober, E., & Wilson, D. S. (1998). *Unto others: The evolution and psychology of unselfish behavior.* Cambridge, MA: Harvard University Press.

Tesser, A. (1988). Toward a self-evaluation maintenance model of social behavior. In L. Berkowitz (Ed.), *Advances in experimental social psychology* (Vol. 21, pp. 181–227). New York: Academic Press.

Thompson, C. W., Cowan, C. L., & Rosenhan, D. L. (1980). Focus of attention mediates the impact of negative affect on altruism. *Journal of Personality and Social Psychology, 38,* 291–300.

Tolsdorf , C.C. (1976). Social networks, support, and coping: Exploratory study. *Family Process, 15,* 407–417.

Trivers, R. L. (1971). The evolution of reciprocal altruism. *Quarterly Review of Biology, 46,* 35–37.

Vaughan, K. B., & Lanzetta, J. T. (1980). Vicarious instigation and conditioning of facial expressive and autonomic responses to a model's expressive display of pain. *Journal of Personality and Social Psychology, 38,* 909–923.

Webley, P., & Lea, S. E. G. (1993). The partial unacceptability of money in repayment for neighborly help. *Human Relations, 46,* 65–76.

Weiner, B., Perry, R. P., & Magnusson, J. (1988). An attributional analysis of reactions to stigmas. *Journal of Personality and Social Psychology, 55*, 738–748.

Williamson, G. M., & Clark, M. S. (1989). Effects of providing help to another and of relationship type on the provider's mood and self-evaluation. *Journal of Personality and Social Psychology, 56*, 722–734.

Wills, T. A. (1990). Multiple networks and substance abuse. *Journal of Social and Clinical Psychology, 9*, 78–90.

Wills, T. A. (1992). The helping process in the context of personal relationships. In S. Spacapan & S. Oskamp (Eds.), *Helping and being helped: Naturalistic studies* (pp. 17–48). Newbury Park, CA: Sage.

Wills, T. A., & DePaulo, B. M. (1991). Interpersonal analysis of the help-seeking process. In C. R. Snyder & D. R. Forsyth (Eds.), *Handbook of social and clinical psychology* (pp. 350–375). New York: Pergammon.

Wolcott, I. H. (1986). Seeking help for marital problems before separation. *Australian Journal of Sex, Marriage and Family, 7*, 154–164.

Wortman, C. B., Battle, E. S., & Lemkau, J. P. (1997). Coming to terms with the sudden, traumatic death of a spouse or child. In R. C. Davis & A. Lurigio, (Eds.), *Victims of crime* (2nd ed., pp. 108–133). Thousand Oaks, CA: Sage.

Yinon, Y., & Landau, M. O. (1987). On the reinforcing value of helping behavior in a positive mood. *Motivation and Emotion, 11*, 83–93.

Zahn-Waxler, C., Robinson, J. L., & Emde, R. N. (1992). The development of empathy in twins. *Developmental Psychology, 28*, 1038–1047.

Roy F. Baumeister
Ellen Bratslavsky

Victim Thinking

The twentieth century has produced more victims of more varied types of trauma and transgression than any other century in world history. Reigns of terror in two Communist countries each killed over 20 million people and exposed many millions of others to less extreme traumas such as imprisonment, torture, and forced relocation. Meanwhile, the categories of victimization have expanded in the United States as more and more offenses are perceived as worthy of legal action, resulting in such incidents as burglars suing homeowners because of injuries sustained during the burglary, companies being sued for sexual harassment because of joke telling or teasing coworkers, a Kansas bank being fined because of not having Braille codes on the drive-through automatic teller (so that blind drivers could not use the machine), and a man who was fired for never bathing suing his employer for discrimination.

The expanding roster of victims of large and small transgressions has sparked some research efforts to understand the psychology of victims, but it is probably safe to say that these efforts remain preliminary and most of the major work on this topic lies ahead. Findings by pioneers such as Janoff-Bulman (1992) and Silver, Boon, and Stones (1983) have indicated that the quest for meaning—that is, the thoughtful effort to arrive at a coherent, plausible, and acceptable interpretation of one's victimization—is a central part of the victim experience for many people, and so it is vitally important to investigate the thought processes of victims. The purpose of this chapter is to cover some of the research findings on how victims think about their transgressions and other matters, so as to offer an assessment of the current state of knowledge and a blueprint for further work.

☐ Are Victims Biased?

Before we cover the specific patterns of victim thinking, it is necessary to ask whether there is anything special or unusual about that thinking at all. If the cognitive processes of victims are similar to those of people who are not in victim roles, then there may be relatively little to say.

The assumption that victimization does not carry major cognitive biases or distortions seems fairly widespread. Many researchers rely heavily on victim accounts, which are often accepted in a rather uncritical fashion. For example, in his well-known and notorious book, Goldhagen (1996) adopted the methodological approach of relying heavily and uncritically on victims' accounts of the Holocaust—despite his stated goal of understanding the psychology of the perpetrators—and disregarding anything perpetrators themselves said, which he felt might be distorted by self-serving efforts to reduce guilt. The resulting work is a summary of victim views, although it masquerades as a dispassionate investigation into the psychology of perpetrators, and any reader of that work should be able to see that it represents more a compilation of victims' efforts to demonize perpetrators rather than any genuine or insightful understanding of the actual perpetrators. Although his work represents an absurd extreme, many other writers about great historical crimes have taken a similar approach of accepting victim accounts at face value while being very skeptical of perpetrators' accounts.

The assertion that perpetrators might be biased by self-serving efforts to conceal or minimize their crimes is uncontroversial. But is it methodologically or epistemologically safe to rely on victims?

There is, in fact, some theoretical basis for suspecting that victims might also offer biased or distorted accounts of events. In many cases, victims have a material interest in portraying the transgression in a certain way. Legal plaintiffs, for example, might maximize or exaggerate their suffering in order to win a larger damage award from the jury. Even outside of a legal context, many victims may desire social support, sympathy, and other benefits from the people around them, and they may find it useful to describe their suffering in maximal or exaggerated terms in order to attract such supportive attentions. After all, even if other people are initially supportive to a trauma victim, it is plausible that their sympathy and support may dwindle before the victim's need for it ends. In order to maintain the claim on continued support, the victim might therefore regard it necessary to communicate his or her suffering in strong and dramatic terms.

The wish to avoid guilt or responsibility may be another reason that victims might provide biased or distorted accounts. Although there are certainly some cases in which victims are wholly innocent, the majority of episodes of violence and transgression contain some degree of shared responsibility and mutual provocation (see Baumeister, 1997, for review). Most instances of domestic violence or acquaintance murder, for example, emerge from episodes in which there is a progressive escalation of mutual hostility—beginning with dispute or criticism, escalating through verbal hostility (e.g., insults and reproaches), followed perhaps by threats of physical aggression, and possibly even some reciprocal pushing and hitting, before the violence reaches its climax. Likewise, in cases of transgressions that do not involve physical violence, transgressors often perceive that they were provoked or threatened by the victim, and so their aggression is (to the perpetrators) a response to victims' acts (e.g., Baumeister, Stillwell, & Wotman, 1990). Victims, obviously, may be reluctant to regard their own actions as part of the causal chain leading toward their eventual suffering, because that interpretation would amount to self-blame. Hence their accounts may be distorted in many cases in order to downplay their own role.

Although these suggestions are plausible, they are difficult to test empirically. Thus, perpetrators may perceive that their aggression is simply a response to provocations from the eventual victims, but it is difficult to know whether such perceptions involve some degree of accurate perception or are simply self-serving fabrications on the part of perpetrators. Psychologists, historians, sociologists, and other students of trauma are well aware that victim and perpetrator accounts differ, and there is general agreement that perpetrators will often bias and distort their accounts, but without some objective criterion it is impossible to know whether victims' accounts are also subject to bias and distortion.

The question of victim bias was investigated in a laboratory simulation by Stillwell and Baumeister (1997). The approach was to provide a fixed body of information (consisting of the facts of a interpersonal transgression) to people who were induced to perceive and retell them from the role of either the victim or the perpetrator. This procedure allowed the researchers to compare both the victims' and the perpetrators' accounts to the original stimulus information, in order to ascertain the degree of bias and distortion. More precisely, subjects were instructed to learn the facts of the incident as if it were happening to them (in one assigned role) and then to write the story in the first person as if it were their own memory of a personal experience. There was also a control group, in which people were to learn and then retell the experience in the third person without identifying with any of the characters.

The results confirmed that victim accounts can be biased too. In fact, to the surprise of the researchers, the victim and perpetrator accounts contained almost identical numbers of errors, based on a sentence-by-sentence comparison of the written, recalled accounts with the original stimulus information. Nor was this finding the result of a floor effect or insensitivity of the procedures: The control subjects, who did not identify with either role, made significantly and substantially fewer errors than either the victims or the perpetrators. One might have thought that the control subjects would be less accurate than the others, because they were less personally involved in the stories they were reading and writing, but personal involvement was apparently no guarantee of accuracy. The uninvolved participants in the control condition were substantially more accurate and thorough than the people who role-played the victims or the perpetrators.

To be sure, the finding that victims and perpetrators distorted to equal degrees did not mean that their distortions were the same. On the contrary, they distorted in opposite directions. Perpetrators tended (as one might expect) to distort the facts in ways that reduced the severity of the transgression and their own responsibility for it, such as by omitting the victim's aversive consequences or exaggerating the mitigating circumstances for their acts. Victims, in contrast, altered the story so as to make the transgression more severe and to shift all the responsibility on to the perpetrator (and off themselves).

How were these distortions done? By far, the majority of them consisted of selective omissions. The original story furnished to participants was a complex one full of facts and details about the context and consequences of the transgression. Leaving out some of these (e.g., mitigating circumstances or provoking acts by the victim) made the transgression seem worse than it originally was, but leaving out others (e.g., the consequences for the victim) would make it seem less severe than what was actually presented.

Two other categories of distortions were found. One involved adding events that were not part of the original stimulus material. Although such fabrications were relatively rare, they did occur. The other category involved slanting or embellishing a fact so as to alter its meaning, such as putting a certain "spin" on events. For example, victims might embellish a perpetrator's "offer" of help into a "promise" to help (thereby making the eventual failure to help more severe), while perpetrators might suggest that even when exhausted they had offered to help but been put off by the victim who was not ready at that time. This type of error was also far less common than selective omission, but it did occur. For the journalist, historian, legal investigator, or other person who is trying to piece together the objective truth out of discrepant accounts, the most challenging problem would presumably be to find out what has been left out, as opposed to trying to catch outright lies and fabrications.

A second study found that the discrepancies between victims and perpetrators remained intact over time (based on a retest three to five days after the initial exposure to the information). A third study found that even when participants were given specific instructions urging them to be as thorough and accurate as possible and to avoid any mistakes, the victim and perpetrator accounts were different. In fact, on most analyses the subjects who had been given the instructions emphasizing accuracy were not significantly different from the other subjects.

The limitations of these studies must be acknowledged. The experiment was a simulation rather than an actual experience. In particular, there were no objective consequences to be faced. Perpetrators did not have the usual reason for lying, which is fear of punishment. Victims also did not have any material motive for distorting, because they were not going to receive any support or restitution. Although we found victims and perpetrators distorted to equal degrees, it is plausible that outside the laboratory perpetrators may distort more than victims, insofar as telling lies may be a strategic ploy to avoid punishment.

Still, the results are important. It is arguably dramatic and surprising that such significant degrees of distortion occurred in the absence of any pragmatic reason to distort. Simply playing the role of victim (or perpetrator) in a hypothetical, make-believe sense was sufficient to generate substantial and significant alterations to the content of the story. Nor were these differences due to demand characteristics such as a belief by the participants that they were expected to try to distort their accounts in predictable ways: Explicit instructions to be accurate and avoid mistakes yielded negligible increments in accuracy.

For the present purposes, the important implication is that the victim role contains significant sources of cognitive bias. College students randomly assigned to identify with a victim in a hypothetical story later furnished versions of that story that departed in predictable and substantial ways from the original information they had been given. Identifying with the victim also led to significantly more distortions than simply telling the story in the third person, without identifying with anyone (i.e., the control condition), so the attrition and distortion of normal memory processes cannot be blamed for the victims' errors.

☐ Transgressions from Victim and Perpetrator Perspectives

Given that victims and perpetrators show equal degrees of distortion, it seems reasonable to assume that victims are at least partly responsible for many of the discrepancies between victim and perpetrator accounts. This allows us to infer some degree of victim bias in research findings that show differences between victims and perpetrators, even when no criterion of objective accuracy is available. We turn now to examine these patterns.

Our primary source for these results is an investigation by Baumeister, Stillwell, and Wotman (1990). This investigation used the procedure of gathering first-person, autobiographical accounts (see Harvey, Weber, & Orbuch, 1990). A large sample of transgression accounts was assembled by asking each participant to report (in writing) two events from his or her life. One was to focus on an event in which someone did something that angered the participant; the other was to describe an event in which the participant angered someone else. People were told to describe the most important and severe episode they could remember in recent years. The order of the stories was counterbalanced, so that half the people wrote the victim story first and half wrote the perpetrator story first. (No order effects were found.) Extensive content coding, based mostly on dichotomous (yes-no) ratings of each story as to many specific features, was the basis for quantifying the stories. The main analyses consisted of chi-square comparisons of the percent of victim vs. perpetrator stories that contained any given feature.

It is important to keep in mind that each participant wrote one victim story and one perpetrator story. Hence these results do not reflect personality differences between victims and perpetrators: The victims and the perpetrators were the same exact people and were writing both memories on the same day. This procedure would probably tend to reduce differences, and so the study's findings may understate actual differences between perpetrators and victims outside the laboratory. Most important, they indicate biases that must reside in the roles themselves rather than in the people's personalities or overall outlook. When the same person shifts from reporting a victim story to reporting a perpetrator story, his or her style of thinking changes in recognizable ways.

☐ Time Span

A striking difference in time spans is potentially quite revealing about the different cognitive styles of victim and perpetrator roles. Victim stories had much longer and more inclusive time spans than perpetrator stories.

The broader time spans of victim stories were apparent in several ways. First, victim stories were more likely to describe events preceding the incident itself, so as to offer background. Perpetrator stories were almost evenly divided between those that offered some prior events and those that began right away by describing the transgression itself, without background information.

Second, victim stories were more likely than perpetrator stories to describe multiple incidents (included repeated provocations and accumulating grievances). Perpetrators tended to describe only one occasion. This difference suggests that victims tend to have cognitive links between various transgressions that have been done to them on multiple occasions, whereas perpetrators do not link such actions together.

Third, victim stories tended to describe how the consequences of the transgression continued to the present time and would likely extend into the future. Perpetrator stories often referred to the present, but usually it was to say that the present circumstances were wholly unaffected by the episode. For example, a victim story might end by saying, "And I was never able to trust my cousin again after that happened," whereas a perpetrator's story would be more likely to end with something like, "We reconciled after that and are now better friends than we ever were beforehand."

The term *temporal bracketing* seems appropriate to describe the time structure of perpetrator narratives. More precisely, they bracket the incident off in time (and in particular disconnect it from the present). The perpetrator role is apparently experienced as a relatively temporary role, which one may occupy briefly but which is soon relinquished in a strong fashion. Perpetrators describe their past transgressions as wholly in the past, as if to say that their present selves should not be judged or punished based on these past actions.

In contrast, the victim role appears to be a much more long-lasting role. Victims were far less likely to distance themselves from the transgression, and in fact they were more likely to connect the past transgression they suffered with some problems or disadvantages in their present circumstances.

Other studies of victimization suggest similar discrepancies in the time perspectives of victims as opposed to perpetrators. Some groups of victims maintain long memories, extending over historical centuries, of grievances that they suffered. Reporting on the conflict in the former Yugoslavia, the magazine *The Economist* (1994) reported that the Serbs, seen by most as the chief aggressors in the bloody conflict, regarded themselves as the victims based in particular on a long historical memory of grievances. "Visitors are lectured about Turkish atrocities against the Serb people going back to 1389 . . . " (p. 49).

In similar fashion, American slavery seems far more recent and relevant to the present to America's African-American citizens, many of whom are descended from victims of slavery, than to the white descendants of slaveowners. Likewise, modern Jews worry frequently that the memory of the Nazi massacres of Jews will fade from historical memory; and "Never forget" is a motto embraced by their efforts to keep the memory alive.

Perhaps the most dramatic illustration of the long-range time span of victim thinking is Maalouf's (1987) assertion that the Arab world of the Middle East continues to perceive the West in a way colored by its victimization during the Crusades, when Europeans made a series of seemingly (to the Arabs, at least) unprovoked invasions of Arab sovereign territory, committed many brutal atrocities, disrupted the political structure of the region, and brought an end to the cultural flowering that was then in progress in the Middle East. The Crusades began almost a millennium ago and ended over five centuries ago, and so one might assume that perpetrator and victim alike would long ago have consigned them to an irrelevant and distant historical past, but apparently they remain far more relevant to the victim group than to the perpetrator group.

Undoubtedly continued suffering and continued rumination contribute to the perseverance of some victims' memories. The difference in time span may be therefore much more than grammatical style or interpretive breadth. Victims may continue to suffer for years afterward, and this pattern seems likely to make the transgression span a much longer period for them than for the perpetrators, for whom there may be few lasting consequences or reminders.

☐ Endings and Consequences

The capacity to see positive consequences from trauma is celebrated in folk wisdom as an appealing strategy of coping, but the stories analyzed by Baumeister et al. (1990) found relatively few instances in which people cited positive consequences of transgressions. Not surprisingly, there were plenty of negative consequences in the stories—and, also not surprisingly, these were far more common in the victim than in the perpetrator stories. Somehow a majority of the perpetrator stories managed to describe the incident without indicating that there were any consequences at all, either positive or negative. In contrast, three quarters of the victim stories contained some allusion to lasting, aversive consequences.

Was the lack of negative consequences in the perpetrator stories a mere oversight or a strategic defense against responsibility for causing some lasting harm? Probably it was both. When the stories were coded for explicit statements denying that there were any lasting negative consequences, a significant difference was found indicating that such denials were more common in perpetrator than victim stories. (In fact, no victim story contained such a denial.) Thus, at least some perpetrators considered the question of lasting consequences but insisted that their transgression had no such effects. Some perpetrators, apparently, are motivated to assert that they did not cause lasting damage. Still, it seems likely that lasting negative consequences are generally more salient to the victim (who suffers from them) than to the perpetrator (who may move on and never be reminded of them), and so the general lack of consequences in perpetrator narratives could well be partly due to simply not knowing or easily forgetting that past actions could have lasting outcomes.

Although hardly any stories reported positive consequences, there were many that at least contained happy endings. The difference between a positive consequence and a happy ending is that the latter may occur despite the transgression (rather than because of it). Thus, there was a transgression, harm was done, but it was repaired, the people involved resumed their good relationship, and so everyone lived happily ever after (or so at least the story would imply). Happy endings were significantly more common in the perpetrator than in the victim narratives.

To be sure, the fact that over half the perpetrator narratives had happy endings may reflect some defensive or strategic attempt to portray one's past wrongdoing as minor and inconsequential. Still, it seems plausible that the greater number of unhappy endings in the victim stories reflects a basic fact about the victim role: It is an unhappy role. The category of "happy victims" is probably a very small one, and indeed the term itself may be an oxymoron. This suggests the possibility that remaining in a victim role over a long period of time may have some cost in terms of subjective well-being.

Undoubtedly many victims see the consequences of transgressions as more enduring and generally more severe than perpetrators. An even broader difference in perceived scale of consequences was proposed by Baumeister (1997), based on an interdisciplinary review of research about many different forms of crime, violence, oppression, and other evils. This difference, which can for convenience be called the magnitude gap, entails that victims perceive transgressions as far more momentous than perpetrators.

The magnitude gap even extends to a comparison of benefits that perpetrators may receive with the costs that victims suffer. In many cases, such as robbery, land conquest, or rape, one person takes or gains at another's expense, and so the evil or violent act is a kind of social exchange. Yet Baumeister (1997) concluded that the exchange does not conform to the zero-sum model: The victim loses more than the perpetrator gains. The magnitude gap is thus likely to be an enduring barrier to reconciliation or even to mutual understanding between victims and perpetrators. Grudges, vendettas, and other patterns may persist even after efforts to reconcile, because the perpetrator and victim may well see the transgression on different scales of magnitude.

The magnitude gap is perhaps most obvious in the case of murder: Nothing the perpetrator gains by murder can really compare with the magnitude of what the victim loses. In fact, in most cases the perpetrator's gain is minimal: Many murders are simply impulsive acts emerging from drunken arguments over minor issues, and when the killer awakens and sobers up the next day (often in jail) he or she may be quick to recognize the murder as fairly pointless and even self-destructive (Gottfredson & Hirschi, 1990).

Although murder may be the most obvious illustration of the magnitude gap, that gap is not hard to document in other instances as well. In rape, for example, victims may suffer anxiety, nightmares, and sexual disturbances for years, whereas for the perpetrators the gains are usually very temporary. Judged in purely sexual terms, rape offers fairly little; in one study, convicted rapists were asked to rate the sexual pleasure they derived on a ten-point scale, with 10 indicating maximum enjoyment; most rated the episode as 3 or less (Groth, 1979). Likewise, with robbery, the resale value of stolen goods is generally far below the replacement value that the victim must address, and the trauma of being robbed far outweighs and outlasts any satisfactions the robber gains from a successful robbery. Even when robbery involves cash, the robber tends to use it up rapidly in a spending binge, resulting in little lasting benefit (Gottfredson & Hirschi, 1990; Katz, 1988).

The magnitude gap may itself constitute a second form of victimization. After everything the victim suffers, he or she may then confront the perpetrator (if only in court or vicariously in research), and this confrontation will drive home the revelation that the transgression was a minor, trivial, or spur-of-the-moment episode in the perpetrator's life. This smallness conflicts with the central importance the event may have for the victim's life, and victims may be reluctant to accept how such a major victimization could mean so little to the perpetrator.

A recent investigation by Mikula, Athenstaedt, Heschgl, and Heimgartner (1998) contained four studies comparing victim and perpetrator ratings of transgressions with different Austrian samples, including married couples, dating couples, and friendship pairs among schoolgirls. Their findings generally converged with what Baumeister et al. (1990) found. Mikula et al. (1998) consistently found that victims perceived the events as more serious than the perpetrators. Such judgments probably reflect both a differential perception of severity of consequences and the broader magnitude gap.

The magnitude gap brings up the issue of perpetrator intentions. We turn to that next.

☐ Perpetrators' Intentions

Victims and perpetratrators offered very different accounts of the reasons for the transgression. The perpetrator's reasons were, in fact, one of the largest gaps in understanding between the two roles, and we suspect that this discrepancy may contribute to many lasting barriers to understanding and reconciliation between perpetrators and victims.

Simply put, many victims refused to see any reason for the perpetrators' acts. They described the perpetrator's actions as arbitrary, gratuitous, or senseless: "There was no reason to do what he did." Along the same lines, many emphasized that the perpetrator's action was in precise contradiction to what the perpetrator had promised or expressed at other times, and the contradiction was itself presented as gratuitous.

Perpetrators, in contrast, generally had an explanation for their actions. This was not always a fully elaborated, consistent, justified explanation, but at least they were able to account for their actions as being reasonable and somewhat well-intentioned within a broad framework. Only a small minority of perpetrators said "I don't know why I did that" or in some other way depicted their transgression as arbitrary or senseless. Many said that the transgression was an unfortunate or unintended outcome of actions that were designed to produce some other, far more reasonable goal. Still, they offered intelligible and often justifiable explanation for their acts. But victims refused to see any such context.

To the victims, the seeming arbitrariness of the act contributed to its wicked nature and to the victimization. Indeed, the popular image of pure evil involves someone whose intent is purely malicious and who inflicts harm on others for no apparent reason other than perhaps the sadistic or perverse glee of causing harm and seeing someone suffer (Baumeister, 1997; see also Darley, 1992). Satan, after all, is not a well-intentioned but misunderstood figure—rather, he is the evil force who enjoys causing pain and seeing people suffer (e.g., Delbanco, 1995; Russell, 1988). Many victims see the perpetrators of their suffering in just such terms.

Sure enough, the data by Baumeister et al. (1990) showed that victims portrayed perpetrators as acting from sheer malice. Deliberate, unjustified, immoral actions were featured in the victim narratives. Meanwhile, victims were far less likely than perpetrators to cite mitigating factors, impulsive actions, extenuating circumstances, and the like. About a third of the perpetrators said or clearly implied that they could not help what happened—whereas all of the victim stories said or implied that the perpetrator could have avoided the transgression.

Similar findings were reported by Mikula et al. (1998). In their studies, victims consistently rated the transgressions as having been done more intentionally than perpetrators rated them. Although the victim perception of perpetrator intention seems to run contrary to the Baumeister et al. (1990) finding in which victims refused to see perpetrator intentions, the difference is readily explainable in terms of the intention to harm. Thus, Baumeister et al. (1990) found that perpetrators reported reasonable, justified intentions for their actions but victims failed to see these. Instead, victims perceived perpetrators as intending to perform hurtful actions because of malicious intentions. Mikula et al. (1998) likewise found that victims perceived perpetrators as intending to cause harm, as opposed to having constructive, justifiable reasons for their actions.

More generally, victims tend to want to see their victimization as resulting from the deliberate and malicious acts of others. The contribution of chance and accident tends to be minimized (Janoff-Bulman, 1992), and victims are reluctant to see their suffering as due to the indifferent luck of happenstance. When they ask "Why?" and especially "Why me?" they are often reluctant to accept that there is no meaningful or coherent answer and that what happened to them was simply due to chance. Perpetrators, in contrast, place much greater emphasis on chance.

When one looks at broader patterns of how victims perceive perpetrators' intentions, one additional pattern becomes apparent. To understand this, it is necessary to recall the magnitude gap: What the perpetrator gains is usually much less than what the victim loses, and as a result the entire incident may seem minor and trivial to the perpetrator even though it may be enormously important and consequential to the victim. If victims begin to understand the perpetrator's point of view, they are likely to be shocked at the loss of importance. It is difficult for a victim to accept how a perpetrator could be relatively casual about something that is so important to the victim.

One result of such dissonance is that victims may be motivated to construct fictitious elaborations of the perpetrator's intentions, such as portraying them as part of a seriously evil program or grand conspiracy. The literature on victimization contains multiple, sad examples of such thinking on the part of victims. For example, many Jewish writers on the Nazi Holocaust have been moved to assert that killing Jews was the central, overriding obsession of the Nazi leaders, more important to them than consolidating political power, fighting a major war against the rest of the world, and creating the utopian society they envisioned (e.g., Goldhagen, 1996). Likewise, Brownmiller (1975) could not accept that men rape out of a short-sighted and petty quest for personal, sexual pleasure, and so she seriously proposed that every individual act of rape is part of a conspiracy by all men to intimidate and oppress all women. In her theory, presumably, even men who do not engage in rape and profess to oppose it are secretly pleased when rape occurs, because they think acts of rape are furthering the cause of all men to maintain sociopolitical superiority over women. A third example is the belief among African-Americans that all white Americans are involved in a conspiracy to oppress and even eradicate their black fellow citizens. AIDS, crack cocaine, and gun sales to African-American young men (and even black youth gang activity) are seen as part of the white conspiracy to destroy black people. Shakur (1993), for example, claimed that the United States government was the driving force behind the ongoing war between the two major conglomerates of black youth gangs in Los Angeles, the "Bloods" and the "Crips."

It is easy for educated people and social scientists in particular to dismiss such grand conspiracy theories as irrational beliefs of uneducated individuals. Their very absurdity however requires a fuller explanation than mere ignorance on the part of believers. The magnitude gap helps explain the motivation to construct such theories. We propose that victims would prefer to believe theories about such grand conspiracies than to accept the alternatives that trivialize the event in the perpetrators' minds: that the Nazis killed Jews because that was the easiest way to get rid of them; that individual men rape women out of selfish desires for transitory sexual pleasure, and to acquire some minor symbolic satisfaction from sexual conquest; that the suffering of African-American citizens is a byproduct of broad social processes and is itself of little concern to the white majority.

☐ Victim as Causal Agent

The victim role is usually defined and understood as a passive role: Things are done to victims, as opposed to victims actively doing things to others or directing the flow of events. Yet the passivity of the victim role may be exaggerated in some respects.

The autobiographical accounts of transgressions assembled by Baumeister et al. (1990) showed that victims and perpetrators disagreed about the victim's role. A third of the perpetrator accounts clearly indicated that the victim had provoked the incident and was thus partly responsible for it. In contrast, only a miniscule 4% of victim accounts depicted the victim as provoking the incident. A broader category involved all stories in which anything about the victim or the victim's actions helped cause the incident (thus not confined to directly provoking the transgression). Over half the perpetrator stories fell in that category, as compared to only about a third of the victim stories. (Again, the difference was significant.)

Clearly, many perpetrators see their own transgressions as being at least partly a response to the victim's provocative actions, whereas victim stories minimize the victims' own role. Victim stories tend to emphasize the victim's own complete innocence and hence the arbitrary, gratuitous, unjustified nature of the perpetrator's acts. Perpetrators tend to depict their own actions as part of a sequence of events in which the victim's prior actions led them to respond and perhaps transgress.

The ratings of transgressions by Mikula et al. (1998) provide converging evidence. In their studies, victims assigned themselves little or no causal role and instead rated the perpetrators as being solely responsible for the events. Perpetrators' ratings disagreed and assigned a greater causal role to victims (than victims assigned to themselves).

Comparison with larger victimizations and traumas reveals a similar pattern. Research shows that many instances of violence do in fact emerge from mutual, escalating provocations, and so there is indeed some validity to the claims made by many perpetrators that their violent acts were simply made in response to provoking or even violent acts by their eventual victims.

To be sure, some violent offenders do falsely or unreasonably claim that their victims are responsible. The most obvious case of this may be the acts of Communist or other totalitarian states. In the Soviet Union, Maoist China, or Khmer Rouge Cambodia, a seemingly endless stream of innocent people were falsely accused of treasonous or counterrevolutionary activity (including sabotage and espionage) and were arrested, tortured, and in many cases executed (e.g., Becker, 1986; Conquest, 1990; Thurston, 1987). A seemingly humorous, but in some ways very depressing, passage in Conquest (1990) involved the discovery by the inmates at a crowded Soviet prison that one of them was actually guilty of the crimes with which he had been charged—a rare novelty that surprised both guards and fellow prisoners. Under such circumstances, perpetrators may claim and even believe that victims are partly responsible for their fate, but such beliefs are unwarranted.

Very commonly, however, there is some validity to the perpetrators' claims of active instigation by victims. Studies of murder and domestic violence, for example, find that the extremes of violence are often reached only at the end of a gradual sequence of escalation that may begin with some dispute or conflict, leading to angry statements, followed by cursing or insults, followed perhaps by minor physical aggression such as shoving someone (Gelles & Straus, 1988; Luckenbill, 1977).

Some causal role for the victim is, after all, generally more plausible than the alternative assumption that perpetrators inflict harm and violence for no apparent reason and out of the blue. It is important to acknowledge that provoking acts by the victim do not provide moral justification for violent acts by perpetrators, even if they do contribute to our psychological understanding of the transgression. Assigning some responsibility to the victim does not exonerate the perpetrator. Still, many victims act as if it were necessary to deny any responsibility on their part in order to blame the perpetrator.

☐ Underreaction and Overreaction

How do victims and perpetrators respond to transgressions? Once again, both accounts diverged sharply.

Victim accounts tended to feature underreactions. Almost half the victim stories in the Baumeister et al. (1990) sample included at least one incident in which the victim suppressed all response and hence expressed none of the anger that was felt. (And all of them did feel angry, because feelings of anger were specified in the study's instructions as a requirement for all stories.) Some perpetrators realized the victims might swallow their anger, but these were a relatively small proportion (19%) and significantly less than the proportion of victims who reported stifling their responses. One implication is that probably most of us have made more people angry than we realize, because so many of those we angered forced themselves to hold their tongues!

In contrast, victim overreactions were far more common in perpetrator accounts. About half the perpetrator accounts, as compared with only a small minority of the victim accounts, portrayed the victim's response as an overreaction. Clearly, victims tend to see their own responses as appropriate and often even restrained, whereas perpetrators perceive things quite differently.

These two patterns may not be as fully contradictory as they seem. If victims often do manage to stifle all expression of their anger, then perpetrators may genuinely fail to realize the anger they have caused. Hence such incidents (in which victims did underreact) would not show up in the reports we got from perpetrators, but only in the victim reports.

The discrepancy in reports of victim overreaction may also have a theoretically interesting and meaningful basis other than mere interpretive bias. As already noted, victim accounts tended to encompass broad time spans and grievances that accumulate from multiple provocations, whereas perpetrator accounts did not. One common sequence of events may therefore involve initial transgressions that cause anger that is not expressed, followed by repeated or escalating transgressions. After all, if the victim expresses no anger or objection at all, the perpetrator may not even realize that he or she has caused offense, and so a repetition of that behavior would not be surprising. Eventually the victim may blow up and express considerable anger at this pattern. To the victim, this may seem a measured and justifiable response to a whole series of provocations. The perpetrator, however, may be genuinely surprised by this reaction, contrasting as it does with the lack of response to similar actions in the past. Thus, the perpetrator may see the angry outburst as an overreaction to a single incident, whereas to the victim that outburst is a long-restrained response to an accumulated sequence of transgressions.

For the psychology of victims, there may be important implications of the high rate of suppressed anger. Research in other contexts has found that acts of self-control deplete some energy resource in the self, and subsequently this resource is unavailable for other acts of volition, decision, and self-regulation (e.g., Baumeister, Bratslavsky, Muraven, & Tice, 1998; Muraven, Tice, & Baumeister, 1998). If victims do have to exert themselves at controlling and stifling their emotional responses, this could well take a toll that might result in subsequent passivity, indecision, and uncontrolled behavior in other contexts.

☐ Is the Victim Role Debilitating?

Our survey of the findings about the victim role suggests a variety of negative, disadvantageous features. It is plausible that if people embrace the victim's role, they may perpetuate an undesirable condition. Weakness, passivity, and unhappiness are all endemic to the victim role, and so people who identify with the victim role could conceivably sustain perceptions of self as having those disadvantages. Moreover, as we speculated, the requirements of the victim role in terms of regulating affect (and possibly other responses) could deplete the self of valuable resources, thereby impairing volition.

One hypothesis is therefore that the victim role is itself a source of weakness and passivity. Causing people to see themselves as victims might therefore cause them to act in a weaker or more passive fashion than they would otherwise. In fact, it is conceivable that even merely activating the idea of the victim role could have such effects.

Preliminary tests of these effects were conducted by Hastings and Tice (1997). In a pair of experiments, subjects were initially given a priming task. They presented with sets of five words and told to make a four-word sentence from each set (thus discarding one word). This task was adapted from recent procedures used by Bargh (e.g., 1997). By random assignment, half the participants received sets in which the superfluous word had to do with victimization (i.e., words such as pain, abused, mistreated, and victim). Other participants received affectively neutral primes that had nothing to do with victimization.

After this, all participants took an ostensibly unrelated test. In both studies, however, it was found that people who had been primed with the victim role performed worse than control subjects. In the first experiment, the test involved solving anagrams (i.e., unscrambling letters to make words), and participants primed with the victim role solved fewer than control participants. In the second experiment, the test consisted of 3-digit multiplication problems. Once again, people in the victim priming condition solved fewer problems correctly than the comparison group.

Although these studies represent only initial findings and clearly need replication, the results do suggest a debilitating effect of the victim role. People primed with victimization performed worse on both verbal (anagrams) and quantitative (multiplication) tasks. The tests were timed, so the poorer performance could reflect greater passivity, lethargic slowness, or cognitive impairment, and these findings do not reveal what mechanism led to the failure. Still, regardless of the causal mechanism, the outcome has troublesome implications for victims.

The findings are especially remarkable when one considers how far from actual victimization the manipulations were. All that was necessary to produce effects was to activate the schema of victimization by a subtle priming mechanism. Participants were unaware of this activation, and they did not show any changes in mood or emotional state (compared to control participants), yet their task performance dropped significantly.

For real victims, therefore, there may considerable reason to worry that multiple and lasting impairments could result from the victim role itself. Many minor cues or daily events might activate the reminder of one's victimization, akin to our priming task, leading to impaired capacity to perform mental tasks. Moreover, many people may find themselves pressured to sustain their victim role, for a variety of reasons. These could include lawsuits or other proceedings for which the victimization remains relevant. Likewise, certain victim groups may feel that asserting their victim status may strengthen or legitimize their claims for remedial treatment, and so they may encourage members to focus on their victim status. Although such benefits may be important and attractive, the Hastings and Tice (1997) results suggest they may come at a high price.

Conceivably the drawbacks of the victim role could encourage some individuals to repudiate the victim status. One well replicated finding that has puzzled researchers is that most women believe that sex discrimination exists but deny that they themselves have been victimized by it (e.g., Crosby, Cordova, & Jaskar, 1993). Researchers sometimes suggest that it would be desirable to raise women's consciousness of their victimization. Yet these results suggest that some women might be better off eschewing the victim role, and efforts to make them see themselves as victims could lead to impaired performance.

The other side of the coin is forgiveness. By forgiving a perpetrator, one may effectively take oneself out of the victim role. Forgiving is a fairly active response that puts past suffering in the past and renounces claims for further restitution. A variety of research suggests that forgiveness can have assorted benefits for mental and physical health (see McCullough, Sandage, & Worthington, 1997). Some of these may well stem from rejecting the victim role.

Thus, the impact of victimization on thinking goes beyond thinking about the transgression or victimization itself. Activating the victim role impaired people's ability to think about tasks having nothing to do with victimization. The victim role may therefore have a broad effect on thought processes generally, at least to the extent that the ability to solve common problems and perform basic cognitive operations is impaired.

☐ Conclusion

This chapter has covered an assortment of findings pertaining to the victim role. It is well established that victims and perpetrators interpret similar transgressions in systematically different ways. These differences include a tendency for victims (as compared to perpetrators) to see events in a broader temporal context, to see more harmful consequences and ones that continue to the present, to fail to see any valid reasons or justifiable intentions (or even mitigating circumstances) behind the perpetrators' actions, to see perpetrators as motivated by malice or even by grandly evil conspiracies, to see their own responses as underreactions rather than overreactions, and to place greater importance on the entire episode.

Moreover, there is some evidence that the victim role is itself a substantial and significant source of interpretive bias. Although no one denies that perpetrators sometimes rationalize, distort, and even lie in order to minimize their guilt or escape punishment, it is becoming apparent that the victim role is also characterized by strong motivations that can alter and distort cognitive processing.

Last, there is some preliminary evidence that the victim role may be debilitating. In laboratory studies, merely activating the concept of victimization caused people to perform more poorly on subsequent verbal and quantitative tests. If the mere idea of victimization can impair mental performance on a laboratory task, it is possible that actual victims might suffer far more important and pervasive impairments.

Although these findings tend to assign more choice and causal influence to victims than they might prefer themselves, we do not want these points to be overstated. In particular, the distortions and biases we have linked to the perpetrator role would encourage them to seize on any active role by victims in order to shift blame onto victims. Blame is a moral category, and our analysis has sought instead to analyze the causal processes as social scientists. The fact that victims may sometimes share responsibility does not necessarily exculpate perpetrators. In general, victims deserve and require sympathy and support. Our hope is that a fuller understanding of victim thinking will facilitate empathic understanding of their suffering and the resulting efforts to help them.

☐ References

Bargh, J. A. (1997). The automaticity of everyday life. In R. S. Wyer (Ed.), *The automaticity of everyday life: Advances in social cognition* (Vol. 10, pp. 1–61). Mahwah, NJ: Erlbaum.

Baumeister, R. F. (1997). *Evil: Inside human violence and cruelty.* New York: W. H. Freeman.

Baumeister, R. F., Bratslavsky, E., Muraven, M., & Tice, D. M. (1998). Ego depletion: Is the active self a limited resource? *Journal of Personality and Social Psychology, 74,* 1252–1265.

Baumeister, R. F., Stillwell, A., & Wotman, S. R. (1990). Victim and perpetrator accounts of interpersonal conflict: Autobiographical narratives about anger. *Journal of Personality and Social Psychology, 59,* 994–1005.

Becker, E. (1986). *When the war was over: Cambodia's revolution and the voices of its people.* New York: Simon & Schuster.

Brownmiller, S. (1975). *Against our will: Men, women, and rape.* New York: Simon & Schuster.

Conquest, R. (1990). *The great terror: A reassessment.* New York: Oxford University Press.

Crosby, F., Cordova, D. I., & Jaskar, K. (1993). On the failure to see oneself as disadvantaged: Cognitive and emotional components. In M. Hogg & D. Abrams (Eds.), *Group motivation: Social psychological perspectives* (pp. 87–104). London: Harvester Wheatsheaf.

Darley, J. M. (1992). Social organization for the production of evil. *Psychological Inquiry, 3,* 199–218.

Delbanco, A. (1995). *The death of Satan: How Americans have lost the sense of evil.* New York: Farrar, Straus and Giroux.

Gelles, R. J., & Straus, M. A. (1988). *Intimate violence: The causes and consequences of abuse in the American family.* New York: Simon & Schuster/Touchstone.

Goldhagen, D. J. (1996). *Hitler's willing executioners.* New York: Knopf.

Gottfredson, M. R., & Hirschi, T. (1990). *A general theory of crime.* Stanford, CA: Stanford University Press.

Groth, A. N. (1979). *Men who rape: The psychology of the offender.* New York: Plenum.

Harvey, J. H., Weber, A. L., & Orbuch, T. L. (1990). *Interpersonal accounts: A social psychological perspective.* Oxford, England: Blackwell.

Hastings, S., & Tice, D. M. (1997). Impairment of cognitive test performance as a result of priming the victim role. Unpublished findings, Case Western Reserve University.

Janoff-Bulman, R. (1992). *Shattered assumptions.* New York: Free Press.

Katz, J. (1988). *Seductions of crime: Moral and sensual attractions in doing evil.* New York: Basic Books.

Luckenbill, D. (1977) . Criminal homicide as a situated transaction. *Social Problems, 25,* 176–186.

Maalouf, A. (1987). *The Crusades through Arab eyes.* New York: Schocken.

McCullough, M. E., Sandage, S. J., & Worthington, E. L. (1997). *To forgive is human: How to put your past in the past.* Downers Grove, IL: InterVarsity Press.

Mikula, G., Athenstaedt, U., Heschgl, S., & Heimgartner, A. (1998). Does it only depend on the point of view? Perspective-related differences in justice evaluations of negative incidents in personal relationships. *European Journal of Social Psychology, 28,* 931–962.

Muraven, M., Tice, D. M., & Baumeister, R. F. (1998). Self-control as limited resource: Regulatory depletion patterns. *Journal of Personality and Social Psychology, 74,* 774–789.

Russell, J. B. (1988). *The prince of darkness: Radical evil and the power of good in history.* Ithaca, NY: Cornell University Press.

Shakur, S. (1993). *Monster: The autobiography of an L.A. gang member.* New York: Atlantic Monthly Press.

Silver, R. L., Boon, C., & Stones, M. H. (1983). Searching for meaning in misfortune: Making sense of incest. *Journal of Social Issues, 39,* 81–102.

Stillwell, A. M., & Baumeister, R. F. (1997). The construction of victim and perpetrator memories: Accuracy and distortion in role-based accounts. *Personality and Social Psychology Bulletin, 23,* 1157–1172.

Thurston, A. F. (1987). *Enemies of the people: The ordeal of the intellectuals in China's great cultural revolution.* New York: Knopf.

CHAPTER 6

Harvey Peskin

The Ranking of Grief: Death and Comparative Loss

The right or permission to grieve is more essential to the process of mourning than we usually let ourselves know. Perhaps it is even a ritual of mourning that notice not be taken. Although clinical discussion abounds in the intrapsychic blocks and inhibitions to grieving, there has been little acknowledgment of the power of social bodies—families, friends, and community collectives—to withhold or grant entitlement to grieve losses openly and equally. By "little acknowledgment" we mean that while the wish and need to mourn may be privately known to oneself, it is not necessarily so easily made known or acceptable to others in the grieving process. The potential gulf between the personal knowing and the public acknowledgment of grieving is the subject of this chapter.

The presumption that grief is free to—and free for—all has a wishful characteristic. Death indeed seems to allow the whole-hearted expression of connectedness that in life was restrained by the weaker claim of our lower personal or social standing. Witness the remarkable nationwide grief over the death of Princess Diana in a country famously known for the class-conscious exclusiveness and privacy of mourning. But the outpouring of grief for the loss of the famous may only momentarily breach and compensate for the restraints dictated by family boundaries or social position that keeps at bay the grief we feel for those we have truly loved.

On certain occasions, of course, social ranking in the grieving process visibly intrudes when we least anticipate it, as when certain deep expectations—what we might call the "natural order" of mourning—are drastically upended. Witness the coded announcement of a sudden leadership change in dictatorships, like China or the former USSR, by the rearranged seating order of persons in the photographs of government leaders at state funerals. Indeed, any visibility of social rank in grieving, beyond a given and appropriate natural order, may be too visible. An exception to the natural order also occurs when religious law, for reasons of purification, requires members of the priesthood caste (as in orthodox Judaism) to stay away from the gravesite or house of the dead. (The absurd humor in the following tale depends on just this breach of invisibility: An uninvited sexton—the low ranking custodian of the church—mounts the podium in an important church funeral to announce with great piety that he, too, like the president and minister of the congregation before him, is merely a nobody in the eyes of the Lord. The president whispers to the minister, "Look who thinks he's a nobody!")

☐ The Ranking of Grief as a Social Construct: Family Vs. Friends

Over a lifetime of implicit socialization for meeting the sorrow of death, one learns to support those whose right to mourn holds a higher rank than our own and to expect support from those with lower rank. Typically, this social learning reflects the customary status of reference groups to which we and the deceased belong. The larger claim to mourn should belong first of all to the primary reference group of the family who grieves a lost member—and then to those of secondary reference groups consisting of friends, colleagues, associates, and others. Loss that triggers severe and persistent grief is taken by Weiss (1988) to indicate the primacy of a relationship (relationships of attachment); distress and sadness that lack the persistence and severity of grief indicate a secondary relationship (relationships of community). This apparent straightforward definition, however, contains a circularity that reveals the very influence of socialization on mourning. For in this definition, there is no provision for the likelihood that friends, in acknowledging the family's priority, reduce the legitimacy of their own depth of grief by backing away from claiming equal (or even greater) loss. That is, by a willingness to seem less aggrieved than the family, the friend accepts a lesser rank of grieving. Thus, what would appear to fit the definition of lesser grief for a lost friend may turn out to be a meaningful, if private, gesture of sacrifice—itself a deeply relational, even altruistic expression of love for the departed friend. Here we see that the natural order of mourning may itself be a social construct of obedience to cultural rules.

As likely as not, however, the act of giving up one's right to mourn may be so unreflectively culture-bound that the actual depth of experienced grief has become muted or otherwise suppressed. Therapists who are not conditioned to such "culture-fulfilling" hypotheses are often helpful to patients who, having acquiesced to a lower ranking of grief, have made themselves unaware of the depth of grief for a lost friend. The lower ranking of grief for friends, it might be pointed out, belongs to a yet larger social construct that places the influence of friends on personality development as second to the influence of family. The veritable surprise that greeted Harris' (1995) evidence to the contrary—that friends have a greater influence than family on personality development—perhaps testifies to society's complicity in our adherence to a false or, at least, simplistic idea. Or, more simply put, the power of friends in shaping personality is one of the best kept secrets of socialization.

But the less structured, more fluid and mutable organization of friendships than of family implies that rules of ranking for bereavement of friends are not so self-evident nor fall so easily into place. Having no entitlement to grieve apart from what the felt state of the relationship merited, friends measure their closeness and intimacy with each other by the right to mourn that is granted them by their friendship. Having the news of a death withheld or unduly delayed by a close friend may signal a reduced ranking of grief and an unexpected sense of personal rejection. Here one may find himself at the difficult choice point of simply accepting the lower rank without argument in compliance with the quietism of socialization for mourning or argue for the deserved higher rank in defiance of such social learning.

Comparative Bereavement

We propose that this same principle of suspending or surrendering one's bereavement to others who are deemed closer to the deceased or otherwise more entitled to the higher rank applies in a wide variety of human conditions, both between and within social groups. Thus, the ranking of grief pertains as well between and among family members. Moreover, the principle of ranking of grief may profitably lead to a larger interest in comparative bereavement that, we also suggest, is mediated by powerful, if implicit, rules of appropriate conduct that mask, sharpen, or alienate personal grief. Here, we are concerned with the prescriptions and proscriptions we carry with us about the worth that we give to our own losses compared to the worth we accord to the losses of others. We all carry within us monologues of comparative bereavement wherein we take measure of our own need to mourn against our own right to mourn, and do so in light of others' needs and rights. Often enough, we conclude our monologues with a decision to suspend our own need out of concern for the more compelling grief of others, as if we believe that grieving requires exclusive and uncompeting expression because its course is so prone to disruption by the forces of guilt, possessiveness, shame, rivalry, or envy.

In the innumerable versions of collective mourning, the qualities of surrender or suspension of grief are legion, but the theme of self-sacrifice is often much the same. Although we have supposed that the magnanimity of friendship might lead a friend to surrender voluntarily the right and rank of grief to the primary family (or to any others appointed to a higher rank), such surrender may also feel unintentional or, indeed, not an apparent surrender at all, because accepting the lower rank could also help fulfill a counter-need of warding off deeper grief. Alternatively, acceding to the lower rank may itself force a deeper grief by keeping it undischarged or unrequited. Such dynamics suggest the reciprocity of intrapsychic and relational factors in grief work.

Within families, accepting the lower rank as proper or all that one is due may fit with dominant family patterns of rights and privileges in other spheres as well, such as decision-making or division of emotional labor. A mother's overriding grief at the death of her spouse may express a greater emotional entitlement than she allows others in the family. That she could be preempting or postponing her child's grief over losing a father may hardly be noticed. Alternatively, such a mother may believe she is protecting the daughter by carrying the emotional brunt of her child's grief. Indeed, the rank of grief may be determined by how much emotion a survivor is deemed able to cope with. On this supposition, a younger child is usually given the lower rank. But whether such children are left with a sense of their grief being appropriated (or expropriated) from them or being kept for them is a consequential question for personality development. In the here-and-now of family grief, it is not a question that children easily know to ask. And yet, much implicit learning about the priorities of grieving takes place just at these mournful times. How or whether we tell a child about a death is obviously confounded by the implicit theories we hold of children's—especially the very young—capacity to grieve. Every act showing that a child accepts his or her lower rank reinforces a sense that the rank is well suited to the child's less developed capacity. Yet, as we said, the seemingly accepted rank may hide the longing for a higher one. Ignoring this possibility gives fuel to the theoretical position of Anna Freud (1952) that young children do not have a full enough hold of an object relationship to grieve its loss. Bowlby's (1973) contrary position maintained that young children have indeed achieved this capacity. Bowlby's position encourages further inquiry into whether a child's seemingly lesser grief is more apparent than real; that is, whether a child's true grief is underestimated due to parents' expectations that an older sibling is more capable of grief.

Beyond this, how parents differentiate grief from other painful experiences and affects will help decide the child's tolerance for bearing fatal losses. It is often illuminating for adults to learn that their fearfulness or detachment in meeting the death of a loved one can be traced to their parents' overprotection from disturbing events presumed to be beyond a child's understanding. What is pivotal, of course, is the parents' own understanding that grief at any age entails disturbance. An adult friend became aware that the fearful distance his parents kept from their own grief had kept him feeling always the outsider, excluding himself from mourning with others over mutual losses. Being overprotected from grief came at the cost of breaking the connection to a lost person that mourning is meant to acknowledge by the presence of others. Hoping to free his own children from this burden helped him grieve openly in their presence at his sister's funeral, as it helped them grieve openly for their aunt in his presence. In this mutuality, preempting another's grief was no longer a brooding reality: grief had indeed become free to all and free for all.

A child's true grief develops as part of the intersubjective construction of selfhood with parents (Stern, 1985). On the one hand, parents' capacity to grieve in the presence of the child releases and organizes the child's own responsiveness to loss; on the other, the child's capacity to grieve is confirmed and affirmed by the parents' empathic witnessing. The subjective character of grief is attuned, then, to its meaning for others; for example, grief as exclusive or inclusive, hidden or open, oppressive or cathartic, depleting or restorative.

The Ranking of Grief for the Death of a Family Member

Three case vignettes have been selected whose family dynamics describe certain prototypical themes of deferred or arrested grieving. In each family, a certain triangulation pitted one member's right to grieve against another. For these cases, individual psychotherapy helped to reveal the underlying family dynamics that proscribed grief and to recover the patient's entitlement to mourn for a lost relationship whose importance had been blunted by family rules.

Case 1. Within families, the order of grief is normally from parents to siblings or equally among all family members. Ranking is more likely among siblings, the higher rank implicitly held by or given to those whose tie to the lost brother or sister has been deemed by the collective voice of the family to have been closer, more loving, or more devoted. Case 1, a 45-year-old physician, entered therapy divulging at the outset strong guilty feelings over the unmourned suicide of his sister many years before. The sister, handicapped with a birth defect, had led a depressive existence with little hope of substantial recovery or rehabilitation. The patient's sense of having been relatively indifferent to her death shows up, he confesses, in his incuriosity about the exact details of her suicide. He gives himself little slack in making atonement through ruthless self-accusation. For example, he is surprised by the therapist's early question about whether his apparent indifference was already an enactment of his guilt and lack of entitlement to a mourner's right to inquire and be interested. The patient's relationship to the sister was, in fact, less close and devoted than that of another brother. Indeed, the brother's obvious higher rank created an impasse for his understanding the depth of his own grief. Since the sister's death, the manifest differences in the brothers' grieving had become curiously operative in their relationship, with the patient being reminded by the brother of his lack of compassion and care for their sister. The therapeutic work paid new attention to a sibling dynamic in which the brother's higher rank held a precondition of excluding the patient, because devotion to the sister also played out a larger sibling rivalry between the brothers. The patient came to realize that he had acceded to his exclusion not only in the sister's death but during her life. Guilt for both her death and life represented making amends to the brother for the patient's larger triumphs over him in their lifetime of rivalry. But beyond guilt, there was the remorseful discovery of a sister relationship never realized in their lifetime together. This unrealized relationship is also mirrored in the lower rank of grief that one receives or accepts.

Case 2.   The correspondence of ranking in life and death in Case 1 is not, of course, always to be taken at face value. In this second case, where the male patient accepted a rank of grief lower than that of an older sister for their mother's early death, the truth of his relationship with mother had been masked by letting his sister define it for him, complying with his sister's need to undermine the patient's grief. This false sense of a weaker grief was reinforced by also letting the sister take command of their grieving, like in demanding that the patient follow her invented rituals of mourning. But as with Case 1, this distortion of his own grief was meant to convince himself that the sister's claim to a higher rank was justified. Here again is the rivalrous theme of exclusiveness in the grieving process. We observe here one sibling's need to appropriate the legitimate grief of the other rather than acknowledge mutual and equal loss. The uncertainty of early memory makes one vulnerable, of course, to distortions by older siblings whose more accurate memory is taken for granted by younger ones. But in Case 2, the sister's need to reduce her younger brother's rank was apparent not only in grieving but elsewhere, as in her claim that living elders in the family felt less love for the patient. In therapy, the patient came to feel that he deserved to give himself a higher ranking than his false belief of being unlovable had allowed. One crucial therapeutic intervention leading to this change was the therapist's remark that "it's unimaginable to me that someone like you could be unlovable to mother." In confronting his inner denial of self-worth to be a mourner, the patient also undid a corollary of his unlovability: that he did not love mother either.

Case 3.   There is often an unspoken agreement that the ranking of nonblood partners in the bereaved's nuclear family is lower than the ranking of full family members. Thus, the son-in-law of the deceased comes to fold his mourning into that of his wife's who has lost a parent. But what if the wife is unable to grieve? Mourning here becomes problematic for the nonblood partner who, if deeply tied to the deceased, is deprived of permission to mourn. This, of course, is stating the case too consciously and knowingly. More likely, this dilemma, especially in the second half of life when death and dying are normative events, is hardly felt as such, but as simply characteristic of partners given, say, to a common emotional restraint. But we suggest that much that is salutary in grieving is lost in such everyday deferences where grieving by the nonblood partner comes to feel inappropriate and, by seeming to preempt the spouse, disrespectful and disloyal.

In Case 3, a middle-aged patient worked to recognize such feelings vis-a-vis his wife in order to acknowledge that he had not yet really mourned the death, years before, of his beloved mother-in-law. Actually, the wife's emotional restraint at her mother's death was a legacy of stoicism transmitted by her father. Father, who in fact was dying at the very time of the patient's therapy, again expected that his daughter be restrained in grieving his death. Indeed, the ranking—including the prohibition—of grief may very well, as in this family, be passed down from generation to generation. The father's values of restraint and the loyalty of the patient's wife to them had been played out for her mother's death as they were again being played out for her father's coming demise. The patient's deference to his wife's unexpressed grief had become a permanent feature of the home, with no thought about the sacrifice of his own—as well as *their* own—need and right to grieve. The therapist interpreted how much his longing to mourn his mother-in-law had succumbed to having to be a partner to his wife's family loyalty. The ranking of grief was presented by the therapist to the patient as a way of capturing this marital dynamic, but with the interpretation that he was passively wishing for his wife to mourn her parents so that he could exercise being next in line. The patient accepted the interpretation as granting him permission to express his long withheld grief to his wife over the death of her mother. Doing so gave his wife, in turn, permission to grieve with him the impending death of her father.

Beyond sharing his private grief with his wife, the therapeutic intervention also had the effect of rousing him to upgrade his ranking by activating a blood-line connection to his late mother-in-law via his own children. In a bemused and softly nostalgic tone, he noticed that his daughter laughed just like her late grandmother. This observation was important because it signaled his daring to approach a long festering but hidden complaint that, in spite of a long marriage, he had never felt fully accepted by his wife's patrician family. Yet asserting this blood-line connection also meant that he himself was now more ready to belong to her family, for he too had his own longheld hesitations. The patient's guilt for marrying into a family of different religion and different blood-line against the wishes of his own parents kept his tie to his inlaws ambivalent and incomplete.

☐ Ranking of Grief as a Determinant of the Life Course: The Case of "French Lessons"

Alice Kaplan's memoir, *French Lessons* (1993), is a subtle and poignant account of the lifetime effect on an eight-year-old girl of unknowingly yielding her grieving for the death of a father to a mother whose own grief seemed narcissistically inconsolable and incomparable. The daughter's right to her own sadness interfered with the exclusiveness of the mother's mourning. On the day of her father's funeral, Alice wanted to wear black. Her mother refused, "You don't need a black dress, you're a little girl" (Kaplan, 1993, p. 21). Alice's mourning became secretive before finally succumbing to her mother's greater claim. Every week or so, if no one was looking, she opened the closet door to see if the American flag received by the family at the father's funeral was still there or if mother had given it away. Literally and figuratively, the child's grief was exiled to a year of high school and college study in Switzerland and France, there to be supplanted by a life-saving mastery of the French language.

The gulf between Alice's need to grieve and her right to grieve, created by her mother's overweening neediness that left no mitigating room to console her daughter, was both filled and hidden by Alice's emerging talent to learn a language "for covering pain, not expressing it" (Kaplan, 1993, p. 58). In retrospect, she knew "that my passion for French helped me to put off what I needed to say, in English, to the people around me" (p. 214) And yet "French had saved me . . . from living alone in the big house with my mother who was sick and unhappy" (pp. 57–59). Indeed, fearing that grief would kill her mother and leave her an orphan, Alice found a margin of safety in living in a self-protective isolation—"in exile from myself" (p. 210)—that renounced her own grief even more. Covering pain and loneliness in the toils of learning a whole new language at least did not demand a "charade of happiness" (p. 58). Her self-soothing identification with Gatsby's self-made isolation (in *The Great Gatsby*, Fitzgerald, 1925) held a secret reminder of her own buried grief for her father, namely, that only two people came to Gatsby's funeral. With the self-revealing and self-healing function of writing a memoir, she dared reclaim the banished sorrow that, years before, she had so quickly given away. "I remembered my father now, not just the monument I built to house him . . . What would it have been like to rebel against a real father, instead of inventing an imaginary one?" (p. 206).

What is the pain once uncovered? At first, Alice knew only that she had come from "a house where the patterns had broken down and the death that had broken them was not understood" (p. 53). Family death indeed may spell the breakdown of a patterned life without any further recognition about why this is so and why it need not have been so. In *French Lessons*, family rupture comes on the heels of the unshared and inequitable mourning of the father's death, as if one's loss will be overlooked unless sorrow is jealously hoarded or rationed. Yet, when grief is kept so furtive and uncommunal, it grows with inordinate strength because it finds no one to help contain it. Alice anguished over her mother's spiralling despair, whereas she herself used a new language to gag the very expression of her own feelings that became ever more frightening with the mother's incapacity and unwillingness to contain them. A child, unlike an adult, cannot long hold on to grief without the assurance that she will be reconnected to the world of the living. But mother could not provide—indeed, even begrudged—the solace that Alice craved because mother, too, suffered from a tragic childhood that had once been ignored as she was now ignoring her daughter's pain. The forfeiture of Alice's right to be consoled for the tragedy of her father's death perversely honored and repeated the mother's own sense of unacknowledged childhood tragedy.

☐ Ranking of Grief as Deference to Greater Loss

So far we have discussed rankings among individuals who grieve the loss of the same friend, partner, or family member. The allowance we give ourselves and others to grieve openly is also the outcome of shared norms and values about the magnitude of different personal tragedies. It is often contended that the loss of a child is perhaps the greatest loss we can experience; then, loss of parents by young people or loss of siblings. The ranking of loss of wanted and unwanted pregnancies has also received recent attention (Wakefield, 1998).

Participants of grief groups know well the hesitancy to express grief when another member is deemed to suffer a more devastating loss. The profound sorrow over the death of one's 80-year-old father who has lived a full life is likely to be restrained or withheld when a mother is sitting in silent despair over her child's death. Such generosity of restraint can easily be mistaken for the waning of mourning for late-aged parents. Indeed, embarrassment or shame for grieving lost love ones beyond expected periods of mourning often drives grief into the underground of unawareness and into the hidden recesses of psychiatric symptoms.

Examples are legion in Holocaust survivor groups. The anguish of having survived in hiding is difficult to acknowledge fully in the presence of death-camp survivors. Or, in child survivor groups, those in hiding whose parents returned after the war are uneasy about recalling their terror in the presence of those whose parents did not return. Or again, the yearning for the return of murdered Holocaust parents is held back in deference to survivors who never knew their parents.

Growing up in families where parents have suffered tragic, especially if traumatic, losses often attenuates or otherwise distorts the grieving process for the real losses of one's own. It is a sign of intergenerational transmission of trauma (Peskin & Auerhahn, 2000) that new losses are pulled into the vortex of prior ones. A report of the psychoanalytic treatment of a child of survivors (Kogan, 1989) reflects the implicit injunction in such traumatized families that every new death joins and feeds an insatiable mourning for the lost family, but lessens the particular identity of the newly lost one. In effect, the ranking of grief for one's own loss has been lowered to accomodate family loyalty to multiple losses.

Kogan's patient, Rachel, came to Israel to reincarnate an extended family lost in the Holocaust, following her living parents' injunction that she stay loyal to their absorption in the world of the dead. For her parents, Rachel was a memorial to the dead children of the family. She had little enough sense of her own personal identity to hold fast to the legitimacy of grieving another loss: the death of her caring partner in the act of making love. An ineffable doom closed rapidly around her; suicide beckoned in the next therapy session. The analyst broke immediately into the dooming vortex with this startling intervention: "his death resembled his birth—he was born from a woman and died, in the midst of love, inside one" (Kogan, 1989, p. 665). To acknowledge such a death as a life-giving experience remarkably lifted the Holocaust shadow of nonrelatedness that for years had consumed the patient. She began thereafter to work on breaking away from her mother and establishing a life of her own. The analyst's intervention was nothing short of a therapeutic rescue (Peskin, Auerhahn, & Laub, 1997) by acknowledging that the patient's loss of her lover evoked and fully earned her own autonomous and regenerative feelings of grief and attachment to a person special to herself. A death, not a murder, a loss of her own, to be protected from the fatalism of unappeasable family mourning. In effect, the ranking of grief had become self-determined rather than enjoined and lowered by parents who insisted on the immutable priority of their grief.

☐ Conclusions

For a last conceptual overview of our thinking, we return to our opening remarks on the place of self-awareness in subordinating one's ranking of grief to others' claims. In our examples and case vignettes, such awareness varied appreciably: from Case 1 where the patient had faint awareness of his need but nothing of his right to mourn his sister's death, to the member of a survivor group who has quite consciously relinquished his right without losing awareness of his need. The calculus of needs and rights in grieving requires clinical acumen no less cogent than more traditional models of intrapsychic barriers to grieving. Perhaps in no other area of therapeutic interest must a therapist monitor the surprising power of so-called empathic feelings to sacrifice personal development. The mustering of one's empathy and altruism, especially when driven by the need to expiate guilt for self-centeredness, may be as much a negative as a positive legacy of grieving. Ironically, the lower ranking of grief as an empathic expression of compassion too often segregates mourners, interfering with the mutuality of self-help by promoting fixed scripts of conduct that obscure the resignation of those who seemingly accept the lower rank without conflict, complaint, or even awareness. A fuller exploration of grieving should thus also include attention to the seemingly negative feelings of narcissistic self-entitlement that loss of loved ones provokes. All too often, the lower ranking of grief that one accepts or even seeks cuts off the chance to recover lost parts (or stimulate new parts) of oneself that, without reflection, are buried with the lost person.

Each of our vignettes has contributed to this overarching conclusion, although none, of course, captures it entirely. We report an unusual group encounter over 30 years ago that embodies our viewpoint with surprising freshness. The small group consisted of young adults at a group-dynamics marathon weekend attached to a conference on post-secondary education. Loss and grief were hardly matters of urgency until a tragedy befell the group on its last day: The group's facilitator, Jane, much liked and respected for her warmth, talent, and maturity, suddenly had to leave the group because of the death of her father. She herself was so compelled to return home that she could not say goodbye. After her departure, a conference organizer informed the group about her father's death. Remarkably, after some moments of awkward silence, the group resumed the very topic under discussion before she left, as if nothing had happened. Fortunately, one member's courage to criticize the group's apparent indifference freed up almost everyone to struggle openly with the far-from-indifferent meaning of the absent facilitator's misfortune. First, someone protested weakly that grief would not have been genuine because the group had no relationship to the dead father, had not lost him, nor had knowledge about what the father's death meant to Jane. The only one, therefore, with a rank to grieve at all was Jane. And, of course, with Jane's sudden departure, there was no chance to find a respectful way to help console her in her grief. The turning point came when another member insisted that the problem was not who Jane lost, but the group's loss of Jane—a premature death, as it were—because a dear and valuable member was gone before the group's own life was finished. Perhaps had she stayed long enough to hear their compassion, the members might have felt the right to feel their loss of her. The group's unexpressed concern for her grief may have silenced its right to know or make known its own loss or indeed, may have shamed and distorted this right into being merely an egoistic demand. In any case, the members could now proceed with some compassion for themselves and express openly and equally the grief over their loss, including frank acknowledgments of their various difficulties in allowing grief to enter their lives or helping others to grieve. Perhaps the most poignant memory of that vivid day is the halting remarks of a shy young nun holding back tears as she acknowledged her anger at losing a warm friendship with Jane who had helped her feel less shy than she could ever remember.

The sum of this group's reflections gives some, but not all, of the many sides of our viewpoint on the ranking of grief.

☐ References

Bowlby, J. (1973). *Separation: Anxiety and anger: Attachment and loss* (Vol. II). New York: Basic Books.

Fitzgerald, F. S. (1925). *The Great Gatsby.* New York: Scribner.

Freud, A. (1952). The mutual influences in the development of ego and id. *Psychoanalytic Study of the Child, 7*, 42–50.

Harris, J. (1995). Where is the child's environment? A group socialization theory of development. *Psychological Review, 102*, 458–489.

Kaplan, A. (1993). *French lessons.* Chicago: University of Chicago Press.

Kogan, I. (1989). The search for the self. *International Journal of Psychoanalysis, 70*, 661–671.

Peskin, H., & Auerhahn, N. (2000). Holocaust transmission: Perverse of life affirming? In J. Harvey and B. Pauwels (Eds.), *Post-traumatic stress theory: Research and application* (pp. 183–210). Philadelphia: Taylor & Francis.

Peskin, H., Auerhahn, N., & Laub, D. (1997). The second holocaust: Therapeutic rescue when life threatens. *Journal of Personal and Interpersonal Loss, 2*, 1–15.

Stern, D. (1985). *The interpersonal world of the infant.* New York: Basic Books.

Wakefield, L. (1998). One in ten thousand. In J. Bialosky & H. Schulman (Eds.), *Wanting a child* (pp. 149–157). New York: Farrar, Straus and Giroux.

Weiss, R. (1988). Loss and recovery. *Journal of Social Issues, 44*, 37–52.

CHAPTER

Aurora Liiceanu

Parallel Selves as the End of Grief Work

People's explanations of past events involving severe stress, especially when presented in a story-like form that includes characterizations of the self and others, have great adaptive function in the account-maker's life and implications for one's personal identity. Weiss (1975) showed that the account in its story-like form contained all the essential features of a short story, having as components a central point, characters, and temporal structure including a beginning, middle, and ending. Introducing the temporal dimension of the personal history shows that the real is transformed by retroanalysis into a succession condensed in present and constitutes an element of the temporal perspective described by Fraisse et al. (1979). This perspective allows people the ability to perceive continuity and the integration of the events in time. Attributional activity is central to plots presented by people confronted with stressful situations, somehow independent of the quality of the listener and the context of communication. It is an activity for one's own use more than for others. Janoff-Bulman and Lang-Gunn (1988) suggest that spontaneous attributional activity should be prominent in connection with accidents, criminal victimization, catastrophic events and the like simply because such events are intensely negative, personally significant, severely stressful, and usually unexpected.

In many occasions Harvey (1996) emphasized that the category of stressor events encompasses a broad spectrum of experiences. The conceptual analysis of two main terms like "trauma" and "bereavement" could evidence it. Indeed, any research in the field of psychology of loss must be based on a recognition of the phenomenological diversity of loss experiences as well as the individual nature of many constructions of loss. However, psychological dynamics show similarities across cultures—in order to develop a new personal identity that incorporates the loss into who the person has become is, after all, a common identity change.

Among the categories of loss, the death of a child is conceded to be one of the harsher, if not the harshest and most restless loss of all. Rando (1993) noted that the unique relationship between the parent and the child made the readjustment to a new world without forgetting the old, particularly difficult. Brabant, Forsith, and

McFarlain (1997) argue that the parents having lost a child are different; they expressed having found new meaning in life.

The material for this chapter is drawn from a larger study of collective and personal memory and the reciprocal nurturing function in a small village community during the last 50 years. Among the life stories collected, one refers to the death of two boys and the process of identity change of their mother. I will use during the text the initial letter of her name when referring to her account-making, namely A. She is about 60 years old and the death happened quite a long time ago—15 years. Bereavement as a central part of her life story seems to be a normal human experience, out of grief complications or pathology.

My purpose was to capture the intersection between the presence of the other as helping agent and the individual subject to the experience of the children's death. The psychology of loss needs to focus not only on people's perceptions and stories of loss, but also on how their perceptions and stories change over time. As Neimeyer (1998) shows, recent research makes emergent the idea that meaning reconstruction in response to a loss is the central process in grieving. The experience of grieving, even treated as a private act, does not happen outside the context of interpersonal interactions. In such contexts, sometimes, the other can strongly contribute to restoration-oriented coping.

☐ The Grieving Process and the Grief Work

A tragedy happened to A and her family. Her two sons, aged 15 and 17 years old, died unexpectedly after being electrocuted in the presence of their playmates during a school holy day. The tragic event can be described as she remembers it:

> The last born boy was terribly naughty. Like a devil. It was he who had the idea. He climbed up an electricity pole a day before, over there, on the pole. And a brother of mine, who was just passing by, chased him away, saying to him to come down because it was very a dangerous place. He told him to come down; maybe he should have died then and the other should be alive now. But, no and no and no. He didn't come back but, just ate walnuts and recited poems. Usually, he did only as he wanted to do. There were many children around. The next day he woke up in the morning, left the bed, ate, and went directly to the same place and climbed up the pole. You see, like a trigger, like being triggered. The children were not surprised because it was just him. But, they were paralyzed when he cried, they were like stones. The older boy wanted to take him away, to save him, and climbed up the pole, too, and they both died, eventually.

The birth of a new identity or redefining her identity after this traumatic event was accompanied obviously by a necessary mourning. The working through refers to both an active mental and emotional process and a reactive one. These processes have dynamics that shouldn't be skipped under similar conditions—even if we admit the existence of interindividual particularities or differences. The operation of giving up an attachment—a partial one as far as A's loss refers to two of her children—in terms of a change in her identity leading to self-awareness is hardly achieved. It implies a redefinition of identity. The Asian metaphor of a vase which has to be filled up—even if it is full—until a replacement of its initial content by a new content occurs is very appropriate for making this change intelligible. This operation is very delicate in psychological terms. The fear of losing a part of one's identity creates an imperious need of inner restructuring which is accompanied by insecurity manifested initially by a refusal—a refusal or a rejection of reality. The grief work, namely the effort to rebuild the identity and the process itself of rebuilding and making room for a major trauma leading to a self-continuity is a difficult process. In A's case it was a matter of years because sudden, traumatic bereavements are frequently considered to be a worse type. In addition to this, a double loss is supposed to be even more stressful. The elaboration of the mourning includes coping with the past and the creation of a project, a scenario which results in a relief and anxiety release.

A reached serenity; and the time between the traumatic event of her sons' deaths and the present reveals an incontestable psychological truth: any suffering well-lived and integrated in life as a whole can stimulate the person to develop a new identity. A senseless event often brings posttraumatic disorders that are sometimes psychologically irreversible. While A suffered badly, she was able to recover.

To A, the crucial instance in the process of redefining herself was meeting The Virgin of Parepa, a highly prestigious person with special premonitious gifts living in a neighboring village. The people attributed the role of a saint to this person and she had the role of a catalyst. The stages of A's identity change as inferred from her story attest to the processuality of the psychological adjustment:

Resistance to Change

Generally, there are two types of resistance to experiencing grief: the shock as a blockage at the level of reality perception, sometimes accompanied by sensorial hallucinations, and the negation, both cognitive—the event did not occur—and emotional. In this last case, the traumatized person is reactionless and soulless. Tata Arcel (1995) reports the case of a mother, who having lost a child and her husband when a neighboring village was attacked in May 1992 in northern Bosnia and Herzegovina, was unable to mourn the losses she experienced and functioned like a "soulless puppet." Bowlby (1982) proposed that loss is followed by three phases of response. First, may be a brief interval of shock or denial, a phase most likely not anticipated. A described vividly the shock she felt:

> From the beginning I was going crazy. I tried to stab my mother. I didn't remember the knife being in my hand at all. For the next two or three months, I was not allowed to go alone anywhere, even to toilette. I was always assisted by somebody so I wouldn't try to kill myself. My husband didn't go to work any more. I would wake up in the middle of the night, and leave the bed to go nowhere or just to go away. My husband suffered silently. It is just like him. He does not speak at all. I was under medical care. Drugs so I wouldn't get mad. I felt like jumping out of the window, to escape, I was restless, agitated. People said that I ran and slept in the cemetery, on the grave. I was not myself.

Expressing the Feelings and the Grief

To the extent that A began to talk and express herself, to describe the dreams and the intense sadness, she gradually achieved a distance from the stressful event and was able to identify her loss and who she was after her experience. The trauma became something exterior to her, it was an exercising reality. It was no longer inside herself but out of her body. Only then was she able to face reality and to change her experience into an object that she looked at and described. Expressing the grief and the struggle to decode her restless dreams was a long process:

> I suffered a lot. Incredibly. My dreams gradually got less and less restless. I use to dream about them [her sons] exactly, vividly, how they were before their death for a long time, for years. Until I became peaceful. When I became like that the dreams disappeared, vanished like an illness. Now, my sons did not haunt me in my dreams. It is finished.

Unfinished Things

Expressing the feelings makes A realize that there are things that endure infinitely because they are unfinished, things that are unaccomplished promises or ideals or unactualized aspirations, conversations, and gestures. One should live more attentively to the very moments of which life is composed so that these things aren't passed over in daily realities. Our duty, A says, is to go on living incorporating the bad things in life which the deceased loved persons do not belong to any more. The readjustment to the new world without forgetting the old one was, in her case, a time consuming process. The loss is not a loss but something which has added to her life experiences: It is necessary to live with the suffering inside you and to work through it. The past has gone. The grief and the life have to be side by side.

Meaning Given to the Loss

Central to the account making are people's memories of the past. Horowitz (1986) describes the role of the completion tendency in people's use of thoughts to adapt to highly troubling events. This tendency refers to people's need to match new information with inner structures based on older information, and the revision of both until they agree. As Harvey, Orbuch, & Weber (1990) mentioned, this tendency is similar to Lewin's (1935) hypothesis about the importance of interrupted events in creating a tension that leads to a completion-oriented drive state (the Zeigarnick effect) and to Mandler's (1984) theory of the negative emotional state following the interruption of action plans.

The memory-cognition component of the process of recovery following a severe stress involves making sense or giving meaning to the loss. The meaning has positive consequences and creates the distance between the person experiencing a trauma and the traumatic event itself. Meaning making actualizes personal experiences, or episodic memories as Tulving (1983) refers to them, and develops new meaningful mental realities. A refers to this solitary and inner process when she said:

> You are quiet, face to face with the terrible reality or you are together with the tragedy and you don't need anybody else.

As predicted by Taylor (1983), making downward comparisons is associated with the ability to find meaning and with better psychological outcomes. Comparing oneself to those who are worse off is a productive way to interpret one's own situation and a cognitive strategy that enabled A to minimize the malevolence of her victimization. Comparing herself with real others who are worse off, she sees her trauma as a cause for reassurance rather than disaster and a very way to access the consolation others offered. The others function as a bridge between inconsolability to a gradual consolability. The collective memories are also encoded in our minds and they are helpful for their high relevance: In our village a more dreadful event happened. Father, son, daughter, son-in-law, and grandchild were in a car—the whole family except the mother, namely the grandchild's grandmother. They went to visit somebody who enrolled in military service. Not very far from Constanta, they had a car accident and four of them died. Only the child remained alive although badly hurt. They were buried in the village cemetery. Near the church are four crosses and graves lying side by side. The child is now a church servant but he grew up and was raised as an orphan with eight other children—his brothers. He spent a long time in a hospital and the relatives bought a coffin for him, too, and dug a grave for him. He recovered eventually and they sold the coffin and filled up the hole.

Relief and Legacy

The last stage in A's recovery could be called "laissez partir." It is a moment of relief and release from the repetitive ruminations, invasion of obsessive thoughts and feelings by memories or awareness, and images that flood the person with distress. The traumatized person separates himself from the beloved dead who do not belong to the life as lived by others in peace and acceptance. Letting go, in A's case, means to be separated from her dead sons but also to reach out and contact them, to be close to them in a separate reality and a different way. This means to accept the physical separation, while continuing to live with them, but in a different way. The bereavement ends with a legacy: revisiting the past and internalizing the past sequences of their togetherness in positive terms, and sharing these experiences with the dead beloved who are absent but not forgotten. Long after the loss, the sons continue to be thought of with affection and a sense of closeness so it may be said that, as Klass, Silverman and Nickman (1996) have shown, the attachment figures continue to be loved. They are forever a part of A's life:

> In the aftermath, now, I am able to go to the cemetery. I don't suffer anymore. They are lying side by side. I go there sometimes twice a day. It's nobody business but mine. There are rumors that I slept over there [at the cemetery]. I couldn't imagine them together. I am talking to them, but to each one, separately. I shared my troubles with them, especially with the older one, I told them news. About my daily work, trifles or real facts. Yes, I am speaking to them and I feel better as if they are listening to me.

☐ The Virgin of Parepa and the Tranquilizing Dream as God's Sign

As I have already mentioned, A contacted a supporting, out-of-family person who lived in a village named Parepa. This woman functioned as a trigger for the change in A's attitude toward the stressful event. A changed from a restless to peaceful mood and experienced acceptance after her dream following the visit to the Virgin of Parepa. This meeting was a founding moment of A's recovery and a marker in the process of the identity dynamics:

> I went to Parepa, to the Virgin of Parepa. She was still alive. And, she told me: "Don't cry for the older boy. He was not inquired after. He had to pass a crossroad and nobody helped him. One has three crossroads during the life, namely places where one is be-

tween good luck and bad luck. Someone may have a chance, but there are crossroads which cannot be passed over. And, the older one was not required. He didn't manage to pass over. And, don't cry for the younger one. He wasn't supposed to pass over because he was required three times and eventually he died of fire. This was his fate and this was his written fate. Having met the Virgin of Parepa, in my dreams the older one appeared. He told me not to cry because he is still my child. He told me: We are your children forever. Don't cry and don't speak of us! So he told me. And, in my dream, I was heading to a large place, a hill, a green empty place, and I saw many doors, they looked like standing coffins. And, suddenly I heard a voice. I remember that dream very well, it is so vivid in my memory that I have goose bumps. And, that voice, telling me: What are you doing here? I say: I am looking for my sons. It was a male voice and when I looked up, so, straight, I saw a very old man, with a long white beard and sitting in a golden chair. He was pale, white-faced. I was trembling in front of him and I am still trembling now when I tell you. I will never forget him until my death! And, he says to me: You are not welcome here. Go away! Let the children alone, they are in peace here. They are all right. Don't worry! And, the older son told me: Don't cry, mother! We are dead but we do well. And this makes me peaceful. And, I turn quietly to my life and to things which I was supposed to do. No more suffering! God sets my mind at rest. I got peace of mind. That voice gave me the joy to go on living. It was a God's sign not a devil's one! That "go away" woke me up. Even separated, we are together.

In this story, the representation of the God is an ordinary one. He is an old man, wearing a white beard and he is a good man and a caregiver. A left her restlessness and returned to life thanks to his tranquilizing message. This moment is critical to normal grieving and according to Stroebe, Schut, and Stroebe (1998); complications or pathology would occur if either oscillation between two coping models—loss- and restoration-oriented coping—does not occur or there is (involuntary) disturbance within this process (which may happen when the bereavement is also a trauma). The oscillation ends when a commuting phase occurs—in A's case her commuting agent is God. Religion can help. Belief in both life after death, which is cosubstantial to the Orthodox religion and its rituals, and in a purpose in life buffers the difficulties of bereavement. A believes wholeheartedly in an afterlife in which she will rejoin the lost sons and so believes that her separation from them is just temporary. According to Smith et al. (1991–1992), belief in life after death is associated with greater recovery, less avoidance, and greater ability to find meaning in the death. A's family and, first of all, The Virgin of Parepa acted as comforters who bolstered the belief in afterlife and helped A in her struggle with personal existential questions and assumptions. Moving the old relationship and mother-children interactions to another reality cannot rely on physical contact. The relationship is no more intense than in the initial period of grieving—regardless of its recurrent presence in A's feelings. Also, the God A met in her dream gave her new dimensions in terms of privacy and secrecy and made A turn back from significant others. The physical separation is gradually minimized in importance and A became ready to accomplish her role as a mother in organizing her children's afterlife. Purpose is associated with a greater social support network that is necessary to accomplish religious rituals. There was no cease of A's motherly role and the self continuity was felt as a living force and new energy bringer:

> For I am peaceful now, I am able to accomplish my tasks. I gave alms like a good and caring mother. I've though of everything for them to be provided with all the comfort in their afterlife. The symbolic behavior is entirely respected and no deviation could occur.

She transfers goods from life to afterlife: I have done and am doing all my best. Each has his own house. I gave two beds, two tables, all the necessary things to live in, furniture, lamps. I doubled everything. They have to make choices but I am careful for not leaving room for any quarrel. I did twice my duties as a good mother for fearing that they are not together and thus not being able to see each other. But, I am content and I set my mind at rest. I did what I am supposed to do and more than that.

The last thing worth mentioning refers to the difference in how she related to each son after their deaths. Obviously, she was upset. The younger one brought his brother to death and A thought regretfully that at least one should remain alive. This is about forgiveness. Working through forgiveness meant to reconvert the negative spontaneous thoughts related to the younger son into positive ones and to feel that the reproaches came to term. She had to accept the last joke of her playful and unpredictable son and his crazy ideas and troubles. In playing with death he didn't want to be alone, he wanted to perform this play to together with his older brother, as A said. But, it was she who added:

I had to forgive him and give up blaming him. He made me mad for a while. It took time to forgive. I haven't forgotten but I forgave. Now I divide my love in two parts because they are two. Equally. This is the last thing that I had to handle and it was not easy at all. Two, and suddenly the death. Who could imagine that this may happen to me! Lastly, I understood that forgiving means love, too.

In the life span, the recurrent memories associated with the loss are present. The events related to the loss are encoded in A's mind and her memory is not separated from the self. In time, she remembers that she was affected by haunting memories which would torment her even when sleeping. These memories, even triggered by cues she encountered in everyday life, came to term in their negative valence. New expectations were learned and her mental arrangements are the subject of the dialectic between the positive and the negative. This calls for reconfiguring the self-schemas.

☐ The Full Life as Therapy, and the Peaceful, Invisible Presence of the Absent, Beloved Ones

The loss remains, but now functions so as to focus A's attention on the amazing fact of existence rather than nonexistence, the wonder of life rather than the absolute terror of death. A's life is appreciated and worthy of substantial investment because it is no longer taken for granted. A knows that everything is transient and ultimately unsafe and yet it is this very awareness that leads her to value life—for life is worth living. A recognizes her effort to create her own meaning close to home, to enjoy all the aspects of her life, to give priority to close relationships and family harmony, and to discriminate among life experiences in terms of importance. It is in this sense that she changes in time—and for her it was a long time—and constructs the meaning of life. She copes and adjusts, but never recovers in the sense of being the woman she used to be. Rather, as Janoff-Bulman and Berg (1998) have convincingly asserted, the traumatic events lead to a new evaluation and appreciation of life. And here is what A learned as a survivor of trauma:

I am busy now, all day long. I do a lot of things. I have to do lots of things around the household, animals waiting to be looked after, grandchildren to be loved and helped to grow up. I go to monasteries, meet people and talk to them, spend time with them, share experiences and feelings. Living is so amazing. My house is my very world. When I think of the fragility of life and its shortness. We do not know what the future has in store for us. Who knows? Life is life. It has to be lived; it is a duty.

In the aftermath, at a moment the world makes sense again and greater importance is given to the present.

☐ Conclusion

In understanding the grief, the loss research is more advanced and models of explaining the dynamics specific to the grieving process are frequently present in the loss literature. Horowitz (1986) stated that the normal phases of stress response syndromes involve a stressor event—a person's outcry such as display of fear, sadness or rage—and the development of denial and intrusion, and working through reactions to the stressor to completion. He shows the role of completion in people adjusting to intense stress. Also, in discussing the transition subsequent to a life crisis, Moos (1986) was interested in establishing a set of phases, finding out that working through and completion are crucial and evidence the intervention of the cognitive instances. Later on, Harvey, Orbuch, and Weber (1990) amplified the theoretical analysis on the psychology of accounts and account-making, elaborating a social psychological model as a revision of Horowitz's (1986) model. They add emphasis on where account-making likely enters the normal reaction pattern and what might be the likely consequence of failure to engage in account-making in terms of possible dysfunctionality. The component of identity or self-concept change and is included in their model as the final stage in the sequence. This puts in evidence the importance of social psychological perspective on loss and the place of beneficial intervention of the cognition.

It seems that death is probably the only type of loss that can never be recovered. Death is forever and is among the most significant first lessons of life. The persons experiencing the death of beloved ones are incontestably different. More precisely, they are no longer the persons they used to be. The case here demonstrates that grief work results in a neutralizing effect. Recall will never trigger intense, insupportable distress as in A's case. Insofar that she develops a twofold identity or two selves, consisting of one for living ones and one for lost ones, she manages successfully her attachment system which in turn gets more complex. This express what Harvey et al. (1990) mean by identity change and shows how their model works. The case which I refer to here is evidence that the work for ameliorating human suffering that attends loss, for curing disrupted attachment bonds, or for emerging the reconstruction of meaning and restoration of a viable sense of identity can be successful. Some people might call it a new vision on death, too. For some people, the lost beloved ones are never lost.

☐ References

Bowlby, J. (1982). Attachment and loss: Retrospect and prospect. *American Journal of Orthopsychiatry, 52,* 664–678.

Brabant, S., Forsith, C. I., & McFarlain, G. (1997). The impact of the death of a child on meaning. *Journal of Personal and Interpersonal Loss 3,* 255–267.

Fraisse, P., Halberg, F., Lejeune, H., Michon, J. A., Montangero, J., Nuttin, J., & Richelle, M. (1979). *Du temps biologique au temps psychologique*. Paris: Presse Universitaires deFrance.

Harvey, J. H. (1996). *Embracing their memories. Loss and the social psychology of story-telling*. Needham Heights, MA: Allyn & Bacon.

Harvey, J. H. (Ed.). (1998). *Perspectives on loss. A sourcebook*. Philadelphia: Taylor & Francis.

Harvey, J. H., Orbuch, T. L., & Weber, A. L. (1990). A social psychological model of account-making in response to severe stress. *Journal of Language and Social Psychology, 9*, 191–207.

Horowitz, M. J. (1986). *Stress response syndromes* (2nd ed.). New York: Jason Aronson.

Janoff-Bulman, R., & Lang-Gunn, L. (1988). Coping with disease, crime and accidents. The role of self-blame attributions. In L. Y. Abramson (Ed.), *Social cognition and clinical psychology: A synthesis*. New York: Guilford.

Janoff-Bulman, R., & Berg, M. (1998). Disillusionment and the creation of values: From traumatic losses to existential gains. In J. H. Harvey (Ed.), *Perspectives on loss. A sourcebook* (pp. 35–47). Philadelphia: Taylor & Francis.

Klass, D., Silverman, P. R., & Nickman, S. L (Eds.). (1996). *Continuing bonds: new understandings of grief*. Washington, DC: Taylor & Francis.

Lewin, K. (1935). *A dynamic theory of personality*. New York: McGraw-Hill.

Mandler, J. M. (1984). *Stories, scripts and scenes: Aspects of schema theory*. Hillsdale, NJ: Erlbaum.

Moos, R. H. (Ed.). *Coping with life crisis*. New York: Plenum.

Neimeyer, R. A. (1998). Can there be a psychology of loss? In J. H. Harvey (Ed.), *Perspectives on loss. A sourcebook* (pp. 331–341). Philadelphia: Taylor & Francis.

Rando, T. A. (1993). *Treatment of complicated mourning*. Champagne, IL: Research Press.

Smith, P. C., Range, L. M., & Ulmer, A. (1991–1992). Belief in afterlife as a buffer in suicidal and other bereavement. *Omega, 24*, 219–227.

Stroebe, M., Schut, H., & Stroebe, W. (1998). Trauma and grief: A comparative analysis. In J. H. Harvey (Ed.), *Perspectives on loss: A sourcebook* (pp. 81–96). Philadelphia: Taylor & Francis.

Tata Arcel, L. (1995). Core experiences of the refugees. In L. Tata Arcel, V. Smalc-Folnegovic, D. Kovacic-Kozaric, & A. Marusic (Eds.), *A psycho-social help to war victims: Women refugees and their families from Bosnia and Herzegovina and Croatia*. Copenhagen: IRCT.

Taylor, S. E. (1983). Adjustment to threatening event: A theory of cognitive adaptation. *American Psychologist, 38*, 1161–1173.

Tulvig, E. (1983). *Elements of episodic memory*. New York: Oxford University Press.

Weiss, R. S. (1975). *Marital separation*. New York: Basic Books.

CHAPTER 8

David J. Mayo

Rational Suicide?

The loss of a loved one is always deeply painful. A loss to suicide can be doubly so. Shock at a preventable, unnecessary death can quickly translate into anger at the person who commited suicide for what he or she has done and perhaps guilt over not having foreseen and forestalled it. Thus the tragedy of death can be compounded when a death is by suicide.

But must death by suicide be a doubly regrettable mistake? Or can suicide perhaps be sometimes rational? The view that it cannot has a long and venerable history, which I'll return to shortly. It has been woven deeply into the ideology of the mental health professions, whose codes of ethics have usually dictated that the only appropriate goal with a suicidal client is prevention—coercive prevention if necessary. Yet many harbor nagging doubts: The suicides of Socrates, of Samson, Judas, or Madame Butterfly strike many of us as tragic, but hardly mad. Instead we see these suicides as sad but perfectly understandable acts, committed in the name of honor, responsibility, or perhaps some other principle. As the national debate over physician assisted suicide swirls in the background, one thinks of those whose lives seem to be drawing to a close in any case. How many would insist that Sigmund Freud was acting irrationally when he ended his life with an overdose of morphine after his terminal cancer had eaten away so much of his jaw that it left him disfigured, in horrible pain, and in the constant presence of a stench so unbearable that even his beloved pet dog would not come near him but instead cowered in the corner of the room? Polls consistently indicate the American public favors legalization of physician-assisted suicide by a margin of two to one. Even Edwin Shneidman, the "father of suicidology," has been heard to remark on a number of occasions that "all suicides are irrational—except my own." This seems to be an opaque way of acknowledging that some suicides can be rational, while at the same time insisting that for the purposes of public policy we must pretend otherwise.

For contemporary mental health professionals the question is, of course, not merely academic; increasing numbers of them are feeling a tension between two competing ideologies, each embodying a way of viewing suicide and hence dictating a proper way of responding to it.

Mental health professionals are not the only people who have a special stake in how society answers the question of rational suicide. Some physicians feel aid-in-dying is only a logical extension of compassionate end-of-life care. Others are horrified by the very suggestion that their traditional roles as healers should now be corrupted by the new job of executioner. Still others are deeply conflicted, convinced on the one hand that some suffering terminal patients might legitimately request their help, but doubting on the other hand that they could ever bring themselves to provide it. And other health care professionals—nurses, pharmacists, social and hospice workers, to name but a few—are stakeholders as well.

First and foremost, however, I believe it is mental health professionals—typically the first to have contact with potentially suicidal persons—for whom the question of rational suicide presents the greatest challenge, both individually and as a profession. Mental health professionals already face the difficult task of having to distinguish genuinely suicidal clients from others who are merely posturing but have no intention of attempting to end their lives. Recognizing the possibility of rational suicide would require them to draw an additional distinction as well—between those potentially suicidal clients for whom suicide would be irrational (and for whom preventative intervention would thus be appropriate) and those for whom it would be rational. This determination would often be literally a matter of life and death.

Mental health professionals reflecting on these considerations have responded in several ways. For some, the prospect of acknowledging that some suicidal clients may be fully rational raises such an overwhelming morass of philosophical, moral, legal, and psychological problems as to prompt a retreat into the comforting and traditional medical wisdom which Shneidman seems to endorse, that we should condemn all suicides as irrational after all. For others this seems dishonest, and hence impossible. Within San Francisco's AIDS community, suicide is regarded as a perfectly honorable and understandable way to end one's life, and the means to do the job are easy to secure. Many counselors of AIDS clients regard as utterly preposterous the suggestion that all their suicidal clients would be well-served by knee-jerk preventative interventions.

More generally, if rational suicide is possible, then competent clients seeking to explore that ultimate option rationally will be ill served by mental health professionals with a visceral bias against it and predisposed to discount the legitimacy of the client's dark view of her world and her options.

Two competing paradigms offer quite different answers to the question of whether suicide can ever be rational. Each paradigm has a long history. In what follows, I will sketch each paradigm briefly, and defend my allegiance to the view that suicide can be rational. I will then argue that our public policies are inconsistent to the extent that they invite terminally ill patients to consider whether and when to refuse life-prolonging therapies on the one hand but tend to discount the rationality of terminal patients who are suicidal on the other,

☐ The First Paradigm

According to the first paradigm, suicide is always a mistake, a product of distorted thinking that violates reason, God's will, morality, and the law. In this view, suicide in general should be discouraged and even condemned, and suicidal individuals stopped whenever possible.

This view has dominated Western thinking for 1400 years. Yet no suicide described in the Bible is spoken of in terms of condemnation, and the historian Gibbon (1947) notes that some early sects of Christians, convinced that martyrs would be gathered under the throne of God, sought martyrdom by taunting Romans until they were executed. This disturbed St. Augustine, who responded in the fifth century with biblical and other religious arguments to the effect that suicide was contrary to God's will. Augustine's condemnation of suicide became Church doctrine at the Councils of Orleans, Braga, and Toldeo in the 6th century, and eventually found its way into law throughout Europe and later, the United States. As recently as a century ago attempting suicide was not only illegal in Great Britain, but a capital offense!

Though these laws have largely been rescinded, this does not reflect a rejection of the paradigm condemning suicide, but only a shift within it. (Laws against assisting suicide remain largely intact.) Thomas Szasz (1970) documents this shift as part of a larger shift which began with the birth of psychology in the nineteenth century, towards substituting medical reasons for religious, moral, or legal condemnations of certain behaviors—usually either sexual behaviors (e.g., masturbation and homosexuality) or what we have now medicalized as "addictive" behaviors (e.g., excessive drinking, gambling, smoking). Szasz refers to this shift as "the medicalization of morals," whereby actions once seen as voluntary and sinful (and often criminal) came to be seen instead as involuntary manifestations of some mental aberration or mental illness. (Thus mental health professionals speak of people "at risk of suicide," which is condemned as mental aberration or "sick," but not of people "at risk of bank robbery," which is still condemned as criminal.)

The paradigm condemning suicide has proved tenacious, particularly among mental health professionals. Until very recently, virtually all mental health professional codes stipulated that the only proper response to suicidal clients was to try to dissuade them, and if that failed, to intervene coercively. One needn't look far in the literature to find "rational suicide" described as a contradiction in terms. As I'll argue shortly, I believe this paradigm is fundamentally flawed and that one's circumstances may become so grim, especially near the end of life, that suicide may indeed be a rational choice.

If this paradigm is flawed, one might well ask what explains its wide acceptance. Three obvious reasons come to mind. The first is the weight of history: Religious taboos die hard. Second, it's undeniable that most actual suicides are tragic mistakes, the result of transient life-crises, for instance, or of treatable depressions. Thus the current medicalized version of the paradigm and the standard preventative crisis intervention measures it advocates are genuinely appropriate in most cases (just as CPR may be an appropriate response to *most* cardiac arrests). It's tempting, then, to infer that all suicides must be irrational. Finally, it makes things much simpler for mental health professionals, in the way I indicated earlier. If rational suicide is acknowledged as a possibility, then we must characterize and then operationalize the distinction between those which are irrational (and should be prevented) and those which are rational (and should be permitted, and perhaps even aided when help is needed). Again, embracing the possibility of rational suicide would require counselors not only to identify genuinely suicidal patients from among those who are merely posturing, but then also to distinguish between those suicidal patients who should be dissuaded or prevented from carrying out their plans, and those whose suicides should be permitted and perhaps even supported.

While this prospect is daunting, the problem involved is not new: The drawing of tough distinctions is at the core of most thoughtful work, including the work of mental health professionals (when a certain treatment plan is appropriate, when confidentiality must be violated, and so on). Indeed it is at the core of tough decision-making generally, and hence at the core of the life of a free and responsible agent. Even the specific task of distinguishing between persons who are competent to make some decision for themselves and those who are not is a completely general one, which health care professionals (and judges) have had to deal with in many other contexts.

☐ The Second Paradigm

The competing paradigm of suicide, which I find more credible, concedes that most suicides are irrational, but insists some may be rational. One underlying presumption of this view is that our lives are not valuable unconditionally, but derive their value from within. That is, they are worth living only because we as individual subjects and agents value certain kinds of experiences or activities. If an individual's capacities for these sources of value dwindle to the point that life is sapped of all meaning, or are outweighed by unavoidable suffering, suicide may become a rational option.

Although this paradigm may seem radical, it too has a long and venerable history. In the first century A.D. the Roman stoic Seneca wrote

> . . . life has carried some men with the greatest rapidity to the harbour, the harbour they were bound to reach even if they tarried on the way, while others it has fretted and harassed. To such a life, as you are aware, one should not always cling. For mere living is not a good, but living well. Accordingly, the wise man will live as long as he ought, not as long as he can. . . . As soon as Fortune seems to be playing him false[,] then he looks about carefully and sees whether he ought, or ought not, to end his life on that account. . . . It is not a question of dying earlier or later, but of dying well or ill.

Even before this, rational suicide had some acceptance in the cradle of Western civilization. Ancient Athens was only one Greek city-state which recognized it. Those who felt their life had run its course could appear before the Senate and make their case. In his discussion of the history of the suicide taboo Alfred Alvarez (1980) quotes Libanius: "If your existence is hateful to you, die; if you are overwhelmed by fate, drink the hemlock. If you are bowed with grief, abandon life. Let the unhappy man recount his misfortune, let the magistrate supply him with the remedy, and his wretchedness will come to an end." Those who failed to persuade the magistrate would be told their case was frivolous and sent home without the hemlock. Even here, then, it was seen that acknowledging rational suicide required a screening procedure for distinguishing it from frivolous suicide.

The meaning of "rational" in this context is straightforward, and applies generally to all decision-making. Decisions generally involve both factual beliefs (about one's options, and about their likely consequences) and values (indicating what is good or bad, permissible or impermissible) and either of these two components can contribute to irrationality. A person who fails or refuses to consider known relevant facts, or to find out important relevant information which is readily available, behaves irrationally. In addition, a person who makes a decision on values which are inauthentic, that are temporary distortions of his or her "true" long-term value—caused for in-

stance by emotional highs or lows—behaves irrationally. In a nutshell, a rational decision is one grounded in known or available facts and one's authentic values.

An advantage of this analysis is that it disentangles the problem of analyzing "rational" from the contentious issue of rational suicide. Seen in this way, suicide can be
rational or irrational in exactly the way any other decision can be.

Surely this squares with common sense: A person facing *any* important decision
does well to delineate all available options, anticipate the likely consequences of each
as carefully and accurately as possible, and then take care to assess each option on the
basis of one's authentic values rather than on the basis of transient feelings and emotions which may temporarily obscure them.

This same point could be made in terms of competence: Fully competent decision-
making requires a command of relevant information, which in turn requires both
access to information about one's circumstances and one's options, and the capacity
to comprehend it in the fullest sense. For (at least) this reason I am not competent to
pilot a 747 (or even an IBM PC). In addition it requires a clear sense of one's goals and
values, a steady grasp of "what one is about." Wise people often defer important decisions if they realize they lack adequate information, or if they're in the grips of unsettling emotions that compromise their ability to reflect coolly. In short, they realize
that, at least for the moment, they are simply not competent to make a rational decision on some issue. Only fools make important decisions while they are uninformed,
or feel confused, intoxicated, exhilarated, or upset.

Against this conception of rationality we see more clearly why some suicides strike
many of us as rational, while most suicides do not. Many of us find the suicides of
Socrates and Madame Butterfly to be as rational precisely because they are grounded
in acceptance of hard reality and based on deep value commitments. At the same
time, we all acknowledge that most actual suicides occur while the suicide victim's
capacity for rational decision-making is compromised. Anxiety, depression, and despair all distort understanding and obscure authentic values. Grief often involves denial, anger, and depression; and all of these can compromise a person's decision-
making competence. At the same time, we mustn't be too quick to dismiss anyone
suffering major losses as incompetent to make important decisions on his or her own
behalf.

☐ Refusing Life-Prolonging Therapy and Rational Suicide in the Face of Terminal Illness

There is, I believe, an inconsistency, or at least an incongruity, between two widely
embraced ways of thinking about end-of-life decisions. On the one hand, mental health
professionals tend to condemn (or dismiss) all suicides as irrational. At the same time,
most of us believe that near the end, as our bodies give out in spite of everything
medicine has to offer and we realize we are approaching death, each of us, if we
remain competent enough to understand the situation, is entitled to say at some point
"enough is enough—I am ready to die." Many of us can easily imagine losses and
afflictions occurring near the end of a slowly progressing terminal illness that would
irreversibly deprive our lives of meaning. Admittedly, someone who feels fit and healthy
who receives a diagnosis of HIV+ may naturally react in shock and panic at the news,
and suicidal impulses at that point may well be irrational. By contrast, consider a

patient near death from full-blown AIDS—frail and bedridden, unable to eat or drink, blind, able to communicate only with difficulty but still clearly lucid, with barely the energy to move, who knows only too well what the future holds, and has had plenty of time to think about it—who only wishes for it all to end.

Such patients will probably have been encouraged to prepare advance directives indicating their treatment preferences should they become incompetent. Radical organizations such as The Hemlock Society are not the only ones that encourage people to consider an advance directive. The federal government has tried to do so as well. The Federal Patient Self-Determination Act of 1992 requires all hospitals receiving federal funding to ask all admitted patients whether they have completed a living will or some other advance directive.

But at the moment an advance directive is irrelevant to our hypothetical dying-but-competent AIDS patient, simply because he is still competent and able to communicate. Were that patient to announce he had decided to forgo further life-prolonging therapies, and was he fortunate enough to have a hospice program available to provide optimal palliative care, it is hard to imagine caring professionals bullying him about giving up on life, or demanding a competency assessment. Instead (one certainly hopes) he would find supportive understanding of his acceptance of the fact that his life has run its course and of his decision that further life-prolonging therapies were inappropriate.

But how different the establishment response might be if this patient, instead of merely standing on his right to refuse further life-sustaining treatment, indicates that he has no wish to endure a final week or month, but wants to be able to end it now and pleads for the means. At this point, a different mental-health mind-set may kick in, the result of the paradigm which rejects rational suicide. Because this patient is suicidal his decision may be instantly suspect. The patient who would decline not only further life-prolonging measures but even our palliative ministrations may be seen as an affront to our professional capacities to care for the dying. Instead of being regarded as the rational choice of someone who has reasonably determined his life has run its course, questions of competence and treatable depression may be raised: The patient may now be seen as "at risk of suicide;" his decision to die is now medicalized and hence discredited.

☐ Erring on the Side of Life

I have painted in bold strokes this hypothetical suicidal client who is rational, of course, and even if I am right about this case there are many others which even I will concede are less obvious, borderline cases. Confronted with these cases, even the professional sympathetic in the abstract to rational suicide may naturally be tempted to err on the side of life. Without denying that there will be tough and heart-wrenching cases, I think there is a danger lurking as one takes refuge in this notion. If it is a good strategy, the same logic should apply equally to both the terminal patient who merely refuses further life-prolonging therapy, and the terminal patient who is similarly situated *except* that he has no wish to linger but would prefer to get it over with. American law and medical ethics are both absolutely clear that the former patient has the right to refuse life-sustaining treatment. Why, then, should the presumption be otherwise for the second patient?

More fundamentally, when one errs on the side of life, we should not lose sight of the fact that *one does err.* The costs of that error—additional human suffering—are routinely ignored, first because they are borne by the already-suffering patient and not by the care providers committing the error, and second because the caregivers may take comfort in the conviction that "we were only doing what we thought was right." But the road to hell is paved with good intentions, which in this case do nothing to offset huge costs for the rational patient or client, whose waning life has come to offer very little, and whose suffering may be immense. As life slips away, one loses control over more and more dimensions of one's existence. These losses, rather than physical pain, are often the greatest source of suffering. For the terminal patient who remains competent and is rationally contemplating suicide, the time and manner of his death is almost certain to be the single most important matter over which he may hope to retain some control. Erring on the side of life paternalistically medicalizes and in effect dismisses this person's final important life project.

☐ Conclusion

I acknowledge that most actual suicides are irrational. I even acknowledge that there are many things both family and health and mental health professionals may be able to do to restore meaning and value to the lives of terminally ill patients who are suicidal. Of course these avenues should be explored. Better pain management immediately comes to mind: In the last several years improved palliative care of the dying has become a top priority of American medicine.

But most terminal patients intent on ending their lives do not do so because of pain. They do so instead because of "suffering," which usually involves a sense of utter loss of control of their destinies.

For many of these patients it is possible to restore enough control to return meaning and value to their lives. Again, we should listen to such patients, and explore all avenues available. However, what may emerge, if we truly set our biases aside and listen closely and openly, is that for some patients the single most important issue of control is control over the time and manner of their deaths. Ironically, assuring that control by providing such patients with the means to end their lives may do more than anything else within our power to dispel their sense of hopelessness and despair, and to restore their interest in embracing life for as long as medicine can sustain it.

☐ References

Alvarez, A. (1980). The background. In M. P. Battin & D. Mayo (Eds.), *Suicide: The philosophical issues* (pp. 3–27). New York: St. Martin's Press.

Gibbon, E. (1947). *The decline and fall of the Roman empire* (Vol. I, Chap. XXI). New York: Heritage Press.

Seneca. (1983). On suicide. In S. Gotovitz (Ed.), *Moral problems in medicine* (2nd ed.).

Szasz, T. (1970). *The manufacture of madness.* New York: Harper and Row.

LOSS AND TRAUMA ASSOCIATED WITH SPECIFIC POPULATIONS

Suzanne C. Thompson
Diana J. Kyle

The Role of Perceived Control in Coping with the Losses Associated with Chronic Illness

Losses and traumas come in many forms throughout life. In this chapter, we focus on the plight of individuals who are living with a chronic illness such as cancer, arthritis, or heart disease. The losses that these types of illnesses bring are, in so many cases, obvious and sudden. But much of the time, the losses due to chronic illness are gradual, progressive, and more subtle, for example, an increasing loss of independence due to disability, a diminishing sense of vitality and energy, and a growing loss of the ability to engage in many occupational and recreational activities. Perhaps most important is the danger of losing the sense that one's life is under one's control at all. For several reasons, our focus here is on the role that perceptions of control play in chronic illness. The idea that people need to have a sense of control in their lives is a major concept in a number of theories of life satisfaction and emotional well-being (Seligman, 1975; Taylor, 1983; White, 1959). Furthermore, having a sense of control and assessing one's control are also an integral part of coping with stressful, traumatic experiences (Janoff-Bulman & Freize, 1983; Lazarus & Folkman, 1991; Taylor, 1983).

Because the loss of control and the role of preserving a sense of control are likely to be particularly salient for those dealing with a progressive disease, it is important to understand how losses due to chronic illness can undermine perceptions of control and how a sense of control can be restored or maintained in these types of circumstances.

First, we present the prevalence and characteristics of chronic illnesses to highlight their psychological and economic importance. Then we review the research that has focused on perceptions of control in chronic illness, with an emphasis on complexities in the relationship between perceived control and psychological and physical outcomes. We then consider how individuals with an ongoing disease maintain a sense of control, and the effectiveness of interventions designed to enhance control.

☐ Chronic Illness: Prevalence and Consequences

According to Maes, Leventhal, and DeRidder (1996) there is not a universally accepted medical definition of chronic illness due to the tremendous variations in causes, progression, and outcomes of these illnesses. Generally, however, the term chronic illness or disease refers to a persistent, unstable, progressive, irreversible, degenerative, and long-lasting disease.

Most of us will develop a chronic illness during our lifetime. It is estimated that over 100 million people in the United States suffer from at least one chronic illness (National Institute of Nursing Research, NINR, 1997). For example, 43 million Americans have some form of arthritis (Arthritis Foundation, 1998) with an additional 2 million more afflicted with rheumatoid arthritis (Mercola, 1996); 12 million Americans have a history of heart disease, angina pectoris, or both (American Heart Association, 1996); and 8.2 million have a history of cancer, and over one million new cases diagnosed each year (American Cancer Society, 1999). Considering the growing elderly population and the concomitant rise in chronic health conditions, the prevalence of chronic illnesses is expected to increase dramatically in the coming decades.

The economic impact of chronic health conditions is enormous. They annually cost the economy over $470 billion in direct medical costs and over $230 billion in lost productivity (NINR, 1997). Moreover, in addition to these costs, over 25 million caregivers provide uncompensated care at an estimated annual market value of $300 billion (NINR, 1997).

The psychological implications for those who are chronically ill are also profound. Because chronic illnesses typically impose day-to-day hassles, unpleasant medical treatments, pain, disability, and a threat to life itself, they entail significant personal losses. For example, because chronic illness intrudes into the patient's daily life, as well as the lives of family members, family routines, and activities are threatened (Devins & Binik, 1996). In addition, those with a chronic illness may be faced with the loss of stamina and physical strength, and undesired changes in physical appearance. In addition to physical disability, the negative biases and stigma of others may lead to losses in the area of occupational and employment roles (Susman, 1994; Wright, 1988).

One of the most central psychological losses associated with ongoing illness is the diminishment of a sense of personal control. While any major life stressor can undermine personal control (Janoff-Bulman & Frieze, 1983), several features of chronic illness magnify this threat: personal responsibility for the stressor, unpredictability, and ongoing dependency. Because lifestyle factors such as diet, exercise, tobacco and alcohol use often play an important role in the onset and course of health conditions, chronically ill individuals may feel personally responsible for their condition and also may be held responsible by family members and medical personnel. A critical factor may be whether the ill individual sees the initial cause and progression of the disease as controllable or uncontrollable. Those who view the illness as avoidable through behavior that they can modify can still maintain a sense of prospective control over disease progression, its recurrence, and the onset of future illnesses. However, others who attribute these lifestyle behaviors to a more change-resistant aspect of their character will feel little personal control over both the current illness and their vulnerability to future illnesses. Research done by Timko and Janoff-Bulman (1985) with breast cancer patients revealed that characterological self-blame was negatively correlated with perceptions of control over chronic illnesses.

The second characteristic of chronic illness, unpredictability, intertwines uncertainty into almost every aspect of one's personal life. Uncertainty can seriously undermine personal control and can be particularly distressing because it blocks active strategies to reestablish control over the illness and to plan and be prepared for the future. Patients often experience unpredictable episodes of exacerbation and remission in many diseases (e.g., cancer, hypertension, multiple sclerosis, rheumatoid arthritis) which can be especially stressful and punctuate their lack of control over the symptoms and outcomes of the disease, especially if the exacerbation occurred even though the patient was complying with medical advice and treatment.

Finally, dependence on others can also decrease personal control by undermining a sense of adult autonomy due to the need for constant medical or personal care. Some caregiving styles on the part of the caregiver can exacerbate the patient's feelings of helplessness. A number of studies have found that overprotective care is associated with a lower sense of control and increased depression on the part of the patient (Thompson & Sobolew-Shubin, 1993). Collectively, these three aspects impose serious threats to the loss of personal control.

☐ The Role of Perceptions of Control in Chronic Illness

The benefits of having a sense of control in a wide variety of circumstances have been thoroughly documented. When facing situations as diverse as problems in the workplace or school, recovery from surgery, handling pain, being the caregiver of an ill spouse, commuting, aging, or post traumatic stress, people are better off if they believe that they have the ability to exert control or improve their situation. The advantages of a sense of control include emotional well-being, increased likelihood of engaging in health promoting behaviors, improved performance, and better health (Thompson & Spacapan, 1991). One theory of how individuals cope with a chronic illness, the control and predictability model, proposes that a sense of helplessness is a major feature of chronic illness and that coping is a process of regaining a sense of control (Krantz, 1980).

A large number of studies have examined the role of perceived control for those who are chronically ill. Many illnesses have been studied including cancer, rheumatoid arthritis, heart disease, stroke, chronic fatigue, AIDS, HIV, spinal cord injury, Parkinson's disease, diabetes, and chronic pain. Both general and specific perceptions of control, as well as control in a variety of domains (e.g., symptoms, general life events, health, medical care) have been assessed. Most of the research covered here consists of well-designed, longitudinal studies that controlled for variables such as disease severity that could cause a spurious relationship between perceived control and outcomes. Despite the tremendous variety in methodology and subject population, almost all of the studies found that control was associated with better psychosocial outcomes. Research has found that cancer patients with a stronger sense of control are better adjusted (Blood, Dineen, Kauffman, Raimondi, & Simpson, 1993; Cunningham, Lockwood, & Cunningham, 1991; Newsom, Knapp, & Schulz, 1996; Thompson, Sobolew-Shubin, Galbraith, Schwankovsky, & Cruzen, 1993). More positive psychological adjustment has also been associated with higher perceptions of control for individuals with rheumatoid arthritis (Chaney et al., 1996), chronic fatigue (Ray, Jefferies, & Wier, 1997), cardiac disease (Helgeson, 1992; Kugler et al., 1994;

Mahler & Kulik, 1990; Moser & Dracup, 1995), HIV or AIDS (Reed, Taylor, & Kemeny, 1993; Thompson, Collins, Newcomb, & Hunt, 1996; Thompson, Nanni, & Levine, 1994), spinal cord injury (Schulz & Decker, 1985; Shnek et al., 1997), multiple sclerosis (Shnek et al., 1997) chronic pain (Turk, Okifuhi, & Scharff, 1995; Wells, 1994), Parkinson's disease (Wallhagen & Brod, 1997), and diabetes (White, Tata, & Burns, 1996).

Far fewer studies have examined physical outcomes associated with perceived control, but several positive effects have been found. A sense of control was associated with less angina pain (Fitzgerald, Tennen, Affleck, & Pransky, 1993) and earlier release from the hospital (Mahler & Kulik, 1990) for coronary artery bypass surgery patients, faster recovery from stroke or wrist injury (Partridge & Johnston, 1989), and better functional activity for osteoarthritis surgery patients (Orbell, Jonston, Rowley, Espley, & Davey, 1998).

Although the overall effects of perceived control appear to be positive, several restrictions on this conclusion need to be noted. A few of the studies of chronically ill individuals have not found a relationship between perceived control and psychosocial adjustment. For example, the control perceptions of cancer patients (Berckman & Austin, 1993; Malcarne, Compas, Epping-Jordan, & Howell, 1995) and those with Parkinson's disease (MacCarthy & Brown, 1989) were not associated with psychological distress. Other studies have found positive effects of perceived control for cancer and Parkinson's patients, so the lack of an effect is not due to the disease, but could be a measurement issue. In the Malcarne et al. (1995) study, a one-item measure of perceived control was used and the dependent variable was a combination of physical and psychological symptoms. In the Berckman and Austin (1993) study, the control measure consisted of one item measuring perceived control and 16 items asking about ways to get control. This measure is likely to have poor construct validity as a respondent could have a strong sense of control but use only one approach to getting control and thus score very low on the scale. In the MacCarthy and Brown (1989) study, the reason for the nonsignificant results could be low power. The correlations that were found between control and adjustment were significant at the .05 level, but the authors used a .001 cut-off level due to the large number of comparisons being made. Thus the negative correlations between perceived control and psychological distress were not reported as significant.

Although these few studies might be dismissed as having measurement or power concerns, it must be noted that a number of the studies that were cited above as finding positive effects for perceived control also measured another type of perceived control (e.g., control in a different domain of functioning) and did not find effects for all of the kinds of control measured or did not find effects for all the outcome measures that were assessed. For example, Wallhagen and Brod (1997) found a positive relationship between control over symptoms and well-being for Parkinson's patients, but no relationship between control over the disease and well-being. Furthermore, two of the studies that found positive effects for some types of perceived control also found negative effects for another type. For cancer patients, perceived control over a recurrence of cancer was positive, but control over the onset of cancer was associated with more depression (Newsom et al., 1996). In another study, pre-operative perceived control for those undergoing osteoarthritis surgery was related to more depression at three months (Orbell et al., 1998). As noted earlier, benefits of perceived control for functional activity were found at nine months, so that by nine months, positive effects of control were found. Hence the overall conclusion is that perceived control is related to good outcomes for chronically ill individuals, but it is not the case that control always shows benefits in all domains of control and there are a few instances in which having a sense of control was related to negative outcomes.

A further restriction on the conclusion that perceived control is adaptive is that almost all of the studies are correlational. It has clearly been established that perceptions of control are associated with positive psychosocial and physical outcomes, but correlational studies can not establish the direction of that relationship. However, because laboratory studies that manipulate perceived control find psychological and physiological benefits from having a sense of control (cf. Thompson, 1981), it seems likely that at least some of the association between control and good outcomes can be attributed to the benefits of having a sense of control.

Complexities in the Control/Outcome Relationship

Although perceptions of control are generally associated with positive outcomes, there has been a concern that the benefits of control may not accrue to everyone or in all circumstances. Here we examine several complexities in the effects of perceived control: the accuracy of control perceptions, groups differences in the effects of control, interactions between desired and actual control, and the distinction between primary and secondary control.

☐ Does Control Have to Be Realistic?

An enduring and important question regarding the effects of having a sense of control is whether or not perceived control is beneficial only if perceptions are accurate. Many writers have suspected that believing that you have control when, in fact, you do not could be harmful, leading to inappropriate and fruitless attempts to change one's situation and difficulties in coping when perceptions are disconfirmed. In the area of chronic illness, this question of whether control has to be realistic to be helpful has been addressed in several ways. One approach to the question is to examine the differential effects of perceived control depending on the severity of the disease or degree of impairment. The reasoning is that the greater restrictions on individuals' actions and poorer prognosis of those with a more severe disease means that their perceptions of control are less realistic.

Despite the reasonable assumption that control needs to be realistic, the empirical results suggest otherwise. Research examining the interaction between severity and perceived control on outcomes finds that that perceived control is just as beneficial for those who are facing more severely restrictive or pessimistic circumstances as it is for those in better circumstances (Helgeson, 1992; Reed, Taylor, & Kemeny, 1993; Thompson et al., 1993). Furthermore, the use of what is considered a high control coping strategy (seeking information) was just as beneficial for those with largely uncontrollable diseases (arthritis and cancer) as it was for those categorized as controllable (hypertension and diabetes; Felton & Revenson, 1984). A low-control coping strategy (wish-fulfillment fantasy) was equally ineffective with both types of diseases. There is one mixed result: Affleck, Tennen, Pfeiffer, Fifield, and Rowe (1987) found that for arthritis patients with more severe symptoms, perceived control over symptoms was associated with less mood disturbance. However, patients with a more severe disease and more perceived control over the disease were more disturbed.

Another indicator that control perceptions do not have to be realistic to be adaptive comes from a study of breast cancer patients whose participants had high perceptions of control over their cancer despite the fact that these perceptions were most likely not accurate (Taylor, Lichtman, & Wood, 1984). The control perceptions appeared to have benefits even when this belief was disconfirmed: Those who had a recurrence found another avenue for believing they had control (Taylor, 1983).

These results indicate that the accuracy of control perceptions is not an important factor, but more research is needed on this important point. Longitudinal studies that assess control beliefs and their effects when the control strategy fails to provide protection are necessary to resolve the issue.

☐ Demographic Factors: Age and Ethnicity

Another concern is that the effects of control may not be the same for all demographic groups. There is not much research on this topic, just some suggestions from various studies that examined interactions of control with demographic factors. For example, Thompson et al. (1996) found no differences in perceived control between African-American and White prison inmates with HIV, but the relationship between control and adjustment was quite different for the two groups. More perceived control was strongly associated with better adjustment for White inmates, but there was no relationship between control and adjustment for African-American inmates.

As a variant on the theme that control has to be realistic to be beneficial, it has been suggested that because older adults are likely to be experiencing increasing restrictions due to age-related impairments, they are likely to have lower levels of control and also find fewer benefits from a sense of control than would younger individuals. However, it has generally been found that judgments of control stay stable throughout the adult years, with declines coming only in the later years (Mirowsky, 1995; Nelson, 1993) or not at all (Lachman, 1991; Peng & Lachman, 1993). The adaptiveness of primary control also holds for older groups (Andersson, 1992; Brandstadter & Rothermund, 1994; Wallhagen, 1992/1993). In fact, Rodin (1986) has suggested that perceived control may have greater benefits for older than younger individuals.

☐ Perceived Control and Desire For Control

It is important to distinguish between perceived control and actual control. Believing that you have control appears to have positive effects, but it does not follow that being in a situation that offers more opportunity for control (from the perspective of another individual) has positive effects. Eitel, Hatchett, Friend, Griffin, and Wadhwa (1995) studied patients with end-stage renal disease who were in one of two conditions: self-administered dialysis which was considered by the researchers to be a high control condition or medical staff administered dialysis which was assumed to be a low control condition. An interaction between condition and severity of illness was found such that for those in the self-administration condition, more serious illness was associated with worse adjustment. The opposite was true for those in the medical staff administered condition. The study did not measure perceived control, so it is possible that self-administration undermined rather than enhanced perceptions of control for the more seriously ill. Another study examined the interaction between cancer patients' desire for control and whether or not they were given a choice of antiemetic treatment for chemotherapy. The choice had no effect for patients who were in the lower third or upper third in desire for control, but for those who had a moderate level of desire for control, being given a choice seemed to reduce anxiety and lessen negative mood (Wallston et al., 1991). In a third study, older adults who were either physically disabled or bereaved were assigned to one of three levels of an intervention: control-enhanced, placebo-contact, or a no-contact group. The control enhancement increased mental health for individuals with a high internal locus of control, but the placebo-contact group worked best for those with a low internal locus. Those who were low in internality were actually better off if they were encouraged to be dependent (Reich & Zautra, 1991).

These three studies vary in many respects, but a common theme is that actual control may be helpful only if it matches recipients' desires and capabilities for exercising control. More seriously ill individuals who do not feel capable of extensive self-care, those whose desires for control greatly exceed or are not up to the actual level of control that is being offered, and those whose preferred strategies are to rely on others rather than take responsibility themselves are less likely to find a situation that requires them to exert control beneficial.

Types of Control: Primary and Secondary

Coverage of all the types of control that have been proposed by various theorists and researchers is beyond the scope of this paper, but we will cover one distinction because it is particularly likely to be important for chronically ill individuals. In an important theoretical paper, Rothbaum, Weisz, and Snyder (1982) suggested that there are two main ways in which individuals get a sense of control. One is by actively working to get what they want (primary control) and the other is by accepting or adjusting to their situation as it is (secondary control). Rothbaum et al.'s insight that accommodation or adjustment can be an important component to an overall sense of control was in contrast to the prevailing notion that acceptance of passive strategies were a sign of helplessness and thus an indicator of low perceived control.

Chronically ill individuals can accept the prognosis and limitations of their situation in a number of ways. Some may be relieved just to have a final diagnosis. In the words of one chronically ill individual:

> "For years I knew something was wrong . . . it came as a relief to give it a name. It wasn't in my head! . . . Any diagnosis is a relief because you know what you've got to fight. If people have proper diagnoses, they know which tiger to fight (as opposed to the whole jungle). Knowledge is power" (National Institute of Health, NIH, 1998).

Another individual stated that "You never get over grief or pain. You recognize it, but you move past it. If you dwell on it, you sink lower and lower, and all there is, is the pain" (NIH, 1998).

Some recent research has examined Rothbaum et al.'s (1982) idea that acceptance of or adjustment to one's situation contributes to a strong sense of control. In an interview study that examined how those with chronic physical disabilities use secondary control, Krantz (1995) found that over 80% spontaneously described a secondary control strategy such as finding a positive meaning in one's current circumstances and that almost all of these comments had a positive or neutral valence, indicating that from the user's perspective the secondary control was seen as helpful. According to Krantz, secondary control functioned to maintain self-esteem, identify new areas for growth or gratification, and give a sense that one was obtaining new knowledge.

Rothbaum et al. (1982) proposed that secondary control is used when primary control efforts have failed. Several studies have explored how primary and secondary control interact. Consistent with the idea that secondary control serves as a back-up strategy when primary control is low, two studies found that secondary control is an adaptive strategy only when perceptions of primary control are low; if primary control is high, a sense of secondary control is not important (Thompson et al., 1994; Thompson et al., 1998). However, some studies have also found a different form of interaction between primary and secondary control: that acceptance is not adaptive unless individuals also have a sense of primary control (Ray et al., 1997; Thompson et al., 1996). The participants in both of the latter studies may have been in circumstances (chronic fatigue syndrome and inmates with HIV in a state prison, respectively) in which accommodating to and accepting one's situation without an accompanying sense of primary control fed into helplessness. So there may be some limits on the adaptiveness of accepting one's situation when the situation is one of very low control unless one also has a strong sense that ways to change the situation for the better are also available.

The combination of maintaining a sense of control over some areas of life and accepting one's lack of control in others seems like a potentially workable strategy for chronically ill individuals. More research is needed to identify when secondary control is and is not adaptive.

☐ Why Control Matters in Chronic Illness

What can account for the positive effects that are generally associated with a sense of control for those who are chronically ill? There are two main routes to better outcomes. First, those with a sense of control are more likely to attempt to make changes to get better outcomes. Those who follow their medical regimen carefully, actively look for ways to reduce stress, and seek out and follow expert advice have a better chance of improving their physical health and eliminating or reducing stressors that impact on emotional well-being. There is some evidence that individuals who have a sense of control are more likely to attempt to solve their problems (Ross & Mirowsky, 1989). It is possible that attempts to directly address problems are frequently effective, although there is no research indicating that this is the case.

Second, a sense of control could have psychological and physical benefits because the perception that one's situation is controllable changes the meaning and emotional flavor of the experience. The sense of helplessness, that one is a pawn of circumstances or other people, is stressful in itself, so those with a sense of control avoid this disturbing view of their situation. In addition, those who feel they themselves have control may be able to relax and find it unnecessary to monitor for potential threats because they have the sense that they can successfully deal with problems that may occur. Thus, they do not experience the psychological consequences of helplessness.

Finally, it is important to note that a sense of uncontrollability has been associated with increased physiological reactivity to stress and with depressed immune functioning (Brosschot et al., 1998; Dantzer, 1989). Those with a sense of control may avoid the potentially health-compromising physiological effects of stress. These benefits may be especially important for chronically ill individuals who are already facing threats to their health.

☐ What Do People Do to Get a Sense of Control?

Given that it may be difficult to maintain a sense of personal control when one has a chronic illness, it is useful to examine how those who keep a sense of control manage to do so. Some research has explored the specific activities that people spontaneously report give them a sense of control. Berckman and Austin (1993) asked lung cancer patients to list "all the ways in which they had control over the course of their cancer." A variety of responses were given including following their physician's medical advice and using diet, nutrition, smoking cessation, exercise, faith, and positive thinking. In another study of cancer patients, respondents also gave varied responses (Thompson et al., 1993). The most frequent responses were to ask questions of their doctor; keep communication open with family and friends, use exercise, rely on faith, and keep active. From these two studies, it does not appear that any one particular strategy is used to help maintain control.

Researchers and theorists in this area have proposed a number of general strategies for maintaining a sense of control in the face of a serious loss (see Thompson & Wierson, in press). These include using acceptance, changing to reachable goals, finding and creating control, and using humor. As discussed earlier in this chapter, acceptance or secondary control involves being satisfied with one's situation as it is and accommodating oneself to the loss. Finding benefits and meaning in the loss and in one's current life situation make it easier to accept one's current circumstances. Although having a chronic illness is overall a negative experience, many individuals are able to find some benefits in their situation. For example, stroke patients state that their stroke helped them appreciate life and their spouse and that they have grown from the experience (Thompson, 1991). Acceptance increases a sense of control because it helps people feel less like helpless victims.

A second way to maintain control, changing to reachable goals, involves disengaging from goals that can no longer be reached in current life circumstances and finding satisfying goals that are attainable. Making progress toward goals can make an important contribution to a feeling of control and mastery in life. Those who downplay the importance of goals that are no longer reachable and cultivate their investment in reachable goals are more likely to keep an overall sense of control. Brandstadter and Rothermund (1994) found that older adults maintain an overall sense of general control by deemphasizing the importance of goals that have become difficult to achieve and focusing instead on more reachable goals. For example, disabled individuals may use their situation as an impetus to switch to a more satisfying career and one that is more attainable in their current circumstances (Krantz, 1995).

A third strategy for maintaining control is to identify and cultivate the areas of personal control that are still available. One avenue is to influence the course of one's illness by obtaining extensive medical information, getting good medical care, following the course of treatment, reducing stress in one's life, improving overall fitness through diet and exercise, and investigating alternate types of treatment. For example, one individual takes an active role in his or her medical care: "I sought out information so that I could be proactive about my illness. I like to know what's being done to me and I like to know the results of the procedures" (NIH, 1998). For some individuals the active role may involve using alternative health care as a way of enhancing a sense of control. Because predictability enhances a sense of control (Thompson, 1981), just getting information on the causes and course of one's disease and treatment options can increase a sense of control.

Some individuals may feel that the course of their illness is not amenable to control, but that they can exert some control over other areas in their lives by keeping a positive attitude or trying to reduce the stress for family members. Areas for control that are unconnected to the illness can also help foster a general sense of control. Any activities that make salient the connection between one's own action and a desired outcome increase perceived control. As an example, one breast cancer survivor joined other women with breast cancer on a rowing team and reported that her involvement helped remind her of the effectiveness of her actions (Mitchell, 1997).

Finally, there is some evidence that a sense of humor may help people retain perceptions of autonomy and self-efficiacy. Solomon (1996) found that older adults who used humor had more perceived control and also were more likely to be aging well. She proposed that humor helps people gain control by redefining the situation as less threatening.

☐ Interventions to Increase Control

An important research focus has been on increasing perceived control among those who are in low control circumstances so that more individuals can experience the positive psychological and physical health benefits associated with having a sense of personal control. Intervention studies to enhance the perceived control of chronically ill individuals have explored a variety of techniques. One approach has been to use a comprehensive intervention with a number of ways to teach stress-reduction and coping skills. The idea is that some success in reducing stress and handling problems could increase a sense of control. Along these lines, Cunningham et al. (1991) exposed cancer patients to a psychoeducational program with seven weekly 2-hour sessions that included coping skills, relaxation, positive mental imagery, stress control, cognitive restructuring, goal setting, and lifestyle change. After the program, participants had higher perceptions of self-efficacy which, the authors suggest, led to their ability to exert control, improved mood, and improved relationships with others. Similarly, Telch and Telch (1986) found that group coping skills instruction improved self-efficacy for cancer patients. Parker et al. (1988) provided rheumatoid arthritis patients with cognitive behavioral therapy and training in coping, problem solving, distraction, and self-management. The group receiving this intervention reported less catastrophizing and stronger perceptions of control over pain. A cognitive behavioral treatment program for pain patients had the positive effect of reducing feelings of helplessness (Katz, Ritvo, Irvine, & Jackson, 1996). Although these studies have found positive effects from these comprehensive interventions, given the variety of techniques used in each study, it is hard to know if it was the enhancement of control per se that produced the positive effects.

Another approach has been to use an intervention that is more closely focused on specifically enhancing control. Several studies have encouraged chronically ill patients to participate more in their treatment or treatment decisions. For example, Johnston, Gilbert, Partridge, and Collins (1992) randomly assigned rehabilitation patients to a group that received a routine appointment letter with the message that their efforts would pay off or to a control group who did not get this message. The group receiving the message had higher levels of perceived control and were more satisfied with the information they received. In a study with ulcer disease patients, participants were taught to read their own medical records and encouraged to ask questions of their medical care providers (Greenfield, Kaplan, & Ware, 1985). Those who received this intervention came to prefer a more active role in medical care and were more effective in obtaining information from their physicians.

An additional two studies, however, found mixed results for interventions that encouraged participants to exert more control over their treatment. In a study by England and Evans (1992), cardiac patients were invited to participate in a decision about their treatment. Although all patients received the invitation, there was considerable variance in how much decision control participants perceived they actually had which led the researchers to question whether encouraging patient participation is an effective control-enhancing strategy. As described earlier, Wallston et al. (1991) randomly assigned cancer treatment patients so that they either had a choice or did not have a choice of antiemetic drug. The choice was effective in reducing anxiety and negative mood only for those who were moderate in the desire for control. Finally, as mentioned earlier in this paper, Reich and Zautra (1991) used a comprehensive control enhancement intervention with at-risk older adults (bereaved or disabled). The intervention used cognitive and behavioral techniques to increase perceived control, for example, participants were helped to identify controllable and uncontrollable events in their lives. These techniques were effective in increasing personal control for individuals who were already internal in locus of control.

Overall, attempts to increase the perceived control of chronically ill individuals have shown some promise, especially if they increase general coping and stress-reduction skills. Interventions that specifically give patients more control may need to be matched to the level of control desired by the patient and may be more effective for those who already are attuned to ways that they control outcomes.

☐ Conclusion

Personal control plays an important role in coping for those with an ongoing illness. Those with a sense of control have better emotional well-being, reduced stress, and perhaps better physical health outcomes. In addition to this general conclusion about the beneficial effects of perceived control when dealing with a chronic illness, research has also identified some restrictions on that conclusion. Some ethnic group members may not derive the same benefits from perceptions of control as majority group members do. This may be due to preferences for a different style of coping that emphasizes group support instead of individual action. Another restriction is that not all individuals want to have control over medical outcomes, perhaps because taking personal action is contrary to their usual coping strategy. Researchers have also discovered that secondary control or acceptance is a strategy that is not antithetical to having personal control. Rather, a sense of acceptance can contribute to an overall sense of control. Finally, despite suggestions that perceptions of control need to be accurate to be useful, there is little evidence that the accuracy of control judgments affects their utility for chronically ill individuals.

Research has made a good start on delineating the role of personal control in the lives of chronically ill adults. More work is now needed to identify practical ways to increase the perceived control of those with an ongoing illness so the benefits of personal control can be more widely available.

☐ References

Affleck, G., Tennen, H., Pfeiffer, C., & Fifield, C., & Rowe, J. (1987). Downward comparison and coping with serious medical problems. *American Journal of Orthopsychiatry, 57,* 570–578.

American Cancer Society. (1999). 1999 facts and figures. Cancer: Basic facts [On-line]. Available: http://www.cancer.org/statistics/cff99/basicfacts.html

American Heart Association. (1996). Coronary heart disease and angina pectoris [On-line]. Available: http://www.amhrt.org/statistics/04cornry.html

Andersson, L. (1992). Loneliness and perceived responsibility and control in elderly community residents. *Social Behavior and Personality, 7,* 431–443.

Arthritis Foundation. (1998). Arthritis—Increasing awareness through the media [On-line]. Available: http://www.arthritis.org/pressroom/awareness.asp

Berckman, K. L., & Austin, J. K. (1993). Causal attribution, perceived control, and adjustment in patients with lung cancer. *Oncology Nursing Forum, 20,* 23–30.

Blood, G. W., Dineen, M., Kauffman, S. M., Raimondi, S. C., & Simpson, K. C. (1993). Perceived control, adjustment, and communication problems in laryngeal cancer survivors. *Perceptual and Motor Skills, 77,* 764–766.

Brandstadter, J., & Rothermund, K. (1994). Self-percepts of control in middle and later adulthood: Buffering losses by rescaling goals. *Psychology and Aging, 9,* 265–273.

Brosschot, J. F., Godaert, G. L. R., Benschop, R. J., Olff, M., Ballieux, R. E., & Heijnen, C. J. (1998). Experimental stress and immunological reactivity: A closer look at perceived controllability. *Psychosomatic Medicine, 60,* 359–361.

Chaney, J. M., Mullins, L., Uretsky, D. L., Doppler, M. J., Palmer, W. R., Wees, S. J., Klein, H. S., Doud, D. K., & Reiss, M. J. (1996). Attributional style and depression in rheumatoid arthritis: The moderating role of perceived illness control. *Rehabilitation Psychology, 41,* 205–223.

Cunningham, A. J., Lockwood, G. A., & Cunningham, J. A. (1991). A relationship between perceived self-efficacy and quality of life in cancer patients. *Patient Education and Counseling, 17,* 71–78.

Dantzer, R. (1989). Neuroendocrine correlates of control and coping. In A. Steptoe & A. Appels (Eds.), *Stress, personal control and health* (pp. 277–294). New York: Wiley.

Devins, G. M., & Binik, Y. M. (1996). Facilitating coping with chronic physical illness. In M. Zeidner & N. S. Endler (Eds.), *Handbook of coping* (pp. 640–696). New York: Wiley.

Eitel, P., Hatchett, L., Friend, R., Griffin, K. W., & Wadhwa, N. K. (1995). Burden of self-care in seriously ill patients: Impact on adjustment. *Health Psychology, 14,* 457–463.

England, S. L., & Evans, J. (1992). Patients' choices and perceptions after an invitation to participate in treatment decisions. *Social Science & Medicine, 34,* 1217–1225.

Felton, B. J., & Revenson, T. A. (1984). Coping with chronic illness: A study of illness controllability and the influence of coping strategies on psychological adjustment. *Journal of Consulting and Clinical Psychology, 52,* 343–353.

Fitzgerald, T. E., Tennen, H., Affleck, G., & Pransky, G. S. (1993). The relative importance of dispositional optimism and control appraisals in quality of life after coronary artery bypass surgery. *Journal of Behavioral Medicine, 16,* 25–43.

Greenfield, S., Kaplan, S., & Ware, J. (1985). Expanding patient involvement in care. *Annals of Internal Medicine, 102,* 520–528.

Helgeson, V. S. (1992). Moderators of the relation between perceived control and adjustment to chronic illness. *Journal of Personality and Social Psychology, 63,* 656–666.

Janoff-Bulman, R., & Frieze, I. H. (1983). A theoretical perspective for understanding reactions to victimization. *Journal of Social Issues, 39,* 1–17.

Johnston, M., Gilbert, P., Partridge, C., & Collins, J. (1992). Changing perceived control in patients with physical disabilities: An intervention study with patients receiving rehabilitation. *British Journal of Clinical Psychology, 31,* 89–94.

Katz, J., Ritvo, P., Irvine, M. J., & Jackson, M. (1996). Coping with chronic pain. In M. Zeidner & N. S. Endler (Eds.), *Handbook of coping: Theory, research, and applications* (pp. 252–278). New York: Wiley.

Krantz, D. S. (1980). Cognitive processes and recovery from heart attack: A review and theoretical analysis. *Journal of Human Stress, 6,* 27–38.

Krantz, S. E. (1995). Chronic physical disability and secondary control: Appraisals of an undesirable situation. *Journal of Cognitive Psychotherapy: An International Quarterly, 9,* 229–248.

Kugler, J., Tenderich, G., Stahlhut, P., Posival, H., Korner, M. M., Korfer, R., & Kruskemper, G. M. (1994). Emotional adjustment and perceived locus of control in heart transplant patients. Journal of *Psychosomatic Research, 38,* 403–408.

Lachman, M. E. (1991). Perceived control over memory aging: Developmental and intervention perspectives. *Journal of Social Issues, 47*(4), 159–175.

Lazarus, R. S. & Folkman, S. (1991). The concept of coping. In A. Monat & R. S. Lazarus (Eds.), *Stress and coping* (3rd ed., pp. 189–206). New York: Columbia University Press.

MacCarthy, B., & Brown, R. (1989). Psychosocial factors in Parkinson's disease. *British Journal of Clinical Psychology, 28,* 41–52.

Maes, S., Leventhal, H., & DeRidder, D. T. (1996). Coping with chronic diseases. In M. Zeidner & N. S. Endler (Eds.), *Handbook of coping* (pp. 221–251). New York: Wiley.

Mahler, H. I. M., & Kulik, J. A. (1990). Preferences for health care involvement, perceived control, and surgical recovery: A prospective study. *Social Science & Medicine, 31,* 743–751.

Malcarne, V. L., Compas, B. E., Epping-Jordan, J. E., & Howell, D. C. (1995). Cognitive factors in adjustment to cancer: Attributions of self-blame and perceptions of control. *Journal of Behavioral Medicine, 18,* 401–417.

Mercola, J. M. (1996). *Protocol for using antibiotics in the treatment of rheumatic diseases.* Paper presented at Annual Meeting of the American Academy of Environmental Medicine, Boston, MA.

Mirowsky, J. (1995). Age and the sense of control. *Social Psychology Quarterly, 58,* 31–43.

Mitchell, J. (May 28, 1997). Paddling toward life. *The Oregonian,* Section D, pp. D1, D3.

Moser, D. K., & Dracup, K. (1995). Psychosocial recovery from a cardiac event: The influence of perceived control. *Heart & Lung, 24,* 273–280.

National Institutes of Health. (1998). Information for clinical patients: Coping with chronic illness [On-line]. Available: http: //www.cc.nih.gov/ccc/patient_education/coping /.html

National Institute of Nursing Research. (1997, March 12). Summary of the Capitol Hill breakfast briefing on women's health and chronic illness [On-line]. Available: http://www.nih.gov/ninr/CapHillFriends_Brief.htm

Nelson, E. A. (1993). Control beliefs of adults in three domains: A new assessment of perceived control. *Psychological Reports, 72,* 155–165.

Newsom, J. T., Knapp, J. E., & Schulz, R. (1996). Longitudinal analysis of specific domains of internal control and depressive symptoms in patients with recurrent cancer. *Health Psychology, 15,* 323–331.

Orbell, S., Jonston, M., Rowley, D., Espley, A., & Davey, P. (1998). Cognitive representations of illness and functional and affective adjustment following surgery for osteoarthritis. *Social Science & Medicine, 47,* 93–102.

Parker, J. C., Frank, R. G., Beck, N. C., Smarr, K. L., Buescher, K. L., Phillips, L. R., Smith, E. I., Anderson, S. K., & Walker, S. E. (1988). Pain management in rheumatoid arthritis patients: A cognitive-behavioral approach. *Arthritis and Rheumatism, 31,* 593–601.

Partridge, C., & Johnston, M. (1989). Perceived control of recovery from physical disability: Measurement and prediction. *British Journal of Clinical Psychology, 28,* 53–59.

Peng, Y., & Lachman, M. E. (1993). Primary and secondary control: Age and cultural differences. Paper presented at the 101st Annual Convention of the American Psychological Association, Toronto, Canada.

Ray, C., Jefferies, S., & Wier, W. R. C. (1997). Coping and other predictors of outcome in chronic fatigue syndrome: A 1-year follow-up. *Journal of Psychosomatic Research, 43,* 405–415.

Reed, G. M., Taylor, S. E., & Kemeny, M. E. (1993). Perceived control and psychological adjustment in gay men with AIDS. *Journal of Applied Social Psychology, 23,* 791–824.

Reich, J. W., & Zautra, A. J. (1991). Experimental and measurement approaches to internal control in at-risk older adults. *Journal of Social Issues, 47*(4), 143–158.

Rodin, J. (1986). Aging and health: Effects of the sense of control. *Science, 233,* 1271–1276.

Ross, C. E., & Mirowsky, J. (1989). Explaining the social patterns of depression: Control and problem-solving—or support and talking? *Journal of Health and Social Behavior, 30,* 206–219.

Rothbaum, F., Weisz, J. R., & Snyder, S. S. (1982). Changing the world and changing the self: A two-process model of perceived control. *Journal of Personality and Social Psychology, 42,* 5–27.

Schulz, R., & Decker, S. (1985). Long-term adjustment to physical disability: The role of social support, perceived control, and self-blame. *Journal of Personality and Social Psychology, 48,* 1162–1172.

Seligman, M. E. P. (1975). *Helplessness: On depression, development, and death.* San Francisco: Freeman.

Shnek, Z. M., Foley, F. W., LaRocca, N. G., Gordon, W. A., DeLuca, J., Schwartzmann, H. G., Halper, J., Lennox, S., & Irvine, J. (1997). Helplessness, self-efficacy, cognitive distortions, and depression in multiple sclerosis and spinal cord injury. *Annals of Behavioral Medicine, 19,* 279–286.

Solomon, J. C. (1996). Humor and aging well. A laughing matter or a matter of laughing? *American Behavioral Scientist, 39,* 249–271.

Susman, J. (1994). Disability, stigma, and deviance. *Social Science and Medicine, 38,* 15–22.

Taylor, S. E. (1983). Adjustment to threatening events: A theory of cognitive adaptation. *American Psychologist, 38,* 1161–1173.

Taylor, S. E., Lichtman, R. R., & Wood, J. V. (1984). Attributions, beliefs about control, and adjustment to breast cancer. *Journal of Personality and Social Psychology, 46,* 489–502.

Telch, C. F., & Telch, M. J. (1986). Group coping skills instruction and supportive group therapy for cancer patients: A comparison of strategies. *Journal of Consulting and Clinical Psychology, 54,* 802–808.

Thompson, S. C. (1981). Will it hurt less if I can control it? A complex answer to a simple question. *Psychological Bulletin, 90,* 89–101.

Thompson, S. C. (1991). The search for meaning following a stroke. *Basic and Applied Social Psychology, 12,* 81–96.

Thompson, S. C., Collins, M. A., Newcomb, M. D., & Hunt, W. (1996). On fighting versus accepting stressful circumstances: Primary and secondary control among HIV-positive men in prison. *Journal of Personality and Social Psychology, 70,* 1307–1317.

Thompson, S. C., Nanni, C., & Levine, A. (1994). Primary versus secondary and disease versus consequence-related control in HIV-positive men. *Journal of Personality and Social Psychology, 67,* 540–547.

Thompson, S. C., & Sobolew-Shubin, A. (1993). Overprotective relationships: A nonsupportive side of social networks. *Basic and Applied Social Psychology, 14,* 363–383.

Thompson, S. C., Sobolew-Shubin, A., Galbraith, M. E., Schwankovsky, L., & Cruzen, D. (1993). Maintaining perceptions of control: Finding perceived control in low-control circumstances. *Journal of Personality and Social Psychology, 64,* 293–304.

Thompson, S. C., & Spacapan, S. (1991). Perceptions of control in vulnerable populations. *Journal of Social Issues, 47*(4), 1–21.

Thompson, S. C., Thomas, C., Rickabaugh, C. A., Tantamjarik, P., Otsuki, T., Pan, D., Garcia, B., & Sinar, E. (1998). Primary and secondary control over age-related changes in physical appearance. *Journal of Personality, 66,* 583–605.

Thompson, S. C., & Wierson, M. (in press). Enhancing perceived control in psychotherapy. In C. R. Snyder & R. E. Ingram (Eds.), *Handbook of psychological change.* New York: Wiley.

Timko, C., & Janoff-Bulman, R. (1985). Attributions, vulnerability, and psychological adjustment: The case of breast cancer. *Health Psychology, 4,* 521–544.

Turk, D. C., Okifuhi, A., & Scharff, L. (1995). Chronic pain and depression: Role of perceived impact and perceived control in different age cohorts. *Pain, 61,* 93–101.

Wallhagen, M. I. (1992–1993). Perceived control and adaptation in elder caregivers: Development of an explanatory model. *International Journal of Aging and Human Development, 36,* 219–237.

Wallhagen, M. I., & Brod, M. (1997). Perceived control and well-being in Parkinson's disease. *Western Journal of Nursing Research, 19,* 11–31.

Wallston, K. A., Smith, R. A. P., King, J. E., Smith, M. S., Rye, P., & Burish, T. G. (1991). Desire for control and choice of antiemetic treatment for cancer chemotherapy. *Western Journal of Nursing Research, 13,* 12–29.

Wells, N. (1994). Perceived control over pain: Relation to distress and disability. *Research in Nursing & Health, 17,* 295–302.

White, R. (1959). Motivation reconsidered: The concept of competence. *Psychological Review, 66,* 297–333.

White, R., Tata, P., & Burns, T. (1996). Mood, learned resourcefulness and perceptions of control in type 1 diabetes mellitus. *Journal of Psychosomatic Research, 40,* 205–212.

Wright, B. A. (1988). Attitudes and the fundamental negative bias: Conditions and corrections. In H. E. Yuker (Ed.), *Attitudes toward persons with disabilities* (pp. 3–21). New York: Springer.

Dieter Ferring
Sigrun-Heide Filipp

Coping as a "Reality Construction": On the Role of Attentive, Comparative, and Interpretative Processes in Coping with Cancer

Years of research have highlighted the impact of exposure to threatening life events on an individual's life, and a diverse set of criteria has been chosen to describe their effects. While an explicit focus on *pathogenic* effects, both on psychological as well as physical well-being, has dominated the beginning of this research paradigm, research during the last two decades has more strongly accentuated the role of adaptive behaviors and, thus, taken a *salutogenic* view (e.g., Antonowsky, 1987). This perspective has led to the study of resources—factors that contribute to resiliency—and, thus, to the health and well-being of people facing stressful events. Besides various stable individual difference variables (such as hardiness, toughness) the process of coping with stressful events itself has been considered an important resource as well (see Filipp & Aymanns, 1996).

The term coping describes the various ways in which people deal with loss and crisis; how the process of becoming gradually adapted to an often dramatically altered life situation may unfold over time, and under which circumstances people's ways of dealing with loss and crisis may ultimately prove to be adaptive. The diversity of phenomena that are subsumed under the concept of "coping" has found its correspondence in the divergent theoretical perspectives that have been adopted here. Thus, it has often been stated that conceptual diversion is the predominant feature within this research area (see Filipp, 1999; Taylor, 1984). Nevertheless, there seems to be some consensus about the functions of coping: All conceptions accentuate that one can either change circumstances and bring them into line with one's wants and needs—changing the world—or one can change one's beliefs, lower one's aspirations, or replace unattainable goals—changing the self (see Rothbaum, Weisz, & Snyder, 1982). Active attempts to change the world are referred to as problem-focused coping, primary control, or assimilative coping and may be a common and adaptive response to many stressful situations experienced in life (Brandstädter & Renner, 1992; Heckhausen & Schulz, 1995; Lazarus & Folkman, 1984). But these attempts are of little use when the major coping task is to come to terms with a situation that cannot be altered and that only allows for little, if any, control. Here, one has to change aspirations, goals, and personal beliefs, and to disengage from unattainable goals— behaviors which have generally been described as strategies of cognitive adaptation (Taylor, 1983).

In the following we will focus on the behavior that individuals show when being confronted with the diagnosis of cancer, a severe, and often life-threatening chronic disease. Needless to say that there is little room for problem-centered coping in its usual sense; rather, cognitive maneuvers may be required in order to not be over-whelmed by one's fears. Accordingly, we will first describe why this situation can be considered a prototype of critical life events. Second, we will present a heuristic model for the conceptualization of coping processes in which the role of cognitive processes in constructing an interpretative reality is accentuated. Third, we will present results from the Trier Longitudinal Study on Coping with Chronic Disease that support propo-sitions derived from this model.

☐ Severe and Chronic Disease as a Prototype of Critical Life Events

The onset of severe and chronic disease represents one of the most traumatic events imaginable, especially when it occurs nonnormatively in earlier phases of the life span. As we already have argued elsewhere, this is due to different reasons (see also Filipp, 1992; Klauer, Ferring & Filipp, 1998). First, people in Western cultures are not nor-mally prepared to deal with disease and death. Second, they do not usually consider the onset of chronic disease as one of the possible realities in their lives. This belief is convincingly demonstrated by research in personal invulnerability and unrealistic optimism (e.g., Taylor & Brown, 1988; Weinstein, 1980). Thus, neither an anticipa-tory socialization with regard to such traumatic experiences has occurred, nor do people, in general, voluntarily engage in ways of anticipatory coping with potential threats to their health or lives. Following the terminology of cognitive psychology, the diagnosis of cancer may therefore be characterized as a weakly scripted situation (Abelson, 1981) for which appropriate responses (let alone behavioral routines) are not readily at hand.

Additionally, whereas other negative life experiences (e.g., loss of a loved one) are embedded, at least partially, into culturally shaped ways of responding (e.g., through public rituals or mourning customs; see Stroebe & Stroebe, 1987) that often facilitate the coping process, the initial diagnosis of cancer clearly lacks this external facilita-tion. Rather, it is usually accompanied by high degrees of behavioral disorganization, and often by the disruption and breakdown of many social bonds. Cancer is not only far beyond the (primary) control of those suffering from it, in many cases it is even beyond physicians' control. Patients are often exposed to their diagnosis in a com-pletely unpredictable way, particularly when it is taken into consideration that the detection of cancer frequently occurs simply by chance. Furthermore, to suffer from cancer usually implies the loss of hopes, goals, and plans, or, at least, it imposes the necessity to disengage from ongoing commitments (Klinger, 1975). Finally, to be diagnosed as a cancer patient nearly always means a threat to fundamental beliefs about the self (e.g., being a strong, powerful, effective, or functioning person) and about the world as a predictable, controllable, and safe place to live. Accordingly, because of the necessity to alter these belief systems, the diagnosis of cancer may well be one of the most negative life experiences in general (see Filipp, 1999).

Thus, the diagnosis of cancer intensely challenges an individual's assumptive worlds (Janoff-Bulman, 1992), imposes heavy threats to psychological and physical survival, and causes dramatic alterations in many, if not all, domains of life. Consequently, it is not too surprising that the process of cognitive adaptation to cancer has been primarily investigated when it comes to the study of patients' coping behaviors (e.g., Klauer, Ferring & Filipp, 1998; Klauer & Filipp, 1997; Taylor, 1983). In the following, we will accentuate these processes by proposing a heuristic model that describes different cognitive processes which in our view constitute the essential part of the coping process and may constitute the basis for further coping attempts.

☐ A Model of Coping with Loss and Trauma

Filipp (1999) has recently pointed out that coping, in its most general meaning, represents all attempts to gradually transform an *objective* reality comprised of bad news, (losses, threats, or trauma) into a *subjective* reality (see Watzlawick, 1976) in which victims can continue to live in relative peace. At first glance, this resembles attempts to bring individual conceptions of "what is" and "what ought to be" into better alignment—a notion that the concept of coping shares with many approaches in which the reduction of discrepancies is the core issue. However, the reduction of discrepancies between the world as it is and the world as it should be by means of control-oriented or palliative coping presupposes that individuals are indeed aware of these discrepancies and perceive the reality (that they have to live in) in a fairly undistorted manner. But, as we all know, this is by no means the rule.

The capacity of human information processing is limited, and individuals cannot perceive all aspects of a given situation. Rather, they focus on specific aspects that are predominant according to their view. In other words, people selectively attend to and perceive reality. In addition, there is much support in literature that objective reality is sometimes so ambiguous and complex ("What did the doctor say?") that individuals have considerable power to define and shape reality through their construals and appraisals. Interindividual differences in evaluating the objective reality are well-documented, especially in the beginnings of cognitive stress research (e.g., Lazarus, 1993).

Accordingly, it is our belief that we need to know more than simply the "is" and the "ought" in order to both understand the process of how victims of life crises gradually come to terms with their lot and to take the large interindividual differences into account more seriously. Coping with loss and trauma can be best understood in terms of a process during which victims of life crises are going to process, step by step, the discrepancies between the "is" and the "ought." Such a notion has long been promoted by Horowitz (1982) and despite some profound criticism of stage-like conceptions of the coping process (see Wortman & Silver, 1992), we consider such an information-processing view of coping to be an extremely useful and theoretically promising approach.

Figure 1 demonstrates the postulated sequence of steps which underlie the construction of an interpretative reality within this heuristic model by describing three fundamental processes that are not necessarily conceived of as being sequential in nature: first, *attentive processes* that contribute to the construction of an individual's perceptive reality, in terms of selectively attending to bad news and, thus, defending positive illusions; second, *comparative processes* that help to shape perceptive reality toward a reality that victims of life crises can gradually tolerate and accept; and third, interpretative processes that help to construe an interpretative reality mainly through attempts to ascribe subjective meaning to what currently makes up one's perceptive reality. Attentive, comparative, and interpretative processes are influenced by the individual's internal model of the self, internal model of the world, and his or her individual motivational system.

Internal models of the self and the world guide our perception and our actions. People perform mental simulations of what might occur, predict events that should happen, and calculate their abilities to control their onset and impact, all of these being reflections of individual beliefs as well as socioculturally shared views of the world as it ought to be. When the predictions are undesirable, or when it appears that little can be done to control the events or, similarly, when the real occurrences are not at all what was expected, emotional responses are likely to develop that directly affect further information processing. Referring to Taylor and Brown's (1988) work on the importance of positive illusions, one can assume that these models of the self and the world are based on and comprised of illusionary beliefs that state that the world is a meaningful, nonrandom place and we ourselves are relatively invulnerable.

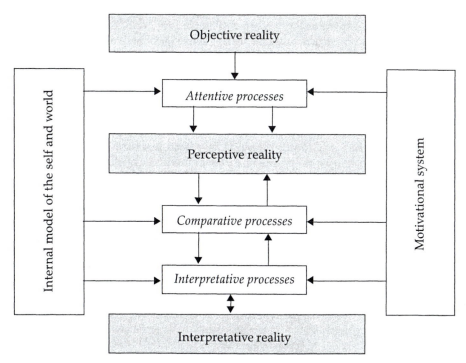

FIGURE 1. A heuristic model for the conceptualization of coping with loss and trauma.

The preservation of these views constitutes an essential part of the individual motivational system. In fact, individuals' views about their selves and the world can be characterized as conservative ones: We are motivated to confirm our views of the self and the world rather than to disconfirm them and, thus, these views become powerful regulators of both cognitive processing and behavioral responding to loss and trauma. This need is, for instance, seen to form the explicit motivational basis for temporal comparisons: People would rather evaluate their selves as stable, before they would be willing to admit that the self has changed in the aftermath of critical life events (see Klauer, Ferring, & Filipp, 1998). Other phenomena such as the self-fulfilling-prophecy or top-down processing represent concepts from different conceptual networks which describe this tendency toward confirming our views. Disconfirming information is painful and avoided, and one does not voluntarily engage in altering one's world and self view, rather we try to immunize ourselves against this kind of information (e.g., Brandtstaedter & Greve, 1994).

At first glance, the transformation of objective reality into one's perceptive reality includes the individual's selective attention to and construals of what has happened to him or her. Furthermore, rumination about whether and how what happened could have been avoided, appraisals of one's resources for dealing with or overcoming what happened, comparisons of one's own current life with that of others or with hypothetically worse worlds, and many other types of intrapsychic coping (Lazarus & Folkman, 1984) may come into motion after this perceptive reality has been established. As an attempt at a conceptual differentiation of these cognitive maneuvers, we will focus on the three processes that were introduced above: 1) attentive processes that lead to the construction of a perceptive reality, 2) comparative processes that serve to shape perceptive reality toward a tolerable form, and 3) interpretative processes that help to construct causal as well as teleological meaning from subjective reality.

Attentive Processes in the Construction of a Perceptive Reality

Let us illustrate the importance of attentive processes in reality construction by the different reactions that patients show when they are informed about their diagnosis of cancer. Initial reactions to this diagnosis have been described by the use of vigilance and avoidance, two independent forms of attention regulation (see Krohne, 1993). Carver and Scheier (1993) studied these phenomena in a sample of cancer patients who were interviewed at the time of diagnosis and before surgery. They concluded that there was considerable divergence in the indices of vigilance used. In other words, patients showed a considerable degree of variability in where they focused their vigilance. Furthermore and with respect to avoidance, the researchers could show that patients were not avoiding in general, but rather were avoiding specific thought contents which differed from one measurement to the other. These results show that patients are selectively attentive and inattentive to certain aspects of the life-threatening situation. In our view it is especially the inattentiveness that supports the thesis of reality construction, since to be selectively *inattentive* to certain aspects implies, by definition, that a person must have some awareness of threatening information in order to know where *not* to look (sometimes referred to as the paradox of denial; see Breznitz, 1986). This finding demonstrates that patients actively negotiate or construe their perceptive reality rather than simply distort it.

Presumably, the main motivational force behind these attentive processes lies in attempts to defend one's positive illusions (i.e., unrealistically positive self-evaluations, exaggerated perceptions of personal control, and unrealistic optimism about the future). The focus on positive illusions or creative self-deception has led to a controversy about fact and fiction when it comes to their assumed functions as a means of regulating one's psychological well-being (Block & Colvin, 1994; Colvin & Block, 1994; Taylor & Brown, 1994). Phenomena like depressive realism have been cited as being supportive of these presumed functions because they circumscribe what happens when these strategies do not work. Recent reviews reveal that although many studies have generated evidence consistent with the depressive realism hypothesis, almost as many have provided evidence inconsistent with this view (see Ackermann & DeRubeis, 1991).

To support our proposition of selective reality monitoring, we will therefore not rely on single studies providing results which can always be criticized due to substantive or methodological issues (e.g., neglect or omission of important third variables, questionable ecological validity of a study). Rather, we rely on a corpus of theory and research derived from cognitive psychology that states that human information processing under threat is extremely limited and, thus, has to be selective and economic. This finding has been repeatedly proven within cognitive psychology since the early works of Broadbent (1958; see also Shiffrin, 1988). In addition, we incorporate phenomenological models that elaborate the positions of social constructivism (and social constructionism) and delineate the consequences for a postmodern epistemology (e.g., Gergen, 1990; von Foerster, 1988; Watzlawick, 1976). Finally, we refer to clinical and consulting psychology where the constructivist view has become very prominent and has been successfully used in interventions. This is done in such a way that a reality that is perceived as painful can be "deconstructed" (e.g., by account making or story telling; Harvey, 1996) into a reality that can be coped with (see Hoyt, 1996).

Comparative Processes in Shaping Perceptive Reality

When speaking of comparative processes that allow for a shaping of one's perceptive reality, we have to consider at least four—not necessarily mutually exclusive—types of reference comparisons: 1) Social comparisons that are comprised of the evaluation of the self on a given dimension compared to (real or fictitious) others; 2) Temporal comparisons, that allow for an evaluation of one's present position on a dimension in question relative to past or anticipated points of reference; 3) Criteria-based comparisons by which the present life situation is evaluated with what is thought to be an appropriate standard of comparison (i.e., functional criteria); and 4) Comparisons with hypothetical worlds that allow for the imagination of any comparison standard. In the following, we will focus on the importance of social comparison processes in shaping perceptive reality (see also Filipp & Ferring, 1998; Klauer, Ferring & Filipp, 1998).

It was Festinger (1954) who pointed out that people have a general preference for evaluating themselves by using three sources of information. Besides objective information and personal standard information (which implies temporal comparisons as well as comparisons with hypothesized or possible selves), he highlighted the importance of social comparison information, and he differentiated this information with respect to its results and its underlying motives. He assumed that lateral comparisons (i.e., comparisons with similar others) are guided by an accuracy motive and should serve the desire to have an accurate sense of oneself, one's abilities, and opinions. These, in turn, should allow for the anticipation and control of future events. Subsequent research focused on downward comparisons (i.e., comparisons with persons who are worse off than oneself) that should serve the desire for self-enhancement (e.g., Hakmiller, 1966; Wills & Suls, 1991). Finally, upward-comparisons were considered (i.e., comparisons with people who are presumably better off than oneself) and conceived of being motivated by the need for self-improvement (see Wayment & Taylor, 1995). The focus on primarily epistemic motives underlying comparison processes gradually gave way to conceptions in which their power in regulating subjective well-being was highlighted.

In particular, the accuracy motive underlying lateral comparisons has been questioned, and it was argued that lateral comparisons should serve another motive aimed at the reduction of perceived discrepancies between oneself and other persons. It has been reported that victims of life crises (e.g., rape victims) do not just use social comparison information that lies at hand; rather, they often tend to actively generate comparison information by construing false consensus (i.e., overestimating the proportion of others with a similar fate) in order to avoid or reduce negative feelings of uniqueness (Goethals, Messick, & Allison, 1991). Thus, lateral comparison may be used to reduce perceived deviance by finding examples of other persons who have the same (but not a worse) problem.

When it comes to the perception of deviance or similarity at least three different types of similarity can be differentiated according to Wills (1992): 1) Fate similarity, involving the question if the target person's status is similar or worse off than oneself; 2) future similarity, an assessment of the probability that one will have a better, similar, or worse status than the target; and 3) personal similarity, which is the perceived similarity of oneself and the target person with respect to personality attributes. Wills suggested that a typical comparison situation provides some mixture of all these types of information and that these types of similarity have quite different effects on the outcome of the comparison process. He showed that the combination of the possible levels of fate similarity (i.e., same status versus worse status) and future similarity (i.e., similar, worse, or better) results in a judgment matrix with 2 × 3 possible outcomes, some of them resulting in positive well-being (e.g., if the person has the same fate than the target, but expects his or her future status to be better) and some in negative well-being (e.g., if the person has a worse fate than the target, and expects his or her future to be even worse). The same can be done for other configurations of the similarity dimensions, and different outcomes on well-being can be predicted for each given configuration of similarity or dissimilarity on a specific dimension. The author concludes that downward comparison information will not always result in enhancement of subjective well-being, and he argues that this will instead depend on the similarity information in a given comparison context.

Interestingly, downward comparisons in laboratory and field studies seem to have a uniformly positive effect, despite the potential negative effects which may be expected in the analytical considerations of similarity information. This implies, in general, that humans are not scientists who collect and weigh information in order to obtain a reliable judgment of their life situation. The motive underlying comparisons is not accuracy, but rather establishing or defending positive states and self-worth. The uniformly positive effect of downward comparisons can be explained as follows (in line with Wills, 1992): First, people actively select those comparison targets that allow for a favorable comparison; second, people combine their similarity ratings in a compensatory way that allows for a favorable outcome (e.g., one's own present life situation may be worse than the target's but one might, nevertheless, expect that the future life situation may be better). Third, people use different indicators within each similarity dimension. When it comes to personality similarity, it may be stated, for example, that one's physical well-being is worse than the target's but may, at the same time, maintain that one is better off with respect to another attribute (for this issue, see Filipp & Ferring, 1998). Fourth, persons can use hypothetical targets with attributes that allow for a favorable comparison. Hypothetical targets may include fictitious persons from the literature or other media as well active mental creations of figures with specific attributes.

These notions show that people are selective and creative in using comparison targets and dimensions, which is clearly indicative of a motivational tendency aimed at defending the self model and preserving emotional well-being. Despite some confusions and also contradictory evidence with regard to how social comparisons are used in response to loss and trauma and with regard to their presumed adaptive value (see, for an overview, Buunk, 1994), the notion of selective (i.e., self-enhancing or self-protecting) comparisons is highly prominent in the literature. Results from numerous studies have highlighted that when coping with loss and trauma, individuals are especially inclined to compare themselves selectively with others who are worse off than themselves (see Taylor & Lobel, 1989).

Interpretative Processes in Shaping Perceptive Reality

When perceptive reality is modulated by comparative processes into an interpretative reality, we have to consider interpretative processes and, in this context, we subsume processes of establishing meaning to an individually perceived reality. Meaning implies answers to the questions of causality as well as finality. In other words, to establish meaning implies the integration of a threatening, harmful experience into one's model of the self and the world by answering questions that reconstruct the causal "why" and the teleological "why" or "what for." The causal why comprises, in its essence, questions of causality, responsibility, and blame, and the teleological why comprises the question of the gains (and losses) which can be derived from the experience (see Emmons, Colby, & Kaiser, 1998).

Since the first studies were published on causal attributions in the real world (e.g., Bulman & Wortman, 1977), it became evident that responsibility and blame for what happened in one's life constitute important issues with respect to psychological well-being. But, like in many other fields, an inconsistent pattern of results has emerged over the years, especially in studies that aimed at identifying the effects that self-blame has on psychological well-being in coping with loss and trauma. Shaver (1985) tried to clarify inconsistent results by proposing a conceptual differentiation of the term self-blame, that implies three components: causation, responsibility, and blameworthiness (see also, Montada, 1992). We will now consider this differentiation.

Shaver and Drown (1986) pointed out that causality involves the production of an effect by internal or external forces, and responsibility implies the consequences or outcomes of this process. According to their view, causality is dichotomous whereas responsibility is variable and multidimensional, and the attribution of responsibility follows causality attribution. Attributed responsibility for an action depends on various factors such as awareness of the action's consequences, volition and intent of the action, and the awareness of the moral wrongfulness of the action (see Montada, 1992). Blame, in Shaver's view, is a disputed social judgment, since it represents the attribution after the perceiver has assessed and refused to accept the validity of the actor's justification for an action the perceiver thinks was intended.

Comparable to the rationale elaborated by Wills (1992) on social comparisons, one again has to admit that—unlike researchers—people in general as well as victims do not necessarily follow these conceptual distinctions. This is most strikingly illustrated in cases where blame is assigned even when it is unwarranted, for example when victims of sexual harassment or AIDS patients are blamed for their lot (Ford, Liwag-McLamb, & Foley, 1998; Herek & Capitanio, 1997). This is also illustrated by studies that show a beneficial effect of self-blame, since it allows for a retro-gnostic establishment of control that one actually did not have. Interestingly, researchers have concluded that individuals do not differentiate among the concepts of responsibility, fault, and blame (see Sholomskas, Steil & Plummer, 1990) that has, for example, led to the development of a blame avoidance program in which the conceptual differentiation of self-blame is taught (Shaver, 1992).

Our point here, again, is that the motive underlying these endeavors is not epistemic but rather hedonic (i.e., regulating one's psychological well-being). If it is—in this line of reasoning—necessary for one to have control, control is reestablished by an attribution of self-blame, regardless of the objective circumstances. Various other motives may be mentioned here that also may result in such a motivated misperception of reality (e.g., the belief in a just world; for an overview, see Montada & Lerner, 1998).

When we consider the answers to the question of a teleological why, we are focusing on a more neglected aspect. In our view, the assignment of meaning always implies construals of purpose, that is, human experiences are meaningful if they serve a purpose. Certainly the purpose of a particular life experience can be inferred from its (real or presumed) consequences. If we are able to state that some critical event has led to some positive outcome, we can conclude that this experience has had a purpose and, thus, is not meaningless. In particular, the construction of positive changes is likely to occur when discrepancies between the perceptive and objective reality can neither be reduced nor neglected. Here, temporal comparisons that primarily serve this goal come into play, since they may result in (subjective) evidence of gains or growth; in addition, ruminative thought aimed at making sense out of what happened represents another category of the interpretative processes that might be involved here (see Filipp, 1999).

Furthermore, the teleological why implies adherence to or (re)formulation of individual goals. In this context, we have to refer to the concept of hope. Hope implies adherence to highly valued goals and desired future events that have some subjective probability of occurrence; in this understanding, "hoping is coping" (Weisman, 1979). In fact, there is a long tradition of considering hope and the quality of survival in cancer patients as mutually related factors. One of the early conceptualizations was formulated by Engel (1968) who differentiated giving up (i.e., helplessness) and given up (i.e., hopelessness) as separate states. Whereas giving up is characterized by the subjective loss of control and lowered contingency expectations in the sense of helplessness, the state given up implies the loss of highly valued goals, signifying the end of past and futile endeavors at adaptation (for more recent work on the concept of hope, see Snyder, 1998). Thus, there are good reasons to use the concept of hope in studying coping with and adaptation to severe disease, because hope, in turn, is also seen to be steady enough to withstand reality (see Snyder, Irving, & Anderson, 1991).

Interpretative as well as comparative processes are both used to bring perceptive reality into a subjectively experienced meaningful form. Processes that may be used to establish meaning to an altered life situation comprise causal constructions as well as the perception of changes and the regulation of hope (for further information on this issue, see Filipp, 1999). All of these processes can be described by the flexible use of the interpretative space which reality leaves. Next, we will present results from our research on coping with cancer, focusing on the role of social comparisons and their relation to hopelessness. Here, we try to provide evidence for the flexible use of objective information and the shaping of a reality in which people are forced to face threats to their lives.

☐ Examples from the Real World: Social Comparisons in Cancer Patients

The data presented were assessed within the Trier Longitudinal Study on Coping with Chronic Disease[1], a study consisting of three general aims (for more detailed descriptions see Filipp, 1992; Filipp, Klauer, Freudenberg, & Ferring, 1990): 1) We were interested in observing the course of coping with cancer over time. Therefore, we used a longitudinal design with repeated measurements over the course of one year and an additional follow-up was conducted two years later. Additionally, patients differing in time elapsed since their diagnosis were recruited in order to construct a cohort-sequential design. 2) Determinants of coping with cancer were investigated as well as determinants of temporal variations in the course of coping over time. Hence, several sets of predictors, such as medical data, were obtained from the patients' physicians at the time of study onset. Moreover, personality variables (such as dispositional self-awareness, self-efficacy) and quantitative as well as qualitative indicators of social integration (e.g., network size, received social support) were included. 3) We wanted to identify adaptive coping behaviors, both in short-term and long-term perspectives. For this purpose, a set of multiple criteria of coping effectiveness was considered; for example, patients' perceptions of disease-related changes, as well as hope, self-esteem, and other indicators of emotional well-being were assessed. During the first year of the study, coping behaviors were assessed four times at intervals from three to four months. All variables presumed to be either predictors or adaptational outcomes were assessed on at least two occasions of measurement.

Patient sampling was conducted in cooperation with several hospitals and institutions for cancer care and rehabilitation in West Germany. Thus, all patients were recruited within medical settings. At the first measurement occasion, the sample consisted of 332 patients (178 females, 154 males) with a mean age of 51 years (age range: 20–74 years). With regard to tumor sites, the four largest subgroups comprised patients with breast cancer ($N = 83$), patients suffering from malignancies in the digestive system ($N = 63$), patients with tumors of mouth, throat, and larynx ($N = 47$), and

---

[1]Research was sponsored by a grant from the German Research Association to the second author.

patients with cancers of the blood or lymphatic system (N = 43). At the initial interview, 50% of the sample had been diagnosed within the previous year, and the amount of time elapsed since diagnosis varied between 1 and 840 weeks (M = 112 weeks). A subsample of 128 patients (38.5%) had already had a cancer recurrence before participating in the study.

In the following we focus on the prevalence of upward, lateral, and downward social comparisons that have been observed for a complete longitudinal sample of 178 cancer patients (71 women, 107 men; M = 52 years, SD = 12.66). This sample was described by comparable medical indicators: time elapsed since diagnosis had a mean of two years and two months, and the largest percentage of the patients suffered from carcinoma (86%; especially breast cancer, cancer of the digestive system, and malignoma of mouth, throat, and larynx).

Social comparisons were assessed by a single-item rating at all four points of measurement: Patients had to complete the sentence *"Compared to other patients, I think that I cope with my disease . . ."* on a 5-point scale comprised of the categories *much better, better, the same, worse,* and *much worse.* The distribution of the resulting judgments is summarized in Table 1. The prevalence of upward social comparisons was quite negligible, because the categories "much worse" and "worse" showed relative frequencies of $1.7 < f_{rel} < 5.0$ across the four occasions of measurement. Lateral comparisons had been selected by approximately 30% of these patients ($26.4 < f_{rel} < 33.7$), and the main part of the sample, namely, over 60% ($64.6 < f_{rel} < 71.9$) compared in a downward manner (i.e., by stating that they coped better or much better with their disease than other patients). Exact χ^2 tests displayed that the category "better" revealed the greatest deviation from the uniform distribution (t_1: χ^2_4 = 149.14, $p < .00$; t_2: χ^2_4 = 113.85, $p < .00$; t_3: χ^2_4 = 168.29, $p < .00$; t_4: χ^2_4 135.09, $p < .00$). Thus, downward social comparisons were most pronounced in our sample.

In order to prove whether comparison judgments had an impact on patients' psychological well-being we computed polyserial correlations with hopelessness, which was assessed at t_2 and t_4 by a German version of the Beck-Scale (see Krampen, 1979). When inspecting the distal relationship (i.e., between comparison ratings and hopelessness measured three month later), we found a correlation of r = –.40 ($p < .00$) between hopelessness at t_2 and the comparison ratings at t_1 and a correlation of r = –31 ($p < .00$) between hopelessness at t_4 and the comparison ratings at t_3. Proximal correlations showed that comparison ratings at t_2 and t_4 both correlated r = –.50 ($p < .00$) with concurrently assessed hopelessness. The relation between comparison ratings at t_1 and hopelessness at t_2 is illustrated in Figure 2. Here, the function of down-

TABLE 1. Absolute and relative frequencies of cancer patients' responses to the sentence *"Compared to other patients I think that I cope with my disease . . . "* at four points of measurement (n = 178).

Category	t_1		t_2		t_3		t_4	
Much worse	2	1.1	2	1.1	2	1.1	—	
Worse	1	0.6	7	3.9	1	0.6	3	1.7
The same	51	28.7	53	29.8	47	26.4	60	33.7
Better	88	49.4	78	43.8	95	53.4	79	44.4
Much better	36	20.2	38	21.3	35	18.5	36	20.2

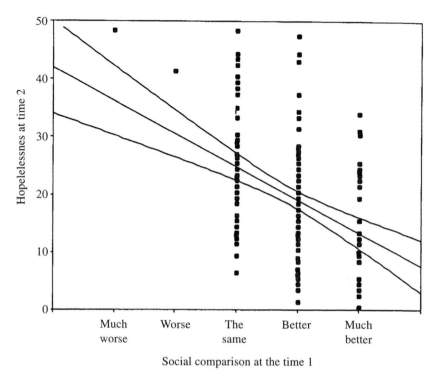

FIGURE 2. Scattergram of social comparison ratings at t_1 and hopelessness measured three months later at t_2.

ward social comparisons is clearly illustrated since hopelessness decreased in those patients who considered their coping behavior to be better or much better than that of other patients.

In a next step of analysis, structural equation modeling was used to inspect the *multivariate* relationship of social comparisons and hopelessness across time within a path model. Comparison ratings were treated here as categorical variables to account for the different semantics of the five response categories as well as for their skewed distribution, whereas hopelessness scores were treated as continuous variables, and a matrix of product-moment, polychoric, and polyserial correlations constituted the input for path analysis (see Joreskog & Sorbom, 1996). The specified path model represented a quasi-experimental test of the distal and proximal causal effects that social comparisons may yield on well-being. Figure 3 shows, that a first-order autoregressive process for comparison ratings was specified by allowing only for first-order correlations between ratings at adjacent measurement points. Furthermore, we specified only unidirectional paths from comparison ratings to hopelessness at t_2 and t_4. The autoregression of hopelessness was taken into account by the correlation of hopelessness residuals.

The model test resulted in excellent fit statistics ($\chi^2_9 = 2.39$, $p = .98$; $AGFI = .99$). However, since the sample size was comparatively low ($N = 178$), we will not overesti-

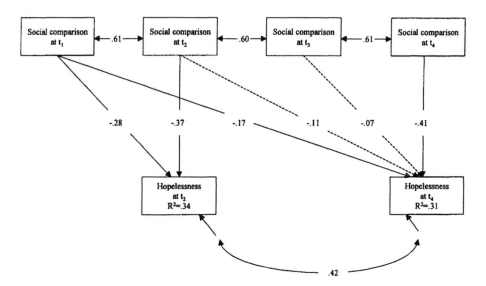

FIGURE 3. Path diagram specifying the interrelation of social comparison ratings and hopelessness.

mate the power of the model, and it certainly has to be cross-validated in other samples. First-order correlation between social comparison ratings showed that these were described by a medium stability of $.60 < r_{tt} < .61$, indicating a common variance of 30% for adjacent ratings which is to be expected for single-item ratings. Interestingly, ratings followed a first order regressive process, since the model fit did not require further subdiagonal correlations between the ratings. When inspecting the effects of comparisons on hopelessness, it became evident that 34% and 31% of variance were explained at t_2 and t_4, respectively; not all paths reached significance as is indicated by the dotted lines. Proximal paths at t_2 and t_4 were all significant, and they describe the above-mentioned relation between comparison and hopelessness. When considering the distal effects, social comparison at t_1 significantly predicted hopelessness at t_2 as well t_4, but the path of ratings at t_2 and t_3 on hopelessness at t_4 barely missed significance. Nevertheless, results indicate that there are comparatively strong effects of social comparison ratings on hopelessness in that downward social comparisons did decrease hopelessness.

To further validate these results we specified a second path model which treated comparison ratings as dependant variables and allowed only for causal paths originating from hopelessness on the respective comparison ratings at t_2, t_3, and t_4. Fit statistics for this alternative model were much worse ($\chi^2_9 = 133.7$, $p = .00$; $AGFI = .61$). Modification indices showed that this was due to the not specified—because theoretically not reasonable—path between hopelessness at t_2 and t_4 and social comparison at t_1. This provides further support for an interpretation of the first model which accentuates the causal effect of social comparisons on psychological well-being and highlights the importance of downward comparisons.

We can only speculate about the comparison targets and the similarity or dissimilarity dimensions which were selected by the majority of patients who judged themselves to be better or much better off than other patients. Our next step of analysis may offer some hints about this. We will consider the group of patients who died while participating or after their participation in the research project, and, thus, were objectively worse off than any other patients with respect to disease progression.

☐ Social Comparison Activity and Distance From Death

The group of deceased participants of the Trier Longitudinal Study comprised 68 patients. This sample size was reduced to 52 patients (27 men, 25 women) with a mean age of 52.63 years (SD = 11.36; range: 20–75 years) when controlling for missing values in medical data, and reduced further to a size of 23 patients who had complete data sets on all four occasions of measurement. This subsample was comprised of 9 men and 14 women with a mean age of 52.25 years (SD = 8.78) and was matched with a group of survivors with respect to age, sex, and medical variables. In particular, tumor site and size, lymph node invasion, metastases, and multimorbidity were used in the matching procedure. In addition, physicians' ratings of their patients' progno-sis, compliance, and coping effectiveness were considered. The matching procedure showed that both groups were comparable with respect to age and gender, as well as to tumor site, lymph node invasion, and multimorbidity. Yet, the groups could not be matched with all variables: Tumor size proved to be larger in the sample of the de-ceased patients; more patients within this sample had had a relapse as well as me-tastases; and physician's prognosis proved to be less favorable. Thus, some indicators of medical status as well as disease progression could not be controlled for. Since we were not interested in predicting survival time that would have required a perfect match between the groups, but rather wanted to contrast deceased patients and sur-vivors in a follow-back approach, we interpret these results to be indicative of the different life situations that existed within the two samples. We can not definitely state the extent that deceased patients were aware of their disease progression, but since physicians' prognoses were comparatively worse, one can assume that there must have been some indication. An open question remains of how much scope there was within the sample of deceased patients for downward or lateral comparisons with other patients (at least with respect to this criterion which might be—from an outside perspective—a powerful one).

In Table 2 we have summarized the social comparison ratings of the deceased pa-tients and survivors across the four points of measurement. In a first step we will focus on the deceased patients' ratings: Not one of these patients compared in an upward way by stating that he or she coped much worse with his or her disease than other patients. Only at the first and second point of measurement did one and two patients, respectively, state that they coped worse with their disease than other pa-tients. Rather, the majority of patients made downward comparisons by referring to the categories "better" or "much better." Overall, 70% did this at t_1, at t_2 and t_3, and even still 52% at t_4. Again, we computed exact χ^2 tests that examined the expected frequencies versus a uniform distribution across the response categories and—comparable to the results observed for the sample of 178 patients—residuals showed that the category "better" (i.e., downward social comparisons) had the greatest re-sidual, indicating that these ratings were predominant at all four occasions of mea-surement (t_1: χ^2_4 = 19.83, $p < .00$; t_2: χ^2_4 = 15.04, $p < .00$; t_3: χ^2_4 = 31.13, $p < .00$; t_4: χ^2_4 = 22.87, $p < .00$).

TABLE 2. Relative frequencies of 25 deceased patients and 27 "matched" survivors on social comparison categories

Category	Deceased				Survivors			
	t_1	t_2	t_3	t_4	t_1	t_2	t_3	t_4
Much worse	—	—	—	—	—	4	—	—
Worse	4.3	8.7	—	—	—	—	—	—
The same	26.1	21.7	30.4	48	26	37	15	33
Better	52.2	47.8	60.9	39	56	44	78	52
Much better	17.4	21.7	8.7	13	18	15	7	15

At first glance and from an objective perspective, these results may be considered contraintuitive; one might ask which comparison targets the patients actually did use since they were worse off with respect to their disease progression than every other patient. But this first inspection of the data has to be reassessed with respect to the temporal distance to death as well as to the ratings of matched survivors. Temporal distance between study onset and death varied between 12 weeks to 190 weeks with a mean of 76 weeks (SD = 46 weeks). In the following, we will consider the ratings of the patients who died during the *first year* of the study. This subsample comprises 19 patients, and distance from death ranged between 12 weeks to 51 weeks (M = 33 weeks, SD = 11 weeks). Due to early drop-out, only data from the first two occasions of measurement are available for this group, and the sample decreases further because two (first measurement) and nine patients (second measurement) had missing values on the ratings. Nevertheless, results are quite striking as can be seen in Figure 4.

The result pattern described in Table 2 receives further support in Figure 4: Most of the patients compared downwardly, stating that they got along better or much better

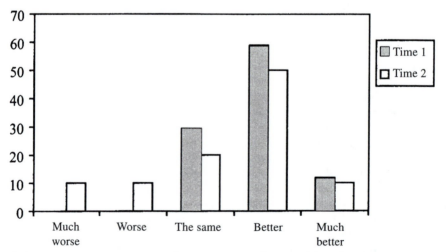

FIGURE 4. Ratings at two times of measurement of n = 17 (t_1) and n = 10 (t_2) patients deceased during the first year while participating at the Trier Longitudinal Study.

than other patients. We can not exclude that this finding is caused by a selective drop-out of patients at t_2, since due to disease progression, these patients could no longer participate in the study. But even then, ratings obtained at t_1 are quite clear since none of the patients did an upward comparison.

In a second step, we compared deceased patients and matched survivors with respect to their ratings, and the resulting distributions are also presented in Table 2. Again, χ^2 tests were performed to test for significant differences between the two samples, but none of the χ^2 values reached significance. This finding indicates that both survivors and deceased patients showed a comparable response pattern in such a way that there was a predominance of downward social comparisons.

What do these results imply? First, they show that objective reality as it may be indicated by disease progression did not have an influence on social comparison ratings. Second, these results indicate that in making comparisons patients used the large interpretative space when asked to make the self-referent judgment *compared to other patients* to construct favorable dissimilarities by presumably relying on other than disease-related comparison dimensions.

☐ Conclusion

The main proposition of this chapter suggests that people actively construe their views of the self and the world and that the impact of cancer (or any other traumatic event) depends largely on how well these experiences can be incorporated into their belief systems. We presented a heuristic model that describes the process by which this can be accomplished. This information-processing approach represents an attempt to account for empirical results, that show that many victims of a life crisis do not appear to become intensely distressed following the experience of loss and crisis, as well as to account for the striking variability that is observed in responses to a single life crisis, such as the diagnosis of cancer (see also Wortman & Silver, 1992). We think that it is the active and, not necessarily, intentional construction of reality that may help to explain the observed variability in these responses. The study of coping with cancer, in our view, yields the most striking evidence with respect to this issue since this disease is associated with a diversity of objective strains (such as medical treatment procedures) and objective changes in life as well (Filipp, 1992; Klauer & Filipp, 1997). But it seems that the degree of threat which may be expected from a researcher's or, more general, an outside perspective is not equally reflected in patients' emotional responses. It is especially these divergences, that led us to focus on attentive, comparative, and interpretative processes by which, in our view, objective reality is transformed into a perceptive and an interpretative one.

Apparently, many cancer patients are highly flexible in using these processes to construct a world still worth living in in order not to lose hope. In our empirical illustration, we presented evidence on social comparison activity that was observed in patients differing in cancer progression. Here we found unequivocal evidence that patients were engaged primarily in downward social comparisons irrespective of their medical status and that these comparisons were associated with the maintenance of hope across time. Even for those patients whose cancer did progress and who ultimately had to face their approaching death, evidence for downward comparisons was nevertheless observed. We do not have data on how veridically these patients' perceived the worsening of their disease, yet they obviously were still strong enough to perceive their coping efforts as more effective than those of other patients. It is this freedom in selecting dimensions on which one may compare oneself that helps to brighten up even the darkest sides of life.

By presenting these results we have only focused on a small segment within the process of coping with cancer. It is important to note that we do not want to give the impression that an information-processing view of coping with cancer necessarily implies that each coping effort will yield a positive end—and thus create a new myth in coping research. Surely there may be times when comparative processes do not work in shaping a perceptive reality. This may happen when one's subjective reality can no longer withstand objective reality, and when the arbitrariness in construing perceptions and interpretations is reduced. As we have reported elsewhere, there was an increase in hopelessness within the sample of terminal cancer patients that was supportive of this view (see Filipp, 1992). A second point which seems to be of crucial importance if reality construction should have positive effects is the exchange and validation of our self and world views in social interaction. When individuals are no longer able to socially verify their construals, to communicate and validate them via social feedback, their confidence in stating that the world is as it is may no longer be supported. Yet as our results from patients near death show, even then there may still be some room for interpretative processes.

☐ References

Abelson, R. P. (1981). Psychological status of the script concept. *American Psychologist, 36,* 715–729.

Ackermann, R., & DeRubeis, R. J. (1991). Is depressive realism real?. *Clinical Psychology Review, 11,* 565–584

Antonovsky, A. (1987). The salutogenic perspective: Toward a new view of health and illness. *Advances, 4,* 47–55.

Block, J., & Colvin, C. R., (1994). Positive illusions and well-being revisited: Separating fiction from fact. *Psychological Bulletin, 116,* 28.

Brandtstaedter, J., & Renner, G. (1992). Coping with discrepancies between aspirations and achievements in adult development: A dual-process model. In L. Montada, S.-H. Filipp, & M. Lerner (Eds.), *Life crises and experiences of loss in adulthood* (pp. 301–319). Hillsdale, NJ: Erlbaum.

Brandtstaedter, J., & Greve, W. (1994). The aging self: Stabilizing and protective processes. *Developmental Review, 14,* 52–80.

Breznitz, S. (1986). Are there coping strategies? In S. McHugh, & T. M. Vallis (Eds.), *Illness behavior: A multidisciplinary model* (pp. 325–329). New York: Plenum Press.

Broadbent, D. E. (1958). *Perception and communication.* London: Pergamon Press.

Bulman, R. J., & Wortman, C. B. (1977). Attributions of blame and coping in the "real world": Severe accident victims react to their lot. *Journal of Personality and Social Psychology, 35,* 351–363.

Buunk, B. P. (1994). Social comparison processes under stress: Towards an integration of classic and recent perspectives. *European Review of Social Psychology, 5,* 211–241.

Carver, C. S., & Scheier, M. F. (1993). Vigilant and avoidant coping in two patient samples. In H. W. Krohne (Ed.), *Attention and avoidance. Strategies in coping with aversiveness* (pp. 295–319). Seattle, WA: Hogrefe and Huber.

Colvin, C. R., & Block, J. (1994). Do positive illusions foster mental health? An examination of the Taylor and Brown formulation. *Psychological Bulletin, 116,* 3–20.

Emmons, R. A., Colby, P. M., & Kaiser, H. A. (1998). When losses lead to gains: Personal goals and the recovery of meaning. In P. T. P. Wong & P. S. Fry (Eds.), *The human quest for meaning: A handbook of psychological research and clinical applications* (pp. 163–178). Mahwah, NJ: Erlbaum.

Engel, G. L. (1968). A life setting conductive to illness: The giving up-given up complex. *Annual International Medicine, 69*, 293–300.

Festinger, L. (1954). A theory of social comparison processes. *Human Relations, 7*, 117–140.

Filipp, S.-H. (1992). Could it be worse? The diagnosis of cancer as a prototype of traumatic life events. In L. Montada, S.-H. Filipp, & M. Lerner (Eds.), *Life crises and experiences of loss in adulthood* (pp. 23–52). Hillsdale, NJ: Erlbaum.

Filipp, S.-H. (1999). A three-stage model of coping with loss and trauma: Lessons from patients suffering from severe and chronic disease. In A. Maercker, M. Schuetzwohl, & Z. Solomon (Eds.), *Posttraumatic stress disorder: A life-span developmental perspective* (pp. 43–78). New York: Hogrefe & Huber.

Filipp, S.-H., & Aymanns, P. (1996). Coping. In T. von Uexkuell, R. H. Adler, J. M. Herrmann, K. Koehle, O. W. Schonecke, & W. Wesiack (Eds.), *Psychosomatic medicine* (5th ed., pp. 277–289). Munich: Urban & Schwarzenberg.

Filipp, S.-H., & Ferring, D. (1998). Befindlichkeitsregulation durch temporale und soziale Vergleichsprozesse im Alter? [Regulation of subjective well-being in old age by temporal and social comparisons?]. *Zeitschrift für Klinische Psychologie, 27*, 93–97.

Filipp, S.-H., Klauer, T., Freudenberg, E., & Ferring, D. (1990). The regulation of subjective well-being in cancer patients: An analysis of coping effectiveness. *Psychology and Health, 4*, 305–317.

Ford, T. M., Liwag-McLamb, M. G., & Foley, L. A. (1998). Perceptions of rape based on sex and sexual orientation of victim. *Journal of Social Behavior and Personality, 13*, 253–262.

Gergen, K. J. (1990). Die Konstruktion des Selbst im Zeitalter der Postmoderne [The construction of self in the age of postmodernism]. *Psychologische Rundschau, 41*, 191–199.

Goethals, G. R., Messick, D. M., & Allison, S. T. (1991). The uniqueness bias: Studies of constructive social comparison. In J. Suls & T. A. Wills (Eds.), *Social comparison. Contemporary theory and research* (pp. 149–176). Hillsdale, NJ: Erlbaum.

Hakmiller, K. L. (1966). Threat as a determinant of downward comparison. *Journal of Experimental Social Psychology* (Suppl. 1), 32–39.

Harvey, J. H. (1996). *Embracing their memory: Loss and the social psychology of storytelling.* Boston: Allyn & Bacon.

Heckhausen, J., & Schulz, R. (1995). A life-span theory of control. *Psychological Review, 102*, 284–304.

Herek, G. M., & Capitanio, J. P. (1997). AIDS stigma and contact with persons with AIDS: Effects of direct and vicarious contact. *Journal of Applied Social Psychology, 27*, 1–36.

Horowitz, M. J. (1982). Stress response syndromes and their treatment. In L. Goldberger, & S. Breznitz (Eds.), *Handbook of stress* (pp. 711–733). New York: Free Press.

Hoyt, M. F. (Ed.) (1996). *Constructive therapies.* New York: Guilford Press.

Janoff-Bulman, R. (1992). *Shattered assumptions: Towards a new psychology of trauma.* New York: Free Press.

Joreskog, K. G., & Sorbom, D. (1996). USREL8: User's reference guide. Chicago: Scientific Software.

Klauer, T., & Filipp, S.-H. (1997). Life change perception in cognitive adaptation to life-threatening illness. *European Review of Applied Psychology, 47*, 181–188.

Klauer, T., Ferring, D., & Filipp, S.-H. (1998). "Still stable after all this ...?": Temporal comparison in coping with severe and chronic disease. *International Journal of Behavioral Development, 22*, 339–355.

Klinger, E. (1975). Consequences of commitment to and disengagement from incentives. *Psychological Review, 82*, 1–25.

Krampen, G. (1979). Hoffnungslosigkeit bei stationären Patienten: Ihre Messung durch einen Kurzfragebogen (H-Skala) [Hopelessness in hospital patients. A German version of the H-scale]. *Medizinische Psychologie, 5*, 39–49.

Krohne, H.-W. (Ed.). (1993). *Attention and avoidance. Strategies in coping with aversiveness.* Seattle, WA: Hogrefe & Huber.

Lazarus, R. S. (1993). Coping theory and research: Past, present, and future. *Psychosomatic Medicine, 55,* 234–247.

Lazarus, R. S., & Folkman, S. (1984). *Stress, appraisal, and coping.* New York: Springer.

Montada, L. (1992). Attribution of responsibility for losses and perceived injustice. In L. Montada, S.-H. Filipp, & M. Lerner (Eds.), *Life crises and experiences of loss in adulthood* (pp. 133–162). Hillsdale, NJ: Erlbaum.

Montada, L., & Lerner, M. J. (Eds.). (1998). *Responses to victimizations and belief in a just world.* New York: Plenum.

Rothbaum, F., Weisz, J. R., & Snyder, S. S. (1982). Changing the world and changing the self: A two-process model of perceived control. *Journal of Personality and Social Psychology, 42,* 5–37.

Shaver, K. G. (1985). *The attribution of blame: Causality, responsibility, and blameworthiness.* New York: Springer.

Shaver, K. G. (1992). Blame avoidance: Toward an attributional intervention program. In L. Montada, S.-H. Filipp, & M. Lerner (Eds.), *Life crises and experiences of loss in adulthood* (pp. 163–178). Hillsdale, NJ: Erlbaum.

Shaver, K. G., & Drown, D. (1986). On causality, responsibility, and blameworthiness: A theoretical note. *Journal of Personality and Social Psychology, 50,* 697–702.

Shiffrin, R. M. (1988). Attention. In R. C. Atkinson, R. J. Herrnstein, G. Lindzey, & R. D. Luce (Eds.), *Stevens' handbook of experimental psychology: Learning and cognition* (2nd ed., Vol. 2, pp. 739–811). New York: Wiley.

Sholomskas, D. E., Steil, J. M., & Plummer, J. K. (1990). The spinal cord injured revisited: The relationship between self-blame, other-blame and coping. *Journal of Applied Social Psychology, 20,* 548–574.

Snyder, C. R. (1998). A case for hope in pain, loss, and suffering. In J. H. Harvey (Ed), *Perspectives on loss: A sourcebook. Death, dying, and bereavement* (pp. 63–79). Philadelphia: Brunner/Mazel.

Snyder, C. R., Irving, L. M., & Anderson, J.R. (1991). Hope and health. In C. R. Snyder, & D. R. Forsyth (Eds.), *Handbook of social and clinical psychology: The health perspective.* (Pergamon general psychology series, Vol. 162, pp. 285–305). New York: Pergamon Press.

Stroebe, W., & Stroebe, M. S. (1987). *Bereavement and health. The psychological and physical consequences of partner loss.* Cambridge, MA: Cambridge University Press.

Taylor, S. E. (1983). Adjustment to threatening events: A theory of cognitive adaptation. *American Psychologist, 38,* 1161–1173.

Taylor, S. E. (1984). Issues in the study of coping: A commentary. *Cancer, 53,* 2313-2315.

Taylor, S. E., & Brown, J. D. (1988). Illusion and well-being: A social psychological perspective on mental health. *Psychological Bulletin, 103,* 193–210.

Taylor, S. E., & Brown, J. D. (1994). Positive illusions and well-being revisited: Separating fact from fiction. *Psychological Bulletin, 116,* 21–27

Taylor, S. E., & Lobel, M. (1989). Social comparison activity under threat: Downward evaluation and upward contact. *Psychological Review, 96,* 569–575.

von Foerster, H. (1988). On constructing a reality. In S. C. Feinstein, A. H. Esman, J.G. Looney, G. H. Orvin, J. L. Schimel, A. Z. Schwartzberg, A. D. Sorosky, & M. Sugar (Eds.), *Adolescent psychiatry: Developmental and clinical studies, Vol. 15. Annals of the American Society for Adolescent Psychiatry* (pp. 77–95). Chicago: University of Chicago Press.

Watzlawick, P. (1976). *How real is real?* New York: Random House.

Wayment, H. A., & Taylor, S. E. (1995). Self-evaluation processes: Motives, information use, and self-esteem. *Journal of Personality, 63,* 729–757.

Weinstein, N. D. (1980). Unrealistic optimism about future life events. *Journal of Personality and Social Psychology, 39,* 806–820.

Weisman, A. D. (1979). *Coping with cancer*. New York: McGraw-Hill.

Wills, T. A. (1992). The role of similarity in coping through downward comparison. In L. Montada, S.-H. Filipp, & M. Lerner (Eds.), *Life crises and experiences of loss in adulthood* (pp. 196–212). Hillsdale, NJ: Erlbaum.

Wills, T. A., & Suls, J. (1991). Commentary: Neo-social comparison theory and beyond. In J. Suls, & T. A. Wills (Eds.), *Social comparison. Contemporary theory and research* (pp. 395–411). Hillsdale, NJ: Erlbaum.

Wortman, C. B., & Silver, R. C. (1992). Reconsidering assumptions about coping with loss: An overview of current research. In L. Montada, S. H. Filipp, & M. J. Lerner (Eds.), *Life crises and experiences of loss in adulthood* (pp. 341–365). Hillsdale, NJ: Erlbaum.

11

CHAPTER

Beth Leedham
Beth Meyerowitz

Loss, Adjustment, and Growth after Cancer: Lessons from Patients' Children

Cancer is a traumatic event that is associated with significant losses in the lives of patients with the disease. A large body of research documents that, in the wake of a cancer diagnosis and treatments, patients often experience emotional distress and upheaval, troubling physical symptoms, and significant disruptions in daily activities (Holland & Rowland, 1989; Meyerowitz, Leedham, & Hart, 1998). Fortunately, these acute difficulties typically abate over the year or two following the end of treatment, if the disease remains in remission. Nonetheless, most patients report that the cancer experience changes their lives forever, leaving them with a recurring sense of loss and vulnerability.

The distress and disruption associated with the diagnosis and treatment of cancer is not limited to the patient. The cancer experience unfolds in the context of one's social support system, and cancer's effects can extend to those around the patient (Germino, Fife, & Funk, 1995; Lewis, 1996). Studies indicate, for example, that the spouses of cancer patients experience considerable emotional distress and mood disturbance, often as great as the distress reported by the patients themselves (Keitel, Zevon, Rounds, Petrelli, & Karakousis, 1990; Northouse & Swain, 1987). Most spouses report a gradual reduction in distress and improvement in mood that is similar to the patient's psychosocial recovery, in that it can take up to two years on average (Hoskins, 1995; Northouse, 1984; Ptacek, Ptacek, & Dodge, 1994).

Common sense would suggest that patients' children, too, are likely to experience the cancer diagnosis as traumatic and to suffer a number of losses as a result of the parents' disease and treatments. However, children have received relatively little attention in the research literature on family sequelae of cancer, with most of the existing data focusing on patients' spouses or on the parents of pediatric cancer patients.

The preparation of this chapter was supported in part by grants from the Spencer Foundation and by the American Cancer Society-California Division.

This relative gap in the literature is most unfortunate, given the prevalence of cancer; the American Cancer Society (1998) estimates that three out of four families in the U.S. will have a member diagnosed with cancer. This means that most families will, at some point, be faced with adjusting to the losses associated with the disease, and many of these families will have children still in the home. How children respond to the losses associated with a parent's cancer diagnosis and treatment is the focus of this chapter.

☐ Parental Cancer as a Traumatic Stressor

Cancer can potentially be even more traumatic for patients' children than it is for the patients themselves. Tedeschi and Calhoun (1995) provide a useful framework for understanding why, drawing on existing literature (Abrahamson, Metalsky, & Alloy, 1989; Calhoun & Allen, 1991; Davidson, Fleming, & Baum, 1986; Downey, Silver, & Wortman, 1990; McCann & Pearlman, 1990; Slaby, 1989; Tennen & Affleck, 1990; Weiss & Parkes, 1983). Four key characteristics of traumatic experiences identified by Tedeschi and Calhoun can be extended to be relevant to the experiences of cancer patients' children[1]. First, traumatic experiences are typically sudden and unexpected, meaning that the individual confronted with such an event is unable to prepare him or herself psychologically. For the cancer patient's child, who (depending on age and history) may come to the experience with limited knowledge or understanding of the fact that people even get seriously ill, the precipitousness of a parent's cancer diagnosis may seem enhanced. This may be particularly true in situations in which a parent fails to communicate prior information about suspicious symptoms, visits to the doctor, or biopsies, in order to avoid worrying the child.

Second, a traumatic event is one that is perceived as out of one's own control. Although the fact of a cancer diagnosis is out of the patient's direct control, the adult patient does have straightforward methods of obtaining control in a secondary fashion (Rothbaum, Weisz, & Snyder, 1982), for example, by obtaining good medical care, seeking information about the disease and treatments, and complying with the medical regimen. Patients' children are deprived of direct behavioral ways of obtaining secondary control, however, and even information about the disease cannot be obtained directly from medical personnel and must be filtered through the parent, who may or may not communicate effectively with the child (this lack of information from physicians is also a problem that has been identified by spouses; Northouse, 1989). Children may therefore experience their parents' cancer as something that is doubly out of their control.

Third, negative events that are out of the ordinary are often experienced as traumatic. As Tedeschi and Calhoun (1995) point out, this is often because such events also tend to be unexpected and out of one's own control, but additionally, if an event is unfamiliar, one is unable to draw on experience as one attempts to cope. Others may be unable to provide effective support because they, too, lack experience with the stressor. In the case of parental cancer in general, the event is statistically not

---

[1]Although parental cancer can affect offspring of all ages, our discussion here is relevant chiefly to those who were children or adolescents at the time of the parent's cancer, who are the focus of most of the empirical research on patients' children.

rare, of course. However, among families with children living at home, and especially among those with the youngest parents and youngest children, only a minority will experience parental cancer. For young children, therefore, this is a highly unusual and, potentially, a correspondingly more traumatic event.

Fourth, a traumatic event is one that creates long-lasting problems. In the case of parental cancer, children can face a number of severe short-term stressors, such as a temporarily disabled or hospitalized parent, less time and attention from the healthy parent, financial pressure on the family, increased household responsibilities, and disrupted family routines. Patients' children also may face more permanent family changes, such as the additional stress of taking on a caregiver role, as well as long-term losses, including the threats of recurrence, parental death, and elevated personal risk for cancer—the likelihood of which can at best only be estimated. The severity and uncertainty of these potential long-term losses can make them a chronic source of stress (Koocher, 1986).

Because children may have a less well-developed array of coping strategies available to them than do adults (Brown, O'Keefe, Sanders, & Baker, 1986; Rowland, 1989), all of these losses, serious by any measure, may be made more profound by occurring in the context of limited coping skills. Nevertheless, many children appear to cope successfully with this traumatic stressor. To discover how children respond to a parent's cancer, we begin by reviewing the research on immediate psychosocial responses to parental cancer and then discuss findings from the few research studies that have examined longer-term responses among patients' children. We then address research on predictors of successful coping with this traumatic stressor, and finally, we identify open questions and directions for future research. The literature on children of cancer patients is sparse, and throughout, we illustrate certain points by describing in some detail selected findings from our own research. We collected interview and questionnaire measures from two samples of young-adult daughters of cancer patients who had lived at home when their parents were treated, as well as from two comparison samples of age-matched women whose parents had not had cancer. In both samples, participants provided data on current psychosocial adjustment, health attitudes, and health behaviors, and those whose parents had had cancer provided descriptive, retrospective data about their parents' experience with cancer and their past and present reactions to it (Leedham & Meyerowitz, 1999).

☐ Responses to a Parent's Cancer

Immediate Responses

Family members confronted with the news that a parent has cancer often experience emotional reactions that mirror those of the cancer patient him or herself: intense fear, anxiety, exhaustion, uncertainty, and confusion. In one early study examining responses among family members in general, Cassileth and colleagues (1985) compared psychological responses of oncology outpatients and their next-of-kin (which included chiefly spouses, as well as some parents, children, and siblings), and found high concordance between the two groups on measures of anxiety, distress, and mental health. In another study of chemotherapy outpatients and their family caregivers, Given and colleagues (1993) documented that patients' physical limitations had a substantial impact on caregivers' daily lives, and depression levels were correlated between patients and caregivers.

Reviews and clinical reports have suggested that parental cancer can result in distress, communication problems, and role reorganization within the family (Lewis, 1990; Northouse, 1984; Northouse & Northouse, 1987; Sales, 1991; Sales, Schultz, & Biegel, 1992; Wellisch, 1979). However, the body of empirical research focusing specifically on children of cancer patients at the time of the crisis is quite small. Lichtman and colleagues (1984) were among the first to document distress and disruption in relationships among the children of cancer patients. A sample of 68 breast cancer patients was interviewed regarding how their children were adjusting to their cancer and how the cancer had changed their relationships with their children, who ranged in age from 12 to 37 at the time of diagnosis. Although many patients reported that their relationships with their children had strengthened after diagnosis, 12% of the sample reported at least some deterioration in their relationships with one or more of their children. The types of problems patients reported in addition to relationship tension included extreme fearfulness on the part of the child, denial of the cancer, rejection of the parent, anger and argumentativeness, and acting-out behavior.

Distress and disruption in families of cancer patients have also been the focus of a program of research conducted by Lewis and colleagues (Armsden & Lewis, 1993; Armsden & Lewis, 1994; Lewis, 1990; Lewis, 1996; Lewis, Ellison, & Woods, 1985; Lewis & Hammond, 1992; Lewis, Hammond, & Woods, 1993; Zahlis & Lewis, 1998). In their longitudinal study of 126 families whose mothers had nonmetastatic breast cancer, children and other family members completed interviews assessing their reactions to this family crisis. Descriptive data suggested that young school-aged children (ages 7–10) commonly reported high levels of fear, sadness, loneliness, worry, and sometimes anger about the cancer. Older school-aged children (ages 10–13) commonly discussed the household disruption and role changes associated with their mothers' illness. Adolescents frequently mentioned coping with the competing demands of wanting to help their mothers and wanting to engage in their own activities (Lewis et al., 1985).

Although for many children these feelings may be manageable, research from Compas and colleagues (1994) has documented clinically elevated levels of psychological symptoms among certain subgroups of patients' children. Data were collected from 117 cancer patients, 76 spouses, and 110 children (including young adults, adolescents, and preadolescents) within the first few months of diagnosis. Compared with normative data, greater than expected levels of anxiety, depression, or both were found among young adult children for whom the same-sex parent was the ill parent and among adolescent girls whose mothers had cancer.

In our research, we have found that these emotional reactions can be among the most vividly-recalled responses to a parent's cancer diagnosis. In our initial sample of 45 daughters of cancer patients, all participants recalled having had strong negative emotional reactions to their parents' illness. The responses recalled most frequently by participants included upset (recalled by 71.1% of the sample), anger (62.2%), fear and worry (51.1%), confusion (51.1%), and surprise (22.2%). Family disruption was not uncommon, but we found that family difficulties often related to problems with the healthy parent, rather than with the sick parent. One-fifth of the women in our initial sample recalled having had negative feelings toward the healthy parent, and one-third reported having had problems with the healthy parent's behavior. The types of problems participants recalled had to do with the severity of the healthy parent's emotional reactions or the demands he or she placed on the child (Leedham & Meyerowitz, 1999). We have also found that a substantial proportion of participants had problems in other areas, including negative changes with friends (cited by one-half of the sample), such as friends growing more distant, and negative changes in one's own health in response to the parent's cancer (cited by 40% of the sample), such as headaches, weight loss, or sleep disturbance.

Lasting Responses

Clearly, a cancer diagnosis and its treatment can exert a powerful short-term impact on patients' children. Whether a parent's cancer continues to affect children over the long term is less clear. Although some clinicians have suggested that parental cancer can permanently alter children's personalities and cognitive performance (e.g., Rait & Lederberg, 1989), very little research has directly examined the lasting psychosocial effects of parental cancer.

In the first empirical study addressing this issue, Wellisch and colleagues (1991) compared 60 adult daughters of breast cancer patients with 60 matched comparison women on psychological symptoms, sexual functioning, and health and coping behaviors. The breast cancer group was similar to controls on psychiatric symptoms and coping. Daughters of cancer patients appraised themselves as more likely to get breast cancer than did comparison women, but they were no more likely than comparison women to obtain mammograms or Pap smears or to perform breast self-examination (Wellisch et al., 1991). However, the distributions of behavioral measures were highly skewed in this study, with most patients engaging in very high levels of protective behavior; additionally, the sample was middle-aged (M = 42 years), meaning that participants' susceptibility appraisals and health behaviors may have been more reflective of knowledge of their actual health status than of prior experience with their parents' disease and treatments.

Data from a study by Lewis and colleagues (1994) also address longer-term responses. Data on family functioning were collected from mothers with diabetes, nonmetastatic breast cancer, or fibrocystic breast disease, and from their young children (ages 6–12). Time since diagnosis averaged several years for all groups. Mothers' ratings of their child's behavior were actually *superior* among the breast cancer group, and nurse observers also rated children of cancer patients as better-adjusted behaviorally than children in the other two groups. However, children of women with breast cancer or diabetes had lower self-rated self-esteem scores (Armsden & Lewis, 1994).

We undertook research on the effects of parental cancer in order to examine further the lasting responses to parental cancer. In both of our samples, we found no differences between daughters of cancer patients and comparison women on measures of psychological adjustment. Mood, distress, self-esteem scores, and even grade-point average did not differ between the groups. Nevertheless, qualitative data taken from participants suggested that almost all continued to experience a lasting subjective impact of their cancer experiences that appeared to be too subtle or existential to be measured by general psychological instruments. Participants spoke eloquently about many types of changes they attributed to their parents' cancer experience, including changes in views about cancer, views of health and death, outlooks on life, and social relationships.

Although the cancer group did not differ from comparison women on quantitative measures of adjustment, in our first sample we did find significant differences on some cognitive appraisal variables. The daughters of cancer patients appraised themselves as more susceptible to cancer than did comparison women ($p < .05$), especially those for whom it was the mother, rather than the father, who had had cancer ($p < .05$). Not surprisingly, women whose parents had died of their cancer were more likely to appraise cancer as highly threatening, and cancer treatments as less effective, than did women whose parents had lived.

We measured a variety of self-reported early-detection or prevention behaviors, including smoking, dietary changes, Pap smears, sun exposure, sunscreen use, seeking medical attention for suspicious symptoms, and seeking information about cancer. Despite differences in cognitive appraisals, we found little evidence that experiencing parental cancer was associated with adherence behavior. Women in the cancer group did report performing slightly more breast self-examinations than did women in the comparison group, but this finding was not strongly significant, and it did not replicate in our second sample. Moreover, although women in the cancer group reported engaging in more cancer information-seeking behavior than did comparison women ($p < .001$), they were no more well-informed about cancer than were comparison women ($p > .25$).

A related literature that indirectly addresses the issue of lasting responses to parental cancer is concerned with populations at high risk for cancer. This research has begun to document some psychosocial difficulties and low levels of cancer-protective behaviors among high-risk individuals (many of whom are the children of cancer patients). Specifically this research, much of which has focused on women at risk for breast cancer, demonstrates that high-risk women tend to have exaggerated perceptions about their true susceptibility to cancer (Lerman et al., 1995), probably because they make the common cognitive error of overestimating the role of genetics in cancer etiology and underestimating the importance of other risk factors. This exaggerated risk perception can contribute to high anxiety levels, with data showing that up to one-third of women at risk for breast cancer have clinically elevated anxiety that can impair general functioning (Kash, Holland, Halper, & Miller, 1992; Lerman et al., 1991; Lerman et al., 1993). Women with high anxiety are less likely than those with moderate anxiety to engage in early-detection behavior (Kash et al., 1992; Lerman et al., 1991; Lerman et al., 1993).

Positive Changes After Parental Cancer

Thus far, we have focused on the distress and disruption that follow a diagnosis of cancer in a parent. There is increasing awareness in the literature of the importance of considering positive outcomes, as well. Several theorists have argued that a central task in adjusting to loss is integrating the traumatic experience into one's life by finding a sense of meaning in the event (Janoff-Bulman, 1992; Taylor, 1983; Thompson & Janigian, 1988). According to this argument, extremely negative events threaten the individual's world view, requiring either a change in outlook or a change in the perception of the event. Several studies have found that a majority of cancer patients and survivors report positive changes as a result of their cancer experience (Andrykowski, Brady, & Hunt, 1993; Collins, Taylor, & Skokan, 1990; Curbow, Somerfield, Baker, Wingard, & Legro, 1993). In fact, it is not unusual for patients to report more positive than negative changes in their relationships and perspective on life.

There is some evidence that benefits also may accrue to family members of cancer patients. Germino et al. (1995) found no differences between patients and their partners on finding a sense of meaning and found that the search for meaning decreased perceived threat for both groups. Similarly, Stetz, McDonald, & Compton (1996) reported that caregivers of bone marrow transplant patients discovered "unanticipated rewards and benefits" (p. 1422), particularly in terms of increased family closeness and greater appreciation of life.

In our own research, we have found that children of cancer patients also find lasting benefits in their experience. Over 90% of the women in both of our samples indicated that cancer had caused at least one positive change in their lives. The most common changes included being more open and expressive, coping better with problems, becoming a stronger person, and developing closer relationships with family and friends. We found that the tendency to report personal growth and benefits was positively correlated with appraising the parent's treatments as difficult and with recalling more emotional upheaval at the time of the parents' illness, suggesting that greater threat may have stimulated greater efforts to find meaning and benefits. Data consistent with this hypothesis have also been reported in a pilot study by Mireault and Compas (1996) comparing adolescents and young adults who had lost their parents to death from cancer with those whose parents had survived; those whose parents were deceased were significantly more likely to report finding positive meaning in their experiences with their parents' cancer.

In summary, then, the research findings on immediate adjustment among patients' children appears generally consistent with our conceptualization of parental cancer as a traumatic stressor. The existing body of qualitative and quantitative literature on responses to parental cancer consistently demonstrates that, over the short term, the diagnosis of cancer in a parent can be highly disruptive for children. The degree to which these disruptions persist over time remains unclear, however. Few lasting differences are apparent on measures of psychological functioning, although among the subgroup of children of cancer patients who are at high risk for cancer themselves (i.e., those with a strong family history of heritable cancers), persistent elevations in anxiety and distress may be more likely. Both the data on children of cancer patients in general and the literature on high-risk groups suggest that these individuals may have a persistently elevated sense of personal susceptibility to cancer, but that this experience does not necessarily translate into elevated levels of cancer-protective health behaviors. Finally, despite the lack of differences among children of cancer patients and comparison groups on measures of general psychological adjustment, limited data suggest that cancer patients' children may have a lasting, subjective sense of being profoundly affected by their parents' cancer experiences. Many of these subjective changes are positive.

☐ Predictors of Successful Coping

The impact that cancer appears to have on patients' children gives rise to questions regarding how children cope effectively with this trauma. A word is warranted regarding how effective coping might be defined. In their seminal work on the topic of coping, Lazarus and Folkman (1984) define coping as "constantly changing cognitive and behavioral efforts to manage . . . demands that are appraised as taxing or exceeding the resources of the person (p. 141)." Within this framework, two general types of successful coping can be identified. Effective problem-focused coping is behavior that manages the stressor, by altering the stressor itself or reducing one's exposure to it. For example, the cancer patient who complies with her chemotherapy regimen is engaging in a problem-focused coping behavior aimed at eliminating the stressor itself. In situations that are not amenable to problem-solving approaches, however, emotion-focused coping strategies aimed at managing emotional reactions to the stressor may be most adaptive (Lazarus & Folkman, 1984).

As noted earlier, a parent's cancer diagnosis constitutes a stressor that is largely beyond a child's control; it is a situation in which children may find few effective problem-focused strategies available to help them cope directly with the stressor. Perhaps for this reason, the limited research on coping with parental cancer has tended to focus on variables related to emotional adjustment, such as behavioral problems among young children, psychological distress, and self-esteem, as the primary outcome variables of interest. A number of variables have been identified as possibly influencing these outcomes. They include variables related to the individual child, variables related to the situation itself, and family variables. These categories do not appear to be distinct, but rather are likely to overlap and influence coping in a dynamic fashion.

Characteristics of the Child

Two studies specifically on the children of cancer patients suggest that two characteristics of the child, age and gender, may influence coping interactively. In the first, more descriptive study, described above, Lichtman and colleagues (1984) found that mothers with breast cancer were more likely to experience problems in their relationships with their daughters than with their sons, and a relatively large proportion of those problem relationships were with adolescent, rather than younger or adult, children. In their quantitative research examining predictors of adjustment among cancer patients' children, Compas and colleagues (Compas et al., 1994) have found that adolescent girls whose mothers had cancer were more at risk for psychological distress symptoms than girls whose fathers were ill or boys whose fathers or mothers were ill.

One mechanism responsible for elevated risk among adolescent girls appears to be the increased household responsibilities that are frequently placed on girls in the family (Grant & Compas, 1995). Coping behavior may serve as another mechanism: using a larger sample that included the adolescent subsample described above, Compas and colleagues (Compas, Worsham, Ey, & Howell, 1996) have identified emotion-focused coping strategies, particularly cognitive avoidance, as predictors of anxiety and depression. This is likely not because emotion-focused strategies in general are ineffective, but rather because avoidance is a particularly ineffective type of emotion-focused strategy. A growing literature confirms that cognitive approach coping strategies can foster effective adjustment after a traumatic stressor, and avoidance strategies can hamper coping efforts (e.g., Carver et al., 1993; Stanton & Snider, 1993).

Characteristics of the Cancer Situation

There are likely a number of factors related to the stressful situation itself that may influence a child's adjustment to the trauma of parental cancer. The variable that has received the most attention has been disease severity. Data indicate that relatively mild forms of cancer and cancer treatments are associated with better adjustment in patients' family members. For example, in their study comparing the concordance of psychological reactions among oncology outpatients and next-of-kin, described earlier, Cassileth and colleagues (1985) found that for both patients and relatives, psychological well-being was best among those receiving follow-up care only, was poorer among those receiving active treatment, and was worst among those receiving palliative treatment.

Lewis and colleagues have postulated that the mechanism responsible for this relationship is the degree to which the disease renders both the ill parent and the healthy parent unavailable (Lewis, Hammond, & Woods, 1993, Lewis, Woods, Hough, & Bensley, 1989, Zahlis & Lewis, 1998). In some cases, parents may become unavailable emotionally; as Zahlis & Lewis (1998) point out, a mother's depression has been linked to impaired parenting (Brody, Stoneman, & Burke, 1987; Goodman & Brumley, 1990; Orvaschel, 1983). In others, the absence may be physical and literal; even when no evidence of depression exists, illness demands, such as hospitalization, illness after chemotherapy, or frequent trips to radiation therapy can limit children's access to a parent (Armsden & Lewis, 1994).

The most extreme case of this, of course, is when the disease is terminal, and the parent dies. A large literature on bereavement includes numerous reports documenting that grief reactions are normal among children. Mood disturbance in bereaved children may be particularly elevated in the first few months after a death and may be especially likely to be marked by anxiety (see Kranzler, 1990, for a review). The degree to which parental death places children at long-term risk for psychological problems is unclear, however.

Early reports suggested that bereaved children in general were at risk for later adult psychiatric diagnoses, including major depression, with parental death exerting the greatest long-term impact on children who are younger than 10 years of age at the time of the parent's death (e.g., Barry & Lindemann, 1960; Brown, Harris, & Copeland, 1977). A few studies have examined children's responses to parental terminal cancer specifically. Seigel and colleagues (1992) compared children whose parents had advanced cancer and children whose parents were not ill on self-report measures of depression, anxiety, self-esteem, and parent-rated behavior problems. All parents in the cancer group eventually died within six months of data collection. Not surprisingly, children of parents with terminal cancer showed relative elevations on all measures of psychological distress and on behavioral problems, although it is unknown how long these elevations persisted. The sole published study directly comparing children of patients who died from cancer to those whose parents survived found no differences between the groups on measures of anxiety and depression collected within the year following the death (although the sample size was very small and included no preadolescents; Mireault & Compas, 1996).

Some recent research on parental death in general has begun to indicate that it may be family variables, such as poor family functioning after the death, rather than the loss itself, that accounts for the relationship between parental death and current or later depression (Breier, Kelsoe, Kirwin, Beller, Wolkowitz, & Pickar, 1988; Harris, Brown, & Bifulco, 1986; West, Sandler, Pillow, & Baca, 1991). Our data are consistent with this view; in both of our studies of women whose parents had had cancer, we found that whether the parent had lived or died was unrelated to contemporary measures of psychological adjustment, but variables related to family communication did predict distress levels. We now turn to a discussion of some of these family variables.

Characteristics of the Family

Within the literature on children of cancer patients, clinical opinion holds that open communication about cancer is beneficial for patients' children (Adams-Greenly & Moynihan, 1983; Grandstaff, 1976; Northouse & Northouse, 1987). Some limited empirical research supports the hypothesis that open communication predicts better adjustment among patients' children, at least in the short term (Lewis et al., 1989; Vess, Moreland, & Schwebel, 1985a, 1985b; Walsh-Burke, 1992). In interviews with 48 fathers with young children whose wives had either nonmetastatic breast cancer, diabetes, or fibrocystic breast disease, Lewis and colleagues (1989) found that fathers reporting higher levels of psychosocial functioning in their children also reported more open communication, higher levels of marital adjustment, and better quality of the father-child relationship. In a study of role functioning in families in which a parent has cancer, Vess and colleagues (1985a, 1985b) documented that parents' ratings of good marital communication were associated with better role management, less role strain, more cohesion, and less conflict within the family over time. Data from an intervention designed to enhance communication and adjustment in 14 families experiencing an adult cancer revealed that higher self-ratings of family communication were associated with improved subjective ratings of adjustment to the cancer (Walsh-Burke, 1992).

Data from our initial study suggested that a variable related to communication about the cancer, namely, satisfaction with how one was told about the parent's cancer, predicted a significant and substantial proportion of the variance in distress above that accounted for by individual and situational variables. We considered that this finding might have been anomalous, and we further explored this issue in the second sample.

We examined a number of variables related to family functioning, including the source of information about the parents' diagnosis, the degree of delay in the child's learning about the diagnosis, ratings of satisfaction with how one was told about the diagnosis, and ratings of past family closeness and communication. Unlike the first sample, which was comprised entirely of White participants, this second sample was ethnically diverse, with over two-fifths being members of ethnic minority groups. In the second sample, the communication finding was replicated, but only among the subgroup of White participants: among this subgroup, cancer-related communication variables predicted a significant amount of the variance in present distress, above that accounted for by individual and situational variables. Those who were more distressed were younger at the time of diagnosis, were less satisfied with how they were told about the diagnosis, had poorer past family communication, were more likely to be told about the diagnosis by a source other than one or both of the parents, and were told about the cancer either before the parent herself knew about the diagnosis or immediately upon diagnosis. Participants who knew about the cancer soonest tended to have been told of the diagnosis by a physician as they waited for their mother to recover from a biopsy, or they learned of the diagnosis immediately because they had accompanied their mothers to doctors' appointments. It is possible that this relationship between the timing of the news and later distress actually represents distress attributable to problems associated with being the primary source of social support for one's mother, rather than to communication issues per se.

Among ethnic minority participants, prior family communication did not bear a relationship to current distress levels. Qualitative data further explored this issue. We had asked participants to describe the types of advice they might offer to other potential cancer patients and their children. Although a majority of participants in both groups endorsed open family communication, we found that ethnic majority participants (40.5%) were significantly more likely than those from ethnic minority groups (17.2%) to recommend to other children that they communicate openly, share their feelings, and think positively. Majority participants were also significantly more likely to recommend to parents that they be honest with their children (83.3% vs. 62.1%), and they were also more likely to endorse the importance of maintaining a positive attitude (35.7% vs. 10.3%). Ethnic minority participants, on the other hand, were significantly more likely to offer the advice that parents spend extra time with their children (24.1% vs. 7.1%).

These data are exploratory, and, to be sure, the designation "ethnic minority" is not conceptually meaningful (unfortunately, our sample sizes were too small to examine individual ethnic groups separately). Moreover, our goal was not to compare ethnic groups to find differences, such efforts being of questionable theoretical and clinical utility (Meyerowitz, Richardson, Hudson, & Leedham, 1998). Rather, these preliminary data illustrate that the predictors of long-term adjustment among cancer patients' children may be numerous, and the relations among predictors may be complex. Family communication is an understudied variable that may be relevant to adjustment for many persons, and variables related to the family context in which this stressor unfolds may play a greater role in predicting later adjustment than do the actual facts of the situation, including whether the parent lives or dies. However, family coping processes in response to cancer differ dramatically across cultures (Gotay, 1996), and the types of family processes that foster adjustment to parental cancer may differ among groups.

Moreover, family process itself may vary across time; as Northouse (1984) discusses, early in the disease process, the chief problems faced by families include managing emotional reactions and interacting with medical staff. As the family adapts to the diagnosis, the challenge is to adjust to changes in roles and lifestyles, meet the needs of well family members, and manage the uncertainty of the situation. Should the disease evolve into a terminal phase, the family faces the tasks of communicating about death, providing care to the dying family member, and managing the separation and loss. The family environment and parental coping can also influence the types of coping strategies children use; for example, children coping with sickle cell disease are more likely to be hopeful and optimistic when they have parents who suggest active coping strategies, and general family cohesion is associated with active coping among children (Kliewer & Lewis, 1995). Thus, the individual child, possessing his or her own strengths, vulnerabilities, and coping skills, copes with a changing stressor in the context of a dynamic family environment, and the individual, the stressor, and the family environment can influence each other in an evolving fashion.

☐ Conclusion

Parental cancer possesses the characteristics of a traumatic event as set forth in the loss and trauma literature, and existing data show that this experience is indeed traumatic for most children. Clinical reports and a relatively small empirical literature confirm that, in response to a cancer diagnosis and its treatment, children have many of the same reactions that patients do, such as emotional distress and social disruption. Also, as is typically the case with patients, most children appear to eventually adjust to this trauma. Some data suggest that over the long term, children of cancer patients may differ from their peers on some attitudinal variables and may have a strong subjective sense of being different, but do not appear to differ on general measures of psychological adjustment. However, existing data on lasting sequelae have been collected from high-functioning samples, and it is possible that a subgroup of patients' children may be at greater risk for lasting adjustment difficulties. A number of additional questions remain unclear; in particular, it is unknown precisely how children achieve good adjustment after parental cancer. Only a few studies have begun to examine the processes by which children adjust. A number of possible predictors of adjustment have been tentatively identified, including variables related to the child, to the cancer situation, and to the social and family context in which the stressor unfolds. A few research studies have begun to examine mechanisms of risk, including cognitive coping and parental support.

In their review of developmental issues in posttraumatic growth, Aldwin and Sutton (1998) point out that the construct of resilience subsumes a number of protective factors identified in studies on vulnerability among children undergoing stress. This literature consistently identifies female gender, high intelligence, easygoing temperament, and positive social interactions as characteristics of resilient children (although the gender relationship appears to reverse in adolescence, when girls are more likely to get depressed in response to stressful events—which may help to explain further the findings in the parental cancer literature on adolescent girls). Research on adult cancer patients also has shown that dispositional variables are significant predictors of psychosocial outcomes, through their relationship to coping behavior (Carver et al., 1993). However, personality or temperamental variables have not been examined as possible predictors of responses to parental cancer. Other possible predictors that have not been empirically examined include financial and other structural resources (e.g., health insurance, childcare, education) available to the family. Research on adults suggests that economically disadvantaged cancer patients experience poorer medical and quality of life outcomes (see Meyerowitz et al., 1998, for a review), and a similar pattern may be found among patients' children.

In addition to a more in-depth examination of possible predictors of good outcomes, future research on responses to parental cancer can benefit from a deeper examination of possible mediators. The process by which children make their adjustment has not been fully explored, although some research teams have begun to identify factors responsible for variation in outcomes. The program of research conducted by Lewis and colleagues, for example, describes parental marital discord and availability of parental support as possible characteristics directly affecting children's outcomes. Another possible variable related to social support that merits examination is support obtained from the medical team; patients who perceive better emotional support, empathy, and communication skills on the part of their physicians report greater satisfaction with their care and higher levels of adjustment (Burton & Parker, 1994; Roberts, Cox, Reintgen, Baile, & Givertini, 1994; Wiggers, Donovan, Redman, & Sanson-Fisher, 1990).

As another example, Compas and colleagues (1996) have described the relationships between approach and avoidance coping strategies and later outcomes; another possible but unexamined cognitive coping strategy that could serve as a mediator is cognitive attribution. As Tedeschi and Calhoun (1995) point out, literature on adults' attributions for traumatic events demonstrate that blaming others for negative events is often associated with worse psychological outcomes over the long term (Abrahamson, Metalsky, & Alloy, 1989; Downey, Silver, & Wortman, 1990; Tennen & Affleck, 1990), probably because it increases a sense of powerlessness; self-blame, on the other hand, can provide a sense of control, however grim, over the event. Blaming oneself for a traumatic event also enables the individual to believe that future similar events are avoidable (as in the case of the rape survivor who blames herself for leaving a door unlocked, and resolves to take better precautions in the future; Janoff-Bulman, 1979). In the case of younger children witnessing a family crisis, however, attributions to self may be easily made and may be highly maladaptive. For example, self-blaming phenomena have been described among young children who are themselves cancer patients (Rowland, 1989) and among school-aged girls whose attributions of self-blame for marital conflict are associated with internalizing behavior problems as rated by the parent (Cummings, Davies, & Simpson, 1994).

In addition to these conceptual issues, future research on immediate and lasting responses to parental cancer must grapple with methodological difficulties. For immediate responses, few existing studies have provided multifaceted and standardized assessments of outcomes. Additionally, some general outcomes that have proved extremely meaningful in research with patients themselves, such as subjective ratings of quality of life, have not been considered at all among patients' children. To be sure, identifying an appropriate battery of measures of quality of life for patients' children would be challenging, because the issues of greatest importance, and the assessment tools best suited to address them, will vary with the developmental stage of the child and the specifics of the cancer situation.

Understanding lasting responses raises a different set of methodological issues. The available literature indicates that children of cancer patients adjust to the trauma in most domains, and standardized measures of overall functioning have not been sensitive to the sense of "being different" that many children report. Thus, although the types of effects that persist may be experienced by the individual as profound, they may not be easily measurable; effective study of lasting responses to parental cancer may therefore require new approaches to measuring such existential changes. Additionally, it seems clear that this trauma, like many others, provides opportunities for growth. Such important reactions may be obscured if research focuses primarily on distress and disruption as the outcomes of interest. A complete description of lasting responses requires consideration of how and when individuals find meaning and accrue benefit to their experience with parental cancer.

Future research that capitalizes on a longitudinal, multivariate, interdisciplinary approach—drawing on the psychosocial oncology, developmental, and trauma and loss literatures—can begin to fill many of these gaps in the literature on responding to the trauma of parental cancer. Further information about the consequences of parental cancer can produce immediate clinical benefits by providing information on how best to help the many parents and children who will face this trauma. Additional research in this area can also broaden our understanding of the impact of trauma on individuals who are not the initial victim.

☐ References

Abrahamson, L. Y., Metalsky, G. I., & Alloy, L. B. (1989). Hopelessness depression: A theory-based subtype of depression. *Psychological Review, 96*, 358–372.

Adams-Greenly, M., & Moynihan, R. T. (1983). Helping the children of fatally ill parents. *American Journal of Orthopsychiatry, 53*, 219–229.

Aldwin, C. M., & Sutton, K. J. (1998). A developmental perspective on posttraumatic growth. In R. G. Tedeschi, C. L. Park, & L. G. Calhoun (Eds), *Posttraumatic growth: Positive changes in the aftermath of crisis* (pp. 43–63). Mahwah, NJ: Lawrence Erlbaum.

American Cancer Society. (1998). *Cancer facts and figures–1998*. Atlanta, Georgia: Author.

Andrykowski, M. A., Brady, M. J., & Hunt, J. W. (1993). Positive psychosocial adjustment in potential bone marrow transplant recipients: Cancer as a psychosocial transition. *Psychooncology, 2*, 261–276.

Armsden, C. G., & Lewis, F. M. (1993). The child's adaptation to parental medical illness: Theory and clinical implications. *Patient Education and Counseling, 22*, 153–165.

Armsden, G. C., & Lewis, F. M. (1994). Behavioral adjustment and self-esteem among school-age children of mothers with breast cancer. *Oncology Nursing Forum, 21*, 39–45.

Barry, H., & Lindemann, E. (1960). Critical ages for maternal bereavement in psychoneurosis. *Psychosomatic Medicine, 22*, 366–381.

Breier, A., Kelsoe, J. R., Kirwin, P. D., Beller, S. A., Wolkowitz, O. M., & Pickar, D. (1988). Early parental loss and development of adult psychopathology. *Archives of General Psychiatry, 45*, 987–993.

Brody, G. H., Stoneman, Z., & Burke, M. S. (1987). Family system and individual child correlates of sibling behavior. *American Journal of Orthopsychiatry, 57*, 561–569.

Brown, G., Harris, T., & Copeland, J. (1977). Depression and loss. *British Journal of Psychiatry, 30*, 1–18.

Brown, J. M., O'Keefe, J., Sanders, S. H., & Baker, B. (1986). Developmental changes in children's cognition to stressful and painful situations. *Journal of Pediatric Psychology, 11*, 343–358.

Burton, M. V., & Parker, R. W. (1994). Satisfaction of breast cancer patients with their medical and psychological care. *Journal of Psychosocial Oncology, 12*, 41–63.

Calhoun, L. G., & Allen, B. G. (1991). Social reactions to the survivor of suicide in the family; A review of the literature. *Omega, 23*, 95–107.

Carver, C. S., Pozo, C., Harris, S. D., Noriega, V., Scheier, M. F., Robinson, D. S., Ketcham, A. S., Moffat, F. L., & Clark, K. C. (1993). How coping mediates the effect of optimism on distress: A study of women with early stage breast cancer. *Journal of Personality and Social Psychology, 65*, 375–390.

Cassileth, B. R., Lusk, E. J., Strouse, T. B., Miller, D. S., Brown, L. L., & Cross, P. A. (1985). A psychological analysis of cancer patients and their next-of-kin. *Cancer, 55*, 72–76.

Collins, R. L., Taylor, S. E., & Skokan, L. A. (1990). A better world or a shattered vision? Changes in life perspectives following victimization. *Social Cognition, 8*, 263–285.

Compas, B. E., Worsham, N. L., Epping-Jordan, J. E., Grant, K. E., Mireault, G., Howell, D. C., & Malcarne, V. L. (1994). When mom or dad has cancer: Markers of psychological distress in cancer patients, spouses, and children. *Health Psychology, 13*, 507–515.

Compas, B. E., Worsham, N. L., Ey, S., & Howell, D. C. (1996). When mom or dad has cancer II: Coping, cognitive appraisals, and psychological distress in children of cancer patients. *Health Psychology, 15*, 167–175.

Cummings, E. M., Davies, P. T., & Simpson, K. S. (1994). Marital conflict, gender, and children's appraisals and coping efficacy as mediators of child adjustment. *Journal of Family Psychology, 8*, 141–149.

Curbow, B., Somerfield, M. R., Baker, F., Wingard, J. R., & Legro, M. W. (1993). Personal changes, dispositional optimism, and psychological adjustment to bone marrow transplantation. *Journal of Behavioral Medicine, 16*, 423–441.

Downey, G., Silver, R. C., & Wortman, C. B. (1990). Reconsidering the attribution-adjustment relation following a major negative event: Coping with the loss of a child. *Journal of Personality and Social Psychology, 59,* 925–940.

Germino, B. B., Fife, B. L., & Funk, S. G. (1995). Cancer and the partner relationship: What is its meaning? *Seminars in Oncology Nursing, 11,* 43–50.

Given, C. W., Stommel, M., Given, B., Osuch, J., Kurtz, M. E., & Kurtz, J. C. (1993). The influence of cancer patients' symptoms and functional states on patients' depression and family caregivers' reaction and depression. *Health Psychology, 12,* 277–285.

Goodman, S., & Brumley, H. (1990). Schizophrenic and depressed mothers: Relational deficits in parenting. *Developmental Psychology, 26,* 31–39.

Gotay, C. C. (1996). Cultural variation in family adjustment to cancer. In L. Baider, C. L. Cooper, & A. K. De-Nour (Eds.), *Cancer and the family* (pp. 31–52). New York: Wiley.

Grandstaff, N. (1976). The impact of breast cancer on the family. *Frontiers of Radiation Therapy and Oncology, 11,* 145–156.

Grant, K. E., & Compas, B. E. (1995). Stress and anxious-depressed symptoms among adolescents: Searching for mechanisms of risk *Journal of Consulting & Clinical Psychology, 63,* 1015–1021.

Harris, T., Brown, G. W., & Bifulco, A. (1986). Loss of parent in childhood and adult psychiatric disorder: The role of lack of adequate parental care. *Psychological Medicine, 16,* 641–659.

Holland, J. C., & Rowland, J. H. (Eds.). (1989). *Handbook of psychooncology: Psychological care of the patient with cancer.* New York: Oxford University Press.

Hoskins, C. N. (1995). Adjustment to breast cancer in couples. *Psychological Reports, 77,* 435–454.

Janoff-Bulman, R. (1979). Characterological versus behavioral self-blame: Inquiries into depression and rape. *Journal of Personality and Social Psychology, 37,* 1798–1809.

Janoff-Bulman, R. (1992). *Shattered assumptions: Towards a new psychology of trauma.* New York: Free Press.

Kash, K. M., Holland, J. C., Halper, M. S., & Miller, G. (1992). Psychological distress and surveillance behaviors of women with a family history of breast cancer. *Journal of the National Cancer Institute, 84,* 24–30.

Keitel, M. A., Zevon, M. A., Rounds, J. B., Petrelli, N. J., & Karakousis, C. (1990). Spouse adjustment to cancer surgery: Distress and coping responses. *Journal of Surgical Oncology, 43,* 148–153.

Kliewer, W., & Lewis, H. (1995). Family influences on coping processes in children and adolescents with sickle cell disease. *Journal of Pediatric Psychology, 20,* 511–525.

Koocher, G. P. (1986). Coping with a death from cancer. *Journal of Consulting and Clinical Psychology, 54,* 623–631.

Kranzler, E. M. (1990). Parent death in childhood. In L. E. Arnold (Ed.), *Childhood stress.*

Lazarus, R. S., & Folkman, S. (1984). *Stress, appraisal, and coping.* New York: Springer.

Leedham, B., & Meyerowitz, B. (1999). Responses to parental cancer: A clinical perspective. *Journal of Clinical Psychology in Medical Settings, 6,* 441–461.

Lerman, C., Daly, M., Sands, C., Balshem, A., Lustbader, E., Heggan, T., Goldstein, L., James, J., & Engstrom, P. (1993). Mammography adherence and psychological distress among women at risk for breast cancer. *Journal of the National Cancer Institute, 85,* 1074–80.

Lerman, C., Lustbader, E., Rimer, B., Daly, M., Miller, S., Sands, C., & Balshem, A. (1995). Effects of individualized breast cancer risk counseling: A randomized trial. *Journal of the National Cancer Institute, 87,* 286–292.

Lerman, C., Trock, B., Rimer, B., Jepson, C., Brody, D., & Boyce, A. (1991). Psychological side effects of breast cancer screening. *Health Psychology, 10,* 259–267.

Lewis, F. M. (1990). Strengthening family supports: Cancer and the family. *Cancer, 65,* 752–759.

Lewis, F. M. (1996). The impact of breast cancer on the family: Lessons learned from the children and adolescents. In L. Baider, C. L. Cooper, & A. K. De-Nour (Eds.), *Cancer and the family.* Chichester, England: Wiley.

Lewis, F. M., Ellison, E. S., & Woods, N. F. (1985). The impact of breast cancer on the family. *Seminars in Oncology Nursing, 1,* 206–213.

Lewis F. M., & Hammond, M. A. (1992). Psychosocial adjustment of the family to breast cancer: A longitudinal analysis. *Journal of the American Women's Association, 47,* 194–200.

Lewis, F. M., Hammond, M. A., & Woods, N. F. (1993). The family's functioning with newly diagnosed breast cancer in the mother: The development of an explanatory model. *Journal of Behavioral Medicine, 16,* 351–370.

Lewis, F. M., Woods, N. F., Hough, E. E., & Bensley, L. S. (1989). The family's functioning with chronic illness in the mother: The spouse's perspective. *Social Science & Medicine, 29,* 1261–1269.

Lichtman, R. R., Taylor, S. E., Wood, J., Bluming, A., Dosik, G., & Leibowitz, R. (1984). Relations with children after breast cancer: The mother-daughter relationship at risk. *Journal of Psychosocial Oncology, 2,* 1–19.

McCann, I. L., & Pearlman, L. A. (1990). *Psychological trauma and the adult survivor: Theory, therapy, and transformation.* New York: Bruner/Mazel.

Meyerowitz, B. E., Leedham, B., & Hart, S. (1998). Psychosocial considerations for breast cancer patients and their families. In J. J. Kavanagh, A. Z. DePetrillo, N. Einhorn, S. Pecorelli, & E. Singletary (Eds.), *Cancer in women.* Cambridge, MA: Blackwell.

Meyerowitz, B. E., Richardson, J. E., Hudson, S., & Leedham, B. (1998). Ethnicity and cancer outcomes: Behavioral and psychosocial considerations. *Psychological Bulletin, 123,* 47–70.

Mireault, G. C., & Compas, B. E. (1996). A prospective study of coping and adjustment before and after a parent's death from cancer. *Journal of Psychosocial Oncology, 14,* 1–18.

Northouse, L. (1984). The impact of cancer on the family: An overview. International *Journal of Psychiatry in Medicine, 14,* 215–242.

Northouse, L. L. (1989). The impact of breast cancer on patients and husbands. *Cancer Nursing, 12,* 276–284.

Northouse, L. L., & Swain, M. A. (1987). Adjustment of patients and husbands to the initial impact of breast cancer. *Nursing Research, 36,* 221–225.

Northouse, P. G., & Northouse, L. L. (1987). Communication and cancer: Issues confronting patients, health professionals, and family members. *Journal of Psychosocial Oncology, 5,* 17–46.

Orvaschel, H. (1983). Maternal depression and child dysfunction. In B. B. Lahey & A. E. Kazdin (Eds.), *Advances in child clinical psychology* (Vol. 6, pp. 169–197). New York: Plenum.

Ptacek, J. T., Ptacek, J. J., & Dodge, K. L. (1994). Coping with breast cancer from the perspectives of husbands and wives. *Journal of Psychosocial Oncology, 12,* 47–72.

Rait, D., & Lederberg, M. (1989). The family of the cancer patient. In J. C. Holland & J. H. Rowland (Eds.), *Handbook of psychooncology: Psychological care of the patient with cancer* (pp. 585–597). New York: Oxford University Press.

Roberts, C. S., Cox, C. E., Reintgen, D. S., Baile, W. F., & Gibertini, M. (1994). Influence of physician communication on newly diagnosed breast patients' psychologic adjustment and decision-making. *Cancer, 74*(1 Suppl.), 336–341.

Rothbaum, F., Weisz, J., & Snyder, S. (1982). Changing the world and changing the self: A two-process model of perceived control. *Journal of Personality and Social Psychology, 42,* 5–37.

Rowland, J. H. (1989). Developmental stage and adaptation: Child and adolescent model. In J. C. Holland & J. H. Rowland (Eds.), *Handbook of psychooncology: Psychological care of the patient with cancer* (pp. 519–543). New York: Oxford University Press.

Sales, E. (1991). Psychosocial impact of the phase of cancer on the family: An updated review. *Journal of Psychosocial Oncology, 9,* 1–18.

Sales, E., Schulz, R., & Biegel, D. (1992). Predictors of strain in families of cancer patients: A review of the literature. *Journal of Psychosocial Oncology, 10,* 1–26.

Siegel, K., Mesagno, F. P., Karus, D., Christ, G., Banks, K., & Moynihan, R. (1992). Psychosocial adjustment of children with a terminally ill parent. *Journal of the American Academy of Child and Adolescent Psychiatry, 31*, 327–333.

Slaby, A. E. (1989). *Aftershock: Surviving the delayed effects of trauma, crisis, and loss.* New York: Villard.

Stanton, A. L., & Snider, P. R. (1993). Coping with a breast cancer diagnosis: A prospective study. *Health Psychology, 12*, 16–23

Stetz, K. M., McDonald, J. C., & Compton, K. (1996). Needs and experiences of family caregivers during marrow transplantation. *Oncology Nursing Forum, 23*, 1422–1427.

Taylor, S. E. (1983). Adjusting to threatening events: A theory of cognitive adaptation. *American Psychologist, 38*, 1161–1173.

Tennen, H., & Affleck, G. (1990). Blaming others for threatening events. *Psychological Bulletin, 108*, 209–232.

Tedeschi, R. G., & Calhoun, L. G (1995). *Trauma & transformation: Growing in the aftermath of suffering.* Thousand Oaks, CA: Sage.

Thompson, S. C., & Janigian, A. S. (1988). Life schemes: A framework for understanding the search for meaning. *Journal of Social & Clinical Psychology, 7*, 260–280.

Vess, J. D., Moreland, J. R., & Schwebel, A. I. (1985a). An empirical assessment of the effects of cancer on family role and functioning. *Journal of Psychosocial Oncology, 3*, 1–16.

Vess, J. D., Moreland, J. R., & Schwebel, A. I. (1985b). A follow-up study of role functioning and the psychological environment of families of cancer patients. *Journal of Psychosocial Oncology, 3*, 1–14.

Walsh-Burke, K. (1992). Family communication and coping with cancer: Impact of the We Can Weekend. *Journal of Psychosocial Oncology, 10*, 63–81.

Weiss, R., & Parkes, C. M. (1983). *Recovery from bereavement.* New York: Basic Books.

Wellisch, D. K. 91979). Adolescent acting out when a parent has cancer. *International Journal of Family Therapy, 1*, 230–241

Wellisch, D. K., Gritz, E. R., Schain, W., Wang, H., & Siau, J. (1991). Psychological functioning of daughters of breast cancer patients. Part I: Daughters and comparison subjects. *Psychosomatics, 32*, 324–336.

West, S. G., Sandler, I., Pillow, D. R., & Baca, L. (1991). The use of structural equation modeling in generative research: Toward the design of a preventive intervention for bereaved children. *American Journal of Community Psychology, 19*, 459–480.

Wiggers, J. G., Donovan, K. O., Redman, S., & Sanson-Fisher, R. W. (1990). Cancer patient satisfaction with care. *Cancer, 66*, 610–616.

Zahlis, E. H., & Lewis, F. M. (1998). Mothers' stories of the school-age child's experience with the mother's breast cancer. *Journal of Psychosocial Oncology, 16*, 25–43.

CHAPTER Amerigo Farina

The Few Gains and Many Losses for Those Stigmatized by Psychiatric Disorders

☐ The Stigma of Mental Disorders

This chapter is concerned with stigma. When someone is stigmatized he or she is undeservedly besmirched and degraded because of some characteristic that makes that individual less worthy in society's estimation and often in the individual's own self-regard. Stigma is an astonishingly pervasive phenomenon. It can be caused by conditions such as ethnicity, skin color, obesity, deformities of the body, physical appearance, criminality, and even pregnancy (Jones et al., 1984). Students of these matters believe that any significant departure, and possibly any noticeable departure, from societal ideals of pedigree, personal history, and appearance can be stigmatizing. Here we will be examining one of the unlimited numbers of conditions that can ruin people's lives and lead to a daily struggle to reduce the stigma's impact. A well-known stigma that will serve as an example is obesity. Being fat can become an individual's major worry in life and it has spawned myriad diets, drug aids, and even radical and dangerous surgical procedures. In this chapter, the concern is the stigma of psychiatric disorders. Like obesity, it is a particularly potent blemish; this chapter will focus upon the kinds and degree of losses psychiatric disorders engender.

First however, a question: why are mental afflictions so demeaning? Perhaps the major factors are the societal beliefs and attitudes that prevail in this and seemingly in every other society (Farina, 1998, p. 253). Among the most important and influential of these beliefs are that mentally disordered individuals are unpredictable, tense, and highly dangerous. They tend to be viewed as qualitatively different from ordinary people and to have an unsavory, occult connection with the spirit world. One source of these present disparaging beliefs are past events, both actual and legendary, involving mental patients. Virtually all of the information from ancient times indicates that throughout history insane individuals were regarded with fear and loathing and imbued with inhuman, demonic characteristics. The Bible, Greek history and mythology, and Roman writings all portray those afflicted with mental disorders as profoundly different from ordinary human beings (Deutsch, 1965; Farina, 1982; Zilboorg & Henry, 1941). These sources tell us they have become (or are possessed by) demons and can be expected to behave accordingly. Thus, Hercules killed his brother's and his own children while possessed by a demon. The popular name for insane people in Roman times was *larvatus,* meaning full of phantoms. During the Middle Ages those who displayed what are now regarded as common symptoms of mental disorders were thought to be witches and in the power of demons. The affected individual was likely to be killed by being burned to death, a procedure that was thought to expel these supernatural entities while saving the soul from eternal perdition. While such burning is in the past, the exorcising of demons is not over, and it is currently practiced by some religious denominations.

More recent beliefs, and the practices to which they lead, surely are also responsible for the present societal repugnance visited on mental patients. During colonial times in America, the insane were thought to be insensitive to heat and cold and even in cold New England they were housed in unheated quarters in the winter. This view seems more appropriate for snakes than disturbed people. The treatments used at those times should be considered to understand contemporary perceptions of the mentally disordered. These included ministrations like beatings, blistering the body, removing parts of their intestines, castrating men and removing the clitoris of women, and transfusing animal blood into their veins. Could these things be done if the patients were regarded as sentient human beings? Quite recently a variety of shock treatments employing drugs and continuous electric shock were used to render patients unconscious. Even more extreme were the various operations that entailed entering the skull in order to surgically remove parts of the brain. The institutions where patients were housed (and, in lesser numbers, continue to be housed) can still be seen at the edges of cities and towns, surrounded by walls, looking like jails rather than places to heal people. Knowledge about these beliefs and practices is transmitted across generations and, even if the entire history is generally not known, the past apparently continuous to convey an image of the mentally ill as fearful, mysterious, and satanic beings.

We should now consider whether mental patients—and the infamous reputation they continue to have now—really are degraded and rejected because of what has happened in the past. That is, would a random sample of normal people be stigmatized simply because they were thought to be mental patients but were otherwise typical individuals? The answer is an unqualified yes, as research, some of which we will examine, convincingly reveals (e.g., Farina & Felner, 1973). But they are stigmatized for other reasons in addition to simply being patients. That perpetuates and adds to the stigma in a complicated interaction. Those individuals who become mental patients display socially objectionable behaviors long before, during, and after their hospitalization. Indeed, it is typically those behaviors that cause them to be identified and hospitalized as mental patients. In a seminal study of this issue, Zigler and Phillips (1961) tabulated symptoms displayed by individuals newly admitted to a psychiatric hospital. The three most common symptoms, all shown by at least 35% of the 793 patients in the sample, were depression, tension, and suspiciousness. Among the 15 most common symptoms were also assaultiveness, drinking, hallucinating, and withdrawal. Ample data exists indicating that people showing such behaviors are disliked (e.g., Gurtman, 1986). Not only are mentally disordered individuals characterized by comportment that make them disliked but they also, as a group, fail to acquire a repertoire of behaviors that are indispensable for continued social interaction. As a result, they are rejected and isolated (Farina, Fisher, & Fischer, 1992). The more severe the mental disorder developed as adults, the more socially incompetent and isolated were people found to be throughout their lives. This association seems to cover the gamut from relatively normal people to the most profoundly mentally disordered. And so mental patients are stigmatized because they display disliked behaviors and lack social skills as well as simply because they are known to be mental patients.

The foregoing are not the only factors leading to the social stigma that is such a painful and ubiquitous problem for people afflicted with mental difficulties. A sizable literature has accumulated that indicates people with mental afflictions are less physically attractive than comparable individuals whose adjustment is good. This research has been summarized several times (e.g., Burns & Farina, 1992). What makes these findings important for this chapter is that unattractive people are themselves strongly disliked and treated less favorably than more comely individuals (e.g., Herman, Zanna, & Higgens, 1986). This lifelong social rejection may be partly responsible for the increased probability that unattractive individuals will develop a mental disorder. An additional variable leading to the social avoidance and isolation of those unfortunates tainted by mental problems is fear of contamination. An overview of the phenomenon of contamination is provided by Posner (1976):

> [I]n our society it is not only the deviant who is stigmatized but also those who are associated or aquainted with the deviant . . . . Even an innocuous or casual walk down the street with the stigmatized other tends to stigmatize a person who accompanies such an individual. (p. 27)

A summary of some of the research on contamination is provided by Mehta and Farina (1988) who also offer hypotheses as to why contamination occurs. Among these hypotheses are: 1) people that appear together are seen as alike, and 2) if someone associates with a marginal person (i.e., someone bearing a social stigma), he or she cannot be worth very much. People are aware that they can be encompassed by someone else's blemish and so avoid stigmatized people thereby heaping further rejection on them. A final reason for the degradation of mental patients is one that is initially surprising: their fear that they will be socially repulsed causes them to behave in an objectionable manner thus producing the very rejection they fear. This will be considered further in a subsequent section but the following illustrative study of this phenomenon should make it clearer. Subjects who had been mental patients were interviewed by an employment interviewer to allegedly rate them for competence as a worker (Farina, Gliha, Boudreau, Allen, & Sherman, 1971). Half the subjects were told the interviewer was aware they were former mental patients while the rest were informed he thought they were former *medical* patients. The interviewer (actually another experimenter) was not aware of what the subjects had been told. When the subjects believed they were viewed as former mental patients, they felt less appreciated, found a task they were asked to do more difficult, and performed more poorly than did subjects in the other condition. The interviewer also rated them as more tense, anxious, and poorly adjusted than subjects in the medical patient group. So we see a diverse set of factors that conspire to poison the social life of those unlucky people who are afflicted with mental disorders.

☐ Losses

Having considered stigma and its causes we now turn our attention to the central concern of this chapter, namely, the losses endured by those who are stigmatized. A helpful way to organize the totality of these losses in order to facilitate understanding of this complex matter is to divide the losses into two categories: subjective losses and objective losses. In the natural course of events these two kinds of losses to the victim do not occur separately. Rather, in most instances they go hand in hand, one being a kind of mirror image of the other. But there are important differences between them. Subjective injuries are done to the internal, personal life of the individual. They hurt self-esteem, confidence, and expectations that the future will be pleasant and manageable. Such injuries are not directly observable and need to be inferred. They are most easily assessed by self-reports and narratives. An example of such losses are reports by an ex-psychiatric patient that he is ashamed to meet acquaintances because they think he is crazy. Objective damage caused by stigma, on the other hand, is the kind that can be observed and measured; generally the data obtained are quantitative rather than qualitative as in subjective losses. As an example, consider a study by Farina and Felner (1973). During an employment interview it was subtly conveyed to applicants for a job who were thought to be ex-mental patients, relative to controls, that they were significantly less likely to be given a job with the company.

Turning first to intrapersonal losses, there are two good sources of information about the destructive effects caused by social stigma. One source is the many autobiographies written by people who have had the misfortune of experiencing a mental disorder. These span a long period of time and encompass many nationalities. Some of these personal histories are well known, such as Clifford Beers' (1948) *A Mind That Found Itself: An Autobiography*. Beers (1876–1943) was a college student at the onset of his disorder and the detailed, careful description of his subjective experiences and the humiliations he encountered had a significant impact on the perception and care of people with psychiatric problems in the United States. As we might expect, even within a small sample of these autobiographies there is a lot of variation from one to another but there is also a strong common theme. For the victims of psychiatric disorders the personal subjective consequences constitute a major part of the suffering caused by a mental breakdown. One such victim, Joan Houghten (1980), provides an eloquent and convincing description of the diminution of her personal worth following her hospitalization. In her view, friends, employers, and even her church subjected her to degrading rebuffs. She writes

> Part of the recovery process from mental illness involves overcoming a problem of even greater magnitude than the illness itself: the negative feelings and attitudes of others toward the mentally ill. For lack of a better word, we call this problem 'stigma.' For me, the stigma of mental illness was as devastating as the experience of hospitalization itself. (1980, p. 7)

Spontaneously written narratives by people who have been in the unwelcome role of psychiatric patients impressively gives us a vivid glimpse into what it is like for the afflicted. However, these sources do not provide the systematic, organized information we would like to have about the nature and degree of the psychic damage that stigma inflicts upon its victims. Some studies have been done that gather specific, if spotty, systematic information and highlight the usefulness of this approach. Obviously, such studies also rely on subjective reports but the reports are directed by the investigator toward securing the desired information. In one of these, Vellenga and Christensen (1994) interviewed patients being treated at a mental health clinic, asking each how their disorder had affected their lives. One cluster of consequences that emerged was a feeling on the part of the patients that they were discredited and shamed. They were conscious of being treated and perceived differently. One patient said, "I feel shunned . . . How do you tell people that you don't work, but there's nothing physically wrong. I wish I'd have a heart attack or some physical problem. Then people would understand" (p. 365). A second cluster of consequences was loss of self-esteem, relationships, and employment. The patients reported a radical separation from others and an impoverishment of their lives. And the patients also experienced the onset of acute distress that did not relent nor even diminish noticeably. One patient put it this way, "Physical suffering goes away, but mental suffering has been going on for 20 years. It's just never ending" (p. 368).

Several studies provide more precise data and paint a picture of life, following a mental disorder, that is very bleak and devoid of those basic satisfactions that are readily available to the average person. Thus, Flanagan (1978) found that a high proportion of American adults, 85%, felt that their most important needs in life were well met. In contrast to that, only 56% of a population with a chronic mental disorder reported being mostly satisfied with their lives (Lehman, Ward, & Linn, 1982). And Perese (1997) reveals that large percentages of a group of 73 chronic mental patients had basic needs that were not satisfied: having no friend was reported by 62%, no role in life or mostly no job, by 60%, not belonging to a group was a problem for 56%, and 55% complained of having no self-identity.

It seems obvious that the internal life of those victimized by mental problems can be truly bad, approaching a living, unending hell. Social stigma may not be the exclusive cause of this horror but it certainly plays a highly important part. Note, though, that the information on which this pessimistic conclusion is based focuses on individuals with severe mental disorders. What is life like for the much larger group troubled by milder conditions? Unfortunately, the lion's share of the data that has been gathered has centered on the more showy serious problems. Not very much direct information is available on which to base a judgment about the mildly affected majority. However, while there is disagreement on this matter, there are good reasons for believing that mental disorders are ranged along a continuum of quantitative differences, rather than consisting of qualitatively different entities. If that is true, as I believe it to be, then the intrapersonal lives of people who have milder disorders are similar to those experienced by those more seriously afflicted. They, too, are in misery but a misery that, in keeping with their more moderate afflictions, probably is less all-encompassing and painful.

Before turning to the demonstrated objective losses that mental problems engender for the victim, there is a general phenomenon of which we must note. As soon as someone is identified as suffering from a psychological disorder, that person is exposed to all the problems caused by that stigma. So those who are least able to cope with the world and are, therefore, helped by mental health practitioners, are immediately degraded by others, and therefore are in some ways worse off than they were before they were helped. People have a general awareness of this pattern of events, including people who are receiving help or are considering getting it. Followers of political events are conscious of the devastating negative effects that involvement in psychiatric treatment can have on politicians. The 1972 Democratic vice-presidential nominee, Thomas Eagelton, was promptly dropped from the ticket when it was revealed that he had undergone such treatment. And in 1998 President Clinton, during his administration, experienced considerable emotional turmoil and sought help in dealing with it. But he chose the clergy to provide that help, and not a mental health professional (Urbinas, 1998). That decision was widely believed to reflect Clinton's fear of being stigmatized as mentally unstable if he saw a mental health professional.

Less anecdotal information regarding this blighting of people treated by mental health workers is available. A group of 47 Israelis who had refused to meet a psychiatrist in a primary care clinic were interviewed to discover why they had refused the help offered (Ben-Noun, 1996). Among the nine types of explanations given, the most prevalent were: "I am afraid people would think I am insane" and "It might interfere with my social relationships and threaten my job." In another study, newly admitted medical and psychiatric inpatients, 30 in each group, were asked their willingness to reveal their admission and diagnosis to friends, family members, and people at work (McCarthy, Prettyman, & Friedman, 1995). The psychiatric patients were less willing to have the information disclosed. And a group of college students, all of whom had been hospitalized for psychiatric conditions, were asked about their feelings regarding the hospitalization (Dougherty et al., 1996). The students feared they would be regarded as mentally ill if the admission became known and were very concerned and anxious about that prospect. A similar pattern was encountered by Hollingshead and Redlich (1958) while they were doing research for their influential book, *Social Class and Mental Illness: A Community Study*. They found that New Haven residents receiving psychotherapy were being treated in large numbers in the city of New York, and not locally. Their therapists were reluctant to give the researchers the information sought about them. The patients had gone to New York because they feared knowledge of the treatment would endanger their jobs and social status. The therapists were hesitant to do anything that might increase the probability of discovery.

And yet, doctors seem to operate under the general rule that, when in doubt, the safest course of action is to assume a morbid condition is present and to treat it accordingly. That certainly appears to be the current practice with Lyme disease where antibiotics are likely to be administered if the disease is merely suspected. Advice columns in newspapers consistently tell readers to consult professionals if there is any possibility of a morbid condition, specifically mental problems. This seems to be a wise approach for conditions like Lyme disease, cancer, or heart problems where quick action might prevent more serious morbidity and even save lives. After all, what is to be lost? There are no serious negative consequences if therapy is started and it is later found that there is no Lyme disease. For psychiatric diagnoses, however, there are negative consequences because of the stigma and they can be very serious. This is illustrated by a case of a young man who was incorrectly given a diagnosis of schizophrenia following an emotional upset and thereafter encountered striking social stigmatization (Witztum, Margolin, Bar-On, & Levy, 1995).

Perhaps the worst aspect of being tainted by a history of mental disorder is that it is virtually impossible for those to whom it happens to remove the stain. A general overview of the problem is provided by Wahl's book (1995) where he points out the damaging consequences of having been mentally ill. Because of the stigma, people are reluctant to seek, accept, or reveal psychiatric treatment. After treatment, they encounter rejection, discrimination, and restriction of opportunity. Link, Struening, Rahav, Phelan, and Nuttbrock (1997) measured the effects of stigma of psychiatric care on the well-being of 84 men, all of whom had psychiatric problems and were drug addicts. The measures were taken on two occasions. The first was at the time they entered treatment, when they displayed many psychiatric symptoms and were addicted to drugs, while the second took place one year later, when they were far less symptomatic and mostly free of drugs. In spite of being essentially cured, the stigma continued to have a strong negative effect on their well-being. And for a cohort of ex-patients discharged from a state mental hospital, it was found that the stigma resulting from the institutionalization went with them into the community with destructive effects (Dewees, Pulice, & McCormick, 1996). They were followed for four years by means of interviews with multiple informants and were found to be poorly integrated into the community. During the study period, 87% of them were again hospitalized for periods ranging from three months to one year. An important factor in creating the unmanageable problems the ex-patients encountered was judged to be social stigma. Using laboratory procedures, rather than field methods, Rodin and Price (1995) did some carefully controlled experiments to determine the permanence of stigma in general. They found that once someone was flawed by a degrading condition, overcoming that flaw did not restore that someone to an unblemished status. Once stigmatized, the individual continued to suffer the degradation of the stigma and was less valued than an otherwise comparable individual who had never been degraded. Interestingly, subjects admired individuals who had overcome some stigmatizing characteristic through their own efforts but, nevertheless, preferred the company of otherwise comparable others who had never been blemished.

We now turn to the objective losses that are caused by the social degradation of psychiatric disorders. Of course, some mental health professionals assert that there is no such degradation (Bentz & Edgerton, 1971; Crocetti, Spiro, & Siassi, 1974) or, at worst, that it is fast disappearing (Segal, 1978). If that is true, there would be no losses to concern us. Unfortunately, the most convincing studies indicate otherwise. Two sets of studies replicated, respectively, about 20 years apart (Farina & Ring, 1965, replicated by Piner & Kahle, 1984) and 25 years apart (Lamy, 1966, replicated by Skinner, Berry, Griffith, & Byers, 1995) found that the stigma continues to be strongly present over those periods of time. Moreover, there is evidence that the authors reporting benign or improving attitudes may be basing their conclusion on artifacts. Brockman, D'Arcy, and Edmonds (1979) classed studies of changes in attitudes toward mental disorders into two groups: those that report attitudes are improving and those that report they are not. These researchers then examined the methodology of the studies and the adequacy of the researcher's training and found that it was the poorer studies and those done by the less well-trained researchers that report attitudes to be improving. The sounder investigations disclose a poorer fate of continued negative social views that faces the victims of mental disorder.

A lot of the research on what happens to psychiatric patients in our society has focused on important facets of community living such as employment and housing. We will consider these facets individually and see a coherent picture that is revealing when the entire mosaic emerges.

Work

Work is a cardinal determiner of someone's identification and status as a person in Western society. It is perhaps of greater importance for a man than a woman but the sexes are becoming similar in this regard. Upon meeting someone or hearing about him or her, a critical thing we seek to know is his or her occupation. Hugely different reactions can occur depending on what the occupation is revealed to be. But our occupational life affects more than how others regard us and our own self-respect, as significant as these are. The kind of work we do determines our income, and having no job generally means virtually no income. So even our physical well-being is dependent on our occupation or lack thereof. No wonder, then, that researchers have been concerned with the possible damage of stigma on the working life of the mentally disordered.

This area of research is very old, rich, and varied, and, except for a few quirks, seemingly quite unequivocal. Some studies have utilized interviews and self-report questionnaires and the subjects have been both employers and former mental patients. In the case of two studies (Olshansky, Grob, & Ekdahl, 1960; Olshansky, Grob, & Malamud, 1958), there being no laws against discrimination toward the mentally ill at that time, 25% of the employers stated flatly that they would not hire former mental patients. And 40% of those who would hire them would do so only if they could be placed in nondemanding, low pressure jobs. More telling, only 26 of 200 employers had knowingly hired an ex-mental patient in the preceding three years and only five were prepared at that time to hire an ex-patient who was fully qualified for the job. A more contemporary study reveals a similar picture of prejudice and stigmatization, particularly in the case of smaller companies (Manning & White, 1995). That study was done in England and the harsh attitudes found may reflect more lenient laws against discrimination there than in the USA.

Behavioral studies yield very similar results (Farina & Felner, 1973; Link, 1987; Link, Cullen, Mirotznik, & Struening, 1992). The first study listed is a particularly realistic one since an experimenter, in the guise of a man trying to find work, actually sought jobs from 32 business establishments. He gave identical work histories in each place but in 16 he also reported having had a psychiatric hospitalization while no such information was given to the other 16. The economy was depressed at the time of the study and not enough jobs were offered to test for differences between the two conditions, although four jobs were offered in the control in comparison to two jobs in the patient condition. Having expected such an outcome, the researchers also surreptitiously recorded the interview between the employment interviewer and the applicant. These tapes were then blindly rated for friendliness of the interviewer and for probability that the applicant would find a job there. The employment interviewers were found to be significantly less friendly and indicated the probability of finding a job was significantly lower in the mental patient than the control condition.

The second study (Link, 1987; Link et al., 1992), although quite different, obtained results consistent with those of Farina and Felner. Former mental patients who expected society to reject people with a psychiatric history were, in fact, more likely to be unemployed than comparable individuals who did not anticipate stigmatization. For a control group free of mental problems, expectations that mental hospitalization would elicit rejection were not related to employment. It appears that, at least for ex-mental patients who are concerned about their employability, some noxious personal or interpersonal processes are generated that interfere with finding work.

Finding a job is not the only problem a man who has suffered from a psychiatric disorder may encounter if he seeks employment. If he is hired, he will find that difficulties engendered by his psychiatric history are by no means over. Please note that the preceding assertion refers to males. That is quite deliberate because research suggests that females may meet with a more generous reception in the workplace and rather clearly shows that women are kinder to coworkers with a psychiatric history than are males (Farina, 1981). But male workers already on the job seem not to welcome someone as a coworker if that person has had a mental problem. In one relevant study (Farina, Felner, & Boudreau, 1973), male VA hospital workers were told that since they knew their own job best, management wanted them to meet a job applicant and evaluate how well he would do if hired to work with them. The applicant was actually a researcher who was presented as an ex-mental patient to half the workers and as an ex-surgical patient to the rest. Those in the mental patient condition, in comparison to the others, expected to get along more poorly with him, they expected him not to do well on the job, they recommended him less strongly for the job, and they imbued him with stereotypic mental patient characteristics such as being unpredictable. That study was replicated with a female researcher who was presented to male workers as an ordinary applicant or as a former mental patient (Farina, Murray, & Groh, 1978). The workers again responded more negatively to the applicant in the mental patient condition although the male researcher/applicant was more decisively rejected.

Housing

Both formal research and societal events convincingly show that ex-psychiatric patients encounter special obstacles in finding housing because of their history. A notorious incident occurred in Long Beach, New York, that was widely reported. In 1974 this seaside Long Island community was no longer attracting tourists and many of its hotel rooms remained unoccupied. State mental hospitals began housing discharged patients in those hotels. The residents of the town were not so keen about this, however, and they passed a law barring anyone in need of continuous psychiatric care and medication from living in those hotels. Quite obviously, this law was aimed at keeping former mental patients away from the community.

A carefully done study by Page (1977) strongly supports the conclusions prompted by the Long Beach incident. Advertisers wishing to rent furnished rooms or flats whose ads appeared in newspapers on a particular day were telephoned by a female researcher. She telephoned a sample of 30 different advertisers in each of several conditions, in each case asking if the property was still available. She said nothing unusual about herself in the control condition, while for another condition she revealed that she was about to leave a mental hospital. In still another condition, she stated that she was inquiring for her brother who was about to be released from jail. Whereas she received 25 positive response in the control condition, not more than 9 such responses were obtained in the other conditions. Both the jail and mental hospital conditions were significantly different from the control but were not different from each other. Twenty advertisers who had been called for either the mental hospital or jail condition and who had reported their property as no longer available were called a second time using the control procedure. On the second call, 18 of the 20 reported that the room or flat *was* available for rent. A subsequent replication of that study confirmed the earlier findings although the results were less striking (Page, 1995). An ex-patient seeking housing certainly faces a dismal situation and has good reason for not disclosing his or her troubled history to a potential landlord.

Neighbors

Why are landlords so cautious about renting to former mental patients? We might reasonably think they expect such individuals to have little money and so refuse them housing to avoid trouble trying to collect the rent. But we saw earlier that residents of Long Beach wanted to keep ex-patients out of their town when the payment of rent was not an issue. Most probably, the answer to the question of why people want those who have had mental problems kept away lies in the stigma society attaches to them. Unfortunately, that answer does not provide very much clarification. Stigma is a perplexing phenomenon that consists more of mystery than enlightenment. What the answer does tell us is that people would not be happy to have ex-patients move near them. A surfeit of evidence makes the truth of the foregoing assertion amply clear. As in the case of housing, this evidence can be gleaned from societal events and can be found in the systematic research done by social scientists.

Some of the former kind of evidence has been conveniently gathered and published as a book (Fink & Tasman, 1992). The book is actually a report of part of the proceedings of the 1989 annual meeting of the American Psychiatric Association, the theme of which was "overcoming stigma." In one of the chapters of that book (Farina, Fisher, & Fischer, 1992), the authors cite newspaper reports that indicate deinstitutionalization is hampered because of the resistance of people to having former patients move near them. A specific item cited by them appeared in the *Hartford Courant* and was based on a reporter's interview with Audrey M. Worrell who was then the Connecticut Mental Health Commissioner. According to Worrell, there were 14 group homes for deinstitutionalized mental patients in Connecticut at that time. In establishing them, community resistance had been encountered in 7 of the 14, in the form of local zoning actions or regulatory delays. At least eight proposed homes could not be opened because of local hostility. Also, three homes were under construction at that time and two of them had met with opposition.

The same chapter describes a notorious event which occurred in Greenwich, Connecticut, that very vividly illustrates how unwelcome as neighbors people known to have mental problems are. A group home for psychiatric patients was opened in that town and residents on the same street asked the Greenwich Board of Tax Review to lower the amount at which their houses were evaluated for tax purposes. They argued that the presence of the shelter housing mental patients reduced the market value of their houses since potential buyers would not want to live near such an establishment. The Board evidently accepted the validity of this argument since the homeowners were granted reductions ranging from $2,960 to $10,270. This event is an unusual one and it was denounced by numerous officials. However, negative societal reactions to those with a history of mental disorder are far from unusual.

Some quite realistic but controlled studies also reveal this same objection that people have to living near ex-mental patients. Two of these studies are very similar and can be described simultaneously (Cutler, 1975; Farina, Thaw, Lovern, & Mangone, 1974). A male in his twenties went to people in their own homes and announced he was investigating the problem of finding a place to live faced by people who had been hospitalized for a prolonged period. Half the subjects were told the patients were hospitalized for medical reasons and half were told that they had been admitted for a nervous disorder. They were asked to listen to a tape-recorded interview between the alleged patient and the investigator in order to get a reasonable idea of what kind of person the patient was. Subjects in the two conditions heard the same recording. The subjects were then asked a series of questions about how they and their neighbors would respond if that particular patient were to move into a house nearby.

The results of two studies show that, relative to the medical patient condition, the former mental patient is expected to have more trouble finding a job, it is anticipated that the neighbors will not accept him, and he is expected to have greater difficulty in various areas of community functioning. Interestingly, respondents interviewed in the mental patient condition were significantly less willing to take part in similar future experiments than subjects in the medical patient condition. This finding may mean that people find it unpleasant to think about a former psychiatric patient moving into their neighborhood, even if they assert that they themselves—if not their neighbors—would welcome him.

What happens when the person afflicted with a mental disorder is a child? Zultowsky and Farina (1989) did a relevant study in much the same manner as the two studies just reviewed. In the Zultowsky and Farina study, researchers (two women in their twenties) went to homes, introduced themselves as students at a nearby university, and asked the resident for permission to interview them about children. It was then explained that children who once were routinely institutionalized were being returned to the community and the researchers wanted to know how they and their neighbors would feel if a home for such children were established near their houses. The home would house about 15 children but one third of the subjects were told the children were orphans, one third that they were emotionally disturbed, and the remaining one third that they were learning disabled. Following this, the homeowners were verbally given a questionnaire that asked for their reactions, as well as their beliefs about their neighbors' reactions, to such an event. The results showed that the response to establishing such a home was more negative in the retarded and disturbed conditions than in the orphan condition. The two former conditions did not differ from each other. The data also indicated that no group homes of any kind were wanted nearby.

The preceding study is consistent with other research in showing that mental problems are strongly stigmatized whether in adults, children, or vice-presidential candidates. Like other studies, this one finds that the public rejects people with learning disabilities and those with emotional maladies equally, although quite aware of the difference between these conditions. A final point about this study should be noted. It is tempting to think people do not want mentally aberrant people nearby because they fear such people might run amuck and attack anyone available, such as the neighbors. This study suggests that fear of violence is not the only possible source of rejection since it does not seem likely that children constitute a physical threat for most people.

A study by Gillmore and Farina (1989), while not specifically focused on the behavior of neighbors, is relevant to the reception children are likely to receive from people who do not know them when their mental condition deviates from the expected.

Fifth and eighth grade boys individually met another boy of their own age at their school. The boy they met was presented as a child who might be coming to their school. The "new" boy was actually one of six confederates, three of fifth- and three of eighth-grade age. Each subject was asked to tell the newcomer about the school and he was also asked to judge how well the new boy would get along there. The confederate was presented to 1/3 of the subjects in each grade as an ordinary child, to another 1/3 as learning disabled, and to the final 1/3 as emotionally disturbed. The confederates were always blind to condition and, after the interaction, the confederates were questioned about the subject by an experimenter, who was also blind to condition. Behavioral measures showed that subjects in the emotionally disturbed and retarded conditions were less friendly and more anxious than those in the control condition. They also wanted more social distance from the "retarded" and "disturbed" child and expected their peers to be more rejecting toward them relative to the control condition. Essentially, the same results were obtained in the two grades and, as in the Zultowsky and Farina study, the subjects responded to the two mental problem conditions with the same degree of rejection.

The Family

Typically our family is a highly important entity for all of us. It consists of people from whom we anticipate acceptance and support, especially during difficult times. For those afflicted with mental problems who are rejected by society as threatening and sullied, their family may assume a critical role. And yet, family members share the unfavorable cultural beliefs and attitudes of society as a whole toward those with mental problems. Moreover, they are usually unable to avoid contact with the afflicted and so are exposed to their frequently disagreeable and disturbing behaviors. The noxious effect of some of these patient behaviors on family members has been documented (Hooley, 1987). In addition, family members face social rejection because of contamination by the affected relative. Consequently, the family is prone to reject the patient. Rejection by the family must constitute an absolutely devastating loss for mentally ill people who are likely to feel totally abandoned. But this rejection does seem to take place, as the research we will consider indicates.

In accordance with the purposes of this chapter, we wanted to know the severity and frequency of the losses experienced by mental patients as a result of alienation from (or outright stigmatization by) their families. We wanted to know about both subjective as well as objective losses. But there is a dearth of studies overtly probing patients and their families about these issues. That is not surprising, given the taboo nature of such topics. Can a mother be asked if her son is an embarrassment to her and if she would like to get him out of the house? However, we do have plethora of information that speaks clearly, if not always directly, about these matters.

There were three large state mental hospitals in Connecticut before deinstitutionalization lead to their consolidation. One of these was the Connecticut Valley Hospital in Middletown. Beginning in 1878 that institution had a cemetery on its grounds in which inmates who died there were buried if their families did not take possession of the body. What is remarkable about that cemetery is that all of its 1,685 tombstones, each marking a grave, are identical and there are no names on them. On each, there is only a single number which makes the identification of the person buried there possible. An article that appeared in the *Hartford Courant* (Hamilton,

1999), a daily newspaper, revealed that tombstone # 1 marks the grave of Curtis Dart, the first person buried there. He died on July 5, 1878. The professionals at the hospital told me that the practice of leaving the name of the deceased off the tombstone was intended to shield the families of the patients from public awareness that one of their members was insane. That was also the opinion expressed in the *Hartford Courant* article. Such a practice speaks volumes about the relations between patients and their families. That even more extreme measures may be taken by some families is suggested by Eugene O'Neil's play, *Strange Interlude*. In that play, a family hides a mentally deranged relative in the attic because they fear being disgraced if people find out about her. Systematic and carefully done research substantiates these anecdotal observations. Phelan, Bromet, and Link, (1998) interviewed family members of first admission psychiatric patients and found that half reported concealing the hospitalization from society. Some families also reported being avoided by others.

The family is unquestionably exposed to embarrassing and painful experiences because of the afflicted member, which is not to say that justifies selfish and immoral behaviors. The social stigmatizing of families of mental patients has been thoughtfully analyzed by Torrey (1988) who believes it has three main causes. The first is the presence in the home of a mentally disordered person which, for the public, makes the home a dangerous, offensive, and embarrassing place. These societal feelings are the basic components responsible for the repudiation of the mentally ill, and the mentally ill arouse these feelings whether they are at home or elsewhere. The second reason is that the public blames the families for causing the member's mental problems. Believing the families are responsible for the disorder may lead society to regard them as pariahs. Mental health professionals have sometimes been blamed for inducing this belief in the citizenry (Lefley, 1992). Clearly, plenty of publications by professionals, including articles in the popular media, imply or assert outright that it is indeed the family that generates the disorder. Illustrative of this pattern is a paper by Fromm-Reichmann (1948). Its publication date indicates how long this finger pointing has been going on. The article is rather well known because in it the term 'schizophrenogenic mother' (the mother who causes schizophrenia) is first used. That is indeed what the author asserts—that some mothers cause that morbid condition in their children. It seems that numerous practitioners are satisfied in their own minds that some families are guilty of producing the disorder in their relatives. Lefley makes the following statement based on studies that she cites: "Many families have reported their anger, despair, and feelings of stigmatization after interacting with clinicians ranging from studied evasion to outright hostility" (1992, p. 131). This state of affairs seems highly likely to interfere with the rapport between patient and family and to lower the patient's acceptability to the family which constitutes a huge loss for him or her.

It may be that mental health workers have promoted public stigmatization of patients' families by attributing the cause of the disorder to them. However, it is also possible that both parties, the public and the workers in the field of mental health, have negative views of such families because of underlying beliefs in the culture they both share. For example, it seems to be a truism in contemporary Western culture that parents are overwhelmingly important in shaping their children's personalities. Regardless of the validity of this belief, it probably results in misery for the family and causes estrangement from the patient which must be very destructive for him or her.

The third and final cause that Torrey (1988) believes is responsible for the social degradation of the families of patients is contamination. This phenomenon has been described previously and some of the research substantiating its reality has been cited. Recapitulating briefly, there is a penalty to be paid by those who associate with individuals who are stained in some manner, be they handicapped, thieves, or mentally disordered. And so the family acquires some of the characteristics of the affected member and is also sullied and devalued.

Our examination of the conditions in which families and their mentally troubled member find themselves suggests that life for them is difficult and unpleasant. Pertinent direct studies bear out these expectations. Rose (1996) reviewed research on the stress impinging on the family caregivers of mentally ill patients. Stress is high for those families and, as expected, a lot of it is due to social stigma. However, fear that people will discriminate against the patient and a lack of professional support and information also contribute to the family's problems. For the parents, the burden is particularly heavy since more factors generate stress for them in comparison to other family members. For example, they face the future responsibility of chronically providing special care for a handicapped offspring and they are plagued by social and personal suspicions that they may have caused the problem. But siblings also encounter exquisitely painful difficulties, especially if they believe the sibling is able to control his or her behavior (Greenberg, Kim, & Greenley, 1997). Gullekson (1992) provides an eloquent personal account of what it is like for a child when an older sibling develops a serious mental disorder (paranoid schizophrenia) and is hospitalized. The lack of skills to cope with the situation made the experience a catastrophe for her.

☐ Stigma—A Pandemic Problem

Even though some mental health professionals disagree, there are compelling reasons for believing that people who have been afflicted by a mental disorder are strongly stigmatized. A question that now emerges is the following: Is this phenomenon present in all societies or is it something unique to America? If it were a local occurrence, then we might begin to search for its causes in the peculiarities of our culture. If it is much more general than that, we might suspect the problem is generated by any kind of human interaction involving a mentally deviant person. Also, there might be cultures and subcultures that could provide a haven for people who suffer the misfortune of a mental disorder, a misfortune society magnifies with its degradation. Or, conceivably, once the process is better understood, a social haven could be constructed for afflicted individuals. Thus, there are both practical and theoretical reasons for being concerned with the generality of this phenomenon.

The clear answer to the question is that we, in the United States, are not the only ones facing this social phenomenon. For one thing, some of the research literature reviewed comes from other cultures such as Canada and England where psychological research has developed to a level comparable to our own. These studies report that rejection of those with mental problems is the same as in the United States (e.g., Page, 1977). In addition, there are quite a number of reports that show stigmatization is present in cultures that are very different from ours. Thus, Davies and Morris (1990) found it present in Bengal and Thailand. Both Koizumi and Harris (1992) and Munakata (1989) report that the mentally disordered are stigmatized in Japan. Pearson and Phillips (1994) tell us that also happens in China while Rodrigues (1992) finds that it is likewise present in Brazil. Whatever causes stigma seems not to be located in the immediate history of society and its social practices but, rather, deeply within the nature of human beings. Since the phenomenon appears to be a facet of basic human nature, we can expect a great deal of difficulty in eliminating or reducing it.

There are some encouraging findings in this rather dark picture and I end this section with a look at one of these reports. The study is costly but quite realistic (Farina, Hagelauer, & Holzberg, 1976). The authors noted that ex-mental patients complained of not being believed by physicians once their psychiatric history was known. Their symptoms tended to dismissed as imaginary, they reported. One female patient asserted that "Your arm has got to be falling off before they believe you." To check this, appointments were made with 32 medical practitioners by a 23-year-old graduate student in the guise of someone suffering from some physical problems. His complaints, in all cases, were of stomach pains suggestive of ulcers. He reported having had a prior attack nine months earlier. However, he told 16 of these doctors that he had been traveling around the country at the time while he told the other 16 that he had been in a mental hospital at the time.

The researcher had a small tape recorder hidden on his body and the entire conversation between doctor and "patient" was recorded and later analyzed by raters blind to condition. Duration of conversation, time in the office, friendliness manifested by the doctor's voice, and the doctor's judged seriousness of the symptoms and their expected duration were all compared across conditions, as were prescriptions, fees charged, and number of examining procedures used. The "ex-mental patient" was treated quite as well as the control. The only significant difference found was that more examinations not directly related to stomach pains (e.g., an eye examination) were done with the mental patient. This might mean that the report of a former psychiatric patient is not likely to be believed and doctors want to check things for themselves. But the important finding is that former mental patients seem likely to receive the same medical care as anyone else.

☐ Gains

The title of this chapter indicates that one of its concerns is personal gains or advantages derived because of having a mental disorder. It seems obvious, when we consider the losses incurred because of mental problems, that nothing comparable is to be gained. As for the benefits, we might expect that they would come from the support systems that society establishes for its afflicted members. In the first half of the 20th century that support was pretty much limited to providing housing in asylums but, thereafter, with the deinstitutionalization movement, it included group homes, outpatient therapy, and other services. Actually, very little research on this topic seems to have been done. It does appear, though, that recipients of such help show a resulting improvement in well-being and in the quality of their life, as we might expect. A neatly relevant study was done by Rosenfeld (1997) whose subjects were 157 chronically mentally ill individuals. They were interviewed and provided information about the services they were receiving as well as measures of the quality of their life. Rosenfeld found a significant relation indicating that the more help they had been given, the better the quality of their life was reported to be.

Of course, when people are selected out for special help from society, they are likely to become aware they are being helped because of their failures. It is generally presumed they have been incapable of taking care of themselves and the provision of aid itself becomes demeaning and stigmatizing. During the Victorian era, English society ladies would bring Christmas baskets to poor families and the donors were puzzled because the recipients seemed ungrateful for the gift (Jones, Farina, Hastorf, Markus, Miller, & Scott, 1984). It does not seem difficult, though, to understand the humiliation of those families who believe the gift givers are looking down upon them. The basket means they are seen as members of the lower classes—being poor, uneducated, dirty, and lacking in proper manners. Research substantiates these common sense conclusions. A study by Blaine, Crocker, and Major, (1995) indicates that favors done to stigmatized individuals because of sympathy with their problem has a negative impact on the receiver's self-esteem, affect, and motivation. This reaction constitutes a barrier to the provision of effective help for mentally troubled individuals who are living in the community.

In spite of this problem, a support system for individuals with poor mental health, in toto, is almost certainly an asset for them. But another kind of effort to aid such individuals, and one of massive proportions, has been underway in our society for decades. That is the campaign to reduce or remove the social stigma from mental illness. No centralized coordination directs this campaign, rather, it is being carried out by many independent and often local organizations. The elements that unite these diverse and scattered groups are two. First, they agree on the need to help afflicted individuals. Second, they agree on how to do it—by convincing society that mental disorders are diseases like any other disease. The central theme of the messages directed at the public is this: You do not blame or look down upon someone who has pneumonia, so why do you view and treat someone with schizophrenia differently? There is a strong moral tone to these messages that implies that whoever does not comply with them misunderstands mental disorders and is acting shamefully. Sometimes highly prominent people lend support to this movement or actually assume a leadership role in it. Thus, on June 5, 1999, the president of the United States, Bill Clinton, teamed with Tipper Gore, wife of the Vice President, to initiate a White House campaign against the stigma of mental illness (*Hartford Courant*, 1999). The president is quoted as saying ". . . mental illness is misunderstood and feared" while Tipper Gore said "One of the most widely believed and most damaging myths is that mental illness is a personal failure, not a physical disease. Nothing could be further from the truth." However, although this effort is certainly well-intentioned and the logic seems compelling, research suggests this entire enterprise should be reconsidered. We will now examine this research.

Persuasive messages are clearly effective in changing the beliefs of targets about the nature of psychopathology, as will be seen. It is also clear that those changes can alter stigmatization. However, it seems that the consequences can be favorable for the mentally ill or they can be harmful to them. Moreover, while the target of the communication may be the general population, special components of society are also likely to be influenced and may be affected in a different and possibly unwanted way. In what follows, the relevant literature will be reviewed separately for the public, for mental health professionals, and for the mentally ill. For each of these population segments, the aim will be to understand the effect on stigmatization of these persuasive messages.

The Public's Beliefs About the Nature of Mental Disorder and the Effect on Stigma

People's beliefs about the nature of psychopathology can be changed very easily, as Nunnally (1961) demonstrated a long time ago. Attending a class, receiving psychiatric treatments, being exposed to the ideas of others, or merely reading a few phrases embedded in a message with an apparently different aim have all been shown to alter beliefs about what mental disorders are (Farina & Fisher, 1982). The earliest research to determine what consequences follow these changes in beliefs appears to be that of Rothaus, Hanson, Cleveland, and Johnson, reported in 1963. Their subjects were hospitalized psychiatric patients. They were coached to present the cause of their hospitalization in two different ways and each patient was then separately interviewed by two people. For one interviewer, they reported that their hospitalization was caused by an illness. They used terms like 'nervous breakdown' and their treatment was described as consisting of tranquilizers and other drugs. For a different interviewer, social problems were cited as having caused the hospitalization. On that occasion each patient described his own particular personality problems (e.g., being shy) and stated his treatments were designed to help him solve his interpersonal difficulties. Otherwise, the patients behaved comparably in the two conditions. The interviewers judged the patients in the social problems condition as more likely to be given a job than the same patients in the illness condition. So the study suggests that medicalizing mental disorders makes the sufferer *less* socially acceptable, rather than more.

Another study using very different procedures and done outside the United States (Norway) supports the findings of Rothaus et al. Ommundsen and Ekeland (1978) told their student subjects that the study in which they were participating was researching traffic accidents. The subjects were then randomly divided into three groups and were given the same description of a driver losing control of a car and running into a tree. One of the groups was told that the driver had been hospitalized for an appendectomy while the other two groups learned that the driver had been in a psychiatric hospital. In addition, for one of the two latter groups the psychiatric condition was presented as an illness by quoting the ex-patient as saying that he had gotten sick, had trouble with his nerves, but that medicine helped him. For the final group, the condition was presented as an interpersonal problem by reporting the ex-patient as saying he had trouble on the job, economic problems, and could not cope with the stress. The subjects were then asked to indicate which of 16 factors, some placing the blame on the driver, others on conditions, were responsible for the accident. When the psychiatric disorder was presented as an illness, the driver was blamed for the accident significantly more than the control (the appendectomy patient) driver. There was no significant difference in blame assigned between the control driver and the ex-patient driver when his psychiatric disorder was presented as an interpersonal problem. The difference between the two psychiatric conditions was also unreliable.

Three separate studies were done by Farina, Fisher, Getter, and Fischer (1978) and Fisher and Farina (1979), all having the same aim, to wit, to induce changes in the subjects' beliefs about mental illness and to examine the effect of the changes on stigmatization. Two of the studies were done identically using college students as subjects. The beliefs were significantly altered as intended by means of a message describing the student mental health clinic. Half the subjects were informed that mental health problems were social, and the remainder that they were medical in nature. The manipulation was radically different in the third study and, since the technique used was successful, the study has engaging implications. The subjects were students enrolled in two abnormal psychology classes and the beliefs about mental disorders of the members of the two classes were comparable at the beginning of the course. But one of the classes was taught by someone who described mental problems as almost exclusively due to social learning, while the other instructor assigned an important role to genetic and somatic factors. As indicated, at the end of the course the beliefs of the students differed significantly and in the expected direction.

In all three of the studies, subjects were asked how degrading they believed mental disorders to be. In none of the three was there a significant difference between those subjects who believed mental disorders were illnesses and those who viewed them as interpersonal problems. Actually, there were directional differences in all three experiments with the social learning groups describing mental disorders as less degrading than the illness groups. An additional finding obtained in all the experiments was that subjects in the social learning groups, relative to subjects in the other condition, believed that people suffering from mental problems had better control over their condition. The meaning of this finding will be considered.

Perhaps the most direct study of the attitudinal and behavioral effects of these messages was done by Mehta and Farina (1997). Subjects were brought to a laboratory in pairs and told they would do a task together after one revealed some personal information to the other. The ostensible purpose of the study was to measure the effect of the information on task performance. The information transmitted was that one of the subjects, actually a confederate, had been either a medical or a mental patient. The mental patient condition was further divided into either a disorder described as a disease (biochemical disorder, treated with medicines) or an interpersonal problem (the way I was raised, now learning how to get along with people). The task involved communicating information by means of electrically connected panels housed in different rooms. One of the pair acted as the teacher and that was always the naive subject who was seemingly chosen for that role by chance. The confederate, in the role of the learner, had to be led to the correct solution by the teacher by means of electric shocks administered when the learner sent an incorrect solution. The shocks' intensity and duration could be varied by the teacher and thus provided a behavioral measure of favorability toward the learner in each of the three conditions.

As expected, the subjects saw large and significant differences between the control and each of the mental patient groups. For example, the mental patient groups were seen as more poorly adjusted, tense, and prone to violent behavior. However, there were no significant differences between the two mental patient groups for any of the self-report measures. Thus, the messages portraying mental disorders as diseases do not improve the social acceptability of people with mental disorders. The results of the shock measures more strikingly raise questions about the wisdom of convincing the public that mental disorders are diseases. The shocks administered in the disease condition were actually significantly *more* painful than those given in the social problems condition.

The foregoing studies have manipulated conceptions of mental disorders and found that viewing them as illnesses neither reduced stigmatization nor improved the perception of the afflicted. Yet, as indicated, that seems to be the cardinal reason for the shower of messages directed at society. That hypothesis could be checked in another way, utilizing individuals whose conceptions of psychopathology inherently lean toward an illness or a learned direction. Some research bearing on this question has been done. Golding, Becker, Sherman, and Rappaport (1975) constructed a scale measuring a dimension quite similar to the learning-to-illness dimension. Subjects holding an illness conception rated mental patients as more disturbed and expressed more reluctance to become friends with them than did subjects holding learning conceptions. In a second study, the researchers showed a videotape of moderately disturbed patients to learning view subjects and to illness view subjects. The latter subjects saw the patients as more deviant and expected greater deviance in social interaction with them than subjects who believed mental illness to be learned. Here we see evidence again that a disease conception of psychopathology does not decrease stigmatization. It seems to do just the opposite.

Mental Health Workers' Beliefs About Mental Disorders and the Effect on Stigma

Quite clearly, what mental health workers (aides, nurses, professionals) think is wrong with their charges can make a large difference in how the afflicted are treated. Those workers typically have considerable power over patients and, if these beliefs affect behavior, the beliefs of the caretakers may be important. Some research focusing on the social learning–illness dimension indicates that beliefs that psychopathology is a learned condition lead to more favorable perception and treatment of patients than a disease view. Cohen and Struening (1964) carried out a major study of this issue. They first devised a questionnaire to measure the degree to which a respondent regards mental disorders as illnesses as compared to learned patterns of behavior. These questionnaires were then administered to representative samples of mental health workers at each of 12 mental hospitals. They then measured favorability of behavior toward the patients by the staffs of the same 12 hospitals. The measure of favorability they used was the number of days the patients spent in the community during their first year of hospitalization: a measure reasonable in those days (early 1960s) when many of the hospitalizations were involuntary and preventing the patients from eloping was a constant problem. The researchers found that, for hospitals where staff beliefs were toward the disease end of the continuum, patients spent fewer days in the community than patients from hospitals staffed by workers with more of a social learning view.

Langer and Abelson (1974) were also specifically interested in beliefs that psychiatric problems are learned or are manifestations of a disease. Their subjects were two groups of mental health professionals, one group believing mental disorders were exclusively learned while the other group thought biological factors played an important role. All subjects were shown the same videotaped interview but half the subjects in each group were told the interviewee was a job applicant while the rest were informed that he was a mental patient. The learning oriented professionals described the interviewee comparably in the two conditions, but those with an illness view described the 'patient' as significantly more disturbed than the 'job applicant.' In interpreting this finding, it should be noted that the more disturbed a patient is perceived to be, the more he or she is stigmatized (Farina, 1998, pp. 256–257). Hence, we see once again that a disease conception of mental disorders appears to have an unfavorable effect on the esteem and treatment of psychiatric patients. In this case, the disease-oriented mental health professionals, perceiving nonexistent disturbed behavior, will have a lower regard for the patient and may cause the administration of unneeded treatments and restrictions of freedom.

Patients' Beliefs About Mental Disorders and the Effect on Stigma

While the main target of the messages that mental disorders are illnesses is the general public, the patients are also certain to hear them. How are they affected? At this time, we know that they *are* influenced, but as to whether, overall, this influence is good or bad is not yet clear.

Mechanic, MacAlpine, Rosenfield, and Davis (1994) divided schizophrenic patients into two groups on the basis of what they thought to be the nature of their affliction. One group leaned toward blaming their condition on a disease or biological process while the second group was not disposed to attribute it to medical factors. This distinction is quite comparable to the social learning–illness continuum that has been our focus. The researchers report that the illness group, relative to the other group, reported better social relations and a higher quality of life. This differs from the results of the studies described above, and was presumably due to patients feeling less stigmatized and having higher self-esteem. And so it would seem that the *illness* conception should be promoted among mental patients.

However, reports from other studies raise serious questions about this conclusion. Morrison, Bushell, Hanson, Fentiman, and Holdridge-Crane (1977) observed that the more outpatients believed psychiatric conditions were illnesses, the more dependent they felt on mental health professionals. That is worrisome since patients who acquire a somatic view may do less to improve their interpersonal functioning and so may become socially isolated, chronic cases. This interpretation is supported by a study (Morrison, 1976) in which a group of psychiatric outpatients had their views of mental disorders shifted in a social learning direction while another group served as a control. Six months after the manipulation, psychiatric hospitalization had occurred less frequently for the experimental group than for the control. Especially relevant is a study by Farina, Fisher, Getter, and Fischer, (1978). Female college students were recruited to receive a psychotherapy session that, they were told, was intended to help them with their own personal problems. Half of them were then induced to view mental disorders as illnesses and the rest to view them as interpersonal problems. Following the therapy, they were asked to make a note in a journal during the subsequent week each time they thought about a personal problem such as was discussed in therapy. The social learning group thought about personal problems significantly more frequently than the disease group. Evidently people with an illness conception of mental disorders not only believe there is little they can do about their problems in adjustment, but actually do little to cope with their difficulties. Thus, the conception patients have of their condition, whether as illness or learned, seems to have good and bad components. When they view their condition as an illness, patients may be more comfortable with themselves and may be more pleasant companions. However, they may also lethargically accept their own defective social behavior, and depend on the experts to 'cure' it.

☐ Conclusion

The concern of this chapter is the stigma of mental disorders. That stigma is one of the many kinds of social degradation that exists and it is a very potent one. The reasons why those who suffer from mental problems are stigmatized are considered and they are numerous, diverse, complex, and not well understood. They surely include remnants of historical events like the gruesome procedures of the past that were used as cures and the personal alienating characteristics—such as tension—of the mental patient population. The major focus of the chapter is on the consequences that are confronted by afflicted individuals and, in keeping with the aims of this book, the losses are selected for special attention.

The losses incurred because someone is mentally disordered can usefully be divided into two kinds, subjective or internal losses, and objective and measurable losses. The former kind of injury is done to the private and personal life of the individual, and it damages characteristics like self-esteem and confidence. There have been numerous eloquent spontaneous descriptions of the acute and unending pain felt by those who develop a mental disorder and find themselves severely stigmatized because of it. There have also been disciplined investigations that reveal the victims have overwhelming general losses in their quality of life. Their basic needs, especially needs for association and interaction with others, that are satisfied as a matter of course for the average person, are unfulfilled in a large proportion of such individuals.

Better researched and documented are the objective deprivations that follow once someone is recognized as having mental problems. These losses occur in many areas of living. Work, which is of basic importance in determining the nature one's life, becomes difficult to find and, once obtained, is fraught with continuing difficulties for the afflicted. Fellow workers avoid them and are mistrustful. Housing is less readily available to them and landlords lie to keep them from renting their property. It is also clear that they are not wanted as neighbors and communities have passed laws transparently designed to keep them away. Fear of being subjected to violence is not the only factor producing this rejection since the public similarly rejects maladjusted children who do not appear to pose that problem. Even elementary school children reject other children thought to suffer from mental abnormalities. Studies done with the families of mental patients reveal that the affected member creates problems for the family both because of his or her disturbed condition and because of the social stigma brought upon the family. Some striking evidence of the family's desire to distance itself from the mentally disordered member exists. This social rejection of the mentally ill is not limited to certain societies but appears to be a very general phenomenon that exists in all societies.

A consideration of the possible gains derived from having a mental problem indicates that condition confers very little that is advantageous. Society does provide some support such as housing and counseling. Additionally, various groups, such as mental health associations, have devoted much effort to free mentally troubled people of stigma. The basic assumption guiding their messages to the public is that if mental illness is viewed as being like any other disease, the afflicted will be better accepted. However, research raises very serious doubts about that and even opens the possibility that they may be harming the people they aim to help. More research and thought is in order concerning the wisdom of continuing this campaign.

☐ References

Beers, C. W. (1948). *A mind that found itself: An autobiography.* Garden City, NY: Doubleday.

Ben-Noun, L. (1996). Characterization of patients refusing professional psychiatric treatment in a primary care clinic. *Israel Journal of Psychiatric and Related Sciences, 33,* 167–174.

Bentz, W. K., & Edgerton, J. W. (1971). The consequences of labelling a person mentally ill. *Social Psychiatry, 6,* 29–33.

Blaine, B., Crocker, J., & Major, B. (1995). The unintended negative consequences of sympathy for the stigmatized. *Journal of Applied Social Psychology, 25,* 889–905.

Brockman, J., D'Arcy, C., & Edmonds, L., (1979). Facts or artifacts?: Changing public attitudes toward the mentally ill. *Social Science and Medicine, 13,* 673–682.

Burns, G. L. & Farina, A. (1992). The role of physical attractiveness in adjustment. *Genetic, Social, and General Psychology Monographs, 118,* 157–!94.

Cohen, J., & Struening, E. L. (1964). Opinions about mental illness: Hospital social atmosphere profiles and their relevance to effectiveness. *Journal of Consulting Psychology, 28,* 292–298.

Crocetti, G. M., Spiro, H. R., & Siassi, I. (1974). *Contemporary attitudes toward mental illness.* Pittsburgh, PA: University of Pittsburgh Press.

Cutler, W. D. (1975). *The relationship of subjects' sex to attitudes and behaviors toward male mental patients.* Unpublished doctoral dissertation. University of Connecticut.

Davies, T. W., & Morris, A. (1990). A comparative quantification of sigma. *Social Work and Social Sciences Review, 1,* 109–122.

Deutsch, A. (1965). *The mentally ill in America* (2nd ed.). New York: Columbia University Press.

Dewees, M., Pulice, R. T., & McCormick, L. L. (1996). Community integration of former state mental hospital patients: Outcomes of a policy shift in Vermont. *Psychiatric Services, 47,* 1088–1092.

Dougherty, S. J., Campana, K. A., Kontos, R. A., Flores, M. K. D., Lockhart, R. S., & Shaw, D. D. (1996). Supported education: A qualitative study of the student experience. *Psychiatric Rehabilitation Journal, 19,* 59–70.

Farina, A. (1981). Are women nicer people than men?: Sex and the stigma of mental disorder. *Clinical Psychology Review, 1,* 223–243.

Farina, A. (1982). The stigma of mental disorders. In A. G. Miller (Ed.), *In the eye of the beholder* (pp. 305–363). New York: Praeger.

Farina, A. (1998). Stigma. In K. T. Mueser & N. Tarrier (Eds.), *Handbook of social functioning in schizophrenia* (pp. 247–279). Boston: Allyn & Bacon.

Farina, A. & Felner, R. D., (1973). Employment interviewer reactions to former mental patients. *Journal of Abnormal Psychology, 82,* 268–272.

Farina, A., Felner, R. D., & Boudreau, L. A. (1973). Reactions of workers to male and female mental patient job applicants. *Journal of Consulting and Clinical Psychology, 41,* 363–372.

Farina, A., & Fisher, J. D. (1982). Beliefs about mental disorders: Findings and implications. In G. Weary & H. Mirels (Eds.), *Integrations of clinical and social psychology* (pp. 48–71). New York: Oxford University Press.

Farina, A., Fisher, J. D., & Fischer, E. H. (1992). Societal factors in the problems faced by deinstitutionalized psychiatric patients. In P. J. Fink & A. Tasman (Eds.), *Stigma and mental illness* (pp. 167–184). Washington, DC: American Psychiatric Press.

Farina, A. Fisher, J. D., Getter, H., & Fischer, E. H. (1978). Some consequences of changing people's views regarding the nature of mental illness. *Journal of Abnormal Psychology, 87,* 272–279.

Farina, A., Gliha, D., Boudreau, L. A., Allen, J. G., & Sherman, M. (1971). Mental illness and the impact of believing others know about it. *Journal of Abnormal Psychology, 77,* 1–5.

Farina, A., Hagelauer, H. D., & Holzberg, J. D. (1976). The influence of psychiatric history on physicians' response to a new patient. *Journal of Consulting and Clinical Psychology, 44,* 49.

Farina, A., Murray, P. J., & Groh, T. (1978). Sex and worker acceptance of a former mental patient. *Journal of Consulting and Clinical Psychology, 46*, 887–891.

Farina, A., & Ring, K. (1965). The influence of perceived mental illness on interpersonal relations. *Journal of Abnormal Psychology, 70*, 47–51.

Farina, A., Thaw, J., Lovern, J. D., & Mangone, D. (1974). People's reactions to a former mental patient moving to their neighborhood. *Journal of Community Psychology, 2*, 108–112.

Fink, P. G., & Tasman, A. (Eds.). (1992). *Stigma and mental illness*. Washington, DC: American Psychiatric Press.

Fisher, J. D., & Farina, A. (1979). Consequences of beliefs about the nature of mental disorder. *Journal of Abnormal Psychology, 88*, 320–327.

Flanagan, J. C. (1978). A research approach to improving our quality of life. *American Psychologist, 33*, 138–147.

Fromm-Reichmann, F. (1948). Notes on the development of treatment of schizophrenia by psychoanalytic psychotherapy. *Psychiatry, 11*, 263–273.

Gilmore, J. L., & Farina, A. (1989). The social reception of mainstreamed children in the regular classroom. *Journal of Mental Deficiency Research, 33*, 301–311.

Golding, S. L., Becker, E., Sherman, S., & Rappaport, J. (1975). The behavioral expectations scale: Assessment of expectations of interaction with the mentally ill. *Journal of Consulting and Clinical Psychology, 43*, 109.

Greenberg, J. S., Kim, H. W., & Greenley, J. R. (1997). Factors associated with subjective burden in siblings of adults with severe mental illness. *American Journal of Orthopsychiatry, 67*, 231–241.

Gullekson, M. (1992). Stigma: Families suffer too. In P. J. Fink, & A. Tasman (Eds.), *Stigma and mental illness* (pp. 127–138). Washington, DC: American Psychiatric Press.

Gurtman, M. B. (1986). Depression and the response of others: Reevaluating the reevaluation. *Journal of Abnormal Psychology, 95*, 99–101.

Hamilton, E. (1999). *Harford Courant*, A1, May 20.

Harford Courant, (1999). A 7, June 6.

Herman, C. P., Zanna, M. P., & Higgins, E. T. (Eds.). (1986). *Physical appearance, stigma, and social behavior: The Ontario Symposium*, Volume 3. Hillsdale, NJ: Erlbaum.

Hollingshead, A. B., & Redlich, F. C. (1958). *Social class and mental illness: A community study*. New York: Wiley.

Hooley, J. M., Richters, J. E., Weintraub, S., & Neale, J. M. (1987). Psychopathology and marital distress: The positive side of positive symptoms. *Journal of Abnormal Psychology, 96*, 27–33.

Houghton, J. (1980). One personal experience: Before and after mental illness. In J. G. Rabkin, L. Gelb, & J. B. Lazar (Eds.), *Attitudes toward the mentally ill: Research perspectives*. Report of an NIMH Workshop, January 24–25, 1980 (DHHS Publication No. ADM 80-1031). Washington, DC: U. S. Government Printing Office.

Jones, E. E., Farina, A., Hastorf, A. H., Marcus, H., Miller, D. T., & Scott, R. A. (1984). *Social stigma: The psychology of marked relationships*. New York: W. H. Freeman.

Koizumi, K., & Harris, P. (1992). Mental healthcare in Japan. *Hospital and Community Psychiatry, 43*, 1100–1103.

Lamy, R. E. (1966). Social consequences of mental illness. *Journal of Consulting and Clinical Psychology, 30*, 450–454.

Langer, E. J., & Abelson, R. P. (1974). A patient by any other name . . . ; Clinician group difference in labeling bias. *Journal of Consulting and Clinical Psychology, 42*, 4–9.

Lefley, H. P. (1992). The stigmatized family. In P. J. Fink & A. Tasman (Eds.), *Stigma and mental illness* (pp. 127–138). Washington, DC: American Psychiatric Press.

Lehman, A., Ward, N., & Linn, L. (1982). Chronic mental patients: Quality of life issues. *American Journal of Psychiatry, 139*, 1271–1276.

Link, B. G. (1987). Understanding labeling effects in the area of mental disorders: An assessment of the effects of expectations of rejection. *American Sociological Review, 53*, 96–112.

Link, B. G., Cullen, F. T., Mirotznik, J., & Struening, E. (1992). Consequences of stigma for persons with mental illness: Evidence from social sciences. In P. J. Fink & A. Tasman (Eds.), *Stigma and mental illness* (pp. 87–96). Washington, DC: American Psychiatric Press.

Link, B. G., Struening, E. L., Rahav, M., Phelan, J. C., & Nuttbrock, L. (1997). On stigma and its consequences: Evidence from a longitudinal study of men with dual diagnosis of mental illness and substance abuse. *Journal of Health and Social Behavior, 38*, 177–190.

Manning, C., & White, P. D. (1995). Attitudes of employers to the mentally ill. *Psychiatric Bulletin, 19*, 541–543.

McCarthy, J., Prettyman, R., & Friedman, T. (1995). The stigma of psychiatric in-patient care. *Psychiatric Bulletin, 19*, 349–351.

Mechanic, D., McAlpine, D., Rosenfield, S., & Davis, D. (1994). Effects of illness attribution and depression on the quality of life among persons with serious mental illness. *Social Science and Medicine, 39*, 155–164.

Mehta, S., & Farina, A. (1988). Associative stigma: Perceptions of the difficulties of college-aged children of stigmatized fathers. *Journal of Social and Clinical Psychology, 7*, 192–202.

Mehta, S., & Farina, A. (1997). Is being "sick" really better? Effects of the disease view of mental disorder on stigma. *Journal of Social and Clinical Psychology, 16*, 405–419.

Morrison, J. K. (1976). Demythologizing mental patients' attitudes toward mental illness: An empirical study. *Journal of Community Psychology, 4*, 181–185.

Morrison, J. K., Bushell, J. D., Hanson, G. D., Fentiman, J. R., & Holdridge-Crane, S. (1977). Relationship between psychiatric patients' attitudes toward mental illness and attitudes of dependence. *Psychological Reports, 41*, 1194.

Munakata, T. (1989). The socio-cultural significance of the diagnostic label "neurosthenia" in Japan's mental health care system. *Culture, Medicine, and Psychiatry, 13*, 203–213.

Nunnally, J. C. (1961). *Popular conceptions of mental health.* New York: Holt, Rhinehart, & Winston.

Olshansky, S., Grob, S., & Ekdahl, M. (1960). Survey of employment experience of patients discharged from three mental hospitals during the perod 1951–1953. *Mental Hygiene, 44*, 510–521.

Olshansky, S., Grob, S., & Malamud, I. T. (1958). Employer's attitudes and practices in hiring ex-mental patients. *Mental Hygiene, 42*, 391–401.

Ommundsen, R., & Ekeland, T. J. (1978). Psychiatric labeling and social perception. *Scandinavian Journal of Psychology, 19*, 193–199.

Page, S. (1977). Effects of the mental illness label in attempts to obtain accommodation. *Canadian Journal of Behavioral Science, 9*, 84–90.

Page, S. (1995). Effects of the mental illness label in 1993: Acceptance and rejection in the community. *Journal of Health and Social Policy, 7*, 61–68.

Pearson, V., & Phillips. M. (1994). Psychiatric social work and socialism: Problems and potential in China. *Social Work, 39*, 280–287.

Perese, E. F. (1997). Unmet needs of persons with chronic mental illnesses: Relationship to their adaptation to community living. *Issues in Mental Health Nursing, 18*, 19–34.

Phelan, J. C., Bromet, E. J., & Link, B. G. (1998). Psychiatric illness and family stigma. *Schizophrenia Bulletin, 24*, 115–126.

Piner, K. E., & Kahle, L. R. (1984). Adapting to the stigmatizing label of mental illness: Foregone but not forgotten. *Journal of Personality and Social Psychology, 47*, 805–811.

Posner, J. (1976). Death as a courtesy stigma. *Essence, 1*, 26–33.

Rodin, M., & Price, J., (1995). Overcoming stigma: Credit for self-improvement or discredit for needing to improve? *Personality and Social Psychology Bulletin, 21*, 172-181.

Rodrigues, C. R. (1992). Comparacion de actitudes de estudientes de medicina brasilenos y espanoles hacia la enfermedad mental. *Actas Luso Espanolas de Neurologia Psiquiatrica y Ciencias, 20*, 30–41.

Rose, L. E. (1996). Families of psychiatric patients: A critical review and future research directions. *Archives of Psychiatric Nursing, 10*, 67–76.

Rosenfield, S. (1997). Labeling mental illness: The effects of received services and perceived stigma on life satisfaction. *American Sociological Review, 62,* 660–672.

Rothaus, P. Hanson, P. G., Cleveland, S. E., & Johnson, D. L. (1963). Describing psychiatric hospitalization: A dilemma. *American Psychologist, 18,* 85–89.

Segal, S. P. (1978). Attitudes toward the mentally ill: A review. *Social Work, 23,* 211–217.

Skinner, L. J., Berry, K. K., Griffith, S. E., & Byers, B. (1995). Generalizability and specificity of the stigma associated with the mental illness label: A reconsideration twenty-five years later. *Journal of Community Psychology, 23,* 3–17.

Torrey, E. F. (1988). *Hidden victims: An eight-stage healing process for families and friends of the mentally ill.* New York: Doubleday.

Urbinas, H. (1998, September 19). Clinton takes his troubles to the clergy, not psychotherapist. *The Hartford Courant,* A10

Vellenga, B. A., & Christensen, J. (1994). Persistent and severely mentally ill clients' perceptions of their mental illness. *Issues in Mental Health Nursing, 15,* 359–371.

Wahl, O. F. (1995). *Media madness: Public images of mental illness.* New Brunswick, NJ: Rutgers University Press.

Witztum, E., Margolin, J., Bar-On, R., & Levy, A. (1995). Stigma, labelling and psychiatric misdiagnosis: Origins and outcomes. *Medicine and Law, 14,* 659–669.

Zigler, E. & Phillips, L. (1961). Psychiatric diagnosis and symptomatology. *Journal of Abnormal and Social Psychology, 63,* 69–75.

Zilboorg, S., & Henry, G. W. (1941). *A history of medical psychology.* New York: Norton.

Zultowsky, D., & Farina, A. (1989). *Community acceptance of mentally retarded and emotionally disturbed children.* Unpublished manuscript, University of Connecticut, Storrs, CT.

CHAPTER

Melvin J. Lerner

The Human Costs of Organizational Downsizing: The Irrational Effects of the Justice Motive on Managers, Dismissed Workers, and Survivors

Technological progress and an economy driven by competition in free markets has transformed the American work place and in the process the lives of many Americans. To successfully compete in global markets companies are replacing employees with more cost effective advanced technology, and whenever feasible transferring production to sites with lower wage scales. In addition, the practice of continually reshaping and tailoring its work force to accomplish specific tasks allows companies to respond more efficiently to market demands. The increased responsiveness to market demands results in employment policies that replace permanent positions with time limited contracts. As a consequence, the typical career path for the American adult will include a series of work periods with several companies. To remain employed people must become entrepreneurs, staying aware of changes in the job market and preparing to find the best deal for themselves in their next contracts.

At the macro level the most visible effects of these changes in the means of production and employment practices include the loss of well-paying, secure, blue and white collar jobs that had provided sufficient one-earner income and job security for a "middle class" life style. The replacement of labor with advanced technology has led to an increase in positions at the highest levels of intellectual skill and income, together with an even greater number of low paying, low skilled jobs (Council of Economic Advisors, 1996). In the resultant productive and profitable economy, that part of the labor force with the ability to design and manage the advanced technology, estimated to be about 20% of the population (Reich, 1991), enjoys great economic benefits. However, a much larger number have lost or been denied access to good well-paying jobs, and as the result of downsizing and plant closures many are at various stages of coping with what sociologists would term downward mobility.

At the micro, individual, level, the displaced-replaced workers and their dependents experience considerable loss in income with little prospect of recovering the life style they had assumed would always be available if they were willing to be faithful, diligent, employees (Newman, 1993). The vast majority, including those who are the survivors in the economic restructuring, must live with the omnipresent specter of job insecurity. This includes the threat of unpredictable future job loss leading to incessant efforts to increase one's market value when it is not at all clear what future forms the job market will take. In essence, as corporate America thrives in this more efficient, profitable, economic world, increasing numbers of citizens can not realize their aspirations for a nice life for themselves and their families (Newman, 1993). For many, a nice life requires a sufficiently stable income to purchase a respectable home in a decent neighborhood and provide continuing support for one's children. In this technology-driven, increasingly global economy, those job aspirants with unremarkable job qualifications can no longer rely on union protected industrial jobs, but must compete for marginally sustaining wages with increasing numbers of people in the global labor market willing to work for even less (Aronowitz & DiFazio, 1994).

Having observed these trends, the economist Paul Krugman (1994) noted that " . . . economic forces are more and more tending to split the society into two: Those with good jobs and a rising standard of living, and those with either falling incomes or the prospect of a more or less permanent life on the dole" (Krugman, 1994, p. 9). He then concluded that "Even an economist can see that such a split demoralizes those on the bottom and coarsens those at the top" (Krugman, 1994, p. 9). Whether or not one agrees with Krugman's psychological insights there are sufficient reasons to raise and attempt to answer basic questions concerning the impact of these economic trends on people's lives. Is it true, for example, that those on the bottom of the economic rung are demoralized by their fates? Why would they not be simply resigned to their fates, angry, or energized to better themselves? And is it possible that many of those who succeeded in obtaining good jobs and a rising standard of living are coarsened by their successes, rather than comfortably satisfied with what they have been able to accomplish, and appropriately sympathetic towards those who are destined to suffer with considerably less?

To generate answers to these and related questions, the remainder of this chapter will examine the ways societal norms and psychological processes influence how people react to having bad things happen to them and to their being involved in bad things happening to other people. Much of the discussion will focus on people's justice motive and how it appears in their reactions to conditions of loss and deprivation.

☐ Societal Norms and Rational Reactions to Important Events

The most commonly accepted descriptions of how people react to terrible things appear in the writings of several social psychologists, such as Shaver (1985), Skitka and Tetlock, (1992, 1993) and Weiner (1993) as well as the conventional morality of our society (Heider, 1958). According to these theories and societal norms, people are morally responsible for their behavior when they are judged to be in control of their acts, and the outcomes of their acts or the consequences of their failing to act, could be anticipated by any reasonable person. If someone is judged to be responsible for something happening, either good or bad, then the assignment of credit or blame depends upon the judged moral worth of the person's intentions (Shaver, 1985). However, according to Piaget (1932), very young children do not go through this process of assessing responsibility and intention in arriving at their moral judgments. Instead, in the earlier stages children seem to reason backwards from outcomes to personal worth or attributes: Their judgments reflect the belief that bad outcomes are caused by bad people, and bad outcomes happen to bad people. Then, in the normal course of development, by adulthood they learn that accidents can happen to or be caused by anyone, and that the true worth of a person is revealed in the value of their intentional efforts, not in the outcomes of their acts, per se. But, contrary both to Piaget's observations and conventional wisdom, there is good reason to believe that adults do not outgrow their earlier outcome-generated blaming reactions. Recent research and theory now recognizes that, depending upon the circumstances, people may employ thoughtful reasoning or they may automatically condemn someone who is simply associated with a bad outcome (Chaiken & Trope, 1999) regardless of their intentions.

From the perspective of conventional morality, the answers to the questions of how competent employees react to losing their jobs, how corporate management reacts to implementing widespread dismissals in response to market pressures, and how the awareness of these events affects remaining employees, are relatively simple. According to the societal norms, what happens to the discharged employees is a tragic but unavoidable consequence of economic realities. By any reasonable analysis the discharged employees are not to blame for losing their jobs or for the subsequent deprivation and suffering because of the relative unavailability of decent paying replacements in the job market. And certainly those who remain employed did no harm in staying with their jobs.

By rational analysis of the circumstances and conventional rules of morality, the unemployed victims are innocent of any wrongdoing, and if they experience any emotional reaction to their fates it should be some form of dysphoria: anxiety, fear, sadness, or anger at those who caused this to happen. But who would that be? The most likely candidate would seem to be the employer who let them go. But it is commonly recognized that in most cases the company's executive and managerial staff were only responding to the demands created by competitive pressures in the marketplace. They were morally and legally obligated to the corporate stakeholders to protect their market share and, typically, after due deliberation the most rational choice required that they downsize or relocate the plant. To do otherwise would have meant intentionally harming the stakeholders in the company including the remaining and future employees. The public consensus is that the managers and executives of the company did nothing morally wrong in dismissing the employees. So what dynamics are set in place when, according to the norms of our society, people (managers) are morally required to cause great harm to other people—competent employees—and their families? How do the participants and observers react when there are obviously innocent victims of undeserved suffering, but according to conventional standards there is no one to blame, no one at fault?

The research literature, self-defined as the study of procedural justice, seems to converge on the importance influence of societal norms concerning fairness on ameliorating people's reactions in such situations. Although the most reliable reaction to being unjustly deprived is anger toward the harmdoer (Smith & Ellsworth, 1985), Brockner and Weisenfeld (1996), who based their review of the available research on procedural justice, concluded that if people believe that their losses and deprivation were the result of the application of fair procedures they will express no more anger than if they had not been deprived. More specifically, several studies have found that if employees had been fully informed, asked for their opinions, and otherwise treated respectfully, they were unlikely to subsequently express resentment toward the companies that had terminated their employment in the process of downsizing. In addition, those employees who were retained showed few if any signs of resentment or demoralization because of what they had witnessed happening to their less fortunate co-workers (Brockner & Weisenfeld, 1996).

It would be a serious error, however, to interpret these sanguine findings of the procedural justice research as also offering the means to eliminate the serious consequences of job loss for the lives and well-being of the employees. Societal norms concerning fair play and moral decision making can justify employers' fair dismissals of workers, and make it less likely that fairly victimized employees will openly express any subsequent anger. That may be useful information for employers, but there is no evidence that losing one's job through a fair process will reduce or soften the effects of the ensuing financial and personal crises associated with being unemployed. The sobering truth is that, after the most fairly and respectfully conducted dismissal, those who find themselves jobless in this competitive job market must still face the potential threats to their identities as providers and productive members of society, while adjusting to the often devastating experiences for themselves and their families stemming from the unmerited and unavoidable losses of income and financial insecurity (Kieselbach, 1997; Kozlowski, Chao, Smith & Hedlund, 1993; Leana & Feldman, 1992).

☐ Irrational Counter-Normative Reactions to Suffering and Loss

Harsh economic realities are not the only, and possibly not the most pernicious, sources of suffering that await both the fairly and unfairly dismissed employees. According to the commonly accepted rules for assigning blame and culpability, the employees who lost their jobs because of corporate downsizing or plant closures are innocent of any wrongdoing. Therefore, they should at least be free, then, from having to deal with any feelings of guilt, shame, or condemnation from others. Considerable evidence, however, suggests that is not the case.

Observers Blame the Victim

Many factors contribute to observers blaming and condemning the victims of unemployment, including the need to believe they live in a just or at least controllable world, where they can avoid being victimized themselves (Reichle, Schneider, & Montada, 1998). The evidence suggests that when observers can not eliminate the victim's unjust fate, and do not believe that the victims will be ultimately compensated for their suffering, they may resort to finding reasons to blame or derogate them (Lerner, 1980). And in circumstances where the objective reality or personal attachment to the suffering victims inhibits finding them personally blameworthy, people may resort to denying the presence of the painfully threatening injustice by simply avoiding the victims. In the absence of the ability to end the victim's suffering, the more similar they are to the victims, the greater the observer's efforts to avoid them (Lerner & Agar, 1972; Novak & Lerner, 1968).

Other, less motivationally based processes may also contribute to finding fault with objectively innocent victims, including hindsight bias, the correspondence effect, and the simple application of common ideologically and culturally supported beliefs (Lerner & Goldberg, 1999), such as "In this country everyone who wants work can find it," "If someone is poor or unemployed that's usually because he doesn't have sufficient ability or motivation to do better for himself: it is basically his fault," and "The only excuse would be that the person is sick, but then again, whose fault is that, and why didn't he prepare for that possibility?" Most people are bothered, upset, and frightened, by the suffering of innocent victims. Their feelings of compassion and concerns with justice may impel them to come to the victim's aid, but failing that, people will find other ways to become more comfortable with the injustices that they can not or will not change. Unfortunately that often leads to creating justice by finding the victims in some way culpable, or at least deserving of their fate, or simply forgetting about them (Herbert & Dunkel-Schetter, 1992).

Victims' Self-Blame

Investigators have identified different levels of victimization inflicted upon the dismissed employees. The primary victimization involves the economic losses; secondary victimization includes the loss of valued social identities and interpersonal contacts as a consequence of the job loss. The blaming, rejection, and avoidance by others becomes the tertiary form of victimization (Kieselbach, 1997). Extending this framework one can find evidence for yet a fourth form of unmerited suffering: the unemployed worker's guilt and depression. The victims often react to their own unfortunate fates in much the same ways as do the observers, for probably very similar reasons. The fact that they are innocent of wrongdoing and can obviously attribute their victimization to the actions of others, or at least the "fates," is no more effective in eliminating their irrational tendency to blame and derogate themselves than equally innocent victims of rape and serious accidents (Bulman & Wortman, 1977; Janoff-Bulman, 1979).

One explanation psychologists offer for this irrational self-blame asserts that people are attempting to preserve a sense of control over future terrible injustices by blaming themselves for having done—or failed to do—something to bring about their present suffering (Janoff-Bulman, 1979). Whether the control explanation is true or not, more primitive, less rational, or functional processes appear to contribute to victims' self-derogation. For example, Rubin and Peplau (1973) found remarkable evidence of an explicitly chance-determined victimization causing sane, reasonable adults to think less of themselves and lower their self-esteem. The participants in this research were young men who had been assembled in small groups to await the outcome of the draft lottery conducted during the latter part of the Vietnam war. The lottery was based on birthdates, and depending upon the order in which a birthdate is randomly selected, the young men would learn the probability of their being drafted and sent to kill and be killed in Vietnam. Just prior to and after the actual drawing Rubin and Peplau (1973) had the young men complete a series of scales and questionnaires including a commonly used measure of self-esteem.

By dividing the men into those whose birthdates indicated they definitely would not be drafted—winners—in this momentous lottery, those who were certain to be drafted—losers—and those whose fates were indeterminate, Rubin and Peplau (1973) discovered an important trend: Immediately after learning their fates, a majority of the winners showed increases in self-esteem, most of the losers revealed significant lowering of self-esteem, and the reactions of the remainder were evenly mixed.

In this natural experiment the explicit role of chance in determining the participants' fates reduces the plausibility that the desire to control future outcomes influenced the young men's subsequently raising or lowering their self-esteem upon learning of their good or bad fortune. What, then, could have led to the signs of self-derogation among those who were the losers in the draft lottery?

One obvious possibility is a simple mood effect: The men became depressed over learning of their terrible fate and this negative mood led them to perceive and evaluate everything negatively, including themselves (Forgas, 1995). But that possibility becomes less tenable given the additional evidence that the losers in the lottery also preferred to meet with winners rather than other losers. They did not indiscriminately react to everyone and everything in negative terms. Mainly, the losers added to their own suffering by condemning themselves. It appears that preconsciously they had reasoned backwards from the outcome to their worth as a person: "I must be a bad person because something terrible just happened to me. Bad outcomes happen to bad people." Although this ressembles the kind of reaction often revealed in people's reactions to victims (Lerner & Goldberg, 1999), it is most remarkable to find it so clearly demonstrated among the victims themselves. Obviously, this clearly irrational reaction is inconsistent with both society's rules for assigning culpability, and the natural motivation to defend one's self-esteem and think well of one's self. It appears likely, then, that the victims may have had no choice in the matter: The awareness of their fate elicited rather simple schemas that automatically, preconsciously, led to their self-derogation—bad things happen to bad people. It is worth noting that in this sense, their moral evaluations closely resembled the moral reasoning of the younger children in Piaget's (1932) seminal research.

Self-Blame Experienced by Well-Intentioned and Inadvertent Harmdoers

There is ample evidence that this irrational self-condemnation does not only appear among victims. People who accidentally cause others harm also often reveal this form of irrational self blame. Several experiments have shown, for example, that clear signs of guilt and attempts to restore a sense of self-worth can be induced in people by making them unwitting accidental harmdoers (Freedman, Wallington, & Bless, 1967). This has been done by the simple procedure of instructing the research participants to take a seat at a table and then upon their pulling out the chair, or leaning on the table, they accidentally spill someone's research material, ostensibly causing the victim to spend hours to reassemble. Although societal norms, and the conventional rules of morality, recognize this kind of event to be an unforeseeable, unintentionally harmful act, and thus absolve the perpetrator of any culpability, that person typically experiences considerable guilt and depression and will attempt to restore his or her self-esteem. Some evidence (see, e.g., McGraw, 1987), suggests that people may experience more guilt following accidental harmdoing than when the harm was foreseeable or intentional. This high level of guilt appeared among the inadvertent harmdoers even when they openly recognized they were not morally responsible in the sense of being blameworthy for accidentally causing the victim's fate (McGraw, 1987).

In this same vein, managers and executives have reported experiencing severe guilt after having dismissed employees rendered redundant by the normatively justified and economically necessary decision to downsize their company. The July 25, 1994 lead article and cover story of *Fortune*, "Burned-Out Bosses," (Smith, 1994) portrays management as the unexpected victims of the restructuring. One executive involved in downsizing reported that "nothing—not over-work, not confusion, not lost perks, not apprehension—is as deadening to a manager's morale as firing subordinates" (Smith, 1994, p. 46). The role of guilty feelings in this demoralization process is explicit in the conclusion: "What makes the flood of dismissals in recent years especially distressing for managers is that so often workers have been fired not for cause but because their skills were no longer needed" (Smith, 1994, p. 2). An IBM executive described the process:

> Every year we'd call it something different—early retirement, reorganization, reengineering . . . it was slow water torture . . . came home every night worried how this one or that one was going to support himself. (Smith, 1994, p. 46)

Although no figures are available for the incidence of guilt and burnout among managers participating in downsizing, experienced consultants have recognized the prevalence of these unanticipated strong emotional reactions following corporate restructuring, and the serious problems they create for management. In his address on receiving a Distinguished Professional Contribution to Knowledge Award from the American Psychological Association, Harry Levinson (1994) observed that:

> the conscious guilt any manager of conscience has about terminating someone else without cause is compounded by the unconscious guilt that arises from the sense that he or she is destroying the other. (Levinson, 1994, p. 429)

Brody (1985),working with an entirely different population, also found a remarkably high incidence of severe guilt feelings following women's adoption of a rational, normatively appropriate course of action. These irrational guilt feelings appeared among daughters after they had placed their infirm elderly parents in nursing homes. As in the case of corporate managers' decisions to downsize their companies, the daughters' decisions were arrived at after extensive consultations with the best available professional experts. Moving the parents into the nursing home typically occurs only after the professional advisors convince all concerned that the parents' increasing needs require continuous custodial and medical supervision. Nevertheless, Brody (1985) found that in spite of all the prior supportive evidence and rational arguments, after the institutionalization actually takes place the daughters unexpectedly feel very guilty. Although they may consciously recognize the irrational bases of their guilt, at the same time they report feelings of having failed their parents in their times of greatest need.

As in the case of the managers who participated in downsizing, the socially accepted rules for assigning culpability did not prevent the emotional anguish of people who, in the course of doing their duty and meeting their obligations, caused others to suffer. Regardless of the justifiability of their intentions the awareness that their acts were the immediate cause of an innocent person's grief and suffering appears to have been sufficient to elicit strong guilt feelings. Apparently, reactions to terrible events can be shaped by the automatic application of a second outcome driven schema: Bad things are caused by bad people. Both schemas—bad things happen to bad people and bad things are caused by bad people—involve the direct association of the valence of outcomes with people's worth, but it is not at all clear what specific events will lead the observer to focus on the victim or perpetrator, or both. However, what remains critically important, and theoretically intriguing is that these schemas can influence people's reactions in spite of their being contrary to conventional rules and norms. And in the process they automatically elicit self-inflicted, unmerited pain.

☐ Moral Reasoning and Moral Intuition: A Theoretical Framework

An interesting image of the moral dimension in peoples' lives begins to take shape as one integrates these findings with what can be observed in the context of societal institutions. People appear to function at two levels of awareness and are capable of two kinds of moral evaluations. On the one hand, they often apply conventionally rational rules for thoughtfully determining causality, culpability, and moral worth, especially in legal encounters, and the institutional settings where economic aid is distributed (Skitka & Tetlock, 1992, 1993). The overriding principle in the fashioning and application of these rules appears to be that people should get what they deserve, often determined by what their accomplishments merit (Weiner, 1993). On the other hand, especially in emotionally arousing situations, people may arrive at moral evaluations based on their intuitive assessment of people's worth. Although these evaluations also involve judgments of deserving, they seem to reflect the kind of simple outcome-driven schemas Piaget (1932) found among younger children: The valence of the outcome determines the judgment of the actor's worth.

Several psychologists have recently generated systematic frameworks encompassing the thoughtful, normatively conventional ways people process information and react to their world with those processes that involve relatively automatic eliciting of simple schemas (see, e.g., Chaiken & Trope, 1999). Of particular relevance, here, Shweder and Haidt (1993) identify the relatively slow, conventionally rational processing of information involved in moral reasoning and the automatically elicited moral intuitions that follow from a rapid appraisal of events. Although people often experience the consequences of those immediate appraisals as emotions of anger, shame, or guilt, the specific schemas underlying those intuitions remain inaccessible to conscious retrieval; they are introspectively opaque. Though their psychological origins typically remain in the unconscious, Shweder and Haidt (1993) describe those emotions as the experienced "self-evident truths of morality" involving "injustice, the right, and the good" (p. 364).

Elucidating the differences between the social-psychological processes involved in moral reasoning and moral intuitions can provide a better understand of how managers and caregiving daughters could be surprised by their unanticipated guilty feelings. Quite understandably, these self-defined harmdoers initially engaged in rational and thoughtful dialogues, both internal and external, to arrive at the most sensible, decent way to meet their obligations to all concerned. Naturally, those dialogues were informed and guided by societal norms that it is reasonable and proper to avoid, or at least minimize, undeserved suffering, in trying to achieve the greatest benefit to all. As a consequence, the managers and caregivers had every reason to believe they had justice and decency on their side. Unfortunately, tragically, they were unable to include in their decision-making the often counternormative and introspectively opaque schemas that generated their intuitive emotional reactions to the subsequently suffering victims of their decisions. Intuitively, irrationally, they then condemned themselves for having caused the suffering.

Since the unexpected guilt and shame they were experiencing had no basis in their understanding of what constitutes good and bad, moral and immoral, they were left with the need to find some appropriate explanation and possibly, means of expiation. The available evidence reveals that people who experience guilt following accidental harmdoing may subsequently engage in extra efforts to be helpful and kind to a third party (Freedman et al., 1967). Presumably, in so doing they may be able to rescue their self-image and restore their sense of being a decent person in a just world. Unfortunately, following accidentally harming someone people may also exhibit less socially desirable reactions, including derogating their victims (Lerner & Matthews, 1967), and increased hostility to outgroup members who appear to threaten their salient social identity (Meindl & Lerner, 1984).

Obviously, the presence of benign and even benevolent intentions can not prevent at least transitory damage to people's sense of self-worth after being either the innocent victim or the cause of undeserved harm. It is also important to note that the desire to maintain a sense of control over future events does not plausibly account for this form of self-inflicted suffering elicited by explicitly accidental, random, uncontrollable events. The immediate lowering of self-esteem appears to be directly elicited by the outcome and occurs prior to, or independently of, the attribution of blame. Similar themes seem to guide the immediate self-condemnatory reaction and the subsequent efforts of self-redemption: judging one's self as a bad person and then finding ways to demonstrate one's worth by additional acts, or redefining the event to illustrate the importance of deserving and justice in people's lives. Apparently, whether motivated or automatically elicited, the theme of deserving can initially override the more comforting influence of societal norms and the presumably basic motivations to avoid pain, and think well of one's self. Then after experiencing the lowered self-esteem, people's efforts to restore their equanimity will reflect attempts to deny any injustice was actually done, and enhance their sense of self-worth by performing good deeds. But, how do these findings fit with what is known about how important and prevalent the theme of justice is in people's lives? How important is it to people that they and others get what they deserve?

☐ The Justice Motive in Social Behavior: Normative and Intuitive Aspects

The theme of justice as a distinct source of human motivation began to gain attention in the social psychology of the 1950s. The early research that led to the concept of relative deprivation documented the observation that people's satisfaction with their lot in life depends less upon what resources they possess than with their assessment of whether or not they have what they deserve (Stouffer, Suchman, DeVinney, Starr, & Williams, 1949). The proposition that having less than deserved would disturb people was easily accepted as common sense. However, equally compelling evidence also revealed that employees would actively alter their efforts, often at considerable financial costs, to avoid being paid more than they thought they deserved (Adams, 1963). Although subject to considerable subsequent efforts to find more profit-oriented motivation, the basic findings remained and emphasized the central importance of people's desired motivation to get what they deserve and see to it that others are not cheated in the process. The motivation to see that justice prevails also appeared in the early research designed to explain the rejection of innocent victims. That research found that observer's would attempt to rescue and compensate innocent victims; however, when that was not possible they would resort to other ways of reestablishing justice (see previous discussion). These findings together with the research identifying the extent of victims' self-blame led to the recognition of a rather central and prevalent justice motive in people's lives that often appeared in ways that were quite distinct from people's efforts to maximize their outcomes.

Normative Theories: Justice as Rational Self-Interest

Subsequent research, beginning in the mid 1970s , attempted to encompass the various manifestations of the justice motive in people's lives within the prevailing normative views of human motivation. That took the form of attributing people's desire for justice to their enlightened attempts to maximize their outcomes. For example, the exchange and the related equity theories (see, e.g., Messick & Cook, 1983; Walster, Walster, & Berscheid, 1978) assumed that people follow rules of justice if and when they believe it is the most rational way to pursue their own self-interest. They also proposed that the concern with maximizing one's rewards guides what rule of fairness or justice people will employ in a particular situation or whether or not they ignore justice entirely. In essence, according to these prevailing normative theories, justice rules are social devices people employ to facilitate their getting other things they desire such as money, power, or social esteem. From this widely shared perspective there is nothing distinct nor terribly compelling about the way justice appears in people's lives. The justice motive is merely a manifestation of rational self-interest (Tyler, 1994).

The vast majority of social psychological research since the mid 1970s has confirmed the image of people in each encounter using their rational faculties to get the best deal for themselves—greatest profit for least cost—while still behaving within the rules of decent conduct (Tyler, 1994). In truth, however, most of the research need not have been done, since the methods employed merely required the research subjects to engage in some form of conscious, relatively thoughtful, moral reasoning. And in so doing, they were recalling and reciting their understanding of various societal norms. Although the subjects often participated in experiments, the experimental situations were explicit simulations of an economic encounter with minimal if any incentives at stake. Or, the experimental subjects were asked to imagine how they would respond to various vignettes containing brief descriptions of an encounter. In essence, virtually all the evidence that was used to infer human motivation was obtained from people role playing or explicitly trying to imagine how they would react were the events actually occurring in the real world (Messick & Cook, 1983; Tyler, 1994).

As a consequence, the data yielded by these methods are essentially people's opinions based upon their lay theories of human motivation and their use of societal norms concerning what is the most reasonable, appropriate way to react in a particular situation. More recently, many social psychologists have not bothered with experimental simulations and instead have employed questionnaires and interviews to directly obtain people's opinions from which they then infer how much and in what ways people care about justice (Tyler, 1994). Within the framework offered by Shweder and Haidt (1993) this body of research can be described as studies of people's thoughtfully generated moral reasoning. Of course, what is absent and sorely missed are studies of how people feel, think, and act when they are fully engaged, emotionally and motivationally, in an important encounter. This body of research used to describe how the justice motive appears in people's lives does not include studies of people's automatically elicited preconscious moral intuitions most often associated with experiencing the emotions of anger, guilt, sadness, or shame.

The net effect has been virtual consensus among social psychologists that people are for the most part engaged in relatively rational efforts to promote their own self-interest (Tyler, 1994). And, in the pursuit of those goals most people generally follow, and are committed to societal norms of sensible decent conduct in terms of what they desire, how they go about meeting those goals and how they react to the behavior of others. People who violate societal norms are deemed clumsy, foolish, or harmful to others, and are derogated and punished when necessary, while everyone else goes about the business of getting what they want within the rules of fair competition and mutually benefiting cooperation. Certainly, the societal norms require that no sane, decent person reject innocent victims, nor blame themselves and others for events beyond their control (Weiner, 1993). But what about the evidence that irrational counternormative reactions to undeserved suffering often appear in people's lives? People often do derogate innocent victims (Reichle et al., 1998; Ryan, 1971), and blame themselves and others for having accidentally (or guided by honorable intentions) caused others to suffer (Brody, 1985; Freedman et al., 1967; Levinson, 1994; McGraw, 1987; Smith, 1994). And people even more often automatically, without conscious planning, shape their efforts, not to maximize their outcomes but, rather, to have themselves and others get what they deserve (Adams, 1963; Simmons & Lerner, 1968).

Rediscovering the Preconscious Aspects of the Justice Motive

Fortunately, social psychologists are beginning to recognize that there are important psychological processes that are preconscious and inconsistent with societal norms and conventional views of human motivation (see, e.g., Chaiken & Trope, 1999). For example, Bazerman, White, and Lowenstein (1995) described several studies where people expressed more satisfaction with a fair outcome than if offered a larger but less fair outcome, but if people were required to make a conscious choice between the two alternatives, they would elect to maximize their pay-offs in preference to having lesser but more fair outcomes. The investigators conclude that when people engage in what Shweder and Haidt (1993) would term moral reasoning, the societal norms of rational self-interest become the compelling factors in their decisions, but if allowed to follow their moral intuitions people automatically prefer fairness. Similarly, Miller and his colleagues (Miller & Ratner, 1996) concluded, with considerable supporting evidence, that people not only overestimate the extent to which others will act in a self-interested manner but, more to the point, people feel it is emotionally risky to publicly display their preferences for other, more principled choices. In other words, most people are aware of the expectation that they and others will act in a rationally self-interested manner, and they recognize that anyone whose acts do not obviously conform with their own best interests is at risk of being labeled a type of irrational deviant.

Experiments explicitly designed to reveal the differential effects of people's conscious and preconscious concerns with justice have reappeared in the social psychological literature. Lerner, Goldberg, and Tetlock (1998) initially aroused their research participants' concerns with justice by having them watch a filmed excerpt vividly depicting an obviously evil character bullying and humiliating a kind, vulnerable person in front of his classmates. After watching the film, ostensibly as part of a second study, the participants then reacted to a series of brief vignettes, each of which portrayed someone whose negligent acts caused others to suffer. The participants then rated the negligent perpetrators' responsibility and assigned levels of punishment. On the basis of prior research (Keltner, Ellsworth, & Edwards, 1993), these investigators predicted and found that witnessing the initial injustice elicited anger in the participants and the extent of their anger carried over into their reactions to the harmdoer in the next situation. The more anger they experienced witnessing the initial injustice, the more punitive their reactions to the negligent perpetrator in the next situation were.

These subsequent punitive reactions, however, did not appear if the participants had been informed that the initial harmdoer, the evil bully, had been apprehended and punished by the courts. Even though the participants who believed the villain had been punished still brought the same level of anger into the next situation, their anger did not influence their subsequent reactions to the negligent harmdoer (Goldberg, Lerner, & Tetlock, 1996). Apparently, their preconscious concerns with issues of justice leading to punishment had been satisfied. In addition, other participants acted more rationally if they expected to be interviewed by a postdoctoral researcher interested in their reactions either to the film or the vignette. The anticipation of having to publicly justify their reactions led these participants to shape their punitive reactions to correspond with their ratings of the second perpetrators' responsibility and negligence, rather than directly to the anger they were experiencing. As expected, the anticipation of the interview made the participants aware of the societal norms concerning the appropriate rules for assessing culpability and punishment, while in the absence of that reminder their moral intuitions let their anger automatically influence their reactions. The findings of this experiment suggest when and how reactions to injustices are expressed either in the form of rational normative moral reasoning or rather primitive moral intuitions.

Other recent experiments have provided compelling evidence of the psychological effects elicited by dramatic portrayals of an injustice. Hafer (1998) presented her participants with a news segment containing a moving description of a criminal assault in which a young man had been robbed and beaten. She then had her participants engage in a simple perceptual reaction time task (a modified Stroop test) that required the subjects to indicate as quickly as possible the color of a word flashed on a screen. Though similar in length and frequency across categories, the words were systematically varied to be either justice-related—for example, *fair, unequal*—or words associated with physical or social harm that weren't story-related, and story-related words that were not related to harm or justice; neutral words were also included. As she expected, her participants took longer to identify the color of justice-related words than any of the other category of words, presumably because of the participants' preoccupation with justice-related issues. She also found that the greater the person's delay in identifying the color of the justice-related words, indicating a greater preoccupation with justice issues, the more negatively they subsequently rated the victim's character. However, these justice-related effects did not appear if the participants had been previously informed that the perpetrators of the injustice had been apprehended and punished. The reactions of the participants who thought justice had been done revealed no particular delay in identifying the color of justice-related words and there was no significant relation between that recognition time and the derogation of the victim.

With these ingenious experiments Hafer (1998) generated compelling evidence that vivid depictions of someone having been victimized elicit justice-related concerns and thought processes in the observers. And, the research findings confirmed the hypothesis that the greater those concerns the more likely the observers will resort to derogating the victim's character, presumably as a way of satisfying the desire to see that justice prevails. Obviously, the participants in these experiments were not consciously aware of how their thoughts about justice issues influenced either their identification of the word's color or their evaluation of the victim's character. Therefore, none of these reactions could have been elicited in the typical research situation involving simulations and emotionally sterile vignettes, nor would people be able to report them in their thoughtfully shaped responses to an opinion survey. Those methods enable emotionally detached, role-playing participants to report only that which is conventionally understood: It is generally agreed that people are concerned with justice issues as a more or less intelligent way to meet their other needs, and of course it is virtually a cultural truism that no sane, decent person would ever derogate an innocent victim (Weiner, 1993). But that is only true some of the time, under specific circumstances.

☐ Another Look at the Human Costs

Although changes occurring in the American workplace have created greater wealth and thus may ultimately raise the overall standard of living, they have also led to many human tragedies. Managers and executives involved in corporate restructuring may suffer from unanticipated feelings of guilt, even though by societal standards they had acted responsibly in meeting their legitimate obligations. Workers, dismissed from their jobs so that their employers can remain competitive in the contemporary markets, experience severe threats to their well-being and self-worth in spite of the obvious fact that they had done nothing to merit their loss of gainful employment. By any objective standard they are merely the innocent victims of economic forces, yet they and their families are often unable to maintain their dignity and self-respect as contributing members of society. Although morally not at fault, the discharged workers are faced with the demeaning reality that they have failed to provide a decent living for themselves and their families. In addition, the employees who hold onto their jobs in spite of the extensive and pervasive downsizing, and those who must accept temporary contracts in order to find work, live with increasing insecurity and threatening prospects concerning what the future holds for them and their families.

The Unanticipated Irrational Costs

The tragic aspects of these events are evident in the amount of human suffering directly attributable to the loss of income and job security. But important additional suffering can be traced to the fact that whenever there is human loss and deprivation the issues of justice, deserving, and fairness become salient in the harmdoers', victims', and observer-survivors' lives. Unfortunately, the private and public dialogues, the way people talk to themselves and one another about the justice considerations in these events, include only the normative, publicly accepted rules for determining culpability and blameworthiness. The tragic truth that has been rediscovered, however, is that this form of moral reasoning about justice, about what is good and bad, may neither incorporate nor influence the intuitive reactions people experience. Considerable evidence reveals that although the societal norms may publicly justify people's acts and exonerate the victims, the salience of the suffering and losses automatically generate outcome driven, normatively irrational, and personally costly blaming reactions. The decision makers may feel guilty, the victims become self-punitive and depressed, or angry at the obvious injustice of it all, the family members and other observers feel that someone must be to blame for their suffering, and eventually find someone to condemn: possibly themselves or their spouses. People's moral intuitions can elicit outrage and anger and serve as a source of concerted efforts; however, when there is no legitimate target available, nor obvious course of remedial action, then these intuitive preconscious aspects of the justice motive may be manifested as cognitively primitive blaming and punitive reactions (Hafer, 1998; Lerner, 1980) with at least temporarily devastating effects on the emotional well-being of all concerned.

Potential Dangers in Efforts to Recover Self-Esteem

Fortunately, most people have considerable ability and the personal resources needed to cope with the losses inflicted upon them. By adulthood they have learned ways to recover from temporary threats to their self-esteem, and over time repair the damage from more severe or chronic losses (Montada, Filipp, & Lerner, 1992). But not all of these coping mechanisms are equally constructive for the individual or society. If it is true that the majority of the labor force will be faced with increasing risk of being declared redundant by the introduction of increasingly sophisticated technology or the availability of a much cheaper labor pool, then that majority will have to find some way other than their position in the economy to derive their dignity and well-being. In effect, the middle class as a dream and lifestyle will become less available, but what will takes its place? Armstrong-Stassen and Latack (1992) reported that many survivor's of corporate downsizing became disillusioned with their identities as good employees working for trustworthy companies. Instead, the survivors turned to their families and religions for their security and sense of self-worth. Unfortuately, despite whatever personal benefits that are gained or disappointments avoided by such identity changes, these changes also include the risk of increased insulary and the rejection of outgroups (Meindl & Lerner, 1984). Political analysts have noted the increased risk of the rise of totalitarian regimes in these socioeconomic circumstances.

The working middle class now takes out their resentments on the very poor, very foreign, or very Democratic. They will discover that this will help them as much as aspirin helps a corpse . . . . Many of them could turn against a society that broke its deal and stuck a 'loser' sticker on their foreheads. They may vote for demagogues who reject the society that has turned against them. (Rosenthal, 1995)

Conclusions

It is commonly recognized among scientists as well as laymen that people are primarily, or at least ultimately, concerned with gaining pleasure and avoiding pain. This leads to the related assumption that people are predominantly motivated by the desire to maximize their outcomes and minimize their costs. Even when people appear to be acting in ways that are altruistic or costly to themselves, the natural reaction is to assume that there must be some form of self-interested motivation underlying their behavior (Miller & Ratner, 1996). In describing how justice appears in peoples' lives, social psychologists point to the observation that people will at times use fairness arguments to promote their own self-interested goals as evidence of everyone's preoccupation with self-maximizing motivation. But an examination of the evidence clearly indicates that people also often sacrifice desired resources including, at times, their own safety and well-being in order to see to it that justice prevails. This insistence on finding an underlying self-interested motive in everything that people do carries with it the risk of failing to recognize systematic differences in what people care about and what motivates their behavior. In the case of the justice motive this risk includes additional hazards because, as the evidence indicates, the justice motive is a very important force in people's lives and its manifestations are not always understood or easily controlled by conventional wisdom.

What this all means, is that when confronted with serious issues involving pain, suffering, deprivation, or loss, people can react at two levels of awareness: Consciously, they may more or less rationally assess culpability and assign blame and punishment according to conventional rules of morality; or, especially when the events are a vivid part of their experience, they are just as likely, if not more so, to automatically dispense blame and punishment to whomever is associated with the suffering and loss. Those intuitive emotional reactions, typically, have little if anything to do with rational, conscious thought processes or sophisticated moral reasoning, except in the effort to justify an individual's initial automatic reactions. In this manner innocent victims get blamed and may hate themselves, innocent, inadvertent harmdoers feel guilty and ashamed, and innocent bystanders can be targeted as the scapegoats responsible for all the suffering. The procedures for neutralizing these potentially destructive manifestations of the justice motive or turning them to more constructive uses cannot be easily identified and implemented. Additionally, that won't occur until the problems are recognized and informed solutions attempted. And unfortunately, that will not happen as long as social psychologists continue to look for the justice motive in people's rationally enlightened efforts to pursue their own self-interest.

☐ References

Adams, J. S. (1963). Toward an understanding of inequity. *Journal of Abnormal and Social Psychology, 67,* 422–436.

Armstrong-Stassen, M., & Latack, J. C. (1992). Coping with work-force reduction: The effects of layoff exposure on survivors' reactions. *Academy of Management, Best paper proceedings*, 207–211

Bazerman, M. H., White, S. B., & Lowenstein, G. F. (1995). Perceptions of fairness in interpersonal and individual choice situations. *Current Directions in Psychological Science, 4*, 39–42.

Brockner, J., & Wiesenfeld, B. M. (1996). An integrative framework for explaining reactions to decisions: Interactive effects of outcomes and procedures. *Psychological Bulletin, 120*, 189–208.

Brody, E. (1985). Parent care as normative family stress. *The Gerontologist, 25*, 19–29.

Bulman, R. J., & Wortman, C. B. (1977). Attributions of blame and coping in the real world: Severe accident victims' reactions to their lots. *Journal of Personality and Social Psychology, 35*, 351–363.

Chaiken, S., & Trope, Y. (Eds.). (1999). *Dual-process theories in social psychology.* New York: Guilford.

Council of Economic Advisors. (1996). *Job creation and employment opportunities: The United States labor market, 1993–1996.* Washington, DC: U.S. Department of Labor.

Forgas, J. P. (1995). Mood and judgment: The affect intrusion model (AIM). *Psychological Bulletin, 117*, 39–66.

Freedman, J. L., Wallington, S. A., & Bless, E. (1967). Compliance without pressure: The effects of guilt. *Journal of Personality and Social Psychology, 7*, 117–124.

Goldberg, J., Lerner, J., & Tetlock, P. (April, 1996). *The psychology of punitive bias in judgments of responsibility.* Paper presented at the meeting of the Western Psychological Association, San Jose, California.

Hafer, C. (1998). Measuring the threat to justice beliefs with a Stroop colour-naming task. Paper presented at the meeting of the International Society for Social Justice Research, Denver, Colorado.

Herbert, T. B., & Dunkel-Schetter, (1992). Negative reactions to victims: An overview of responses and their determinants. In L. Montada, S. Filipp, & M. J. Lerner (Eds.), *Life crises and experiences of loss in adulthood* (pp. 497–521). New York: Plenum.

Janoff-Bulman, R. (1979). Characterological versus behavioral blame: Inquiries into depression and rape. *Journal of Personality and Social Psychology, 37*, 1798–1809.

Keltner, D., Ellsworth, P. C., & Edwards, K. (1993). Beyond simple pessimism: Effects of sadness and anger on social perception. *Journal of Personality and Social Psychology, 64*, 740–752.

Kieselbach, T. (1997). Unemployment, victimization, and perceived injustices: Future perpectives for coping with occupational transitions. *Social Justice Research, 10*, 127–152.

Kozlowski, S. W. J., Chao, G. T., Smith, E. M., & Hedlund, J. (1993). Organizational downsizing: Strategies, interventions, and research implications. In C. L. Cooper & I. T. Robertson (Eds.), *International review of industrial and organizational psychology.* New York: Wiley.

Krugman, P. (1994, September 25). Long-term riches, short-term pain. *The New York Times*, p. 9.

Leana, C. R., & Feldman, D. C. (1992). *Coping with job loss.* New York: Lexington.

Lerner, J., Goldberg, J., & Tetlock, P. (1998). Sober second thought: The effects of accountability, anger, and authoritarianism on attributions of responsibility. *Personality and Social Psychology Bulletin, 24*, 563–574.

Lerner, M. J. (1980). *The belief in a just world: A fundamental delusion.* New York: Plenum.

Lerner, M. J., & Agar, E. (1972). The consequences of perceived similarity: Attraction and rejection, approach and avoidance. *Journal of Experimental Research in Personality, 6*, 69–75.

Lerner, M. J., & Goldberg, J. H. (1999). When do decent people blame victims? The differing effects of the explicit rational and implicit/experiential system. In S. E. Chaiken & Y. Trope (Eds.), *Dual process theories in social psychology.* New York: Guilford.

Lerner, M. J., & Matthews, G. (1967). Reactions to suffering of others under conditions of indirect responsibility. *Journal of Personality and Social Psychology, 5*, 315–325.

Levinson, H. (1994). Why the behemoths fell: Psychological roots of corporate failure. *American Psychologist, 49*, 428–436.

McGraw, K. M. (1987). Guilt following transgression: An attribution of responsibility approach. *Journal of Personality and Social Psychology, 53*, 247–256.

Meindl, J. R., & Lerner, M. J. (1984). Exacerbation of extreme responses to an outgroup. *Journal of Personality and Social Psychology, 47,* 71–84.

Messick, D. M., & Cook, K. (Eds.). (1983). *Equity theory: Psychological and sciological perspectives.* New York: Praeger.

Miller, D. T., & Ratner, R. K. (1996). The power of the myth of self-interest. In L. Montada & M. J. Lerner (Eds.), *Current societal issues in justice* (pp. 25–49). New York: Plenum.

Montada, L., Filipp, S., & Lerner, M. J. (Eds.). (1992). *Life crises and experiences of loss in adulthood.* Hillsdale, NJ: Erlbaum.

Newman, K. S. (1993). *Declining fortunes: The withering of the American dream.* New York: Basic Books.

Novak, D. W., & Lerner, M. J. (1968). Rejection as a consequence of perceived similarity. *Journal of Personality and Social Psychology, 9,* 147–152.

Piaget, J. (1932). *The moral judgment of the child.* New York: Harcourt Brace.

Reich, R. (1991). *The work of nations: Capitalism in the 21st century.* New York: Knopf.

Reichle, B., Schneider, A., & Montada, L. (1998). How do observers of victimization preserve their belief in a just world cognitively or actionally? Findings from a longitudinal study. In L. Montada & M. J. Lerner (Eds.), *Responses to victimizations and belief in a just world* (pp. 55–87). New York: Plenum.

Rosenthal, A. M. (1995, January 7–8). Profit up and employment down, anger up and civility down. *International Herald Tribune,* p. 5.

Rubin, Z., & Peplau, L. A. (1973). Belief in a just world and reactions to another's lot: A study of participants in the national draft lottery. *Journal of Social Issues, 29,* 73–93.

Ryan, W. (1971). *Blaming the victim.* New York: Pantheon.

Shaver, K. G. (1985). *The attribution of blame: Causality, responsibility, and blameworthiness.* New York: Springer-Verlag.

Skitka, L. J., & Tetlock, P. E. (1992). Allocating aid: The roles of scarcity, ideology, causal attributions, and distributive norms. *Journal of Experimental Social Psychology, 29,* 397–409.

Skitka, L. J., & Tetlock, P. E. (1993). Providing public assistance: Cognitive and motivational processes underlying liberal and conservative policy preferences. *Journal of Personality and Social Psychology, 65,* 1205–1223.

Shweder, R. A., & Haidt, J. (1993). The future of moral psychology: Truth, intuition, and the pluralist way. *Psychological Science, 4,* 360–365.

Simmons, C. H., & Lerner, M. J. (1968). Altruism as a search for justice. *Journal of Personality and Social Psychology, 9,* 216–225.

Smith, C. A., & Ellsworth, P. C. (1985). Patterns of cognitive appraisal in emotion. *Journal of Personality and Social Psychology, 48,* 813–838.

Smith, L. (1994). Burned-out bosses. *Fortune, 130,* 44–52.

Stouffer, S. A., Suchman, E. A., DeVinney, L. C., Starr, S. A., & Williams, R. M., Jr. (1949). *The American soldier: Adjustment during army life* (Vol. 1.). Princeton, NJ: Princeton University Press.

Tyler, T. R. (1994). Psychological models of the justice motive: Antecedents of distributive and procedural justice. *Journal of Personality and Social Psychology, 67,* 850–863.

Walster, E., Walster, G. W., & Berscheid, E. (1978). *Equity: Theory and research.* Boston: Allyn & Bacon.

Weiner, B. (1993). On sin versus sickness: A theory of perceived responsibility and social motivation. *American Psychologist, 48,* 957–965.

Janet L. Ramsey
Rosemary Blieszner

Transcending a Lifetime of Losses: The Importance of Spirituality in Old Age

Stressful life events may later be recognized as blessings (Snorton, 1999), but during the time we experience them, they threaten our coping capacities and the meaning systems by which we live. Old age especially may present stressful life events or multiple losses that injure one's sense of self-identify. Examples are chronic health problems, the death of a partner or friends, changes in vocational identity, economic difficulties, reduced capacity for social involvement, and difficulties in dealing with a rapidly changing technological and bureaucratic world. Comorbidity and psychogenic stress leading to physical health problems are common, further complicating one's efforts to return to a full and happy life after difficult experiences (Smyer & Qualls, 1999).

There are tremendous individual differences in coping abilities among those in the elderly population. Biological variabilities, present and past life stressors, and differences in protective factors, such as types and amounts of resources available, combine to produce these variations. Some seniors can navigate their ways through traumas and losses and emerge stronger and wiser; others get stuck in despair and lose not only hope but also their sense of self.

Typically, clinical treatment and casework with old adults has responded to these variabilities by focusing on the elimination of as many external stressors as possible. For example, efforts are made to modify the environment, provide social support, and improve health practices (Smyer & Qualls, 1999). Equally important, however, are the internal conclusions about meaning that a person ascribes to a stressful life event. These interpretations, in turn, contribute significantly to how he or she will react emotionally, somatically, and behaviorally. All clinicians know that some persons appear to be emotionally overwhelmed by events that most people would consider minor and unimportant—the tinge of pain in a leg, a small quarrel with a spouse, the stare of a stranger. When transitions or heavy losses, such as the death of a parent or a late-life divorce, occur in the lives of these persons, they are likely to experience severe depression or debilitating anxiety. Other people are able to go through both daily life and heavy losses and even appear to benefit from and be strengthened by their ordeals. Still others are somewhere in between and can survive many losses and transitions but not every trauma.

This ability to survive adversity, and sometimes to transcend it, is often referred to as resiliency. Like many other contemporary terms in psychotherapy, this word is borrowed from the world of the physical sciences. Resiliency is described as the ability to rebound after being hurled down to a hard reality. Although the term resiliency is often used in psychology to refer to behaviors aimed at maintaining levels of functioning in the face of challenge or returning to previous levels after a loss (Baltes, Lindenberger, & Staudinger, 1996), we use it more inclusively here to include posttraumatic behaviors and attitudes that lead beyond survival to growth and development.

In order to try to instill resiliency through the learning of new coping skills, clinicians have emphasized strategies such as assertiveness training (Hashimi, 1991), cognitive restructuring for depression and anxiety (Teri, Curtis, Gallagher-Thompson, & Thompson, 1994), and interventions to increase clients' locus of control over significant aspects of their lives (Rodin, 1986). Usually neglected, however, is the coping resource typically cited by elders themselves: their religious beliefs. "I couldn't have done it without the Lord" is a commonly heard remark after a loss (Ramsey & Blieszner, 1999). But, trained to avoid the topic of religion for fear of offending someone's beliefs (Crossley, 1995; Neeleman & Persaud, 1995), clinicians ironically avoid any discussion of spiritual faith, the very aspect of coping that elderly survivors themselves most often mention.

Indeed, scholars have demonstrated, through quantitative and qualitative research, that religious faith is a significant factor for successful coping in both men and women. As early as 1979, David Moberg wrote of what he called "spiritual well being." Since then, many researchers, for example Koenig, George, and Siegler (1988), have found that elder adults spontaneously mention religion as their most frequently used coping strategy. Recently, and reflecting a trend in society, a change in terminology has occurred and "spirituality" rather than "religion" or "religiosity" has been used to describe the lived experience that includes those attitudes, beliefs, and practices that give spirit to the lives of faith-filled people. During the past decade, ethnographic studies (e.g., Sung, 1999), feminist approaches (e.g., Burke, 1999), cross-cultural research (e.g., Ramsey & Blieszner, 1999), and interpretations of personal journals (e.g., McFadden, 1999) have explored the spiritual factor in trauma and loss during the later years.

How does spirituality function in the lives of older adults to enable them to cope successfully and age well? As the works just cited reveal, it is often helpful to interview strong and successful elderly survivors themselves in order to learn the answer to this question. Such men and women are models of resiliency whose lives can offer inspiration and encouragement both to younger persons and to their contemporaries. They live among us as persons who have transcended a lifetime of losses, learned to cope with incredible difficulties, and gained deep understandings of life.

☐ An Illustrative Study of Spirituality and Resilience

Curiosity about the contributions of spirituality to aging well led to a cross-cultural investigation of elderly women who were nominated by their pastors and peers as outstanding examples of individuals with deep faith that permeated their daily life (Ramsey & Blieszner, 1999). We selected participants for in-depth interviews from one denomination, Lutheranism, to avoid the potential confounds with theological differences that appear in other research on aging and spirituality. Four American and four German women, all 65 years of age or older, spoke at length about their spirituality in the context of their life experiences. Questions focused on how their faith helped them to manage anxieties about growing older, difficulties in relationships, health problems, and a variety of other losses and daily challenges. Past traumas they had survived included World War II, the death of a spouse, and loss of physical mobility.

We found great richness, depth, and complexity in the narrative accounts provided by study participants and we learned much from them about the meaning of resiliency. These spiritually hardy old women exhibited courageous honesty and were still seeking deeper personal integrity. They were not spiritual superwomen who, with the power of God, could hurdle over the handicaps of life in a single bound. In fact, they wept often—but they did not mourn endlessly. The failures and losses in their lives were not seen as unmanageable catastrophes, but were viewed as opportunities for growth, for increased maturity, and for trust in the promises of God. Thus, emotional maturity was matched by spiritual maturity. In their later years, these women had a lively sense of personal identity, heightened through the clarity of honest, ongoing self-examination. They recognized in their suffering the potential for growth beyond their own doing; they discerned a process not of reason alone, but one of Spirit.

Even though, for methodological reasons, we interviewed only Lutheran women, we believe that their experiences apply to members of many faith groups. They discussed universal matters of loss and joy and life and death. They told us of triumphs and failures, of false starts and of spiritual homecomings. A reoccurring theme in their narratives was the importance of personal relationships with family, members of their faith community, and God.

☐ Relationships and Spirituality in Old Age

Most old people participate in personal relationships, which, though sometimes stressful, contribute greatly to their psychological well-being. Elders who are aging well place great emphasis on contacts with their relatives and friends (Adams & Blieszner, 1995; Day, 1991; Johnson & Barer, 1997). Indeed, socially isolated elders are at risk for both poor physical functioning and reduced morale (Andersson, 1998; Newsom & Schulz, 1996).

Likewise in our research, study participants spoke in detail about the value of relationships with family members and friends. Indeed, their spirituality was closely interwoven with relationships that buoyed their morale and gave meaning to their lives. As they talked about faith, their children, husbands, parents, grandparents, nieces, pastors, and friends appeared, disappeared, and reappeared in their stories. The women cared deeply about other people and learned from them, they appreciated other members of the community who were their role models, they nurtured and assisted community members when needed, and they hoped that their children and grandchildren would find the joy and strength they found in spirituality. They suffered over conflict in their families and rejoiced over the successes of special people in their lives. Children were particularly important to these women, and those who were or had been married spoke often about their husbands. Within their congregations, the personal relations they had with others were multifaceted and interdependent. Clearly, relationships with others, both daily and in times of trouble, were very much a part of their spiritual lives and integrated into their experiences of God's presence.

However, although they enjoyed other people and felt it necessary to be part of a faith community, these women were not clingy or dependent. Their relationships are better described as interdependent because they can give and take in an atmosphere of shared support and acceptance. They lived according to a belief in mutuality, a back and forth between giving and taking, and thus they were able to receive gifts and assistance from others graciously as well as do acts of kindness for others in their community. One German woman, whose husband died and left her indigent, spoke of how wonderful it was that God was able to act through her church friends: They purchased clothing and a car for her and now she could use those gifts to visit the sick and shut-ins!

The women's relational style did not preclude their thinking abstractly or making decisions objectively, as has been assumed in previous writing about women's stages of faith development (e.g., Stokes, 1990). Although relational imagery and language dominated their accounts, they also spoke about studying and praying to find God's will for their daily lives. Theologically they had questions about infant baptism, universal salvation, and theodicy, the meaning of suffering. But they unanimously expressed the conviction that it was their relationship with God that gave them strength to cope with suffering, which, in turn, led to greater faith for the next challenge.

☐ Applications for Clinical Practice

Concepts from cognitive-behavioral, existential, and narrative therapies have particular relevance for the study of resiliency. Coping ability during stressful times, along with growth and increased maturity afterwards, signify that one has learned how to think rationally, come to terms with the meaning of one's own existence, and integrated life events into an ongoing personal narrative that is positive and helpful. Practitioners with cognitive, existential, or narrative perspectives all raise questions of how we interpret ourselves to ourselves, how we narrate our life experiences to our own interior audience. We briefly review these therapeutic approaches in order to note their clinical appropriateness in working with elders and encouraging spiritual resiliency.

Cognitive Therapy

An approach often used to treat depression and anxiety, cognitive therapy is actually one component of a very effective combination, cognitive and behavioral therapies. Practitioners of cognitive therapy seek to modify a client's thoughts and perceptions about events in order to bring about healthy changes in her or his behavior. Beck, one of cognitive therapy's founders, proposed that it is not so much the activating events of our lives that disturb us as it is the catastrophic thoughts (cognitions) we have after those activating events occur (Beck, Rush, Shaw, & Emery, 1979). Clients are, therefore, taught to identify irrational thinking, dispute it in an ongoing internal argument, and replace it with thoughts and behaviors that are more rational and more helpful in developing an attitude of problem solving (Goldenberg & Goldenberg, 1996). This approach, combined with appropriate modifications in behavior, is a highly effective therapy for depressed elderly people and is often maintained at follow-ups, even by clients with chronic illness or dementia (Teri et al., 1994). Its success echoes the bounce-back factor described earlier in that it emphasizes the importance of self-talk for determining whether personal losses and transitions will lead to worry, sadness, and fear or to new growth, confidence, and feelings of mastery—what we are calling resiliency. A resilient person, proposes cognitive therapy, is one who has learned how to think.

Like those who have successfully concluded cognitive-behavioral therapy, the women we met are experts both at reframing and follow-through actions. They do not engage in self-talk that inspires irrational fears and contributes to the vicious cycle of anxiety. They combine calm, rational thinking with faith as a *felt* experience, including the experience of God's presence. Skilled at decisive thinking, they have learned to state a situation for what it is—a problem to be solved, not a disaster. They argue with themselves and with their own fears and go on, eventually, to replace anxiety with hope and confidence. They engage in lives of active serving and find ways to contribute to the community at whatever activity level they can manage.

One American woman, for example, has learned to reframe the frightening experience of going away from or returning home alone. She asks the Lord "to take care of me and bring me home safe." Although it is hard for her not to have her loved ones with her, she manages her anxieties through her interpretation that God is present as she opens the door to go out or in. Similarly, another woman reported how, because of her faith, her feelings about being alone differ from those of her sister, who, according to our respondent, worries needlessly. For both of these women, who no longer have family members living in their homes, spiritual resiliency allows them to reframe a potentially frightening situation as one that, though not ideal, is tolerable. They can do this because the experience of God's presence leads them to feel secure.

Although sometimes conceding the need to combine faith and cognitive therapies, counselors frequently do not understand how powerful this combination can be in working with elderly clients. We suggest that, whether or not a therapist shares clients' beliefs, it is important to recognize spiritual strength when one sees it and to be willing to help clients explore ways in which their faith in God's presence might lessen anxieties. Many faith traditions are rich in beliefs that can aid in reframing catastrophic thoughts. "It's terrible that I am alone now" might be transformed through hopeful substitutions congruent with spirituality into "But I'm not really alone because God is with me." One of the women we studied explained why this sense of God's presence has kept her from despair by speaking of God as "right here; I know He's always there. I don't get bitter like some people."

Other worries expressed by these women are common in old age, including the fear of dying alone, anxieties about the next generation, and concerns about increasing disability. They each found different ways to deal with their uneasiness, but all revealed some element of reliance on God's presence in their lives. Counselors spend much time and energy working with clients on expanding their support systems, but how often do they speak with comfort and naturalness about the spiritual support system on which so many elderly people rely?

Perhaps the most commonly mentioned concern of aging people is the fear of becoming dependent on others. But this anxiety, too, is reframed by spiritually the resilient elderly women in our study. Neither dependence nor independence but interdependence becomes the focus of their lives. Their sense of interdependence is based on a lifestyle that embraces the spiritual community. They see themselves neither as objects of care nor as fiercely individualistic and self-reliant. They need each other and they need God; they give to each other and they work for God. At one end of the activity spectrum was one of the American woman. She is blind, almost deaf, and can go nowhere without the help of others. Yet she views her need for help not as an alarming dependency but as a natural opportunity for the church family to participate in mutual support and reciprocity. When she spoke of her situation, it was without self-pity or fear. Similarly, the monetarily poor German woman described previously was able to accept financial gifts from others without injury to her sense of dignity. For her, these were signs of God at work; she spiritually reframes as "God's gift" what others would dread as economic dependency. Referring to money given to her so that she could attend a retreat, she said, "And then she [a friend] sent me that! And that was indeed a gift from God."

On the other hand, one American woman's life appears at first glance to be amazingly independent. She cares for herself and her farm with tremendous energy and with little outside assistance. Yet she became almost angry when we asked if she felt self-sufficient; she insisted on acknowledging her reliance on God: "I truly feel that anything we do we should do it as a praise to God, 'cause He has given us the strength to do these things."

Many examples of spiritual reframing go beyond personal belief to incorporating a sense of spiritual community. When one of the German women writes her poetry, not only is she able to move from despair into confidence in God, but she feels she is writing for the whole community. Another's visitations to sick and homebound persons are not for her own sanctification so much as her acting on behalf of the congregation's outreach. Her effort is anchored firmly in a sense of community.

We saw, too, that assuaging fears is not the only conceivable result of learning spiritual reframing—joy is also a reality. One woman, who has moved past what she believes to be a German propensity for overseriousness, professes that this joy is hard-won: "But, no, that one goes there [to Holy Communion] with joy and takes part in the Lord's Supper, that He is there and says to us, 'Yes, I have died for you, and I have given Myself up for you,' that is a joy."

As these examples show, the eight women we met are resilient because they have learned how to think.

Existential Therapy

Existential therapies, including logotherapy and some family therapy models, are also useful in resiliency building because of the focus they place on one's experience of one's internal world. What meaning does someone attribute to his or her life? Suffering does not have to have the final word, according to Victor Frankl (1969), a Viennese psychiatrist and a survivor of the Nazi Holocaust; the "will to meaning" one gives sufferings can promote transcendence of any ordeal. The counselor using Frankl's logotherapy confronts a person with his or her life purpose and, in partnership with the client, enters into in a healing process leading to the discovery of new meaning. Frankl's personal experiences as a prisoner in Auschwitz taught him that the health of one's inner self is far less dependent on external circumstances or psychological abnormality than it is the result of making a free decision. He witnessed, in that grotesque place, a fascinating process: Prisoners who held fast to their moral and spiritual values survived emotionally intact. They filled what seemed to be a terrifying vacuum with the discovery of beauty and with spiritual meaning. This same process, said Frankl, can help clients discover meaning through spiritual reinterpretations of suffering. Similarly, family therapists with a constructivist view, including solution-oriented therapists, believe that there is no single, proper view of reality and that neither the therapist's view nor the family member's view is correct. Therefore, they encourage clients to define their own goals and search out their own meaningful solutions. For example, Gestalt therapist Walter Kempler urged family members to become more intensely aware of what they were doing or saying or feeling, more in touch with what was going on in everyday family discussions in order to look beyond the surface, to uncover and own the basics of their human experience (Goldenberg & Goldenberg, 1996). The resilient person, for the existential therapist, is someone who knows how to be.

The questions of meaning that are the foci of existential therapies were richly evident throughout the interviews we conducted, confirming the appropriateness of this therapeutic approach for working with older persons. Here, too, relationships with others were consistently interwoven in the picture of resiliency that emerged. Illustrating this perspective is the German interviewee who finds pleasure and significance in being able to do simple things, such as dancing, being with others, and gazing at the beauty of the church interior. Also, the 93-year-old American woman who is blind, weak, and no longer able to leave her chair, believes that God is in charge of her life and that her ministry of prayer is important to the whole community. She lives to pray and to fulfill whatever God has in mind for her; she is God's servant and finds meaning in what she believes to be a morally upright, theologically sound life. Reminiscent of Frankl's (1969) stories of persons who watched the stars in the concentration camps, another American finds meaning in her appreciation of nature, in looking at the world God made. Along with her love for friends and family, she finds sufficiency in taking part as a creature in the Creator's world. Still another has discovered meaning revolving around her farm work, and in defining herself as a worker in God's Kingdom. These four metaphors for self, "minister," "servant," "nature-lover," and "worker," are powerful meaning givers, helping greatly to compensate the women for the losses they have sustained.

The women in our study did not hesitate to share emotional aspects of their search for meaning. As they sought to explain themselves and the meaning of their lives, they cried, laughed, and sighed; there was no gap between their existential questions and powerful human feelings. Because they felt safe in their communities, they could share what M. Scott Peck (1987) referred to as the lost art of crying. One interviewee demonstrated this as she cried when speaking of her mother's illness and death, but she also articulated how the caretaking role had given meaning to her life.

> When my husband died in '79, my mother lived next door. So she was getting old and I felt like she needed to be with me, and I was alone so I brought her down here to live with me. Then she died in '86. But the last three years she was almost bedfast. So I had it real hard again, but I came through it, and I feel like I've been enriched by it.

This caretaker's emotional and existential courage cannot be understood apart from the community in which she lived and from which she drew strength.

The search for meaning is often characterized as a solitary matter, yet these women's endeavors were definitely communal. One vivid example of how the community functions to support those who are searching for meaning occurred in Germany after a focus group meeting the first author conducted as part of this project. An emotionally fragile woman (not one of the spiritually resilient women we interviewed) broke down as she talked about her World War II experiences, crying and speaking bitterly about her spiritual doubts. "Where was God? Why did God do this to us Germans?" she asked. The stronger women in the community responded by offering various opinions about responsibility for the war and its meaning for Germany. They took it upon themselves to invite her over for coffee later, so that they could support her during her time of hurt and doubt.

Thus, we found that through incorporating spirituality in their interpretations of life events, these women have learned how to be.

Narrative Therapy

Narrative therapists believe that we live in a "destoried" world (White & Epston, 1990) and, as a result, suffer an impoverishment of meaning in our lives. Feelings of emptiness and dissatisfaction, expressed especially by those in younger cohorts, may result from what was, at first, their lost belief that objective, scientific truth would supply all the answers to life's questions (Bateson, 1972). When illness or other losses occur that cannot be remedied by technology, despair or at the least feelings of disempowerment can occur. Chronically ill people, many of whom are old, tend to have problem-saturated descriptions of their lives; they have difficulties separating themselves from their illnesses. Thus, clients in narrative therapy are encouraged to externalize their problems and create new and more hopeful narratives for themselves. The therapist helps them search for exceptions, for times when they were able to manage and cope during transitions, thereby increasing their feelings of empowerment, responsibility, and choice. Language is framed in positive modes such as, "When your life is better, how will that be?" Narrative therapists help those who come to them recognize that their problems may actually be the property of society, not of the ill or old or "different" person who is the client. Together, therapist and client deconstruct reality and its dominant narrative and rewrite self-descriptions anchored in more authentic plot lines for the past, present, and future (White & Epston, 1990). For narrative therapists, resilient persons are those who have learned how to narrate their own life stories.

The worlds of the spiritually resilient women in our study are anything but destoried. They are able to externalize their problems, rewrite their plot lines, and visualize their narratives within a larger, ongoing story. They create and re-create personal histories with heart as well as mind, and they have a sense of the many ways in which their individual stories intersect with those of others to whom they relate, including friends and family. They view their stories as part of the larger story of God's People, and they are, therefore, able to move along the path of spiritual development—*der Weg*, as a German woman called it, "the way." Rather than telling problem-saturated stories in which they appear as victims, they tell stories rich in choices, empowerment, and second chances.

There is no question that even as they spoke, the women were actively participating in reconstructing the reality of their experiences. We cannot know all the ways in which our interviews encouraged a narrative process that was helpful and healing, for there is no way to unweave the women's narratives into the parts that became different in the telling. The women's stories created them as much as they created their stories. Although such restorying was not the goal of the project, it certainly occurred, as it does in narrative therapy, and had a tremendous healing potential. Letters and notes we continue to receive from the women confirm our impression that the telling of their life stories strengthened them. After reading the book that recounted this research project (Ramsey & Blieszner, 1999), one of the German women recently sent a poem, dedicated to the first author, that began, "If you are praised, and the good in you is revealed, then beats the heart so strongly . . . . " Of course "the good" was her own spiritual resiliency, revealed as she quietly told the story of her life.

When one considers the external events the women in this research experienced, it is easy to see ample reasons for them to write stories with the theme, "Poor Me!" Like so many others, the women have suffered the deaths of children, spouses, and parents. They told of alcoholic husbands and sons, or daughters and stepmothers who belittled them. War, poverty, and illness shattered life as they knew it. One example is the 93-year-old homebound woman whose narrative is totally lacking in self-pity; she sees her physical ailments as just one part of who she is, not as the defining element of her self. She has vision problems; she is not "the blind woman." Similarly, the impoverished German woman's story line suggested a faltering immediately after the death of her husband. But as she explained her reactions to widowhood, she came to see the love and concern of her adult children as God's way of helping her acquire a new story line. "Get a life," they told her, and the life she got was one so new and hopeful that she was almost sheepish in telling how much happier she is now. She became more active in the Christian community and her days are filled with Bible groups, worship, and calling on the homebound. Her *Weg,* her faith pilgrimage, is now the theme of her life, and the time after the loss of her spouse may be viewed as a new chapter in her story entitled, "A Second Chance."

The women's narratives were full of continuity as well as change. Their stories already contained important themes that they had retained over time. Only revisions are needed, in keeping with new situations, better insights, and increased maturity. This is consistent with emphases in narrative therapy. Wrote Parry and Doan (1994), "If these themes are important in the old story, there is no need to assume that they must be totally abandoned or labeled as bad or ineffective in the new version. Rather, they need to be reinterpreted" (p. 50). An example is the trusting, almost childlike persona one German woman has created for herself within her community. Now, however, she is no longer the child of the family of origin where she was once adored; rather, she defines herself as a child of God, a member of His family of believers.

Perhaps the most dramatic rewrite told in this project was provided by one of the German women who had been a member of the Hitler youth movement. Her narrative now is anchored in community, but her early chapters had been filled with the theme, "Me." Her youthful persona was, she said, overly individualistic and rebellious. As an adult she found an active role in the Christian community, where a *Geländer* (handrail) was available to guide her. She did not rewrite her story to excuse herself or deny that she had made bad choices in her youth. Instead, she encouraged her whole community to participate in a rewrite of the typically ignored World War II period, and one result was discussion of the Nazi era in her town's jubilee book (Kurtz, 1982). This woman's spirituality allows her to externalize evil, such as the evil that came with Hitler, and go on to work against corruption in a variety of ways—as her town's first woman mayor, as an activist in ecology and world peace movements, and as a courageous host who brings up the topic of the Holocaust in social settings to those who would prefer to forget. When she says, in effect, "never forget," she is also saying, "evil will never write my story again."

As shown by the thoughtful analyses of even the most difficult situations that the women in our study provided, a spiritually strong person knows how to tell life's story.

☐ Conclusion

We believe that the interpersonally grounded spiritual resiliency found in the women we interviewed offers important correctives to the individualistic and overly rationalistic themes sometimes emphasized by therapists, even by those who employ cognitive-behavioral, existential, or narrative approaches. Being effective in work with elderly people does not involve fixing or curing. Rather, there is a kind of patient presence involved that is more at home with questions of meaning, spiritual reframing, and life stories than with the diagnostic inquisition and an emphasis on the symptoms of psychopathology. Listening to metaphors and plot lines that have resulted in the client's becoming stuck, and helping elderly clients replace their broken records of despair and powerlessness with empowering metaphors that have a spiritually healthy component is geriatric counseling designed for the values and mind-set of today's elders. Listening for how old persons describe their lives, including not changing the subject when they speak of their faith, is crucially important. Counseling for spiritual resiliency is certainly not about evangelizing the beliefs of the counselor; one must consistently and carefully work within the faith traditions of the clients. But ignoring religion as an ingredient of strength ignores aspects of resiliency most precious to many older clients.

We further suggest keeping in mind the importance of personal relationships as a vital ingredient in an older person's spirituality. The clinician who understands this component of elders' spiritually will recognize the value of the therapeutic relationship itself as a potential aspect of recovery, and will listen attentively for helpful and healthy family and friendship themes nestled within the complex and diverse narratives that aged clients tell. He or she may also find it helpful to share with older clients some empowering stories of strong survivors such as those described above.

It could be argued that hearing stories of resilient women would only discourage old people who are not coping successfully with difficulties in their lives. Might exposure to examples of strength make those who are currently having difficulties with losses or transitions feel even more inadequate? Certainly, sharing stories of resilient persons must be done with the same care, good timing, and tact required by any therapeutic intervention. It is important, too, that models not be held up as perfect saints. For example, the women in this study did not claim spiritual perfection; in fact they do not have a sense of being special or unusual in any way. Women similar to the eight we met in our research could no doubt be found everywhere. These women have felt, at times, nearly overwhelmed by their circumstances and exigencies. Transitions and losses have been difficult, and the women in our study have not found supernatural ways to escape the pain and ambiguities of life. But through the strengths they gained from loving relationships, they found the power to travel on journeys out of difficulties and into joyous life for the larger community. Along the way, they integrated their emotional and religious experiences to focus on strength-giving relationships with others.

People who hurt are, indeed, thirsty for encouraging stories of survivors. The vulnerability risked by those in who share stories of their journey can be more than an inspiration for those who are slowly moving out of denial. It is also an embodiment of what survivorship looks like. Often it is the loss of hope, the impossibility of moving past despair and seeing alternative outcomes, that overwhelms those who are aging. If narratives of strong people are told with a light, nonmoralistic, and empathetic touch, they can impart inspiration and fresh optimism to those who previously foresaw only catastrophe. Such stories can also work towards re-creating a positive idea of what it can mean to grow old.

☐ References

Adams, R. G., & Blieszner, R. (1995). Aging well with friends and family. In P. E. Fontane & J. C. Solomon (Eds.), *Aging well in contemporary society* [Special issue]. *American Behavioral Scientist, 39,* 209–224.

Andersson, L. (1998). Loneliness research and interventions: A review of the literature. *Aging & Mental Health, 2,* 264–274.

Baltes, P. B., Lindenberger, U., & Staudinger, U. M. (1996). Life-span theory in developmental psychology. In W. Damon (Ed.), *Handbook of child psychology* (5th ed., pp. 1029–1143). New York: Wiley.

Bateson, G. (1972). *Steps to an ecology of mind.* New York: Ballantine.

Beck, A. T., Rush, A. J., Shaw, B. F., & Emery, G. (1979). *Cognitive therapy of depression.* New York: Guilford.

Burke, P. C. (1999). Spirituality: A continually evolving component in women's identity development. In L. E. Thomas & S. A. Eisenhandler (Eds.), *Religion, belief, and spirituality in late life* (pp. 113–136). New York: Springer.

Crossley, D. (1995). Religious experience within mental illness: Opening the door on research. *Bristish Journal of Psychiatry, 166,* 284–286.

Day, A. T. (1991). *Remarkable survivors: Insights into successful aging among women.* Washington, DC: Urban Institute.

Frankl, V. E. (1969). *The will to meaning: Foundations and applications of logotherapy.* New York: World.

Goldenberg, I., & Goldenberg, H. (1996). *Family therapy: An overview* (4th ed.). New York: Brooks/ Cole.

Hashimi, J. (1991). Counseling older adults. In P. K. H. Kim (Ed.), *Serving the elderly: Skills for practice* (pp. 33–49). New York: Aldine de Gruyter.

Johnson, C. L., & Barer, B. M. (1997). *Life beyond 85 years: The aura of survivorship.* New York: Springer.

Koenig, H. G., George, L. K., & Siegler, I. C. (1988). The use of religion and other emotion-regulating coping strategies among older adults. *Gerontologist, 28,* 303–310.

Kurtz, J. (1982). *700 Jahre Stadt Wilster (700 years of the City of Wilster).* Hamburg, Germany: Verlagsbuchbinderei Ladstetter.

McFadden, S. H. (1999). Surprised by joy and burdened by age: The journal and letters of John Casteel. In L. E. Thomas & S. A. Eisenhandler (Eds.), *Religion, belief, and spirituality in late life* (pp. 137–149). New York: Springer.

Moberg, D. O. (Ed.). (1979). *Spiritual well being: Sociological perspectives.* Washington, DC: University Press.

Neeleman, J., & Persaud, R. (1995). Why do psychiatrists neglect religion? *British Journal of Medical Psychology, 68,* 169–178.

Newsom, J. T., & Schulz, R. (1996). Social support as a mediator in the relation between functional status and quality of life in older adults. *Psychology and Aging, 11,* 34–44.

Parry, A., & Doan, R. E. (1994). *Story re-visions: Narrative therapy in the postmodern world.* New York: Guilford.

Peck, M. S. (1987). *The different drum: Community-making and peace.* New York: Simon & Schuster.

Ramsey, J. L., & Blieszner, R. (1999). *Spiritual resiliency in older women: Models of strength for challenges through the life span.* Thousand Oaks, CA: Sage.

Rodin, J. (1986). Aging and health: Effects of the sense of control. *Science, 233,* 1271–1276.

Smyer, M., & Qualls, S. H. (1999). *Aging and mental health.* Malden, MS: Blackwell.

Snorton, T. (1999, March). *Each day a blessing, each year a gift.* Presentation at the 45th Annual Meeting of the American Society of Aging, Orlando.

Stokes, K. (1990). Faith development in the adult life cycle. *Journal of Religious Gerontology, 7,* 167–185.

Sung, K-t. (1999). Filial piety: The traditional ideal of parent care in East Asia. In J. Ellor, S. McFadden, & S. Sapp (Eds.), *Aging & spirituality: The first decade* (pp. 33–39). San Francisco: American Society on Aging.

Teri, L., Curtis, J., Gallagher-Thompson, D., & Thompson, L. (1994). Cognitive-behavior therapy with depressed older adults. In L. S. Schneider, C. F. Reynolds, II, B. D. Lebowitz, & A. J. Fridhoff (Eds.), *Diagnosis and treatment of depression in late life* (pp. 279–291). Washington, DC: American Psychiatric Press.

White, M., & Epston, D. (1990). *Narrative means to therapeutic ends.* New York: Norton.

Paul L. Toth
Rex Stockton
Frederick Browne

College Student Grief and Loss

Every relationship ends in death or separation. Grief is well known to anyone who has lived long enough to experience a yearning for another. In spite of grief being well studied and ubiquitous it can affect survivors with such profound emotional and, at times, physical pain that normal everyday functioning is suspended. Following a significant loss, grief and grief recovery become the central focus of one's experience. University students, especially traditional students (ages 18–23) who tend to be less experienced with death and loss, may suffer the loss of an important relationship with a heightened sense of isolation and hopelessness. Young adults are challenged to experience the intensity of grief, perhaps for the first time, as well as their own vulnerability and mortality. This chapter will discuss dynamics of grief and loss, examine college students' grief and loss, share some clinical observations that inform us about grief and grief recovery, and make recommendations regarding grief counseling with the college population.

☐ Grief and Loss

Early work related to grief focused on death as the major initiator of grief (Bowlby, 1973; Kübler-Ross, 1969). However, the causal factors of grief have been expanded to include things such as the loss of attachment relationships. As an example, Kaczmarek, Backlund, and Biemer (1990) found the suddenness of a breakup, the perceived closeness of the relationship, and the duration of the relationship had a significant impact on the level of depression resulting from the loss of a romantic relationship (p. 323). A loss of this nature and the ensuing grief can adversely affect "academic performance, life satisfaction, and mental health" (Okun, Taub, & Wittmer, 1986, cited in Kaczmarek, Backlund, & Biemer, 1990, p. 319). Grief resulting from the breakup of a romantic relationship can be very serious. It has been related to suicide in young adults (Santrock, 1981).

For the purpose of this chapter, we have defined loss as the loss of an object of love through death or divorce, or from separation, or the ending of significant relationships. For example, loss may be experienced in the death of a parent, sibling, or friend, the end of a romantic relationship, parental divorce, or another experience of separation that seriously alters a person's social network, perceptions of self, and perceptions of the world. Grief is our emotional, psychological, and physical response to loss. Bereavement and sorrow are expressions that represent physical and emotional feelings related to the loss. Grief is a serious matter, with potentially damaging consequences. LaGrand (1989) stated that the ten most reported feelings accompanying loss were depression, anger, emptiness, loneliness, frustration, disbelief, shock, helplessness, loss of self-confidence, and guilt. Worden (1991) and Raphael (1984) added a number of other feelings associated with the manifestation of normal grief. These included sadness, self-blame, despair, anxiety, fatigue, yearning, emancipation, relief, and numbness. Worden also listed a number of physical sensations associated with grief that parallel symptoms of anxiety or panic. These include dry mouth, tightness in the chest and throat, breathlessness, weakness, and a sense of unrealness. Moreover, people react to significant loss by experiencing inhibition of pleasure, confusion, deadening of emotions, loss of physical and sexual energy, and lack of interest in life (Toth, 1997). In its intensity and longevity loss is like no other emotional response to a life event.

Traditionally, in Western thought, grief resolution is accomplished by the withdrawal of bonds with the object of the grief. In terms of psychoanalytic theory, this allows for emotional energies to be redirected towards new healthy attachments (Worden, 1991). However, Marwit and Klass (1995) in a study designed to identify and describe the inner representation of death and its relationship to grief resolution, found that a positive representation and relationship with the deceased individual related to successful grief resolution. In effect, this means that grief resolution is not simply a matter of loosening bonds with the deceased, but a matter of reframing the relationship.

Much of the grief literature is developmental in nature. The process of grieving is explained as a serious of stages. It has sometimes been assumed that the bereaved must pass through a sequence of stages in order to complete his or her grief process. The developmental model is most useful, however, if it is seen as a guide in our effort to understand the grief process and not a doctrine to be followed lock-step or thrust upon anyone. Clinicians argue against adhering to the developmental model at the expense of remaining sensitive to individual differences (Sprang & McNeil, 1995). Indeed, the notion that one stage model fits all is incompatible with the importance of individual experience in grief. With this in mind, we will examine stages of grief to help elucidate our understanding of grief recovery.

Lamb (1988) explained the developmental aspects of grief by dividing the process into three stages. Lamb's model maximizes flexibility and allows for utility of interpretation. The first stage of grief allows time for the bereaved to adjust to the reality of loss. It is a kind of moratorium on the more commonly acknowledged symptoms of grief: tears and sadness, for example. Symptoms in this initial stage include "shock, acute crisis, numbness, protesting (and) denial" (Lamb, 1988, p. 563). This early stage of grief provides time for the bereaved to develop a cognitive framework in which they begin to make sense of the loss experience. It can also help delay an onslaught of emotions. Delaying emotions allows the "individual to sustain the impact of the loss without being overwhelmed by the pain and sorrow" (p. 563). Lamb's first stage is like that of Parkes' (1970, as reported in Worden, 1991) first phase of grief: a period of numbness. Worden (1991) wrote that this first phase helps the survivor "disregard the fact of the loss at least for a brief period of time" (p. 35). This first stage/phase usually lasts several weeks after the socially sanctioned mourning period.

Lamb (1988) referred to the second period of grief as the intermediate stage. Much like Parkes' (1970) second phase, this stage is, perhaps, the most difficult for the survivor. In this stage, which lasts from two to twelve months after the loss, the person experiences distress, disorganization, despair, and yearning for the object of loss. These feelings and thoughts are frequently experienced in isolation. Acquaintances and friends close to the grieving person may withdraw previous support since the loss becomes less central to their lives. According to Lamb, two overlapping processes mark this stage. First, the person obsessively reviews the situation around the loss. He or she may become stuck on one particular thought that may have effected the outcome of the loss. Second, the bereaved individual becomes involved in making new meaning out of the loss.

The final stage of grief includes involving oneself in preloss activities without the one who is being grieved. It may mark the beginning of new activities and initiatives the person had not been able to do with his or her significant other. In this stage the person makes a "conscious decision" to no longer dwell on death while acknowledging that he or she must go on with life in spite of their loss (Lamb, 1988). Like Lamb, Parkes (1970) stated that it is highly important that the bereaved reorganize his or her behavior and begin to set life back on track (in Worden, 1991).

☐ College Student Grief

Both literature and clinical experience point to the significant impact of grief and loss on college students. Traditionally-aged undergraduate students (18–23 years old) who have experienced loss may be vulnerable to additional stressors due to their maturational stage and the environment in which they are left to grieve.

Though death among college-aged peers is less than the norm, death is well known within this age group as well as on college campuses. Floerchinger (1991) reported that significant loss through death among college students is more pervasive than was commonly thought. She collected information from a number of resources, including U.S. census reports, to describe the prevalence of grief among college-age persons. She stated that as many as 15% of certain populations would lose a parent to death by the time they are 16 years old. Five percent of the families surveyed by the U.S. Census Bureau (1971–1986)* reported the death of a parent. Wener and Jones (1979) estimated that 10% of families economically positioned to afford college would lose a parent to death (in Floerchinger, 1991). Moreover, students are affected by the deaths of peers. By some estimates, between four and fifteen deaths occur for every 10,000 college students. According to Floerchinger, this would mean that between 5,000 and 19,000 college students die each year. This figure appears even more daunting if the death of relatives (especially grandparents, given the age of the college student population) were to be counted along with peers. LaGrand (1986) surveyed over 3,500 university students. Of those surveyed 28.5% reported that their most recent major loss was the death of a loved one. Over 24% said that their loss involved the end of a love relationship, 10.1% reported the end of a friendship, and 9.8% reported separation from a loved one. Just over 1% stated that their most recent major loss was

*(as reported in Floerchinger, 1991)

divorce. Nearly 75% of students surveyed by LaGrand, then, described a loss of a significant other due to some type of separation or end of a relationship. Balk and Vesta (1998) reported a Kansas State University study that found ". . . at any point in time 25–30% of the students are within the first 12 months of the death of a family member or of a friend" (pp. 24–25). Most young adults on college campuses will experience significant loss during their college experience. However, many will be dealing with loss through death for the first time.

Developmental theorists take note that young adults have entered into a stage in life where separation through death or loss can provide particular challenges. Janowiak, Mei-Tal, and Drapkin (1995) stated that "college students are struggling with breaking away from their families of origin and developing independent identities. It may be especially difficult for young adults to cope with the loss of a loved one at the same time they are attempting to become autonomous individuals" (p. 56). In addressing young adults, the experience of a traumatic loss has been found to be related to a greater amount of general psychological distress and less individuation from the family over the course of a lifetime (Bradach & Jordan, 1995).

Balk (1996) reported that higher levels of attachment to the deceased produced more psychological distress and acute grief in bereaved students. He found that greater attachment led to less comfort. In fact, the stronger the attachment, the more distressed the bereaved. This would suggest that college students' grief and drive toward individuation could interact to produce a catalyst for heightened distress. However, autonomy and individuation may not be as important for some students as for others. Kuk (1990) pointed out that women's development might not be as dependent upon individuation as their male counterparts. She stated that identity development in women has more to do with connectedness and compassion than it does with individuation and separation. Moreover, studies where bereaved young adults continued to remain attached to their deceased siblings, and where bereaved children and adolescents continued an attachment to their deceased parents indicate the bereaved find some level of comfort in remaining attached to the deceased. Tyson-Rawson (1993) found that 10 of 14 young women who reported continued attachment to their dead fathers were comforted by this ongoing emotional relationship (in Balk, 1996). It stands to reason that young women who experience a significant loss are likely to have a different kind of developmental crisis than men. "Their crisis may focus on the difficulty of redefining and developing an identity apart form the love object to which they were connected" (Toth, 1997, p. 88).

Traditionally-aged college students encounter an additional developmental challenge when facing grief and loss due to the death of a close relative or loved one. For many college students this type of loss will be their first experience of separation due to the death of a significant other. These students may not have experienced the intense emotions death brings. Students whose parent, sibling, or close friend has died may say things like, "I've never felt such pain," "I can't imagine ever feeling better," and "how long will this pain go on?" Laments and questions such as these reveal not only students' intense pain but also their uncertainty or tentativeness of making sense out of the experience. Intensity of emotions combined with a lack of experience with grief can make it additionally difficult for young adults to move through their loss.

Many persons who have studied bereavement in college students point out that both the developmental stage of late adolescents and the college environment can be unfriendly to the tasks of grieving (Balk & Vesta, 1998; Sklar & Hartly, 1990; Toth,

1997). Sklar and Hartly (1990) wrote that young adults are particularly vulnerable to difficulties arising from a close friend's death. This is because young adults who are individuating from their family are connected to friends to a deeper degree than they had experienced in the past. This makes a friend's death all the more traumatic.

Also, death for young adults is generally due to a sudden, violent, or shocking event instead of a more predictable illness—as with older adults. This type of death can leave survivors with a great degree of emotional trauma. When loss occurs because of deaths that are "sudden, violent, premature, or stigmatized, they are likely to be associated with a more problematic course of recovery and life adjustment" (Bradach & Jordan, 1995, p. 316). Reporting results from a number of studies, Bradach and Jordan noted that families are changed and at times can become seriously disturbed (particularly in the case of early parent loss) by the death of a member (Bradach & Jordan, 1995). The level of coping skills they gain at this juncture may affect their future ability to deal with other deaths or family illnesses (Rolland, 1990).

Furthermore, Toth (1997) wrote that the home and college environments often present different responses to the bereaved. The death of a close relative—especially a parent, sibling, or grandparent—will bring a student from the university to the home setting. At home, students are often steeped in mourning rituals that can enhance the grief process. Toth noted from clinical experience that some students encounter home as ". . . the place where death can be discussed and the grieving student experiences some affirmation for thoughts and feelings. In this case, students may long to be home where they can be sad, angry, or irritable and not have to worry about what their college peers think" (Toth, 1997, p. 88).

Many students return to school to face an environment that goes about life as usual without making room for the bereaved to take the time he or she needs for emotional recovery. Robak and Weitzman (1995) addressed the topic of disenfranchised grief, defined by Doka (1989) as the experience of loss without socially sanctioned support and expression. According to Robak and Weitzman, losses such as "perinatal death and abortion, death of a pet, death of a lover (including same-sex lovers), and death of a divorced spouse" are examples of disenfranchised grief (p. 269). The support network of the grieving individual is viewed as important to the ability of the grieving individual to overcome his or her grief. However, with disenfranchised grief, the support network does not conceptualize the grief experience as having a great degree of severity, which often keeps the grieving individual from receiving appropriate support. This adds to the difficulty of recovering from the grieving process. Balk and Vesta (1998) stated that "bereaved students find few if any persons in the university willing to mention the death, to acknowledge the importance of this event in the student's life, or to recognize the significance for the griever of the person who died" (p. 25).

One exploratory study (Vickio, Cavanaugh, & Attig, 1990) found that the study's nongrieving participants (123 undergraduate students) possessed ". . . substantial awareness of the various facets of the grief process, including the emotional, physical, interpersonal, and temporal features. Many also demonstrated sensitivity to the wide diversity that can exist in grief reactions, rather than having a narrowly circumscribed view of what grief entails" (p. 239). However, even if students are aware of the grief process, this does not indicate that they apply their knowledge when confronted with a bereaved friend or peer. The college campus—where youthful celebration is demonstrated in many ways, and expectations to achieve academic success are the norm, may easily become a troublesome environment when one experiences significant loss.

Two additional challenges most students negotiate when grieving are academic difficulties and the loss of personal identity that often follows. The symptoms of grief, as stated above, include loss of energy and motivation, loss of concentration, and heightened emotional experiences. These symptoms can make the work of being a student quite difficult. Students are often at a loss as to how they might proceed with course work when faced with loss. They say things like: "I can't study any longer," "I just want to be with my family," and "How will I ever finish my semester?" Berson (1988) wrote, "academic work is the college student's job in life, and the inability to do the job can prove painfully disruptive" (p. 105). Grief interferes with students doing their "job." And along with this may come a loss of sense of self. Persons whose lives have centered on academic progress are challenged to reassess their self-perceptions when this progress is arrested by grief. A student, then, is not only confronted by the reality of a significant loss, but also must deal with the loss of his or her internalized image as a successful student (Toth, 1997).

☐ Clinical Observations

The authors gathered information from a number of persons who work with college students in the area of grief, loss, and trauma. These persons represented a number of professions including counselors, psychologists, clergy, and educators. Many of these professionals worked with grieving students or taught courses that focused on grief and loss.

Counselors who work with students in clinical settings and educators who work with students in classrooms both agree that students who have experienced significant loss need, above all, to talk and be heard (LaGrand, 1986; Price, Dinas, Dunn, & Winterowd, 1995; Toth, 1997; Worden, 1991). And, many students seem to indicate that talking to friends and family about their loss is quite helpful. It stands to reason, given the large numbers of students experiencing loss, that only few will seek out professional counseling. Students who have difficulty readjusting to life without their object of loss—or students who have other psychological difficulties, such as depression, exacerbated by the loss—may seek help from a counselor. Those who adjust with the help of others seldom need professional services.

The types of losses students encounter is wide ranging (LaGrand, 1986). Professionals who work in the areas of counseling and education see a variety of people who have experienced many different types of losses. Student losses vary in both nature and intensity. Much like LaGrand's survey, professionals report seeing students who struggle with loss due to death and with the loss of romantic partners. Professionals also report working with students who experience the loss of nonromantic relationships, changes in self or others that constitute an interpersonal or internal loss, loss when parents divorce, loss of a job, loss of a good grade, and loss due to the death of pets. Interpersonal loss, loss due to death and ending relationships, is the most prevalent (LaGrand, 1986). Interpersonal loss seems to cause the highest degree of disruption in students' lives. Curiously, not many students identify parental divorce as a recent significant loss (only 28 out of 3,510 students [1.2%] in LaGrand's study identified divorce as a significant major loss). This may be because many adults tend to divorce while children are younger than college age. Perhaps, then, by the time students come to college, they will have had years to adjust to the divorce. Or, perhaps, in a nation such as the United States with a substantial divorce rate most young people find a built-in support network of friends who may also come from divorced families.

Harvey, Orbuch, Weber, Merbach, and Alt (1992) discussed the importance of bereaved persons confiding in others about his or her grief. They stated that loss is an experience that diminishes a person's sense of self. In order to pass through this pain and confusion, the bereaved must build a new identity.

> Essentially, through this identity change, each of us becomes a new person—all of life, indeed, is filled with much change and the resultant new selves. Loss, broadly defined . . . is the chief stimulant or catalyst. In its noblest form, major loss can force one to think and feel along new and useful dimensions and to achieve a reconciliation of the deepest and most stable kind. (p. 102)

However, unless a bereaved person meets someone with an empathic ear he or she is likely to withdraw from society. An empathic listener can provide a grieving person with an opportunity to begin to make sense out of the loss. The bereaved needs a trusted other in which to confide.

Confiding in another is usually done by talking (which seems to fit nicely into the therapeutic setting). However, confiding can be done in ways other than talking. The process of confiding may begin by writing, drawing, or other displays of artistic creativity as well as through avenues of expression more traditional to counseling (Harvey et al., 1992). Therapists who work in university settings see many creative individuals in their practice. Counselors can experiment with different ways of confiding that go beyond talking. One of our colleagues discussed such an encounter with a student. He asked the student to bring material to the session that reminded the student of a deceased friend. The student more than complied. He brought a collection of pictures and artifacts he created (this in itself was a work of art) that included creative works done by both the student and the friend. This was an important opportunity for the student to confide in the counselor about his love for the deceased and how this death changed his life.

Confiding in another is central to the healing process because it helps a bereaved person begin to find meaning or make account of his or her loss. Account-making is central to reducing stress brought on by grief. "Finding meaning in death, maintaining morale in its wake, and our own negotiating with immortality represents major steps confronting us all when those close to us die" (Harvey et al., 1992, p. 108).

As with all counseling, perhaps even more so with grief counseling, it is important to engage students' values and beliefs in the therapeutic process. Late adolescence is an important time in the development of values and ideals for traditionally aged college students. Most students are experiencing life away from their parents for the first time. They may be questioning parental values and authority. They may be struggling with what they believe to be true about themselves, their family, and the world. They often are asking existential questions and finding themselves in what Erikson has termed a crisis of identity, and later, a crisis of intimacy (Erikson, 1968). When loss, and especially loss through death, occurs, questions about life, death, and purpose become even more compelling. It is important to ask the bereaved what meaning he or she finds in the loss. This can be done in a number ways. The counselor can ask how the student's view of the world has changed since the death of his or her loved one. Or, the counselor can ask if he or she believed that God or some higher power had a role in the loss or in recovery form the loss. The counselor can ask if or how personal beliefs or spiritual sustenance are incorporated into the bereaved person's self care. These types of questions may encourage comfort in some persons and anger in others. Whatever is expressed, it is important to examine the origin of the feelings. What thoughts are behind them? How has the loss challenged and changed or entrenched the student's belief? And also, what does this mean to the student? Is the student left to grieve not only a significant loss of a person, but also the loss of a long cherished belief? Loss, especially loss through death, can shake people at their core. Careful and considerate investigation of values and beliefs during recovery from grief can help students develop in new and helpful ways.

Although many students would probably agree that talking to friends and family is helpful in working through loss, it is also true that what friends and family members sometimes say can feel quite insensitive. Several studies and clinical data have suggested that comments made to persons struggling with loss can have an important impact (Balk & Vesta, 1998; LaGrand, 1986). When people make comments to those in mourning, the comments that are most helpful pertain to validating the feelings of the bereaved. Those that are least helpful seem to attempt to rationalize the loss. When a friend or family member offers platitudes or easy answers to ontological inquiries, the bereaved often feels unheard and unimportant. Words appearing to be a comfort from the helper's point of view can appear judgmental and insensitive to the bereaved. Counselors will often hear clients say something like "can you believe that my uncle told me not to be angry? He has no idea what I'm feeling." Or, "I don't know how to handle it when my roommate keeps telling me 'you've got to move on.'" There are many kinds of remarks that are not helpful. These include remarks that are judgmental or direct the bereaved to feel or act a certain way. Attempts to keep the grieving person from remembering his or her experiences with the deceased and attempts to keep the bereaved from his or her emotions are also perceived as unhelpful (Vickio, Cavanaugh, & Attig, 1990).

Grieving students need to talk. But, to whom do they go for help? Even though students may feel quite badly, they may not feel their problem is one that merits the attention of a professional counselor. Moreover, there continues to be stereotypes and assumptions about going to counseling that may be difficult for the average traditional undergraduate to breach. Grief education for college and university resident hall staff and students can be an important element to aid students in working through their sorrow. Students need to talk about the pain surrounding their loss. But they also need an empathic and nonjudgmental ear. Most students, at one time or another, will look to their peers for solace. A grief education program for students and resident hall staff can focus on how to best provide support to grieving students. A study by Kubitz, Thorton, and Robertson (1989) examined students' expectations about grief on their assessment of the bereaved. They found that students who have a moderate amount of social contact with the bereaved are the ones influenced most by their own expectations about grief. People most likely to dismiss or avoid a grieving person, then, are those who have everyday casual interaction with him or her. This would suggest that residents living on the same dormitory floor as the bereaved, with the exception of those who are most close—like a roommate or a few close friends—might be the ones to shun and reject the student. Being treated in such a way could increase the student's grief due to the loss of a familiar and secure place—the residence hall floor on which the student lives. By educating resident hall staff and students about the importance of being supportive of bereaved peers rather than distancing themselves from them, a more welcoming and supportive environment may be created.

LaGrand (1986) wrote that social support in grief and loss offers the following help to college-aged adults. Social support acts as a listening post that students can use to measure others' acceptance of their emotional behavior. Social support provides an outlet for the student to share the burden of grief. Social support from peers can stand in the place of broken relationships. Support from other students can be used to help examine the bereaved's relationship with the person he or she is grieving. It can also provide the student with encouragement to go on with his or her daily tasks.

☐ Therapeutic Tasks and Principles

There are a number of important therapeutic principals or tasks of which to take note when working with grieving students in a counseling setting. One of the first and most important tasks is to provide students with ongoing support (Worden, 1991). Although students often receive support from family and friends, the counselor should examine their support systems and attempt to provide what might be missing. Even though bereaved persons desire social support and turn to friends and family for help (LaGrand, 1986), it might not always be there. Students may want their bereaved friend to move on and a counselor would then need to pick up where the person's friends left off. In this case, a counselor would likely have to deal with the bereaved's sense of abandonment and added loss when friends no longer desire to listen.

Lamb (1988, 1999) discussed three assessment tasks important in grief counseling. The counselor needs to 1) identify and reframe the client's symptoms, 2) assess the stage of grief and 3) determine if the client's symptoms are normal or complicated. What Lamb calls reframing the symptoms, others refer to as normalizing behaviors (Worden, 1991). Clients are not always aware that the distress they feel is associated with grief. It is not uncommon, for example, for a person whose father has recently died to see glimpses of his image or hear his voice. However, if this is a student's initial experience with significant loss he or she may think this is a sign of "going crazy" or "losing it." The therapist can help unburden the student of this fear by informing the student that he or she is not going crazy but having a normal reaction to a significant loss. Lamb (1999) provided a number of questions to assess complicated grief. The counselor should determine whether or not the student had time to grieve. Was he or she able to return home for the funeral (in the case of loss due to death) and reestablish connections with family members? Did he or she not go home or return to school too soon after the death and become over involved in studies? Did the student ever grieve? Worden (1991) wrote that persons who experience prolonged grief are aware that they have not been able to work through the loss and feel as if it should have been resolved months or even years earlier. Moreover, determining what role guilt plays in grief helps assess whether or not it is pathological. Is the bereaved's guilt focused on the time of death (as in uncomplicated grief) or is it chronic, unresolved guilt (often with complicated bereavement?; Lamb, 1999).

An important early task of grief counseling is to establish a therapeutic agreement (Lamb, 1988, 1999; Worden, 1991). The client and counselor should overtly agree to explore the client's loss experience. It is helpful for the counselor to provide the student with a general framework for what grief counseling will be like. Lamb suggested that a time limit around the counseling experience is important. A time limit will help the client understand that his or her counseling will not go on forever, and implicitly, that the intensity of this pain will not continue forever.

Another early task in grief counseling is to help the student bring the loss object to the present (Lamb, 1988, 1999; Worden, 1991). Because loss can be so painful, many people push the emotional experience out of their immediate awareness. In so doing they also distance themselves from the object of loss. So, ". . . an early task of grief is to come to a more complete awareness that the loss actually has occurred . . . . Survivors must accept this reality so they can deal with the emotional 'impact of the loss" (Worden, 1991, p. 42). Lamb (1999) suggested that students bring an item into therapy that reminds them of the person they grieve. Bringing the object of loss directly into the client's awareness will heighten the client's arousal and encourage him or her to express feelings. Any reminder of loss—such as a photo of the deceased relative or a piece of clothing that the client connects with the person—will serve to connect the client with feelings about the one who is grieved.

Helping students accept and express feelings is a fundamental aspect of grief work (Worden, 1991). Worden reported a number of feelings that are especially expressive of grief. These include anger, guilt, sadness, helplessness, and anxiety. Depending upon the psychological needs of the student and where the student is in his or her grief recovery, the counselor can make a number of interventions that will assist in expressing feelings. Worden asserts, however, that in working with feelings focus is essential.

> Sadness must be accompanied by an awareness of what one has lost; anger needs to be properly and effectively targeted; guilt needs to be evaluated and resolved; and anxiety needs to be identified and managed. Without this focus, the counselor is not being effective, regardless of the amount or degree of feeling that is being evoked. (p. 47)

Another important task of grief recovery is encouraging persons to tell the story of their loss (Sedney, Baker, & Gross, 1994; Toth, 1997). Telling the story provides emotional relief. It also helps the bereaved discover meaning in the midst of the loss and cultivates concern between the people with whom the story is shared (Sedney et al., 1992). Toth led a therapy group for college students who experienced loss through death. He encouraged group members to tell their loss story. They kept a journal of this experience. Reflected in the journals were a number of therapeutic factors that related to the act of storytelling. These factors included a sense of universality or hope in the midst of shared pain, the importance of cathartic expression, the importance of being heard by others, and learning from one anothers' experiences.

Although the grief process never completely ends, one must eventually leave the heart of grief behind and enter into new relationships with others and a new association with the world. Lamb (1988) discussed a final task of grief, the importance of saying goodbye and developing new significant relationships. A counselor could help initiate saying goodbye, in the case of loss through death, by encouraging a visit to the cemetery where the client could speak to the loved one about joys and regrets and end with goodbye. The therapist could help the bereaved role play a discussion with the significant other to help facilitate a symbolic parting. Worden (1991) suggested that the client practice saying a temporary goodbye to the deceased at the end of each counseling session. This can be done in gradual steps eventually leading to the client saying a final goodbye. But Worden cautions that goodbye does not mean the bereaved will forget his or her significant other or that the process of grief is over. Saying goodbye does not end the relationship with the deceased, but it allows the survivor to emotionally relocate the deceased and continue on with life. Worden wrote, "I view saying goodbye as saying goodbye to the desire for the deceased to be alive, to be here with me, and goodbye to the fantasy that I can ever recover the lost person" (p. 87).

Conclusion

Loss is final and initiates the painful process of grief through which we all must travel. Even for those of us who have had a good deal of experience with major loss, grief changes our personal perspectives and, at times, stops us in our tracks. For many adolescents and young adults, entering into grief and wrestling with the subsequent emotions can feel like an overwhelming task. It is our hope that this chapter has provided insights into this experience and presented some ideas as to how to think about and respond to college student grief and loss.

References

Balk, D. E. (1996). Attachment and the reactions of bereaved college students: A longitudinal study. In D. Klass, P. R. Silverman, & S. L. Nickman (Eds.), *Continuing bonds: New understandings of grief* (pp. 311–328). Washington, DC: Taylor & Francis.

Balk, D. E., & Vesta, L. C. (1998). Psychological development during four years of bereavement: A longitudinal case study. *Death Studies, 22,* 23–41.

Berson, R. J. (1988). A bereavement group for college students. *Journal of Group Psychotherapy, Psychodrama and Sociometry, 41,* 101–117.

Bradach, K. M., & Jordan, J. R. (1995). Long-term effects of a family history of traumatic death on adolescent individuation. *Death Studies, 19,* 315–336.

Bowlby, J. (1973). *Separation.* New York: Basic Books.

Doka, K. J. (1989). *Disenfranchised grief: Recognizing hidden sorrow.* New York: Lexington.

Erikson, E. H. (1968). *Identity, youth and crisis.* New York: Norton.

Floerchinger, D. S. (1991). Bereavement in late adolescence: Interventions on college campuses. *Journal of Adolescent Research, 6,* 146–156.

Harvey, J. H., Orbuch, T. L., Weber, A. L., Mergach, N., & Alt, R. (1992). House of pain and hope: Accounts of loss. *Death Studies, 16,* 99–124.

Janowiak, S. W., Mei-Tal, R., & Drapkin, R. G. (1995). Living with loss: A group for bereaved college students. *Death Studies, 19,* 55–63.

Kaczmarek, M. G., Backlund, B. A., & Biemer, P. (1990). The dynamics of ending a romantic relationship: An empirical assessment of grief in college students. *Journal of College Student Development, 31,* 319–324.

Kubitz, N., Thornton, G., & Robertson, D. U. (1989). Expectations about grief and evaluation of the griever. *Death Studies, 13,* 39–47.

Kübler-Ross, E. (1969). *On death and dying.* New York: Macmillan.

Kuk, L. (1990). Perspectives on gender differences. In M. J. Barr (Series Ed.) & L. V. Moore (Vol. Ed.), *New directions for student services. Evolving theoretical perspectives on students,* (no. 31, pp. 15–28). San Francisco: Jossey-Bass.

LaGrand, L. E. (1986). *Coping with separation and loss as a young adult.* Springfield, IL: Thomas.

LaGrand, L. E. (1989). Youth and the disenfranchised breakup. In K. J. Doka (Ed.), *Disenfranchised grief: Recognizing hidden sorrow.* New York: Lexington.

Lamb, D. H. (1988). Loss and grief: Psychotherapy strategies and interventions. *Psychotherapy, 25,* 561–569.

Lamb, D. H. (1999, February*). Therapeutic strategies with grieving college students.* Paper presented at the meeting of the Big Ten Counseling Centers, Evanston, Illinois.

Marwit, S. J., & Klass, D. (1995). Grief and the role of the inner representation of the deceased. *Omega, 30,* 283–298.

Okun, M., Taub, J., & Witter, R. (1986, March). Age and sex differences in negative life events and student services usage. *Journal of College Student Personnel,* 160–164.

Parkes, C. M. (1970). The first year of bereavement: A longitudinal study of the reaction of London widows to death of husbands. *Psychiatry, 33,* 444–467.

Price, G. E., Dinas, P., Dunn, C., & Winterowd, C. (1995). Group work with clients experiencing grieving: Moving from theory to practice. *Journal for Specialists in Group Work, 20,* 159–167.

Raphael, B. (1984). *The anatomy of bereavement: A handbook for the caring professions.* London: Hutchinson.

Robak, R. W., & Weitzman, S. P. (1995). Grieving the loss of romantic relationships in young adults: An empirical study of disenfranchised grief. *Omega, 30*(4), 269–281.

Rolland, J. S. (1990). Anticipatory loss: A family systems developmental framework. *Family Process, 29,* 229–244.

Santrock, J. (1981). *Adolescence* (2nd ed.). Dubuque, IA: Brown.

Sedney, M. A., Baker, J. E., & Gross, E. (1994). "The story" of death: Therapeutic considerations with bereaved families. *Journal of Martial & Family Therapy, 20,* 287–296.

Sklar, F., & Hartley, S. F. (1990). Close friends as survivors: Bereavement patterns in a "hidden" population. *Omega, 21,* 103–112.

Sprang, G., & McNeil, J. (1995). *The many faces of bereavement: The nature and treatment of natural, traumatic, and stigmatized grief.* New York: Brunner/Mazel.

Toth, P. L. (1997). A short-term grief and loss therapy group: Group members' experiences. *Journal of Personal & Interpersonal Loss, 2,* 83–103.

Tyson-Rawson, K. (1993). *College women and bereavement: Late adolescence and father death.* Unpublished doctoral dissertation, Kansas State University, Manhattan, Kansas.

Vickio, C. J., Cavanaugh, J. J., & Attig, T. W. (1990). Perceptions of grief among university students. *Death Studies, 14,* 231–240.

Wener, A., & Jones, M. D. (1979). Parent loss in college students. *Journal of the American College Health Association, 27,* 253–256.

Worden, W. J. (1991). *Grief counseling and grief therapy: A handbook for the mental health practitioner* (2nd ed.). New York: Springer.

Gary A. Morse

On Being Homeless and Mentally Ill: A Multitude of Losses and the Possibility of Recovery

Homelessness has become all too commonplace within contemporary American culture. In the early 1980s media and research reports first became prominent that an increasing number of people were literally homeless (that is, sleeping in shelters for the homeless, the streets, parks, abandoned buildings and the like; see Rossi, 1989). By 1994, Link and his colleagues reported the results of a rigorous, landmark research study that found 13.5 million (7.4% of the United States population) had been homeless at some point in their lives. The sheer number of people who experience homelessness was far greater than earlier estimates. Also disturbing were data that homelessness disproportionately affects poor and disabled persons (see Morse, 1986) especially those with severe mental health disorders. About one-third of people who are homeless suffer from a severe mental illness (see Dennis, Buckner, Lipton, & Levine, 1991).

Despite these statistics, public interest in homelessness has waned. In the 1980s, media images of people living on the streets and shelters evoked compassion, and homelessness became a crise celibrae (Hopper, 1984) of public policy. This concern has appeared to fade, the crise celibrae response replaced with compassion fatigue (Ferguson, 1990; Uzelac, 1990). While some government funding and private programs continue to serve people who are homeless, there is less governmental and media interest in the homeless. The homeless, it appears, have become increasingly forgotten. Within this context, there has also been a consistent failure to recognize that people who have been homeless and mentally ill experience lives affected by a multitude of losses, even while they possess the possibility of recovery.

The issues of loss and recovery among people who have been homeless with a severe mental illness are poorly understood. There has been little scholarly attention or empirical research on this topic, despite extensive research in other areas of homelessness. The purposes of this chapter are twofold: 1) to review and describe the nature of loss for people who are homeless and mentally ill, and 2) to examine the concept and possibilities of recovery for these individuals.

☐ Loss

We need to fully recognize that this group of individuals experiences significant losses related both to being homeless and to having a serious mental health disorder. Homelessness and mental illness each involve direct and associated losses; undoubtedly, these two variables interact, creating additional complications in loss. The next two subsections will examine losses related to the experiences of homelessness and mental illness, respectively.

Homelessness and Loss

Inherent in homelessness is material loss. Most obvious and paramount, is the loss of one's home, which, regardless of the type of dwellings, serves as a place of shelter from environmental and social threats. Typically, however, people who become homeless also lose a number of other significant material objects, including pets, furniture, and valued personal belongings. A home also provides for physical comforts—a favorite chair, a quiet room, one's own bed and blankets—that are usually not available in shelters or street locations.

Homelessness involves losses of the most basic resources—material supports that most people take for granted—but equally significant are the social and psychological losses involved in homelessness. For many, a home is the primary arena for experiencing companionship and for receiving social support from family and loved ones. A home promotes a sense of social connectedness and belonging. Becoming homeless typically creates losses or serious disruptions in all of these social domains; even in the relatively infrequent instances when families remain fully intact after losing their home, significant interpersonal disruptions and losses often occur.

The psychological effects of a home are also profound. For many, a home facilitates a sense of security, well-being, and peace—it provides a psychological as well as physical sanctuary from the stresses of the external world. Losing one's home is an emotionally traumatic event that often precipitates fear, anxiety, and insecurity as well as loss. Feelings of anger, bitterness, mistrust, and alienation also are common, especially as people endure prolonged homelessness. Most deleterious, perhaps, are the losses of hope and meaning that often pervade people who become homeless. The extreme poverty that characterizes homelessness contrasts starkly with individual aspirations and culturally-induced expectations about "the good life." As homelessness persists, there appears to be the loss of a sense of control over the situation and a loss of personal meaning—factors which lead to hopelessness and despair. These losses of hope, meaning, and control undoubtedly explain in part the rather startling finding from one large study that more than one in five homeless people had thought about suicide in the past seven days (Morse et al., 1985). The loss of hope, meaning, and control is not unique to people who are homeless, but instead appears to be a common dynamic involved in the phenomena of loss (Thompson, 1998).

Closely intertwined with the losses of hope, meaning, and control is a loss of self-identity. Again, being homeless collides violently with self-expectations; few if any, aspire to be homeless. Consequently, self-blame often occurs, and self-concepts often change for the worse as individuals become unable to accommodate their present social realities with views of the self as successful. Prehomeless identities are often lost, self-concepts are negatively affected, and some report feeling less than human, forgotten, or overlooked.

As discussed previously (Morse, 1998b), losing one's home and becoming homeless is only one, albeit the most direct, type of loss involved in homelessness. People who become homeless have typically experienced a number of associated losses. Although limited empirical research has been conducted, it does appear that people who become homeless as adults are likely to have suffered significant, early developmental losses. For example, people who are homeless are more likely than others as children to have experienced a loss of a family or home environment (such as being placed in foster care or an institutional setting as a child—see, for example, Piliaviin, Sosin, & Westerfelt, 1989; Sosin, Colson, & Grossman, 1988). Qualitative and case study reports (e.g., Morse, Calsyn, & Wolff, 1996; Spencer, Zawier, Templehoff, Morse, & Calsyn, 1994) also suggest that homeless people have frequently suffered the losses of premature deaths of parents or siblings.

People who are homeless are also more likely than the general population or a psychiatric population to have experienced other stressful or traumatic life events in the year prior to becoming homeless (Morse et al., 1985). Particularly common events involved the death of family or friends, losses of a job and income, and traumatic and abusive events.

Severe Mental Illness and Loss

Apart from being homeless, a serious and persistent mental illness (e.g., schizophrenia, bipolar disorders) also involves multiple losses for the affected individual. Severe mental health disorders typically cause losses or impairments in personal functioning in a variety of areas, including vocation, social relations, self-care, and independent living skills. Closely associated with impaired functioning are concomitant losses of social roles. For example, all too often a severe mental illness damages or robs an individual of their social roles as a student, employee, or parent. Similar to homelessness, and to other losses (see Thompson, 1998), people with severe mental illness often experience a loss of purpose and meaning in their life. There is often an acute sense of a loss of opportunity, a painful awareness of the discrepancy between their preillness goals and aspirations and their current abilities and life situations. Despite attempts, some feel hopeless about their ability to control their illness and lives (see also Thompson, 1998). Most serious, perhaps, people who face a persistent, major mental illness often feel as if they lose their very selves. A loss of self-identity and personal humanness are common (Davidson, 1992). Self-esteem suffers and self-concepts are often altered by a heightened sense of negativity, illness and failure. A global loss of pleasure and joy in life often results.

Implications

Although there has been little research and attention, it is clear that both homelessness and severe mental illness are experiences laden with loss. Each condition involves multiple and severe losses, and, it is likely that there is a negative interaction between homelessness and mental illness. Although research is currently lacking, people who experience both conditions are probably more prone to suffer greater levels of despair, and more serious losses in functioning, social roles, meaning, hope, and personal identity. The extent and nature of these losses undoubtedly pose significant challenges for the individuals and for service providers.

Unfortunately, however, there seems at present to be little awareness and attention focused on the loss experiences of people who are homeless and severely mentally ill. Service providers tend to focus their assessments and interventions on the most obvious needs: social resources, such as housing and income, and medication and psychosocial services for the mental health disorders. Clearly, these needs are important and should remain a priority of service and treatment efforts. However, it is ironic that people who are homeless and mentally ill, who experience a multitude of severe losses, receive few inquiries or services for their issues of loss. It is rare that a shelter worker or even a mental health provider will ask about specific losses that may have occurred, or about the individual's own emotional and cognitive experience of the loss. In this way, the common social service response may further reinforce the experience of being overlooked and forgotten, inadvertently contributing to the developing sense of alienation and depersonalization.

This inattention by service providers is consistent with one of the most striking contemporary issues in homelessness: compassion fatigue. The notion of compassion fatigue has been advanced to explain dwindling public and governmental concern for people who are homeless. It suggests a disinterest in the problems of the homeless, a passive acceptance of homelessness itself as a feature of our current cultural life. The consequence of this reaction allows homelessness to persist as a prevalent social problem. This compassion fatigue constitutes a secondary loss (see Harvey, 1996) among the general public. A secondary loss occurs when individuals who have not directly experienced loss react by shutting down their awareness and sympathy toward those who have experienced a specific trauma; this is thought to often occur because of an unwillingness to bear and acknowledge the painful situation. In general, as Harvey wrote, this involves a secondary loss of feeling and wisdom (1996). In the present topic area, there appears to be a similar closing down or denial of the pain which is involved in being homeless as well as the pain of severe mental illness. It involves losses of our mindfulness or awareness about disturbing social realities, of our moral sensibilities (Hopper, Mauch, & Morse, 1990) about what is socially acceptable, and also a loss of connection within our own heart, with our own compassion. In this way, we lose a bit of our humanity as we close our eyes and hearts to the humanity of those who are homeless and mentally ill; and we lose sight not only of their losses and pain, but also to the possibilities of healing and recovery.

☐ Recovery

Just as the issue of loss is a largely unrecognized issue for people who are homeless and mentally ill, so too has there been little attention to how people cope, adjust, and, in some instances, recover from these experiences and conditions. The remainder of this chapter will explore these issues, with an emphasis on the possibilities of recovery.

Adjustment and Outcomes

Precious few studies have examined how people who are homeless and mentally ill cope and adjust to their circumstances. A classic work in this area was the early account by Baxter and Hopper (1981) who reported that people who are homeless and mentally ill use a number of creative strategies in order to survive the rigors of being homeless. They stated, for example, that some extreme and overt behaviors labeled as psychotic, such as loud talking to one's self or gesturing wildly, were self-defense mechanisms that functioned to ward off potential attackers on the streets, since potential assailants would be less likely to assault an unpredictable crazy person. They also reported that some of the severe hygiene problems common among "bag ladies" were strategies employed to decrease their vulnerability on the streets; for example, if a woman appeared unkept and smelled badly, she would be less likely to be raped.

Baxter and Hopper's work was a landmark study in several respects, including for identifying the unique and innovative coping techniques that homeless people with mental illness use for surviving and adapting to homelessness. Unfortunately, however, there have been few longitudinal studies examining how people cope and adjust over time, especially as they may exit homelessness and become housed again. Further, there are other indicators that despite some creative strategies, there are still a significant number of adjustment problems. Alcohol and drug abuse has become exceedingly common, affecting 50% or more of people who are homeless and mentally ill (Drake, Osher, & Wallach, 1991; Federal Task Force on Homelessness and Mental Illness, 1992). While substance abuse often preceded homelessness (Morse et al., 1985), in other cases homeless people may begin to abuse alcohol or street drugs as a way of trying to cope, or to self-medicate from despair or mental health symptoms. In this way, the co-occurring substance abuse for some is a reflection of unresolved problems, pain, and losses in the individual's life.

In addition to substance abuse, the literature also suggests a number of other adjustment problems and poor outcomes associated with homelessness. These include poor physical health, victimization, incarceration, and premature death (see Morse, 1986). Further, observers have noted that some of the skills used by homeless people to survive homelessness may have unattended, negative side effects. For example, not taking a shower or maintaining grooming may help prevent sexual abuse, but it impairs the person's likelihood of obtaining a job; thus, some adaptive behaviors may unwittingly perpetuate homelessness.

By contrast, evaluation research indicates improved adjustment over time, especially for persons who received specialized services, such as assertive community treatment or assertive case management (see Morse, 1999). People who are homeless with a severe mental illness often improve in multiple domains, including housing, service utilization, and symptoms. The research data indicate that services can meaningfully assist people who are homeless and mentally ill to improve their adjustment, but the quantitative statistics do not adequately capture the nature of the changes that occur for some people. First person accounts, clinical experiences, and case study reports suggest that people who are homeless and mentally ill sometimes undergo significant, profound changes in their lives (Morse, 1998a; Morse et al., 1996). The concept of recovery, rather than outcome data alone, may more adequately describe the changes and growth that occur for some.

The Concept of Recovery

There has been little discussion of recovery from homelessness but the topic has become an important concept within the field of mental health. One leading scholar in the area has suggested that the emerging concept of recovery will become the guiding vision of the mental health service system (Anthony, 1993). At present, recovery is a much discussed issue, especially within the realm of mental health policy and politics in the public sector. However, it is sometimes used as a buzzword without a clear understanding of the concept, and Curtis (1999), has warned that the term can become simple rhetoric, used without associated, meaningful policies. Similarly, there is controversy over the value of the term recovery within the general field of loss. Some have cautioned that terms like recovery are used too quickly while the individual is still in the throes of struggling with the painful aspects of the loss, and that the term itself connotes an overly positive picture of adjustment (Harvey and Weber, 1998; Rando, 1993). Given these divergent points of view, and the fact that terms are sometimes bandied about with little conceptual attention and less empirical research, it is necessary to review the concept of recovery in closer detail.

Despite its popularity, there are relatively few scholarly or research studies on recovery from mental illness. Longitudinal studies (e.g., see Harding, Zubin, & Strauss, 1987) examining the course of schizophrenia give some empirical support that a significant percentage (about one-half to two-thirds) of people experience a substantial improvement or recovery over the long-term (e.g., 25–35 years). The limited published literature also draws heavily from first person accounts of individuals who have described their illness and progress (e.g., Deegan, 1988; Lovejoy, 1984), with very few conceptual formulations (for exceptions, see Anthony, 1993) or empirical studies (Davidson, 1992; Young & Ensing, 1999). Few have offered definitions of recovery within the field of severe mental illness. Anthony (1993) provided one attempt, describing recovery as

> a deeply personal, unique process of changing one's attitudes, values, feelings, goals, skills and/or roles. It is a way of living a satisfying, hopeful, contributing life even with limitations caused by illness. Recovery involves the development of new meaning and purpose in one's life as one grows beyond the catastrophic effects of mental illness. (p. 15)

Deegan, a psychologist who has described her own struggles and recovery from mental illness, described it succinctly: "Recovery refers to the lived or real life experience of persons as they accept and overcome the challenge of the disability" (Deegan, 1988, p. 11).

A review of the limited literature suggests other important features or characteristics of recovery in mental illness. These include the development of insight about one's condition (Young & Ensing, 1993), the development of new hope or meaning and purpose (Anthony, 1993; Deegan, 1988; Young & Ensing, 1999), the reconstitution of a changed and more valued sense of self (Deegan, 1988; Davidson, 1992; Young & Ensing, 1999), a greater sense of choice and self-direction (Davidson, 1992; Young & Ensing, 1999), and enhanced coping or adjustment, including greater self control of symptoms (Davidson, 1992c).

A recent research study by Young and Ensing (1999) used qualitative methods to attempt to understand the experience of recovery from the perspective of the person with severe mental illness. They reported a three-phase model of recovery, the first phase of which involved what was termed "overcoming 'stuckness.'" Common aspects of this phase included acknowledging and accepting the illness, developing the desire and motivation to change, and finding a source of hope or inspiration. They described the middle phase as "regaining what was lost and fostering self-empowerment." Common key features of this phase included discovering and fostering self-empowerment, which involved taking control and responsibility for one's own life, recovery, and actions; learning about and redefining the self, which included recapturing parts of the old self, discovering new aspects of self, and learning there is more to the self than one's illness; and regaining basic functioning. Finally, Young and Ensing (1999) described a third or later phase as improving the quality of life. This included common features of striving to attain an overall sense of well-being and trying to reach new levels of potential and functioning, especially in meaning and purpose in life, sometimes through spirituality.

The concept of recovery from mental illness has parallels to a similar concept for people with physical disabilities and illnesses. The similarities are rarely acknowledged (for an exception, see Anthony, 1993; see also Harrison, 1984; Wright, 1983), and the labels for the concepts sometimes vary, with terms like "healing," "wellness," and "wholeness," more common than recovery in the physical health fields, but regardless of the nomenclature, key elements are common. Freeman (1998), for example, a health care professional with long-term Multiple Sclerosis and disability, described healing as learning lessons from one's illness, separating the self from the illness, and gaining a larger and more spiritual perspective on one's life and purpose. Similar accounts are common from people suffering from cancer, AIDS, and other illnesses and in the fields of mind-body health and psychoneuroimmunology (see, for example, Borysenko & Borysenko, 1994).

Aspects of the concept of recovery from severe mental illness also bear strong resemblance to fundamental processes discussed within the general literature on loss. Thompson (1998), for example, described reestablishing meaning and control as common and successful ways of coping with losses. Changing one's self-identity and goals are also described as common, effective tactics toward these ends (Thompson, 1998), just as they are common acts in the process of recovery from mental health disorders. There are also strong parallels between the descriptions of recovery in the literature on severe mental illness and Janoff-Bulman and Berg's (1998) discussion of those who have suffered traumatic losses. In each area regaining meaning and value in life become more prominent. Janoff-Bulman and Berg's description of the process of rebuilding the self, the importance of relationships, and gaining new perspectives of one's personal strengths fits closely with the recent research on recovery reported by Young and Ensing (1999).

To summarize, recovery from severe mental illness, despite a paucity of research and scholarly attention, is an important concept. Fundamental elements of the experience of recovery parallel other areas of loss, including physical illness and disability, and trauma. Key aspects of the recovery concept include:

- The individual obtains some improvement in functioning, attitude, or well-being;
- The person plays an active, participating role in that improvement, including in symptom management;
- The individual develops a stronger sense of self, one that includes some degree of separateness and autonomy from the mental illness;
- Improvement includes a broad span of possibility, not only of symptom reduction or role functioning, but also of well-being and meaning;

- Recovery from the illness is a process, a journey of trials, losses, and difficulties as well as growth and well-being;
- Critically important in that process are core facets of being human: finding hope, recognizing possibility, discovering or creating meaning, and exercising courage and choice.

Two caveats deserve further attention. First, the limited literature reviewed is drawn primarily from severe mental illness. Knowledge is lacking on the process of recovery from homelessness and, more precisely, the twin and interacting conditions of being homeless and experiencing a severe mental illness. The losses may be even greater for people who face both severe mental illness and homelessness, and the recovery process more complicated. While extensive or detailed information is lacking, limited case study reports suggest recovery also occurs for people who are both homeless and severely mentally ill (Morse et al., 1996), with similar, profound, qualitative personal changes apparent.

Second, the nature of the relationship between loss and recovery is ill-defined and deserves further attention. Especially salient are criticisms that terms like recovery and healing connote overly positive images of the individual's experiences (Harvey & Weber, 1998). Indeed, a review of the literature on recovery from severe mental illness typically suggests that most scholarly reports are dominated by descriptions of the positive aspects of growth and improvement. First person accounts help to restore a balanced perspective that acknowledges the pain as well as the potential involved in loss and recovery. Deegan (1988), for example, wrote:

> Recovery does not refer to an absence of pain or struggle. Rather, recovery is marked by the transition from anguish to suffering. True suffering is marked by an inner peace, i.e., although we still felt great pain, we also experienced a peace in knowing that this pain was leading us forward into a new future. (p. 15)

As Miller and Omarzu (1998) among others (e.g., Harvey & Weber, 1998) note, losses are an integral part of living, and, as individuals survive loss, they integrate their experiences into new social and personal identities. Janoff-Bulman and Berg (1998) describe an alternative but complimentary process in discussing trauma, that the "victimization is regarded as a teacher, providing important lessons and benefits" (p. 44). Harvey and Weber (1998) put the more general point in a similar point of view: "Our losses become, in a sense, a lesson and a gift" (p. 326). Both perspectives are accurate, we learn from our losses, and these lessons change who we are, including our self-identity. In this way, homelessness and loss are intimately interwoven into wholeness. Experiencing and confronting loss, thus, has the potential for change, for growth. As Harvey and Weber (1998) aptly put it: "Loss and growth form a remarkable dialectic" (p. 325). The outcome, as Janoff-Bulman and Berg (1998) note, is a transformation of the individual. Some individuals are able not only to survive and cope well but also to create new meaning and value in their lives not in spite of their losses, but "*because* of their losses" (Janoff - Bulmon & Berg, 1998, p. 35).

Research Issues

There is a need for much more research to increase our understanding about loss and recovery from homelessness and severe mental illness. Given the paucity of conceptual articles and empirical studies, considerable attention needs to be directed toward the most fundamental question: "What is happening when someone talks about "recovery" from a loss; what has changed?" (Miller & Omarzu, 1998, p.7). Further as noted previously, most of the current publications come from the area of severe mental illness alone. Basic research is needed to describe the issues of loss and recovery and their interrelationships with homelessness and severe mental illness. Unanswered questions currently arise as to the similarities and differences in the experiences of loss and recovery from both conditions, as compared to severe mental illness alone. Of particular interest is whether the stage model of recovery from severe mental illness (Young & Ensing, 1999) can be replicated. There is growing controversy over the validity of stage models in loss and recovery in general (see Miller & Omarzu, 1998), and Young and Ensing's model was based on a very small, select sample. Whether their findings will generalize to other groups of people with severe mental illness, especially those who have also lost their homes, is open to further investigation.

Other fundamental questions also need further study. There is little information currently, for example, on the percentage of people who are homeless with a severe mental illness who experience recovery. Even more important is a better understanding of the process of how someone recovers. This is likely to be a complicated and controversial area of investigation, and even now there is some difference of opinion among loss researchers on what constitutes process factors versus the outcome indicators of recovery (see, for example, Janoff-Bulman & Berg, 1998).

Future knowledge will be enhanced if the research literature is based on both quantitative and qualitative methods. Basic questions, such as the prevalence of recovery over time, will ultimately be best addressed by quantitative methods. In the interim, however, research that is qualitative, or that combines both methods, will deepen our understanding and advance the research agenda (see Davidson, 1992; Young & Ensing, 1999 for two exemplary studies). Across time, narrative research that conveys individuals' stories of loss and recovery will add a richness and wisdom to our knowledge. We expect that such research, as Harvey and Weber stated it for the field of loss as a whole, will "tell us much about people's courage and resiliency as it will their susceptibility to stress and breakdown due to serious losses" (1998, p. 320).

Particularly important will be research that illuminates the personal actions and external factors that facilitate coping with losses and recovery. Other researchers have suggested some critical factors for people with severe mental illness or for people who experience trauma or other losses (e.g., Davidson, 1992; Deegan, 1988; Janoff-Bulman & Berg, 1998; Thompson, 1998; Young & Ensing, 1999). Factors suggested have included accepting the illness or confronting the loss, finding new hope and meaning, reconstructing one's beliefs about self and the world, receiving social support, being able to tell one's story to another person, and feeling the consistent support and hope from a service provider. Further research is needed in this area, again attempting to clarify the relationships between factors that create recovery and those that are characteristics of the outcome. Additionally, more attention needs to be directed toward interventions that human service workers can provide to effectively facilitate recovery from mental illness and homelessness.

Service Considerations

The current literature provides little direction on how to facilitate people's recovery from homelessness and mental illness. Standard best practice patterns suggest the necessity of providing outreach and engagement, housing and basic resource assistance, psychotropic medications to stabilize psychotic symptoms, and psychosocial support and case management services (HUD/HHS, 1998). Such approaches have been effective for improving client outcomes in some important domains, such as housing and psychiatric symptoms (see Morse, 1999). However, improvements have not been observed in all areas of outcome domains, and there is little quantitative data of the impact on recovery. Recent research (Burger, Calsyn, Morse, & Klinkenberg, 1999) has found an enduring prevalence of depressive profiles among clients, despite significant reductions in homelessness and psychotic symptoms. These results suggest the possible lingering effects of loss and inadequate service attention to well-being and recovery. Unfortunately, the larger literature on severe mental illness has offered relatively little information on how service providers may facilitate recovery; this lack of service implications is surprising, given the growing popularity of the recovery concept.

People with severe mental illness who are homeless will probably be best served by a multifaceted set of services. The remainder of this subsection provides a preliminary sketch of these services, identifying first the service objective and then briefly discussing corresponding methods of practice. Several underlying service principles are also assumed. One, recovery-oriented services are incorporated within a comprehensive set of interventions, such as outreach and engagement, housing and resource assistance, medication services, and psychosocial supports. Two, the services are individualized, tailored to each person's unique needs and preferences. Three, these recovery services are provided within the context of a caring relationship with a service provider that persists over time—a factor that consumers have consistently identified as crucial in their own stories of recovery (e.g., see Anthony, 1993). And, fourth, efforts to facilitate hope and recovery must be grounded in an empathic exploration and understanding of the person's unique experiences of loss. These experiences are likely to be multifaceted and to surface at various points throughout the recovery work. Rather than seen as setbacks, feelings and discussions concerning losses must be viewed as fundamental — and potentially transforming — aspects of recovery.

Instilling Hope.   Russinova (1998) has suggested a number of strategies to inspire hope. These include accepting, valuing, and believing in the person; assisting the person to recall previous accomplishments and experiences and to set current goals; and supporting the person's spiritual beliefs. While conveying a realistic and personalized sense of hope, it is especially important to recognize an individual's historical and current pain and losses.

Imagining and Planning for Recovery.   Service providers need to assist clients not only in developing hope for recovery but also in begining to imagine what recovery would mean in their own lives and to consider the process for achieving recovery. The "recovery roadmap" has been used in helping individuals overcome substance addictions (Merit Behavioral Care, undated) and it is also applicable to people with severe mental illness and homelessness. A recovery roadmap helps individuals to articulate their hopes and to create an expectation of recovery. A recovery roadmap may include written or graphic visualizations of goals and statements or diagrams of actions, supports, and services needed to reach the goals. Recovery roadmaps may also indicate potential problems or relapse triggers, and provide concrete planning on how to cope with threats and problems. A recovery roadmap is broader than a typical individualized treatment plan and helps to facilitate the imaginations and energies of clients and service providers toward greater improvement and recovery. Copeland (1997) has developed a slightly more narrow but compatible tool called a Wellness Recovery Action Plan (WRAP) that is consistent with a recovery roadmap. The WRAP includes self-guided components on describing "how you feel when you feel well" (p. 3) as well as listings of actions that promote wellness; triggers for emotional imbalance and accompanying coping plans; early warning signs and corresponding actions plans to cope; and symptoms that indicate the need for external help.

Developing Social Resources.   As noted, assertive community treatment or active case management is needed to assist individuals in obtaining basic social resources, including income, furniture, utilities, and, most importantly, housing.

Accepting Limitations.   A key aspect of recovery for many involves acknowledging and accepting their illness (Young & Ensing, 1999) and probably also their immediate, if temporary, socioeconomic condition. Psychoeducation concerning the person's disorder can be useful in this regard. It is important that providers follow the general advice from Remen (1996), that education and prognoses be given very carefully, in a manner that acknowledges wide individual variability, and promotes rather than destroys hope and possibility.

Fostering a Positive Sense of Self.   Davidson (1992) has identified four steps that are important in people developing a sense of self and recovering from mental illness. Step one is to help the individual to identify a sense of self which is separate from the illness; as Davidson explains, this process can be intuitive or a rational, cognitive-educational process. A second step is to assist the individual to "take stock of the self." This involves the individual reflecting on their perceived strengths and limitations before returning to old projects or initiating new ones. A third phase is "putting the self into action," accompanied by "reflection and incorporating the results of these actions into a revised sense of self" (p. 10). For some individuals, it is critical that small steps are undertaken, giving an opportunity to develop successes and build a stronger sense of self. The fourth step is learning to appeal to the self. As Davidson described it, "Once a person has developed a consistent sense of self beyond the illness s/he can appeal to this self as enduring in the midst of symptoms and as a reminder that the symptoms are in fact representative only of an illness and thus need not be threatening or interminable" (p. 11). Narrative therapy techniques (e.g., Parry & Doan, 1994) can also be effective for helping clients to identify a sense of self.

Fostering Symptom Management Skills.   Some degree of self-control of psychiatric symptoms is a hallmark characteristic of recovery. Studies of the natural coping of people with severe mental illness indicate that many people report some ability to manage or reduce psychotic symptoms (Breier & Strauss, 1983). Common symptom management patterns include practicing some form of self-instruction (self-evaluation, coupled with self-talk or self-direction), and behavioral strategies of either reducing involvement in order to decrease stress and stimuli, or increasing activity ("keeping busy"; Breier & Strauss, 1983). Copeland and McKay (1992) have also studied, and reported in a self-help treatment manual, extensive coping strategies used by people with bipolar disorder and major depression. To facilitate recovery, service providers can assist clients to develop symptom management skills in a variety of ways, including eliciting and reinforcing an individual's own but infrequently used skills, especially using solution-oriented therapy techniques (O'Hanlon & Weiner-Davis, 1988); teaching skills directly; and by facilitating peer-support exchanges on coping techniques. In all cases, it is important to be mindful that whether a given technique is effective for a particular person is very individualistic.

Building Additional Client Skills. Many clients, especially those with an adolescent or early adult onset of their mental illness, may be lacking crucial interpersonal and intrapersonal skills. Assisting clients to learn skills in areas such as handling anger, conflict, relationships, and social interactions can facilitate growth and recovery. Structured interventions (e.g., see Liberman & Evans, 1985) can be adopted to assist clients in these areas. Also important are stress reduction and relaxation behaviors. Stress often precipitates problems or exacerbates symptoms, but clients are often offered little in terms of coping or stress reduction and relaxation techniques. A number of effective stress reduction methods may be helpful for clients (see Copeland & McKay, 1992). Beyond these specific content areas, many clients could also benefit from learning general problem-solving skills (e.g., Spivak & Shure, 1974) which they can apply to various difficulties that arise in their lives.

Developing Healthy Social Support Networks. Social network therapy techniques (Bebout & Harris, 1993) can be used to help clients repair and reestablish old social supports or to construct new support systems.

Creating Alternative Social Roles. For many people with a persistent illness, the disorder has become their identity and social career (Goffman, 1961). In addition to assisting clients to develop an alternative sense of self, it is also crucial to help people create alternative social identities through new roles. A variety of roles are possible (e.g., as a friend, student, partner, etc.), but vocational roles are especially important given the priority placed on jobs in our society and clients' own high levels of interests in obtaining jobs (e.g., Morse & Calsyn, 1986). Work is a meaningful activity for many people in our culture, and recovery is often facilitated when people with severe mental illnesses can obtain jobs. Assisting individuals to obtain normalized community jobs while providing specialized supports through the individual placement and support (IPS) program is one promising approach to helping individuals find the restorative effect of employment (Becker & Drake, 1993).

Building Meaning. Meaning has a central role in the recovery process for many people. Service providers can foster meaning through different approaches. In addition to helping create social support networks and jobs—activities that are often infused with personal meaning—psychotherapeutic approaches that draw upon narrative therapy techniques (e.g., Parry & Doan, 1994) or existential strategies (e.g., Yalom, 1980) can be effective for helping individuals construct personal meaning in their lives. Providers also need to be aware and respectful of individuals' religious and spiritual beliefs and experiences that can foster meaning and spirituality.

Preventing Relapse.   Part of recovery is anticipating and preventing crises and relapses. Service providers should assist clients to develop crisis or relapse prevention plans. These tools are similar to the recovery roadmap or WRAP but are more narrow, developed from research and clinical work that suggest that many people with severe mental illness follow fairly predictable, sequential patterns that lead to psychiatric decompensation or rehospitalization (see Curtis, 1993; Mendel, 1989). For people who are also homeless, the plans should be broadened to include preventing re-occurrences of homelessness or associated conditions, such as alcohol or substance abuse. Similar to Copeland's (1997) WRAP, the crisis or relapse prevention pattern is developed in collaboration with the individual, assisting the person to identify: the sequence of behaviors and situations that have lead to crisis in the past; antecedent stressors and triggers; early warning signs and indicators of relapse (in behavioral, emotional, and symptomatic domains); and possible alternative ways of coping and obtaining assistance to prevent a full relapse or crisis. Solution-oriented techniques, (O'Hanlon & Weiner-Davis, 1988) such as identifying exceptions and what has helped in the past, are often useful for devising alternative coping plans

Interventions in the above areas can be made in individual or group modalities and in community-based or office settings. Experimentation and evaluation of these methods will be useful over time.

Perhaps more important than any specific intervention method is the way which people with severe mental illness and homelessness are viewed. As noted earlier, interventions have traditionally focused on psychosocial resources or medication. While these are clearly important, a broader view of the person is needed, one that includes but extends beyond pure biochemical or social-political conceptions. Ironically, as others have described, the person is too often ignored in the services (Davidson & Strauss, 1992; Deegan, 1988). The foundation for services needs to be person-centered and holistic, one which understands the bio-psycho-social-spiritual nature of the person, with specific attention to understanding both the individual's unique mosaic of losses and grief, and the very real possibility of recovery.

☐ Conclusion

Despite a remarkably high prevalence rate, there has been less attention and concern directed in recent years to the problem of people being homeless, including those who also have severe mental illness. This phenomena, termed compassion fatigue, constitutes a secondary loss within our culture. Further scholarly and policy work needs to be directed to raise awareness about homelessness, especially to findings that people who are homeless experience a multitude of losses even while they possess the potential of recovery. Further research concerning loss in this area may be especially important since, as Harvey and Weber (1998), indicated, the experience— or, rather, even the *awareness*—of losses can lead "people to become more passionate, more compassionate, more humane, and . . . . empathic and available to others" (p. 328). "Recovery," Anthony (1993) wrote, "is a truly unifying human experience. Because all people (helpers included) experience the catastrophes of life (death of a loved one, divorce, the threat of severe physical illness, and disability), the challenge of recovery must be faced" (p. 15). Similarly, Deegan (1988) observed how both psychiatric clients and staff experience losses and have the potential of recovery. She further observed the illusory "us/them" dichotomy between people with severe mental illnesses and staff, and the fact that "we all share a common humanity" (p. 18). Loss and recovery are universal aspects of experience that can serve to reduce stigma and remind us of a common thread which connects all people. In this way, a greater understanding of loss and recovery may function as an antidote to compassion fatigue, restoring some of our collective humanity, and helping us to better serve people who are homeless and mentally ill.

☐ References

Anthony, W. A. (1993). Recovery from mental illness: The guiding vision of the mental health service system in the 1990s. *Psychosocial Rehabilitation Journal, 16*(4), 11–23.

Baxter, E., & Hopper, K. 1981. *Private lives/public spaces: Homeless adults on the streets of New York city.* New York: Community Service Society.

Bebout, R. R., & Harris, M. (1993). *The community connections social support network intervention model.* Washington, DC: Community Connections, Inc.

Becker, D. R., & Drake, R. E. (1993). *A working life: The Individual Placement and Support (IPS) program.* Concord, NH: New Hampshire-Dartmouth Psychiatric Research Center.

Borysenko, J., & Borysenko, M. (1994). *The power of the mind to heal.* Carson, CA: Hay House.

Breier, A., & Strauss, J. S. (1983). Self-control in psychotic disorders. *Archives of General Psychiatry, 40*, 1141–1145.

Burger, G. K., Calsyn, R. J., Morse, G. A., & Klinkenberg, W. D. (1999). Protypical profiles of the Brief Psychiatric Rating Scale. Paper submitted for publication.

Copeland, M. E. (1997). *Wellness Recovery Action Plan.* Brattleboro, VT: Peach Press.

Copeland, M. E., & McKay, M. (1992). *The depression workbook: A guide for living with depression and manic depression.* Oakland, CA: New Harbinger.

Curtis, L. (1993, May). Crisis prevention—The cornerstone of crises response. *In Community,* 6– 7. (Newsletter published by the Center for Community Change, Trinity College of Vermont, 208 Colchester Avenue, Burlington, Vermont 05401.)

Curtis, L. (1999, May 10–12). Recovery and psychiatric disability: What are we learning? Workshop presented at 1999 Spring Training Institute, Missouri Department of Mental Health, Branson, Missouri.

Davidson, L. (1992). Developing an empirical-phenomenological approach to schizophrenia research. *Journal of Phenomenological Psychology, 23*(1), 3–15.

Davidson, L., & Strauss, J. S. (1992). Sense of self in recovery from severe mental illness. *British Journal of Medical Psychology, 65*, 131–145.

Deegan, P. E. (1988). Recovery: The lived experience of rehabilitation. *Psychosocial Rehabilitation Journal, 11*, 11–19.

Dennis, D. L., Buckner, J. C., Lipton, F. R., & Levine, I. S. (1991). A decade of research and services for homeless mentally ill persons. *American Psychologist, 46*, 1129–1138.

Drake, R. E., Osher, F. C., & Wallach, M. A. (1991). Homelessness and dual diagnosis. *American Psychologist, 46*, 1149–1158.

Federal Task Force on Homelessness and Severe Mental Illness. (1992). *Outcasts on Main Street.* Washington, DC: HHS/Interagency Council on the Homeless.

Ferguson, S. (1990, September/October). Us vs. them: America's growing frustration with the homeless. *Utne Reader,* 50–55.

Freeman, C. (1998, July 24–26). Physically challenged and empowered. Presentation given at the Body & Soul Conference, Boulder, Colorado.

Goffman, E. (1961). *Asylums.* Garden City, NY: Doubleday.

Harding, C. M., Zubin, J., & Strauss, J. S. (1987). Chronicity in schizophrenia: Fact, partial fact or artifact? *Hospital and Community Psychiatry, 38*, 477–486.

Harrison, V. (1984). A biologist's view of pain, suffering, and marginal life. In F. Dougherty (Ed.), *The depraved, the disabled, and the fullness of life*. Wilmington, DE: Michael Glazier.

Harvey, J. H. (1996). Editorial and commentary: On creating the "Journal of Personal and Interpersonal Loss" and the nature of loss. *Journal of Personal and Interpersonal Loss, 1*(1), iii–ix.

Harvey, J. H., & Weber, A. L. (1998). Why there must be a psychology of loss. In J. H. Harvey (Ed.), *Perspectives on loss: A source book* (pp. 319–330). Philadelphia: Brunner/Mazel.

Hopper, K. (1984). Whose lives are these, anyway? *Urban and Social Change Review, 17*(2), 12–13.

Hopper, K., Mauch, D., & Morse, G. (1990). *The 1986–1987 NIMH-funded CSP demonstration projects to serve homeless mentally ill persons: A preliminary assessment*. (Unpublished government report.) Rockville, MD: National Institute of Mental Health.

Housing and Urban Development (HUD) & Health and Human Services (HHS). (1998). *National symposium on homelessness research: What works?* Arlington, VA: Author.

Janoff-Bulman, R., & Berg, M. (1998). Disillusionment and the creation of values: From traumatic losses to existential gains. In J. H. Harvey (Ed.), *Perspectives on loss: A source book* (pp. 35–48). Philadelphia: Brunner/Mazel.

Liberman, R. P., & Evans, C. C. (1995). Behavioral rehabilitation for chronic mental patients. *Journal of Clinical Psychopharmacology, 5*(Suppl. 3), 8S–14S.

Link, B. G., Susser, E., Stueve, A., Phelan, J., Moore, R. E., & Struening, E. (1994). Lifetime and five-year prevalence of homelessness in the United States. *American Journal of Public Health, 84*, 1907–1912.

Lovejoy, M. (1984). Recovery from schizophrenia: A personal odyssey. *Hospital & Community Psychiatry, 32*, 809–812.

Mendel, W. M. (1989). *Treating schizophrenia*. San Francisco: Jossey-Bass.

Merit Behavioral Care (undated). *Drug abuse and prevention workshop* (Vol. 2). Author.

Miller, E. D., & Omarzo, J. (1998). New directions in loss research. In J. H. Harvey (Ed.), *Perspectives on loss: A source book* (pp. 3–20). Philadelphia: Brunner/Mazel.

Morse, G. (1998a). A different field of dreams: Outreaching and serving homeless people. *The Journal, 9*(1), 41–43.

Morse, G. A. (1998b). Homelessness and loss: Conceptual and research considerations. In J. H. Harvey (Ed.), *Perspectives on loss: A source book*. Philadelphia: Brunner/Mazel.

Morse, G. (1999). A review of case management for people who are homeless: Implications for practice policy and research. In L. B. Fosburg & D. L. Dennis (Eds.), Practical lessons: The 1998 *national symposium on homelessness research* (pp. 7-1 through 7-34). Washington, DC: U.S. Department of Housing and Urban Development and U.S. Department of Health and Human Services.

Morse, G. A. (1986). *A contemporary assessment of urban homelessness: Implications for social change* (Published Report, 1986). Center for Metropolitan Studies, University of Missouri-St. Louis.

Morse, G., & Calsyn, R. J. (1986). Mentally disturbed homeless people in St. Louis: Needy, willing, but underserved. *International Journal of Mental Health, 14*, 74–94.

Morse, G. A., Calsyn, R. J., Allen, G., Tempelhoff, B., & Smith, R. (1992). Experimental comparison of the effects of three treatment programs for homeless mentally ill people. *Hospital and Community Psychiatry, 43*, 1005–1010.

Morse, G. A., Calsyn, R. J., Klinkenberg, W. D., Trusty, M. L., Gerber, F., Smith, R., Tempelhoff, B., & Ahmad, L. (1997). An experimental comparison of three types of case management for homeless mentally ill persons. *Psychiatric Services, 48*, 497–503.

Morse, G., Calsyn, R. J., & Wolff, N. (1996, March). *Final report: Cost effectiveness of case management for the homeless* (unpublished manuscript). Gerontology program, University of Missouri-St. Louis.

Morse, G., Shields, N. M., Hanneke, C. R., Calsyn, R. J., Burger, G. K., & Nelson, B. (1985).

Homeless people in St. Louis: A mental health program evaluation, field study, and followup investigations. St. Louis, MO: State of Missouri, Department of Mental Health.

O'Hanlon, W. H., & Weiner-Davis, M. (1988). *In search of solutions: A new direction in psychotherapy.* New York: Norton.

Parry, A., & Doan, R. E. (1994). *Story re-visions: Narrative therapy in the post-modern world.* New York: Guilford.

Piliavin, I., Sosin, M., & Westerfelt, H. (1989). *Conditions contributing to long-term homelessness: An exploratory study* (unpublished manuscript). Institute for Research on Poverty, University of Wisconsin-Madison.

Rando, T. A. (1993). *Treatment of complicated mourning.* Champaign, IL: Research Press.

Remen, R. N. (1996). *Kitchen table wisdom: Stories that heal.* New York: Riverhead Books.

Rossi, R. H. (1989). *Down and out in America: The origins of homelessness.* Chicago: University of Chicago Press.

Russinova, Z. (1998). Promoting recovery from serious mental illness through hope-inspiring strategies. *Community Support Network News, 13*(1), 1, 4–7.

Spencer, R., Zawier, B., Tempelhoff, B., Morse, G., & Calsyn, R. J. (1994). *Incorporating integrated treatment approaches in the continuous treatment team model: A manual for working with dually-diagnosed homeless individuals* (unpublished manuscript). Gerontology Program, University of Missouri-St. Louis.

Spivack, G., & Shure, M. B. (1974). *Social adjustment of young children.* San Francisco: Jossey-Bass.

Sosin, M. R., Colson, P., & Grossman, S. (1988). *Homelessness in Chicago: Poverty and pathology, social institutions and social change* (unpublished manuscript). School of Social Service Administration, University of Chicago, IL.

Thompson, S. C. (1998). Blockades to finding meaning and control. In J. H. Harvey (Ed.), *Perspectives on loss: A source book* (pp. 21–34). Philadelphia: Brunner/Mazel.

Uzelac, E. (1990, December 9). Turning cold. *Miami Sun Sentinel*, 1G, 6G.

Wright, B. (1983). *Physical disability–A psychosocial approach.* New York: Harper & Row.

Yalom, I. D. (1980) *Existential Psychotherapy.* New York: Basic Books.

Young, S. L., & Ensing, D.,S. (1999). Exploring recovery from the perspective of people with psychiatric disabilities. *Psychiatric Rehabilitation Journal, 22,* 219–231.

PART

III

LOSS AND TRAUMA ASSOCIATED WITH CLOSE RELATIONSHIPS

Stevan E. Hobfoll
Nicole Ennis
Jennifer Kay

Loss, Resources, and Resiliency in Close Interpersonal Relationships

Loss of a loved one is often the most painful of life's experiences. It plays so close to the heart that it is the mainstay of poetry, literature, and film, all of which attempt to capture the poignancy, despair, and essence of departure, death, and separation from those people whom we love most. In the social sciences as well, loss and separation from loved ones have been a pivotal area of study. Bowlby (1980) was among the first to see loss and separation as a central defining point for development of the infant and child. Parkes (1972) incorporated the inevitable process of death and grief into mainstream psychology, emphasizing that grief reactions could produce severe reactions even in healthy individuals. Given that the social sciences and our culture have accepted this idea—that grief reactions can be severe and require treatment even when the individual is otherwise psychologically healthy—so unequivocally now it is easy to forget that at the time of its introduction this thought was seen as radical. Mourning was seen as a normal process of little interest to psychology and melancholy was seen as a deep-seated psychopathology, having little to do with life events occurring after early childhood (Freud, 1915/1917).

Most of the interpersonal theorizing on loss speaks to the psychological and social attachments that are central and therefore likely to be damaged if not lost entirely when loss of a loved one occurs (Harvey & Miller, 1998; Parkes, 1972; Stroebe & Stroebe, 1987). However, theories have tended to address interpersonal loss as separate from other kinds of losses, or apply theories of interpersonal loss to other kinds of loss. Hence, theories might see loss of a loved one as qualitatively different from retirement, loss of one's home, or job loss. Alternatively, some theories might tend to extrapolate from interpersonal loss to these other categories. In such instances, job loss is viewed in terms of grief and grief resolution based on a model of interpersonal grief.

☐ Conservation of Resources Theory

Conservation of Resources (COR) theory is a comprehensive motivational theory that speaks to the role of resource loss, its impact on stress, and the part it plays in goal-oriented behavior. In this chapter we will explore how COR theory applies to interpersonal loss in particular, and examine how interpersonal loss impacts a multitude of resources that are central to people's sense of self, attachment to others, economic viability, and day-to-day functioning. We will make the case that loss of a loved one must be removed from Western individualistic notions if it is to be understood beyond its poetic, literary boundaries. With this fuller understanding should come an increased ability to predict the consequences of loss and an understanding of how to address it therapeutically.

Relationships: Their Historical Purpose and Their Current Manifestation

Before explicating the principles of COR theory it is helpful to understand the history of relationships. When we think of close personal ties we think of love and use the term loved ones. We must recognize, however, the recency of love's primacy in relationships, and in doing so come to appreciate that love is only one aspect of close ties, and one whose primacy is only recently acquired. Instead, the *functional* basis of close ties is the primary evolutionary and cultural component.

Surely, romantic love has existed in love relationships from time immemorial. The Old Testament sings Solomon's "Song of Songs,"

Set me as a seal upon thy heart,
As a seal upon thine arm:
For love is strong as death,
Jealousy is cruel as the grave; the flashes thereof are flashes of fire,
A very flame of the Lord. (Song of Sol. 8:6)

Nevertheless, for the tribe, the functional nature of relationships was primary and it is this functional level that has contributed to our genetic stock to produce our species' need for attachments. Members of the tribe needed each other for hunting, planting, protection, and procreation. Loss of any individual could spell loss of a vital role and could place the tribe, and its shared genetic pool, in a precarious role. As the institution of marriage was codified, marriage was seldom a product of love or individual decision making. Instead, marriage in its early forms was more closely related to property rites, propagation, protection, and division of labor.

Relationships between a child and parent are more likely to possess both an historical-cultural and genetic love bond. However, even here, it is readily apparent that the love bond fortifies the functional bond. The attachment of a parent to child and child to parent must be strong enough to ensure biological preservation on both sides of the attachment. A strong love bond ensures dedication, loyalty, and the willingness to incur sacrifice.

The veracity of this message is made clear in the Ten Commandments in the West and in Confucianism (Eliot, 1980) in the East, which say nothing of love, but much of the functional relationships between people. Of those commandments that pertain to relationships between people, they concern property (stealing and coveting), false testimony against one's neighbor, honor of father and mother, adultery, and murder (Kaplan, 1981). Likewise, the biblical marital contract (called Ketuba) contains provisions for the protection of the wife and the disposition of her property (Kaplan, 1981). Similarly, it is only very recently (post World War II) that loss of love and incompatibility can be grounds for divorce in Western nations, and still are not recognized as legitimate grounds within many religious communities.

Love has become increasingly central in our cultural views toward romance, and even family members, as the likelihood of protection against functional difficulties and survival itself become less of an issue. It can be said that love has replaced functional intent as the predicate of relationship formation and sustenance. Current cultural imperatives suggest that we should not marry without love and we should not be having children for "the sake of the farm" or to support us in our old age. The primacy of love is still not a worldwide phenomena even now, however, as many cultures still have arranged marriages. Yet, it is nevertheless clear that love has become a central facet of close relationships. Love is left out of few theories of relationship loss, whereas the more functional aspects of relationships are likely to be minimized.

Conservation of Resources Theory and Interpersonal Relationship Loss

COR theory begins with the basic motivational tenet that people strive to obtain, retain, protect, and foster those things they most value (Hobfoll, 1988, 1989). Those things that people value are termed resources and they are either directly valued, such as home, family, or health, or instrumental in the acquisition of basic valued resources (e.g., insurance, money, knowledge). Resources are further understood in that they are tied to the nexus of individual-nested in family-nested in group-nested in tribe (Hobfoll, 1998). What this means is that we cannot separate resources of the individual from those that are linked to the family, group, or tribe. For example, even such a basic self resource as self-efficacy entails success within social settings and is inferred by the greater culture. An executive feels self-efficacy probably only in small part by his actual behavior, but instead by the sociocultural implications of having a position that is deemed a success by the greater social milieu. If this broader linking is true of self-efficacy, how much more is it the case for such resources as social support, employment and good marriage? Each of us may individuate our understanding of resources, but few resources are circumscribed solely within an individual and his or her self boundaries.

In our research (Hobfoll & Lilly, 1993), we found 74 key resources (see Table 1) nominated by a series of dozens of community groups. Freedy, Saladin, Kilpatrick, Resnick, and Saunders (1994) noted that from this greater list, a subset were especially relevant in the wake of natural disaster. Stoll (1999) in a series of studies in sport and rehabilitation found a more specific group of resources, but again a rather finite number were nominated by individuals who shared a social setting or challenge (e.g., back injury, long distance sports). These studies suggest that the number of key resources may be tailored from the broader group of resources that hold in most situations to a subset of finite resources that are more specific. However, in virtually all cases the more finite resources are merely particular examples of the original 74 resources found. For example, health is a basic resources, but a back injury group will relate it to health concerning their back injury.

Resources can also be better understood by dividing them categorically. There are several reasonable ways to divide resources. One breakdown is by type: object resources, personal characteristics and skills, condition resources, and energy resources (Hobfoll, 1988). Object resources pertain to those key physical resources such as home,

TABLE 1.   COR Resources

Personal transportation (car, truck, etc.)	Ability to organize tasks
Feeling that I am successful	Extras for children
Time for adequate sleep	Sense of commitment
Good marriage	Intimacy with at least one friend
Adequate clothing	Money for extras
Feeling valuable to others	Self-discipline
Family stability	Understanding from my employer/boss
Free time	Savings or emergency money
More clothing than I need*	Motivation to get things done
Sense of pride in myself	Spouse/partner's health
Intimacy with one or more family members	Support from coworkers
Time for work	Adequate income
Feeling that I am accomplishing my goals	Feeling that I know who I am
Good relationship with my children	Advancement in education or job training
Time with loved ones	Adequate financial credit
Necessary tools for work	Feeling independent
Hope	Companionship
Children's health	Financial assets (stocks, property, etc.)
Stamina/endurance	Knowing where I am going with my life
Necessary home appliances	Affection from others
Feeling that my future success depends on	Financial stability
me	Feeling that my life has meaning/purpose
Positively challenging routine	Positive feeling about myself
Personal health	People I can learn from
Housing that suits my needs	Money for transportation
Sense of optimism	Help with tasks at work
Status/seniority at work	Medical insurance
Adequate food	Involvement with church, synagogue, etc.
Larger home than I need*	Retirement security (financial)
Sense of humor	Help with tasks at home
Stable employment	Loyalty of friends
Intimacy with spouse or partner	Money for advancement or self-
Adequate home furnishings	improvement (education, starting a
Feeling that I have control over my life	business)
Role as a leader	Help with child care
Ability to communicate well	Involvement in organizations with others
Providing children's essentials	who have similar interests
Feeling that my life is peaceful	Financial help if needed
Acknowledgment of my accomplishments	Health of family/close friends

*Groups repeatedly admitted investing more in these two luxury resources than other resources they deemed more important.

transportation, cooking appliances, and clothing. Personal characteristics and skills include those resources that are contained within the self, such as having a job skill, sense of mastery, self-esteem, and optimism. Condition resources include social positions that give individuals links them to resources within society. These include employment, tenure, marriage, and being attached to loving others (i.e., a support system). Finally, energy resources have no value in and of themselves, but are conferred value by virtue of their availing individuals to other resources. These include money, credit, and knowledge. Knowledge, for example, has no value other than when it is used to achieve some other end such as status, better employment, or problem solving. Indeed, knowledge is often jealously guarded so that it remains "owned" by those who possess it and not shared.

COR Principles.   COR theory posits a number of central principles that have particular implications for the circumstances of resource loss and gain and their relevance to the stress process. We will discuss two of these principles in this chapter. *The first principle of COR theory is that resource loss is more impactful than gain.* This first principle distinguishes COR theory from general reinforcement theory which makes no statement as to the relative weight of gain and loss and indeed suggests that loss and gain of the same object or reinforcer are of equal value. Instead, COR theory proposes that resource loss has decidedly more magnitude than resource gain. In studies comparing resource loss and gain, it has repeatedly been found that loss is more impactful, and that resource gains have little impact outside of the context of loss (Hobfoll & Lilly, 1993; Wells, Hobfoll, & Lavin, 1997, 1999). Hence, in a relationship context it can be said that losing a relationship will have more psychological impact than gaining a relationship. A child's birth is celebrated for a day before one psychologically turns one's attention back to work and other aspects of life, whereas a child's death is devastating and its effects are felt for a lifetime. This same principle seems to hold for loss and gain as mundane as a cup in a laboratory experiment (Tversky & Kahneman, 1974). In this regard, it was found that participants in an experiment would expend more effort to avoid losing a cup that they were just given; then they would expend to gain the same cup! Moreover, there is recent evidence that this first principle is a basic cognitive bias that exists on the neurological level (Ito, Larsen, Smith, & Cacioppo, 1998). In studying the impact of disaster, Ironson et al. (1997) found that resource loss was the best predictor of not only psychological sequelae, but also immunological compromise.

Resource gain should not, however, be viewed as trivial by any means. Research suggests that resource gain is particularly important when loss has occurred (Cohen & Hoberman, 1983; Wells et al., 1999). That is, resource gain has a protective effect such that it buffers the otherwise negative impact of resource loss. For example, Wells et al. (1999) found that the existence of gains in intimacy had little effect for pregnant women who experienced few resource losses during pregnancy. However, for those who experienced such losses as job setbacks, health problems, and economic difficulties, the gain of intimacy and other resources during that period had an offsetting effect on depression.

The second principle of COR theory is that people must invest resources in order to obtain, retain, protect, and foster other resources. This might seem circular, but can be seen, for example, in the use of money (one resource) to protect other money through insurance or investing in education. On the interpersonal level, we may use social support, and by doing so exchange and expend favors, in order to forestall the loss of self resources such as self-esteem or hope. Relationships demand the investment of time, energy, and the loss of other potential resources because of lost opportunities when we invest in a relationship. This principle was first observed and carefully studied by Schönpflug (1985). He noted that in order to cope with challenges people consider not only the direct outcomes of their efforts, but the resources they have to expend to achieve those ends. People might choose not to act or to act in some minimal fashion because the resource costs of coping are too high. For instance, when a marriage is threatened individuals often see the investment of resources (such as time, trust, and effort) as too steep compared to the ultimate value of the marriage, given the likelihood of failure in saving the marriage even after significant resource investment. Add to this equation the possibility of some second relationship, and the resource loss-gain balance may favor not investing resources, or at least a temporary "wait and see" period.

Such a view of relationships may appear too economic and cold, but COR theory does not see this in terms of straightforward resource exchange as might Kelley (1979). Communal ties have been shown to have long-term involvements that cause people to be willing to sacrifice beyond a simple gain-loss accounting (Clark & Mills, 1979). Moreover, because the resources are held by individuals-nested in family-nested in group-nested in tribe, individual effort and valuation in the above marriage example can be seen as allowing for the esteem of resources of the couple over the individual. Moreover, the sense of love and attachment that increased effort brings is itself a central resource (Bowlby, 1980), making the very sense of having love and being loved as primary. Nevertheless, the economics of COR theory may increase our ability to understand such behavior as staying in a bad marriage, remaining with an abusive partner, or dedicating oneself to love even in a case where love is unrequited. In other words, close relationships involve both romantic resources and more practical ones and we ignore either type at the peril of being unable to predict behavior and psychological states.

Loss Cycles.   Given that resource loss is critical and people must invest other resources to protect and preserve resources, those who lack resources are more vulnerable to stress (Ennis, Hobfoll, & Schröder, 2000; Holohan, Moos, Holohan, & Cronkite, 1999; Wells et al., 1999). This leads to a critical corollary of COR theory for the understanding of interpersonal loss. Specifically,

> Once an initial loss occurs, it follows that further loss will have even greater impact as the individual, family, or group will have fewer remaining resources available to forestall the negative impact of secondary loss. This then creates loss cycles that increase in impact and speed and increase the likelihood of severe negative psychological and functioning sequelae.

Studying the aftermath of Hurricane Hugo, Kaniasty and Norris (1993) noted that not only did the disaster most negatively impact those who lacked close supportive ties, but that the initial disaster impact further reduced resources and set the stage for rapidly expanding cycles of resource loss. Similarly, Wells et al. (1999) found that women had initial resistance to resource loss, but as losses mounted there was an accelerating negative impact.

There is not room here to expand further on COR theory or on the supporting research. Readers are referred to other work for this purpose (Hobfoll, 1988, 1989, 1998). The key points, however, are valuable and we expand upon them in the coming pages for understanding how relationship loss impacts individuals and families and how we might intervene to minimize its negative effect on people, their functioning, and their other relationships.

☐ The Interweaving of People's Resource Webs

In this section we explore the resource webs that exist among people in three major domains. The three areas of interest are those that connect people biologically, economically, and psychologically. Because of this interconnectiveness, resource loss and the stress that results impact more than just the individual. We explore how the interconnections of resources leads to a powerful synergistic impact of interpersonal loss.

Biological and Cultural Connectiveness

Individuals' first goal is survival because without survival, there is no continuation of the self, family, or species. Survival is biologically not an individualistic concept, but instead is communal. Sacrifice of the self for the family or tribe is as much a part of survival as survival of the individual. From a biological standpoint, those events or circumstances that prevent or impede survival create stress. Survival refers also to survival of one's kin as well as one's culture. The joint survival of the individual-in-group is the fundamental motivation of our species. The loss of an individual has no influence on the species' domination of a niche, and individual survival does not ensure the transfer of a group's genes unless those genes are shared by enough members of the group to allow creation of a new genetic template for the species. In support of the collective nature of variation, Darwin (1859/1959) wrote:

> Natural selection will modify the structure of the young in relation to the parent, and of the parent in relation to the young. In social animals it will adapt the structure of each individual for the benefit of the whole community; if the community profits by the selected change. (p. 93)

Biologically, people are connected in families and tribes. These social structures allow for a decrease in individual effort for goal acquirement, while emphasizing goals for the group. Society creates institutions and customs around marriage, work, education, and other important domains that facilitate individual and societal advancement. As culture advances, individual resources and social resources become more closely enmeshed. Individual, familial, tribal and social goals are linked closely. "Individuals set tasks for themselves, distilling from the many culturally prescribed and biologically based demands of social life and survival a set of personal life task goals for which to strive" (Cantor, 1990, p. 736). Through this sociocultural distillation process, how a person behaves in reaction to stress is matched to situations largely derived from social norms and constraints.

Through biological and communal processes, stress is largely enmeshed with family organizations and society as a whole. COR theory widens the study of stress from an individual appraisal to one that incorporates social interconnections. Stress occurs in circumstances that represent a threat of loss or actual loss of the resources required to sustain the individual-nested-in-family-nested-in social organization (Hobfoll, 1998). Individual-nested-in-family-nested-in-social organization emphasizes that although it is possible to separate these levels for study, they are inevitably linked. Without individuals, there is no organization or family, and individuals must rely on social attachments for well-being, self-esteem, and survival. This implies that resources are not only valued by the individual but are intertwined with group membership. COR emphasizes people striving to regulate their resource reserves in order to support survival, preserve well-being, and retain their social ties.

Following this logic, stress, at its most primary level, is created by events or circumstances that hinder survival. For example, loss of a partner is biologically stressful because it hampers procreation. This loss has more impact on surviving female spouses because men can procreate until much later in life. In this regard, after the death of a spouse, men have a higher probability of remarriage than do women of the same age (Kaeaer, Jokela, Merilae, Helle, & Kohola, 1998; Wu, 1995). Further, Kaeaer et al. (1998) found that remarried men had higher lifetime reproductive success than women who remarried. Kaeaer et al. (1998) hypothesized that this may be due to men's longer reproductive lifespan as compared to women. Since the institution of marriage is so closely connected with bearing children, women suffer greater procreational loss than men in the event of spousal loss.

A further function related to biological underpinnings is the role of the partner for protection of the young. This might seem to be an outdated need, but for much of the economically underdeveloped world, including many Western nations, the issue of physical protection is still vital. Moreover, if we understand that protection means having a secure household, having medical insurance, and having income that will ensure maintenance of the provision of food, shelter, and employment, then we can see how loss of one's partner may mean the difference between biological preservation and risk of that preservation. In the United States, loss of one's partner is likely to bring a working or even middle class family into poverty and may bring a poor family into homelessness (Morgan, 1981; Lopata, 1973).

In this manner we are not arguing that the stress of partner loss is primarily biological or even that sociobiological factors are in themselves predictive of the sequelae of partner loss. Rather, our point is that biological patterns endemic to the species are related to the social institutions that are part and parcel of culture, such as the institution of marriage. This, in turn, means that partner loss, and indeed loss of any loved one, has bio-psycho-social implications that impact on the conservation of resources that are central to the stress process. If we ignore the biological roots of culture, we simplify the stress process and in so doing produce more limited models to explain the impact of loss of a loved one and the potential interventions to limit such impact.

Economic Interdependency

For spouses, their economic resources are so intertwined it is often difficult to separate them for each individual. The family's resources are a product of the investments made by each spouse, whether in paid labor or the unpaid contribution of a homemaker. Hence, when there is a loss of a spouse, economic threats to the family are likely to arise. The extent of the impact of the overlap of couple's economic resources is illustrated in a study by Shapiro (1996). Shapiro examined the differences in psychological and economic distress between remarried and divorced people, and investigated whether differences in economic distress explained differences in psychological distress. He found that those who remarried had significantly lower rates of economic and psychological distress than those who were currently divorced. He also found that economic distress explained a large proportion of the impact of marital status on psychological distress. Interestingly, he found no differences in psychological distress between the remarried and divorced after controlling for income differences. This means that loss of economic resources accounted for much of the psychological distress people were experiencing, and that marital status was only a proxy for economic loss.

Economic resources of the couple cannot be evaluated only in terms of paid labor. Whether or not household labor is traditionally divided, each spouse is likely to make an economic contribution either in dollar form or in kind. For example, in a relatively traditional family, the wife may be in charge of tasks such as cooking and cleaning, whereas the husband may handle maintenance of the car and house. In the event of one of these spouse's death, there are many household tasks that may not get accomplished or that will require substantial dollar investment to offset. Because of the roles that each spouse filled, when one dies, there is an extreme strain financially on the surviving spouse as well as the family as a whole. Nevertheless, because financial income is critical and because men earn more, the loss of a husband is typically more economically devastating than the loss of a wife. Women who do not work in the paid labor force, are likely to be especially vulnerable because they may lack not only income but also the requisite skills relevant to current employment conditions. In this light, James (1996) found that women who devoted themselves to childcare and unpaid work in the home, suffered greater economically following separation or divorce.

Consequently, when examining spousal loss, it is important to take into account the economic interdependency that exists in most families. Income will be a major factor, but unpaid labor will also be a factor that will require creative means of assessment. Although economic losses are more likely to result from the loss of a male partner, the omnipresence of dual career families makes this an increasingly challenging factor for both men and women.

Culture and Psychological Connectiveness

Stress then is not just an individual experience, but takes into account the sociobiological context, family economics, and culture. This means that both individual and broader environmental perspectives are vital to understanding the concept of stress and its ultimate psychological experience. Margaret and Paul Baltes (1982, 1990) emphasize in their theory of Compensation with Optimization that psychological stress is a function of broader sociocultural phenomena. They suggest that individuals' stress experiences are a derivative of social and cultural processes involving their resources and the resource demands of the culture. Society creates institutions and traditions around work, marriage, education, health care, and other important life domains that facilitate both individual and societal advancement. This leads to individuals being tied to a social group where individual resources, such as self-esteem, become intertwined with group membership. In this manner, resources to a large extent are established and operate from being part of certain social systems; the couple is a primary building block of these social systems within society. This also translates to the fact that society creates regulatory systems at work, for raising children, and for social situations, that are supportive of the institution of couples, not singles. Hence, stress is more likely to occur after interpersonal loss, because social structures are in place to support couple and two-parent families, and not single adults or single-parent families.

With attachment, the most primary of which is with one's partner, comes an interdependence that is at once both cultural and psychological. Rather than solely acting independently of others according to self-interest, people act in their own self-interest in cooperation with others, and against others (Van Lange, Otten, De Bruin, & Joireman, 1997). This collectivist orientation implies that people will often act in a self-sacrificing manner if it will benefit their spouse, family, social group, or society. In this way, interpersonal contacts provide a roadmap for understanding and navigating the complexities of the world around us. Interpersonal ties define and demarcate individuals' roles in that web of relationships.

A major psychological resource that is gained and lost on the basis of having and losing one's partner has been conceptualized under the general heading of social support. Parkes, Burgess and McKenzie (1926) in their classic book, *The City*, proposed that health and well-being, versus deviancy and ill-health, were direct consequences of the extent to which individuals were nested in social relationships in which they held a sanctioned place and position; marriage is one key to this sanctioning process. Cassel (1974) later reawakened this earlier theme, theorizing that the strengths of primary social contacts provide a protective, health-enhancing influence. Antonovsky (1979) further built on this idea and identified the nesting of individuals within social networks as general resistance resources. He stated that intimate relationships provided access to a greater web of supportive ties and a sense of community. Berkman (1977) identified the importance of social ties in the maintenance of health and well-being in his landmark examination of adults in Alameda County, California. She found that those individuals who were married, had close friends and relatives, church membership, and informal and formal group association had the lowest mortality rates.

If we understand that the ties created as a couple is a primary linkage upon which many of these other relationships are predicated, then the importance of having and losing a partner can be more fully appreciated. When people lose their partner, they not only lose the social support they once received from their partner, but they may also lose social support from the formal and informal social groups to which the couple once belonged. For example, Smith and Zick (1996) found that for nonelderly men (less than 65 years of age), there was an elevated morality risk when their wives died suddenly and they had a harder time adjusting. They hypothesized that perhaps this was due to the fact that wives were the critical link to their husbands' social support network. However, if their spouses' death was not sudden, they had an easier time adjusting, perhaps because they had time to redefine their connection to their social networks. As long as they continued to define themselves as a couple, they may not even have felt justified in seeking individual support.

It is also important to note the deleterious effects of social support that may be exacerbated when people lose their partner. When people rely on or offer social support, they are making themselves vulnerable to stress contagion (Riley & Eckenrode, 1986) and "pressure cooker" effects (Hobfoll & London, 1986). This occurs because social support translates into sharing stress exposure among others for whom consequences may be jointly experienced or empathically shared (Hirsch, 1980). For example, Miller, Smerglia, Gaudet, and Kitson (1998) found that following the loss of a spouse, widowed and divorced women experienced stress associated with increased social support from family and friends. However, the authors found that social support had mixed effects on distress, depending on the type of support. Advice did not affect distress for either group, but widows and divorcees who received material support experienced increased distress. COR emphasizes that people strive to regulate their resource reserves in order to preserve well-being and retain the fabric of their social ties. People are motivated to sustain themselves and their core social groups which can become difficult in the face of loss because they are sharing stress and pain in the support process.

The loss of love is still one of the least understood psychological concepts. On one level loss of love can be understood in Bowlbian terms of loss of a loving attachment (Bowlby, 1980). However, this still loses some of the romantic element of love as it is so poignantly expressed in music, literature, and poetry (Hendrick, Dicke, & Hendrick,

1998; Meeks, Hendrick, & Hendrick, 1998; Taraban, Hendrick, & Hendrick, 1998). COR theory is too large scale to aid in a specific understanding of love, however, the concept of resource substitution in COR theory may prove relevant. Specifically, COR theory suggests that resources may be substituted following loss in order to limit loss's negative impact (Hobfoll, 1988, 1998). This translates into loss of love having greater impact the greater the love, not only because the loss is greater, but because the belief that a new love will substitute will be evaluated as less likely. Some cross-substitution is possible, such as obtaining love from other relationships following loss of a partner. Similarly, finding a new partner may prove a key remedy after some period of mourning transpires. Nevertheless, if loss of love is painful, then loss of great love may create special challenges for those involved.

☐ Resilience and the FALL Model

This section addresses the concept of resilience in the context of the Fitting, Adaptation, Limitation, and Leniency (FALL) model. This model is an extension of the ideas from the Conservation of Resources theory (Hobfoll, 1998) and refers specifically to how resources interact to counteract stress' impact.

The nature of resiliency can be defined as the possession and sustaining of key resources that prevent or interrupt loss cycles. For example, money can be invested to prevent financial loss outright, and time and energy can be invested to prevent the loss of love by contributing to one's family. If initial loss occurs, strong resource reservoirs can offset or minimize the impact of the loss. Rejection by a partner may be painful, but turning to family for support can help an individual feel nurtured and cherished. Hence, the key to resilience in the face of loss is the sustaining of resource reserves. The active process of stress and coping must be developed in the context of how resources are used based on an individual's nesting in families and social organizations. Using this premise to understand the process requires us to take into account how people's environment will impact their use and sustenance of key resources in preventing loss cycles. A better understanding of the FALL model may provide the context that will allow for the development of ideas about the active processes of stress and coping in the face of interpersonal loss.

Fitting

Fitting is the first step in the FALL model and it posits that individuals actively and reactively engage in the fitting of their resources to the demands of their environments in order to promote resiliency. This has typically been understood in static terms of resource "fit." For example, in a sample of widowed and divorced women Miller et al. (1998) found social support had mixed effects on distress depending on the type of support provided. Practical support was more beneficial in reducing distress for widows, and having someone to listen to personal problems was more beneficial for divorcees. Therefore, the resource of social support decreased distress only if it fit the demands of the environment.

The theoretical work of Thoits (1994) offers a foundation upon which to build an understanding of resource fitting, a more dynamic concept than static fit. In her work, Thoits proposed that certain higher level resources act as resource managers thereby allowing them to have a greater impact by providing individuals the ability to use other resources more effectively. Thoits' ideas combined with the COR principle that individuals' resources contribute to the gain of additional resources provides us a more action oriented framework with which to view the process of stress and coping. When resources are examined in this context, individuals are provided more degrees of freedom to demonstrate their ability to engage in resiliency promoting strategies. The key point of these findings is that we must move to the older concept of resource fit (French, Caplan, & Van Harrison, 1982) to the more dynamic concept of resource fitting, which implies that resources are managed to respond to demands and that the greater the ability to exercise this fitting, the more resiliency will be expressed. There are a number of strategic steps in the act of fitting resources:

Shaping One's Resources to Increase Invulnerability, Irrespective of Circumstances. The main idea in this first step is that individuals proactively fashion their resources in order to protect themselves against potential stress. Work done by Taylor, Pham, Rivkin, and Armor (1998) on mental simulation is one instance of shaping resources in order to achieve desired goals. By using mental simulation individuals can move themselves from a current situation toward an envisioned future; in doing so they manage emotions and fundamental tasks that will produce successful completion of their goals. The process of mental simulation promotes resilience in that it can be used proactively in order to engage in self-regulatory behavior that will help people better manage their resources in a variety of situations.

Positioning Oneself such that One Cannot be Easily Threatened with Resource Loss or Lose Resources. This kind of fitting promotes ideas that are in line with what might be called stage setting. The emphasis here is on actively positioning oneself in circumstances that limit loss or potential loss. For example in interpersonal relationships people often provide nurturance to others who may in turn provide love or support. Through this process people are also more insulated from the pain of isolation. In addition, providing nurturance increases the chance that social support will be available when needed (Miller et al., 1998).

Accurate Estimating of Threat of Loss or Actual Loss if it Occurs. This is the next critical phase in the fitting of resources and it involves an appropriate assessment of the stressor in order to employ resources in the most useful manner (Lazarus & Folkman, 1984). An appropriate assessment of the stressor allows an individual to mobilize resiliency-promoting strategies that may garner him or her certain degree of protection.

Assessing of the Adequacy of the Resources that may be Employed to Offset Loss or Increase Gain of Resources. After an accurate assessment of the situation, an understanding of those resources that can be used to address the situation is needed (see also Lazarus & Folkman, 1984). For example, Schut, Stroebe, and van den Bout (1997) examined coping in a sample of widows and widowers who were suffering from elevated levels of distress 11 months after their loss. They found that widowers benefited more from emotion-focused interventions and widows from problem-focused interventions. Due to gender differences in coping styles, these opposite gender strategies were the most adequate resources that could be used to offset the loss and consequent stressors experienced.

Deciding Whether Internal Resources are Adequate to Address Situational Demands or Whether External Resources are Warranted. A prudent appraisal of resource need is important because using external resources could deplete them and not using them could deplete internal ones. The key to resilience here lies in understanding how to coordinate resources for maximum benefit. These last three strategies involve understanding the demands of the situation and accessing those resources that are appropriate.

Adaptation

Adaptation is the second step in the FALL model and promotes an integrative approaches to the dynamic processes of stress and coping. The core ideas behind the process of adaptation encourage a widening of the lens when examining the coping process. In other words, a broader temporal span is emphasized in order to provide a more accurate view of the process. Therefore, instead of looking at stress and coping during the crisis, it becomes necessary to examine the subsequent adjustments made after the crisis has abated. In references to the latter we might find that one has learned something vital or gained support that contributes to overall resiliency. However, it should also be kept in mind that coping resources that promote resiliency may have been accrued long before the crisis began. For example, Moos, Cronkite, and Moos (1998) found that having family resources led to a better prognosis in the treatment of depression. The adaptive process that should be recognized is that—despite a diagnosis of clinical depression—individuals were able to maintain their existence as part of the family unit. It is important to note that Moos and his colleagues found that those resources (i.e., family support) that were better indicators of resilience were the resources acquired prior to and irrespective of the problem.

The process of adaptation is accomplished through the process of selective optimization with compensation (SOC; Baltes, 1987, 1997). SOC is a process that involves the use of particular strategies that enables individuals or groups to select out of or into circumstances that match or do not match their strengths and weaknesses thereby promoting resilience. The process also involves readjusting, changing, increasing, and honing resources to meet changed environmental circumstances or personal resources. SOC has three features that are indicative of a gain/loss relation: 1) adaptation as a general feature of life span development; 2) adaptation to biological and social aging with its limitations of plasticity; and 3) selective and compensatory efforts dealing with evolving deficits for purpose of life mastery and effective aging (Baltes, 1987). The process of SOC provides a view of individuals' life history and personal development in which to examine individuals use and sustenance of key resources that enable them to offset loss cycles. In other words, when given the opportunity to examine individual development within the context of family and social organizations, we gain a better perspective on how the individual orchestrates the resources in his or her environment in order to optimize the process of adaptation—a much broader and more inclusive concept than coping.

To understand that coping is a dynamic process it is important to keep in mind that in times of loss or when there is a threat of loss the possession of resources or resource gain increases in meaning (Frankl, 1963). For example, when a family member is diagnosed with a serious illness we find that people begin to take stock of their resources. This is necessary because people must decided how it is they are going to cope with the current crisis and in doing so must find those resources from which they can profitably draw. It is important to note that during times of loss we become increasingly aware of our resources as they are set in contrast to the things around us. Therefore, even in the face of personal tragedy, such as the loss of a loved one, we find that people tell of and remember their blessings (Hobfoll, 1998). Similarly, Smith and Zick (1996) suggest that having the opportunity to emotionally prepare for the loss of a spouse promotes resilience. What becomes apparent is that people enact gain cycles in the wake of loss in part to offset current resource loss, but also because they become aware of future losses and seek to prevent them. Hence, resource loss serves the function of drawing attention to the consequences that may occur if loss cycles continue or a more pervasive loss occurs in the future. After having experienced loss, gain strategies that might shelter the individual or social group on future occasions are learned and people seek to implement them.

In the process of adaptation individuals use available resources to create an environment that is conducive to their success. Resource gain is critical in this regard because it is interwoven with loss. Although loss may have more of an impact; the extent of loss's negative impact may be prevented or forestalled though resource gain. People must invest resources in order to protect against resource loss, recover from losses, and gain resources (Hobfoll, 1989). Resource investment promotes resilience, making it a key component in the dynamic adaption process (Schönpflug, 1985). Paradoxically, the cost of resource investment also means that the decision not to act based upon assessment of resource reservoirs is an indication that individuals understand the need to have resources in order to offset losses. The act of evaluating resource stores and choosing not to employ them because they are needed for the minimal protection that must be sustained following a crisis or for later crises that may be forthcoming provides an illustration of the dynamic process of adaptation and distinguishes it from coping, which addresses the here and now without much reflection on past or future circumstances.

Limitations and Leniency

The last two Ls in the FALL model refer to limitations and leniency. A basic assumption inherent in work on coping with stress in general, and coping with interpersonal loss in particular, is that people's resiliency resources have equivalent value for people of different status. As such, it is assumed that a given level of money, self-efficacy, social support, or insurance will have equal value for different people in the same setting. In fact, this assumption is highly questionable as environments and people interact differently based on individuals' social status, gender, and ethnicity. In other words, the rules are different for different people based on their status.

Limitations.   Limitations involve taking into account the environment's role in enabling individuals to use and sustain their valued resources. Resources will promote resiliency provided that the environment allows this to occur. This aspect of the

FALL model highlights an area that can often be overlooked in resource based models, that is the limits placed on individuals by their environment. In other words, knowing someone's resources and objective demands does not provide information on the fitting of the resources to the demands due to the fact that the biases of the social structures individuals are operating in need to be acknowledged. The limits placed on individuals due to race, class, or gender profoundly influence the fitting of resources to the demands in the adaptation process. It is important to note that not only does bias itself create stressful demands but it also limits the application of resources.

The purchasing of a house can be used to demonstrate of this aspect of the model. The purchase price and the availability of credit for a mortgage are the demands and a family's finances are the key resources. However, in many regions of the United States an African-American family will need a greater amount of capital to purchase a home, because in order to obtain a mortgage they will require more money than a comparable white family. Henceforth, $100,000 becomes a relative, not an absolute, amount as a resource and an African-American family will therefore have a more difficult time fitting their resources to the environmental demands.

One difficult scenario that follows women's loss of their partner is their having to re-enter or upgrade their place in the paid labor force. The lack of recent experience or their need to invest in child care may be seen by employers as negating the strength of their educational resources, talents, and other life experiences. One could contend that they, in fact, might lack recent experience, but then one would expect that these women might be given extra credit, for example, for their need to work which will make them more loyal employees and less likely to miss work than someone in a dual-career relationship. It is diagnostic of the limitations process that those with low status (African-Americans, women, Jews) are only discredited for their status, never over-credited. For example, a widow who has gone back to school may actually have an advantage over her male counterpart who has long since been away from retraining experiences. She will have the advantage then of a combination of past experience and recent training, whereas her male counterpart might be said to have the advantage of past training and recent experience. His combination, however, is given greater credit than hers, not because it is empirically better, but because lowered status results in a devaluing of her combination of resources.

Leniency. Leniency is the final step in the FALL model and in this step the role of ennoblement is examined in reference to the use of resources. The concept of ennoblement suggests that there is conferred dominance and privilege by being a member of the ennobled group. Leniency is a positive bending of the rules in order to lower the obstacles in the environment or an artificial overvaluation of resources to benefit the ennobled. Ennoblement eases the strain of fitting resources to demands. The ennobled generally hold the power in society and deny their rule breaking abilities. This is, in some ways, the opposite of limitations, but not its direct opposite.

In the process of limitations, obstacles are placed in the path of the successful investment of resources. In the process of leniency, rules and impediments are relaxed in order to facilitate resource investment. In a sports analogy, the rookie is sanctioned for each mistake, whereas the star player can transgress any number of rules to score a goal. In the stress process, ennobled groups are sometimes willing to see that others have been prevented from opportunities because of limitations. It is more difficult, however, to accept that one achieved one's successes because of favoritism. This would translate not only to others' achievements, but also to accepting that we may more properly have failed.

In work settings, the consequences of stress for men and women may facilitate our understanding of both limitations and leniency. Alcoholism is disproportionately a problem for men (American Psychiatric Association, 1994), and one that is likely to be exacerbated by interpersonal loss. However, alcohol problems have achieved a special status at work where people receive understanding and special allowances. In this way, men are likely to be forgiven their psychological transgressions. In contrast, women may receive punitive feedback for appearing depressed, a more typical reaction to stress for women (Rehm & Tyndall, 1993).

Limitations and leniency can be generally applied to the process of stress following any loss, but have particular implications for interpersonal loss. In this regard, men seem to come out of divorce and widowhood with partially enhanced status. The single man is perhaps even envied because he can do the things that men are assumed to want to do, and these have little to do with family. He can go out with the boys when he pleases, watch all the sporting events he wishes, and see younger women. A woman who is divorced or widowed is seen as having lost her link to status. Her primary purpose is assumed to be family which is disrupted by spousal loss. She is perceived as less attractive because of her years and less sexual, therefore, her mate value has decreased (Buss & Shackelford, 1997).

The legal system has responded to this dual process of limitations and leniency in areas like the mortgage market, hiring, and financial credit by making bias in these matters illegal. However, even in these areas, bias is difficult to monitor. In the more interpersonal areas of remarriage and social acceptance, legislation and law is not possible. Research on interpersonal loss must move status variables such as age, ethnicity, education, and gender to center stage, rather than the more typical process of using them as controls. By uncovering how status interacts with resources we will achieve a clearer understanding of the patterns of resiliency and the generalizability of resiliency theories for different status groups.

☐ Conclusion

In this chapter we have presented COR theory and applied it to the realm of interpersonal loss. We have highlighted that stress is a process that has biological, economic, social, and psychological components. The elements of stress are interwoven because we are biologically social animals and live in socially derived cultures. Likewise resiliency must be seen as a multifaceted concept that involves the process of adaption, not just coping with stress in the acute fashion that has typically been done.

COR theory makes specific predictions as well. First, resource loss is depicted as more powerful than resource gain. In the case of interpersonal loss, this principle means that losses will have a decisive impact and long-term ramifications. Second, people will need to invest resources to offset the negative sequelae of interpersonal loss. However, because of their loss their resource reservoirs may be severely depleted at precisely the time they need them most. This, in turn, leads to a process of loss cycles, such that initial losses cascade into multiple losses that have widening impact outside the initial realm of the interpersonal loss, into the economic, biological, and psychological realms.

Resource gain and the ability to manage resources in the recovery process must also be broadened. Psychology has tended to focus on the mental health aspects, and most specifically on psychological distress. However, COR theory points to the importance of functioning in a more general sense that includes family, economic, sexual, social, and psychological aspects. Indeed, because many individuals who experience interpersonal loss have increased responsibilities in the familial and economic arenas, these domains will have special importance. This is not to say that psychological ramifications are not important, they are paramount, but they are most critical in their interrelationship to these other realms. COR theory allows for a means of disentangling these processes and understanding them in their broader ecological context.

☐ References

American Psychiatric Association. (1994). *Diagnostic and statistical manual of mental disorders* (4th ed.). Washington, DC: Author.

Antonovsky, A. (1979). *Health, stress, and coping.* San Francisco: Jossey-Bass.

Baltes, M. M., & Baltes, P. B. (1982). Microanalytic research on environmental factors and plasticity in psychological aging. In T. M. Field, A. Huston, H. C. Quay, C. Troll, and G. E. Finley (Eds.), *Review of human development* (pp. 524–539). New York: Wiley.

Baltes, M. M., & Baltes, P. B. (1990). Psychological perspectives on successful aging: The model of selective optimization with compensation. In P. B. Baltes, & M. M. Baltes (Eds.), *Successful aging: Perspectives from the behavioral sciences* (pp. 1–34). New York: Cambridge University Press.

Baltes, P. B. (1987). Theoretical propositions of life span developmental psychology: On the dynamics between growth and decline. *Developmental Psychology, 23*, 611–626.

Baltes, P. B. (1997). On the incomplete architecture of human ontogeny: Selection, optimization, and compensation as foundation of developmental theory. *American Psychologist, 52*, 366–380.

Berkman, L. F. (1977). *Social networks, host resistance and mortality: A follow-up study of Alameda county residents.* Unpublished doctoral dissertation, University of California, Berkeley.

Bowlby, J. (1980). *Attachment and loss* (Vol. 3): *Loss.* New York: Basic Books.

Buss, D. M., & Shackelford, T. K. (1997). From vigilance to violence: Mate retention tactics in married couples. *Journal of Personality and Social Psychology, 72*, 346–361.

Cantor, N. (1990). From thought to behavior: "Having" and "doing" in the study of personality and cognition. *American Psychologist, 45*, 735–750.

Cassel, J. (1974). An epidemiological perspective on psychosocial factors in disease etiology. *American Journal of Public Health, 64*, 1040–1043.

Clark, M. S., & Mills, J. (1979). Interpersonal attraction in exchange and communal relationships. *Journal of Personality and Social Psychology, 37*, 12–24.

Cohen, S., & Hoberman, H. M. (1983). Positive events and social support as buffers of life change stress. *Journal of Applied Social Psychology, 13*, 99–125.

Darwin, C. (1859/1959). *The origin of species: By means of natural selection or the preservation of favoured races in the struggle for life.* New York: New American Library.

Eliot, C. W. (Ed.). (1980). The saying of Confucius, *Sacred writings: Confusion, Hebrew, Christian, Part 1.* Danbury, CT: Grolier.

Ennis, N., Hobfoll, S. E., & Schröder, K. E. E. (2000). Money doesn't talk, it swears: How economic stress and resistance resources impact inner-city women's's depressive mood. *American Journal of Community Psychology, 28*, 149–173.

Frankl, V. E. (1963). *Man's search for meaning.* Boston: Beacon.

Freedy, J. R., Saladin, M. E., Kilpatrick, D. G., Resnick, H. S., & Saunders, B. E. (1994). Understanding acute psychological distress following natural disaster. *Journal of Traumatic Stress, 7,* 257–273.

French, J. R. P., Jr., Caplan, R. D., & Van Harrison, R. V. (1982). *The mechanisms of job stress and strain.* Chichester, UK: Wiley.

Freud, S. (1915/1917). *Mourning and melancholia* (Standard ed.), *14.* London: Hogarth Press.

Harvey, J. H., & Miller, E. D. (1998). Toward a psychology of loss. *Psychological Science, 9,* 429–434.

Hendrick, S. S., Dicke, A., & Hendrick, C. (1998). The relationship assessment scale. *Journal of Social and Personal Relationships, 15,* 137–142.

Hirsch, B. J. (1980). Natural support systems and coping with major life changes. *American Journal of Community Psychology, 8,* 159–172.

Hobfoll, S. E. (1988). *The ecology of stress.* New York: Hemisphere.

Hobfoll, S. E. (1989). Conservation of resources: A new attempt at conceptualizing stress. *American Psychologist, 44,* 513–524.

Hobfoll, S. E. (1998). *Stress, community and culture: The psychology and philosophy of stress.* New York: Plenum.

Hobfoll, S. E., & Lilly, R. S. (1993). Resource conservation as a strategy for community psychology. *Journal of Community Psychology, 21,* 128–148.

Hobfoll, S. E., & London, P. (1986). The relationship of self-concept and social support to emotional distress among women during war. *Journal of Social and Clinical Psychology, 4,* 189–203.

Holahan, C. J., Moos, R. H., Holahan, C. K., & Cronkite, R. C. (1999). Resource loss, resource gain, and depressive symptoms: A 10-year model. *Journal of Personality and Social Psychology, 77,* 620–629.

Ironson, G., Wynings, C., Schneiderman, N., Baum, A., Rodriguez, M., Greenwood, D., Benight, C., Antoni, M., LaPerriere, A., Huang, H. S., Klimas, N., & Fletcher, A. (1997). Postratumatic stress symptoms, intrusive thoughts, loss, and immune function after Hurricane Andrew. *Psychosomatic Medicine, 59,* 128–141.

Ito, T. A., Larsen, N., Smith, K., & Cacioppo, J. T. (1998). Negative information weighs more heavily on the brain: The negativity bias. *Journal of Personality and Social Psychology, 75,* 887–900.

James, S. (1996). Female household investment strategy in human and non-human capital with the risk of divorce. *Journal of Divorce and Remarriage, 25,* 151–167.

Kaeaer, P., Jokela, J., Merilae, J., Helle, T., & Kojola, I. (1998). Sexual conflict and remarriage in preindustrial human populations: Causes and fitness consequences. *Evolution and Human Behavior, 19,* 139–151.

Kaniasty, K., & Norris, F. (1993). A test of the social support deterioration model in the context of natural disaster. *Journal of Personality and Social Psychology, 64,* 395–408.

Kaplan, A. (1981). *The living torah hebrew: The five books of Moses and the Hafforah.* New York: Moznaim.

Kelley, H. H. (1979). *Personal relationships: Their structures and processes.* Hillsdale, NJ: Erlbaum.

Lazarus, R. S., & Folkman, S. (1984). *Stress, appraisal, and coping.* New York: Springer.

Lopata, H. Z. (1973). Living through widowhood. *Psychology Today, 7,* 87–92.

Meeks, B. S., Hendrick, S. S., & Hendrick, C. (1998). Communication, love and relationship satisfaction. *Journal of Social and Personal Relationships, 15,* 755–773.

Miller, N., Smerglia, C., Gaudet, D., & Kitson, G. C. (1998). Stressful life events, social support, and the distress of widowed and divorced women: A counteractive model. *Journal of Family Issues, 19,* 181–203.

Moos. R. H., Cronkite, R. C., & Moos, B. S. (1998). The long term interplay between family and extrafamily resources and depression. *Journal of Family Psychology, 12,* 326–343.

Morgan, L. A. (1981). Economic change at mid-life widowhood: A longitudinal analysis. *Journal of Marriage and the Family, 43*, 899–907.

Parkes, C. M. (1972). *Bereavement*. New York: International Universities Press.

Parkes, R. E., Burgess, E. W., & McKenzie, R. D. (1926). *The city*. Chicago: University of Chicago Press.

Rehm, L. P., & Tyndall, C. I. (1993). Mood disorders: Unipolar and bipolar. In P. B. Sutker & H. E. Adams (Eds.), *Comprehensive handbook of psychopathology* (pp. 235–261). New York: Plenum.

Riley, D., & Eckenrode, J. (1986). Social ties: Subgroup differences in costs and benefits. *Journal of Personality and Social Psychology, 51*, 770–778.

Schönpflug, W. (1985). Goal directed behavior as a source of stress: Psychological origins and consequences of inefficiency. In M. Frese & J. Sabini (Eds.), *The concept of action in psychology* (pp. 172–188). Hillsdale, NJ: Erlbaum.

Schut, H. A., Strobebe, M. S., & van den Bout, J. (1997). Interventions for the bereaved: Gender differences in the efficacy of two counseling programs. *British Journal of Clinical Psychology, 36*, 63–72.

Shapiro, A. (1996). Explaining psychological distress in a sample of remarried and divorced persons: The influence of economic distress. *Journal of Family Issues, 17*, 186–203.

Smith, K., & Zick, C. (1996). Risk of mortality following widowhood: Age and sex differences by mode of death. *Social Biology, 43*, 59–71.

Song of Songs. Old Testament, 8(6).

Stoll, O. (1999). *Die theorie der ressourcenerhaltung in der sportwissenschaftlichen forschung–studien zur wirksamkeit von sport, spiel und bewegung auf die psyche* (Conservation of resources theory in sports science research—studies to the effect of sport, games and movement on psychological well-being). Leipzig: Habilitationsschrift, Universität Leipzig. Post doctoral habilitation. University of Leipzig.

Stroebe, W., & Stroebe, M. S. (1987). *Bereavement and health*. New York: Cambridge University Press.

Taraban, C. B., Hendrick, S. S., & Hendrick, C. (1998). Loving and liking. In Peter Andersen & L. Guerrero (Eds.), *Handbook of communication and emotion: Research, theory, applications, and contexts.* (pp. 331–351). San Diego, CA: Academic Press, Inc.

Taylor, S. E., Pham, L. B., Rivkin, I. D., & Armor, D. A. (1998). Harnessing the imagination: Mental simulation, self-regulation, and coping. *American Psychologist, 53*, 429–439.

Thoits, P. (1994). Stressors and problem-solving: The individual as psychological activist. *Journal of Health and Social Behavior, 35*, 143–160.

Tversky, A., & Kahneman, D. (1974). Judgment under uncertainty: Heuristics and biases. *Science, 185*, 1124–1131

Wells, J., Hobfoll, S. E., & Lavin, J. (1997). The effects of resource loss, resource gain and communal coping on anger during pregnancy among women with multiple roles. *Psychology of Women Quarterly, 21*, 645–662.

Wells, J., & Hobfoll, S. E., & Lavin, J. (1999). When it rains, it pours: The greater impact of resource loss compared to gain on psychological distress. *Personality and Social Psychology Bulletin, 25*, 1172–1182.

Van Lange, P., Otten, W., De Bruin, E., & Joireman, J. A. (1997). Development of prosocial, individualistic, and competitive orientation: Theory and preliminary evidence. *Journal of Personality and Social Psychology, 73*, 733–746.

Wu, Z. (1995). Remarriage after widowhood: A marital history study of older Canadians. *Canadian Journal on Aging, 14*, 719–736.

CHAPTER

Carolyn Ellis

Negotiating Terminal Illness: Communication, Collusion, and Coalition in Caregiving

Communication about illness is not a static quality as presented in most research; instead participants and the quality and direction of their communication may change over time as illness worsens and relationships intensify or retreat. This chapter inserts the family caregiver into what health communication researchers usually view as a patient-physician centered process. My work examines the trajectory of communication and decision-making as it moves from dyadic and patient-centered (patient-physician and patient-caregiver) to a triadic process of communication among the patient, family caregiver, and physician, and finally to the caregiver-physician dyad (see Beisecker et al., 1997). My goal is to study communication about illness and dying as it occurs in the changing situations of people's lives over time. Thus I focus on private communication that took place in a variety of contexts about the illness of my partner and my involvement as primary caregiver rather than on interactions between patients and physicians observed in formalized research settings or retrospective reports. What does it mean, I ask, to say that we should be truthful with people who are dying?

☐ A Narrative, Autoethnographic Approach

"We have to intubate Gene. The conservative treatment isn't working," Dr. Townson says quickly and apologetically as I enter the emergency room.

"Might he die?" I ask. The doctor nods yes. "Even if he's intubated?"

"Yes, possibly. But we won't feel guilty about it, not you or me. We are doing everything we can. We'll make it as comfortable as possible. And if he doesn't die now, he will die soon anyway."

After the intubation, Dr. Townson comes to Gene's room. "I hate the tube," Gene mouths. "It hurts." On a pad, he writes, "I think this happened because I wasn't getting enough oxygen."

"No," says Dr. Townson. "Your body can't get rid of CO_2."

With eyes blazing and anger and pain etched on his face, Gene mouths as a statement and a question, "Then I'm dying."

"You're not dying," says Dr. Townson, with an edge of a nervous chuckle. "There are some radical things to try."

Gene mouths to me, "He's not being straight with me." Since Gene already knows he's dying, I wonder why he asks.

When Dr. Townson leaves, I say to Gene, "He doesn't want you to give up hope."

"I just want him to be straight with me."

"It's hard to tell someone he's dying."

"I want the truth."

"Basically he's telling you the truth. They don't know anymore."

The proceeding excerpt comes from *Final Negotiations: A Story of Love, Loss, and Chronic Illness* (Ellis, 1995, pp. 188–192), a narrative, autoethnographic account about my experience of caring for my critically-ill partner Gene, a middle-aged adult with emphysema accompanied by dementia in the final stage. With Gene's verbal consent, the daily field notes I kept about our personal relationship during the last year of his life included my thoughts and feelings; verbatim recorded conversations between us; day-to-day descriptions and analyses of activities in the hospital; and stories of contacts and conversations with health care providers. Events that occurred earlier in our nine-year relationship were recreated systematically through recording our chronological history from memory, assisted by notes, interviews, physicians' records, tape recordings of conversations, diaries, and personal calendars (see Ellis, 1991). Written from these notes, the published story serves as the source for this chapter, which focuses on triadic communication about illness and dying. As in the original work, names of physicians are pseudonyms.

While constructing an index for the book project, I discovered that I had 22 episodes classified under the heading of doctor–caretaker communication, which made me aware for the first time of how much of my life had been involved in communication with Gene's physicians. These excerpts, in addition to the nine entries under doctor-patient communication and the more than dozen entries describing conversations Gene and I had during or immediately after each doctor's visit and hospital stay, form the basis for this chapter. After examining these entries, I was intrigued by the intricacies of these conversations, the different ways we talked to each other, and how important these conversations were in showing the negotiation of illness and dying over time and in different communication contexts. Juxtaposing these conversations showed the role of the caregiver in the dance of hope, secrecy, ambivalence, and trust that occurred in the fluctuating contexts of awareness (see Timmermans, 1994), communication, negotiation, and control.

First-person, autoethnographic accounts, such as *Final Negotiations*, open an important avenue to exploring the intricacies of intimate communication that are left out or ignored in most social science research. In prior studies, researchers have relied on observing public dyadic interaction between health care providers and patients. With the exception of a few ethnographic and videotaped studies, subjects are viewed at one point in time solely in public contexts, such as doctors' offices and hospital rooms, which permit access to researchers. Researchers obtain information through questionnaires or interviews that ask doctors and patients to reconstruct unilaterally after the fact how they sent or received messages. But when patients are terminally ill and near death, communication usually occurs privately in patient rooms, in one-on-one phone conversations between health providers and caregivers, and in the hallway outside patients' hospital rooms. Many of these conversations would not take place, or would be stifled, if patients, doctors, or family caregivers were aware of being observed or recorded by outsiders. Likewise, it would be difficult, after the fact, for most people to reconstruct systematically how these events occurred, even if they were comfortable revealing this intimate detail to a stranger in a brief interview, which they usually are not.

The point is that our theoretical, practical, and empirical understandings of health communication have been based primarily on a partial and situated focus that leaves out some of the most crucial and intimate aspects of the process, particularly in cases of extended and chronic care. In this chapter, I attempt to bring private communication over time into the public eye by presenting excerpts recorded from my own experience as a long-term caregiver. I portray discussions with four different doctors over a period of approximately eight years. As a case study, my particular story is affected by factors that impact communication, including personality and style of interaction of each doctor, psychological and social characteristics of all interactants, and characteristics of the relational context (Glasser, Rubin, & Dickover, 1990; Haug, 1994; Haug & Ory, 1987), for example, severity of the patient's illness, and length and quality of all of the involved dyadic relationships (Glasser, Rubin, & Dickover, 1990).

The case I present has unique characteristics that readers should keep in mind: Gene and I were both academic sociologists, and our educational status undoubtedly impacted the amount and kind of information we received together and individually from doctors (see Haug & Ory, 1987, p. 24; Krant & Johnson, 1977–78); I kept notes on this experience and planned to write about it, and my introspection about and involvement in Gene's case may have increased as a result; I obtained power-of-attorney about three months before Gene died and we were married six weeks prior to his death though we had been partners for nine years, and these events may have affected matters of informed consent.

☐ Contextualizing the Project

The literature on communication about illness for the most part describes dyadic exchange between doctors and patients (Glasser et al., 1990; Ong et al., 1995; Sharf, 1993), and usually presents patients as the passive recipients of messages sent by powerful and knowledgeable providers (Vanderford, Jenks, & Sharf, 1997). Social scientists and physicians have investigated such topics as flow of information (Glaser & Strauss, 1965), the hierarchical (Drass, 1981), sequential, and asymmetrical (Fisher & Groce, 1985) nature of speech exchange (Mishler, 1985; West, 1983), cultural demands on doctor-patient communications (Cicourel, 1981), as well as the relationship of patient satisfaction to patterns of communication (Ley, 1988). Research on patient communication with other health care providers and on communication between health care providers has been limited (Sharf, 1993).

Similarly, family caregivers often are left out of the conversation (Adelman, Green, & Charon, 1987; Hardwig, 1995). As Miller and Zook (1997, p. 60) and others point out, casting our understanding beyond the patient-physician relationship net is particularly important given that our aging population is putting pressure on our traditional modes of care, and the increasing chronicity of disease and the AIDS epidemic require continuing care by friends and family. Though there are insightful in-depth interview studies of the experiences of caring for elderly parents and the public policy that surrounds it (for example, Abel, 1991), their emphasis tends not to be on health care communication. The work available on communication with caregivers, for the most part, views caregivers as "patient support systems," as a means to the goal of well-being of patients (Hardwig, 1995), and focuses on caregiver stress, health, tasks, social support, and satisfaction with the doctor's role (Haug, 1994, pp. 5–6; see also Abel, 1991). Usually these studies are composed of self-assessed health, symptom, or satisfaction checklists. Recent observations of physician-caregiver relationships have offered a new angle from which to study support (see, for example, Council on Scientific Affairs, 1993; Eisendorfer & Cohen, 1981; Glasser & Miller, 1998; Vitaliano, 1990). Yet, as Haug (1994, p. 6) points out, these researchers have not taken as their task the objective of explaining how support from a physician is sought and communicated.

Two situations in particular would seem to lend themselves to examining health communication in a triadic context—parents accompanying children with mental problems and adult children accompanying elderly parents with Alzheimer's (cf. chapter in this volume by Williamson & Shafer) to doctors' offices. The former has yielded little in the way of understanding triadic communication since those involved tend to assume that parents rather than children are the only active agents (Adelman, Green, & Charon, 1987; Korsch, Gozzin, & Francis, 1968; Stewart, Pantell, Dias, Wells, & Ross, 1981; Turnbull & Turnbull, 1986). Although some researchers have encouraged physicians to involve the child (Pantell, Stewart, Dias, Wells, & Ross, 1982; Vaughan, 1957), Maynard (1991) reported that doctors and parents tend to construct children as clinical objects (see also Baker, Yoels, Clair, & Allman, 1997).

The latter context of elderly patients accompanied by caregivers, however, has offered the primary site for the few studies that exist of health communication in a triadic context (Adelman et al., 1987; Beisecker, 1989; Beisecker et al., 1997; Coe & Prendergast, 1985; Haug, 1994; Rosow, 1981, Silliman, 1989). In most of these encounters, the parents who have been diagnosed with Alzheimers (Glasser, Rubin, & Dickover, 1990; Haug, 1994). Examining interaction in doctors' offices, these researchers estimate that 20–50% of older patients are accompanied to the doctor by a third person, usually a family member (Greene, Adelman, Charon, & Hoffman, 1986; Prohaska & Glasser, 1996), setting the structural conditions for the caretaker-patient-physician triad.

Sociologists, in particular Georg Simmel, have long noted the distinctions between triadic and dyadic interaction (see Wolff, 1950). Mills (1953) found that triads tend to break down into dyads of the two most active members and the third isolated person. In studies of triadic communication in medical care, researchers have demonstrated that this kind of coalition formation occurs (Rosow, 1981; Silliman, 1989), and some researchers have developed models for assessing the forms of the coalitions and the roles the third person may play (Adelman et al., 1987). Patterns in coalition formation may fluctuate even during a single episode, and coalitions vary depending on factors such as characteristics of the membership of the triad and length of time the coalition has been in existence (Coe & Prendergast, 1985), as well as whether the coalition is observed early or later in the illness progression (Glaser et al., 1990, p. 324). Several researchers, such as Adelman, Greene, and Charon (1987), have examined the impact of family presence on physician-cancer patient interaction. Third person presence may facilitate the physician-patient relationship: for example, LaBrecque, Blanchard, Ruckdeschel, & Blanchard (1991) showed that when family members are present, physicians are likely to spend more time with the patient and provide more information. Or family presence may be associated with questionable effects: for example, LaBrecque et al. (1991) and Greene, Majerovitz, Adelman, and Rizzo (1994) have noted decreased emotional support from physicians to patients, physicians' increasing difficulties dealing with clients with different and sometimes conflicting needs, and less involvement by patients.

While this research offers insight into the communication process, it is important to consider contexts of communication outside doctors' offices with other kinds of patients and to examine what gets communicated and how. In my experience, which I describe below, communication between Gene, his doctors, and me shifted radically between dyadic and triadic coalitions. Messages that were sent and received by participants in the triad often were contradictory, changing over time and by context. As we spoke, our words and actions were surrounded and affected by ethical and moral concerns about awareness, decision making, collusion, control, hope, secrecy, and truth telling.

☐ Patient–Doctor, Patient–Caregiver Communication

I first accompanied Gene to his New York physician, Dr. Silverman, in 1976 about a year after I met him. At each visit, after pulmonary testing, I joined Gene as he and his doctor reviewed results and discussed treatment. While we were in the doctor's office, communication took place almost solely between Gene and his doctor of several years, while I listened, playing the role of "passive supporter" (Adelman et al., 1987, p. 731). Dr. Silverman treated Gene as a colleague; Gene took part in the analysis of his disease, and they shared research projects and details of their lives.

Dr. Silverman's strategy, which Timmermans (1994, p. 332) described as an "uncertain open awareness context" where hope is sustained while information is given, was to move between candidly laying out the bad news and optimism. At one visit, he told Gene how much the numbers on tests had decreased, and then said, "But look at what you can still do. Most people in your condition are home in bed, but you're traveling around the world. A new drug is being tested in Canada. Let's see if we can figure out a way to obtain it."

Gene listened attentively, hopefully. Then a cloud passed over his face. "But, Doc, it's not a cure, is it?"

"No," the doctor replied, holding eye contact with Gene. "There is no cure. Maybe in the future, but not in your lifetime."

Gene's shoulders sagged farther into his chair as Dr. Silverman looked away, busying himself with altering Gene's many medications: "I think changing your antibiotic will help. Try taking one four times a day, instead of two twice a day."

After Gene and I left the office, we tried to interpret how he was doing and how we felt. Gene often turned his anger at his condition toward his doctor, while I tried to be supportive yet understand the doctor's position. After this visit, Gene said angrily, "Why does Silverman pretend there's hope, when there isn't any? Why doesn't he just say so?"

"He does, Gene. He said there was no cure in your lifetime."

"But then he says the shuffling of the medicine will help. It won't," replied Gene. "That's true. But think of his position. He wants to be honest, yet not depress you or make you feel there's no hope for improvement. So he confronts us with the stark reality of your deterioration, and then gives us a ray of hope to hang on to. It isn't dishonest. He wants to have hope too."

"I guess," Gene replied, softening with resignation. "At least we have each other," he continued, now changing sides. "And who knows. Maybe I'll live longer than anybody thinks. There's always the possibility of a lung transplant."

"Anything is possible," I replied. "I'm just glad to have this time now. I guess our situation is not really worse than others. Everybody will die." We vowed that together we'd "beat this disease," though we were unsure what that meant.

The doctor's candid opinion, supported by decreasing numbers, confronted us with the reality of Gene's impending death. Afterwards, we began to relate to the disease much as the doctor had—facing the inevitable and then looking for some reason to be hopeful. Ambivalence as a coping mechanism helped all of us integrate hope and reality. Without fully realizing it at the time, the two of us were being socialized in the doctor's office and in our conversations afterwards into the roles of dying and grieving. I rehearsed how to show Gene love, yet shut out pain and fear; Gene practiced how to face his illness, yet escape living as a dying person.

Later I began to take more of a role in these visits, though the primary communication continued to occur between Gene and Dr. Silverman. More and more, Gene's case was presented as "our case." More and more, I pushed Gene, sometimes in the doctor's presence, to probe for answers to questions about our daily lives together, such as exertion, home remedies, and finally longevity.

"You know these things can't be accurately predicted," Dr. Silverman replied to Gene's question about his future. When Gene said he wanted his opinion anyway and the doctor looked my way, I nodded my head affirmatively for him to continue. "Emphysema is a plateau disease. As you have experienced, when you drop a level you never come back to where you were before. How long you stay on a plateau depends on many variables, such as whether you get an infection. But I'm going to give you a guess anyway. If you don't catch a bad cold, you'll probably be able to work for three to five years and live from seven to ten." The doctor quickly returned to writing prescriptions, touching Gene's shoulder affectionately as he left the room. Even though we acknowledged that there was no way to predict what actually would happen, these projected numbers took on a reality and were useful in calculating the feasibility of future plans.

Approximately a year later, Gene had deteriorated considerably and rode an electric wheel chair and used oxygen during his visit to the doctor. As a result of a conversation Gene and I had, Gene asked the doctor, "Would you be willing to talk to Carolyn alone? I want her to know what she's getting in to, since I'm moving to Florida to live with her."

The doctor responded, "Certainly, but there's nothing I don't tell you." Gene said he wanted to give me the opportunity to ask questions without his being there.

Once in the room with the doctor, I asked, "I know you can't be sure, but what can I expect from here on? What will the deterioration be like? And the end? How will he die?"

Taking a deep breath, Dr. Silverman's eyes focused directly on mine. With piercing intensity, he said, "It won't be pleasant. He'll continue much like in the past. More and more he'll be unable to move around, and will probably just sit in a comfortable position. If he ever gets groggy and confused, get him to the hospital immediately."

When I asked if Gene's brain would deteriorate, he replied, "Thankfully, the brain is the last thing to go. He'll probably be mentally active way after his mobility goes. But at some point, his body won't be able to get rid of carbon dioxide and it will impair him mentally. It could happen any time, but it will be temporary. As soon as doctors regulate his blood gases, his mental faculties will come back 100%." I asked if a respirator would help, and he responded, "Yes, but the issue is quality of life."

"Could he talk on it?"

"He would have to cover a hole in his throat when he spoke and speak slowly between breaths."

"Could he come home with it?"

"He could," he replied slowly. I shake my head to get rid of the image of Gene in bed with a machine hooked to a hole in his throat.

In this open awareness conversation, for the first time I faced the details of the physical reality of what would happen to Gene, and *I faced it without Gene*. While the doctor told me nothing he wouldn't tell Gene, it would have been difficult for Gene and the doctor if Gene had asked these questions directly. I would not have broached these topics if Gene had been present and the doctor probably would not have been as explicit if I had. And, I have to believe that Gene sent me in alone because on some level he could not or did not want to face this information nor put the doctor in the uncomfortable position of giving the answers to him.

This conversation served to pass on important information to us. Yet it gave me some control of what Gene got told, when, and how. Open awareness contexts often are ambiguous and complex (Glaser & Strauss, 1965). They involve the messiness of emotional response as well as cognitive information management, and often change from day-to-day, moment-to-moment (Timmermans, 1994; Mamo, 1999). Chronic illness is an unfolding drama where the patient and caregiver get prepared emotionally and cognitively to handle the next step by first confronting a prior step. It is not just information that must be handled; the emotions of hope and despair must be successfully juxtaposed as well (Good, Good, Schaffer, & Lind, 1990; Mamo, 1999; Timmermans, 1994). There are advantages to breaking bad news slowly (Seale, 1991). At the same time, the patient and caregiver must have some awareness of what to expect in the future so that plans can be made and the future can be coped with realistically. The doctor is not always in the best position to know when the time is right (Glaser & Strauss, 1965, p. 119; Timmermans, 1994). Too much too soon might overwhelm clients, leaving them with no room for hope or optimism, which might speed the demise and make the situation worse than it would have been otherwise. As the caregiver, I would become an important orchestrator of when and how awareness would occur.

After receiving information from the doctor, my mood was solemn. I felt close to Gene, yet I also felt apart as I contemplated what would happen to him, and me. After leaving the doctor's office, I asked Gene if he wanted to know what I talked to the doctor about. "Only if you want to tell me. It was your private conversation," he responded.

I told him what he already knew about gradual deterioration, loss of mobility, and the problem with steroids. I wondered whether I should tell him everything. How would he handle information about mental deterioration? That at some point he would not be able to think clearly? Gene and I already knew his brain would be the last organ to be affected, and we thought that it would happen, if at all, only at the very end. But now it sounded like the confusion would come and go. I thought about the slight bewilderment that accompanied Gene's last change in medication. Is that what it would be like?

Gene interrupted my thoughts, "I know all that. Did you ask about the respirator?" When I repeated what the doctor said, Gene replied, "It doesn't sound as good as I thought. I guess it will be hard to talk."

"Would you want to live like that?" I asked, wanting him to say no and then afraid that he would.

"If I could talk and still work with graduate students, I think so. But would *you* want it?"

"I don't know. I would want you to live as long as you could, as long as you wanted to. But it's hard to imagine what it would be like. Would you be in an institution or at home? If you were home, who would take care of you all the time? Could you go out with the respirator? Could we still have conversations?"

"Maybe I could handle being in bed all the time," Gene responded, addressing his own concerns. "But when I can't read and think clearly anymore, I'll want to kill myself."

This was the first time I had information about Gene's illness that he didn't have. Thus, it was the first time I confronted what to tell him and whether he wanted to know everything. When I didn't reveal everything about the mental deterioration, I got a preview of how our relationship, which always had explored openly all aspects of intimacy, would change in the future. Gene and I always had colluded on how to live life fully, not as though he were dying, yet organize and plan for contingencies of his illness. Having a private conversation with Dr. Silverman opened up the possibility of colluding with someone other than Gene about Gene. Yet it also made me feel a more vital part of the triadic communication.

☐ Triadic Communication: The Doctor–Caregiver Coalition in Formation

In 1984, after we had moved to Florida, Gene was hospitalized for respiratory failure while visiting in Stony Brook, Long Island. Since Gene was light-headed, in pain, and in and out of reality, it seemed appropriate from the start that his physician, Dr. Simpson, and I had conversations apart from Gene. My first conversation with the doctor was a long distance phone call before I arrived at the hospital. The doctor talked about the possibility of Gene having a tracheotomy and being on a respirator. After a discussion about Gene and I being unmarried, the doctor agreed that he would consider me to be Gene's common-law wife, and then he asked for permission to proceed with radical treatment. I responded, "I want to discuss it with Gene. We make decisions together."

As soon as I arrived at the hospital, I told Gene about the conversation, but I played down the possibility of a tracheotomy and respirator, rationalizing that in his condition this was the best strategy. Along with Gene's friends, I played out a facade to some extent, pretending to tell Gene everything, but in reality I smoothed out rough edges to make his condition appear better than the messages we received. It seemed the best thing to do, though I felt disloyal when I remembered we were dealing with his body and making decisions about his life.

The doctor and I monitored the information we gave Gene. When the doctor told me new medication would upset Gene's stomach, I suggested not telling Gene, and Dr. Simpson agreed. The doctor told Gene he was cautiously optimistic about his condition, and then a few minutes later in a private conversation in the hall advised me, "He's not out of the woods yet," which I assumed meant he might die. It wasn't so much that the doctor told me much he didn't tell Gene, it was the way he told me. There was always hope when he talked to Gene; with me, he admitted that Gene faced possible death. With Gene, he always had something else to try; with me, he was pessimistic that there was anything, short of intubation, that would work.

Sensing the coalition forming between me and the doctor, Gene began to demand that doctors talk to him. "I'm not a *him*," he said when a doctor spoke to me about his condition. "My name is Gene and I can talk and hear."

This experience gave me my first real taste of colluding with doctors. I rationalized that it was a temporary condition and that once Gene recovered from this episode without intubation that we again would talk openly about everything that happened. But once back in Tampa, it became increasingly difficult to carry out my rationalization.

Dr. Townson had become Gene's doctor in Tampa about a year prior to the hospitalization in Stony Brook. In his early to mid-forties, Dr. Townson was almost two decades younger than Dr. Silverman, and he worked in a university and clinic setting instead of private practice. Much more removed from his patients than Dr. Silverman, he never touched Gene, showed emotion, had direct eye contact, or revealed anything about his own life. At first, I had little interaction with Dr. Townson since Gene often went to the doctor's office alone, now that he had an electric wheelchair and a van lift. When I accompanied Gene, I usually stayed quiet.

From the beginning, Gene questioned whether Dr. Townson was open and honest with him. When asked early on about Gene's prognosis, the doctor flippantly replied, "It's possible you could still be like this in ten years. Some people are. Or you could die tomorrow."

"He really doesn't tell me anything," Gene told me, showing anger. "It frustrates me. Maybe he doesn't know anything. But he's seen people at this stage before. I want the whole truth."

I agreed, but much later when Gene again asked the same questions and complained that Dr. Townson refused to answer them, I again found myself in the role of interpreting the doctor's position. "But most of your questions—how long do I have, what happens next—have no answers," I said, as we walked to the car from the office visit.

"But he doesn't even give me time to formulate questions; he just rushes through."

Gene's health deteriorated quickly after his initial hospitalization in Stony Brook. Because Dr. Townson was part of a university clinic, we could not always count on his being on rounds when Gene had an emergency. The first time I took Gene in acute distress to a Tampa hospital, just a few weeks after he returned from Stony Brook, we had to deal with unfamiliar doctors who wanted to intubate Gene. Although I tried to convince Gene to go along with them, he refused treatment. After consulting with other doctors, I found one at another hospital who was willing to treat Gene more conservatively. Since staff there refused to listen to me because I was not a relative, I told Gene I wanted power-of-attorney. Afterwards, Gene was angry with me for siding with the doctors and said he wasn't sure he wanted me to have power-of-attorney because of the position I took. "You cried and pleaded with me to be intubated," he accused.

"Only because I thought you'd die without it. But I always wanted to do what you wanted. I was confused and you weren't lucid. I didn't know what to do." I felt hurt by his accusations and sad not to have a doctor like Dr. Silverman that Gene and I knew and trusted.

A few weeks later, Gene was hospitalized again. This time Dr. Townson was on rounds, and this time Gene was not lucid. In the emergency room, when the nurse shook him, he opened his eyes wide. Looking startled, his head moved from person to person like a periscope in a Popeye cartoon, and he laughed shrilly like a mad man. Never before had I seen him so out of touch with the outside world.

In the waiting room, Dr. Townson told me that intubation was necessary to save Gene's life and that Gene might die even if intubated. Giving consent, I did not ask how Gene felt, since this time I was certain he would not be able to respond. Until this moment, I had never engaged in a significant one-on-one conversations with Dr. Townson. Immediately I now felt a bond as he and I decided Gene's fate. I listened as Dr. Townsend pointed out the inevitability of Gene's death. Emotionally distraught, I agreed with his decision, and felt we were on the same side.

In the hospital later, Dr. Townson came into Gene's room, and said he had tried to call me. We started for the door to talk in the hall, then stopped ourselves, but not before Gene caught the movement. "I want to know," angrily mouthed Gene, who could not speak because of the tubes, "absolutely everything." When Dr. Townson responded by explaining the intubation, Gene wrote, "I think this happened because I wasn't getting enough oxygen," a problem that had a solution. Dr. Townson responded that it happened because "your body can't get rid of CO2," a problem that had no solution. Gene then mouthed, "Then I'm dying."

"You're not dying," said Townson, with an edge of a nervous chuckle. I caught my breath. Dr. Townson wasn't being truthful. But Gene already knew he was dying, so why did he ask? Dr. Townson continued, "There are some radical things to try," but he hadn't told me about anything else.

Gene mouthed to me, "He's not being straight with me." I felt caught in the middle of a spider web, entangled in deception every which way I turned, including inward, and I didn't know a way out. Whose side was I on anyway? I wondered. I had no idea what to do. Why was it so important for Gene to hear from the doctor that he was dying? The more important question now was "Will it be soon?", a question Gene seemed unwilling to ask and Dr. Townson seemed unwilling to answer (see Glaser & Strauss, 1965, p. 80). As he had in the past, Gene sought to play out the worst case scenario, so he could figure out how to cope and stay in control. But if he accepted that the question was not "Am I dying?" but "When will I die?" this meant that there was nothing to try and no control to regain. I felt in a bind because this time, unlike before, I knew there would be no staying in control; still, I tried to be truthful, explain the doctor's position, yet not take away Gene's last shred of hope.

When Dr. Townson left, Gene turned his face to the wall. I gently turned it back, and said, "Baby, he doesn't want you to give up hope."

"I just want him to be straight with me."

"It's hard to tell someone he's dying."

"I want the truth."

"Basically he's telling you the truth. They don't know anymore."

From this time on, Dr. Townson and I would clearly form a coalition, because we were faced with the same task—how to tell Gene the truth yet still support his illusion that there was hope that he might still regain control of his life. I began to feel that taking away his hope completely, even when he asked us to, was unethical. Perhaps this strategy also meant that I spent less time facing Gene's mortality, and consequently my own. Perhaps the same was true for Dr. Townson.

Later, when Dr. Townson called me at home, his style was much softer than his flippant style with Gene and the conversation was much more open and informative. While I had no direct knowledge of his conversations with Gene when I wasn't present, I assumed from Gene's descriptions that they were similar to the conversations he had with Gene in my presence. With me alone, Dr. Townson not only talked about "when," we also discussed "how" Gene would die, a question that, to my knowledge, Gene never asked (see Glaser & Strauss, 1965, p. 80). Dr. Townson's message to me was so hopeless, that I had to believe he was telling me the truth, though I'm sure he omitted what he felt were the unnecessary gory details.

"I want to know everything," I told Dr. Townson on the phone. "I can handle it."

"Yes, I think you can. And it's good you're being realistic." I didn't think then to question why that was so good.

"How long do you think he has?"

"We don't really know, but data show that someone who has been intubated usually has about a year. And since Gene has not been doing well, it's safe to say he has less than that."

"So we're talking weeks or, at the best, months?"

"Yes," he said kindly.

"What will happen?" I asked. "Will his lungs just stop working?"

"No, he'll get weaker and weaker and we'll have to intubate him again."

"What happens when intubation doesn't work?"

"We can give him a tracheotomy to connect him directly to a respirator."

"Can he come home?"

"Yes," the doctor said, then, "but would you want him to?"

"No, I don't think so," I said, without knowing what I wanted. "And I don't think he would either," I continued, basing my conclusion on his not wanting to be intubated again; surely he wouldn't want to live attached to a machine. "So what do you do then?" I asked.

"At some point," he said, a little nervously, "we just don't intubate him. And I'll make sure it's all comfortable," he hurried to assure me. Though I didn't know in reality what that meant, I assumed it referred to controlling pain as much as possible.

"I think Gene wants to know all this."

"I feel that intellectually Gene wants to know everything, but deep inside he doesn't," Dr. Townson responded.

I had assumed Gene wanted to know, but would he want to hear what I just heard? "I'm not sure he wants to hear that there is no hope," I said.

"Exactly," Dr. Townson responded in relief. Did I let the doctor lead me to this wanted conclusion? Did I know what Gene wants? Did Townson? How could he? Though I was confused, this conversation stimulated me to think that the doctor and I were in charge now of what Gene got told because Gene was "incompetent," and I questioned what he really was able to know and how much he wanted to know.

Then Dr. Townson said, "I'm going to try some experimental drug that might leach CO_2. But it will make his stomach worse and might negatively affect his breathing."

I realized that all we could do was prolong the dying process. How did one handle the hell of no hope? By fantasizing hope. There is no other way that works. If I needed to have hope so desperately, I rationalized, certainly Gene did too. As Timmermans (1994) and Mamo (1999) suggest, awareness contexts consist of more than cognitive processing; they also include emotion work and emotional response. Neither Gene nor I was ready emotionally to accept his dying.

I was anxious the next day when I saw Gene, wondering what he would ask, and how I would answer. Gene inquired about his prognosis. When I didn't respond, he said questioningly, "I know anyway. I think probably less than a year?"

I offered to tell him what the doctor told me, and when he nodded, I repeated: "The prognosis for someone who has been intubated is about a year. Since you had problems, you probably have less than that. It depends on your body."

Sadly, but seeming to accept the news, Gene replied, "I wanted to have a year left or at least live until my birthday in June."

"Maybe you will," I replied, renewing his and my hope.

This discussion led us to talk about death, not our first discussion of this topic, but one of the first to cut through the myth of a romantic death. When Gene said he wanted to die at home, I suggested it might be better for him to die in the hospital where I'd have help, especially given his mental confusion. When he asked about a respirator, I told him that Dr. Townson said he could live at home on one.

"Well, if I still could talk maybe I could tolerate lying in bed, but I don't want to live attached to a machine. And, I would have to feel decent." I shared Gene's vacillation; I didn't want him to die, but I also couldn't imagine his living for an extended time on a respirator.

When he asked what I wanted, I responded, "I guess I'd want you to be intubated one more time if you're willing. I want to feel we still have something left to try," I said, echoing Gene's usual refrain. "I don't want to think that the next time you are hospitalized could be it."

"That sounds reasonable. But if I'm back in the hospital in a week, then what's the use of being intubated one more time? Maybe I'll fight this thing," he then said.

I responded, "We haven't lived like you're dying in the past, and I don't want to do it now."

We then agreed that he would make out a living will saying he didn't want to be attached to machines. This conversation led me to believe that Gene and I together were coming to accept his dying. Thus, I was surprised the next day when he once again pursued the same conversation with the doctor, as though our discussion never had taken place. Awareness contexts were anything but stable.

"I told the doctor that he and I needed to talk," Gene said on the telephone from the hospital. When I asked what he said, Gene replied, "He said he had an open talk with you. And I said, but you haven't had one with me. When he asked what I wanted to know, I asked again if I were dying and he said no, that there were things to try."

Did Gene want Dr. Townson to openly admit he was dying? Should I tell the doctor to be candid with Gene? Or maybe the three of us should talk. Or did Gene need someone to be mad at? What more was there to know?

Gene's conversations with me were much different from the conversations I observed, and he reported having, with Dr. Townson. With the doctor, he often sought confirmation of his dying as though it was something he was unsure of; with me, Gene seemed more aware of his mortality and we started the process of readying for his death. When I asked him if his life was worthwhile, he responded, "There have been some good times lately. It's still worth it because we're together. Is it all too much for you? If so, I could just turn up the oxygen and quit taking medication and go out on CO_2."

"Not yet," I responded.

In the next week, we had a living will notarized; Gene signed a power-of-attorney form to make sure I would have no trouble making decisions when he couldn't. Together we called funeral homes to arrange for his embalming, and signed a form donating his body to a medical school. He called friends to say goodbye, admitting he wouldn't live long. Not long after this, we were married. Though we married primarily because we wanted to be family and to signal to others that we had been, we were reassured by the legal solution this provided for decision-making.

We both lived in dual liminal realities between life and death. I felt like I must experience everything I could and like I was inactive at the same time, waiting for something to happen. "There are two realities here," Gene explained. "One is that I think I could die anytime. Then I get better and have to orient myself to living."

"I live in the same duality," I replied, surviving and dying—two halves of the circle.

As Gene's physical illness worsened and his mental confusion began to increase, realistic conversations about his health and our relationship became virtually nonexistent, and Gene turned his energy and passion instead toward figuring out how he could live longer. No longer were we "on the same page." Most of the time, Gene was plotting to live, while the doctor and I were plotting how he might die. Gene's and my lives were no longer connected in the ways they always had been, as partners sharing daily life and goals. Our relationship, which had always rested on a foundation of naked openness, now seemed to require a protectiveness against knowing or sharing the truth. I now held a power over information that I had never wanted but now understood as necessary. I lived in the dual reality of wanting to meet Gene's goal of living as long as he could and my own of wanting a meaningful ending I could endure. Often these felt like competing goals and I was confused about how to act and think.

Dr. Townson saw as his job now to gently lead me to the realization and acceptance of Gene's death; at the same time I knew Gene would die soon, I continued to act as though Gene would live for a long time. To do otherwise seemed immoral. As Gene's illness grew worse and his determination to live increased, I had more one-on-one phone calls with Dr. Townson from whom I sought advice on daily problems regarding Gene's discomfort and reassurance that I was doing the right things. In our conversations, the doctor continually reminded me that Gene's dying was inevitable and that we shouldn't feel guilty. My acceptance of Gene's dying grew deeper, but occasionally my questions to the doctor demonstrated that I still had hope that his condition might improve. Or perhaps the reality I lived daily with Gene made it increasingly difficult to accept fully the reality I had come to share with the doctor. The doctors' stark replies to my inquiries continued to move me toward accepting the inevitable.

"Are we doing harm by not bringing him in now?" I asked Dr. Townson.

"No," he replied. "There isn't much we can do."

In another call, Dr. Townson said. "You know he might die this time?" I tell him I do.

At a later hospitalization, Dr. Townson reminded me, "He might make it through this one or he might die during this hospital stay. But he won't get better."

Dr. Townson and I planned how to proceed and also negotiated decision making. "We have a living will," I said, "to be used after one more intubation."

"Don't show it to anyone," he instructed. "We'll take care of it. Don't worry." In another conversation, I said, "He's decided against intubation, but he doesn't want to die either."

"I will tell the other doctors on duty not to intubate unless you or Gene say to."

"I want Gene to make the decision," I replied, seeking to return the decision about life and death to Gene.

"By the time he gets here he can't always make it. I'll make it."

"No, I can make it," I insisted, feeling that it was inappropriate to relinquish my power to the doctor and that he had inappropriately tried to take it. I knew he was trying to save me from making the decision, but I also wondered if he also was trying to make his life easier. But would it really have made it easier? To decide to let someone die? Do doctors ever get used to that? (see Seale, 1991)

As partners, Dr. Townson and I began to play each scenario by ear. There were no rules anymore. "Gene asked me to find out if he might die if he went to sleep," I said.

Dr. Townson laughed nervously, "Well, that wouldn't be so bad, would it? Let him sleep. Turn up his oxygen to 11/2. If you can't arouse him from sleep, don't be alarmed. Do whatever you think best. We're in no man's land now. We can't do things by the book."

No longer was our joint task to make Gene well. Each of us sought in our own way to get through this experience, or what Gene referred to as the task of dying. Gene worked on dying without giving up hope of regaining control, uttering contradictory comments one after the other: "I might die. It's getting close. But I don't think so. I have to get stronger. I need a rest." I worked on dealing with the reality that existed after giving up hope of control, in order to face the things that had to be done and prepare myself for life without Gene. Yet, I looked to the doctor to collude with me in allowing Gene to hope, and I sought his help through the transition. "There are still things to try," the doctor continued to tell Gene, and I was glad when his optimism gave Gene hope. More and more the doctor moved back and forth between maintaining Gene's illusions and comfort and helping me face reality. More and more he concentrated on my well-being. "How are you doing? That's just as important now," Dr. Townson asked me. I too began to focus on my own sanity and appreciated Dr. Townson's praise for the good job I was doing. Perhaps there was a better way to have gotten through this phase, but given what had to be accomplished and how difficult it had become to talk to Gene about the reality we lived in, I didn't know any other option.

☐ Doctor–Caregiver Collusion

Dr. Townson and I reached a new level of collusion when Gene began spending more time in his version of reality than in ours, hallucinating he was a variety of people and demanding that something be done to make him better.

"He wants to do isometrics to walk again," I told the doctor. When he reminded me that Gene was never going to walk again, I replied, "But we don't have to tell him that," and the doctor agreed. Instead Dr. Townson and I both praised Gene for his imagined accomplishments.

When Gene's discomfort increased, I asked Dr. Townson whether we should give him pain killers, to relieve his physical pain and our agony, though I knew they might slow down his respiration. Dr. Townson left the decision to me, then later suggested I give him a codeine if I felt it necessary.

"But he's already confused."

"Then don't give it to him. Do whatever you have to. It's a collapsed vertebrae, from the steroids. There's nothing that can be done."

When I called Dr. Townson to discuss Gene's obsessiveness—he spent his whole day and night planning and demanding, and even attempted to buy a new car—the doctor replied, "It might be CO_2, or steroids, or just being confined. People almost never live this long in his condition, so this is all unusual, although not unheard of. Take away control," he instructed. "You have to. Call the bank."

"I'm ready for this to be over," I said quietly, though I would change my mind many times after that whenever I confronted the vast difference between having the little piece of Gene still left versus having no physical or conversational presence at all.

"I knew it," he replied, and I couldn't help but think he sounded almost triumphant. "Don't feel guilty about feeling this way."

"I don't," I said, though putting my thoughts into words sent a pang of guilt up my spine.

Gene now often lived in a fantasy world. Sometimes he acted crazy; then, seconds later, rational. This stage would be the hardest, for with it, Gene lost his status as "person." When I limited Gene's access to the phone to prevent him from buying a new car and a myriad of other things, he turned to Dr. Townson. "I appreciate your keeping me alive doc," he said on the phone. ". . . yeah, and everything everybody is doing. But Carolyn and I don't always agree on values. I need someone to represent my interests. . . . No she doesn't always do that. You need to call Larry [who was a fantasized lawyer]. . . . Please." Frustrated, Gene handed me the phone after Dr. Townson asked to talk to me.

"Yes, he does sound crazy. I'm prescribing an antidepressant for him. It is mild and won't hurt him as much as codeine. But it still might do him in," he cautioned. My heart twisted. "But at this point we have to calculate what will happen if he stays like he is without eating and taking medications." I agreed, though in retrospect I wonder what the difference would have been. The antidepressant, Haldol, might have made it easier for us, but did it make dying easier or better for Gene?

That night before I could pick up the Haldol, Gene began continually screaming for police, then endorphins, then "I'm being kidnaped." Somehow he managed to give himself a breathing treatment, yelling between breaths. Exhausted and not knowing what else to do, I hid two Valium in with his other pills and tried to force him to take them, but he resisted. Finally, the horrible truth sank into my soul. We weren't at all on the same side anymore; we were enemies. I wanted him to die; he wanted to live. This was the final negotiation for control—control, which always had been an important dynamic in our relationship, from the early days when I was a student and he was a professor who controlled when and how we saw each other, until now when decisions about his life were in my hands. While now he saw me and everyone around him—including the nurses we hired—as the enemy, he sought one last time to regain collusion with his doctor.

At his request, I called Dr. Townson for him and listened in on the extension. "I've got to get out of here, Doc," he said. "They're abusing me. I've got to get help."

"Carolyn wouldn't abuse you."

"Yes, she is, Doc. I've got to get out of here."

"Let's put you in the hospital. We can do more for you there."

"Like do the physical therapy?" Gene said, with such hope in his voice that my defenses melted. When the doctor said yes, Gene continued, "Okay, but someone has to call the ambulance."

"Carolyn will."

"No, she won't. You don't understand the situation here."

"If she doesn't, then we'll take care of it. Don't worry."

At the hospital, the doctors wanted to give Gene the prescribed Haldol. Asking if the pill would bother Gene's respiration, I didn't know what I wanted the answer to be.

"It shouldn't. But who knows. We're not usually working with anyone this far along in the disease. If the Haldol does slow it down, that might be the best thing that could happen."

"I agree. As far as I'm concerned, Gene Weinstein is dead and that's just a shell there," I replied, sounding much more sure of my statement than I felt.

"Unfortunately that's true," said Dr. Townson almost wistfully. I swallowed with difficulty.

Gene's personhood broke through in one final episode. I was not prepared for this last triadic scene in the hospital with Gene on the verge of death and an unfamiliar doctor in charge.

Dr. Colter, as associate of Dr. Townson's, commanded, "You must take your Haldol, Mr. Weinstein."

"See how short of breath I am. They're trying to kill me," Gene said, his eyes beseeching me to do something. My heart filled with tears as I looked at this vulnerable and scared little man who used to be my powerful and confident Gene.

Dr. Colter and I stepped into the hall. "I don't see Haldol making any difference in his breathing," the doctor said coldly. "Without it, he's going to be back where he was when you brought him in here."

Although aware that pain killers might slow down his respiration, I asked, "Can you give him Valium or codeine or something to calm him down if he won't take Haldol? He has pain in his chest."

"Does his daughter feel that way too?" Dr. Colter asked.

When I responded yes, my voice was calm, but there was a roar churning, like I had plunged into ocean waves right before a hurricane. Then it went away, and what I said had little impact on me.

Dr. Colter paged Dr. Townson and then said, "I'm going to go in and make Gene take the Haldol, unless you object. You can stay out here if it would be easier."

"No, I want to be there," I said, following him. The play I was in seemed to be in fast forward. Was this the right thing to do? Though we had stopped Gene from doing things he wanted to do, such as driving and buying a new car, this was the first time we had forced him to do anything against his will.

"Mr. Weinstein," the doctor said loudly, as if he was talking to a recalcitrant child or a hearing-impaired person, "here is your Haldol."

"I don't want it. It's killing me," Gene insisted, turning his mouth away, remembering the dose he had been given in the emergency room when he arrived.

"If you don't take it, I'm going to stick you with it," the doctor threatened, holding the pill and water next to Gene's puckered mouth. I saw the doctor as a large face with distorted features, like in a cartoon, when the bad guy balloons and occupies the whole screen. I screamed, but no sound came out.

Gene pleaded, "Please don't. You said you wouldn't. You bastard." I tried to make a sound, but when I saw Gene was about to give in, I held back and let the drama unfold.

"I didn't say I wouldn't."

"Stop," the sound escaped. "This is awful." I cried out the words, but softly, hoping the doctor wouldn't hear and would continue in his mission.

Dr. Colter kept going. I was surprised when Gene opened his mouth, whimpering softly. Colter held the water glass for him while he drank.

"Dr. Townson is coming, baby," I said to Gene, my voice breaking, after Colter left, "and we can talk to him about all this."

What a system. Here we were, Gene close to death, and we had to deal with a doctor we hardly knew. Dr. Townson would not have forced Gene to take the Haldol. But how could I complain? I had tried to give him Valium.

I described the forced Haldol to Dr. Townson, who listened to me thoughtfully outside Gene's door. "It was awful. Can't we give him Valium or something to calm him and ease his pain? He thinks the Haldol is killing him."

"You know what the Valium will probably do?" When I shook my head yes, he continued, "He's living from sheer will. The planning keeps him alive." After consulting with Dr. Colter, he said, "I think it's best not to give Gene anything else right now. It's unclear whether he is competent and has the right to refuse Haldol. Until the therapist says he isn't, he can refuse it. To add something to this now would complicate matters. Let's just deal with the Haldol and see what happens. We can talk about other things later."

"Okay," I said, disappointed and relieved. "One more thing—could you order the physical therapy, if only for a placebo effect?" He nodded and smiled. "And would you talk to him again? He feels better talking to you."

I followed him back into Gene's room. "The Haldol is killing me," Gene said softly.

"I don't think it's affecting your breathing," Dr. Townson reassured. "And it seems to be keeping you calm." Then Dr. Townson told Gene about the physical therapy, and Gene perked up slightly.

When Dr. Townson left, Gene lay slumped down in bed, broken. My child. "He made me take it," he said quietly.

I made one more try to collude with Gene. It would be our last. Draping myself over him, I shrouded my face in his still broad and hairy chest. I hugged him, careful not to exert too much pressure. My body heaved from buried sobs. "You don't have to take it again if you don't want to, ever," I declared, my voice coming from deep in my gut. "I'm sorry I let that happen, baby. It won't again." I would see to it. I would protect him. Those bastards. I felt brain-washed. What had we done to him? That spirit, so wonderful and irascible, I felt it leave the room when he swallowed the Haldol.

I was surprised when rather nonchalantly Gene said, "Well, they think it's helping and I want to cooperate." A childlike expression replaced the agony of before.

The anger drained quickly from my body. Okay, maybe this was better. At least easier. What did I want anyway?

With this, we were all in collusion. Since Gene became "sane" and calm from the Haldol, we once again were able to express love for each other. When he died three days later, the doctors and I agreed it was for the best. After Gene was pronounced dead, Dr. Townson called me in Gene's room and asked if I had any questions.

Any questions? What questions could I possibly have now?

☐ Conclusion

This work has examined the relationships that evolved among a patient, his doctors, and the primary caregiver over the course of a terminal illness. As the primary caregiver, I have used my unique vantage point to portray the communicative patterns and emotional complexities that developed as my partner became sicker and I became intricately involved with doctors in medical decision making. The main issue around which these interactional episodes turn is the question: "What does it mean to tell the truth?" While a norm of openly informing patients about their condition now prevails as an ethical standard in the United States and other countries (Seale, 1991; Timmermans, 1994), my experiences show that the epistemology of chronic care is one in which the conditions of truth encompass both cognitive and emotional dimensions. Awareness contexts are complicated by messy emotions that affect how people take in information, what it means to them, and how they process it on different occasions (Mamo, 1999; Timmermans, 1994). Given these complexities, what does it mean to say that we should be truthful with people who are dying?

Gene and I continually designed new frames about his illness, and we moved deftly from one definition of the situation to another attempting to maintain the most hopeful frame possible. We began early in our relationship to live in uncertainty and ambivalence and, following the lead of Gene's doctors, to keep hope and the despairing truth of his physical condition in balance. We tried to live fully in the moment every day, yet take periodic time-outs to discuss how to cope with his physical deterioration and its impact on our relationship, and plan for future contingencies. We felt it was important to feel and show love without constantly being overtaken by the pain and fear of loss, and to live as though Gene were not dying in order to squeeze as much happiness out of our limited time together as possible.

As we moved through the emotional and physical plateaus of the illness experience, our conversations became more and more framed by the reality of his physical deterioration and I became more involved in triadic discussions involving Gene, his doctors, and myself. For a while both Gene and I lived in two realities simultaneously—that he would die and that there was still something to try—and we began to shift at about the same pace toward the truthful framing of his illness as terminal. But as reality became too much to bear in its day-to-day physical, emotional, and psychological manifestations, Gene moved more toward hope that something still could be done while I was forced to understand and confront his declining medical prognosis. No longer feeling that I could turn to Gene to help work out how we should feel about all this, yet not wanting to replace his hope with despair, I found myself depending more on discussions with the doctors (and they on me) to decide how to accomplish Gene's dying the best we knew how. While in the end Gene stayed more consistently in the frame of hope, I had to move repeatedly between hope and practicality. The story I tell of this process presents a far more complex picture of communication and truth telling than the one-shot doctor-patient studies that take place in doctors' offices.

In demonstrating the importance of examining first-person narrative studies to understand the intricacies of the lived experience of communication in terminal illness, this case dovetails with the work of Howard Brody (1987) who argues that it is important to examine patients' stories of sickness, both real life stories and literary accounts, and with Arthur Kleinman (1988) who examines suffering through patients' life histories. Similar to *Final Negotiations* (Ellis, 1995), many other personal illness narratives already exist that could provide information and comparisons about communication between patients, caregivers, and health professionals, for example narratives by Frank (1991) and Lerner (1978). Theorists, such as Couser (1997), Frank (1995), and Hawkins (1993), offer a summary of many of these narratives and provide analysis of the themes in them, including how illness stories are communicated. In this analysis, the original data offer in-depth stories that are contextualized within the whole illness process with which the patient, caregiver, and medical staff are coping. Likewise, several sociologists, such as Mamo (1999), Timmermans (1994), and Weitz (1999), have begun to include their own stories in their articles about communication in health care settings to provide in-depth perspectives from caregivers and family members and insights to expand or amend existing theory. These stories present caregivers as care partners (Miller & Zook, 1997), who are active, caring participants and whose lives are affected deeply as they share in the illness, making them more than patient support systems (Hardwig, 1995) who are the means to the patients' well-being. In exploring health communication more holistically, processually, and personally, our research can provide deeper insights and broader illustrations of how to talk about illness and death.

☐ References

Abel, E. (1991). *Who cares for the elderly? Public policy and the experiences of adult daughters.* Philadelphia: Temple University Press.

Adelman, R., Green, M., & Charon, R. (1987). The physician-elderly patient-companion triad in the medical encounter: The development of a conceptual framework and research agenda. *The Gerontologist, 27,* 729–34.

Baker, P., Yoels, W., Clair, J., & Allman, R. (1997). Laughter in triadic geriatric medical encounters: A transcript-based analysis. In R. Erickson & B. Cuthbertson-Johnson (Eds.), *Social perspectives on emotion,* Vol. 4 (pp. 179–207). Greenwich, CT: JAI.

Beisecker, A. E., Chrisman, S. K., & Wright, L. J. (1989). The influence of a companion on the doctor-elderly patient interaction. *Health Communication, 1,* 55–70.

Beisecker, A. E. (1997). Perceptions of family caregivers of persons with Alzheimer's disease: Communication with physicians. *American Journal of Alzheimer's Disease, 12,* 73–83.

Brody, H. (1987). *Stories of sickness.* New Haven, CT: Yale University Press.

Cicourel, A. (1981). Notes on the integration of micro and macro levels of analysis. In K. Knorr-Cetina & A. Cicourel (Eds.), *Advances in social theory and methodology: Toward an integration of macro- and micro-sociologies* (pp. 1–40). London: Routledge & Kegan Paul.

Coe, R., & Prendergast, C. (1985). The formation of coalitions: Interaction strategies in triads. *Sociology of Health and Illness, 7,* 236–247.

Council on Scientific Affairs. (1993). Physicians and family caregivers: A model for partnership. *Journal of American Medical Association, 269,* 1282–1284.

Drass, K. (1981). *The social organization of mid-level provider-patient encounters.* Unpublished doctoral dissertation, Indiana University.

Eisendorfer, C., & Cohen, D. (1981). Management of the patient and family coping with dementing illness. *Journal of Family Practice, 12,* 831–837

Ellis, C. (1991). Sociological introspection and emotional experience. *Symbolic Interaction, 14,* 23–50.

Ellis, C. (1995). *Final negotiations: A story of love, loss, and chronic illness.* Philadelphia: Temple University Press.

Fisher, S., & Groce, S. (1985). Doctor-patient negotiation of cultural assumptions. *Sociology of Health and Illness, 7,* 72–85.

Glaser, B., & Strauss, A. (1965). *Awareness of dying.* Chicago: Aldine.

Glasser, M., & Miller, B. (1998). Caregiver and physician perspectives of medical encounters involving dementia patients. *American Journal of Alzheimer's Disease, 12,* 70–79.

Glasser, M., Rubin, S., & Dickover, M. (1990). The caregiver role: Review of family caregiver-physician relations and dementing disorders. In S. Stahl (Eds.), *The legacy of longevity: Health, illness and long term care in later life* (pp. 321–337). Newbury Park, CA: Sage.

Good, M.-J. D., Good, B., Schaffer, C., & Lind, S. (1990). American oncology and the discourse on hope. *Culture, Medicine and Psychiatry, 14,* 59–79.

Greene, M., Adelman, R., Charon, R., & Hoffman, S. (1986). Ageism in the medical encounter: An exploratory study of the doctor-elderly patient relationship. *Language and Communication, 6,* 113-124.

Greene, M. G., Majerovitz, S. D., Adelman, R. D., & Rizzo, C. (1994). The effects of the presence of a third person on the physical-older patient medical interview. *Journal of the American Geriatrics Society, 42,* 413–419.

Hardwig, J. (1995). SUPPORT and the invisible family. *Hastings Center Report, 25* (Special Supp.), S23–S25.

Haug, M. (1994). Elderly patients, caregivers, and physicians: Theory and research on health care triads. *Journal of Health and Social Behavior, 35,* 1–12.

Haug, M., & Ory, M. (1987). Issues in elderly patient-provider interactions. *Research on Aging, 9,* 3–43.

Kleinman, A. (1988). *The illness narratives: Suffering, healing, and the human condition.* New York: Basic Books.

Krant, M., & Johnston, L. (1977–1978). Family members' perceptions of communications in late stage cancer. *International Journal of Psychiatry in Medicine, 8,* 203–216.

Krieger, S. (1984). *Social science and the self: Personal essays on an art form.* New Brunswick, NJ: Rutgers University Press.

Korsch, B. M., Gozzi, E. K., & Francis, V. (1968). Gaps in doctor-patient communications: Doctor-patient interaction and patient satisfaction. *Pediatrics, 42,* 855–870.

LaBrecque, M., Blanchard, C., Ruckdeschel, J., & Blanchard, E. (1991). The impact of family presence on the physician-cancer patient interaction. *Social Science Medicine, 33,* 1253–1261.

Ley, P. (1988). *Communicating with patients: Improving communication, satisfaction and compliance.* London: Chapman & Hall.

Mamo, L. (1999). Death and dying: Confluences of emotion and awareness. *Sociology of Health and Illness, 21,* 13–36.

Maynard, D. W. (1991). Interaction and asymmetry in clinical discourse. *American Journal of Sociology, 7,* 448–495.

Miller, K., & Zook, E. (1997). Care partners for persons with AIDS: Implications for health communication. *Journal of Applied Communication Research, 25,* 57–94.

Mills, T. M. (1953). Power relations in three person groups. *American Sociological Review, 18,* 351–357.

Org, L. M. L., De Haes, J. C. J. M., Hoos, A. M., & Lammes, F. B. (1995). Doctor–patient communication: A review of the literature. *Social Science and Medicine, 7,* 903–918.

Pantell, R., Stewart, T., Dias, J., Wells, P., & Ross, A. (1982). Physician communication with children and parents. *Pediatrics, 70,* 396–402.

Prohaska, T., & Glasser, M. (1996). Patients' views of family involvement in medical care decisions and encounters. *Research on Aging, 18,* 52–69.

Rosow, I. (1981). Coalitions in Geriatric Medicine. In M. R. Haug (Ed.), *Elderly patients and their doctors* (pp. 137–146). New York: Springer.

Seale, C. (1991). Communication and awareness about death: A study of a random sample of dying people. *Social Science Medicine, 32,* 943–952.

Sharf, B. (1993). Reading the vital signs: Research in health care communication. *Communication Monographs, 60,* 35–41.

Silliman, R. (1989). Caring for the frail older patient: The doctor-patient-caregiver relationship. *Journal of General Internal Medicine, 4,* 237–241.

Stewart, T., Pantell, R., Dias, J., Wells, P., & Ross, A. (1981). Children as patients: A communications process study in family practice. *The Journal of Family Practice, 13,* 827–835.

Timmermans, S. (1994). Dying of awareness: The theory of awareness contexts revisited. *Sociology of Health and Illness, 16,* 322–339.

Turnbull, A., & Turnbull, H. R. (1986). *Families, professionals, and exceptionality.* Columbus, OH: Merrill.

Vanderford, M., Jenks, E., & Sharf, B. (1997). Exploring patients' experiences as a primary source of meaning. *Health Communication, 9,* 13–26.

Vaughan, G. F. (1957). Children in hospital. *Lancet, 1,* 1117–1120.

Vitaliano, P. (1990). Commentary. *The Journal of Family Practice, 30,* 437–440.

Weitz, R. (1999). Watching Brian die: The rhetoric and reality of informed consent. *Health, 3,* 209–227.

Wolff, K. (Ed.). (1950). *The sociology of Georg Simmel.* New York: Free Press.

Gail M. Williamson
David R. Shaffer
The Family Relationships in Late Life Project

Caregiver Loss and Quality of Care Provided: Preillness Relationship Makes a Difference

Family caregivers represent society's primary line of defense against institutionalization of frail elderly persons (e.g., Himes, 1992), but many are uniquely challenged by a role they are ill-prepared to assume (e.g., Allen, 1994; Hinrichsen & Niederehe, 1994). Although it is perhaps the case that most provide care of acceptable quality, virtually no empirical evidence documents this assumption (Barer & Johnson, 1990). Our thesis is that quality of the relationship between caregiver and care recipient before illness onset is a critical determinant of the subsequent quality of care. Moreover, we propose that providing care affects caregivers in predictable ways in qualitatively different kinds of relationships and that these factors then influence the quality of care they provide.

It is important to point out that in our view, poor quality of care covers a great deal more than abuse, neglect, or exploitation. Because these more extreme types of maltreatment have received the most attention, care more broadly defined as low in quality has yet to be studied systematically, even though it is doubtless more common than actual legally-defined cases. Our work in this area centers largely around specifying the complex systems of factors that are likely to place caregiver–care recipient dyads at risk for poor quality care, with early identification serving as a primary prevention strategy.

The Family Relationships in Late Life Project is an ongoing study conducted through the Department of Psychology at the University of Georgia (L. S. Miller and C. E. Lance, coinvestigators), in collaboration with the University of Pittsburgh (R. Schulz, coinvestigator) and the University of Texas Southwestern Medical Center (M. F. Weiner, coinvestigator). The study is supported by the National Institute on Aging (AG15321, G. M. Williamson, principal investigator). Manuscript preparation was facilitated by a fellowship to the first author from the Institute for Behavioral Research at the University of Georgia.

☐ A Review of the Literature

The Elder Abuse Literature

Although plagued by methodological and conceptual shortcomings, the literature most directly relevant to quality of informal care is that on elder abuse and neglect. It is estimated that each year, between 1.5 and 2 million older adults in the United States are victims of abuse, neglect, or exploitation (Administration on Aging, 1991). Even after adjusting for factors commonly related to death in old age, a history of abuse and neglect puts elders at increased risk of mortality (Lachs, Williams, O'Brien, Pillemer, & Charlson, 1998). Elder abuse may be almost as common as child abuse (Heisler, 1991; but see Sigler, 1989, for a differing opinion), with incidence rates likely to increase as the proportion of elderly persons in our population rises (Santos & Walker, 1993). Most maltreatment of elders living in the community occurs at the hands of a family member acting as caregiver (Block & Sinnott, 1979; Bookin & Dunkle, 1985; Hwalek, Neale, Goodrich, & Quinn, 1996; Quinn & Tomita, 1986; Shiferaw et al., 1994), and a frequently cited contributing factor is the emotional status of the caregiver (e.g., Fulmer, 1991; Hirst & Miller, 1986; Lachs & Pillemer, 1995; Paveza et al., 1992).

Although the first reports of elder maltreatment were published over 20 years ago (e.g., Block & Sinnott, 1979; Burstone, 1975; O'Malley, Segel, & Perez, 1979), knowledge remains far from definitive. While research in other areas of gerontology, including issues related to caregiving, has mushroomed during this period, a similar trend is not evident for quality of care received by community-residing older adults. The 1992 Report from the Secretary's Task Force on Elder Abuse, stated that ". . . there is insufficient information and understanding about the nature and extent of the problem, how it is changing over time and its causes" (Department of Health and Human Services, 1992, p. 1). Our ongoing review of the literature leads to the conclusion that this is still the case today.

To make matters worse, it is likely that existing research presents a picture of elder maltreatment that is potentially based on misclassification (i.e., false-negative and false-positive errors; Shiferaw et al., 1994). Santos and Walker (1993) flatly stated that "[m]ost of the assertions about the nature and magnitude of elder abuse are speculation" (p. vii). Indeed, even the most conceptually sophisticated of these studies indicate wide variability in incidence rates. For example, Steinmetz (1988) found that 23% of caregivers admitted to acts having the potential to produce severe injury. Pillemer and Suitor (1992) reported that 5.2% of a sample of Alzheimer's disease (AD) caregivers had "hit or tried to hurt" the care recipient. A substantially larger percentage (17.2%) admitted to being afraid they *might* hit or try to hurt the care recipient, and caregivers in this group were more likely to say they would place the patient in an institution in the near future.

Despite the dearth of empirically-grounded evidence, federal, state, and community agencies expend already scarce resources in a "kitchen sink" approach to combating the problem of inadequate elder care (Wolf & Pillemer, 1994). As noted by Shiferaw et al. (1994), the critical next step involves conducting "methodological studies which employ comprehensive and rigorous definitions of abuse, and which thoroughly investigate all individuals in the sample, regardless of whether abuse is reported or not" (p. 125). The data reported in this chapter come from such a study.

Limited as it is, the literature on elder maltreatment nevertheless provides some guidance in identifying factors potentially relevant to the study of quality of care. For example, a stressed or emotionally disturbed caregiver is more likely to be an abusive or neglectful caregiver (e.g., Fulmer, 1991; Godkin, Wolf, & Pillemer, 1989; Goodstein, 1987; Wolf, 1997). Pillemer and Finkelhor (1989) reported that a consistent predictor of abuse is "the deviance and dependence of the abusers." Similarly, emotional problems appear to be more common in families of abused elders (Godkin et al., 1989). The much larger, more methodologically and conceptually sophisticated literature on caregiver distress provides additional clues about factors that may lead to poor quality care.

The Caregiving Literature

Early caregiving research focused primarily on describing the caregiving experience and its impact on the individuals who provide informal care to impaired elderly family members (in most studies, victims of dementia). However, it soon became apparent that caregivers varied widely in the extent to which they were distressed (e.g., Haley, Levine, Brown, & Bartolucci, 1987; Williamson & Schulz, 1993). A flurry of research activity ensued mostly aimed at identifying factors that distinguished those who were distressed from those who were not. In this process, a number of obvious variables fell by the wayside, most notably, severity of the elder's impairment. Specifically, how much help elders need and how much help caregivers provide are only slightly (and often, not at all) linearly related to caregiver distress (e.g., Pruchno, Kleban, Michaels, & Dempsey, 1990; Williamson & Schulz, 1993). Does this mean that the amount of help caregivers must provide is of little or no consequence? We think not. Rather, we suspect that a number of variables intervene in the association between objective caregiving burden and caregiver adjustment. Of particular interest is quality of the relationship between caregiver and care recipient before illness onset, a variable directly associated with caregiver affective reactions (Williamson & Schulz, 1990; 1995; Williamson & Shaffer, 1996, 1998; Williamson, Shaffer, & Schulz, 1998).

What do we know about how detrimental caregiving is to caregivers? It is clear that caregivers are subject to increased levels of depressive symptomatology, even after controlling for incidence of depressive disorders in existence before assuming the caregiving role and psychiatric disorders among caregivers' first-degree relatives (Dura, Stukenberg, & Kiecolt-Glaser, 1990, 1991). These findings are particularly disturbing in light of evidence indicating that many depressed people experience ongoing or recurring episodes of depression (Alexopoulos, Young, Abrams, Meyers, & Shamoian, 1989) as well as compromised immune function (e.g., Kiecolt-Glaser, Dura, Speicher, Trask, & Glaser, 1991). All this does not, however, provide definitive information about how caregiver emotional reactions impact the care they provide. Many individuals continue functioning as caregivers of elderly family members despite experiencing high levels of emotional distress (e.g., Schulz & Williamson, 1991), but clues about the quality of the care they provide are scarce.

In addition, because depression is by far the most frequently studied reaction to caregiving, much less is known about other affective reactions, although some research indicates that caregivers also experience more anger and hostility than their noncaregiving peers (e.g., Anthony-Bergstone, Zarit, & Gatz, 1988). An understudied aspect of caregiver affect is the resentment caregivers feel toward their care recipients and the burdens they assume by providing care.

Integrating the Elder Abuse and Caregiving Literatures

Elder abuse researchers and those who work in the more general area of caregiving typically pay little attention to each other's results. This is most likely due to the fact that researchers in each field tend to belong to different disciplines and, consequently, publish their findings in different journals. Our orientation has been toward generalized caregiving research, specifically aimed at determining social and psychological factors that influence caregiver adaptation. Several years ago, we noted that although a substantial literature documented that caregivers are at risk for poorer mental health outcomes compared to their noncaregiving peers (see reviews by Bookwala, Yee, & Schulz, in press; Schulz, O'Brien, Bookwala, & Fleissner, 1995; Schulz, Visintainer, & Williamson, 1990), researchers in our field had not taken what seemed to be the next logical step. That is, how does caregiver emotional distress influence the quality of care impaired elders receive? A thorough review of the caregiving literature revealed virtually no relevant studies. We then turned to the elder abuse literature, and our review indicated that the vast majority of these studies were based on social service and other archival records dealing with identified cases of severe abuse and neglect. In other words, there was little empirically-based information available on poor quality care that is not necessarily so abusive or neglectful (at least initially) that it warrants social service or legal intervention. This is the emphasis of our research. In the following sections, we attempt to integrate the literature on caregiving with that dealing specifically with abuse and neglect to the extent that the literatures relate to our variables of interest. With regard to the abuse and neglect literature, we considered this research not so much for its accuracy or validity as for the link it provides between caregiver emotions and cases of poor quality care that are severe enough to somehow get into the system. In actuality, our research encompasses a wider range of emotional reactions, such as resentment, and less severe indicators of quality of care, both of which are likely to be found in large percentages of caregivers.

☐ Factors Influencing Quality of Care

Preillness Relationship Quality

It is often assumed that qualitative aspects of the interpersonal relationship between caregiver and care recipient influence caregiving outcomes and may, in fact, have an impact on the decision to take on or continue caregiving responsibilities (e.g., Brody, 1990; Cicirelli, 1993). Research tends to support this view. For example, caregivers perceive caregiving as less stressful when they feel high levels of affection toward the care recipient (Horowitz, 1979; Horowitz & Shindleman, 1983). Similarly, stronger attachment and greater relationship closeness have been associated with lower levels of caregiver burden (Cicirelli, 1993; Lund, Pett, & Caserta, 1985). On the other hand, it is clear that some family members will assume the role of caregiver despite having had a relatively poor relationship with the care recipient in the past (Williamson & Clark, 1989a; Williamson & Schulz, 1990). In this situation, providing care is likely to be motivated by duty, obligation, and fear of societal sanctions. These individuals may not be happy about providing care nor may they provide the best quality of care.

Indeed, aspects of the interpersonal relationship between caregiver and care recipient have been implicated in maltreatment. For instance, situations in which a caregiver is financially dependent on an impaired older person may foster abusive behavior (Fulmer & O'Malley, 1987; Godkin et al., 1989; Hwalek & Sengstock, 1986; Hwalek et al., 1996; Pillemer & Finkelhor, 1989) as may unresolved family conflicts and poor conflict resolution skills (Steinmetz, 1988; Wolf, 1988). Thus, a history of troubled relationships is associated with inadequate care (e.g., Galbraith & Zdorkowski, 1984; Giordano & Giordano, 1984; Pittaway, Westhues, & Peressini, 1995), and, in fact, Marriott (1997) noted that individual differences in both caregivers and care recipients are probably subsumed by aspects of the interpersonal relationship and interactions between the two parties.

Amount of Care Provided

Perhaps because data are available in archival sources (e.g., medical records), elder status is the most frequently studied correlate of maltreatment. Research consistently indicates that (contrary to popular belief) indicators of the amount of stress caregivers should experience (e.g., how much assistance the elder requires) are poor predictors of abuse and neglect (Griffin & Williams, 1992; Pillemer & Suitor, 1992; Steinmetz, 1988; Wolf, 1988). In other words, there is not a substantial direct association between care recipient impairment and likelihood of poor quality care.

Similarly, it is not uncommon for caregiving researchers to find that degree of patient impairment and amount of care provided by caregivers are related modestly, if at all, to caregiver distress (e.g., Schulz et al., 1990, 1995; Schulz & Williamson, 1991; Williamson & Schulz, 1990, 1993). Nevertheless, it is important to assess the care recipient's functional impairment because it is the elder's dependency on a family member for care that sets the stage for maltreatment to occur (e.g., Fulmer, 1991; Kosberg, 1988; Steinmetz, 1988; Wolf, 1988; Wolf, Godkin, & Pillemer, 1986).

Caregiver Resentment

With but a few exceptions (i.e., Thompson, Medvene, & Freedman, 1995; Williamson, Shaffer, & Schulz, 1998), previous research has ignored the common observation that caregivers may resent their obligations. Consequently, we know very little about the factors that predict caregiver resentment or how resentment may affect quality of care. However, some information may be gleaned from the few studies that have considered psychological constructs—such as anger and hostility—that are relevant to resentment.

Many aspects of providing care to a frail elderly family member can foster anger, hostility, and resentment. Among these are problem behaviors and aggressiveness on the part of care recipients (Pillemer & Suitor, 1992). According to Hinrichsen and Niederehe (1994), caring for an elderly family member with dementia is not unlike caring for a younger family member with a psychiatric disorder. Specifically, relative to families low in expressed emotion (EE), high EE families (e.g., those in whom hostility and criticism are frequently expressed) appear to foster higher rates of relapse among psychiatric patients (Koenigsberg & Handley, 1986). High EE dementia caregivers are more distressed (Vitaliano, Becker, Russo, Magana-Amato, & Maiuro, 1989) and more likely to have care recipients whose negative behaviors increase over time (Vitaliano, Young, Russo, Romano, & Magana-Amato, 1993). Caregivers who interact with their care recipients in a critical, angry, threatening way are also highly frustrated and emotionally upset, and management by criticism (e.g., yelling, criticizing, and threatening) is associated with greater desire to institutionalize the patient (Hinrichsen & Niederehe, 1994). Moreover, anger can compromise a caregiver's ability to cope with stress (Gwyther, 1991).

An implication of these findings is that angry, hostile (and perhaps, resentful) caregivers are less able to manage difficult caregiving situations—not only to their own detriment but also to that of the patient. Thus, it is likely that caring for a difficult-to-manage elder not only leads to anger and resentment in some caregivers, but also that these emotions further exacerbate the situation—an escalating pattern that may lead to poor quality care and perhaps, maltreatment.

Indeed, pilot research indicated that caregiver anger predicts poor quality care (Williamson & Miller, 1998). That is, angry caregivers report more frequently threatening the elder with nursing home placement, a behavior commonly acknowledged as psychologically abusive. Caregiver anger also is associated with signs of neglect. Specifically, caregiver-reported anger is related to elder reports of not usually having enough food in the house and needing more help than they receive. We propose that compromised care is especially likely to appear among those who resent having to provide care to someone with whom they have not previously enjoyed a satisfying interpersonal relationship (Williamson et al., 1998).

☐ The Theory of Communal Relationships

The focus of our research has been not on current feelings of affection toward the impaired elder, but on historical quality of the caregiver-elder relationship. Results indicate that caregivers evidence more burden, depression, and resentment when their relationship with the patient before illness onset was not characterized by feelings of closeness (Williamson & Schulz, 1990) or frequent instances of mutually responsive behavior (Williamson & Schulz, 1995; Williamson & Shaffer, 1996, 1998; Williamson et al., 1998). The retrospective nature of such assessments does not appear to compromise their validity. For example, Uchino, Kiecolt-Glaser, and Cacioppo (1994) reported that caregivers' retrospective ratings of preillness affection for a family member with AD predicted cardiovascular reactivity in response to stress-inducing laboratory tasks performed two years after the affection data were collected. In addition, multivariate analyses indicate that the apparent effects of relationship history on caregiving outcomes are not attributable to retrospective reporting bias or a wide variety of potential confounding factors including task performance, health-related behaviors, progression of the patient's illness, or caregiver negative affect (Uchino et al., 1994; Williamson & Schulz, 1990, 1995).

A primary objective of this research was to identify individual differences in reactions to providing care. Which caregivers are more inclined to be resentful? Are resentful caregivers likely to provide poorer quality care? Answers likely revolve around the antecedents of resentment, and one such antecedent is quality of the relationship that existed between caregivers and care recipients prior to onset of recipient illness or disability (e.g., Uchino et al., 1994; Williamson & Schulz, 1990, 1995; Williamson et al., 1998). In our work on preillness relationships, we have relied heavily on Clark and Mills' (e.g., 1979, 1993) theory of communal relationships because it is particularly germane to individual differences in caregiving outcomes.

Communal relationships are characterized by behaviors on the part of both partners that are responsive to (or indicative of a desire to respond to) their partner's needs. Although communal relationships are most likely to be found among close friends, romantic partners, and family members (e.g., Clark & Mills, 1979, 1993; Mills & Clark, 1982), these types of relationships can vary in exactly how communal they are (e.g., Clark & Mills, 1993). In highly communal relationships, partners routinely are concerned about and attend to each other's needs as these needs arise. Less communal relationships are characterized by low levels of feelings of responsibility for the other's welfare and less responsiveness to one another's needs.

The theory of communal relationships has fostered a variety of interesting predictions about how people allocate benefits and how they react to helping situations, and numerous empirical studies support these predictions (e.g., Clark & Mills, 1979; Clark, Mills, & Corcoran, 1989; Clark, Mills, & Powell, 1986). Several findings are particularly relevant to reactions to caring for a seriously ill or disabled family member. For example, communal partners do not feel exploited when the other cannot reciprocate their aid (Clark & Waddell, 1985). Moreover, in the context of communal relationships, partners are more inclined to experience elevated affect after having helped their partners (Williamson & Clark, 1989b, 1992) and analogous declines in affect after failing to help (Williamson, Clark, Pegalis, & Behan, 1996).

These data imply that the psychological impact of providing care to an ill or disabled family member can vary dramatically according to the preillness relationship between caregiver and care recipient. In historically communal relationships, responding to care recipient needs should be perceived as a continuation of inrole behavior rather than a distasteful responsibility to be endured. These caregivers most likely display genuine concern for the recipient's welfare while still missing rewarding interactions that may be less apparent in the relationship. Consistent with this notion, distress among caregivers in highly communal relationships is directly predicted by deterioration in the couples' interpersonal behavior and interactions (Williamson & Shaffer, 1998). Similarly, distress among caregivers in historically high communal relationships seems to be a function of the loss of activities associated with a decline in expressions of intimacy and affection (Williamson et al., 1998).

In contrast, caregivers whose pre-illness relationship with the care recipient was characterized by few mutually communal behaviors may provide care more out of duty or obligation than concern for the recipient's welfare (Williamson & Schulz, 1995). Providing care, then, may induce resentment because it qualifies as a highly communal but "out of role" activity for people unaccustomed to placing their partners' needs ahead of their own (or having their partners behave in kind toward them). Indeed, distress among caregivers in less communal relationships is more closely related to perceived burdens associated with providing care than to declines in expressed intimacy and affection (Williamson & Shaffer, 1998). Moreover, resentment in these caregivers appears to result from the loss of idiosyncratic activities brought on by severity of patient symptoms rather than a decline in intimacy and affection (Williamson et al., 1998).

Consistent with these results, reactions to losses in activities most valued by individuals in high and low communal relationships should revolve around whether their partners were an integral part of these activities. In highly communal relationships, many (but probably not all) valued activities should be those shared with the partner. In less communal relationships, partners probably share some important activities, but those that do not involve the partner may be more valued than would be the case in more communal relationships. Thus, if a relationship was communal in the past, the amount of care needed (and provided) may impede, or make impossible, pastimes previously enjoyed with the care recipient, resulting in loss of valued activities for the caregiver. Among caregivers in less communal relationships, the amount of care provided may interfere with idiosyncratic pastimes that caregivers enjoy (e.g., recreation outside the home, socializing with friends) that did not include the patient, also resulting in loss of valued activities, but for a different reason. Our point is that loss of valued activities should reflect variations in past communal behaviors between partners.

Clearly, routine activities can change in many ways when an individual provides care for an ill or disabled family member. Intuitively, the extent to which activities are restricted may play a central role in influencing adjustment to providing care, with major losses in normal activities resulting in poorer adjustment (see Krause, 1998, for a similar opinion). An empirical basis for this hypotheses comes from research investigating the impact of activity loss on psychosocial adjustment of chronically ill and disabled patients (see Williamson, 1998, for a review) and caregivers (Williamson & Shaffer, 1996, 1998; Williamson et al., 1998). Specifically, stressors affect emotional health largely to the extent that they restrict ability to conduct routine activities (see Williamson, 1998; Williamson & Shaffer, in press, for reviews).

We propose that the losses in routine activities that caregivers experience are predicted by factors directly resulting from providing care in low and high communal relationships. For reasons outlined previously, activity loss in low communal relationships should operate as a function of a decline in activities not associated with the care recipient, but, in high communal relationships, activity loss should reflect declines in rewarding aspects of the relationship between caregiver and care recipient.

☐ Hypotheses

Taken in the context of communal relationships theory, our synthesis of the literatures on elder abuse and caregiving led to several testable hypotheses. Because partners in highly communal relationships are accustomed to routinely meeting each others' needs while those in less communal relationships are not accustomed to these behaviors, it was expected that caregivers in more communal relationships provide at least as much (and possibly, more) assistance as those in relationships historically characterized by infrequent mutually communal behaviors. Despite providing equal or greater amounts of care, however, caregivers in more communal relationships should still be less resentful and provide better care than their less communal counterparts.

A distressing aspect of providing care to a frail elderly person is the extent to which caregiving results in a loss of valued activities. We suspected that activity loss occurs in both high and low communal relationships. However, according to the theory of communal relationships, loss of valued activities should reflect differential types of changes in caregivers' lives that depend on how communal their relationship with their partner was prior to illness onset. Specifically, in less (but not more) communal relationships, providing more care should directly affect pastimes that did not previously involve the care recipient, and being less able to indulge in these pastimes should then predict perceptions of activity loss. By contrast, in more (but not less) communal relationships, care recipient impairment, as indicated by the provision of more care, should directly influence rewarding aspects of the interpersonal relationship between caregiver and care recipient, and fewer of these rewards should then predict perceptions of activity loss.

Thus, for different reasons, caregivers in both low and high communal relationships are likely to experience losses in previously valued activities. Moreover, we do not propose that caregivers in highly communal relationships never resent the loss of their previous activities or that their resentment is not related to providing poorer care. In fact, we suspected that when loss of valued activities is high, resentment is a natural reaction that, in turn, forecasts compromised care, regardless of past communal relationship. In other words, although we expected that resentment would be lower and quality of care higher in more communal relationships, we nevertheless suspected that caregivers in these relationships would sometimes resent losses in their normal activities and that, even in highly communal relationships, more resentment would lead to poorer quality of care.

☐ Testing the Communal Relationship Hypotheses

Procedure

As part of a larger ongoing longitudinal study, data reported in this chapter represent preliminary analyses of information provided by the first 200 caregivers interviewed in the first wave of data collection. Participants were recruited from various community sources and medical facilities in areas served by the University of Georgia, the University of Pittsburgh, and the University of Texas Southwestern Medical Center in Dallas. Caregivers were eligible to participate if 1) they were primarily responsible for the care of an impaired elderly (i.e., 60 years of age or older) family member without receiving pay for their services, and 2) the care recipient resided in the community (either with the caregiver or in his or her own home). Structured interviews lasted, on average, about 1.5 to 2.0 hours and were usually conducted in respondents' homes. Each participant was paid $20 per interview.

Sample

Similar to national estimates of caregivers (e.g., Select Committee on Aging, 1987), the proportion of women in this sample was 78%, and mean age of caregivers was 60.7 years (SD = 15.3, range 18–88). Care recipients were, on average, 77.6 years of age (SD = 8.7, range 60–98). The sample was predominantly White (79.5%), but 16.6% were Black, 2.4% were Hispanic, and 1.5% were classified as Other. Patients had a wide variety of disabling conditions with 45.4% diagnosed with AD or a related dementia. In terms of kinship, 43.4% of caregivers were spouses, 31.2% were adult children, and 25.4 % were other relatives or friends of the care recipient. Median caregiver household income was $25,000–30,000 per year ($SD$ = $10,000, range < $5,000 to > $40,000).

Measures

Past Communal Behavior.   The 10-item Mutual Communal Behaviors Scale (MCBS; Williamson & Schulz, 1995; Williamson & Shaffer, 1996, 1998; Williamson et al., 1998) retrospectively assessed frequency of behavioral expressions of communal feelings between caregiver and care recipient prior to illness onset. Specifically, caregivers were instructed to think about "the type of interactions you had with (care recipient) *before* she/he became ill." Five items evaluated caregiver communal behaviors toward the patient (e.g., "If she/he was feeling bad, I tried to cheer her/him up," "I went out of my way to help her/him"). Five additional items evaluated patient communal behaviors toward the caregiver (e.g., "She/he seemed to enjoy responding to my needs," "She/he did things just to please me"). Caregivers indicated frequency of these behaviors (1 = never, 4 = always), and responses were summed to yield a measure with Cronbach's alpha of .86 in this sample. The MCBS has good psychometric properties and is stable over time (e.g.,Williamson & Schulz, 1995). Because hypotheses focused on the distinction between low and high communal relationships, the sample was split at the MCBS mean. That is, caregivers with scores of 31 or lower were classified as having had a past relationship with the care recipient low in mutual communal behaviors (low MCBS; n = 96); those with scores of 32 or higher were classified as having had a relationship high in mutual communal behaviors (high MCBS; n = 104).

Amount of Help Provided.   As in numerous earlier studies, caregiver stress was operationalized as the amount of assistance provided with activities of daily living. Specifically, caregivers responded to18 items (e.g., personal grooming, taking care of personal business) taken from the Activities of Daily Living instrument (ADL; Duke University, 1978) on a scale of 0 (care recipient never did this) to 5 (complete help, I do this for him/her all the time). Responses were summed to yield a measure of amount of help provided with a possible range of 0–90 and Cronbach's alpha of .91. Mean ADL score for the total sample was 49.0 (SD = 18.2, range 3–88) indicating moderate average levels of provided assistance.

Pastimes Without the Care Recipient.   Two instruments were devised for this study to assess frequency (1 = never, 4 = always) of pastimes not shared with the care recipient. First, caregivers were asked how often they 1) visited friends, and 2) participated in hobbies or sports on their own without the care recipient since illness onset; these ratings were summed to create a measure of pastimes currently conducted without the patient. Second, analogous items rating independent participation in these pastimes before illness onset were summed to form a measure of pastimes that did not include the patient in the past. Means for the current and past measures were 5.1 (SD = 1.3, range 2–8) and 5.0 (SD - 1.2, range 2–8), respectively, indicating little average change in independent pastimes.

Rewarding Aspects of the Relationship.   Caregivers responded to items that assessed frequency (1 = never, 4 = always) of rewarding aspects of the interpersonal relationship with their care recipients. First, they indicated how often, since illness onset, 1) they felt happy with their relationship with the patient, 2) the patient made them feel good about themselves, 3) they felt very emotionally close to the patient, and 4) they felt bored or in a rut being with the patient [reverse scored]. Scores were summed to create a measure of the extent to which the current relationship was rewarding. Second, the same four items also were rated according to how things were prior to care recipient illness, and the sum of responses to these items formed an index of how rewarding the relationship was in the past. Cronbach's alphas were .83 and .80, respectively. Mean current reward score was 12.1 (SD = 2.8, range 4–16); mean past reward score was 13.2 (SD = 2.4, range 8–16), indicating a slight average decline in relationship rewards.

Caregiver Activity Loss. A measure previously employed in research on both patients (e.g., Williamson & Schulz, 1992) and caregivers (Williamson et al., 1998) was used in this study. The Activity Restriction Scale (ARS) asked caregivers to indicate the extent to which nine areas of normal activity (e.g., going shopping, visiting friends, participating in sports and recreation, maintaining friendships) were restricted by their caregiving responsibilities (0 = never or seldom, 4 = greatly). Prior research (e.g., Williamson & Schulz, 1992; Williamson et al., 1998) has shown ARS items to be highly intercorrelated, and in this study, alpha for internal reliability was .88. Mean ARS score was 15.8 (SD = 7.4, range 0–35), suggesting that the average caregiver perceived moderate losses in his or her normal activities as a result of providing care.

Caregiver Resentment. Caregiver resentment was operationalized as the sum of 17 items adapted from work by other researchers. Specifically, seven items were drawn from the Caregiver Burden Scale (CBS; Zarit, Reever, & Bach-Peterson, 1980), including three excessive dependence items shown in previous research to discriminate caregiver resentment toward care recipients in relationships varying in closeness (Williamson & Schulz, 1990)—these were, "The patient is overly dependent," "The patient makes requests of me that are over and above what he/she needs;" and "The patient expects me to take care of him/her as if I were the only one he/she could depend on." The other ten items were taken from a resentment scale devised by Thompson et al. (1995)—for example, not having enough time for oneself, having to give up plans for the future, having to care for an invalid. Caregivers indicated how often they felt resentful of each of the 17 situations (1 = never, 5 = almost always), and responses were summed to yield a measure with Cronbach's alpha of .93. Mean resentment score was 36.3 (SD = 14.1, range 17–73), indicating moderate levels of resentment, on average, in this sample.

Quality of Care. At the broadest conceptual level, we have defined poor care as *any act (whether of commission or omission) by a caregiver that harms or has the potential to harm the care recipient.* Our present focus is on behaviors that are potentially detrimental to the elder's physical and psychological well-being. In designing a quality of care measure for this study, we adapted some items from the Conflict Tactics Scale (CTS; Straus, 1979), research by Pillemer and Suitor (1992), and added some items of our own. The resulting instrument contained five psychological items (screamed and yelled; threatened with nursing home placement; threatened to use physical force; threatened to abandon; used a harsh tone of voice, insulted, called names, or swore at him/her) and five physical items (withheld food; hit or slapped; shook; handled roughly in other ways; been afraid you might hit or try to hurt) indicating compromised quality of care. Because of the sensitive nature of these questions, the instrument was placed near the end of the structured interview with carefully worded instructions intended to decrease reactance. Specifically, caregivers were asked to rate how often (0 = never, 4 = all of the time) they employed "methods that caregivers often use when elderly people won't follow the doctor's orders or do what caregivers feel they should do. When you have these kinds of problems with (care recipient), which of these methods have you used?" Responses were summed to create a measure with higher scores representing poorer quality of care and Cronbach's alpha of .69. Indicators of poor quality care were, on average, low in this sample (M = 1.6), but there was adequate variability (SD = 2.2, range 0–13). The most frequently cited indicators of compromised care were psychological in nature—i.e., at least occasionally, screaming and yelling (43.6%), using a harsh tone of voice, insulting, calling names, swearing (28.8%), and threatening to send care recipient to a nursing home (8.9%). However, 3.5% of caregivers admitted to hitting or slapping their patients and handling care recipients roughly in other ways. Six percent reported being afraid that they might hit or hurt the elder.

☐ Results

Preliminary Analyses

We evaluated the possibility that caregivers in low and high communal relationships might differ demographically. However, a multivariate analyses of variance (MANOVA) determined that there were no significant differences between MCBS groups in caregiver age, care recipient age, or annual household income (Wilks's lambda = 0.99, F = 0.79, ns). In addition, as evaluated in chi-square analyses, the two groups did not differ according to caregiver gender, ethnicity, familial relationship to the care recipient, or whether the elder had been diagnosed with dementia (all ps > .32, ns). Consequently, demographic factors were not included in subsequent analyses.

MCBS Differences in Study Variables. A MANOVA for differences between the two MCBS groups revealed a significant multivariate effect for the variables of interest in this study (Wilks's lambda = .70, F = 9.81, p < .0001). Subsequent univariate tests (shown in Table 1) indicated that this effect was attributable to differences in activities conducted without the patient (both current and past), rewarding aspects of the relationship (both current and past), resentment, and quality of care. As predicted, compared to those in less communal relationships, caregivers in highly communal relationships less frequently indulged in pastimes that excluded their partners, more often found their relationships with the patient rewarding, were less resentful, and provided better care. Although high MCBS caregivers appeared to provide slightly more help than their low MCBS counterparts, this difference was not significant. Levels of activity loss were essentially the same in both groups. In sum, high MCBS caregivers provided at least as much care and experienced the same amount of activity loss as did low MCBS caregivers. However, they continued to participate less frequently in pastimes that did not involve the elder and to find their relationship more rewarding. In addition, they remained less resentful and provided better quality care.

Differences between MCBS groups in individual items of the quality of care measure were evaluated with an additional MANOVA that revealed a significant multivariate effect (Wilks's lambda = .87, F = 2.69, p < .004). Univariate tests indicated significant differences for six of the ten behaviors. Specifically, compared to high MCBS caregivers, low MCBS caregivers more reported more frequently 1) screaming and yelling at the elder (p < .001), 2) using a harsh tone of voice, insulting, calling names,

TABLE 1. Differences Between Caregivers Whose Pre-Illness Relationship with Care Recipient Was Low or High in Mutual Communal Behaviors (MCBS)

	M		F
	Low MCBS	High MCBS	
Amount of care provided	47.8 (14.9)	50.8 (20.5)	1.35
Preillness relationship rewards	12.0 (2.6)	14.3 (1.8)	55.59***
Preillness pastimes without care recipient	5.4 (1.1)	4.7 (1.2)	16.16***
Current relationship rewards	10.9 (2.7)	13.1 (2.6)	33.55***
Current pastimes without care recipient	5.3 (1.3)	4.9 (1.2)	4.40*
Activity loss	16.3 (6.9)	15.4 (7.6)	0.68
Resentment	39.6 (13.7)	34.0 (13.5)	16.50***
Quality of care[a]	2.3 (2.7)	1.0 (1.6)	8.19**

[a]Higher scores = poorer quality care.
Note. Values in parentheses represent standard deviations.
* $p < .05$. ** $p < .01$. *** $p < .001$.

or swearing ($p < .0001$), 3) threatening with nursing home placement ($p < .05$), 4) being afraid they might hit or hurt the care recipient ($p < .01$), 5) hitting or slapping ($p < .04$), and 6) shaking the patient ($p < .03$).

Path Analyses

Standard path analyses (e.g., Darlington, 1990) were conducted to examine the antecedents of quality of care in high and low communal relationships. For each MCBS group, current pastimes without the patient and current rewarding aspects of the relationship first were regressed, in separate equations, onto the amount of care provided. In the second step, activity loss was the outcome variable with amount of care, current independent pastimes, and current relationship rewards as predictors. The third step treated caregiver resentment as the outcome, and activity loss was added to the list of predictors. Finally, quality of care was regressed onto the full list of predictor variables.

Low MCBS Relationships. Path analyses of the data reported by low MCBS caregivers revealed the significant pathways shown in Figure 1A. The path model accounted for significant portions of the variance in activity loss ($R^2 = .27$, $p < .001$), resentment ($R^2 = .40$, $p < .001$), and quality of care ($R^2 = .20$, $p < .001$). Higher levels of care contributed to more activity loss which then predicted more resentment and, in turn, poorer quality of care. Fewer rewarding aspects of relationships with care recipients was related to higher levels of both activity loss and resentment. As expected, providing more care predicted fewer activities conducted without the care recipient (but not fewer relationship rewards), which in turn, predicted more activity loss.

High MCBS Relationships. Significant pathways emerging in the path analyses of data reported by high MCBS caregivers are diagramed in Figure 1B. In several respects, these results were similar to those for low MCBS caregivers. First, as in the low MCBS group, the path model accounted for significant portions of the variance in

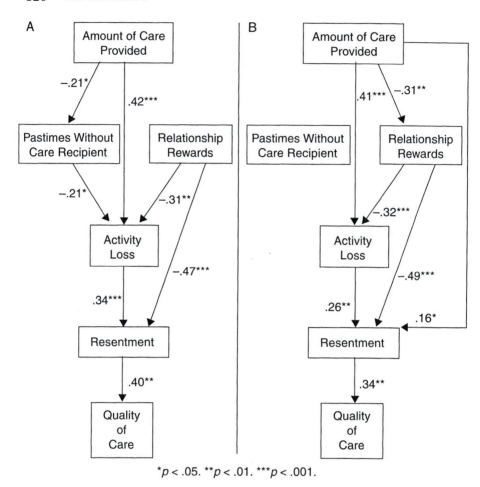

$*p < .05. **p < .01. ***p < .001.$

FIGURE 1. Results of path analyses for caregivers in low (panel A) and high (panel B) communal relationships.

activity loss ($R^2 = .35$, $p < .001$), resentment ($R^2 = .53$, $p < .001$), and quality of care ($R^2 = .20$, $p < .001$). Second, like data for less communal caregivers, among those in highly communal relationships, providing more care predicted more activity loss, more activity loss predicted more resentment, and more resentment predicted poorer quality care.

In both groups, more activity loss and higher resentment were predicted by fewer relationship rewards. There were, however, notable differences between the two groups in these analyses. Amount of care provided was modestly related to resentment in high MCBS caregivers, but there was no analogous association in low MCBS caregivers. More importantly, unlike caregivers in less communal relationships, amount of care provided by caregivers in more communal relationships was not related to current pastimes that did not include the elder nor were these pastimes related to activity loss. Rather, in contrast to results for the low MCBS group, high MCBS caregivers who provided more care were likely to experience fewer relationship rewards. Thus, among caregivers in highly communal relationships, the impact of providing care on caregiver activity loss did not appear to be due to a decline in pastimes that excluded the patient but instead, at least in part, to a decline in relationship rewards.

☐ Discussion

Consistent with hypotheses derived from communal relationships theory, caregivers in relationships historically characterized by frequent mutually communal behaviors reported more rewarding aspects in their relationships with their care recipients, both concurrently and before illness onset, than did those in relationships historically characterized by less frequent mutually communal behaviors. Also consistent with the theory, caregivers in less communal relationships reported more frequently indulging in recreational activities that did not include their partner, both concurrently and before illness onset. Moreover, as expected, despite providing at least as much care and experiencing equal loss of routine activities, caregivers in highly communal relationships were less resentful and provided better care than did those in less communal relationships.

Additional differences consistent with the theory of communal relationships emerged in multivariate analyses with respect to antecedents of activity loss. In high (but not low) communal relationships, more care provided appeared to result in caregivers perceiving fewer rewarding aspects in their relationship with the care recipient which, in turn, led to more activity loss. In low (but not high) communal relationships, providing more care predicted fewer pastimes conducted without the patient, and loss of valued activities was directly predicted by less frequently being able to do things independent of the care recipient. Thus, as expected, the antecedents of activity loss varied according to level of preillness communal behaviors on the part of both caregiver and care recipient.

Also as anticipated, caregivers in low and high communal relationships were not entirely different. That is, regardless of past communal relationship, providing more care led to higher levels of activity loss; more activity loss fostered more resentment, and more resentment then predicted poorer quality care.

In interpreting our results, we consider three issues. First, caregivers faced with providing care to individuals with whom they had a mutually communal relationship before onset of the illness requiring care clearly differ from those who did not have such a relationship. Second, there is one particularly striking and unanticipated similarity between low and high MCBS caregivers that requires further comment. Finally, we speculate about ways that our results can inform interventions aimed at decreasing caregiver resentment and improving the quality of care they provide.

Differences Between Low and High MCBS Caregivers

Analyses for differences between MCBS groups provided clear evidence that when one has had a relationship in which both partners routinely were concerned about and responsive to each others' needs, a disabling condition in one partner is less burdensome for the other partner. Compared to those in relationships not historically characterized by such behaviors, these caregivers reported less frequent leisure pastimes that excluded the care recipient and more often experienced rewarding behaviors from their partners. This was the case both before and after illness onset, a pattern of results that suggests at least two things. The first is that, even when a partner is disabled or severely ill, caregivers in these highly communal relationships are unwilling to engage (and perhaps, uninterested) in pastimes that exclude their partners. Confirmatory evidence comes from research indicating that caregivers in intimate and loving relationships are significantly less likely to use the respite care services that could enable independent pastimes than are those in dysfunctional relationships (Braithwaite, 1998).

The second implication is that, even when they are ill and disabled, individuals in highly communal relationships are still concerned about their partners' needs and, to the extent they are able, responsive to those needs. For example, these care recipients probably find ways to demonstrate their appreciation of caregivers' efforts, express concern about the negative impact that providing care has on caregivers' valued activities, and encourage caregivers to participate in those pastimes. How might these behaviors affect caregivers in highly communal relationships? We envision that highly communal caregivers appreciate being given the choice to engage in pastimes without the care recipient but still are less likely to do so. This interpretation is reminiscent of traditional social psychological research showing that having the freedom to escape a stressful situation results not only in fewer adverse reactions to stress but also in less desire to escape the situation (e.g., Pennebaker, Burnam, Schaeffer, & Harper, 1977). In addition, evidence that their efforts are valued and that their partner cares about their needs should, as our data indicate, lead these caregivers to feel less resentment and provide better quality care. This situation is in direct contrast to what should happen in caregiver–care recipient relationships historically lower in mutual communal behaviors. These care recipients may not behave in ways indicating that they recognize or support caregivers' needs for outside diversion and, as suggested by our data, continue to provide few rewards that could ameliorate their caregivers' feelings of entrapment. Thus, caregivers in less communal relationships may feel resentful and less inclined to provide high quality care.

Our theoretical approach and interpretation of the results could have been totally confounded had caregivers in less communal relationships provided more care or experienced greater loss of activities than those in more communal relationships. But this was not the case. Highly communal caregivers provided at least as much (and, perhaps, slightly more) assistance as those in less communal relationships, and activity loss did not differ between the two groups. The overall pattern of results suggests that it is the *process* through which normal activities are lost that matters in relationships differing in preillness communal behaviors.

We hypothesized that loss of valued activities would depend on the meaning that providing care has in relationships that varied in level of mutually communal relationships prior to illness onset. When both parties have not routinely demonstrated concern for each others' needs, it is likely that each partner has acquired a social network and a set of leisure activities that were independent of the other partner. It seems logical then that a major impact of having to provide care would be on how often one can engage in these pastimes. Although, on average, caregivers experienced little decline in their independent pastimes, there was enough variability in the concurrent measure to show that low MCBS caregivers who were currently less able to indulge in idiosyncratic pastimes perceived more loss in their normal activities, resented the loss, and provided poorer quality care.

In direct contrast, when both parties have routinely demonstrated concern for each others' needs, it is likely that social networks and leisure activities have involved both partners. Thus, as our results indicate, provision of care by high MCBS caregivers does not have a major impact on engaging in pastimes that exclude the care recipient. Rather, it seems that how ill or disabled the care recipient is (as indexed by the amount of care provided) influences the extent to which caregivers' partners are able to continue providing rewards that have characterized the relationship in the past and that fewer rewards in historically high communal relationships then influence loss of caregivers' valued activities.

An Unanticipated Similarity Between Low and High MCBS Caregivers

In view of the anticipated commonalities and differences we observed in the processes influencing quality of care provided by our low and high MCBS caregivers, there is one particularly striking similarity that warrants more discussion. That is, fewer perceived relationship rewards were associated with greater activity loss and higher levels of resentment in both groups. Yet, we believe the similarity in associations among relationship rewards, activity loss, and resentment does not have the same meaning for caregivers who have had a relationship in which both partners routinely were responsive to each other's needs as it does for their counterparts who have not shared such a relationship.

Our original thinking was that highly communal caregivers would resent an illness-induced loss of relationship rewards. This is precisely what the data from this group imply. Not only was the amount of care provided (a proxy for seriousness of recipient illness) negatively associated with relationship rewards but it also directly predicted caregiver resentment. Our interpretation is that although caregivers in communal relationships clearly resent losing relationship rewards, they are inclined to make *situational* attributions for this loss, placing greater blame on care recipient illness than on the care recipient. Indeed, deflecting blame from the care recipient to the unfortunate circumstances may help explain why high MCBS caregivers, who experienced just as much activity loss as their low MCBS counterparts, were less resentful overall and less likely to provide inadequate care.

By contrast, the heightened activity loss and resentment that low MCBS caregivers associated with lower levels of relationship rewards are not so easily linked to care recipient disability. That is, illness severity, as indexed by care provided, predicted neither relationship rewards nor resentment reported by this group. In truth, we suspect that caregivers in less communal relationships have always experienced relatively low levels of relationship rewards from their care recipients and have always resented this state of affairs. Thus, resentment may focus as much, or more, on the care recipient as on the illness situation.

Indeed, a casual inspection of caregivers' responses to individual items comprising the resentment scale provides some tentative support for this differential attributions hypothesis. Four of these items could clearly be labeled personal attributions for which the locus of resentment is the care recipient (i.e., feeling unappreciated by the care recipient, that the care recipient is overly dependent, makes unreasonable requests, and has unreasonable expectations). Another four items could be categorized as situational attributions for which locus of resentment centers on circumstances surrounding and resulting from the illness (i.e., not having enough time for oneself, how much longer it takes to do things, how difficult it is to go anyplace, and feeling responsible for patient well-being). As anticipated, high MCBS caregivers tended to agree more with these situational attribution items (M = 8.37) than with the personal attribution items (M = 7.04). By contrast, low MCBS caregivers, who expressed significantly more resentment overall, were nominally more inclined to blame the care recipient (M = 9.78) than the situation (M = 9.29).

Clearly, a tendency to resent the *situation* more than the *care recipient* is what communal relationships theory might anticipate of a caregiver who has a history of 1) routinely attending to his/her partner's needs, and 2) having a partner who has reciprocated these considerations. And the heightened personal resentment that caregivers in less communal relationships expressed is perfectly understandable when their independent activities are restricted by the needs and demands of care recipients who have not been especially attentive or responsive to them in the past. Nevertheless, we caution that our thinking on this issue is post hoc. Moreover, the comparisons reported above utilized resentment scale items that were not intended to assess (and are hardly optimal for) personal versus situational loci of blame for caregiver resentment. Thus, a strong test of the merits of our differential attributions hypothesis must await future research.

Implications for Identification, Prevention, and Intervention

What can our results tell us that those of other studies have not? These results (and those that subsequently will emerge from this longitudinal project) have implications for treatment outcome research focused on decreasing caregiver resentment and preventing poor quality care. Early identification of the problems likely to occur in low and high communal relationships can serve as a primary preventative measure. Our research also should help identify critical levels of resentment necessary to impact quality of care and, thereby, foster interventions aimed at reducing caregiver resentment, and effects of such strategies on quality of care can then be evaluated.

We also suggest that loss of normal activities is a major contributor to resentment which, in turn, predicts poorer quality of care. Thus, increasing ability to conduct valued activities appears to be an important area for intervention with efficacious strategies likely to vary according to how mutually communal the caregiver–care recipient relationship was in the past. As we have suggested elsewhere (Williamson et al., 1998), our findings provide some clues about the kinds of support that might decrease caregiver vulnerability to feelings of resentment. Specifically, in historically low communal relationships, caregivers may profit most from support with actual caregiving tasks. We suspect that such support will reduce the likelihood that caregiving will seriously restrict idiosyncratic activities of low MCBS caregivers and consequently, lessen their resentment.

This is not to say that caregivers in more communal relationships would not also benefit from caregiving support. However, the activity loss that predicted their resentment was predicted by fewer rewarding aspects of their relationship with the care recipient. The implication here is that high MCBS caregivers may profit most from compensatory support—that is, contacts with friends and family members that focus less on caregiving assistance per se and more on replacing some interpersonal rewards (e.g., feeling good about oneself) that the recipient can no longer provide. Although compensatory support can obviously neither eliminate the sadness that high MCBS caregivers may experience over the decline of a loved one nor replace all valued aspects of a previously close and mutually supportive relationship, it should nonetheless moderate the direct impact of these losses and decrease resentment.

☐ Conclusion

An important question in conducting the type of research reported in this chapter is whether individuals who agree to participate after being informed, as specified by human subjects regulations, that abuse, neglect, or exploitation will be reported to authorities will provide valid, representative data. These concerns have been adroitly discussed by Pillemer and Suitor (1992) who argue that informed consent surveys of "violence and related types of anti-social behavior have been conducted extensively by social scientists. . . . direct interview studies of this kind have been conducted of abusive behaviors specifically against or by elderly persons. . . . numerous studies have found abusive individuals to be surprisingly willing to reveal and discuss their actions" (p. 167). Exact mechanisms responsible for willingness to disclose these behaviors remain unclear. However, a viable explanation derived from the substantial literature on family violence is that many perpetrators of maltreatment do not self-select out of research projects because they do not label themselves "abusers" or "neglectors" (Mikish, 1993). This explanation is consistent with observations that many abusive caregivers see themselves (not care recipients) as the victims (Steinmetz, 1988). In addition, caregivers may lack adequate training and sincerely be doing their best in a very difficult situation (Fulmer & O'Malley, 1987; Steinmetz, 1988).

As in prior research, a certain degree of underreporting is to be expected in studies of this type. However, even with this drawback, previous caregiver studies have found that up to 23% of community samples were freely willing to admit engaging in abusive behavior (Steinmetz, 1988). From the onset of this project, we suspected that cases of severe abuse would not be encountered at intake but, rather, that these cases are more likely to be identified in other ways—for example, protective agency data (Pillemer & Finkelhor, 1989; Steinmetz, 1988). Consistent with this expectation, to date, no severe cases of abuse have emerged in our study. However, we have identified several cases that warranted further investigation. For example, the elders in our study had recently experienced 41 instances of cuts, bruises, falls, and other injuries severe enough to require medical attention, suggesting that they may not receive the level of care and supervision they need.

Finally, we strongly advocate measuring past mutual communal behaviors at or near the onset of caregiving to help identify individuals who are likely to adapt poorly as well as ways that poor adaptation is likely to be manifested. A particularly appealing aspect of using the MCBS in this context is that it appears to apply to all types of kinship associations between caregiver and care recipient. That is, we found no differences according to familial relationship in preillness mutual communal behaviors. Clark and Mills (1993) have proposed that, in general, people feel more obligated to provide large amounts of help to those with whom they have close kinship ties than to those whose ties are less close. Our sample is consistent with this notion—in that, almost 75% of these caregivers were either spouses or adult children. Still, a substantial percentage were extended family members or friends, and these individuals provided as much care as immediate family members. Moreover, preillness relationships with their care recipients were neither more nor less mutually communal than were those of spouses and adult children. It is worth noting that, on average, caregivers in this sample reported relatively high levels of past mutual communal behaviors, and we suspect this reflects a threshold for these behaviors that governs taking on the burdens of providing care. Specifically, it seems likely that people whose relationship with an impaired elder has historically fallen below the threshold, regardless of kinship ties, are extremely unwilling to become caregivers and will do everything in their power to avoid doing so, including premature nursing home placement. We also suspect that when a relationship has met or exceeded this hypothetical threshold, kinship category makes little difference when it comes to assuming the caregiving role, particularly if no spouse or adult child is available. Although our data do not directly address these speculations, they represent interesting directions for future research.

However, at this point, our data clearly indicate that once the caregiving role has been assumed, the less communal the preillness relationship, the less likely people are to adapt well to providing care. Identifying those individuals most likely to adapt poorly means that they can be targeted early on for interventions aimed at lessening their resentment and thereby, improving the quality of care they provide.

References

Administration on Aging. (1991). *Federal Register, 56*(82), 19656–19657.

Alexopoulos, G. S., Young, R. C., Abrams, R. C., Meyers, B., & Shamoian, C. A. (1989). Chronicity and relapse in geriatric depression. *Society of Biological Psychiatry, 26,* 551–564.

Allen, S. M. (1994). Gender differences in spousal caregiving and unmet need for care. *Journal of Gerontology, 49,* 187–195.

Anthony-Bergstone, C., Zarit, S., & Gatz, M. (1988). Symptoms of psychological distress among caregivers of dementia patients. *Psychology and Aging, 3,* 245-248.

Barer, B. M., & Johnson, C. L. (1990). A critique of the caregiving literature. *The Gerontologist, 30,* 26–29.

Block, J. M., & Sinnott, J. (Eds.). (1979). *The battered elder syndrome: An exploratory study.* College Park, MD: Center on Aging, University of Maryland.

Bookin, D., & Dunkle, R. E. (1985). Elder abuse: Issues for the practitioner. *Social Casework, 66,* 3–12.

Bookwala, J., Yee, J. L., & Schulz, R. (in press). Caregiving and detrimental mental and physical health outcomes. In G. M. Williamson, D. R. Shaffer, & P. A. Parmelee (Eds.), *Physical illness and depression in older adults: A handbook of theory, research, and practice.* New York: Plenum.

Braithwaite, V. (1998). Institutional respite care: Breaking chores or breaking social bonds? *The Gerontologist, 38,* 610–617.

Brody, E. M. (1990). *Women in the middle: Their parent care years.* New York: Springer.

Burstone, G. (1975). Granny battering. *British Medical Journal, 3,* 592.

Cicirelli, V. G. (1993). Attachment and obligation as daughters' motives for caregiving behavior and subsequent effect on subjective burden. *Psychology and Aging, 8,* 144–155.

Clark, M. S., & Mills, J. (1979). Interpersonal attraction in exchange and communal relationships. *Journal of Personality and Social Psychology, 37,* 12–24.

Clark, M. S., & Mills, J. (1993). The difference between communal and exchange relationships: What it is and is not. *Personality and Social Psychology Bulletin, 19,* 684–691.

Clark, M. S., Mills, J., & Corcoran, D. (1989). Keeping track of needs and inputs of friends and strangers. *Personality and Social Psychology Bulletin, 15,* 533–542.

Clark, M. S., Mills, J., & Powell, M. C. (1986). Keeping track of needs in communal and exchange relationships. *Journal of Personality and Social Psychology, 51,* 333–338.

Clark, M. S. & Waddell, B. (1985). Perception of exploitation in communal and exchange relationships. *Journal of Social and Personal Relationships, 2,* 403–413.

Darlington, R. B. (1990). *Regression and linear models.* New York: McGraw-Hill.

Department of Health and Human Services. (1992). *Report from the Secretary's Task Force on Elder Abuse.* Washington, DC: U.S. Government Printing Office.

Duke University, Center for the Study of Aging and Human Development. (1978). *Multidimensional functional assessment, the OARS methodology: A manual* (2nd ed.). Durham, NC: Duke University Press.

Dura, J. R., Stukenberg, K. W., & Kiecolt-Glaser, J. K. (1990). Chronic stress and depressive disorders in older adults. *Journal of Abnormal Psychology, 99,* 284–290.

Dura, J. R., Stukenberg, K. W., & Kiecolt-Glaser, J. K. (1991). Anxiety and depressive disorders in adult children caring for demented parents. *Psychology and Aging, 6,* 467–473.

Fulmer, T. (1991). Elder mistreatment: Progress in community detection and intervention. *Family and Community Health, 14,* 26–34.

Fulmer, T. T., & O'Malley, T. A. (1987). *Inadequate care of the elderly: A health care perspective on abuse and neglect.* New York: Springer.

Galbraith, M. W., & Zdorkowski, R. T. (1984). Teaching the investigation of elder abuse. *Journal of Gerontological Nursing, 10,* 21–25.

Giordano, N. H., & Giordano, J. A. (1984). Elder abuse: A review of the literature. *Social Work, 29,* 232–236.

Godkin, M. A., Wolf, R. S., & Pillemer, K. A. (1989). A case-comparison analysis of elder abuse and neglect. *International Journal of Aging and Human Development, 28,* 207–225.

Goodstein, R. K. (1987). Violence in the home: II. Battered parents and the battered elderly. *Carrier Foundation Letter, 126,* 1–4.

Griffin, L. W., & Williams, O. J. (1992). Abuse among African-American elderly. *Journal of Family Violence, 7,* 19–35.

Gwyther, L. (1991, November). *Individualized approaches to anger in Alzheimer's family caregivers.* Presented at the 44th Annual Meeting of the Gerontological Society of America, San Francisco, California.

Haley, W. E., Levine, E., Brown, L., & Bartolucci, A. (1987). Stress, appraisal, coping and social supports as mediators of adaptational outcomes among dementia caregivers. *Psychology and Aging, 2,* 323–330.

Heisler, C. J. (1991). The role of the criminal justice system in elder abuse cases. *Journal of Elder Abuse and Neglect, 3,* 5–15.

Himes, C. L. (1992). Future caregivers: Projected family structures of older persons. *Journal of Gerontology, 47,* 17–26.

Hinrichsen, G. A., & Niederehe, G. (1994). Dementia management strategies and adjustment of family members of older patients. *The Gerontologist, 34,* 95–102.

Hirst, S. P., & Miller, J. (1986). The abused elderly. *Journal of Psychosocial Nursing and Mental Health Services, 24,* 28–34.

Horowitz, A. (1979). Families who care: A study of natural support systems of the elderly. *Aging International, 6,* 19–20.

Horowitz, A., & Shindleman, L. (1983). Reciprocity and affection: Past influences on current caregiving. *Journal of Gerontological Social Work, 5,* 5–20.

Hwalek, M. A., Neale, A. V., Goodrich, C. S., & Quinn, K. (1996). The association of elder abuse and substance abuse in the Illinois Elder Abuse System. *The Gerontologist, 36,* 694–700.

Hwalek, M. A., & Sengstock, M. C. (1986). Assessing the probability of abuse of the elderly:

Toward development of a clinical screening instrument. *Journal of Applied Gerontology, 5,* 153–173.

Kiecolt-Glaser, J. K., Dura, J. R., Speicher, C. E., Trask, O. J., & Glaser, R. (1991). Spousal caregivers of dementia victims: Longitudinal changes in immunity and health. *Psychosomatic Medicine, 53,* 345–362.

Koenigsberg, H. W., & Handley, R. (1986). Expressed emotion: From predictive index to clinical construct. *American Journal of Psychiatry, 143,* 1361–1373.

Kosberg, J. I. (1988). Preventing elder abuse: Identification of high risk factors prior to placement decisions. *The Gerontologist, 28,* 43–50.

Krause, N. (1998). Stressors in highly valued roles, religious coping, and mortality. *Psychology and Aging, 13,* 242–255.

Lachs, M. S., & Pillemer, K. (1995). Abuse and neglect of elderly persons. *New England Journal of Medicine, 332,* 437–443.

Lachs, M. S., Williams, C. S., O'Brien, S., Pillemer, K. A., & Charlson, M. E. (1998). The mortality of elder mistreatment. *Journal of the American Medical Association, 280,* 428–432.

Lund, D. A., Pett, M. A., & Caserta, M. S. (1985, March). *Institutionalizing dementia victims: Some caregiving considerations.* Paper presented at the Western Gerontological Society Annual Meeting, Denver, Colorado.

Marriott, A. (1997). The psychology of elder abuse and neglect. In P. Decalmer & F. Glendenning (Eds.), *The mistreatment of elderly people* (2nd ed., pp. 129–140). London: Sage.

Mikish, J. E. (1993). Abuse and neglect: The adult and elder. In B. Byers & J. E. Hendricks (Eds.), *Adult protective services: Research and practice* (pp. 33–60). Springfield, IL: Charles C. Thomas.

Mills, J., & Clark, M. S. (1982). Communal and exchange relationships. In L. Wheeler (Ed.), *Review of personality and social psychology* (pp. 121–144). Beverly Hills, CA: Sage.

O'Malley, H. C., Segel, H. D., & Perez, R. (1979). *Elder abuse in Massachusetts: A survey of professionals and paraprofessionals.* Boston: Legal Research and Service for the Elderly.

Paveza, G. J., Cohen, D., Eisdorfer, C., Freels, S., Semla, T., Ashford, J. W., Gorelick, P., Hirschman, R., Luchins, D., & Levy, P. (1992). Severe family violence and Alzheimer's disease: Prevalence and risk factors. *The Gerontologist, 32,* 493–497.

Pennebaker, J. W., Burnam, M. A., Schaeffer, M. A., & Harper, D. C. (1977). Lack of control as a determinant of perceived physical symptoms. *Journal of Personality and Social Psychology, 35,* 167–174.

Pillemer, K., & Finkelhor, D. (1989). Causes of elder abuse: Caregiver stress versus problem relatives. *American Journal of Orthopsychiatry, 59,* 179–187.

Pillemer, K., & Suitor, J. J. (1992). Violence and violent feelings: What causes them among family caregivers? *Journal of Gerontology, 47,* 165–172.

Pittaway, E. D., Westhues, A., & Peressini, T. (1995). Risk factors for abuse and neglect among older adults. *Canadian Journal on Aging, 14,* 20–44.

Pruchno, R. A., Kleban, M. H., Michaels, J. E., & Dempsey, N. P. (1990). Mental and physical health of caregiving spouses: Development of a causal model. *Journal of Gerontology, 45,* 192–199.

Quinn, M. J., & Tomita, S. K. (1986). *Elder abuse and neglect: Causes, diagnosis, and intervention strategies.* New York: Springer.

Santos, J. F., & Walker, V. R. (1993). *Elders at risk.* Washington, DC: American Psychological Association.

Schulz, R., O'Brien, A. T., Bookwala, J., & Fleissner, K. (1995). Psychiatric and physical morbidity effects of Alzheimer's disease caregiving: Prevalence, correlates, and causes. *The Gerontologist, 35,* 771–791.

Schulz, R., Visintainer, P., & Williamson, G. M. (1990). Psychiatric and physical morbidity effects of caregiving. *Journal of Gerontology, 45,* 181–191.

Schulz, R., & Williamson, G. M. (1991). A two-year longitudinal study of depression among Alzheimer's caregivers. *Psychology and Aging, 6,* 569–578.

Select Committee on Aging, U.S. House of Representatives. (1987). *Exploding the myths: Caregiving in America.* Washington, DC: U.S. Government Printing Office.

Shiferaw, B., Mittelmark, M. B., Wofford, J. L., Anderson, R. T., Walls, P., & Rohrer, B. (1994). The investigation and outcome of reported cases of elder abuse: The Forsyth County aging study. *The Gerontologist, 34,* 123–125.

Sigler, R. T. (1989). *Domestic violence in context: An assessment of community attitudes.* Lexington, MA: Lexington Books.

Steinmetz, S. K. (1988). *Duty bound: Elder abuse and family care.* Newbury Park, CA: Sage.

Straus, M. (1979). Measuring intrafamily conflict and violence: The Conflict Tactics (CT) scales. *Journal of Marriage and the Family, 41,* 75–88.

Thompson, S. C., Medvene, L. J., & Freedman, D. (1995). Caregiving in the close relationships of cardiac patients: Exchange, power, and attributional processes on caregiver resentment. *Personal Relationships, 2,* 125–142.

Uchino, B. N., Kiecolt-Glaser, J. K., & Cacioppo, J. T. (1994). Construals of preillness relationship quality predict cardiovascular response in family caregivers of Alzheimer's disease victims. *Psychology and Aging, 9,* 113–120.

Vitaliano, P. P., Becker, J., Russo, J., Magana-Amato, A., & Maiuro, R. D. (1989). Expressed emotion in spouse caregivers of patients with Alzheimer's disease. *Journal of Applied Social Sciences, 13,* 215–250.

Vitaliano, P. P., Young, H. M., Russo, J., Romano, J., & Magana-Amato, A. (1993). Does expressed emotion in spouses predict subsequent problems among care recipients with Alzheimer's disease? *Journal of Gerontology, 48,* 202–209.

Williamson, G. M. (1998). The central role of restricted normal activities in adjustment to illness and disability: A model of depressed affect. *Rehabilitation Psychology, 43,* 327–347.

Williamson, G. M., & Clark, M. S. (1989a). The communal/exchange distinction and some implications for understanding justice in families. *Social Justice Research, 3,* 77–103.

Williamson, G. M., & Clark, M. S. (1989b). Providing help and desired relationship type as determinants of changes in moods and self-evaluations. *Journal of Personality and Social Psychology, 56,* 722–734.

Williamson, G. M., & Clark, M. S. (1992). Impact of desired relationship type on affective reactions to choosing and being required to help. *Personality and Social Psychology Bulletin, 18,* 10–18.

Williamson, G. M., Clark, M. S., Pegalis, L., & Behan, A. (1996). Affective consequences of refusing to help in communal and exchange relationships. *Personality and Social Psychology Bulletin, 22,* 34–47.

Williamson, G. M., & Miller, L. S. (1998). *Caregiver mental health and quality of elder care.* Unpublished data, The University of Georgia.

Williamson, G. M., & Schulz, R. (1990). Relationship orientation, quality of prior relationship, and distress among caregivers of Alzheimer's patients. *Psychology and Aging, 5,* 502–509.

Williamson, G. M., & Schulz, R. (1992). Pain, activity restriction, and symptoms of depression among community-residing elderly. *Journal of Gerontology, 47,* 367–372.

Williamson, G. M., & Schulz, R. (1993). Coping with specific stressors in Alzheimer's disease caregiving. *The Gerontologist, 33,* 747–755.

Williamson, G. M., & Schulz, R. (1995). Caring for a family member with cancer: Past communal behavior and affective reactions. *Journal of Applied Social Psychology, 25,* 93–116.

Williamson, G. M., & Shaffer, D. R. (1996). Interpersonal loss in the context of family caregiving: Implications of communal relationships theory. *Journal of Personal and Interpersonal Loss, 1,* 249–274.

Williamson, G. M., & Shaffer, D. R. (1998). Implications of communal relationships theory for understanding loss among family caregivers. In J. H. Harvey (Ed.), *Perspectives on loss: A sourcebook* (pp. 173–187). Philadelphia: Taylor & Francis.

Williamson, G. M., & Shaffer, D. R. (in press). The Activity Restriction Model of Depressed Affect: Antecedents and consequences of restricted normal activities. In G. M. Williamson,

D. R. Shaffer, & P. A. Parmelee (Eds.), *Physical illness and depression in older adults: A handbook of theory, research, and practice.* New York: Plenum Publishing.

Williamson, G. M., Shaffer, D. R., & Schulz, R. (1998). Activity restriction and prior relationship history as contributors to mental health outcomes among middle-aged and older spousal caregivers. *Health Psychology, 17,* 152–162.

Wolf, R. S. (1988). Elder abuse: Ten years later. *Journal of the American Geriatrics Society, 36,* 758–762.

Wolf, R. S. (1997). Elder abuse and neglect: Causes and consequences. *Journal of Geriatric Psychiatry, 30,* 153–174.

Wolf, R. S., Godkin, M. A., & Pillemer, K. A. (1986). Maltreatment of the elderly: A comparative analysis. *Pride Institute Journal of Long Term Home Health Care, 5,* 10–17.

Wolf, R. S., & Pillemer, K. (1994). What's new in elder abuse programming? Four bright ideas. *The Gerontologist, 34,* 126–129.

Zarit, S. H., Reever, K. E., & Bach-Peterson, J. (1980). Relatives of the impaired aged: Correlates of feelings of burden. *The Gerontologist, 20,* 649–655.

20
CHAPTER

Antonia Abbey

Adjusting to Infertility

Being a parent is a cherished life goal. Individuals rarely question that they will be able to have children. Infertility, however, is more common than most people realize. Approximately 8% of all married couples in the United States in which the woman is of childbearing age and is not contraceptively sterile are infertile; about 18% of U.S. married couples without children are infertile (Mosher & Pratt, 1990). Infertility is typically defined as the failure to conceive after one year of regular sexual intercourse without the use of contraceptives (Speroff, Glass, & Kase, 1994). Approximately half of infertile couples eventually conceive and deliver a child; the other half remain infertile (Collins, Garner, Wilson, Wrixon, & Casper, 1984; van Voorhis, Stovall, Sparks, Syrop, Allen, & Chapler, 1997).

Rates of infertility have increased slightly in recent years (Abma, Chandra, Mosher, Peterson, & Piccinino, 1997). The demand for infertility services, however, has risen dramatically. This is due to an improvement in the available medical technology and the large cohort of women in their 30s and 40s who have delayed childbearing. Infertility is equally common in individuals from different races and socioeconomic groups, however, higher income whites are most likely to use medical infertility services (Wilcox & Mosher, 1993). Infertility treatments are expensive and not covered by most insurance plans. For example, the average cost incurred per successful delivery with in vitro fertilization (IVF) ranges from $50,000, for couples with the most easily treated diagnosis (tubal disease), to $160,000 for couples with the most difficult to treat diagnoses (male factors, Neumann, Gharib, & Weinstein, 1994).

☐ Emotional Responses to Infertility

Members of infertile couples experience a wide variety of negative emotions, including anxiety, fear, isolation, depression, guilt, frustration, and helplessness (Berg & Wilson, 1995; Eugster & Vingerhoots, 1999; Kirk, 1963; Menning, 1977; Seibel & Taymor, 1982). Members of infertile couples frequently report feeling inadequate, damaged, and defective as women or men. They often perceive their inability to reproduce as evidence that they are not physically whole and are a failure. Infertile women have reported feeling as if they were "hollow," whereas infertile men have stated that they felt they were "shooting blanks" (Kirk, 1963; Seibel & Taymor, 1982). This diminished sense of femininity or masculinity reduces self-esteem and perceived physical attractiveness (Menning, 1977). Infertile individuals feel helpless regarding an important component of their lives and identity that they had expected to be able to control (McCormick, 1980; Whiteford & Gonzalez, 1995).

Early research on infertility was based on the clinical impressions of physicians, nurses, and psychologists who worked with infertile couples. These studies often took a pathologizing approach and concluded that the psychological distress evident in infertile couples, especially women, were the cause of their infertility (Eiser, 1963). Recent studies with comparison groups, longitudinal designs, and pretreatment—posttreatment analyses have demonstrated that psychological functioning is in the normal range for the vast majority of infertile women and men and that most of the negative affect exhibited among the infertile are a consequence of their infertility, rather than a cause (Berg & Wilson, 1995; Edelmann, Connolly, & Bartlett, 1994; Eugster & Vingerhoets, 1999).

This chapter reviews the literature on psychosocial factors that influence how couples adjust to infertility. Although the quality of infertility research has improved, there are still many studies conducted with small sample sizes, unstandardized measures, and no comparison group or normative information. Rather than providing an exhaustive review, this chapter emphasizes the most theoretically and empirically important studies.

☐ Gender Differences in Response to Infertility

Many authors have reported that women experience more stress in response to infertility than men (Collins, Freeman, Boxer, & Tureck, 1992; Ulbrich, Coyle, & Llabre, 1990; Wright, Bissonnette, Duchesne, Benoit, Sabourin, & Girard, 1991). For example, half the women in one study reported that their infertility was the most upsetting experience in their lives; in contrast, 15% of the men felt that way (Freeman, Boxer, Rickels, Tureck, & Mastroianni, 1985).

There are several reasons why women are more upset by infertility than are men. Cultural norms emphasize the importance of motherhood to a woman's identity. Although societal norms have become more accepting of working women, the majority of women report that having a child is one of their most important life goals (Matthews & Matthews, 1986; Nock, 1987). Miall (1985) vividly described how childlessness disqualifies women from being part of the "ingroup of mothers" (p. 391) and how isolated this makes many infertile women feel. As Whiteford and Gonzalez (1995) observed, "To be childless in a pronatalist society is to run against the norm, with all it's concomitant sanctions" (p. 28).

American society's emphasis on women's youth and physical appearance places an additional burden on infertile women. They feel as if their bodies have betrayed them and that their defect must somehow shine through and affect their physical attractiveness and femininity (Cooper-Hilbert, 1998). Other people typically assume that the infertility is the woman's fault, and this adds to the social stigma infertile women experience.

The majority of infertility tests and treatments focus on the woman's body, even if she is not the source of the problem. The woman needs to keep track of when she is ovulating and when they should have sex; she also receives direct evidence every month of failure with the onset of menstruation. Furthermore, women make the majority of the decisions about which treatments to pursue, which adds to the stress they experience (Greil, 1991).

Abbey, Andrews, and Halman (1991a) compared the responses of infertile and presumed fertile wives and husbands. Results from this study are described in several sections of this chapter, thus a brief overview of its methodology is presented here. Separate in-person interviews were conducted with both wives and husbands in 275 couples (550 individuals) in 1988. Members of 185 of these couples were infertile; the members of the other 90 couples were presumed to be fertile. All participants were married, childless, White, and middle class (defined as having at least a high school education and a 1987 household income in the range of $20,000 to $100,000). White, middle-class couples were selected because this is the sociodemographic profile of couples most likely to seek treatment for infertility (Mosher & Pratt, 1990). Having a relatively homogeneous group of participants also allows more sophisticated analyses to be completed with a smaller number of cases. Infertile couples were principally recruited through infertility specialists; fertile couples were primarily recruited through gynecological practices and marriage license applications. Eighty-one percent of eligible nominees participated in the study. Follow-up telephone interviews were conducted both one and two years after the initial in-person interview. Members of infertile couples were asked a variety of questions about the amount of stress their infertility caused them and how they coped with it; members of presumed fertile couples were asked parallel questions about the biggest problem in their life. The primary outcome measures in this study were marital and global well-being (Andrews & Withey, 1976). Strengths of this study include the large sample of wives and husbands, longitudinal design, and comparison group. Limitations include the lack of minority couples, low income couples, and couples not seeking medical treatment for their infertility.

The inclusion of a comparison group in infertility research allows gender differences to be placed in context; are they unique to the infertile or do they represent more general differences between men's and women's self-reports? Abbey and colleagues (1991a) examined gender differences across a variety of psychosocial variables including stress, self-esteem, depression, life quality, coping strategies, social support, attributions, perceived control, and attitudes about children. Some differences were found between infertile wives and husbands that were not found among the fertile couples. As compared to their husbands, infertile women experienced significantly more stress due to their infertility and they valued children more. Infertile women, as compared to men, used more problem-solving coping and felt more in control over the solution to their problem; yet they also made more self attributions and found less satisfactory meaning in the experience than did their husbands.

Other gender differences were found among both types of couples. Both infertile and fertile women reported lower self-esteem, greater sexual dissatisfaction, greater depression, more escape coping, and more network social support than did men. Husbands reported more confidence that they would have a biological child than did wives. Neither gender nor fertility status was related to global life quality, marital life quality, or spouse social support.

This study's findings demonstrate the importance of including a comparison group in infertility research. Many of the gender differences which were found occurred among fertile as well as infertile couples, and reflect general gender differences in how men and women experience and report on their emotional well-being (Spence, Deaux, & Helmreich, 1985). There were, however, some unique responses among infertile couples. As compared to their spouses, infertile women desire a child more, yet feel less confident that they will have one. Infertile women experience more stress, engage in more coping efforts, and feel more responsibility and control than their husbands. Thus, infertility seems to be more central to women's lives and more frequently on their minds. A woman in the study stated, "The infertility is always there casting a shadow over everything in my life." (p. 310). In contrast, a man reported, "It's not that big a deal to me, what happens happens . . . " (p. 310).

☐ Determinants of the Amount of Stress Infertile Couples Experience

Although most infertile women find their inability to have a child more stressful than do their husbands, individuals vary in the amount of stress they experience, and for some men infertility is a devastating experience (Band, Edelmann, Avery, & Brinsden, 1998; Berg & Wilson, 1995). For example, Cooper-Hilbert (1998) quotes an infertile male client who stated, "I feel like my masculinity is threatened because I can't get my wife pregnant . . . my very essence has been attacked . . . I don't feel very smart or effective in my office . . . I feel powerless and impotent even on the tennis court" (p. 72). Societal pressures for men to appear strong and stoic can cause them to hide their feelings, thus men's emotional distress may not always be as obvious as women's. What factors influence the amount of stress male and female members of infertile couples experience?

Using multiple regression, Abbey, Halman, and Andrews (1992) found that the strongest demographic and treatment predictors of fertility problem stress for men were income, anticipated future treatment costs, and number of physicians seen. The lower men's incomes, the more the anticipated future treatment costs, and the more physicians seen (each of whom presents a bill), the more stress infertile men experienced. Men's traditional responsibility for wage earning may explain these findings. Infertile men may experience stress if they feel unable to afford the treatments needed to achieve parenthood.

Although the vast majority of women in the study worked, financial concerns were less salient to them. The strongest demographic and treatment predictors of women's fertility problem stress were the number of tests received and attributions of responsibility to the physician. The greater the number of tests and the more women attributed responsibility for their problem to physicians, the more stress women experienced. Women receive the majority of infertility tests and treatments even if it is their husband who is infertile. Even a relatively routine procedure, such as taking one's basal body temperature, serves as a daily reminder to women of their inability to have a child. During a month in which a woman is undergoing medical treatment, there are frequent medical appointments to monitor hormone levels and administer the treatment. Because infertile women spend so much time with physicians and are so dependent on them for success, feeling that physicians aren't doing enough or have made diagnostic mistakes can be extremely stressful. Research across a variety of life problems demonstrates that blaming others for one's problems is not adaptive (Tennen & Affleck, 1990), thus it is not surprising that these attributions create stress.

☐ Effects on Well-Being

As described above, Abbey et al. (1991a) found no differences in the mean levels of global life quality or marital life quality of infertile men and women; nor were their differences between levels of life quality among infertile and fertile couples. Members of infertile couples frequently experience emotional distress, however, most are just as satisfied with their lives and their marriages as are other couples (Callan & Hennessey, 1989; Eugster & Vingerhoets, 1999; Hearn, Yuzpe, Brown, & Casper, 1987).

Beyond comparing mean levels of well-being, a second type of research question addresses the relationship between the stress produced by infertility and individuals' life quality. There is an enormous literature that examines the relationship between stress and physical, psychological, and social well-being. It is well documented that stress reduces well-being, and that much of its impact is mediated by a variety of psychosocial variables including preexisting personality traits, self-esteem, and mental health; responses to the stressor including attributions, perceptions of control, and coping strategies; and sociocultural factors, such as social network members' responses and cultural norms (Aldwin & Revenson, 1987; Cohen & Edwards, 1989; Folkman & Lazarus, 1980; Frazier, 1990; Holahan & Moos, 1991; House, Landis, & Umberson, 1988; Pearlin, 1982; Sarason, Sarason, & Gurung, 1997; Taylor, 1983; Tennen & Affleck, 1990). Socio-economic factors are also important (Lachman & Weaver, 1998), however, there is relatively little variance in income and education among the infertile patients included in most research studies.

The stress and coping research literature provides a rich source of hypotheses for infertility researchers. To what extent does adjustment to infertility depend on the same types of factors which influence adjustment to other major life events such as cancer, sexual assault, or death of a loved one? In what ways is infertility unique in its consequences? Results from the infertility literature are described below based on the types of mediating variables examined.

Sexual and Marital Functioning

Infertility strikes at the heart of a marriage. Most women and men marry with the expectation of having children and view parenting as a central life role (Nock, 1987). Thus, infertility challenges the basic traditional function of marriage which is to produce children. Many religious couples feel that sex is sinful if procreation is not achievable. The stress associated with needing to have sexual intercourse on specific days causes sex to become a chore rather than a pleasure. As one member of an infertile couple stated, "I feel like I must *produce* at a specified clinical predetermined moment, when the act of sharing love . . . is something that should be spontaneous" (Menning, 1977, p. 126). Viewing sex as a test or homework assignment can produce impotence, sexual dissatisfaction, and less frequent sexual intercourse (Sabatelli, Meth, & Gavazzi, 1988). "Infertility treatment only intensifies the loss of control over the most private aspect of a couple's life together—their sexual relationship" (Matthews & Matthews, 1986, p. 643).

Andrews, Abbey, and Halman (1992) examined the relationship between stress and well-being among infertile and fertile couples using structural equation modeling. Four marital functioning variables were hypothesized to mediate the relationship between stress and marital well-being: sexual self-esteem, sexual dissatisfaction, intercourse frequency, and marital arguments. For both women and men in fertile and infertile couples, the basic stress and coping paradigm was supported: higher levels of stress, regardless of whether that stress was due to infertility or another problem, had negative effects on marital functioning and life quality. For men, the strengths of the linkages did not depend on the source of the stress. For women, however, infertility had a stronger effect on sexual self-esteem and sexual dissatisfaction than did other types of stress. Thus, for men, infertility acts like any other life stressor. In contrast, for women, infertility has especially strong effects on sexual esteem and satisfaction. As described earlier, there are many reasons to expect infertility to have unique effects for women. Many infertile women report feeling unfeminine and sexually unattractive. They feel that their inability to have a child makes them undesirable sex partners and that their husbands must want to be married to someone who can provide them with a biological child. A woman interviewed by Whitehead and Gonzalez (1995) said, "I felt like a pariah. I thought that even an amoeba can reproduce. Why can't I?" (p. 33).

Perceptions of Control and Attributions

Social psychology has a long tradition of looking at the role of perceptions of control and causal attributions in adjustment to life crises. In general, perceptions of personal control are associated with good adjustment. Attributions to others are associated with poor adjustment, but there are mixed results and great controversy regarding the effects of self-attributions (Frazier, 1990; Janoff-Bulman, 1979; Taylor, 1983; Tennen & Affleck, 1990).

Americans expect to be able to control when they have children and how many children they have (McCormick, 1980). There are many anecdotes about professional couples who spent years worrying about birth control and how to avoid having a child and the irony of their realization that they were unable to achieve a pregnancy when they finally wanted a child. For example, Tennen, Affleck, and Mendola (1991) quoted an infertile woman who stated, "You expect that the day you throw away your diaphragm you're going to be able to get pregnant . . . Then suddenly you realize . . . that you might have a problem. It's shocking!" (p. 110). About 40% of infertility is due to female factors, 30% to male factors, and 30% to a combination of male and female factors or unexplained causes (Speroff et al., 1994). Individuals often feel responsible if they are the member of the couple physically unable to reproduce, although most of these physical conditions (e.g., damaged fallopian tubes, low sperm count) are uncontrollable. In a relatively small percentage of cases, infertility can be linked to damage produced by previous abortions, sexually transmitted diseases, or birth control devices. Anecdotal reports suggest that these circumstances evoke guilt and remorse (Andrews, 1984). Ceballo (1999) interviewed an infertile woman who was unwilling to seek medical treatment because she was certain she would not be taken seriously due to her past drug use.

Only a few studies have looked at control and attributions among infertile couples.

Campbell, Dunkel-Schetter, and Peplau (1991) found that infertility-specific and general perceptions of control were positively related to the well-being of 38 women receiving in vitro fertilization. In contrast, Mendola, Tennen, Affleck, McCann, and Fitzgerald (1990) found that perceptions of personal control over the outcome of their infertility was not significantly related to emotional distress among 65 infertile women. However, feeling that the infertility had strengthened their marriage, which the authors conceptualized as a form of secondary control, was negatively associated with emotional distress. Litt, Tennen, Affleck, and Klock (1992) examined the adjustment of 36 women two weeks after an unsuccessful IVF attempt. The more women felt they had contributed to their IVF failure, the more distress they experienced.

Abbey and Halman (1995) examined the relationship between well-being and 1) perceptions of general control, control over the cause of the infertility, and control over the solution to the infertility; 2) attributions to self, spouse, physicians, God's will, and chance; and 3) finding meaning in one's marriage and religion. In cross-sectional analyses, the more control women and men felt over their lives in general (but not over aspects of their infertility), the greater their well-being. The more men and women felt their infertility was due to chance, the lower their well-being. For women only, the more meaning they found in their marriage and the less they attributed responsibility to physicians, the greater their well-being. For men only, finding meaning in religion was positively related to well-being. Surprisingly, holding oneself or one's spouse responsible for the infertility was unrelated to well-being. The most common reason given for self or partner responsibility concerned physical abnormalities typically viewed as outside of people's control. For example as one husband stated about his wife's cervical problems, "It is not her fault that she has these physical problems."

In longitudinal multiple regression analyses, one's own general perceptions of control and spouse's general perceptions of control were the strongest predictors of well-being one year later for both women and men. In summary, perceptions of control over one's life as a whole and finding meaning in the infertility were consistently linked to well-being in this sample. The authors note that past studies have produced mixed results regarding the importance of domain specific-perceptions of control and self-attributions. The importance of different types of causal attributions may depend on the type of health problem experienced and issues such as whether the final outcome is certain or ambiguous, whether it is an event that can recur, whether voluntary personal behaviors contributed to the health problem, and whether the desired outcome requires the involvement of other people.

Coping Strategies

How individuals handle life crises can affect both their likelihood of resolving the problem and their emotional well-being. Most people use a variety of problem and emotion focused strategies to handle health problems; the amenability of the problem to change affects the mix of strategies selected (Folkman & Lazarus, 1980; Vitaliano, Maiuro, Russo, Katon, DeWolfe, & Hall, 1990). Research demonstrates that active problem-solving and cognitive restructuring are usually associated with good adjustment, whereas denial and escapism are usually associated with poor adjustment (Aldwin & Revenson, 1987; Billings & Moos, 1981; Folkman & Lazarus, 1980).

Depending on a couple's diagnosis and how long they have been trying to have a child, the likelihood of active problem-solving affecting their ultimate outcome varies tremendously. The ambiguity associated with infertility can make it extremely difficult for individuals to know what efforts they should make. For example, the likelihood of success with a medical intervention such as IVF decreases with each attempt; a small percent of couples are successful with a third or fourth IVF attempt but most are not. Because there is always a slight chance that another medical intervention will be successful, it is impossible for couples to know how long they should pursue medical treatment and when they should consider other strategies such as adoption or a child-free lifestyle. In many areas of life, hard work is rewarded with success but that it not necessarily the case with infertility. As Cooper-Hilbert (1998) suggested, "a couple can become like a gambler who continues to put his coins into the slot machine, thinking that the next one will surely be the jackpot!" (p. 14). When is hope still realistic? When is it time to mourn? Physicians, who are themselves enamored with medical technology, rarely tell a couple that there is nothing more that can be done; the couple must evaluate the emotional and financial costs and make their own decision.

Only a few studies have systematically examined members of infertile couples' coping strategies. Stanton, Tennen, Affleck, and Mendola (1992) surveyed 96 infertile women and 72 infertile men. Approximately 90% had used at least seven different types of coping strategies, which indicates that individuals try a variety of approaches to handle the stress associated with infertility. For men, only avoidance coping was associated with emotional distress. For women, avoidance and taking responsibility for the infertility related to increased distress, whereas seeking social support was related to decreased distress. Several other researchers have found that escapism is related to increased emotional distress among infertile women and men (Litt et al., 1992; Morrow, Thoreson, & Penney, 1995).

Edelmann and colleagues (1994) surveyed 152 couples receiving IVF and found that taking direct action and accepting their infertility issues were associated with better adjustment. Terry and Hynes (1998) examined the coping strategies used by 171 women whose IVF attempts failed. Participants were assessed at the clinic prior to the IVF procedure, two weeks after learning the attempt failed, and six weeks later. Using structural equation modeling, they found that escapist strategies, such as hoping for miracles or refusing to believe what happened, in the weeks after the failed IVF attempt was strongly related to increased psychological distress at the later follow-up. In contrast, trying to handle emotions through talking with others and letting one's feelings out, were negatively related to psychological distress. Cognitive strategies, such as trying to see the positive and accepting the outcome, were related to better task performance. Within this short time frame, active problem-solving strategies such as setting goals and planning future steps, were unrelated to adjustment. In an earlier study by these authors using a similar research design, a measure of problem-focused coping that combined behavioral and cognitive strategies was positively related to well-being (Hynes, Callan, Terry, & Gallois, 1992).

In sum, results from the infertility literature confirm those regarding other life problems. Escapism is negatively related to adjustment, whereas cognitive reappraisal is positively related to adjustment. When direct action is warranted, behavioral problem-solving is adaptive.

Reactions of Others and Social Support

Hundreds of studies have examined the effects of positive and negative responses from one's social network on the way in which people cope with chronic and acute stress (Burman & Margolin, 1992; House, Landis, & Umberson, 1988; Sarason, Sarason, & Gurung, 1997). In the infertility literature, many authors have provided anecdotes about the insensitive comments that infertile couples often hear. Because many infertile couples keep their infertility a secret, some comments such as, "Are you too selfish to have children?" are made by individuals unaware of couples' reasons for being childless. Miall (1985) interviewed 71 infertile women and found that 52% had been asked uncomfortable questions by friends and family unaware of their situation. When network members are aware of the infertility, they often provide advice that is perceived as unhelpful, such as "just relax." Lalos, Lalos, Jacobson, and von Schoultz (1985) interviewed 29 couples receiving infertility treatment and found that more that 85% felt that they received no genuine emotional support from friends or family. This discontent leads many infertile individuals to self-help groups such as Resolve or the Endometriosis Association, and in recent years, to internet chat rooms which can meet very specific social comparison niches such as gay men searching for surrogate mothers.

Almost all of the participants in Abbey, Andrews, and Halman's (1991b) study had discussed their infertility with a friend or family member. Both women and men reported feeling somewhat better after talking to others, although their explanations for their ratings were quite different. Women indicated that they only felt somewhat better after talking to others because their friends and family had made both positive and negative comments. In contrast, men reported that they only felt somewhat better because they were not influenced by what others had to say. About half of the men and three-quarters of the women had talked to someone else experiencing infertility. Women found these discussions somewhat more helpful than men did. Anecdotal evidence from members of self-help groups suggested that it is difficult to remain in these groups once one becomes pregnant because one no longer has insider status. Satisfaction with network support was positively related to well-being for both women and men.

Support from one's spouse is particularly important with a shared crisis such as infertility. McEwan, Costello, and Taylor (1987) found that perceiving one's husband as a confidant enhanced infertile women's emotional and social adjustment (there were not enough men in the sample to conduct parallel analyses). Abbey, Andrews, and Halman (1995) used structural equation modeling to examine the longitudinal, mediating effects of spouse support and conflict on the relationship between stress and marital well-being for infertile and fertile couples. Overall, the pattern of results was extremely similar for the different types of couples indicating that the stress of infertility acts in ways similar to other stressors. Participants' perceptions of the amount of support and conflict they received from their spouse were only moderately correlated with their spouses' perceptions of the amount of support and conflict they provided. This suggests that many couples are not effectively communicating with each other so that messages intended to be supportive are not always perceived that way. As expected, the greater the amount of social support and the less the amount of conflict received from one's spouse, the greater marital well-being for women and men. The relationship between support and well-being was slightly weaker among infertile couples who were still childless after three years as compared to infertile couples who eventually became parents and couples who were presumed fertile. Although sharing a crisis can bring couples closer together, it can also be difficult to be supportive when coping styles differ or one member of the couple wants to give up treatment and the other wants to continue. Based on interviews with infertile clients, Mahlesdt (1985) wrote, "because both the man and the woman are hurt, tired, and under great pressure, they may become less able to fulfill each other's needs" (p. 337).

☐ The Effects of Becoming a Parent

Do the negative effects of infertility disappear after a child enters the family or does some of the stress and negative affect persist to the detriment of the parent or child? Garner (1985) provided anecdotal evidence that previously infertile couples were uncomfortable acknowledging any negative aspects of parenthood because it "would make them appear ungrateful and less than perfect parents" (p. 60). Other authors have suggested that infertile parents may be overly protective because they put so much effort into having a child (Greenfeld, Ort, Greenfeld, Jones, & Olive, 1996).

By the two year follow-up interview, 42% of the infertile couples in Abbey and colleagues' study had become parents, primarily through the wife's pregnancy but also through adoption (Abbey, Andrews, & Halman, 1994a, 1994b). Among the presumed fertile couples, 36% had become parents, all through the wife's pregnancy. Multivariate analyses of covariance were computed to examine the effects of parental status on initially infertile and presumed fertile women and men. The transition to parenthood is difficult for all couples and frequently reduces marital satisfaction and intimacy (Belsky & Pensky, 1988). This finding was replicated for couples in this study. New parents, whether or not they were previously infertile, experienced less intimacy in their marriage and less frequent sexual intercourse. Despite the difficulties associated with learning to care for an infant, infertile women who became parents over the course of the study experienced several positive effects as compared to infertile women who did not become parents: decreased stress and negative affect and increased personal control and global life quality, as compared to infertile women who did not become parents. Previously infertile mothers were the only group to show these positive effects; such effects were not found among their husbands or comparison group mothers or fathers. Thus, infertile women, who were more distressed by their infertility than their husbands', experienced the greatest psychological benefits of parenthood.

A few studies have followed children conceived through in vitro fertilization. For example, Olivennes, Blanchet, Kerbrat, Fanchin, Rufat, and Frydman (1997) surveyed the families of 370 IVF children who were 6–13 years of age. Compared to existing norms, the children's height, weight, and physical health were normal and they performed well in school. A few studies have found modest parenting differences between previously infertile and fertile parents, usually in the direction of greater warmth and involvement among the previously infertile; however other studies have found no differences (see Eugster & Vingerhoets, 1999 for a review). For example, the mother of a 9-year-old conceived through IVF stated, "I was very concerned about his personal safety and found it difficult to trust caregivers when he was an infant, but he's turned out to be a very active kid who won't allow me to be overprotective" (Greenfeld et al., 1996, pp. 273–274). Thus, infertile parents who initially feel overprotective are likely to relax as their child matures.

☐ Conclusion

For most couples, infertility is an extremely stressful life event which has a negative impact on their emotional, physical, and social well-being. Overall, infertile individuals handle their infertility in ways comparable to how individuals adjust to other types of major crises. A variety of psychosocial resources including social support, perceptions of control, attributions, and coping strategies influence how well infertile women and men maintain their physical and mental health. Women tend to be more upset by infertility than men, although the vast majority maintain normal levels of psychological functioning. For couples who are able to have a child, there appears to be no long-term detrimental effects; in fact, previously infertile mothers experience great joy.

Systematic research is lacking for many important infertility subgroups. Little is known about the long-term effects of never having a child or the effects of infertility on couples who never seek medical treatment, on low-income couples, and on minority couples. Ceballo (1999) provides anecdotal evidence that infertile African-American women experience isolation and disbelief because of stereotypes about black fecundity. Different religious and cultural groups vary in their emphasis on childbearing and their acceptance of reproductive technology, yet little systematic research has been conducted to examine how such factors influence infertile couples' adjustment (Cooper-Hilbert, 1998). Another important understudied issue concerns how couples decide when to stop treatment and to pursue adoption or embrace a child-free lifestyle. Some couples stop medical treatment after a year; others continue more than 10 years. What personality, social, and cultural factors explain these differences? Most couples who have a child using reproductive technology choose to keep this information a secret from the child (Braverman, Boxer, Corson, Coutifaris, & Hendrix, 1998; van Berkel, van der Veen, Kimmel, & te Velde, 1999). Research has not been conducted to explain how couples make this choice and what its implications are for the child's long-term adjustment. Systematic research has not been conducted on single individuals or gay and lesbian couples who experience infertility. These are just a few of the aspects of infertility that require further psychological research.

☐ References

Abbey, A., Andrews, F. M., & Halman, L. J. (1991a). Gender's role in responses to infertility. *Psychology of Women Quarterly, 15,* 295–316.

Abbey, A., Andrews, F. M., & Halman, L. J. (1991b). The importance of social relationships for infertile couples' well-being. In A. L. Stanton & C. Dunkel-Schetter (Eds.), *Infertility: Perspectives from stress and coping research* (pp. 61–86). New York: Plenum.

Abbey, A., Andrews, F. M., & Halman. L. J. (1994a). Infertility and parenthood: Does becoming a parent increase well-being? *Journal of Consulting and Clinical Psychology, 62,* 398–403.

Abbey, A., Andrews, F. M., & Halman, L. J. (1994b). Psychosocial predictors of life quality: How are they affected by infertility, gender, and parenthood? *Journal of Family Issues, 15,* 253–271.

Abbey, A., Andrews, F. M., & Halman, L. J. (1995). Provision and receipt of social support and disregard: What is their impact on the marital life quality of infertile and fertile couples? *Journal of Personality and Social Psychology, 68*, 455–469.

Abbey, A., & Halman, L. J. (1995). The role of perceived control, attributions, and meaning in members' of infertile couples well-being. *Journal of Social and Clinical Psychology, 14*, 271–296.

Abbey, A., Halman, L. J., & Andrews, F. M. (1992). Psychosocial, treatment, and demographic predictors of the stress associated with infertility. *Fertility and Sterility, 57*, 122–128.

Abma, J., Chandra, A., Mosher, W. D., Peterson, L. S., & Piccinino, L. J. (1997). Fertility, family planning, and women's health: New data from the 1995 national survey of family growth. *Vital and Health Statistics, 23*(19), 1–11.

Aldwin, C. M., & Revenson, T. A. (1987). Does coping help? A reexamination of the relation between coping and mental health. *Journal of Personality and Social Psychology, 53*, 337–348.

Andrews, F. M., Abbey, A., & Halman, L. J. (1992). Is fertility-problem stress different? The dynamics of stress in fertile and infertile couples. *Fertility and Sterility, 57*, 1247–1253.

Andrews, F. M., & Withey, S. B. (1976). *Social indicators of well-being: Americans' perceptions of life quality.* New York: Plenum.

Andrews, L. B., (1984). *New conceptions.* New York: St. Martin's.

Band, D. A., Edelmann, R. J., Avery, S., & Brinsden, P. R. (1998). Correlates of psychological distress in relation to male infertility. *British Journal of Health Psychology, 3*, 245–256.

Belsky, J., & Pensky, E. (1988). Marital change across the transition to parenthood. In R. Palkovitz & M. B. Sussman (Eds.), *Transitions to parenthood* (pp. 133–156). New York: Haworth.

Berg, B. J., & Wilson, J. F. (1995). Patterns of psychological distress in infertile couples. *Journal of Psychosomatic Obstetrics and Gynecology, 16*, 65–78.

Billings, A. G., & Moos, R. H. (1981). The role of coping responses and social resources in attenuating the impact of stressful life events. *Journal of Behavioral Medicine, 4*, 139–157.

Braverman, A. M., Boxer, A. S., Corson, S. L., Coutifaris, C., & Hendrix, A. (1998). Characteristics and attitudes of parents of children born with the use of assisted reproductive technology. *Fertility and Sterility, 70*, 860–865.

Burman, B., & Margolin, G. (1992). Analysis of the association between marital relationships and health problems. *Psychological Bulletin, 112*, 39–63.

Callan, V. J., & Hennessey, J. F. (1989). Psychological adjustment to infertility: A unique comparison of two groups of infertile women, mothers and women childless by choice. *Journal of Reproductive and Infant Psychology, 7*, 105–112.

Campbell, S. M., Dunkel-Schetter, C., & Peplau, L. A. (1991). Perceived control and adjustment to infertility among women undergoing in vitro fertilization. In A. L. Stanton & C. Dunkel-Schetter (Eds.), *Infertility: Perspectives from stress and coping research* (pp. 133–156). New York: Plenum.

Ceballo, R. (1999). The only Black woman walking the face of the earth who cannot have a baby: Two women's stories. In M. Romero & A. J. Stewart (Eds.), *Women's untold stories: Breaking silence, talking back, voicing complexity* (pp. 3–19). New York: Routledge.

Cohen, S., & Edwards, J. R. (1989). Personality characteristics as moderators of the relationship between stress and disorder. In R. W. J. Neufeld (Ed.), *Advances in the investigation of psychological stress* (pp. 235–283). New York: Wiley.

Collins, A., Freeman, E. W., Boxer, A. S., & Tureck, R. (1992). Perceptions of infertility and treatment stress in females as compared with males entering in vitro fertilization treatment. *Fertility and Sterility, 57*, 350–356.

Collins, J. A., Garner, J. B., Wilson, E. H., Wrixon, W., & Casper, R .F. (1984). A proportional hazard's analysis of the clinical characteristics of infertile couples. *American Journal of Obstetrics and Gynecology, 148*, 527–532.

Cooper-Hilbert, B. (1998). *Infertility and involuntary childlessness: Helping couples cope.* New York: Norton.

Edelmann, R. J., Connolly, K. J., & Bartlett, H. (1994). Coping strategies and psychological adjustment of couples presenting for IVF. *Journal of Psychosomatic Research, 38,* 355–364.

Eiser, B. G. (1963). Some psychological differences between fertile and infertile women. *Journal of Clinical Psychology, 19,* 391.

Eugster, A., & Vingerhoets, A. J. J. M. (1999). Psychological aspects of in vitro fertilization: A review. *Social Science and Medicine, 48,* 575–589.

Folkman, S., & Lazarus, R. S. (1980). An analysis of coping in a middle-aged community sample. *Journal of Health and Social Behavior, 21,* 219–239.

Frazier, P. A. (1990). Victim attributions and post-rape trauma. *Journal of Personality and Social Psychology, 59,* 298–304.

Freeman, E. W., Boxer, A. S., Rickels, K., Tureck, R., & Mastroianni, L., Jr. (1985). Psychological evaluation and support in a program of in vitro fertilization and embryo transfer. *Fertility and Sterility, 43,* 48–53.

Garner, C. H. (1985). Pregnancy after infertility. *Journal of Obstetric and Gynecologic Neonatal Nursing, 14,* 58–62.

Greenfeld, D. A., Ort, S. I., Greenfeld, D. G., Jones, E. E., & Olive, D. L. (1996). Attitudes of IVF parents regarding the IVF experience and their children. *Journal of Assisted Reproduction and Genetics, 13,* 266–274.

Greil, A. L. (1991). *Not yet pregnant.* New Brunswick, NJ: Rutgers University Press.

Hearn, M. T., Yuzpe, A. A., Brown, S. E., & Casper, R. F. (1987). Psychological characteristics of in vitro fertilization participants. *American Journal of Obstetrics and Gynecology, 156,* 269–274.

Holahan, C. J., & Moos, R. H., (1991). Life stressors, personal and social resources, and depression: A 4-year structural model. *Journal of Abnormal Psychology, 100,* 31–38.

House, J. S., Landis, K. R., & Umberson, D. (1988). Social relationships and health. *Science, 241,* 540–545.

Hynes, G. J., Callan, V. J., Terry, D. J., & Gallois, C. (1992). The psychological well-being of infertile women after a failed IVF attempt: The effects of coping. *British Journal of Medical Psychology, 65,* 269–278.

Janoff-Bulman, R. (1979). Characterological versus behavioral self-blame: Inquiries into depression and rape. *Journal of Personality and Social Psychology, 37,* 1798–1809.

Kirk, H. D. (1963). Nonfecund people as parents—some social and psychological considerations. *Fertility and Sterility, 14,* 310–319.

Lachman, M. E., & Weaver, S. L. (1998). The sense of control as a moderator of social class differences in health and well-being. *Journal of Personality and Social Psychology, 74,* 763–773.

Lalos, A., Lalos, O., Jacobsson, L., & von Schoultz, B. (1985). Psychological reactions to the medical investigation and surgical treatment of infertility. *Gynecologic and Obstetric Investigation, 20,* 209–217.

Litt, M. D., Tennen, H., Affleck, G., & Klock, S. (1992). Coping and cognitive factors in adaptation to in vitro fertilization failure. *Journal of Behavioral Medicine, 15,* 171–187.

Mahlstedt, P. (1985). The psychological component of infertility. *Fertility and Sterility, 43,* 335–346.

Matthews, R., & Matthews, A. M. (1986). Infertility and involuntary childlessness: The transition to nonparenthood. *Journal of Marriage and the Family, 48,* 641–649.

McCormick, T. M. (1980). Out of control: One aspect of infertility. *Journal of Obstetric, Gynecologic, and Neonatal Nursing, 9,* 205–206.

McEwan, K. L., Costello, C. G., & Taylor, P. J. (1987). Adjustment to infertility. *Journal of Abnormal Psychology, 96,* 108–116.

Mendola, R., Tennen, H., Affleck, G., McCann, L., & Fitzgerald, T. (1990). Appraisal and adaptation among women with impaired fertility. *Cognitive Therapy and Research, 14,* 79–93.

Menning, B. E. (1977). *Infertility: A guide for childless couples.* Englewood Cliffs, NJ: Prentice Hall.

Miall, C. E. (1985). Perceptions of informal sanctioning and the stigma of involuntary childlessness, *Deviant Behavior, 6,* 383–403.

Morrow, K. A., Thoreson, R. W., & Penney, L. L. (1995). Predictors of psychological distress among infertility clinic patients. *Journal of Consulting and Clinical Psychology, 63,* 163–167.

Mosher, W. D., & Pratt, W. F. (1990). Fecundity and infertility in the United States, 1965-88. *Advance Data, 192,* 1–9.

Neumann, P. J., Gharib, S. D., & Weinstein, M. C. (1994). The cost of a successful delivery with in vitro fertilization. *New England Journal of Medicine, 331,* 239–243.

Nock, S. L. (1987). The symbolic meaning of childbearing. *Journal of Family Issues, 8,* 373–393.

Olivennes, F., Blanchet, V., Kerbrat, V., Fanchin, R., Rufat, P., & Frydman, R. (1997). Follow-up of a cohort of 422 children aged 6 to 13 years conceived by in vitro fertilization. *Fertility and Sterility, 67,* 284–289.

Pearlin, L. I. (1982). The social contexts of stress. In L. Goldberger & S. Breznitz (Eds.), *Handbook of stress* (pp. 367–379). New York: The Free Press.

Sabatelli, R. M., Meth, R. L., & Gavazzi, S. M. (1988). Factors mediating the adjustment to involuntary childlessness. *Family Relations, 37,* 338–343.

Sarason, R. B., Sarason, I. G., & Gurung, A. R. (1997). Close personal relationships and health outcomes: A key to the role of social support. In S. Duck (Ed.), *Handbook of personal relationships* (2nd ed., pp. 547–573). New York: Wiley.

Seibel, M. M., & Taymor, M. L. (1982). Emotional aspects of infertility. *Fertility and Sterility, 37,* 137–145.

Spence, J. T., Deaux, K., & Helmreich, R. L. (1985). Sex roles in contemporary American society. In G. Lindzey & E. Aronson, (Eds.), *Handbook of social psychology* (3rd ed., Vol 2, pp. 149–178). New York: Random House.

Speroff, L., Glass, R. H., & Kase, N. G. (1994). *Clinical gynecologic endocrinology and infertility* (5th ed.). Baltimore: Williams & Wilkins.

Stanton, A. L., Tennen, H., Affleck, G., & Mendola, R. (1992). Coping and adjustment to infertility. *Journal of Social and Clinical Psychology, 11,* 1–13.

Taylor, S. E. (1983). Adjustment to threatening events: A theory of cognitive adaptation. *American Psychologist, 38,* 1161–1173.

Tennen, H., & Affleck, G. (1990). Blaming others for threatening events. *Psychological Bulletin, 108,* 209–232.

Tennen, H., Affleck, G., & Mendola, R. (1991). Causal explanations for infertility. In A. L. Stanton & C. Dunkel-Schetter (Eds.), *Infertility: Perspectives from stress and coping research* (pp. 109–131). New York: Plenum.

Terry, D. J., & Hynes, G. J. (1998). Adjustment to a low-control situation: Reexamining the role of coping responses. *Journal of Personality and Social Psychology, 74,* 1078–1092.

Ulbrich, P. M., Coyle, A. T., & Llabre, M. M. (1990). Involuntary childlessness and marital adjustment: his and hers. *Journal of Sex and Marital Therapy, 16,* 147–158.

van Berkel, C., van der Veen, L., Kimmel, I., & te Velde, E. (1999). Differences in the attitudes of couples whose children were conceived through artificial insemination by donor in 1980 and in 1996. *Fertility and Sterility, 71,* 226–231.

van Voorhis, B. J., Stovall, D. W., Sparks, A. E. T., Syrop, C. H., Allen, B. D., & Chapler, F. K. (1997). Cost-effectiveness of infertility treatments: A cohort study. *Fertility and Sterility, 67,* 830–836.

Vitaliano, P. P., Maiuro, R. D., Russo, J., Katon, W., DeWolfe, D., & Hall, G. (1990). Coping profiles associated with psychiatric, physical health, work, and family problems. *Health Psychology, 9,* 348–376.

Whiteford, L. M., & Gonzalez, L. (1995). Stigma: The hidden burden of infertility. *Social Science and Medicine, 40,* 27–36.

Wilcox, L. S., & Mosher, W. D. (1993). Use of infertility services in the United States. *Obstetrics and Gynecology, 82,* 122–127.

Wright, J., Bissonnette, F., Duchesne, C., Benoit, J., Sabourin, S., & Girard, Y. (1991). Psychosocial distress and infertility: Men and women respond differently. *Fertility and Sterility, 55,* 100–108.

CHAPTER 21

Robert O. Hanson
Bert Hayslip, Jr.

Widowhood in Later Life

Because most conjugal bereavements occur in later life, older persons have frequently been included as respondents in studies of bereavement. We have learned much, therefore, about the nature and course of bereavement among older people. Four general issues, for example, have received particular attention: 1) the consequences of bereavement and widowed status among older persons, 2) age as a risk factor for poor outcome of conjugal bereavement, 3) the experience of widowhood in later life from a sociological perspective, and 4) adaptive process to conjugal bereavement in later life. Limited attention, however, has been paid to the role of *aging theory and research*, as it might help us to understand the experience of losing a spouse in later life. It is our sense that in later life, defining life-events and stressors such as becoming widowed must be viewed in the context of the aging experience more broadly.

Various theorists have proposed elements that should be involved in the adaptation process. Weiss (1993), for example, views successful adaptation to bereavement to require a degree of cognitive acceptance, wherein the bereaved arrives at an adequate and hopefully comforting explanation for the death; emotional acceptance, requiring confrontation and eventually neutralization of one's memories and connections to the deceased; and identity change, moving to a new sense of self, locating memories and connections to the deceased more comfortably in a past-self, and to beginning to move on to new relationships. Our concern, however, and the premise of this chapter, is that generic prescriptions for adaptive process in response to conjugal loss must be tempered by a sense for developmental contexts, and (for purposes of this chapter) by consideration of age-related change in 1) the meaning and consequences of the death, and 2) motivation and capacity to adapt. We have two goals, then, for this chapter. First, we briefly summarize the kinds of research conducted, to date, on older widowed persons, and findings. Second, we will discuss some of the major theoretical and research frameworks from the study of aging that may offer insight into the experience of widowhood in later life.

☐ Extant Research Findings

In 1997, there were approximately 34 million Americans age 65 and older. Three million of these were among the fastest growing age group in the population (age 85 and older). Forty-six percent of women age 65 and older and 16% of men are widowed. Population figures also indicate that women tend to outlive men, they are three times more likely than men to become widowed, they are less likely than widowed men to remarry, the duration of their widowhood is typically longer, and they are more likely to spend their later years (when health management concerns become more complex) living alone (U.S. Census Bureau, 1999).

Consequences of Bereavement and Widowed Status

The bereavement experience of older persons is in many ways quite similar to that of younger adults, involving emotional and physical distress, increased use of physician services, medications and so on (Stroebe & Stroebe, 1987; Stroebe, Stroebe, & Hansson, 1993). Like younger adults, however, older bereaved persons exhibit considerable resilience following spousal bereavement. In uncomplicated bereavements, at least, by approximately two years postloss, measures of psychological distress, depressive symptoms, health complaints, and quality of daily functioning generally return to preloss levels, although measures more specific to one's grief for the individual lost (e.g., loneliness, yearning) may remain elevated for some additional time (Byrne & Raphael, 1994; Lund, Caserta, & Dimond, 1993; McCrae & Costa,1988; Mendes De Leon, Kasl, & Jacobs, 1994; Thompson, Gallagher-Thompson, Futterman, Gilewski, & Peterson, 1991). A small percentage of elderly bereaved appear to exhibit a more complicated grief experience and associated depressive symptoms, and these persons may be candidates for clinical treatment (e.g., Prigerson et al., 1995).

Longer-term, however, there is concern for older widowed people. From a sociological perspective, for example, the issue of what is lost in spousal bereavement broadens. In addition to the emotional trauma of losing a beloved attachment figure, there may be important disruptions of social structure and status. Over a long marriage, couples develop understandings, roles, traditions, interdependencies, and a shared social identity. These are an important source of personal rewards, and they are lost with the death of the spouse (Lopata, 1996; O'Bryant & Hansson, 1995).

Older widowed persons are also at increased risk for social isolation and loneliness. In our culture, widowhood is a roleless social status. Widows are more likely to live alone. Their income may drop, reducing opportunities to socialize. They may have to move to a new residence, leaving long-time neighbors and friends. They may be excluded from former patterns of activity and friendship in couple-companionate society. Among older women, especially, there are few potential new male partners, and such relationships tend to be inhibited, anyway, by attitudes among the widow's family (Lopata, 1996; Moss, Moss, & Hansson, in press).

Social isolation, in turn, implies a number of additional concerns. The likelihood of effective social support, for example, reflects one's access to a caring and effective social network (Hansson & Carpenter, 1994). The loss of a partner also alters the nature and meaning of the most basic daily routines, such as food preparation and mealtimes. In this connection, for example, Rosenbloom and Whittington (1993) found that widowed respondents living alone enjoyed mealtimes less, paid less attention to the quality of their diet, were less likely to take nutrient supplements, and experienced unintended weight loss. Similarly, an isolated widow may lack assistance and encouragement with respect to staying fit, managing chronic health conditions, monitoring medications, promptly seeing a physician, and so on (Rowe & Kahn, 1997). Widowhood and associated reduction of social and cognitive stimulation even appear to be indicated as a risk factor for continued intellectual functioning in later life (Schaie, 1994).

Age as a Risk Factor for Poor Outcome of Conjugal Bereavement

Comparisons across broader population samples suggest that, initially, the bereavement reactions of older widows may be less intense than that of younger persons who become widows (e.g., Sanders, 1993; Stroebe & Stroebe, 1987). This pattern is thought to reflect a sense that death in old age is less unexpected, and is viewed as less unfair than when it occurs in younger families. However, grief-related emotional and physical symptoms appear to be resolved more slowly among older widows (e.g., Sanders, 1981; Thompson, et al., 1991). Such a pattern is consistent with the circumstances of bereavement in later life. Losing a long-time partner should have a greater disorganizing effect on the roles, patterns, and activities in one's life (Lopata, 1996). Moreover, losing a spouse in old age may become a triggering event for a variety of stressful life events that tend to cluster in later life. The difficulties of bereavement might be expected to interact with or intensify the consequences of such events, which may include chronic illness or disability, declines in income, support networks, independence, and so on (O'Bryant & Hansson, 1995). Loss of a long-time spouse may also take on symbolic proportions, as does the first onset of an age-related physical disability, in that it may come to symbolize a "line between not being old and being old" (Kemp, 1985, p. 655).

There may be important age-related differences, however, among the older population itself. For example, a longitudinal study by Mendes De Leon et al., (1994) found that widowed persons age 65–74, as compared to those age 75 and over, exhibited increased depressive symptoms into the second and third year post-bereavement.

Adaptive Processes

The gerontological literature provides a variety of examples of successful adaptive process (communal and self-directed) among older widows. Widows benefit from support that matches their needs (O'Bryant & Hansson, 1995). Recent widows also appear to increase the number of widows (who have been through what they have been through) in their social networks. The value of doing so, however, may be more at the level of companionship, as the still-married members of their networks remain their most effective source of support (Morgan, Carder, & Neal, 1997).

For the majority of elderly widows, there is some forewarning of the impending death, because of a spouse's lingering illness, and some of these appear able to use that time to prepare to deal with the consequences of the death. One study, for example, assessed the degree to which older widows had engaged in cognitive rehearsal (thinking through the emotional, financial, family, and life-change implications of the impending death), and behavioral rehearsal (engaging in social comparison with other widows; actually planning and making decisions with respect to housing, financial, and legal matters; making new friends, increasing personal involvements in one's community, and learning to get around on their own). Increased participation in such activities prior to the spouse's death was associated with reports of less emotional disruption in the months immediately after the death, more positive resolution of grief, and more success in handling the practical tasks of adjusting to widowhood (Remondet, Hansson, Rule, & Winfrey, 1987).

Mastering the demands and challenges involved in caregiving for an elderly spouse may also have a positive influence on widows who have been caregivers. One recent study, for example, found widowed respondents who were former spouse caregivers were less likely to be classified as depressed than either married current caregivers or widows who had not previously served as their spouse's caregiver (Wells & Kendig, 1997). These data suggest that the sequence of spousal caregiving and widowhood should not be interpreted simply as an accumulation of stressors. Instead, the experience of caregiving may be a life transition that allows new perspectives, alters the meaning of widowhood, and buffers against the consequences of this all-important life event (Wells & Kendig, 1997).

☐ Explorations of the Role of Gerontological Theory and Research

In this section, we introduce a variety of topics from the aging literature that are relevant to the experience of widowhood in late life. These include 1) physiological aging, 2) heterogeneity in aging, 3) successful aging, 4) emotion-regulation in old age, 5) aging and self-concept, 6) convoy theory, 7) person-environment fit, 8) everyday intelligence, and 9) lifespan theory. Each of these topics provides useful insights into age-related change in the meaning and consequences of the death, and into one's continuing motivation and capacity to adapt.

Age-Related Changes in Physiological Functioning

In combination, the physiological consequences of normal aging and a disease process substantially alter one's capacity to cope with significant life stressors, including bereavement and widowhood. Acknowledging immense diversity, older persons experience cumulative degeneration across the major biological systems (e.g., cardiovascular, skeletal, immune, endocrine, sensory, and central nervous system; Hayflick, 1994). Such changes impact important areas of physiological and cognitive function (strength, endurance, ability to walk, metabolic function, lung function, vision, hearing, waste removal, resistance to disease, memory, and so on). They result in a greater incidence of chronic illness and disability, and diminished adaptive reserves and capacity for self-repair (Rowe, 1985). And increased disability in later life increases rapidly as a predictor of social isolation (Johnson & Troll, 1994).

Increased Diversity in Resources/Competence/Health Experience

Although the elderly are often viewed in stereotypic terms, adult development and aging are actually associated with increased variability in physical, social, and psychological experience. Genetically, we begin life with a unique mix of traits and possibilities. Thereafter, our development is differentially influenced by a wide range of biological and environmental variables. In late adulthood, any age-related declines in function, well-being, or performance also appear to reflect substantial individual variability (Hayflick 1994).

Older adults also exhibit highly diverse reactions to the death of a spouse. Reactions range from being able to take the experience in stride, learning new skills, and adjusting quite well in time, to those who are devastated by the experience (Lund, Caserta, & Dimond, 1993). Important predictors of response include time since the death, intensity of initial psychological reactions (depression, anxiety, physical complaints), and the enduring competencies and traits one brings to the situation (e.g., self-esteem). In addition, individuals vary in the length of time it takes to adapt to widowhood. Factors likely to influence this process include intensity of spousal attachment and dependency, experience of concurrent and cumulative losses in old age, extent to which the death provided gains, e.g., relief for the deceased from lingering pain, or relief for the widow from caregiver burden (Blieszner & Hatvany, 1996). There is also considerable diversity of reaction within individuals, in that a recent widow may function well in some areas of her life, but report lingering loneliness, depression, inability to perform certain activities of daily living (e.g., shopping, home maintenance), and so on (Lund, Caserta, & Dimond, 1993).

Successful Aging

Increasing heterogeneity in old age has resulted in attention to those older adults who appear to be aging more successfully than the norm, and who may be more resilient to the stresses of old age, including bereavement and widowhood. The literature suggests that criteria for successful aging be broadly construed, to include indicators of the quality of later life (e.g., personal control, life satisfaction, social competence) in addition to the more objective indicators of physiological and cognitive function (Baltes & Baltes, 1990). A central theme in this research concerns the identification of modifiable factors that predict avoidance of disease and disability, high cognitive and physical functioning, and continued active engagement with life (Rowe & Kahn, 1997). Such factors of course include available external supports as a buffer to the consequences of decline, disability, or stress. But they also incorporate a sense for older adults' capacity for continued growth and positive change (plasticity), even in the face of age-related decline or stress. A wide variety of self-directed lifestyle changes (e.g., in diet, exercise, continued social and cognitive involvements), and interventions (e.g., therapeutic, educational, social) appear to be useful in this regard. Rowe and Kahn (1997, p. 439) have therefore proposed that "resilience" be added to our list of criteria for successful aging, to encourage a research focus on the speed and effectiveness of an older person's recovery from disabling physical, cognitive, or social events, in order to learn more about the circumstances under which we should expect such resilience. In this connection, Wortman and Silver (1990) have proposed that bereavement researchers also should add to their assessments of recovery or adaptation measures of personal growth, ability to cope, and heightened mastery.

Researchers have noted positive changes in the lives of older widowed persons, as they find ways to adapt to their loss. For example, many report having learned important new skills for independent living (Lund, Caserta, & Dimond, 1993). In this process, older widows have also been found to report new areas of self-discovery. They may learn, for example, that they can master new areas of competence, doing their own taxes, managing investments, repairing things around the house. They may also experience a renewed sense of social autonomy and self-direction, for example, selecting new life goals and making new friends. This experience of resilience and accomplishment, then, may provide a sense of increased personal control and meaning in life (Fry, 1998).

Another body of research has focused on strategies that older persons use for life management that contribute to successful aging and resilience in the face of age-related decline or loss. Acknowledging that in the face of age-related change, it becomes more difficult to continue to maintain one's goals and performance levels across all previous domains of endeavor, one such approach involves the processes of selection, optimization, and compensation (SOC; Freund & Baltes, 1998). Selection strategies involve developing priorities regarding one's most important goals and commitments, and then concentrating on these priorities. In the face of loss, the focus goes to realistically adapting one's goals and standards with respect to potential for recovery. Optimization strategies, then, involve a narrowing of attention to one's priorities, increasing skill acquisition, practice, and persistence in the area of these priorities. Finally, compensation strategies focus on redressing areas of age-related loss of competence that would undermine performance in priority areas of life management. These strategies might include acquiring substitute resources or skills, external or prosthetic aids, devoting more time and energy, asking for help, and so on. Use of SOC strategies among older adults has been found to be associated with satisfaction with aging, increased positive emotions, and decreased loneliness (Freund & Baltes, 1998).

Emotion Regulation in Later Life

At the heart of the bereavement reaction, of course, is an emotional reaction to the loss of a loved one. It is therefore especially interesting that recent gerontological research has focused on the relationships between age and affect generally, and on apparent age-related differences in emotional responses to life stressors. There is a growing body of evidence, for example, that in old age, subjective reports of well-being increase, even though this is a time of increased risk for disability, decline, and loss (Mroczek & Kolarz, 1998). A variety of explanations appear feasible.

For example, Aldwin, Sutton, Chiara, and Spiro (1996) found that older persons may appraise life stressors differently, resulting in differences in experienced emotion and in patterns of coping. This study found that older men, as compared to their middle-aged counterparts, reported fewer life problems, and being less challenged or annoyed by recent problems. They were also dealing, to a greater extent, with the deaths of significant people, but were not more likely to view their bereavement experience in terms of threat or loss. Nor were they more likely to adopt active coping strategies. They felt as confident in their ability to cope with any future problems as did men in the middle-aged group.

It has been suggested also that older adults experience a dampening of emotional responsiveness. Lawton, Kleban, Rajagopal, and Dean (1992) found reports among older persons of reactions to fewer worries, but also to fewer pleasures, and reports of fewer positive and negative emotions. Among these older persons, there was also a reduced physiological responsiveness to upset or excitement. This may reflect in part an increased acceptance of the nature of aging, involving for example the onset of chronic and progressive health conditions. It may also be that older people learn with experience how best to prevent or manage late life troubles, and therefore are less often faced with the need for reactive coping (Aldwin et al., 1996). Given the context, this would represent a more effective coping style.

A number of other explanations also seem feasible with respect to ways in which older persons learn to manage their emotions. For example, they may become more adept at using cognitive strategies in regulating their emotions (Carstensen, Gross, & Fung, 1997; Schulz & Heckhausen, 1998). They may alter their goal-standards for coping with stress, they may engage in social comparison primarily with age-peers and with those who have similarly suffered. They may reappraise difficult life events to find positive consequences to balance the negatives. They also appear to selectively reduce the size of their social networks, retaining contact with emotionally close members, but dropping contact with peripheral members, the result being an increase in the proportion of emotionally close persons in their network. Such shifts in coping style are consistent with Shulz and Heckhausen's (1998) lifespan theory of control. This theory suggests that in our youth we have available more resources with which to exert primary (instrumental) control over our environment, but that in old age, the emphasis shifts toward secondary control, involving for the most part adaptive cognitive processes that focus internally. They note that as we age, the general pattern of our experience is one of increasing losses and decreasing new positive experiences. It is therefore adaptive that our regulatory systems would diminish negative affective responses and increase positive responses.

Aging, Widowhood and Self-Concept

Lopata (1996) views the reconstruction of one's self-concept as a primary task of adaptation to spousal loss. She notes, however, that widows lose a number of social role identities (wife, married friend in couple-companionate relationships, economic partner, and so on). It is important, therefore, to begin to develop new social connections and roles that are rewarding and provide a sense of place and identity. However, older widows, especially, would be expected to have fewer options in this regard, and Lopata would view them to be at increased risk for disengagement and isolation.

Psychologists have viewed this issue in terms of the structure and function of one's self-concept. Markus and Herzog (1991), for example, describe the self-concept as containing schemas for one's past, current, and possible or future selves. These self-schemas are knowledge structures for how we construe and evaluate ourselves in our various and distinct social and life roles. They provide a sense of place and identity, they enable us to organize and interpret our experience. They incorporate an integrated sense for where we've been, who and what we are; and our possible selves, especially, reflect expectations and images regarding who we would like to become and who we are afraid of becoming. In this connection, then, and consistent with Lopata's proposal above, it is instructive that evidence is accumulating to suggest that individuals with a potentially more complex self-concept, containing a greater variety of current and possible selves are less threatened by the loss of one of their important identities (e.g., spouse). To the extent that one's social roles and identities become more constricted in later life, conjugal loss should become a more threatening event (Markus & Herzog, 1991). Here, too, however, a considerable literature has emerged regarding the adaptive functions that are centered in the self. As we age, we increasingly acquire life-experience and self-understanding, and the maturity of perspective that allows greater comfort in the process of sifting among alternatives, finding ways to compensate for loss, and engaging in the kinds of emotion-regulation processes described above (Markus & Herzog, 1991).

Convoy Theory

The concept of the convoy (Antonucci, 1989) suggests that a person's social network of support can be understood in terms of a multilayered matrix of individuals who provide unique types of support that are, in varying degrees, independent of role-specificity. Those whose relationship is less role-dependent, specifically close friends or family, provide help that is more stable than those whose relationship, while no less important to the recipient's well-being and health, is more role-specific and situationally anchored, such as coworkers, neighbors, and health care professionals. Convoys of support vary across persons in a variety of ways, for example, size, density, homogeneity, and stability over time, and persons also vary in terms of their ability to elicit support from others when it is needed.

The importance of social support during bereavement has long been recognized (see Hansson & Carpenter, 1994). However, researchers have not yet focused on the construct of the convoy to more carefully describe and predict widowed persons' functional relationship needs. For example, gender differences in the experience of conjugal bereavement may in part be explained by variations in the convoy of support for widows and widowers (Allen & Hayslip, in press). For men, especially, the social context of widowhood is likely to be more nonnormative (Baltes, 1987). Men's convoys are likely to differ substantially from those of women. For example, they are less likely to be defined by same-sex age peers and more likely to be composed of children, grandchildren, or health care professionals. Also, the support provided by this convoy has to be more timely to be effective, given men's more advanced age, poorer health, and greater isolation at their wives' deaths. Moreover, being able to describe changes in the convoy over time (predeath versus postdeath) may provide insight into the course of bereavement adjustment. There may also be important differences in the convoys of those persons' whose bereavement adjustment is complicated and those for whom bereavement adjustment is less so.

In these respects, Carstensen's (1992) Socioemotional selectivity theory may elucidate the nature of changes in the convoy over time for widowed persons. This theory predicts that as individuals age, they narrow their social networks so that emotional resources are more carefully utilized with close friends and family (Carstensen, 1992, Carstensen, Gross, & Fung, 1997). Lansford and Sherman (1997) found older persons to be more satisfied with the current composition (size) of their support networks than younger persons. These findings, and those of Carstensen (1992), however, were not controlled for either bereavement status or gender. Campbell and Silverman (1996) however, found widowers to be less likely than widows to have close intimate relationships that could otherwise serve as a buffer against loneliness and isolation. Because women tend to outlive their husbands, widowers are less likely to have friends whose wives have died. (Cook & Oltjenbruns, 1998). Moreover, widows are more likely than widowers to report a larger number of persons in their social group and to feel more positively toward such persons (Farberow, Gallagher-Thompson, Gilewski,

& Thompson, 1992). Further analyses of changes in the support convoys of older widowed persons over time (with an eye to how they choose to include or exclude others, and to how persons are added or removed due to ill health, relocation, or death) and of the consequences of such changes could be especially interesting.

Person–Environment Fit

The construct of person–environment fit (Lawton, 1989) suggests that personal adjustment and everyday functioning among older persons is best understood in light of the match between the demandedness or press of their environment (novelty, complexity, rate of change) and the skills and resources of the individual. In this respect, the environment can enhance functioning by providing the opportunity for personal growth, the improvement of one's skills, or the broadening of relationships. Alternatively, for older persons with impoverished cognitive, interpersonal, or health resources, the environment can serve as a buffer if its demands are properly calibrated. In this respect, successful adjustment to the primary loss of a relationship through death, and to secondary losses in one's role in the community, financial, or health status, lifestyle, and other relationships requires that adequate person–environment fits be maintained. The above losses may disrupt this balance, and for persons whose physical or mental health is directly tied to support from their former spouses or family, one might predict that bereavement would have a more deleterious effect on postdeath adjustment and functioning. In this light, widowed persons' functioning over time has been explained in terms of the joint effects of experienced competence, perceived impact of the loss, and perceived resources (Hayslip, Allen, & McCoy-Roberts, in press), a finding which is consistent with a person-environment fit perspective. As person-environment fits may be less than optimal, widowed persons may also have to cope with such mismatches. Klass (1996) has discussed bereavement in terms of efforts to reconstruct the meaning of the loss, and by implication, continuous attempts to restore person-environment congruence. Thus, the perception of the loss as irreplaceable (Stenback, 1980) as well as the quality of attachment to the deceased spouse must be (re)defined (Ainsworth, 1989; Bowlby, 1980). Critical to understanding this process is the appraisal of the meaning of the death in terms of one's ongoing view of the self and the world, which must also be considered as dynamic in nature (see Pearlin & Skaff, 1995).

Everyday Intelligence

Relative to Piagetian and psychometric views of intelligence in later life (Blackburn & Papalia, 1992; Schaie, 1994), the study of everyday intelligence may play a key role in understanding how bereaved persons deal with the many and varied ill-structured problems and choices confronting them both before and after a spouse's death, many of which are highly personal and emotional in nature (see Blanchard-Fields, 1986). Because many such events are ill-structured (Sinnott, 1989), they may require the use of cognitive skills that are qualitative in nature, wherein one must gather information, derive and test hypotheses, and respond to problems with the knowledge that the resulting solutions are temporary (Baltes, Smith, Staudinger, & Sowarka, 1990; Sinnott, 1996). Everyday intelligence is adaptive and dynamic in nature. It may therefore allow widows and widowers to successfully appraise and act upon choices regarding end-of-life issues, funeral planning, resuming a career, returning to school, remarriage, or raising one's grandchildren. Each of these choices is by definition contextual (Lerner, 1996). Equally important is the widowed person's estimates of the adequacy of his or her everyday skills (Schaie, Willis, & O'Hanlon, 1994).

A second and somewhat narrower view of everyday intelligence reflects an emphasis on Instrumental Activities of Daily Living (IADLs; money management, medication and phone use, housekeeping, using transportation; Schaie & Willis, 1999). For widowed persons, the exercise of everyday competence defined in this manner has obvious everyday functional benefits in terms of promoting independence and self-efficacy in the face of threats to one's well-being and autonomy.

Lifespan Theory

A last perspective relevant to widowhood in later life is that of lifespan development (Baltes, 1987; Baltes, Reese, & Nesselroade, 1986). This perspective emphasizes emerging individual differences that reflect a diversity of normative and nonnormative developmental influences. It calls attention to bereavement risk factors and outcomes in terms of their complexity and relationship to one another, rather than singly or in isolation. It also suggests the possibility of historical shifts in the experience of widowhood in light of demographic changes in longevity, mortality, gender roles, and perceptions of appropriate bereavement behaviors in later life (see Kalish, 1976). One implication, then, is that generational changes in the experience of widowhood might require new sets of adaptive skills for future generations of men and women whose spouses have died (see Schaie & Willis, 1999).

☐ Conclusion

We have proposed in this chapter, that in later life, defining life events and stressors such as becoming widowed must be viewed in their developmental context, and in the context of the aging experience more broadly. Three further points deserve emphasis. First, the emotional experience of older persons (including reactions to the loss of a spouse) is at once similar, yet different from that of younger persons (Butler, Lewis, & Sunderland, 1998). Such losses tend to cluster in old age, they may differ in their implications for the widowed person's social and economic status, and older persons are likely to have fewer adaptive reserves. However, recent research now suggests that age brings new perspective on loss and an emergence of adaptive coping responses. Second, it will be important for researchers to take into account the contextual nuances of late life that help to define for an older adult the meaning and implications of the death of a spouse. This will require, for example, greater attention to the changing nature of supportive social relationships across the lifespan, and to the increasing importance with age of the person–environment fit. With increasing age, we become less adaptable in the face of a support network or environment that poorly matches our needs. Finally it is important to remember that older people are highly heterogeneous with respect to their health and psychological status, and also their response to life stressors like widowhood. Many older adults age quite successfully, even in the face of late life adversity, and from them we have much to learn.

☐ References

Ainsworth, M. (1989). Attachments beyond infancy. *American Psychologist, 44*, 709–716.

Aldwin, C. M., Sutton, K. J., Chiara, G., & Spiro, A. (1996). Age differences in stress, coping, and appraisal: Findings from the Normative Aging Study. *Journal of Gerontology: Psychological Sciences, 51B*, 4, P179–P188.

Allen, S., & Hayslip, B. (in press). Research on gender differences in bereavement outcome: A model of experienced competence. In D. Lund (Ed.), *Men coping with grief*. Amityville, NY: Baywood.

Antonucci, T. (1989). Understanding adult social relationships. In K. Kreppner & R. L. Lerner (Eds.), *Family systems and life span development* (pp. 303–317). Hillsdale, NJ: Erlbaum.

Baltes, P. B. (1987). Theoretical propositions of life span developmental psychology: On the dynamics of growth and decline. *Developmental Psychology, 23*, 611–626.

Baltes, P., B., & Baltes, M. M. (1990). Psychological perspectives on successful aging: The model of selective optimization with compensation. In P. B. Baltes & M. M. Baltes (Eds.), *Successful aging: Perspectives from the behavioral sciences* (pp. 1–34). Cambridge, MA: Cambridge University Press.

Baltes, P. B., Reese, H. W., & Nesselroade, J. R. (1986). *Life span developmental psychology: Introduction to research methods*. Hillsdale, NJ: Erlbaum.

Baltes, P. B., Smith, J., Staudinger, U., & Sowarka, D. (1990). Wisdom: One facet of successful aging? In M. Perlmutter (Ed.), *Late life potential* (pp. 63–82). Washington, DC: The Gerontological Society of America.

Blackburn, J. A., & Papalia, D. (1992). The study of adult cognition from a Piagetian perspective. In R. Sternberg & C. Berg (Eds.), *Intellectual development* (pp. 141–160). New York: Cambridge University Press.

Blanchard-Fields, F. (1986). Reasoning in adolescence and adults on social dilemmas varying in emotional saliency: An adult developmental perspective. *Psychology and Aging, 1*, 325–333.

Blieszner, R., & Hatvany, L. E. (1996). Diversity in the experience of late-life widowhood. *Journal of Personal and Interpersonal Loss, 1*, 199–211.

Bowlby, J. (1980). *Attachment and loss: Loss, sadness, and depression* (Vol. 3). New York: Basic Books.

Butler, R. N., Lewis, M. I., & Sunderland, T. (1998). *Aging and mental health*. Needham Heights, MA: Allyn & Bacon.

Byrne, G. J. A., & Raphael, B. (1994). A longitudinal study of bereavement phenomena in recently widowed elderly men. *Psychological Medicine, 24*(2), 411–421.

Campbell, S., & Silverman, P. R. (1996). *Widower: When men are left alone*. Amityville, NY: Baywood.

Carstensen, L. L. (1992). Social and emotional patterns in adulthood: Support for socioemotional selectivity theory. *Psychology and Aging, 7*, 331–338.

Carstensen, L. L., Gross, J. J., & Fung, H. H. (1997). The social context of emotional experience. *Annual Review of Gerontology and Geriatrics, 17*, 325–352.

Cook, A. S., & Oltjenbruns, K. A. (1998). *Dying and grieving: Life span and family perspectives*. Ft. Worth, TX: Harcourt Brace.

Farberow, N. L., Gallagher-Thompson, D., Gilewski, E., & Thompson, L. (1992). The role of social supports in the bereavement process of surviving spouses of suicides and natural deaths. *Suicide and Life Threatening Behavior, 22*, 107–124.

Freund, A. M., & Baltes, P., B. (1998). Selection, optimization, and compensation as strategies of life management: Correlations with subjective indicators of successful aging. *Psychology and Aging, 13*, 531–543.

Fry, P. S. (1998). Spousal loss in late life: A 1-year follow-up of perceived changes in life meaning and psychosocial functioning following bereavement. *Journal of Personal and Interpersonal Loss, 3*, 369–391.

Hansson, R. O., & Carpenter, B. N. (1994). *Relationships in old age*. New York: Guilford.

Hayflick, L. (1994). *How and why we age*. New York: Ballantine.

Hayslip, B., Allen, S., & McCoy-Roberts, L. (in press). The role of gender in a three-year longitudinal study of bereavement: A test of the experienced competence model. In D. Lund (Ed.), *Men coping with grief*. Amityville, NY: Baywood.

Johnson, C. L., & Troll, L. E. (1994). Constraints and facilitators to friendships in late late life. *The Gerontologist, 34*, 79–87.

Kalish (1976). Death and dying in a social context. In R. Binstock & E. Shanas (Eds), *Handbook of aging and the social sciences* (pp. 483–506). New York: Van Nostrand Reinhold.

Kemp, B. (1985). Rehabilitation and the older adult. In J. E. Birren & K. W. Schaie (Eds.), *Handbook of the psychology of aging* (2nd ed., pp. 647–663). New York: Van Nostrand Reinhold.

Klass, D. (1996). Grief in Eastern culture: Japanese ancestor worship. In D. Klass, P. Silverman, & S. Nickman (Eds.), *Continuing bonds: New understandings of grief* (pp. 59–70). Washington, DC: Taylor & Francis.

Lansford, J. E., & Sherman, A. M. (1997, August). *Satisfaction with social networks: A test of socioemotional selectivity theory*. Paper presented at the Annual Convention of the American Psychological Association. Chicago, Illinois.

Lawton, M. P. (1989). Behavior-relevant ecological factors. In K. W. Schaie & C. Schooler (Eds.), *Social structure and aging: Psychological processes* (pp. 57–78). Hillsdale, NJ: Erlbaum.

Lawton, M. P., Kleban M. H., Rajagopal, D., & Dean, J. (1992). Dimensions of affective experience in three age groups. *Psychology and Aging, 7*, 171–184.

Lerner, R. (1996). *Concepts and theories of human development*. New York: Random House.

Lopata, H. Z. (1996). *Current widowhood: Myths & realities*. Thousand Oaks, CA: Sage.

Lund, D. A., Caserta, M. S., & Dimond, M. R. (1993). The course of spousal bereavement. In M. S. Stroebe, W. Stroebe, & R. O. Hansson (Eds.), *Handbook of bereavement: Theory, research, and intervention* (pp. 240–254). Cambridge, MA: Cambridge University Press.

Markus, H. R., & Herzog, A. R. (1991). The role of self-concept in aging. *Annual Review of Gerontology and Geriatrics, 11*, 110–143.

Mendes De Leon, C. F., Kasl, S. V., & Jacobs, S. (1994). A prospective study of widowhood and changes in symptoms of depression in a community sample of the elderly. *Psychological Medicine, 24*(3), 613–624.

McCrae, R. R., & Costa, P. T. (1988). Psychological resilience among widowed men and women: A 10-year follow-up of a national sample. *Journal of Social Issues, 44*, 129–142.

Morgan, D., Carder, P., & Neal, M. (1997). Are some relationships more useful than others? The value of similar others in the networks of recent widows. *Journal of Social and Personal Relationships, 14*(6), 745–759.

Moss, M. S., Moss, S. Z., & Hansson, R. O. (in press). Bereavement and old age. In M. S. Stroebe, W. Stroebe, R. O. Hansson, & Schut, H. (Eds.), *Handbook of bereavement research: Consequences, coping, and care*. Washington, DC: American Psychological Association.

Mroczek, D. K., & Kolarz, C. M. (1998). The effect of age on positive and negative affect: A developmental perspective on happiness. *Journal of Personality and Social Psychology, 75*, 1333–1349.

O'Bryant, S. L., & Hansson, R. O. (1995). Widowhood. In R. Blieszner & V. H. Bedford (Eds.), *Handbook of aging and the family* (pp. 440–458). Westport, CT: Greenwood.

Pearlin, L. I., & Skaff, M. M. (1995). Stressors and adaptation in late life. In M. Gatz (Ed.), *Emerging issues in mental health and aging* (pp. 97–123). Washington, DC: American Psychological Association.

Prigerson, H. G., Frank, E., Kasl, S. V., Reynolds, III, C. F., Anderson, B., Zubenko, G. S., Houck, P. R., George, Ch. J., & Kupfer, D. J. (1995). Complicated grief and bereavement-related depression as distinct disorders: Preliminary empirical validation in elderly bereaved spouses. *American Journal of Psychiatry, 152*(1), 22–30.

Remondet, J. H., Hansson, R. O., Rule, B., & Winfrey, G. (1987). Rehearsal for widowhood. *Journal of Social and Clinical Psychology, 5*, 285–297.

Rosenbloom, C. A., & Whittington, F. J. (1993). The effects of bereavement on eating behaviors and nutrient intakes in elderly widowed persons. *Journal of Gerontology: Social Sciences, 48*, S223–S229.

Rowe, J. W. (1985). Health care of the elderly. *New England Journal of Medicine, 312*(13), 827–835.

Rowe, J. W., & Kahn, R. L. (1997). Successful aging. *The Gerontologist, 37*, 433–440.

Sanders, C. M. (1981). Comparison of younger and older spouses in bereavement outcome. *Omega, 11*, 217–232.

Sanders, C. M. (1993). Risk factors in bereavement outcome. In M. S. Stroebe, W. Stroebe, & R. O. Hansson (Eds.), *Handbook of bereavement: Theory, research and intervention* (pp. 256–267). Cambridge, UK: Cambridge University Press.

Schaie, K. W. (1994). The course of adult intellectual development. *American Psychologist, 49*, 304–313.

Schaie, K. W., & Willis, S. L.(1999). Theories of everyday competence and aging. In V. L. Bengtson & K. W. Schaie (Eds.), *Handbook of theories of aging* (pp. 174–195). New York: Springer.

Schaie, K. W., Willis, S. L., & O'Hanlon, A. M. (1994). Perceived intellectual performance change over seven years. *Journal of Gerontology: Psychological Sciences, 49*, P108–P118.

Schulz, R., & Heckhausen, J. (1998). Emotion and control: A life-span perspective. *Annual review of gerontology and geriatrics, 17*, 185–205.

Sinnott, J. D. (1989). A model for the solution of ill-structured problems: Implications for everyday and abstract problem solving. In J. D. Sinnott (Ed.), *Everyday problem solving: Theory and applications* (pp. 72-99). New York: Praeger.

Sinnott, J. D. (1996). The developmental approach: Postformal thought as adaptive skill. In F. Blanchard-Fields & T. Hess (Eds.), *Perspectives on cognitive change in adulthood and aging* (pp. 358–386). New York: McGraw-Hill.

Stenback, A.(1980). Depression and suicidal behavior in old age. In J. E. Birren & R. B. Sloane (Eds.), *Handbook of mental health and aging* (pp. 616–652). Englewood Cliffs, NJ: Prentice-Hall.

Stroebe, W., & Stroebe, M. (1987). *Bereavement and health*. New York: Cambridge University Press.

Stroebe, M. S., Stroebe, W., & Hansson, R. O. (1993). *Handbook of bereavement: Theory, research, and intervention*. New York: Cambridge University Press.

Thompson, L. W., Gallagher-Thompson, D., Futterman, A., Gilewski, M. J., & Peterson, J. (1991). The effects of late-life spousal bereavement over a 30-month interval. *Psychology and Aging, 6*, 434–441.

U.S. Census Bureau (1999). *Sixty-five plus in the United States*. [On-line]. Available: www.census.gov/socdemo/www/agebrief.html

Weiss, R. S. (1993). Loss and recovery. In M. S. Stroebe, W. Stroebe, & R. O. Hansson (Eds.), *Handbook of bereavement: Theory, research and intervention* (pp. 271–284). Cambridge, UK: Cambridge University Press.

Wells, Y. D., & Kendig, H. L. (1997). Health and well-being of spouse caregivers and the widowed. *The Gerontologist, 37*, 666–674.

Wortman, C. B., & Silver, R. C. (1990). Successful mastery of bereavement and widowhood: A life-course perspective. In P. B. Baltes & M. M. Baltes (Eds.), *Successful aging: Perspectives from the behavioral sciences* (pp. 225–264). Cambridge, UK: Cambridge University Press.

Brock Boekhout
Susan S. Hendrick
Clyde Hendrick

The Loss of Loved Ones: The Impact of Relationship Infidelity

Bob looked out the window of the plane at the wispy clouds floating by and the green Midwestern farms thousands of feet below. He and Emily had been looking forward to this trip for so long. What an adventure—a week in San Francisco to celebrate their 30th wedding anniversary. The real adventure was not the trip, however, but the 30 years they had spent together. This anniversary was a miracle—a miracle that almost didn't happen. Although it had been nearly 20 years since he had told Emily of his affair with an office coworker, he had never forgotten the pain on her face or the icy anger that followed. That was a very difficult time for both of them. But somehow, against all odds, they had worked through the pain, the anger, the sense of betrayal, until they forged a bond that had lasted 30 years. What a celebration this was!

For many people in the United States, their emotional and psychological well-being is often greatly reliant on the satisfaction derived from a committed relationship with a significant other. People in committed relationships (exclusive dating, cohabitation, and marriage) appear to have a preference for romantic relationships that are exclusive. That is to say, people expect to have many of their needs (e.g., emotional and sexual intimacy) and the needs of their partner met solely within the relational bond. Violations of this expectation for exclusivity will likely have a significant impact on both members of the relationship, as in the case of Bob and Emily. Most of us know Bob—or Emily. Some of us *are* Bob—or Emily. Yet probably many more of us know of people less fortunate than Bob and Emily, people whose relationships did not survive the anguish of unfaithfulness. Why are people faithful or unfaithful? What are the effects of unfaithfulness? Can people recover from the pain of unfaithfulness? These are a few of the questions explored in the current chapter.

Humans are social beings, drawn into groupings and pairings by a need to belong (Baumeister & Leary, 1995). Though the distal causes of such bonding may well be

Parts of this chapter are drawn from the dissertation of the first author and from: Relationship Infidelity: A Loss Perspective, by B. A. Boekhout, S. S. Hendrick, & C. Hendrick, 1999, *Journal of Personal and Interpersonal Loss.*

evolutionary in nature (e.g., Mellen, 1981), facilitating pair bonding, reproduction, and provisioning of the young, as well as defense of and by the group, the proximal evidence of bonding is palpable. We live it every day. Lovers, partners, family, and friends—all are important to our daily well-being as well as our very survival.

The intense, hard-wired nature of our bonds with others is evidenced dramatically in romantic, partnered, sexual relationships. It is in these relationships, and in our relationship partners, that we put our physical, emotional, and economic resources as well as our trust, and hopes for the future. And it is the loss or feared loss of these aspects of life that make infidelity such a powerful type of loss.

☐ Conceptualizing Loss

Janoff-Bulman (1992) proposed a particularly useful theoretical perspective on trauma and loss, one that lends itself well to an examination of infidelity. Janoff-Bulman and her colleagues (Janoff-Bulman, 1992; Janoff-Bulman & Frantz, 1996; Morgan & Janoff-Bulman, 1994) discuss the aftermath of trauma as the loss of illusions. Based on our earliest experiences as infants and young children, we develop fundamental assumptions or core representations about the world (Janoff-Bulman, 1992). "These fundamental assumptions reside at the core of our inner world: (a) my world is benevolent, (b) my world is meaningful, and (c) I am worthy" (Janoff-Bulman & Frantz, 1996, p. 135). Based on these assumptions, we overestimate the likelihood of positive events happening to us, even as we underestimate the likelihood of experiencing negative life events. That is how assumptions become illusions.

These positive, overgeneralized assumptions are resistant to change, even in the face of overwhelming disconfirming evidence. Indeed, research by Gluhoski and Wortman (1996) revealed that people's world views were only partially influenced by losses such as life-threatening illness or the death of a loved one. People who had incurred such losses perceived themselves as more vulnerable than others who had not experienced traumatic losses, and also reported less positive views of the self. However, aspects of their world view concerned with fatalism (life experiences as predestined and thus unavoidable) and justice (the world as essentially fair) were not affected by significant losses (Gluhoski & Wortman, 1996).

Stories abound of well-meaning persons who attempt to tell a friend about the infidelity of the friend's relationship partner, only to be met with incredulity, denial, and a tendency to blame the messenger. Part of this resistance to changing our assumptions is a recognition that at some level, acceptance of a trauma (in this case, the partner's unfaithfulness) means that our world (i.e., our assumptions or illusions) will never be the same again. There is terror in recognizing some basic uncertainties in the world, because such recognition emphasizes our personal vulnerability (Janoff-Bulman, 1992). Yet, this very recognition appears to be necessary for our working through and recovering from traumatic loss.

To maintain a balanced perspective, it is important to highlight the considerable usefulness of our positive assumptions or illusions about the world. They feed our optimism, undergird our hopefulness, and augment the quality of our lives. These assumptions are not by definition problematic; rather, it is the overgeneralizing of the assumptions, the lack of qualifiers to the positivity of our assumptions, that can blind us and keep us unprepared for trauma and loss (Janoff-Bulman, 1992).

The relevance of Janoff-Bulman's (1992) fundamental assumptions to the conceptualization of an intimate relationship is obvious when we transform her assumptions into relationship terms: My partner is benevolent, my relationship is meaningful, and I am worthy. These are the beliefs governing many relationships; however, at the time that one relationship partner learns of the other's infidelity, the statements become: My partner is a betrayer, my relationship is meaningless, and I am worthless. It is then that one's loss of faith is dramatic, one's illusions are torn, and one's world is turned upside down (Boekhout, Hendrick, & Hendrick, 1999).

Part of this extreme sense of loss due to a partner's unfaithfulness is because of all that we have committed to our partner. As noted earlier, we have very likely been physically and emotionally intimate with our partner, displaying a vulnerability that is reserved only for someone very close and trusted. We may also have committed ourselves to a partner economically, sharing our resources and even sacrificing our own wants and needs in order to help a partner achieve some important objective (e.g., finish college, open their own business). The reason we invest so much energy into our partner and our relationship is that we trust our partner to care for us as we care for her or him. So trust is a key factor for intimacy (e.g., Holmes & Rempel, 1989). And part of that trust is a hope for and belief in a future for us, our partner, and our relationship.

But hope may be shattered when we learn of a partner's infidelity. No longer does a future together seem assured or even possible. No longer do we believe we can trust our partner. Our physical and emotional intimacy seems a sham—we have been betrayed. Our personal and economic sacrifices seem at best naive and at worst, we feel used. How could this have happened? What do we do next?

Relationships are both reality and illusion; they include what we have, what we believe we have, and what we hope we have. But when a partner's infidelity becomes apparent to us, these illusions are jarred and often lost. It is within the context of relational illusions and their loss that the current chapter considers issues of relationship infidelity.

This general theory of loss provides a framework to consider infidelity and other types of extradyadic involvements—how they occur, why they occur, and what we believe about them. Research has shown that many people believe that extrarelationship sexual activities are unacceptable. However, there is a lack of consensus over which types of nonsexual involvements are acceptable. These emotional and sexual involvements often have negative personal and relational consequences, including a sense of loss. Studies have also found that women and men have different types of, reasons for, and reactions to extrarelationship involvements. Finally, the accuracy of people's perceptions regarding the meaning of their partner's infidelity has been shown to have important implications for the outcome of the committed relationship. These are the issues of loss with respect to relationship infidelity that we consider in the following sections.

☐ Infidelity and Extrarelationship Involvement

Relationship commitment does not automatically imply relationship exclusivity. Yet, most people behave as if such exclusivity is implied. Before examining facets of infidelity, it is useful to consider briefly some possible hypotheses as to why most humans prefer exclusivity in their romantic relationships.

Theoretical Reasons for Exclusivity

Specialness and Sharing. An exclusive relationship provides a very unique and unifying context in which partners share intimate aspects of their lives with each other in ways that are not expressed or experienced with anyone else (Weis & Felton, 1987). This hypothesis is supported by the finding that over 90% of people across the world get married at least once during their life (Buss, 1985). Partners are interdependent, attempting to meet each other's needs in a balanced, reciprocal relationship (Hupka et al., 1985). They receive attention, affirmation, and satisfaction from each other, and their special bond acts as a buffer, protecting the relationship from negative external factors (Eldridge, 1983).

Mate Guarding and Jealousy. Shackelford and Buss (1997) noted that partners who display either excessive mate guarding or no mate guarding are using ineffective strategies that lead to greater relationship dissatisfaction. Thus, partners need to practice some moderate level of mate guarding to show that the mates are of value and that the guarders are invested in the relationship. Furthermore, it appears that some mate guarding tactics produce greater relationship satisfaction than others. Tactics that make the relationship more attractive (e.g., giving gifts, expressing love) produce greater relationship satisfaction, particularly in women. On the other hand, tactics that impose or threaten to impose costs on the partner (e.g., emotional manipulation, threat of infidelity) are more likely to lower relationship satisfaction. Thus, an optimal level of mate guarding with the proper strategies will help evoke feelings of relationship satisfaction in exclusive relationships. According to evolutionary theory, unsuccessful attempts to combat infidelity will likely lead to lower reproductive success, limiting people's ability to pass on their genes (Buss, 1994).

Jealousy has some similarity to mate guarding. Jealousy is evoked when a partner's behavior threatens the specialness or even the existence of the relationship (Bringle & Boebinger, 1990). Similarly, Hansen (1985) reported that there are two components that must be present in order to provoke feelings of jealousy in couples: Partners have to value the relationship, and they must see their partner's behavior as violating their own definition of the relationship. Romantic jealousy has been associated with threats to the primary relationship as well as threats to one's self-esteem, due to the partner's selection of another person over oneself (Nadler & Dotan, 1992). Diminished self-esteem can be a key aspect of the feelings of loss that may occur in response to a partner's infidelity. Buunk (1984) reported that the level of intensity of spouses' jealous reactions was determined, in part, by the attributions that they made for the causes of their partners' extramarital sexual involvement.

The relationship between jealousy and attitudes toward exclusivity is a serious issue due to the potential consequences of jealousy, particularly male sexual jealousy. Sexual jealousy of husbands is the most frequent cause of violence against their wives (Buss, 1994). It is a powerful emotion that has often led men to kill their partners and male rivals. Historically, infidelity could be punishable by death, and many contemporary societies across the world still accept the killing of an unfaithful spouse as justified (Buss; 1994; Johnson, 1972). "In Texas until 1974, for example, it was legal for a husband to kill his wife and her lover if he did so while the adulterers were engaging in the act of intercourse; their murder was considered a reasonable response to a powerful provocation" (Buss, 1994, p. 129). Male sexual jealousy is also a common factor in homicides committed by women defending themselves against men accusing them of being unfaithful. Perhaps the ultimate loss resulting from infidelity is the loss of life.

Incidence of Extrarelationship Involvements

Most studies examining extrarelationship involvements have looked exclusively at extramarital relationships and, in particular, extramarital sexual intercourse. An analysis of the literature indicates that 70% to 85% of Americans disapprove of extramarital sex (Pestrak, Martin, & Martin, 1985). Smith (1994) cited relatively recent data from the General Social Survey (GSS) indicating that approximately 79% of respondents said "that extramarital sexual relations were 'always wrong'" (p. 68). Although some couples have consensual agreements that sanction extrarelationship behaviors with others (i.e., swinging or open marriages), we focus primarily on nonconsensual extrarelationship involvements that violate a partner's expectations for exclusivity in the relationship. The incidence rates of extrarelationship involvements vary from study to study, depending on the sample and the range of behaviors investigated (Thompson, 1983). However, typical of most estimates, a recent survey by Boekhout et al. (1999) found that 59% of college men and 44% of college women who had ever been in a committed relationship reported being sexually or emotionally unfaithful at least once while in the committed relationship. This and similar studies have shown that while the percentages (of unfaithfulness) for men have remained relatively stable since the ground-breaking studies by Kinsey and his colleagues, the percentages for women have risen steadily over the past 50 years (Kinsey, Pomeroy, & Martin, 1948; Kinsey, Pomeroy, Martin, & Gebhard, 1953). Kinsey and his colleagues found that approximately half of all married men and a quarter of all married women had engaged in extramarital intercourse by the age of 40. Thus, the rates of extrarelationship involvements for women are catching up to the rates for men, particularly when both sexual and emotional involvements are included.

As noted earlier, reported incidence rates do vary. For example, in a large scale study of U.S. sexual practices (Laumann, Gagnon, Michael, & Michaels, 1994), "Over 90 percent of the women and over 75 percent of the men in every cohort report(ed) fidelity within their marriage, over its entirety" (p. 214). However, Thompson (1983) contended that most reported incidence rates are conservative estimates for at least two reasons: social desirability in reporting and the inability to ascertain lifetime incidence. However, these conservative estimates illustrate the contradiction that exists: Whereas the majority of people disapprove of these relationships, a sizable percentage of people still participate in them, and without their partner's consent (Thompson, 1983). Accordingly, this type of relational behavior may pose a real threat to the primary relationship.

Attitudes Toward Extrarelationship Involvements

Although the majority of people disapprove of extramarital *sexual* relationships, studies have found that some extramarital situations are more acceptable than others. Weis and his colleagues (Weis & Felton, 1987; Weis & Slosnerick, 1981) found that approximately 80% of the participants in their two studies reported that going to a movie or spending an evening in the living room with an opposite-sex friend while their spouses were out of town was acceptable, but as the activities became more suggestive of sexual behavior (e.g., spending a few days at a secluded cabin), the percentage of participants who rated the activity as acceptable declined. Activities that included specific sexual behaviors were accepted by 4% to 15% of the participants. Those who were most accepting of the sexual and nonsexual extramarital relationships were men and individuals who disassociated sex, love, and marriage (Weis & Slosnerick, 1981). This research also found roughly equal percentages of participants who accepted or rejected some nonsexual activities such as having dinner at a secluded place or dancing to the stereo. Thus, although the majority of participants in both studies believed that sexual behaviors should be exclusive to the primary relationship, they were less certain about which *non*sexual extramarital activities were acceptable or not acceptable. The implication of both studies is that partners might come into conflict if they disagree about what activities should be exclusive to their relationship (Weis & Felton, 1987; Weis & Slosnerick, 1981).

In addition, if a partner views a transgression as a strong breach of their personal beliefs, they may terminate the relationship (Roloff & Cloven, 1994). So a couple may need to formulate or reformulate the rules of their relationship so that such behaviors are prevented. It also seems that some people do not want to discuss their attitudes and extrarelationship behaviors in order to avoid hurting their partner and possibly having the relationship terminated (Pestrak et al., 1985). Yet, it is this very secrecy that often has the most negative effects on those who have been deceived (DePaulo & Kashy, 1998). Some affairs are kept secret for a variety of reasons and often for many years. The multitude of lies often produces a feeling of disillusionment (an aspect of loss) in partners who had placed unconditional faith in their cheating mates (Kaslow, 1993).

Models of Extrarelationship Involvement

Since extrarelationship sex is perceived as unacceptable by most people (Pestrak et al., 1985; Weis & Felton, 1987; Weis & Slosnerick, 1981) and since it often has extremely negative consequences (e.g., Boekhout et al., 1999; Reiss, Anderson, & Sponaugle, 1980), it is important to understand the determinants of such behaviors and why many people still participate in them. Further understanding might provide a basis for comprehending other types of relationship exclusivity issues.

There are two primary models that attempt to explain why some married couples choose to engage in nonexclusive behaviors (Thompson, 1984b; Weis & Slosnerick, 1981). According to the deficit model, partners participate in extramarital behavior due to problems in their marriage. For example, Glass and Wright (1985) found that marital dissatisfaction was correlated positively with both sexual and emotional extramarital involvements for men and women, particularly if the individuals were both sexually and emotionally involved. Similarly, Whitehurst (1983) concluded that "since there is a very high probability that most people will not experience the long-term satisfactions anticipated from marriage, many will toy with deviance of some sort to achieve substitute satisfactions" (p. 122). Similar levels of minor and major deviance are likely to be present in other types of committed relationships as well. In addition, compared to married participants, single participants were more likely to believe that they would not engage in extramarital sex, and they were less likely to feel that marital deficits were adequate reasons for such an involvement, suggesting that they may have more idealistic views of marriage that do not fit with reality (Meyering & Epling-McWherter, 1986).

Buunk (1987) also found that, compared to couples who remained intact after one partner's sexual affair, couples who broke up after a partner's affair reported higher levels of dissatisfaction with the primary relationship and more conflict due to the extrarelationship involvement. Additionally, the couples who broke up tended to be involved in extrarelationships that were more often motivated by aggression and deprivation, potentially leading to a greater experience of loss. However, the breakup group did not rate the alternatives to the primary relationship more positively than did the intact group. Therefore, Buunk contended that those who broke up were not pulled away by alternative attractions but were pushed away by conflicts with their partner that resulted from the affair or escalated with the addition of the affair. This result would suggest that few people enter into nonexclusive relationships out of a desire to find better mates. However, Buss (1994) reported that people regularly assess whether potential partners might offer more benefits than the current partner. Either way, both the push and the pull views indicate that there are deficits in the current relationships that lead people to enter into nonexclusive relationships.

According to the personal growth model, spouses engage in extramarital behaviors to enhance their sense of self, not because they are dissatisfied with their marriages (Thompson, 1984b). These partners are interested in self-discovery through sharing a wider range of activities and companions. For example, college students who projected that they expect to engage in extramarital sexual behaviors in the future predicted that such involvements would increase their feelings of independence and inner security while providing them with adventure and greater social status (Bukstel, Roeder, Kilmann, Laughlin, & Sotile, 1978). In his review of extramarital sex literature, Thompson (1983) described three broad categories of predictors of extramarital sexual involvement. They were: social background, marital characteristics, and personal readiness variables. The social background and personal readiness variables include factors that represent the realization and fulfillment of extrarelationship involvement.

Thus, the deficit and personal growth models differentially affect both where the couples focus their efforts at resolving conflicts regarding relationship exclusivity and whether partners experience a sense of loss due to infidelity. The reasons for engaging in these nonexclusive behaviors may also often incorporate some combination of relationship deficit and personal growth in a given relationship.

☐ Justifications for Extrarelationship Behavior

Glass and Wright (1992) delineated four main categories of justifications for having romantic extrarelationship involvements. The first is a sexual category that includes novelty, excitement, and curiosity. The second category, emotional intimacy, is encompassed by intellectual sharing, understanding, companionship, and respect. The researchers noted that the same set of items can be used to describe a close friendship, and it is important to distinguish between this type of friendship and one that crosses into romantic love and other intimate feelings and behaviors. Love justification (category three) includes receiving love and affection and falling in love. Finally, extrinsic motivation (category four) includes reasons such as getting even with the partner and seeking career advancement. Interestingly, only 20% of men and 30% of women disapproved of all reasons as justifications for an extramarital relationship, suggesting that approval is strongly associated with the exact type of justification (Glass & Wright, 1992).

Gender Differences in Justifications

Some strong gender differences seem to be present for the first three justifications. For example, 77% of women and only 43% of men reported that falling in love would be a justification for an extramarital relationship, but 75% of men and only 53% of women reported that sexual excitement would be a satisfactory justification (Glass & Wright, 1992). Glass and Wright (1985) also found that men are more likely to be involved in sexual affairs without emotional involvement, whereas women are more inclined to have greater emotional involvement in their extramarital relationships. However, men and women may add the other component (emotional for men, sexual for women) after the relationship is established. Several studies have shown that women desire a feeling of closeness and affirmation through talking and sharing prior to engaging in sex, and women see the act of sexual intercourse as an extended expression of this already established feeling of togetherness (Bergner & Bergner, 1990; Mansfield, McAllister, & Collard, 1992). On the other hand, men perceive the sexual act as a means for establishing these feelings of closeness, affirmation, and relatedness.

In addition, Glass and Wright (1985) contended that "women appear to approach extramarital involvement from the perspective of their marital relationships, while men appear to approach involvement from a more individualistic perspective" (p. 1115). Women were more likely than men to link their extrarelationship involvements with marital dissatisfaction, which implies that either women enter such relationships only when they are not content with their marriage, or women's deeper extramarital involvement creates greater marital dissatisfaction (Glass & Wright, 1985; Prins, Buunk, & VanYperen, 1993). However, men may view an affair as having little consequence for their primary relationship, because it appears that they are more likely than women to separate sex from love and marriage (Glass & Wright, 1992). Research also shows that men who refrain from extrarelationship sex do so, not because of a lack of desire, but because of their attitudes and beliefs (Pestrak et al., 1985; Prins et al., 1993). Therefore, it appears that their level of marital satisfaction often has little to do with whether or not men have an affair. Women, on the other hand, may believe that they have to have a good reason (e.g., being dissatisfied with the relationship) for engaging in extramarital relationships (Prins et al., 1993). Overall, these findings suggest that women are more likely to subscribe to the deficit model as a reason for nonexclusive behaviors, whereas men are more likely to engage in nonexclusive behaviors for personal growth.

Similar results were also reported by Thompson (1984a). Compared to women, men engaged in significantly more "sexual only" extrarelationship involvements, and women reported more "emotional only" involvements than men, though the difference was not statistically significant. In a recent study, Boekhout et al. (1999) also found that more men than women reported having sexual only involvements, and though the discrepancy was smaller, more women than men reported engaging in extrarelationship involvements that were emotional only. Interestingly, the most common type of involvement reported by women contained both sexual and emotional elements (Boekhout et al., 1999). Glass and Wright (1985, 1992) would suggest that women are becoming more willing to add the sexual component once an emotional involvement is established. In addition, the least common type of involvement reported by women was sexual only; the least common reported by men was emotional only (Boekhout et al., 1999).

Gender differences were also found in Meyering and Epling-McWherter's (1986) proposal of an ongoing decision-making model that people use to determine if they will participate in extramarital sex. The model included preconditions of permissive attitude and opportunity, perceptions of the payoffs and risks of getting involved, and mediating factors of personal meanings and practical considerations that lead to decisions of whether or not to engage in the behaviors. The study found that men were more influenced by the payoffs and were less likely to believe that the risks would occur, and they had more expectations for involvement. On the other hand, women's decision-making was more strongly influenced by the risks that were seen as more destructive and more likely to occur. Women's identities were more associated with their feelings of relatedness to their primary relationship. Men's identities appeared to be more strongly linked to their feelings of autonomy, and "they are more likely to think they can psychologically separate relationships and enhance their identity through experiences and roles which they view as complementary" (Meyering & Epling-McWherter, 1986, p. 126).

Disclosure, Gender, and Justifications

As noted earlier, Pestrak and his colleagues (1985) contended that some people may keep their involvement a secret to protect their partner from hurt feelings because they fear that their partner will not understand why they had the affair. This reason may be particularly poignant for men who fear that their partner will misattribute their extrarelationship activity as a rejection of the primary relationship. Similarly, Boekhout et al. (1999) found that participants' reasons for not telling their partner when they had been unfaithful tended to reflect an effort to protect their partner and their relationship (e.g., "If I would have told her, I knew she would have broken up with me"). Interestingly, more men reported that they did not tell their partner, whereas more women did tell their partner (Boekhout et al., 1999). This is consistent with the finding that, compared to men, women have a greater tendency to disclose (Winstead, Derlega, & Rose, 1997). Reasons for telling their partner centered around feelings of guilt and a desire to make amends and set the record straight (e.g., "Because I felt guilty and I didn't want to keep the secret inside any longer, I wanted him to know") (Boekhout et al., 1999). This may help explain why some people in extrarelationship involvements had lower self-esteem than uninvolved individuals (Sheppard, Nelson, & Andreoli-Mathie, 1995) and why guilt is negatively related to satisfaction with extramarital sex (Spanier & Margolis, 1983). Only three participants told their partner about their infidelities because they wanted to break up (Boekhout et al., 1999), which supports Buunk's (1987) contention that few people are lured away by possible alternatives to being in the relationship, but they may be pushed away by conflicts with their partners after the infidelity is revealed. It is interesting to note that infidelity has been linked to lower self-esteem for both the unfaithful person (Sheppard et al., 1995) and the original partner (Nadler & Dotan, 1992).

☐ Consequences of Infidelity

These emotional and sexual involvements often, though not always, have negative personal and relational consequences (Boekhout et al., 1999). Although some researchers have reported positive effects of extramarital relationships (e.g., Weil, 1975), most have found that such relationships are likely to have negative consequences (e.g., Buunk 1995; Thompson, 1984b). As noted previously, participants in one study who projected that they would have extramarital sexual relationships in their future marriages were more likely than participants who did not make these predictions to expect that these involvements would have positive outcomes, including increased self-esteem, independence, adventure, and increased social status (Bukstel et al., 1978). However, people anticipating positive outcomes may not be aware of the possible negative results that may affect their partners and their relationships, as well as themselves, or they may be trying to reduce their dissonance by not considering these outcomes. Unwillingness to consider possible negative outcomes may also explain why people who are involved in extramarital sex are more likely to justify such behavior than are uninvolved people (Johnson, 1970).

However, participants in another study, even those who had been involved in an intimate extrarelationship, believed that such extrarelationship involvements would detract from the primary relationship (Thompson, 1984b). In addition, the participants believed that extrarelationship involvements that were both emotional and sexual, as opposed to emotional only or sexual only, were more wrong and detracted more from the primary relationship than either sexual only or emotional only involvements, and they were less likely to pursue such combined relationships. Also, people who were asked to imagine that their partner had admitted having sex with another person reported that they would react with betrayal, anger, disappointment, and self-doubt (Buunk, 1995). Such reactions are congruent with our earlier discussion of infidelity as resulting in disillusionment about the relationship, the partner, and the self.

Gender Differences in Reactions to Infidelity

As noted earlier, men and women have different reasons for their own involvement in extrarelationships. Women and men also appear to have different reactions to a partner's extrarelationship involvement. Overall, men and women may not differ in the intensity of their jealous responses (Buunk, 1995). However, in a study in which participants were asked to rate their perceptions of male and female reactions to a partner's infidelity, compared to men, women were perceived as more likely to react with disappointment and self-doubt to a partner's infidelity, and women were also perceived to be more willing to protect the relationship (Boekhout et al., 1999). Additionally, women were seen as more likely to deny their partner's involvement and yet more willing to confront their partner and find out the reason for the infidelity. These findings appear somewhat contradictory, which illustrates the complexity of attitudes toward infidelity.

Participants believed that men would react with more destructiveness and aggression. In addition, significantly more women than men believed that a feeling of betrayal is a common female reaction to a partner's infidelity (Boekhout et al., 1999). Buunk (1995) also found that, when asked to imagine their reactions to a partner having a sexual affair, men and women were similar in reporting feelings of betrayal-anger. However, significantly more women than men reported that they would also feel disappointment and self-doubt. Finally, compared to men, women whose partners had actually been in extrarelationship sexual involvements were less likely to react with disappointment and anger, which suggests that women may be more resigned to adapting to the unfaithful behaviors of their partners (Buunk, 1995).

Some interesting conclusions can be drawn from these perceived different reactions. For example, since men are more able to separate sex from love (Glass & Wright, 1992), they may not see their affair as a betrayal because it has no consequences for their feelings towards their current relationship. This possibility is also supported by the finding that men felt less guilty than women after engaging in extramarital sex (Spanier & Margolis, 1983) and that men who had been in extrarelationship sexual relations had fewer negative reactions than men who had not been unfaithful, when imagining that their partner had been unfaithful (Buunk, 1995). However, involved men may also be trying to reduce their cognitive dissonance because their extrarelationship behavior is inconsistent with their attitudes and beliefs, and they actually do feel guilty. Furthermore, the perception of females' greater willingness to try to preserve relationships, along with their greater feelings of betrayal, are consistent with sociobiological explanations indicating that women seek stable mating relationships in order to increase their reproductive fitness (e.g., Buss, 1994). Males' sexual reasons for, and aggressive reactions to, infidelity are also consistent with male reproduction strategies and mate guarding (Buss, 1994). Gender role socialization and social learning perspectives can also account for these perceived differences.

Level of jealousy for men and women also appears to be related to a partner's sexual versus emotional extrarelationship involvement. Buss and his colleagues (Buss, Larsen, Westen, & Semmelroth, 1992) asked participants to choose whether a partner's emotional attachment or sexual intercourse with another person would be more distressing. They found that 60% of the men believed they would be more upset with their partner's sexual involvement; however, 83% of the women reported that a partner's emotional infidelity would be more distressing. Similar results were produced from physiological measures (e.g., pulse rate) of participants who were asked to imagine their partner having a sexual affair and to imagine their partner falling in love with another person. Finding this difference in both psychological and physiological measures demonstrates the magnitude of this effect (Buss et al., 1992). Therefore, it seems that men and women do have different reasons for, and reactions to extrarelationship involvements.

In some of our earlier research, the majority of the participants reported experiencing negative consequences due to their infidelity or their partner's infidelity (Boekhout et al., 1999). Almost 80% of the partners of unfaithful participants did learn about the infidelity, and many of these relationships were terminated or characterized as irreversibly damaged (e.g., "I feel bad, my stomach is always in knots, and it causes much unknown tension between us"). However, many couples also eventually worked out their differences and reconciled, usually after experiencing a variety of negative consequences and separation (e.g., "We talked it out—he was very upset but forgave me and wanted to stay together"). Similar results were also found when participants' partners had been unfaithful, although more of these relationships were reportedly terminated (Boekhout et al., 1999).

Along with these negative reactions, several other potentially difficult outcomes have been outlined. For example, one national survey found that less than 12% of the respondents who were engaging in extramarital sex reported that they always used condoms with their primary and secondary relationships (Choi, Catania, & Dolcini, 1994). This behavior puts many people at risk of contracting the AIDS virus and other sexually transmitted diseases. For example, the first author vividly recalls having a discussion on HIV/AIDS with one of his classes, when a student tearfully reported that her father had secretly cheated on her mother and had recently contracted the HIV virus. Both she and her mother feared the possibility that her mother had contracted the virus from her father.

Unless other forms of birth control are being used, the lack of condom use may also lead to pregnancies as a result of these extrarelationship involvements. Kaslow (1993) provided several case examples of affairs that led to the birth of children, and the crushing effects that these reminders of the affairs have had on the lives of all those involved. For example, one married man with three children had a child as a result of an affair and eventually wanted that child to be a member of his family. The wife and children were devastated and enraged, and their once stable family became very chaotic and tenuous. In another case, a woman committed suicide after having a child who was obviously racially different from her and her husband. The tragedy left her husband and children in therapy searching for answers and understanding. In these situations, the child of the affair, an innocent victim, is often blamed for the family's disruption (Kaslow, 1993). Thus, the losses continue.

Perspective on the Models

Although the deficit and personal growth models offer different perspectives on the phenomenon of extradyadic relationships, they are not competing explanations. As we noted earlier, any given affair may contain elements of both a flight from deficits and a movement toward growth. It is also likely that some people almost stumble into such relationships, neither driven nor pulled, but rather responding almost reflexively to an immediate situation. Someone might have a one-night stand without a lot of complexity. A longer-term affair, however, would likely involve more complex aspects of deficit or personal growth or both.

What is more clear is that the high mindedness of the personal growth model doesn't mitigate against a painful aftermath. If one partner is unfaithful, his or her reasons for doing so—whether based on deficit or personal growth—might not matter a great deal to the aggrieved partner. Affairs appear to cause pain, even when they do not cause relational destruction.

Theory development on the topic of infidelity has been largely in the direction of an evolutionary approach, which offers a distal meta-perspective on infidelity that complements the more proximal deficit and personal growth models.

More central than theory to increasing the research on this topic, however, is the willingness of researchers (and participants) to confront a topic that is very private and very painful. Given the *great* discrepancy between our attitudes and values about infidelity and our actual behavior, scholars will need to move beyond their own and their participants' comfort levels if they are to explore this topic more fully.

☐ Coping with the Trauma of Infidelity

As we have noted previously, and as our data confirm, infidelity does not always lead to relationship dissolution. In addition, whether or not the relationship bonds are severed, the person whose partner has been unfaithful must cope actively with the loss of relationship illusions in order to heal and move on with their lives.

In discussing the adjustment to traumatic loss, Janoff-Bulman (1992) points out that the degree of adjustment required will depend on the degree of disillusionment experienced. Since human-induced traumas (e.g., rape, assault, infidelity) are more humiliating, whereas nature-induced traumas (e.g., floods, hurricanes) are more humbling, victims of infidelity are likely to be hurt, angry, and humiliated. In addition, when a trauma has been perpetrated by a family member or someone else very close, losses are potentially even more damaging (Janoff-Bulman, 1992).

The adjustment process involves the reconciliation of old, overly positive, invalid assumptions about the world and new, extremely negative, questionably valid assumptions about the world. There can be a tendency to move from overly-positive generalizations to overly-negative generalizations, and neither extreme is satisfactory for the long term. The typical process involves some alternation of denial and emotional numbing (that relieves emotional pressure and allows the individual to function), and intrusive thoughts (that facilitate habituation to the traumatic event and a complete working through of the emotions surrounding it; Janoff-Bulman, 1992). This alternating of coping strategies allows a person to work through events at a pace that is manageable.

As part of interpreting the traumatic experience, people may cope in a variety of ways, including comparisons with others (She had an affair, but at least she didn't leave me), blaming the self in an effort to maintain control (If I had paid more attention to him, he wouldn't have had the affair), or seeing some benefits from the trauma (This was a wake-up call; now I know how important she and our relationship are to me).

During the period of coping and adjustment, social support from others close to the person who has been betrayed is extremely important. Of course the one single person whose support is likely to mean the most is the one who has been the betrayer, so infidelity presents a rather unique situation where social support is concerned. However, the support and assurance given by family and close friends is very important to an individual's healing. Some people may feel uncomfortable with the victim because infidelity in another relationship highlights the possibility of infidelity in their own relationship (e.g., If his wife can have an affair, my wife can too.), while other people almost seem to blame the victim (e.g., She should have seen this coming and done a better job of tending to her marriage.). But fortunately, most people are likely to be supportive. And therapists can also be very helpful in providing support.

Clinical Implications of Infidelity

Therapists are often called upon to help people deal with the pain of infidelity. Clients may be the betrayed partner, the partner having the affair, or the affair partner. All three are likely to experience pain and loss. Gass and Nichols (1988) characterized an affair as "a coping mechanism for personal, individual problems or for expressions of individual wishes and needs of various kinds as well as a reaction to marital relationship problems" (p. 4). Thus, therapists need to look at why an affair was chosen as the method for coping with these various problems. Ellis (1969) suggested that there are both healthy and disturbed reasons for engaging in extramarital sexual relationships, and according to his classification, some relationship deficit and personal growth reasons appear to be healthy and acceptable, while others are more dysfunctional. Marett (1990) reported that it is also important for therapists to determine whether a mate's extrarelationship involvement serves the function of getting distance from the primary relationship or the function of achieving closeness with the affair partner, which again supports the centrality of the deficit and personal growth models.

It is also important for therapists to ascertain the type of extrarelationship involvement and the justification for the involvement. Findings have shown that partners who are in extrarelationship involvements that are sexual only are able to disengage from these relationships more easily than partners who are in emotional only or combined sexual and emotional extrarelationship involvements (Glass & Wright, 1992). For example, women who were more in love with their affair partners were more likely to stay in the extrarelationship for a longer period of time (Hurlbert, 1992). In addition, justifications and excuses provide cues to the involved persons' cognitions, blame-placing, and reasons for involvements (Atwater, 1979). As we have shown, infidelities can have different meanings, because the involved partners may be solely seeking excitement and personal growth, or may be dissatisfied with various aspects of their relationship. These differences will likely influence the strategies that therapists use.

A number of scholars have reviewed the dynamics involved in conducting therapy with couples who wish to work through problems surrounding extrarelationship involvements. For example, Eldridge (1983) reported that therapists are faced with the challenge of reframing extramarital relationships as functional efforts for growth that can be channeled back into marriages with couples who desperately want to save the relationship. While not condoning the maintenance of extramarital affairs that will harm uninvolved partners, this approach suggests that couples maintain an open-minded perspective (i.e., moving away from rigid traditional beliefs of irreversible damage from participating in nonexclusive behaviors), which can aid interpersonal growth by reducing feelings of guilt in the involved partners and alleviating feelings of victimization in the uninvolved partners.

Accordingly, therapists can help some spouses take the positive growth and new self-awareness stemming from extramarital sexual encounters and assimilate these experiences into previously restrictive marriages, which will help both partners become more aware of and responsive to each other's needs (Eldridge, 1983). Thus, incorporating both personal growth and deficit models, the discovery of increased identity and the development of personal growth in another relationship can be integrated into the primary relationship to overcome the previous deficits and broaden the functioning and fulfillment to be found in that system. While not denying the losses incurred by infidelity, this nonnegative approach emphasizes possible positives that can result. Thus, clinicians face a difficult task in deciding how to treat couples in ways that benefit all concerned parties, inside and outside the primary relationship.

When all is said and done, the experience of infidelity, as with the experience of any trauma and loss, leaves successful survivors who are neither the persons they were immediately preceding the discovery of infidelity nor the persons they were immediately after the discovery of infidelity. They have coped with and ideally transcended the traumatic experience, emerging positive but more guarded on the other side (Janoff-Bulman, 1992). "Rather than overgeneralize from the trauma to all aspects of the world and the self, over the course of successful coping, survivors reestablish positive, yet less absolutely positive, core assumptions. . . . They have made their peace with the inevitable shortcomings of our existence and have a new appreciation of life and a realization of what is really important" (Janoff-Bulman, 1992, pp. 174-175).

☐ References

Atwater, L. (1979). Getting involved: Women's transition to first extramarital sex. *Alternative Lifestyles, 1,* 33–68.

Baumeister, R. F., & Leary, M. R. (1995). The need to belong: Desire for interpersonal attachments as a fundamental human motivation. *Psychological Bulletin, 117,* 497–529.

Bergner, R. M., & Bergner, L. L. (1990). Sexual misunderstanding: A descriptive and pragmatic formulation. *Psychotherapy, 27,* 464–467.

Boekhout, B. A., Hendrick, S. S., & Hendrick, C. (1999). Relationship infidelity: A loss perspective. *Journal of Personal and Interpersonal Loss, 4,* 97–123.

Bringle, R. G., & Boebinger, K. L. G. (1990). Jealousy and the 'third' person in the love triangle. *Journal of Social and Personal Relationships, 7,* 119–133.

Bukstel, L. H., Roeder, G. D., Kilmann, P. R., Laughlin, J., & Sotile, W. M. (1978). Projected extramarital sexual involvement in unmarried college students. *Journal of Marriage and the Family, 40,* 337–340.

Buunk, B. (1984). Jealousy as related to attributions for the partner's behavior. *Social Psychology Quarterly, 47,* 107–112.

Buunk, B. (1987). Conditions that promote breakups as a consequence of extradyadic involvements. *Journal of Social and Clinical Psychology, 5,* 271–284.

Buunk, B. (1995). Sex, self-esteem, dependency and extradyadic sexual experience as related to jealousy responses. *Journal of Social and Personal Relationships, 12,* 147–153.

Buss, D. M. (1985). Human mate selection. *American Scientist, 73,* 47–51.

Buss, D. M. (1994). *The evolution of desire: Strategies of human mating.* New York: Basic Books.

Buss, D. M., Larsen, R. J., Westen, D., & Semmelroth, J. (1992). Sex differences in jealousy: Evolution, physiology, and psychology. *Psychological Science, 3,* 251–255.

Choi, K. H., Catania, J. A., & Dolcini, M. M. (1994). Extramarital sex and HIV risk behavior among US adults: Results from the national AIDS behavior survey. *American Journal of Public Health, 84,* 2003–2007.

DePaulo, B. M., & Kashy, D. (1998). Everyday lies in close and casual relationships. *Journal of Personality and Social Psychology, 74,* 63–79.

Eldridge, W. B. (1983). Therapists' use of information and dynamics from extramarital relationships to stimulate growth in married couples. *Family Therapy, 10,* 1–11.

Ellis, A. (1969). Healthy and disturbed reasons for having extramarital relations. In G. Neubeck (Ed.), *Extramarital relations* (pp. 490–501). Englewood Cliffs, NJ: Prentice-Hall.

Gass, G. Z., & Nichols, W. C. (1988). Gaslighting: A marital syndrome. *Contemporary Family Therapy, 10,* 3–16.

Glass, S. P., & Wright, T. L. (1985). Sex differences in type of extramarital involvement and marital dissatisfaction. *Sex Roles, 12,* 1101–1120.

Glass, S. P., & Wright, T. L. (1992). Justifications for extramarital relationships: The association between attitudes, behaviors, and gender. *The Journal of Sex Research, 29,* 361–387.

Gluhoski, V. L., & Wortman, C. B. (1996). The impact of trauma on world views. *Journal of Social and Clinical Psychology, 15,* 417–429.

Hansen, G. L. (1985). Dating jealousy among college students. *Sex Roles, 12,* 713–721.

Holmes, J. G., & Rempel, J. K. (1989). Trust in close relationships. In C. Hendrick (Ed.), *Close relationships* (pp. 187–220). Thousand Oaks, CA: Sage.

Hupka, R. B., Buunk, B., Falus, G., Fulgosi, A., Ortega, E., Swain, R., & Tarabrina, N. V. (1985). Romantic jealousy and romantic envy: A seven-nation study. *Journal of Cross-Cultural Psychology, 16,* 423–446.

Hurlbert, D. F. (1992). Factors influencing a woman's decision to end an extramarital sexual relationship. *Journal of Sex and Marital Therapy, 18,* 104–113.

Janoff-Bulman, R. (1992). *Shattered assumptions: Towards a new psychology of trauma.* New York: Free Press.

Janoff-Bulman, R., & Frantz, C. M. (1996). The loss of illusions: The potent legacy of trauma. *Journal of Personal and Interpersonal Loss, 1,* 133–150.

Johnson, R. E. (1970). Some correlates of extramarital coitus. *Journal of Marriage and the Family, 32,* 449–456.

Johnson, R. E. (1972). Attitudes toward extramarital relationships. *Medical Aspects of Human Sexuality, 6,* 168–191.

Kaslow, F. (1993). Attraction and affairs: Fabulous and fatal. *Journal of Family Psychotherapy, 4,* 1–34.

Kinsey, A. C., Pomeroy, W. B., & Martin, C. E. (1948). *Sexual behavior in the human male.* Philadelphia: Saunders.

Kinsey, A. C., Pomeroy, W. B., Martin, C. E., & Gebhard, P. H. (1953). *Sexual behavior in the human female.* Philadelphia: Saunders.

Laumann, E. O., Gagnon, J. H., Michael, R. T., & Michaels, S. (1994). *The social organization of sexuality: Sexual practices in the United States.* Chicago: University of Chicago Press.

Mansfield, P., McAllister, F., & Collard, J. (1992). Equality: Implications for sexual intimacy in marriage. *Sexual and Marital Therapy, 7,* 213–220.

Marett, K. M. (1990). Extramarital affairs: A birelational model for their assessment. *Family Therapy, 17,* 21–28.

Mellen, S. L. W. (1981). *The evolution of love.* San Francisco: Freeman.

Meyering, R. A., & Epling-McWherter, E. A. (1986). Decision-making in extramarital relationships. *Lifestyles, 8,* 115–129.

Morgan, H. J., & Janoff-Bulman, R. (1994). Positive and negative self-complexity: Patterns of adjustment following traumatic versus non-traumatic life experiences. *Journal of Social and Clinical Psychology, 13,* 63–85.

Nadler, A., & Dotan, I. (1992). Commitment and rival attractiveness: Their effects on male and female reactions to jealousy-arousing situations. *Sex Roles, 26,* 293–310.

Pestrak, V. A., Martin, D., & Martin, M. (1985). Extramarital sex: An examination of the literature. *International Journal of Family Therapy, 7,* 107–115.

Prins, K. S., Buunk, B. P., & VanYperen, N. W. (1993). Equity, normative disapproval and extramarital relationships. *Journal of Social and Personal Relationships, 10,* 39–53.

Reiss, I. L., Anderson, R. E., & Sponaugle, G. C. (1980). A multivariate model of the determinants of extramarital sexual permissiveness. *Journal of Marriage and the Family, 42,* 395–411.

Roloff, M. E., & Cloven, D. H. (1994). When partners transgress: Maintaining violated relationships. In D. J. Canary & L. Stafford (Eds.), *Communication and relational maintenance* (pp. 23–43). New York: Academic Press.

Shackelford, T. K., & Buss, D. M. (1997). Marital satisfaction in evolutionary psychological perspective. In R. J. Sternberg & M. Hojjat (Eds.), *Satisfaction in close relationship* (pp. 7–25). New York: Guilford.

Sheppard, V. J., Nelson, E. S., & Andreoli-Mathie, V. (1995). Dating relationships and infidelity: Attitudes and behaviors. *Journal of Sex and Marital Therapy, 21,* 202–212.

Smith, T. W. (1994). Attitudes toward sexual permissiveness: Trends, correlates, and behavioral connections. In A. S. Rossi (Ed.), *Sexuality across the life course* (pp. 63–97). Chicago: University of Chicago Press.

374 Loss and Trauma

Spanier, G. B., & Margolis, R. L. (1983). Marital separation and extramarital sexual behavior. *The Journal of Sex Research, 19,* 23–48.

Thompson, A. P. (1983). Extramarital sex: A review of the research literature. The *Journal of Sex Research, 19,* 1–22.

Thompson, A. P. (1984a). Emotional and sexual components of extramarital relations. *Journal of Marriage and the Family, 46,* 35–42.

Thompson, A. P. (1984b). Extramarital sexual crisis: Common themes and therapy implications. *Journal of Sex and Marital Therapy, 10,* 239–254.

Weil, M. A. (1975). Extramarital relationships: A reappraisal. *Journal of Clinical Psychology, 31,* 723–725.

Weis, D. L., & Felton, J. R. (1987). Marital exclusivity and the potential for marital conflict. *Social Work, 32,* 45–49.

Weis, D. L., & Slosnerick, M. (1981). Attitudes toward sexual and nonsexual extramarital involvements among a sample of college students. *Journal of Marriage and the Family, 43,* 349–358.

Whitehurst, R. (1983). Sexual behavior in and out of marriage. *Marriage and Family Review, 6,* 115–124.

Winstead, B. A., Derlega, V. J., & Rose, S. (1997). *Gender and close relationships.* Thousand Oaks, CA: Sage.

Jacqueline L. Karkazis
Sharon L. Lazaneo

Unyielding Custody Disputes: Tempering Loss and Courting Disaster

When intimate relationships or marriages disintegrate and families fall apart, adults, and children alike face loss. For some, loss engendered by an ending of a meaningful relationship is so traumatic, so wounding, so threatening, that it kindles—or rekindles— a near unbearable sense of personal and social vulnerability. Nearing the end, at the end, and after the ending some wrestle with a sense of failure, a flagging sense of self-worth or self esteem; more than a few look back and mourn the loss of their hopes and dreams, and many ruefully wonder what they could have—or should have—done to prevent the break-up. (Gottman, 1994) While the days, weeks, months, and, for some, years following the loss of a significant relationship can be a time when unresolved feelings from the past coalesce with present despair to create a dam in the path of development, most muddle through the difficult, sometimes agonizing, process of saying goodbye on the way toward achieving a renewed sense of trust in self and others, prerequisite steps toward forming new, perhaps deeper attachments.

Other more vulnerable and less-reflective ex-partners may interpret or experience the loss of an important relationship as wholesale rejection. Feeling demeaned and belittled, they keep their focus fixed on the "rear view mirror," ruminatively redoing and reworking the lost relationship in an effort to retain a positive image of self and to ward off what potentiates as uncontrollable hopelessness, helplessness, and humiliation. In an effort to wall off or dispel intolerable or unwanted feelings, some particularly wounded ex-partners or former spouses obsessively deconstruct their lost lives, revise history, and reconstruct the longed for family of the past by giving the cast of characters new, untoward personas and images, well on the way to externalizing the conflict and internalizing a new, reconstructed view of a shared history, injured ex-partners may recast former partners, former lovers (the children's parents) as traitors, abusers, as disordered, and, perhaps most insufferably, as flawed, unfit, or uncaring parents.

☐ Revisionism as a Defense Against Loss

Revisionism as a defense against loss of self, loss of others, and intolerable feelings of shame prompts, drives, and energizes many a protracted and intractable litigation over child custody. Needing validation as a worthwhile person and a good enough parent, some desperate and fragile ex-spouses good enough parent, in the aftermath of an irreconcilable, traumatic separation pursue custody of their children and in the process begin to publicly vilify their former mates—their children's other parent. With legal representation or without, they initiate judicial proceedings motivated, so it seems, to obtain full, sole, or primary custody of the children. When motions are filed, former partners and coparents become instant litigants in a lawsuit that serves to distinguish parents as polarized combatants ready to do battle over who is parentally fit and who is not. New disputants and repeat litigants frequently attach explanatory, self-supportive, and self-serving narratives to their motions. While some narratives are bipartisan and clothe a marriage or a coparenting relationship in familiar words peppered with recognizable images, typically these testimonials are replete with postseparation revisions and vulnific distortions of former partners and family relationships. Such public vulnerations have the capacity to undermine, perhaps shatter, the integrity of one's identity and negate the probity of one's experiences and life story.

While legally declarative reformulations negating the significance and meaning of past relationships between partners, partners as parents, and between parents and children can be compelling, they are often shaped from an angry remolding of the past articulated in self-defense when one feels under attack. Thus, former partners reincarnated as combative parents may describe each other as manipulative, callous, vengeful, controlling, and violent. As litigants, fathers who held mothers in high esteem during the course of a marriage may now project her mothering as typically distant, disinterested, characteristically inadequate, disturbed, reckless—even dangerous. In the midst of an adversarial process, some mothers who once depicted their husbands as loving and supportive, now project a malignant image of his fathering by using such adjectives as absent, unavailable, threatening, violent, abusive, or, in the vernacular, dead beat.

As antagonists in a serious drama played out in the shadow of the Court, already vulnerable mothers and fathers step into the public arena of the courtroom stigmatized as bad objects, discredited as parents, and distressed by the awareness that a reality held in common during a marriage can be a reality so completely denied or lost in the process of a divorce. While litigation captures the attention of those involved and may provide a raison d'etre in the midst of despair, it is never palliative and it is never, ever, a circumscribed, short lived experience. Disputes motivated by an underlying need for personal vindication or parental affirmation are chaffed and aggravated when they unfold within an adversarial system dedicated to the polemics of distinguishing truth from fiction and guilt from innocence. Applied to the family and to child custody disputes in particular, courtroom polemics—controversial arguments and controversial refutations—challenge the integrity of one's percipient understanding of reality, exacerbating (wittingly and unwittingly) family conflict by casting parents into contrasting and invariably conflicting positions of good or bad, fit or unfit, guilty or not guilty. The use of an institutionalized, intrinsically disputatious process in response to a traumatic divide in the family increases the possibility that parent litigants will be iatragenically, if not otherwise, induced to live up to their labels as polarized and high-conflict. Sadly, some parents deplete their supply of emotional resources and pass through financial bankruptcy trying to correct the record and obtain a judicial rendering that can be used as evidence to support a verdict of not guilty by reason of parental competency.

☐ Relentless Litigation Traumatizes Parents and Children

Though it may, for some short period of time, serve as an ego-syntonic, socially acceptable way of expressing outrage, or provide a forum in which to restore a sense of parental competency, or operate to keep one connected to a lost other, relentless litigation over custody ultimately destabilizes parents and holds them hostage to what all too frequently turns out to be a barren, depleting, and debilitating process. Since it is widely thought that the resolution of postseparation conflict is intricately tied to children's positive development and overall well-being (Buchanan, Maccoby, & Dornbush, 1991; Camara & Resnick, 1988; Emery, 1988; Johnston & Roseby, 1997; Wallerstein & Blakeslee, 1989; Wallerstein & Kelley, 1980), unabated postdivorce conflict played out through the course of a childhood can disrupt or interrupt children's development. What may well have been initiated for psychological preservation, postseparation dramatically and traumatically translates to the child (and to the parent) as more risk, more loss, and less protection.

> Eighteen months into a nonstop battle with her ex-husband, a mother of three adolescent boys became momentarily paralyzed by the memory of being in the third grade when her parents, in the midst of their own hotly contested divorce, arbitrarily decided she should live with her mean aunt Molly. Desperately wanting to spare her children from a similar, precipitous loss, and from the developmentally impeding and undermining effects of powerlessness, this mother is unyielding when it comes to insisting that her children have a voice in shaping their own custodial destiny.
>
> With her history in mind, holding a complex view of her former partner, and for the first time, mourning the loss of the best part of her marriage, she hopes her children's arrant, explicitly voiced desire to reside in her care will be empathically received. In the absence of a sensitive and compound understanding of her children's preferences, she worries their voice will be the instrument that prompts an imposed, precipitous and arresting custodial solution. An arbitrary decision negating the importance of her children's attachments and self-determination would be the evidence to convince her that as a mother she could not protect her children from abrupt, unwanted, and traumatizing disruptions. The notion that her children could be summarily and without warning ordered to live with their father, recreates a painful and defining moment of her history and leaves her vulnerable in the course of feeling powerless to secure the ties that bind her children. [From author's experience]

Children of all ages are impacted in some way, large or small, by parental conflict. Many have postulated, and research has confirmed, that doggedly intense, unyielding, pernicious, or violent conflict distresses and injures children (Japel, Tremblay, Vitro, & Boulerice, 1997; Johnston & Campbell, 1988; Johnston & Roseby, 1997). Conflict explicitly supported by overly simplified, rigidly held, nonempathic, negative images of ex-mates tears at the integrity of children who cannot help but personalize and internalize the rage-sated perceptions litigating parents have of one another. Some children resolve the ambiguity inherent in such high-conflict situations by becoming closely identified with the seemingly more embattled, beleaguered parent/litigant and, in an urgent rush to bolster the esteem of the languishing parent, sacrifice some part of self or some internal ingredient necessary in the recipe for normal development. When children get wind of—and they always do no matter how hard parents consciously try to shield them—of just how their mother has vilified their father and just how their father has demonized their mother, they often become self-conscious and circumspect about their birthright, questioning their own intrinsic value and security as the progeny of two flawed parents.

> On a Friday night, in the middle of October, reeling from the death of her father, a middle aged divorced mother of 14-year-old boy, said "no" when her son asked to spend two hours of her custodial time attending a rock concert with his father. She explained, "his father could pull his arm off and watch while he bleeds . . . Robert is at great risk in his father's care . . . I hope you and the Judge will finally understand." When confronted with his ex-wife's characterization of him as heartless and sadistic, Robert's father tried to stay a rapid decline in self-esteem and correct the record by reiterating the truth, "she burned him with scalding water when he was two." Caught between a mother desperately trying to hold on to a good mother image by presenting a case for his father's cruelty and a father desperately trying to defend his good fathering by undermining his faith in his mother's mothering, Robert wonders if he will ever find a womb of neutrality where he can find the words, to create the narrative, to answer the question, "who am I?" After a lifetime of exposure to his parent's dispute over his custody and their corrosive and dehumanizing views of one another, he is not optimistic. [From author's experience]

We have worked with parents and children in the context of custody conflicts for over three decades and can attest to how cautious, how studied children can be when it comes to managing the war zone between their contentious and hostile parents. One creative and yet very constricted seven-year-old child, squeezed between her parents' wholesale conflict over the correct pronunciation of her first name, successfully navigated the harsh and forbidding landscape by rigidly thinking of herself as Eve in her mother's home (her mother's preference) and as Eva (her father's preference) when she was in her father's care. The necessity of maintaining two distinct identities was so fixed, so important, so crucial that when she slept at her father's house she dreamt of herself as Eva and when she stayed overnight with her mother she dreamt of herself as Eve.

Countless children handle parental conflict by vigilantly leaving the heartstrings that bind them to their absent parent at the threshold of their custodial parent's door. Receiving parents often seem to accept the child's silence on the subject of her mother or father or his other home as a sign of contentment, or as evidence that she is only minimally invested in the absent parent. In place of worry or instead of offering a query about the missing piece of the child's experience, parents explicitly or implicitly congratulate themselves on being "enough" for their child, and become amnesiac and unempathic about the child's multiple attachments, wide range of experiences, and dimension of feeling. Puffed up with undisguised pride the father of a three-year-old boasted that his daughter "didn't ask for her mother once" when the mother was denied access to her child for over a month; and the mother of a six-year-old boy seemed pleased if not relieved when she told the child custody evaluator that her son "doesn't mention his father when he's with me . . . He's happy here" and sadly, the father of five-year-old Joy was able to demonstrate he was the "perfectly" preferred parent by asking his daughter to measure with her fingers how much she loved her mother. When she offered a modest two inches worth of love between thumb and forefinger, he queried with rancor, "How much?" and she quickly snapped her fingers closed, leaving nary a trace of space between. To say that Joy had to abandon her feelings and her tie to her mother at the threshold of her father's door is to understate the reality. We hasten to add that each time she stood on the welcome mat outside her mother's door Joy had to "quit claim" any visible signs of her attachment to her father.

Other children overwhelmed by chronic custody conflicts become strangely silent about their parents, keeping perspectives and opinions and reflections about their fathers and mothers to a bare-bones minimum. With flat affect, these children offer colorless and undimensional descriptions of their childhood experiences and render lifeless, limited, and constrained portrayals of family life and family relationships. Parents in turn may narrowly attribute symptoms evident in these constricted children (i.e., enuresis, encopresis, headaches, stomach aches, overt and covert aggression, poor academic performance, depressive affect, and so on) to the other parent's failings, reinforcing for the child the notion that silence is truly golden given that a renegade complaint, or an off-the-cuff remark, or a symptom can quickly become the ammunition to malign, marginalize, or permanently sideline a beloved parent.

> Nine-year-old Bernice had been the subject of a persistently loud custody dispute since her parents' divorce five years earlier. Her verbal descriptions of life with mother and life with father (her parents shared custody a week on and a week off) were religiously bland and heedfully innocuous. Her play, dramatically and poignantly suggested a more dimensional yet harsher reality.
>
> Hunkered down on the office floor, Bernice picked up the basket of Leggos and constructed the Titanic with a throng of doomed passengers. As Bernice navigated the fated ship around the tip of her mother's feet, it hit an iceberg and began to sink. Suddenly afraid, panicked passengers clutching tiny life rafts jumped overboard and floated precariously in the turbulent water surrounding the sinking ship. As one tiny raft after another began to take on water and one passenger after another began to sink into the sea, Bernice successively summoned and orchestrated a rescue. Each harrowing rescue was followed by another crisis and another rescue, ad infinitum. [From author's experience]

Yet other, perhaps more vulnerable and fragile, children wither in the crucible of punishing custody conflicts. Unable to endure the no man's land between their parents, they form alliances or alignments with one parent and distance themselves from the other, In extreme cases, wounded children may at once completely and unequivocally idealize and embrace one parent and devalue and reject the other. Parent–child estrangements that emanate from very complicated and problematic predivorce dynamics involving parents and children, can crystallize into parent–child alienation in the aftermath of a traumatic separation. Predivorce dysfunction and separation crises notwithstanding, some children, in the service of managing intolerable family dilemmas, resort to casting out a previously loved parent in an effort to restore equilibrium and recapture security.

Parent–child estrangements embody a continuum of affects and adaptations, with symptoms ranging from mild to extreme. Exhibiting symptoms of mild estrangements are children who predictably voice varying degrees of rather shallow and illogical criticisms of the more distanced parent ("Mom makes me do homework" and "Dad won't give me junk food"), preserving for the other the status of the idealized or trustworthy nurturer. However, these children do not relinquish their attachments or abandon family ties and though they may appear guarded, underneath they remain open and responsive to genuine, heartfelt, and tenacious nurturing.

At the extreme end of the continuum, we find nine-year-old Philip who expressed his intense hatred for his mother (the parent to whom he had, as an infant and a toddler, been most dependent upon for care and nurturing), by imagining that she would be set afire and he would roast marshmallows in her flames. Seven-year-old Julienne, fashionably attired and stylishly coiffured, split her parents into striking personifications of good and bad. Thus she complained:

> "My mom is always yelling at me, something my dad never does, and she hits me in the face and she locks me out of the house when it is raining. She slaps me because she knows it hurts . . . . I know my Mom works, but she never plays with me. She never buys me anything; when we go to the toy store it is always 'no, no, no!' I'm tired of my toys at my mom's, they're boring. My mom won't let me buy my own clothes. One time she made me clean up the mess I made and then I didn't have time to play with my friends. I know you should like your real mom best, but I don't. I like my dad's wife."

Once she started, Julienne could not stop saying nice things about her father:

> "I am *never* mad at my dad. His friends are nicer to me than my mom's friends. My dad spanks me on the bottom but it never hurts and he never scares me. My dad buys me a lot and that's why I like to be with him. He buys me anything I want. I don't have to clean my room when I am with him and he never yells at me. I have many toys at my daddy's and I never get tired of them. He is always buying me new clothes or surprising me with a new toy. My stepmom brushes my hair and she puts it up in a pony-tail tied with bright colored ribbons."

Always a bit too distant from her mother, over indulged by her father, and crushed by her parent's unending litigation, Julienne eked out a survival that depended upon her willingness to devalue her mother and idealize her father.

For a variety of complex sociopsychological reasons, some parents, mental health professionals, and Court personnel fail to recognize that while the formation of an alignment can operate to resolve unbearable ambiguity for a child, it can also engender distress, anxiety, fear, and, in some extreme situations, terror. A failure to understand parent–child alignments as problematical (we are herein referencing pathological alignments rather than normative, as for example, developmental, age-related preferences and refusals to visit), will at once place some children at risk for solidifying a compromised adaptation while depriving that child of potentially ameliorative relief. The idealized parent, for instance, may well feel gratified, or vindicated in being chosen by the adoring child, thereby subsidizing the anger or the hostility the child expresses toward the devalued parent, viewing it as perfectly reasonable and justified. With an image of the other, less openly valued, parent in mind, the child's anger or fear may solidify and harden as he or she anticipates from the devalued parent a retaliatory response to unmitigated rage and a quieted paralyzed conscience. Certain that his father is right when he says his mother is mean and sadistic, Philip lives in expectation and dread of his mother's retaliation for his unbridled anger.

Mental health professionals, like mothers and fathers, can also err by interpreting the aligned child's hostility and morbidly candid descriptions of the alienated parent as contextually reasonable responses to presumed maltreatment, and by so doing offer no challenge to the defensive distortions that drive a parent–child estrangement.

(We are excluding from this discussion a child's legitimate withdrawal from a parent who has been unduly harsh, distant, or abusive). A child-therapist, for instance, may write a letter to the Court asking that her patient's visitation with her sexually abusive father be terminated without ever considering that her patient has become the repository of her mother's fear and anger as evidenced by the fact that the father has never seen his daughter outside the confines of supervised visitation and her mother has been legally sanctioned for promulgating and promoting false allegations of sexual abuse. By indiscriminately supporting and endorsing the aligned child's harsh, severe descriptions of the estranged parent by focusing on parental guilt (or innocence), the mental health professional may unknowingly aid in mirroring and furthering the very pathology that originally served to split family members. Such errors, while understandable, operate to widen and cement family rifts and to intensify a child's sense of helplessness.

Children plagued by chronic helplessness or depression all too often take flight, missing an opportunity to fight, that is, to strive for mastery and to feel effective by, for example, examining and working through problematical attachments and detachments. Custody litigants, one or the other, frequently retain the services of expert mental health professionals to listen to, understand, and honor what they project as their child's pain, fear, or anger related to the devalued parent. In some instances, seemingly sensitive and extending professionals push the boundaries of their work beyond the limits of impartiality, cede their neutrality, and advocate for but one voice in a chorused custody proceeding. In this regard it is not uncommon for therapists who have listened to, understood, and honored children to compromise their position or contaminate their role by sending unsolicited letters to the Court advancing partisan recommendations related to how parents should or should not share time. Opinions offered in the absence of a comprehensive dynamic understanding of the family, fan the fires of conflict, place the postdivorce family at increased risk, and compromise both the legal and the mental health professions.

One should not underestimate the desperation that aligned (and nonaligned) children may feel in response to their parents' conflict, or their parents' antecedent and ever present vulnerabilities. Some children threaten to run away if their refusal to visit is not supported. Others threaten to harm themselves or a parent. Eleven-year-old Michael, for example, threatened to jump off his mother's roof if she forced him to spend the weekend with his father. Ten-year-old Anna has been protesting spending time with her father for four years and the intensity of her resistance has left her already very anxious mother more anxious and more frightened for Anna's physical safety and emotional well-being. During piques of temper and fits of rage exhibited on the eve of visits with her father, Anna has, aloud in her mother's presence, voiced a wish to die. Wanting to underwrite her daughter's safety, the mother presents herself as the arbiter and the advocate of Anna's needs since she knows from her history and experience the dangers that can beset one in interaction with the father. Anna's mother wants to rescue Anna from her father, a sincerely devoted but frightened man limited by a constricted capacity for the expression of warmth and empathy.

While Anna's expressed aversion to her father was palpable, what was not clear in the absence of ongoing clinical observation and psychological testing was Anna's rage-imbued, pervasive, but highly secret, struggle to separate from her mother. With this additional piece of the psychological puzzle in hand, one could avoid the seductive inclination to endorse the child's desire for distance from her father and rearrange the custody schedule to afford her more time with her mother. Averting this course prevented what surely would have been a traumatic, threatening developmental regression-in the wake of Anna's hidden desire for increased independence and relief from her mother's overwhelming anxiety. A program of family therapy designed to help Anna simultaneously master and manage her father's reclusiveness and the mother–daughter symbiosis has bolstered her overall functioning and afforded family members the best possible opportunity to balance her waning need for dependence against her growing need for independence.

☐ Courtroom Conflict Assaults Integrity

The presumption that loss has been assuaged and disaster mediated can be made when ex-partners have storied the ending of their relationship absent the necessity of engaging in evidentiary arguments and projections over who owns the reality. In contrast, when courtroom narratives assault integrity and undermine the authenticity of personal experience, parent litigants, driven by a desperate need to be believed, endlessly search for the right words and the right moment to present the incontrovertible proof of their legitimacy. Fragmented in response to such existential disputations and negations, combatants often turn to mental health authorities or to the Court in what all too frequently becomes a futile effort to acquire support for their reality, both past and present, through corroborating mental health testimony or a validating judicial rendering. Acquisition of external support for an internal truth in the midst of an adversarial process that often operates to obscure reality is a contradiction in terms that ultimately dampens and dashes the hopes of nearly all litigants who, whether consciously or unconsciously, seek affirmation. While judicial acknowledgment might impeach revisionism, it often resonates as a hollow, empty substitute for an integrated narrative that affirmatively recognizes a separately shared history and the authenticity of individual reality.

☐ Conclusions

Conflict that endlessly threatens integrity and interpersonal and intrapersonal identity, and potentiates sudden, unwanted separations prompts parents and children to guard their borders against traumatic loss: of a relationship; the ability to protect oneself in the midst of danger; of control over an unwanted or overwhelming feeling; or, loss of confidence in the reliability of one's beliefs about themselves and their world. Cautionary tactics employed to defend against the threat and the reality of loss in the middle of a custody dispute hem the edges of internal and external experience and inevitably limit the complexity and depth of human relationships. For example, parents who feel forcibly hobbled to the ongoing threat of losing their child to their ex-partner may steel themselves against the pain of such an unwanted separation by withdrawing. Other parents, emotionally and financially bankrupt in the wake of depleting litigation, have little left over for their children. Other parents, blinded by a need for vindication in the aftermath of a traumatic separation, lose an empathic identification with their child's subjective experience as, for example, occurs when a combative parent self-righteously and blindly works to sever or insidiously weaken the child's tie to and trust in the other parent. When mothers or fathers hand off parenting to conflict, parents become childless and children become parentless and feel orphaned. Dependent upon parents for survival, lacking sophisticated knowledge about causality, and imbuing fathers and mothers with absolute authority, children also formulate simple, self-blaming and ultimately self-undermining explanations to account for lost connections and may, in desperation, evince provocative behavior or exhibit symptoms to recapture a sense of belonging.

A father who sadly identifies himself as a man without a country, and a mother who wants to return to her homeland (Japan) with their four-year-old daughter have been involved in a custody battle for over two and a half years. Devastated in the aftermath of what he defined and experienced as his wife's infidelity and betrayal, the father was convinced that if his child was placed in the custody of her mother she, like his country and his wife, would be lost to him forever. Describing the father as vindictive, the mother refuted the father's characterization and attributed it to an anger laden, punitive strategy to keep her homeless or childless or both. Attuned to her father's emptiness and hopelessness; impoverished and frightened in the vortex of her mother's impassable, impossible dilemma, four-year-old Michiko has become preoccupied with an intrusive worry that she will be orphaned. [From author's experience]

Many parent litigants traumatized by the ubiquitous threat of loss and the futility of attempting to temper vulnerability with anger or rage may need help before they can integrate the notion of meaning beyond the knowable experience of conflict. If help comes in the form of support for one side against the other, or by way of a short-sighted, formulaic mental health renderings based on a single cause-theory; or if its offering is stalled in the turbulent waters of litigation, the underlying dynamics driving the fight will remain obscure and the conflict will continue. In spite of a pull to line up behind one parent or the pressure to align with one camp, one must look beneath and beyond psychological defenses, revisionism, and courtroom polemics to obtain an accurate picture of the complex, kinetic forces that underlie, motivate, and eternalize post-divorce conflict. The odds that fragmenting divisions and schisms will be mediated, that children's heartstrings will span the distance of divorce, and that litigants will find new meaning increase when mental health professionals approach undying conflict with a understanding of causality. To do otherwise is to place in relief the projections that polarize parents and to stretch the threads of a child's attachment to the very edge of security and beyond.

☐ References

Buchanan, C., Maccoby, E., & Dornbusch, S. (1991). Caught between parents: Adolescents' experience in divorced homes. *Child Development, 62,* 1008–1029.

Camara, K., & Resnick, G. (1988). Interparental conflict and cooperation: Factors moderating children's post-divorce adjustment. In E. M. Heatherington & J. D. Arasteh (Eds.), *Impact of divorce, single-parenting, and stepparenting on children* (pp. 169–195). Hillsdale, NJ: Erlbaum.

Gottman, J. M. (1994). *What predicts divorce, The relationship between marital processes and marital outcomes.* Hillsdale, NJ: Erlbaum.

Japel, C., Tremblay, R. E., Vitaro, F., Boulerice, B. (1997). Early parental separation and the psychosocial development of daughters 6–9 years old. *American Journal of Orthopsychiatry, 69,* 49–61.

Johnston, J. R., & Campbell, L. E. G. (1988). *Impasses of divorce: The dynamics and resolution of family conflict.* New York: The Free Press.

Johnston, J. R., & Roseby, V. (1997). *In the name of the child: A developmental approach to understanding and helping children of conflicted and violent divorce.* New York: The Free Press.

Lewis, M. (1992). *Shame: The exposed self.* New York: The Free Press.

Lansky, M. R., & Morrison, A. P. (Eds.). (1997). *The widening scope of shame.* NJ: The Analytic Press, Inc.

Wallerstein, J. S. & Blakeslee, S. (1989). *Second chances: Men, women and children a decade after divorce.* New York: Ticknor & Fields.

Wallerstein, J. S. & Kelley, J. B. (1980). *Surviving the break-up: How children and parents cope with divorce.* New York: Basic Books.

CHAPTER

Christopher R. Agnew

Cognitive Interdependence and the Experience of Relationship Loss

Close relationships with other people are a hallmark of human social life. They begin to develop from the very first moments of life and may last until one's dying day (Bowlby, 1969, 1980). Given their ubiquity and prominence, social psychological interest in the study of close relationships has risen markedly in the past three decades (cf. Berscheid & Reis, 1998). Topics such as relationship satisfaction, love, trust, and commitment have all been the targets of extensive and growing research attention (Sternberg & Hojjat, 1997; Aron & Westbay, 1996; Weiselquist, Rusbult, Foster, & Agnew, 1999; Agnew, Van Lange, Rusbult, & Langston, 1998). As social psychology has become more cognitive in its theoretical and empirical emphases (cf. Devine, Hamilton, & Ostrom, 1994; Markus & Zajonc, 1985), so too has social psychological inquiry into close relationship processes. Bias in retrospective memories concerning one's romantic relationship, positive idealization about one's relationship partner, the transference of significant-other mental representations to new social acquaintances, and models of closeness involving degree of self-other inclusion are all examples of social psychological research on close relationship processes with a decidedly cognitive emphasis (McFarland & Ross, 1987; Murray & Holmes, 1997; Andersen & Glassman, 1996; Aron & Aron, 1997). The present chapter reviews a recent theoretical construct offered to increase our understanding of the cognitive underpinnings of relationship commitment—*cognitive interdependence*—and outlines how this construct may be useful in understanding and characterizing the experience of relationship loss.

The end of a romance can be a particularly devastating emotional experience. Individuals invest considerable time, effort, and energy into their intimate relationships, whether marital or nonmarital, and coming to grips with the finality of dissolution can be enormously difficult (as anyone who has been dumped by a dating partner can attest). Although the affective consequences of relationship dissolution have been well documented (cf. Kitson & Morgan, 1990), relatively little attention has been paid to the cognitive underpinnings of relationship loss. In this chapter, the concept of cognitive interdependence is used to help explain particular aspects of the mindset that characterizes relationship participants.

☐ Relationship Loss: Distinguishing Stayers, Leavers, and the Abandoned

Before proceeding, it is helpful to make some distinctions among the component parts of a dissolved romantic relationship and the differing experiences of loss that are likely to emerge. In the general psychological research literature on loss, the term often refers to the affective, cognitive, and behavioral experience that accompanies the permanent departure of a loved one (Harvey, 1998; Harvey & Miller, 1998). Loss is often the result of death or the onset of a serious health issue (e.g., Alzheimer's disease), events that are generally not under the control of the experiencing individual (Nolen-Hoeksema, McBride, & Larson, 1997). In contrast, within the context of a romantic relationship, the experience of loss resulting from relationship dissolution (or break-up) often originates with the deliberate actions of at least one of the relationship partners (Kitson & Morgan, 1990).

Responsibility for the break-up plays a critical role in determining the nature and experience of relationship loss. In any given relationship, the decision to break-up may be reached by mutual agreement or may be more unilateral in nature. If the decision to end the relationship is truly mutual, the experience of loss is likely to be significantly weaker than if only one relationship partner reached the decision. After all, in this scenario both partners agree with the decision to end the relationship. However, if the decision to terminate the relationship is more unilateral, the two former couple members are likely to possess vastly different thoughts and feelings in the wake of the break-up (Arriaga & Agnew, 1999): those of the "leaver" and those of the "abandoned." The current chapter compares the cognitive experiences of those who unilaterally choose to leave their romantic relationship (leavers) with those who were left by their partner (the abandoned). Leavers and the abandoned can be contrasted with those who are involved in relationships that remain intact (stayers).

Prior to relationship dissolution, all three of these categories of relationship members (stayers, leavers, and the abandoned) may be presumed to have experienced at least some degree of commitment to their relationship, or a close relationship would not be said to have existed. Break-up, by definition, entails a breach of commitment. Thus, it is important to have at least a basic understanding of the concept of commitment. I begin by describing one approach to understanding relationship commitment, inspired by interdependence theory (cf. Kelley & Thibaut, 1978; Rusbult, Arriaga, & Agnew, in press). By understanding how commitment to a relationship literally changes the way an individual comes to think about him- or herself, it becomes possible to better understand why relationship loss can be such a powerful emotional experience.

In our recent work, my colleagues and I have asserted that relationship commitment is accompanied by a restructuring of self-in-relationship mental representations, including the tendency to perceive oneself less as an individual and more as part of a pluralistic self-and-partner collective. We refer to these collective mental representations of the self-in-relationship as cognitive interdependence (Agnew, Van Lange, Rusbult, & Langston, 1998). We use interdependence theory constructs to help delineate and understand self-in-relationship mental representations (Rusbult, 1983; Rusbult, Martz & Agnew, 1998).

☐ Interdependence Theory, Relationship Commitment, and Cognitive Interdependence

Interdependence theory is a broad yet flexible theory of human social behavior. It provides a set of concepts for characterizing any given dyadic or group situation, and it describes the ways in which different situations shape motivation and behavior in dyads, including romantically-involved couples (Kelley, 1979; Kelley & Thibaut, 1978). Within the theory, the concept of dependence plays a pivotal role. Dependence level describes the degree to which each of two interacting individuals needs a specific relationship for the fulfillment of subjectively important outcomes. According to the theory, dependence is greater to the degree that the outcomes available in alternative relationships are poor. To illustrate, consider the relationship of David and Susan. According to interdependence theory, David's dependence on Susan will be greater to the extent that he relies uniquely on Susan for the fulfillment of his needs. These needs may include the need for security, for emotional intimacy, for sexual fulfillment or any combination of the three. In contrast, David's dependence on Susan is reduced to the extent that he believes his needs could be gratified elsewhere (e.g., in an alternative relationship).

Rusbult's investment model (1983; Rusbult, Martz, & Agnew, 1998) extends interdependence propositions by suggesting that the structural state of dependence produces the psychological experience of commitment. The psychological experience of commitment is held to include conative, cognitive, and affective components. The conative component of commitment is manifest in an individual's intention to persist in a given relationship. For example, David is committed to his relationship with Susan to the extent that he actively intends to remain in the relationship. The cognitive component of commitment is manifest in an individual's long-term orientation toward the relationship: David is committed to Susan to the extent that he envisions himself as involved in the relationship for the foreseeable future, and considers the implications of his current actions for their future outcomes. The affective component of commitment is the degree to which an individual forms a psychological attachment to the partner and the relationship: David is committed to Susan to the extent that he experiences life in dyadic terms, such that his emotional well-being is linked to Susan and their relationship.

The three components of commitment are theoretically and empirically distinguishable but tend to co-occur (Arriaga & Agnew, 1999). Overall, commitment may be best thought of as the subjective state that dependent individuals experience on a daily basis. In this sense, commitment may be construed as the subjective sense of allegiance that is established with regard to the source of one's structural dependence. Because David is dependent on his relationship with Susan, he develops intentions to persist in the relationship, he foresees long-term involvement with Susan, and he feels affectively linked to Susan and their relationship. From this perspective, a committed individual clearly sees the world differently than does a noncommitted individual.

Strong commitment to a relationship has been shown to be associated with a wide range of relationship-promoting behaviors, such as 1) disparagement of tempting alternative partners (Simpson, Gangestad, & Lerma, 1990); 2) willingness to sacrifice desired behavioral options for the good of a relationship (Van Lange, Rusbult, Drigotas, Arriaga, Witcher, & Cox, 1997); and 3) tendencies to accommodate rather than retaliate when a partner behaves poorly (Rusbult, Verette, Whitney, Slovik, & Lipkus, 1991). In addition to behaving in ways that promote the maintenance of a relationship, committed individuals tend to think in a relationship-enhancing manner. For example, individuals who are more committed to their partner are more likely to evidence strong trust toward their partner than those who are less committed. Trust, in turn, leads to increasingly strong commitment (Wieselquist, Rusbult, Foster, & Agnew, 1999). In sum, the extant social psychological literature supports the contention that committed individuals are willing to exert significant behavioral and cognitive effort toward the goal of maintaining their relationships.

How is it that committed individuals come to act and think in a relationship-enhancing manner? The distinction between the *given situation* and the *effective situation*, as delineated by interdependence theory, provides a framework for understanding how committed individuals come to think and behave in this way. According to Kelley and Thibaut (1978), the *given situation* refers to each partner's immediate, personal well-being in a specific situation, describing each person's self-centered preferences. Although self-centered behaviors occur in everyday life, behavior is often shaped by broader concerns, including long-term goals or desires to promote both one's own and a partner's well-being. Movement away from given preferences results from a transformation of motivation, a process that leads individuals to relinquish their immediate self-interest and act on the basis of broader considerations. For committed relationship partners transformation of motivation often involves movement away from the desire to maximize one's own immediate self-interest (referred to in interdependence terminology as MaxOwn), coming to see the situation instead on the basis of what is good for the partner (MaxOther) or good for both partners (MaxJoint). The *effective situation* refers to the modified preferences resulting from the transformation process. The theory holds that dyad members' behaviors are based on the transformed, effective situation.

Interdependence theory assumes that the transformation process is shaped by internal processes accompanying an interpersonal event (cf. Kelley, 1979). Unfortunately, few studies have explicated the role of internal events in the process of adaptation to interdependence structure, and knowledge of the mental concomitants of commitment is very limited. We introduced the concept of cognitive interdependence to help fill some existing theoretical gaps. In our view, as individuals become increasingly committed to a relationship they come to think of their partners as part of themselves, and come to regard themselves as part of a collective unit that includes the partner. Consider David and Susan once again. Over time David may become increasingly committed to continuing his involvement with Susan, foreseeing an extended future with her in which his well-being rests on Susan and their relationship. Accordingly, increased commitment is likely to instigate more frequent relationship-relevant cognitive activity, along with a shift in the nature of personal identity and self-representation. David is likely to develop a relatively couple-oriented identity and a relatively pluralistic representation of his self-in-relationship. David no longer thinks of himself simply as David, but comes to regard himself as part of a collective

DavidandSusan unit. This pluralistic, collective mental representation of the self-in-relationship is referred to as a state of cognitive interdependence. Cognitive interdependence may be thought of as a habit of thinking that supports prorelationship motivation and behavior. The existing literature supports the assertion that cognitive interdependence characterizes committed relationships. For example, actor-observer differences in attribution are attenuated for close partners in comparison to strangers, with such attenuation presumably occurring because the distinction between self and partner becomes blurred (Sande, Goethals, & Radloff, 1988). Similarly, individuals tend to reflect others' successes when the other is close, but not when the other is a stranger (Tesser, 1988). The existence of reflected experiences of success and parallel patterns of self-partner attribution is compatible with the notion that commitment results in cognitive restructuring, including incorporation of a close partner into one's sense of self.

☐ Research on Cognitive Interdependence

To test whether strong commitment to a relationship is associated with a relatively pluralistic, other-inclusive cognitive representation of the self-in-relationship, we conducted two empirical studies, a cross-sectional survey study and a two-wave longitudinal study (Agnew, Van Lange, Rusbult, & Langston, 1998). Of course, to examine commitment-inspired changes in the self, we first had to identify valid methods of measuring the cognitive interdependence construct. We employed three operational definitions of the construct: 1) the spontaneous use of plural pronouns in relationship-relevant cognitions (i.e., exhibiting greater use of first person plural personal and possessive pronouns such as "we," "us," "our," or "ours"); 2) the Inclusion of Other in the Self Scale (IOS; Aron, Aron, & Smollan, 1992); and 3) self-reported centrality of one's relationship to one's life. These measures have the advantage of being psychometrically diverse: The pronoun measure provides a covert means of tapping relationship-relevant thought structures; the IOS Scale is a graphical measure that assesses how an individual mentally perceives the amount of self-partner overlap in a relationship; and the centrality of relationship measure is a paper-and-pencil self-report of the degree to which a relationship is considered an essential, highly central element of one's life. Collectively, these measures psychometrically triangulate on mental representations of the self-in-relationship.

For romantic relationships, we found that cognitive interdependence increased hand in hand with increases in commitment level. The more romantically committed individuals became, the greater was the tendency to think about the relationship in a pluralistic, other-inclusive manner, as reflected in the spontaneous use of plural pronouns to describe oneself and one's relationship. In addition, the more romantically committed individuals became, the more they came to regard themselves as "blended" with the partner, as revealed in perceived overlap in mental representations of self and partner. Furthermore, romantically committed individuals tended to regard their relationships as relatively central to who they are and what their lives are about.

We also found in our longitudinal study of romantic relationships that the effects of commitment and cognitive interdependence were reciprocal: Earlier commitment was significantly associated with increases over time in levels of cognitive interdependence and earlier cognitive interdependence was significantly associated with increases over time in commitment level. We anticipated such reciprocal causal associations, in that key processes in ongoing relationships unfold over extended periods of time. Such cyclical patterns could have considerable adaptive value in the context of a generally healthy ongoing involvement. Although the field of social psychology has tended to emphasize models of unidirectional cause-and-effect, models of mutual cyclical influence may be a more suitable means of understanding causal processes in ongoing relationships.

Cognitive Interdependence and the Experience of Loss

Given that commitment to a relationship entails a fundamental restructuring of one's cognitive representation of the self-in-relationship, it stands to reason that an unexpected or unwanted breech in commitment would have profound implications for an individual's sense of self. This is precisely the situation faced by an abandoned individual: One partner has unilaterally decided to terminate the relationship, despite the fact that the other partner still desires the relationship to continue. The abandoned partner is still mentally committed; that is, he or she has cognitively incorporated their now-former partner into their sense of self. In this way, abandoned individuals are quite similar to stayers: Both remain cognitively in the relationship, although only the stayers are still involved in an ongoing involvement. The experience of loss for the abandoned is likely to be quite devastating, as they discover that a fundamental part of the self that was once present is now absent.

Leavers may be assumed to possess quite different thoughts regarding the relationship. Over time, it might be expected that any sense of cognitive incorporation of the partner into the self would have either ceased or failed to develop in the first place. The tendency to possess plural thoughts with respect to the relationship would be displaced by more singular thinking (e.g., from "we complement each other" to "she and I are very different people"). Thus, the experience of loss for leavers is less likely to be characterized by strong emotions, as the fundamental sense of self is less likely to have experienced the same degree of change.

Cognitive Interdependence Over Time: New Longitudinal Findings

We sought to further document the existence of cognitive interdependence in committed romantic relationships and to trace the different cognitive patterns that we believe characterize the thinking of stayers, leavers, and the abandoned. To that end, we used data collected from college students involved in relatively newly-formed dating relationships. The advantage of utilizing a sample of new romances to study cognitive interdependence is largely pragmatic: there is a great likelihood that many of these relationships will end in a reasonably short period of time, and thus we can readily obtain the thoughts of all three categories of relationship members: leavers, stayers and the abandoned. Moreover, even in relatively new relationships, the experience of relationship loss can be quite intense.

Design and Participants. The data are from a multi-wave longitudinal study that was principally designed to investigate the stability of satisfaction level and development of commitment in recently initiated dating relationships (cf. Arriaga, 1999).

However, measures of cognitive interdependence were also collected. There were ten measurement occasions (or "Times") conducted one week apart and a follow-up session conducted approximately four months after Time 10. Measures of cognitive interdependence were collected on every other measurement occasion, during Times 2, 4, 6, 8, and 10. Participants were undergraduates who volunteered to participate in fulfillment of the requirements for introductory psychology courses at the University of North Carolina at Chapel Hill. In order to study the initial development of commitment, participation was limited to individuals who had been involved in a dating relationship of no less than two weeks and no more than three months. Sixty-five individuals began the study at Time 1, with 47 participants (31 females and 16 males) completing all eleven sessions. Data from these 47 participants were analyzed.

Participants were 19 years old on average and were mostly White (64%, with 26% African-American, 4% Asian-American, and 4% Latino). At Time 1, the relationships were, on average, eight weeks in duration and the majority of relationships were exclusive in nature: 74% of participants reported that they and their partner were dating exclusively and 26% reported that they were dating casually. At follow-up (four months after Time 10), 16 participants continued to be in their relationships (stayers) while 31 were no longer dating their Time 1 partners. Of the 31 relationships that ended, 20 of the breakups were participant-initiated (leavers), and 7 were partner-initiated (abandoned). Four participants reported that their relationships had ended by mutual agreement and are, thus, not included in the analyses presented here. Although not large, this data set provides a sufficient number of leavers, stayers, and abandoned to test the study hypotheses (outlined below).

Data collection sessions were conducted on a weekly basis in a small classroom, with up to 10 participants taking part in any given session. Upon arrival, the experimenter reviewed the activities for the day's session, assured participants that their responses would remain confidential, and distributed questionnaires. Because the study involved repeated visits, in addition to fulfilling a requirement for an introductory psychology course, participant names were entered in a raffle for a dinner certificate to the restaurant of their choice. At follow-up participants were debriefed and thanked for their assistance. Each session lasted approximately fifteen minutes.

Measuring Cognitive Interdependence. As in our past research we used three distinct indicators of cognitive interdependence. Of particular interest are the pronoun-based measures. A number of social psychological researchers have linked language use with interpersonal processes. For example, the number of first-, second-, and third-person singular and plural pronouns occurring during natural interaction has been found to be associated with empathic accuracy (Ickes, Stinson, Bissonnette, & Garcia, 1990). Similarly, language use has been analyzed in studies of attributional bias in relationships (Fiedler, Semin, & Koppetsch, 1991). Researchers have also made use of spontaneous verbalization procedures to investigate self-verification processes, on the assumption that spontaneous verbalization stands as "one means of laying bare the complex processes that mediate people's choice of interaction partners . . . . " (Swann, Stein-Seroussi, & Giesler, 1992, p. 399). In parallel fashion, our work examines language use in order to obtain a covert and unobtrusive sampling of mental structure. As in our earlier research (Agnew, Van Lange, Rusbult, & Langston, 1998), we reasoned that to the extent that a partner is regarded as part of the self, the individual should describe the relationship in more pluralistic terms (i.e., exhibit greater use of first-person plural personal and possessive pronouns such as "we," "us," "our," or "ours"). Accordingly, it was hypothesized that individuals who are more strongly committed will exhibit greater plural pronoun use in spontaneous verbalizations about their relationships.

Using an open-ended, spontaneous thought-listing procedure (cf. Brock, 1967; Greenwald, 1968), participants were asked to record their thoughts about their current relationship. The directions for the thought-listing task asked participants to "share some of your thoughts concerning your relationship." Participants were asked to record "any thoughts you have . . . . They can be positive or negative . . . . For each thought, we ask that you write a complete sentence. . . . Please use one line per thought. . . . You can write as many or as few thoughts as you'd care to. Keep in mind that there are no right or wrong answers . . . . " To help participants understand the task, four examples were provided—two positive and two negative—of which two included only plural pronouns (e.g., "We were made for one another") and two included only singular pronouns (e.g., "Sometimes I feel the need for more space"). Given that no order effects have been observed in past administrations of this measure, the examples provided in the instructions were presented in a standard mixed order. In order to maximize the odds that each thought listed by participants would include a subject (and hence, possibly a pronoun), participants were asked to write complete sentences. The instructions were followed by 12 numbered spaces on which participants were to record their thoughts. The questionnaire was self-paced, so participants could spend as much time as they wished recording their thoughts (in fact, participants spent no more than 5 minutes on this measure). No information was provided about why these verbalizations were requested; participants were not told that their thoughts would be coded for plural pronoun usage.

Each thought was later coded by two trained research assistants. Thoughts were coded as including only plural pronouns ("we," "us," "our"), only singular pronouns ("I," "me," "mine"), both plural and singular pronouns (e.g., "I think our relationship is good"), or no personal or possessive pronouns (e.g., "The relationship is good"). Interrater reliability was good ($\kappa = .93$). Coding disagreements were discussed and correct codes were determined. The proportion of plural thoughts (i.e., the number of thoughts that contained only plural pronouns relative to the total number of thoughts) was used as a measure of cognitive interdependence.

The IOS scale (Aron et al., 1992) was also used to assess cognitive fusion of partner with the self. The IOS scale was developed on the assumption that closeness can be conceptualized as overlapping selves, and that the scale taps the individual's "sense of being interconnected with another" (Aron et al., 1992, p. 598). The IOS scale presents seven Venn diagrams representing varying degrees of overlap; one circle is labeled as representing the self, the other circle is labeled as representing the other (or relationship partner). The respondent is asked to select the diagram that "best describes" the relationship. Diagram choices range from completely separate, nonoverlapping circles (1) to nearly complete overlap (7). We propose that this sense of interconnectedness—the tendency literally to perceive the self as overlapping with the partner—provides evidence of the state of cognitive interdependence. Accordingly, it was hypothesized that individuals who are more strongly committed to their relationships would perceive the partner as more integral to the self.

To the degree that a close relationship is regarded as an integral component of the self, the relationship should be regarded as central to one's life—as integral to what makes life important and meaningful. Thus, the tendency to describe one's relationship as central can be regarded as yet another manifestation of cognitive interdependence (cf. Lin & Rusbult, 1995). In addition to the covert language measure and the graphical IOS measure, we obtained an overt self-report measure to capture the more conscious and accessible manifestations of cognitive interdependence. It was predicted that individuals who are more committed to their relationships would report greater centrality of the relationship.

Centrality of relationship was measured with three self-report items: 1) Compared to your school activities, family, friends, etc., how central is this relationship to your life?; 2) How much time do you spend thinking about your relationship?; and 3) Among the things that give your life meaning, how important is your relationship? Each item was answered using a nine-point response scale (e.g., 0 = other things are of some importance, 8 = nothing else is of any importance). Inter-item reliability for the three items was high at each time period (average α = .81), so an averaged measure of centrality of relationship was computed as a third indicator of cognitive interdependence.

The three separate measures of cognitive interdependence obtained were found to be largely and significantly intercorrelated at each time period. Moreover, maximum-likelihood factor analyses indicating the presence of only one underlying factor in any given period. Therefore, we standardized each measure (setting the mean equal to 0 and the standard deviation equal to 1) and created a superordinate measure of cognitive interdependence for use in the analyses reported here.

Measuring Commitment. At each time period, participants also completed self-report measures of relationship commitment. Three items were used to measure each of the three components of commitment: intent to persist in the relationship (e.g., "I intend to stay in this relationship"), long-term orientation regarding the relationship (e.g., "It is likely that I will date someone other than my partner within the next year"), and psychological attachment to the relationship (e.g., "I would feel very upset if our relationship were to end in the near future"). In addition, one item measured general commitment level ("I am committed to maintaining my relationship with my partner"). Each item was answered using a nine-point response scale (0 = do not agree at all, 8 = agree completely). Item analyses revealed evidence of good reliability within each time period (with α-levels between .75 and .80), so an averaged commitment measure was constructed for each time period.

Distinguishing Between Groups. To measure break-up status, participants were asked whether they were still dating the person they were dating at Time 1. Participants who reported that their relationships had ended were also asked who was responsible for the breakup—the participant, the partner, or both participant and partner in mutual agreement. On the basis of responses to this question, participants were categorized into three groups: 1) those individuals whose relationships endured: stayers (n = 16); 2) those individuals who ended their relationships, or leavers (n = 20); and 3) those individuals whose partner ended the relationship, or abandoned individuals (n = 7).

Results Highlights

Only key findings are presented here. Of primary interest is the association between commitment and cognitive interdependence within each time period as well as the pattern of commitment level and of cognitive interdependence exhibited by the three groups over time. The longitudinal pattern of cognitive interdependence for stayers, leavers, and abandoned was traced to determine whether levels of this construct changed over time in similar ways for each group, or whether the changes varied by group.

Association between Commitment and Cognitive Interdependence. To determine whether commitment was associated with cognitive interdependence, correlations were computed between the two measures at each time period. Consistent with our theoretical position, commitment level was found to be associated with degree of cognitive interdependence within each time period (Time 2 r = .80, Time 4 r = .84 , Time 6 r =.75, Time 8 r = .77 , Time 10 r = .80, all ps < .001) as well as across time periods (average r = .82, p < .001). Although these results are qualified by the small sample size, they provide suggestive evidence of the link between degree of relationship commitment and degree of cognitive incorporation of one's relationship partner into the self.

Commitment and Cognitive Interdependence By Group. Figure 1 presents the level of commitment for each of the three groups over time. As the figure illustrates and as the results from analyses of variance demonstrate, the three groups initially did not differ in their levels of commitment. However, over time, leavers be-

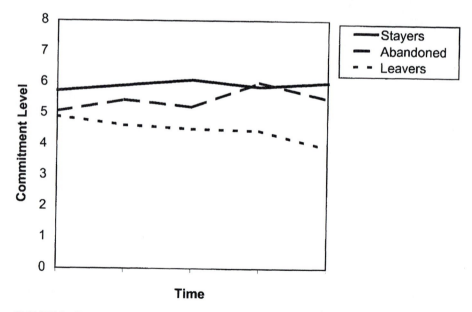

FIGURE 1. Commitment to a relationship over time among stayers, the abandoned, and leavers.

come increasingly less committed than stayers, differences that are statistically significant by Time 6. That these two types of relationship members would differ in commitment is not particularly surprising given the respective fates of their relationships. The results for abandoned individuals are more noteworthy: They did not differ significantly from stayers at any point in time and were marginally more committed than leavers by Time 8. In other words, abandoned individuals were just as committed to their partners over time as those individuals whose relationships remained intact.

Figure 2 presents the pattern of cognitive interdependence for stayers, leavers, and abandoned for each time period. Consistent with the results for commitment level, results from analyses of variance show that individuals in the three groups did not differ in their initial degree of cognitive interdependence. However, over time, stayers exhibited increasingly more cognitive interdependence than did leavers. More interestingly, abandoned individuals did not differ from stayers at any point in time. Thus, the abandoned evidenced the same degree of cognitive interdependence over time as stayers. From a cognitive perspective, their relationships appear to have never ended.

☐ Implications for Understanding the Experience of Relationship Loss

These current results suggest that, for all intents and purposes, abandoned individuals have the same hopes and aspirations for their relationships as do stayers—these two groups exhibited similar levels of commitment over time. The obvious, but important, difference between these two groups is that abandoned individuals are faced

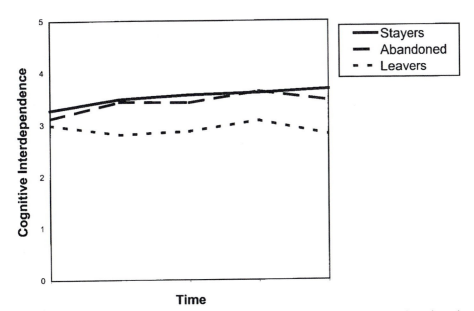

FIGURE 2. Cognitive interdependence over time among stayers, the abandoned, and leavers.

with the loss of their relationship. This is not to say that their relationships were perfect. Indeed, other analyses of these data have shown that the abandoned individuals' relationships were as poorly functioning as those of leavers (Arriaga, 1999). However, rather than focus on such objective qualities as relationship functioning, the current research examined the cognitive experiences of this group. These results help illustrate why certain people are so strongly affected by the loss of a specific relationship or relationship partner: Abandoned individuals think in terms of an intact relationship, seeing themselves still as one with the partner. Their thoughts include the partner, despite the ill fate of their relationship. It is the residual traces of cognitive interdependence that often result in a devastating emotional experience.

Although it may be obvious that abandoned individuals have a more difficult time with their situation than do leavers, documenting the course of recovery for abandoned individuals would be a fruitful direction for future research. Part of identifying the essential qualities of well-functioning, long-term relationships involves noting what is missed once a relationship is no longer intact. By examining abandoned individuals following their loss, more can be learned about what helps make a relationship work. This point is consistent with Berscheid's (1983) view that partners are not aware of the strength of their bonds until their relationship is disrupted, at which time they experience strong affective reactions to the loss of their partner and relationship.

It would also be of interest to follow abandoned individuals over significantly longer periods of time to determine if they become less likely to cognitively incorporate a future relationship partner given their past negative experience (following the adage, "once burned, twice shy"). Such a tendency, of course, would have implications for one's ability to form a committed relationship in the future. However, what at one point may be a negative effect of relationship loss may at a later point turn into a positive effect. For instance, it is possible that the loss experience makes individuals more able to face future relationship challenges (following the adage "what doesn't kill you makes you stronger"). Thus, longitudinal studies spanning significant periods of time would greatly enrich our knowledge of both the immediate and long-term effects of relationship loss.

☐ Conclusion

Research on individuals who experience relationship loss stands to make important contributions to the larger literature on loss. For instance, research on abandoned individuals may uncover effective coping mechanisms that transcend not only relationship loss but also other forms of loss. Although more needs to be learned about the etiology of relationship loss, it is hoped that the concept of cognitive interdependence will be regarded as useful in the continuing quest to understand the mental underpinnings of breaking-up and helpful for practitioners who work with those who suffer from its consequences.

☐ References

Agnew, C. R., Van Lange, P. A. M., Rusbult, C. E., & Langston, C. A. (1998). Cognitive interdependence: Commitment and the mental representation of close relationships. *Journal of Personality and Social Psychology, 74,* 939–954.

Andersen, S. M., & Glassman, N. S. (1996). Responding to significant others when they are not there: Effects on interpersonal inference, motivation, and affect. In R. M. Sorrentino & E. T. Higgins (Eds.), *Handbook of motivation and cognition* (Vol. 3, pp. 262–321). New York: Guilford.

Aron, A., & Aron, E. N. (1997). Self-expansion motivation and including other in the self. In S. Duck (Ed.), *Handbook of personal relationships: Theory, method, and interventions* (2nd ed., pp. 251–270). Chichester, England: Wiley.

Aron, A., Aron, E. N., & Smollan, D. (1992). Inclusion of other in the self scale and the structure of interpersonal closeness. *Journal of Personality and Social Psychology, 63,* 596–612.

Aron, A., & Westbay, L. (1996). Dimensions of the prototype of love. *Journal of Personality and Social Psychology, 70,* 535–551.

Arriaga, X. B. (1999). *The ups and downs of dating: Fluctuations in satisfaction in newly-formed romantic relationships.* Manuscript submitted for publication.

Arriaga, X. B., & Agnew, C. R. (1999). *Being committed: Affective, cognitive, and conative components of relationship commitment.* Manuscript submitted for publication.

Berscheid, E. (1983). Emotion. In H. H. Kelley, E. Berscheid, A. Christensen, J. H. Harvey, T. L. Huston, G. Levinger, E. McClintock, L. A. Peplau, & D. R. Peterson (Eds.), *Close relationships* (pp. 110–168). New York: Freeman.

Berscheid, E., & Reis, H. T. (1998). Attraction and close relationships. In D. T. Gilbert, S. T. Fiske, & G. Lindzey (Eds.), *The handbook of social psychology* (4th ed., pp. 193–281). New York: McGraw-Hill.

Bowlby, J. (1969). *Attachment and loss, volume 1.* New York: Basic Books

Bowlby, J. (1980). *Attachment and loss, volume 3.* New York: Basic Books

Brock, T. C. (1967). Communication discrepancy and intent to persuade as determinants of counterargument production. *Journal of Experimental Social Psychology, 3,* 269–309.

Devine, P. G., Hamilton, D. L., & Ostrom, T. M. (1994). *Social cognition: Impact on social psychology.* San Diego, CA: Academic Press.

Fiedler, K., Semin, G. R., & Koppetsch, C. (1991). Language use and attributional biases in close personal relationships. *Personality and Social Psychology Bulletin, 17,* 147–155.

Greenwald, A. G. (1968). Cognitive learning, cognitive response to persuasion, and attitude change. In A. G. Greenwald, T. C. Brock, & T. M. Ostrom (Eds.), *Psychological foundations of attitudes* (pp. 147–170). San Diego, CA: Academic Press.

Harvey, J. H. (1998). *Perspectives on loss: A sourcebook.* Philadelphia: Brunner/Mazel.

Harvey, J. H., & Miller, E. D. (1998). Toward a psychology of loss. *Psychological Science, 9,* 429–434.

Ickes, W., Stinson, L., Bissonnette, V., & Garcia, S. (1990). Naturalistic social cognition: Empathic accuracy in mixed-sex dyads. *Journal of Personality and Social Psychology, 59,* 730–742.

Kelley, H. H. (1979). *Personal relationships: Their structure and processes.* Hillsdale, NJ: Erlbaum.

Kelley, H. H., & Thibaut, J. W. (1978). *Interpersonal relations: A theory of interdependence.* New York: Wiley.

Kitson, G. C., & Morgan, L. A. (1990). The multiple consequences of divorce: A decade review. *Journal of Marriage and the Family, 52,* 913–924.

Lin, Y. H. W., & Rusbult, C. E. (1995). Commitment to dating relationships and cross-sex friendships in America and China: The impact of centrality of relationship, normative support, and investment model variables. *Journal of Social and Personal Relationships, 12,* 7–26.

Markus, H., & Zajonc, R. B. (1985). The cognitive perspective in social psychology. In G. Lindzey & E. Aronson (Eds.), *The handbook of social psychology* (3rd ed., pp. 137–230). New York: Random House.

McFarland, C., & Ross, M. (1987). The relation between current impressions and memories of self and dating partners. *Personality and Social Psychology Bulletin, 13,* 228–238.

Murray, S. L., & Holmes, J. G. (1997). A leap of faith? Positive illusions in romantic relationships. *Personality and Social Psychology Bulletin, 23,* 586–604.

Nolen-Hoeksema, S., McBride, A., & Larson, J. (1997). Rumination and psychological distress among bereaved partners. *Journal of Personality and Social Psychology, 72,* 855–862.

Rusbult, C. E. (1983). A longitudinal test of the investment model: The development (and deterioration) of satisfaction and commitment in heterosexual involvements. *Journal of Personality and Social Psychology, 45,* 101–117.

Rusbult, C. E., Arriaga, X. A., & Agnew, C. R. (in press). Interdependence processes. To appear in M. Clark & G. Fletcher (Eds.), *The Blackwell handbook of social psychology, Vol. 2: Interpersonal processes.* Oxford, UK: Blackwell.

Rusbult, C. E., Martz, J. M. & Agnew, C. R. (1998). The Investment Model Scale: Measuring commitment level, satisfaction level, quality of alternatives, and investment size. *Personal Relationships, 5,* 357–391.

Rusbult, C. E., Verette, J., Whitney, G. A., Slovik, L. F., & Lipkus, I. (1991). Accommodation processes in close relationships: Theory and preliminary empirical evidence. *Journal of Personality and Social Psychology, 60,* 53–78.

Sande, G. N., Goethals, G. R., & Radloff, C. E. (1988). Perceiving one's own traits and others': The multifaceted self. *Journal of Personality and Social Psychology, 54,* 13–20.

Simpson, J. A., Gangestad, S. W., & Lerma, M. (1990). Perception of physical attractiveness: Mechanisms involved in the maintenance of romantic relationships. *Journal of Personality and Social Psychology, 59,* 1192–1201.

Sternberg, R. J. & Hojjat, M. (Eds.). (1997). *Satisfaction in close relationships.* New York: Guilford.

Swann, W. B., Jr., Stein-Seroussi, A., & Giesler, R. B. (1992). Why people self-verify. *Journal of Personality and Social Psychology, 62,* 392–401.

Tesser, A. (1988). Toward a self-evaluation maintenance model of social behavior. In L. Berkowitz (Ed.), *Advances in experimental social psychology* (Vol. 21, pp. 181–227). San Diego, CA: Academic Press.

Van Lange, P. A. M., Rusbult, C. E., Drigotas, S. M., Arriaga, X. B., Witcher, B. S., & Cox, C. L. (1997). Willingness to sacrifice in close relationships. *Journal of Personality and Social Psychology, 72,* 1373–1395.

Wieselquist, J., Rusbult, C. E., Foster, C. A., & Agnew, C. R. (1999). Commitment, pro-relationship behavior, and trust in close relationships. *Journal of Personality and Social Psychology, 77,* 942–966.

CONCLUSION

25
CHAPTER

Robert A. Neimeyer
Heidi M. Levitt

What's Narrative Got to Do With It?
Construction and Coherence
in Accounts of Loss

My mother's death was a central experience with all of the associated ripplings. There are times when I simply miss her being on the planet, and would like to sit beside her for a good chat and sense her tenderness. Those moments of longing are usually unexpected, accompanied by a free flow of tears, and filled with remembrance. My relationships with my brother and sister, immeasurably deepened during the course of my mother's illness and death, continue to be a source of support as I absorb the reality of my mother's absence. I am particularly grateful for the surprising changes in openness and connection between my sister and myself. I am also struck by the realization that my mother was the last surviving member of the generation before me, and that only one niece, with whom I have little contact, follows me in the next generation. This leaves me with a feeling of discontinuity, as if I were in a somewhat timeless place. My mother's death has me revisiting the loss I feel around not being a mother, and amplifies questions I have about sources of meaning in my life given that the story I had written for myself has not taken form. So, I'm trying to imagine and make sense of my life differently. This is all quite unsettling, at times unnerving, and at times quite liberating. I am grateful that I have the resources and opportunity to pause and consider possibilities at this important juncture in my life.

—Barbara, age 43, (personal communication)

As constructivist/narrative theorists and therapists (Neimeyer & Mahoney, 1995), we read the foregoing contributions to this volume with a sort of double vision. On the one hand, we were inexorably drawn toward organizing the varied chapters in terms of a constructivist vision of human beings as active, meaning-making agents, struggling, like Barbara in the passage above, to assimilate disruptive experiences within frames of significance that are themselves challenged by loss. On the other hand, we also found ourselves attempting to envision ways of assisting persons whose life stories have been rewritten by these often critical or traumatic losses, as they attempted to make sense of them, and again move toward a meaningful future. This brief chapter is the result of this dual focus. We will begin by viewing selected contributions of previous authors through the wide-angle lens of a narrative model of loss, and periodically focus more narrowly on some illustrative psychotherapeutic interventions that we believe fit within this larger picture. In so doing, we hope to offer a provisional way of integrating some of the previous contributions into a broader view, and suggest areas in need of closer examination. In addition, we hope to invite attention to the therapeutic potential of a narrative model for those readers interested in the practical yield of academic studies of loss for their own lives and those of their clients.

☐ Stories We Live, and Stories that Live Us

For many people, the idea that human beings are inveterate storytellers has intuitive appeal. Whether we are reading bedtime stories to our children, telling a joke to a colleague, reading a book, watching a movie, or relating a disturbing event to our partner or friend, we seem to both organize and assimilate experience spontaneously in storied form. Indeed, cognitive scientists have adduced considerable evidence that the declarative memory we use to impart order to temporally distributed experiences is fundamentally narrative, consisting of scripts, event structures or story schemas (Barsalou, 1988; Mandler, 1984). By extension, the self is similarly constructed through an endless series of micronarratives of daily events, eventually abstracting these into an overarching macronarrative of our lives that winnows out those relatively stable features of plot and theme upon which we build a sense of identity (Angus, Levitt, & Hardke,1999).

In both cases, individuals can be viewed as the authors of the stories they live, in the sense that they actively impose a story structure on inchoate experience, relate such stories to others, and ultimately compose themselves in the process (Neimeyer, 2000). In parallel terms, molecular social groupings such as couples (Harvey, 1996), friendship networks (Neimeyer, Brooks, & Baker, 1996) and families (Nadeau, 1997) also seek coherent identities through composing a joint narrative account of who they are and the experiences they have shared. At the most molar level, whole societies, peoples or nations establish a sense of their tradition and distinctiveness through the explicit creation of culture tales (Howard, 1991) that capture and preserve their unique history.

All too often, however, these personal, interpersonal, and cultural attempts at constructing a coherent account are challenged by both normative and traumatic losses (e.g., bereavement, divorce, war) that render individual or collective attempts at meaning-making chaotic or conflicted. As Ferring and Filipp (Chapter 10, this volume) note, the reestablishment of meaning in such cases involves "the integration of a threatening, harmful experience into one's model of the self and the world by answering questions reconstructing the causal 'why' and the teleological 'why' 'what for'" (p. 153). Even appropriate losses tend to stimulate an attempt to restore some measure of coherence and continuity to the personal or shared narrative, perhaps by authoring a new identity that incorporates the loss. Barbara, the writer of the letter with which this chapter opened, seemed to be struggling with something of this sort, as she tried to make sense of the losses (e.g., of her mother's tenderness) and gains (e.g., the surprising changes in connection to her sister) associated with her mother's death.

Although the human attempt to author adequate life stories is obvious, what is less obvious is that people are sometimes "lived by" stories for which they feel no authorial responsibility, or even editorial control (Mair, 1988). Sometimes these stories seem imposed upon them by others, while at other times, they seem to have originated in a once chosen life script that now seems ill-fitting, constraining, or no longer viable. At such times, the discursive resources (e.g., definitions of appropriate social roles, gender identities, cultural ideals) on which people inevitably draw in constructing a sense of self, relationship, or collective identity (Burr, 1995) can come to feel suffocating, inhibiting the personal and social transformations required at times of transition. Something of this sort seemed to be hinted at by Barbara as she reflected on "the loss she felt around not being a mother," a culturally dominant script that she had unreflectively taken up, and that was made salient upon her mother's death. Although she described the generational discontinuity that resulted as unsettling, it was also "liberating," as she began to review the story she had written for herself and began to envision her life differently. Significantly, although these changes were deeply personal, they were also inherently interpersonal, insofar as they entailed shifts in relationship narratives involving significant others both named and unnamed in the letter.

As a way of understanding difficulties arising in the narrative construction of identity in the face of loss, we will outline a general model for analyzing both disrupted and dominating narratives, and suggest their relevance to various contexts ranging from the intrapsychic, through the interpersonal, to the intercultural. This matrix of narrative problems and contexts will also provide a framework for our consideration of some of the conceptual and empirical contributions made by other authors in this volume, as well as our reflection on therapeutic strategies that could prove useful at each of these levels.

☐ Coherence and Complication in Narrative Formation

Stories of loss are often polyvocal, spoken differently from the perspective of the many participants in a grief system, or even from the vantage point of the many voices that issue from a given individual, simultaneously or across time. This raises the possibility—indeed, the probability—of conflict among these accounts of the same loss event. At an individual level, such conflict can take the form of incoherence in one's life story across time, as when a traumatic loss precipitates changes in one's guiding assumptions or sense of self that are radically at odds with what came before. It can also take the form of simultaneous incoherence, as when one voice in the griever incriminates the self for not having averted a loved one's suicide, while another blames the victim. The dialectical tension between these opposing stories is not easily held, and tends to push the narrator toward some form of resolution or integration of the split (Greenberg & Pascual-Leone, 1995).

At a more interpersonal level, the process of narration can be understood as a social or political act, which posits one's own account of an event as true at the possible expense of others. Stories, in this view, stake a claim, they position self and others in a particular (and frequently self-serving) moral discourse (Neimeyer, 2000). Thus, stories of the meaning of any particular loss can be sites of significant conflict, as when two of the fifteen trees planted for the children who died in the Littleton, Colorado, high school shootings were cut down by families who could not abide 'honoring' the killers. Such actions can be understood as the confluence of two clashing stories, in the absence of a narrative frame large enough or durable enough to contain both. This is particularly problematic when the potentially integrative frame is more weakly scripted (Ferring & Filipp, this volume) or less widely held than the conflicting stories it attempts to supplant. In the case of the trees in Littleton, a black-and-white narrative of moral outrage and condemnation easily trumps a shades-of-gray narrative of psychological understanding.[1]

At an abstract level, complicated grief might be understood in terms of the dialectics of coherence or incoherence of the stories being told or enacted about the loss. The pursuit of such coherence, while having deeply personal aspects, is not fundamentally an individualistic process, but is situated within the complexly interdependent resource webs in which human beings are embedded (Hobfall, Ennis, & Kay in Chapter 17 of this volume). For example, problems can arise when incommensurable narratives of the same loss exist: 1) within persons, 2) among persons (e.g., within the same family or community), or 3) among any of the above and broader cultural frames of reference. At such times, it can be therapeutic to work toward a more inclusive narrative that permits such competing accounts to be integrated into a larger whole, or that at least permits each to be respected in its own right. The need to articulate conflicting stories may be most obvious in family therapy, but it may apply equally forcefully at larger community or even cultural levels.

At other times, a given story of loss can become in a sense *too* coherent, too demanding of allegiance, as when family members are subtly pressured toward a false consensus about the meaning of an ambiguous death of one of its members. In such cases, the therapist may need to use circular questions (Selvini-Palazzoli, Boscolo, Cecchin, & Prata, 1980) to point to and support the differences in a family account that threatens to become dominant, marginalizing those who construe the loss in other terms. Cultures can also enforce or fail to question a dominant narrative, as when a story of a recent church shooting was formulated uncritically in the words of one of its survivors: "We are God's people, and expect to contend with Satan." Here, the failure to inquire into the ambiguous meaning of the tragedy stands in stark contrast to the endless conjecture about the causes of the Littleton shootings.

To provide a more systematic framework for organizing the different levels of narrative complication resulting from loss, we have nested the two major categories of difficulties (narrative disruption on the one hand, and dominance on the other) within three contexts ranging from the intrapersonal to the intercultural. The resulting matrix is depicted in Table 1, and will be used to guide the discussion of research and clinical issues that follows.

☐ Disrupted Narratives

Disrupted narratives take two forms: those that are chaotic, and those that are conflictual. In both cases, an existing and previously adequate life narrative is challenged by the loss, and ceases to provide a coherent structure for integrating past experience, enacting a meaningful social role in the present, and projecting into the

---

[1]This thought developed in conversation between one of the authors (R.A.N.) and fellow members of the International Work Group on Death, Dying, and Bereavement, held in Boulder, Colorado, in September of 1999. We would like to especially acknowledge the contributions of Dennis Klass, Julie Edwards, and Janice Nadeau to this narrative elaboration.

TABLE 1. Examples of problematic narratives organized by type and context.

Context	Disrupted Narratives		Dominating Narratives	
	Chaos Intrusion of loss into previously coherent narrative	**Conflict** Collision of two incompatible narratives	**Consistency** Foreclosure of a preexisting narrative	**Conformity** Subordination of a narrative to one more powerful
Intrapersonal	Suicide of partner shatters narrative of relationship, activating unfinished business	Clashing stories of self as victim-survivor versus self as cause of partner's murder of child	Graduate student's self-narrative will not accommodate threatening diagnosis of a learning disability	Stayer in a disintegrating relationship remains committed to narrative of good relationship and ignores problems
Interpersonal	Loss of a special child disrupts family narrative of parents	Conflicting accounts of meaning of miscarriage between husband and wife	Prior marriage narrative complicates accommodating reality of affair	Accounts of loss by friends of deceased subordinated to those of family
Cultural	Ethnic genocide undermines account of a nation's collective identity	Discordant African-American and Euro American grief scripts clash in hospital setting	Subculture struggles with revising its death rituals with acculturation to new country	Subcultures of butch and femme lesbians marginalized in androgynous culture of 1970s

future. In the first instance, the narrative is thrown into a state of confusion by the loss, at any of three levels—intrapersonal, interpersonal, and cultural—as follows.

Intrapersonal chaos occurs when a loss intrudes into an individual's heretofore coherent story of the self or significant others, in such a way that it cannot easily be assimilated. This form of disruption was experienced poignantly by Karen, a 28-year-old woman, who returned from work one day to discover the faceless corpse of her partner, who in a depressive state had committed suicide by placing a shotgun against the roof of his mouth and pulling the trigger. Although Karen's story of their relationship accommodated her partner's moodiness and increasing withdrawal, she found his final act of self-destruction incomprehensible, and was caught up in a whirlwind of questioning about not only his suicide, but also her potential responsibility for the tragedy. Significantly, the personal chaos triggered by the death reverberated deeply into her biography, as it ushered in flashbacks to another murder by gunshot she had witnessed at age 10, and had nearly forgotten. Therapy in Karen's case took the form of first writing an account of her relational struggles with her partner, and then attempting to place them into the broader context of a life story of stoic survivorship in the face of multiple losses. More detailed presentations of narrative techniques in the context of psychotherapy for traumatic assault have been provided by Neimeyer and

Stewart (1998), and the growth-promoting possibilities of assumption-shattering experiences have been outlined by Janoff-Bulman and Berger (Chapter 2, this volume).

Interpersonal chaos refers to the jarring disruption of a shared or communal narrative that leaves two or more persons struggling to make sense of the destabilizing transition, without access to any clear means of doing so. This aptly described the experience of George and Mary, a middle-class couple whose only son, Michael, died of asthma during his second year of college. For over a decade, Michael had seemed to embody all that was special in their family, as represented by his love of books, his command of world events, his musical precocity, and the way in which he had provided the glue that held his parents together through their vicarious investment in his pursuits. Now, cruelly deprived of his participation in their lives, Mary and George felt that their own lives ended with his. Compounding this emotional anguish was their inability to conceive of a way of rewriting their family narrative that made sense, having lost his presence in the family story as the leading character. The way forward seemed to involve their symbolic identification with Michael's best characteristics, in a sense giving him a continued existence through cultivating these same possibilities in themselves. This form of reconnection with the inner representation of a deceased child is sensitively explored by Klass (1999), and various models for understanding the quest for a stable and viable cognitive interpretation of the loss are summarized by Updegraff and Taylor (Chapter 1, this volume).

Cultural chaos ensues when the narrative continuity of a people or nation is disrupted by natural or human-made disasters.[2] As we are writing, the people of East Timor are contending with the arduous task of reweaving an account of their collective identity that somehow gives meaning to the outbreak of pro-Indonesian violence that left its capital city in ruins, and its population displaced. As in similar ethnic uprisings, the task of constructing a jointly held story of the tragedy and the history into which it is inserted is played out on a political stage rather than a therapeutic one, but it nonetheless entails a process of narrative repair on a collective scale. The failure to initiate a healing story of this kind can result in a deviation-amplifying cycle of recrimination, triggering the sort of escalating loss cycles posited by Hobfall and his colleagues (Chapter 17, this volume).

In contrast to chaotic disruption, when those affected by the loss struggle to piece together a once coherent story now shattered by the loss, narrative conflict arises when two or more internally coherent stories vie with one another for assent or acceptance. As is true of narrative chaos, narrative conflict can occur on any level of the self or system.

Intrapersonal conflict refers to discordance between two antagonistic voices within

---

[2]Technically, disruption at the level of "culture tales" could be subdivided into intra- and intercultural contexts, paralleling the subdivisions we proposed for persons above. Thus, a random mass shooting that calls into question the ethos of a society would introduce a chaotic disruption of an intracultural narrative, while an outbreak of genocidal retribution between two warring tribes would be intercultural in the strict sense. However, we are adopting the general designation of "cultural" to refer to both of these circumstances, as well as instances in which the narrative of a given individual or group fails to square with that of the broader culture, as illustrated below. Such a usage sacrifices some precision for the sake of brevity in this short exposition of the narrative coherence model.

the self about an experience. For example, Barry, a 47-year-old father of two children, was torn between two competing narratives of his wife's breakdown, which ended dramatically in her killing of their 4-year-old daughter and her own subsequent suicide. On the one hand, he wanted desperately to explain these incomprehensible acts using a narrative of mental illness, which offered the cold comfort that his wife was driven by a disease process that he at worst abetted through failing to get her professional help. On the other hand, he vacillated between this medical account and a more private one, which emplotted the deaths within a history of marital tension and accusations of infidelity that he shared with no one else. To restore a sense of wholeness to his account of the loss, it was necessary to first articulate the strands of each competing narrative, and then reach for a more inclusive story of the family tragedy that accredited the emotional truth of both. Narrative procedures for promoting this form of therapeutic integration have been reviewed by Neimeyer (2000).

Interpersonal conflict arises when the discordant voices regarding the narrative of an event are situated in different people, rather than within the same individual. This form of incoherence typified the conversations of Mark and Rita, a couple striving to conceive their first child in the face of years of infertility and miscarriage. Whereas Mark was willing to accommodate his wife's powerful desire to bear a child, for Rita doing so represented the fulfillment of her identity as a woman. Thus, each storied the event of the miscarriage differently. For Mark it was unfortunate, to be sure, because it fit within a narrative of mutual failure and portended more clinical regulation of their sexual relationship to increase the odds of successful task completion in the future. For Rita, on the other hand, the spontaneous abortion represented the loss of a real child, whose movements she had felt within her, and who she had invested with a name and identity. Thus, in a real sense, each suffered a very different loss in connection with the same objective event, which might be viewed as occasioning stress on Mark's part, and genuine grief on Rita's. Therapeutic movement was restored when each was able to recognize and validate the complementary narrative of the partner, and begin to collaborate on coauthoring an account that acknowledged the validity of both perspectives. Research on adjustment to infertility has been reviewed by Abbey (Chapter 20, this volume), and the extreme case of interpersonal narrative conflict between perpetrators and their victims has been considered by Baumeister and Bratslavsky (Chapter 5, this volume).

Cultural conflict can arise when two or more narratives, each of which is valid in its own right, collide in the context of a specific loss. Such conflict arose at the bedside of Ophelia, the 82-year-old matriarch of an African-American family who was dying of progressive heart failure in a large urban hospital. In this case, the European-American script for grieving valued stoicism, restraint, and personal leave taking by individuals or small family groups, a script that was endorsed by the predominantly white medical caregivers, and—not incidentally—the hospital code of procedure. However, such a script was strongly at odds with the preferences of Ophelia's loved ones, which cohered with a cultural narrative of extended family and even community involvement in the passing, marked by suitably respectful and emotionally vivid wailing at the point of death. Psychological consultation was requested by nursing staff when these two cultures collided, leading to the negotiation of a private space on the unit in which the culturally appropriate ways of recognizing and ritualizing Ophelia's loss could be enacted by her mourners. Sensitive exploration of such culture clashes has been provided by Hebért (1998), and an ethological narrative of an African-American grief system has been offered by Dula (1997).

☐ Dominating Narratives

Just as difficulties can occur when life stories are disrupted by loss and trauma, likewise complications can arise when the narrative into which the loss is forced is too constraining. Such dominating narratives can be seen as demanding excessive coherence, restricting narrative innovation and development. As a result, these narratives appear prematurely to halt the process of storying a disturbing event by blocking the recognition of new meanings, or disallowing the recognition of divergent plots or themes that could contribute to an alternative narrative. We consider these forms of narrative dominance, respectively, as due to excessive consistency or conformity.

Intrapersonal consistency becomes problematic when narratives do not allow for the changes that occur within the reality of lived experience (e.g., Goncalves, Korman, & Angus, 2000). These foreclosed narratives can prevent individuals from developing adaptive self-narratives, leaving critical experiences outside the range of their explicit self-concept (Arciero & Guidano, 2000). An example of this dilemma occurred when Carl, a student in his first semester of graduate school, was diagnosed as having a learning disability. He was terribly pained by the threat of carrying this "lifelong burden," and refused any assistance or support for his disability, despite his poor grades. His dominant narrative of a competent self was simply too rigid to accept an understanding of himself as needing support. Farina's (Chapter 12, this volume) description of difficulties that clients can have when they language their self-perception in terms of mental illness reflects the flip side of this constraint in an intrapersonal narrative. When individuals become dominated by a progressively reinforced identity as mentally ill, they may resist a more optimistic narrative of independence, as reflected in findings that such terminology increases dependency on mental health workers. Thus, a consistent self-narrative can be dominating if it is either so foreclosed as to preclude useful acknowledgement of a loss, or if it becomes monolithically organized around one's status as victim or sufferer, in a way that blocks more hopeful elaboration of one's life story. In such cases, therapy might assist individuals to recognize how they construct and restrict their experience through the analysis of their metaphors (e.g., Angus & Rennie, 1989; Levitt, Korman & Angus, in press). For instance, Carl's metaphor of a learning disability as a "lifelong burden" might be critically deconstructed by prompting him to visualize the shape and weight of the burden, considering how it might be carried, when it might be laid down, and so on. Ultimately, the goal of intervention might be to help him view his learning difficulties as only one micronarrative in his larger story of self, which could be revised without jeopardizing the central themes of his identity.

Interpersonal consistency occurs when individuals have dominating relationship-narratives that do not allow for shifts that occur within their relationship across time. For instance, Linda, a recently divorced woman, suddenly found herself questioning her inclusion in her friendship circle—one that was entirely composed of still-married friends. Her shift in marital status conflicted with the group identity narrative (married women) and their history, particularly as their discussions usually focused upon marital issues. Even though Linda felt comfortable in the group herself, the group members struggled to reconceptualize their relational-narrative to continue to include Linda as a valid group member. The history of groups can act as a powerful force that militates against change in group identity narratives.

Accommodating inconsistent plot developments in a relational narrative can be a challenging process. Regarding the process of healing from extramarital affairs, Boekhout, Hendrick, and Hendrick (Chapter 22, this volume) observe that the "adjustment process involves the reconciliation of old, overly positive invalid assumptions about the world and new, extremely negative, questionably valid assumptions about the world" (p. 361). Couples vacillate between these world views and denial and renegotiation of experience in the process of creating a more realistic marital story. In couples therapy, it could be useful to understand and to label these cycles as part of the reconstruction of the relationship narrative.

Cultural consistency causes difficulty when a culture or subculture struggles to adapt its dominant narrative to changes occurring over time or in different contexts. For example, many Asian-American populations are currently facing significant challenges to their traditional beliefs and practices regarding grief and mourning as they become increasingly acculturated to life in the United States. Adaptive revision of these loss narratives requires a delicate bridging of the old and new, rather than a wholesale preservation of the old or its outright rejection, both of which create intergenerational tensions (Braun & Nichols, 1997). Moreover, the failure of a dominant cultural narrative to accredit the unique losses sustained by an oppressed group can be viewed as an effort to preserve the consistency of a culture's macronarrative at the expense of many of its members. Raphael and Dobson's (Chapter 3, this volume) discussion of how bereavement can be passed on across generations in the case of marginalized groups illustrates the narrative gap left by the failure to incorporate such losses into the historical account of a people. In dealing with this type of loss, empowerment may be sought by incorporating into cultural narratives greater recognition of their losses and changes that have been made across time, allowing for a clearer validation of the story of the community.

Conformity in narratives occurs when one narrative is so powerful that it does not allow for the emergence of competing narratives. Difficulties in conformity occur, not because of difficulty adapting to changes within a narrative across time, but because of the presence of a strong narrative that forces a compliance of perspective. Problems of conformity can result in difficulty recognizing or developing germinal narrative themes.

Intrapersonal conformity results from an individual's over-investment in one narrative at the expense of others, creating one aspect of self-identity or experience that becomes too powerful to admit competing narratives. For instance, Cara, a 25-year-old woman, entered therapy to explore her pattern of conflictual relationships. In therapy, she presented a narrative of self that focused on herself as a protector. Her role in her family of origin had been to defend her siblings against paternal abuse and her identity appeared to have been organized around this central function. Prior to therapy, however, this identity had precluded the development of a story that represented her very significant experiences of victimization. The absence of a personally relevant account of her own abuse prevented her from recognizing times when she was abused in the present and kept her overly invested in all-too-familiar protective roles, sometimes at the expense of her own development. Similarly, the stayers discussed by Agnew (Chapter 24, this volume) can become so committed to the narrative of having a good relationship that they end up being abandoned without having developed an awareness of relationship difficulties that might have seemed evident to their partners. When confronting intrapsychic conformity in psychotherapy, Gendlin's (1996) focusing can be useful in allowing clients to differentiate and voice fragile self-narratives that might otherwise be subordinated to the pull for conformity to a dominant account.

Interpersonal conformity occurs when social pressure leads individuals to suppress their own story in order to maintain their alliance with others' narratives, forcing the individuals into a position of pseudomutuality. These coconstructed narratives can be quite powerful, and at times can overshadow or obscure the unique experiences of individuals within the system who otherwise might have developed more idiosyncratic stories to describe the significance of their experience of loss. Peskin (Chapter 6, this volume) provides a telling description of interpersonal conformity in which friends of a deceased individual are expected to subordinate their experiences of loss to those of the family, posing the risk that their own accounts of the meaning of the loss will go unvoiced or invalidated.

In interpersonal situations, it might be important to introduce mediation to give power to the disempowered individual and his or her account of experience. Based upon Boekhout, Hendrick, and Hendrick's (Chapter 22, this volume) descriptions of narratives of infidelity, one easily might imagine a situation in which a domineering spouse defends a narrative of extramarital relationships in terms of their role in personal growth. The weaker spouse may find it difficult to articulate and defend conflicting ideals and, without the help of a couples therapist to negotiate these differences in perspective, may find his or her own ideal relationship narrative overshadowed. It can be important to encourage clients in these situations to legitimate their experience and to ensure that their own accounts receive equal attention.

Cultural conformity results from coercive forces by a dominant culture that can limit the development of alternative narratives of an individual, a subculture or a less powerful culture. Political action can be a useful way to unite individuals. It can help them to both resist pressures to conform to dominating cultural narratives and form new collective stories of their experience. For instance, butch and femme lesbians, whose subcultures were discredited by an androgynous feminist culture, suffered through the disintegration of their own communities, as well as alienation from feminist lesbians, in the 1970s. Recently, however, they have been reclaiming their identities and forming modern day narratives of their gender expressions that validate their current experiences (e.g., Feinberg, 1993). When considering personal or political change, the organization of individuals with similar experiences can facilitate the process of developing counter-cultural narratives. This same spirit of resistance against a dominating narrative animates many procedures in White and Epston's (1990; Monk, Winslade, Crocket, & Epston, 1996) style of narrative therapy, which accentuates new plot features that contribute to a preferred identity and recruits an audience for its performance.

☐ Loss and Grief: What's Narrative Got to Do With It?

At first blush, the elemental human phenomena of loss and grief seem so primordial, so raw in their emotional intensity, that a consideration of their narrative dimensions seems abstractly academic. Gripped by the anguished loss of a loved one or struggling against cultural forces that marginalize one's unique experience, a person might reasonably ask: What's narrative got to do with it?

Our answer is: everything. In a fundamental sense, losses cannot even be recognized as such except against the backdrop of a presumed narrative of continuity over time, a continuity imposed by the human need to organize experience along a temporal dimension. At a social level, the subtle and obvious processes of developing, sharing, and seeking validation for a particular account of loss begins as soon as such a perturbation of our life story is acknowledged, forming the central dynamic of our sense-making around the event (Harvey, 1996). Inevitably, such sense-making draws upon a cultural and linguistic matrix of resources—in the form of grief scripts, rituals, metaphors, and changed social roles—that both constrain and enable the integration of loss by any given individual or community (Neimeyer, 1998b).

Our argument in this chapter has been that many of the existing models and findings regarding loss in its variegated forms can be organized within the broad framework of a narrative model. In particular, we have been concerned with the dialectics of coherence of loss narratives, arguing that difficulties arise when life stories are rendered chaotic or conflictual by narrative disruption, or when scripts of identity are bent to the demands of consistency with or conformity to dominating accounts. While not intended to offer a comprehensive or unified theory of loss,[3] such an approach seems to offer an intriguing organizing heuristic that encompasses some of the tensions or problems in account-making that play out on different levels of the self and social system. Equally important, such a model offers at least a suggestive framework for psychotherapeutic, social, and political practices that can foster more healing stories in the wake of profound loss. Developing an adequate and evolving narrative of life's unbidden transitions does not assuage the pain associated with them, but it does permit them to be articulated in a way that encourages both personal integration of such experiences and social validation of their meaning.

References

Angus, L., & Rennie, D. L. (1989). Envisioning the representational world: The client's experience of metaphoric expressiveness in psychotherapy. *Psychotherapy, 25,* 552–560.

Angus, L., Levitt, H., & Hardke, L. (2000). Narrative processes and psychotherapeutic change: An integrative approach to psychotherapy research and practice. *Journal of Clinical Psychology, 55*(10), 1255–1270.

Arciero, G., & Guidano, V. (in press). Experience, explanation, and the quest for coherence. In R. A. Neimeyer & J. C. Raskin (Eds.), *Constructions of disorder* (pp. 91–118). Washington, DC: American Psychological Association.

Barsalou, L. W. (1988). The content and organization of autobiographical memories. In U. Neisser & E. Winograd (Eds.), *Remembering reconsidered* (pp. 193–243). Cambridge, UK: Cambridge University Press.

---

[3]Indeed, we believe that such a theory is conceptually unworkable, and even potentially oppressive, for reasons considered at length elsewhere (Neimeyer, 1998a). Our intent here is more modest: to view a broad range of typically unrelated loss phenomena through the lens of narrative theory, in a way that reveals a few otherwise hidden commonalities among them, and suggests some practical implications.

Braun, K. L., & Nichols, R. (1997). Death and dying in four Asian American cultures. *Death Studies, 21,* 327–359.

Burr, V. (1995). *An introduction to social constructionism.* London: Routledge.

Dula, A. (1997). The story of Miss Mildred. In K. Doka (Ed.), *Living with grief: When illness is prolonged* (pp. 83–95). Washington, DC: Hospice Foundation of America.

Feinberg, L. (1996). *Transgender warriors: Making history from Joan of Arc to Dennis Rodman.* Boston: Beacon Press.

Gendlin, E. T. (1996). *Focusing-oriented psychotherapy.* New York: Guilford.

Goncalves, O. F., Korman, Y., & Angus, L. (2000). Constructing psychopathology from a cognitive narrative perspective. In R. A. Neimeyer & J. D. Raskin (Eds.), *Constructions of disorder: Meaning-making frameworks for psychotherapy.* Washington, DC: American Psychological Association.

Greenberg, L., & Pascual-Leone, J. (1995). A dialectical constructivist approach to experiential change. In R. A. Neimeyer & M. J. Mahoney (Eds.), *Constructivism in Psychotherapy* (pp. 169–191). Washington, DC: American Psychological Association.

Harvey, J. H. (1996). *Embracing their memory.* Needham Heights, MA: Allyn & Bacon.

Hebert, M. P. (1998). Perinatal grief in its cultural context. *Death Studies, 22,* 61–78.

Howard, G. S. (1991). Culture tales: A narrative approach to thinking, cross-cultural psychology, and psychotherapy. *American Psychologist, 46,* 187–197.

Klass, D. (1999). *The spiritual lives of bereaved parents.* Philadelphia: Brunner/Mazel.

Levitt, H., Korman, Y., & Angus, L. (in press). A metaphor analysis in treatments of depression: Metaphor as a marker of change. *Counselling Psychology Quarterly.*

Mair, M. (1988). Psychology as story telling. *International Journal of Personal Construct Psychology, 1,* 125–137.

Mandler, J. (1984). *Scripts, stories, and scenes: Aspects of schema theory.* Hillsdale, NJ: Erlbaum.

Monk, G., Winslade, J., Crocket, K., & Epston, D. (1996). *Narrative therapy in practice.* San Francisco: Jossey-Bass.

Nadeau, J. W. (1997). *Families making sense of death.* Newbury Park, CA: Sage.

Neimeyer, R. A. (1998a). Can there be a psychology of loss? In J. H. Harvey (Ed.), *Perspectives on loss: A sourcebook* (pp. 331–341). Philadelphia: Brunner/Mazel.

Neimeyer, R. A. (1998b). *Lessons of loss: A guide to coping.* New York: McGraw Hill.

Neimeyer, R. A. (2000). Narrative disruptions in the construction of self. In R. A. Neimeyer & J. Raskin (Eds.), *Constructions of disorder: Meaning making frameworks for psychotherapy* (pp. 207–242). Washington, DC: American Psychological Association.

Neimeyer, R. A., Brooks, D. L., & Baker, K. D. (1996). Personal epistemologies and personal relationships. In B. Walker & D. Kalekin-Fishman (Eds.), *The construction of group realities* (pp. 127–160). Malabar, FL: Krieger.

Neimeyer, R. A., & Mahoney, M. J. (Eds.). (1995). *Constructivism in psychotherapy.* Washington, DC: American Psychological Association.

Neimeyer, R. A., & Stewart, A. E. (1998). Trauma, healing, and the narrative emplotment of loss. In C. Franklin & P. S. Nurius (Eds.), *Constructivism in practice* (pp. 165–184). Milwaukee, WI: Families International.

Selvini-Palazzoli, M., Boscolo, L., Cecchin, G., & Prata, G. (1980). Hypothesizing-circularity-neutrality. *Family Process, 19,* 3–12.

White, M., & Epston, D. (1990). *Narrative means to therapeutic ends.* New York: Norton.

INDEX

DATE DUE
